University of Plymouth
Charles Seale Hayne Library
Subject to status this item may be renewed
via your Voyager account

http://voyager.plymouth.ac.uk
Tel: (01752) 232323

NP68

ADMIRALTY SAILING DIRECTIONS

EAST COAST OF THE UNITED STATES PILOT VOLUME 1

East Coast of the United States from
Great Wass Island to Barnegat Inlet

FOURTEENTH EDITION
2013

IMPORTANT - SEE RELATED ADMIRALTY PUBLICATIONS

Notices to Mariners (Annual, Permanent, Preliminary and Temporary); **Symbols and Abbreviations used on Admiralty Paper Charts** (NP5011); **Admiralty Guide to ENC Symbols used in ECDIS** (NP5012); **The Mariner's Handbook** (NP100, especially Chapters 1 and 2 on the use, accuracy and limitations of charts); **Sailing Directions** (Pilots); **List of Lights** and **Fog Signals**; **List of Radio Signals** and **Tide Tables** (or their digital equivalents).

KEEP CHARTS AND PUBLICATIONS UP TO DATE AND USE THE LARGEST SCALE CHART APPROPRIATE

PUBLISHED BY THE UNITED KINGDOM HYDROGRAPHIC OFFICE

© British Crown Copyright 2013

This document is protected by international copyright law. No part of this document may be reproduced, stored in a retrieval system or transmitted in any form or by any means, electronic, mechanical, photocopying, recording or otherwise without the prior written permission of The UK Hydrographic Office, Admiralty Way, Taunton, Somerset, TA1 2DN, United Kingdom (www.ukho.gov.uk)

DIRECTIONS FOR UPDATING THIS VOLUME

This volume is kept up to date in a "Continuous Revision" cycle. This means that it will be continuously revised by its Editor for a period of approximately three years using information received in the Hydrographic Office, and then republished. Publication is announced in Part 1 of *Admiralty Notices to Mariners,* and a listing of all current editions is updated and published quarterly in Part 1B of *Admiralty Notices to Mariners* and six-monthly in NP234 *Cumulative List of Admiralty Notices to Mariners*. Additionally, this list is continuously updated and available on the UKHO website at www.ukho.gov.uk/msi

During the life of the book, it is updated as necessary by notices published weekly in Section IV of *Admiralty Notices to Mariners*.

A check-list of all extant Notices, but not the text, is published quarterly at Section IB of *Admiralty Notices to Mariners*. NP247(2) *Annual Summary of Notices to Mariners - Updates to Sailing Directions and Miscellaneous Publications* is published annually in January and contains the full text of all extant Section IV Notices.

These updates will normally be restricted to those critical to the safety of navigation, and information required to be published as a result of changes to national legislation affecting shipping, and to port regulations.

It is recommended that updates issued in this way are cut out and pasted into the book. Mariners may, however, prefer to keep updates in a separate file, and annotate the text of the book in the margin to indicate the existence of an update. This latter method may be more appropriate in some volumes where significant numbers of updates, sometimes overlapping, may make the cut-and-paste method unwieldy and confusing.

Sub-paragraph numbers in the margin of the body of the book are to assist the user when updating this volume.

RECORD OF UPDATES

The table below is to record Section IV Notices to Mariners updates affecting this volume.

Weekly Notices to Mariners (Section IV)

2013	2014	2015	2016

CONTENTS

	Pages
Directions for updating	ii
Record of updates	ii
Contents	iii
Preface	v
Purpose of Sailing Directions	vi
Reporting new dangers to navigation	vi
Feedback	vi
UKHO contact details	vii
How to obtain Admiralty Charts and Publications	vii
Related Admiralty Publications and their contents	viii
General information	x
Abbreviations	xii
Index chartlet	xiv

CHAPTER 1

Navigation and regulations
- Limits of the book (1.1) 1
- Navigational dangers and hazards (1.2) 1
- Traffic and operations (1.7) 2
- Charts (1.14) 2
- Aids to navigation (1.21) 3
- Pilotage (1.28) 3
- Radio facilities (1.29) 4
- Regulations (1.35) 4
- Signals (1.54) 6
- Distress and rescue (1.57) 7

Countries
- United States of America (1.62) 9

Natural conditions
- Maritime topography (1.89) 11
- Currents (1.92) 11
- Sea level and tides (1.97) 11
- Sea and swell (1.99) 11
- Sea water characteristics (1.104) 17
- Ice conditions (1.108) 17
- Climate and weather (1.112) 22
- Climate information (1.139) 41

CHAPTER 2

North Part of Gulf of Maine 53

CHAPTER 3

West Part of Gulf of Maine 81

CHAPTER 4

Massachusetts Bay, Boston Harbor and approaches 117

CHAPTER 5

Nantucket Shoals to Providence 141

CONTENTS

CHAPTER 6

Block Island Sound and Long Island Sound 173

CHAPTER 7

New York Harbor and approaches, including south coast of Long Island 201

APPENDICES AND INDEX

Appendix I —Vessel Bridge-to-Bridge Radiotelephone Regulations	226
Appendix II —United States - Ports and Waterways Safety - General	227
Appendix III —United States - Vessel Traffic Management	232
Appendix IV —United States - Navigation Safety Regulations	236
Appendix V —United States - Regulated Navigation Areas - Extracts	241
Appendix VI —United States - Danger Zones and Restricted Area Regulations	247
Appendix VII —United States - Inland Waterways Navigation Regulations	249
Appendix VIII —United States - Wildlife, Fisheries and the North Atlantic Right Whale	260
Appendix IX —United States - Navigation Regulations - Cape Cod Canal	267
Appendix X —United States - Shipping Safety Fairways	271
Index	272

PREFACE

The Fourteenth Edition of the *East Coast of the United States Pilot, Volume 1* has been prepared by Captain R M McDonald MNM FNI Master Mariner. The United Kingdom Hydrographic Office has used all reasonable endeavours to ensure that this Pilot contains all the information obtained by and assessed by it at the date shown below. Information received or assessed after that date will be included in *Admiralty Notices to Mariners* where appropriate. For details of *Admiralty Notices to Mariners* and guidance on their use, see *The Mariner's Handbook*.

This edition supersedes the Thirteenth Edition (2009), which is cancelled.

Information on climate and currents has been based on data provided by the Met Office, Exeter.

Copyright for some of the material in this publication is owned by the authority named under the item and permission for its reproduction must be obtained from the owner.

The following sources of information, other than UKHO Publications and Ministry of Defence papers, have been consulted:

United States
Charts
United States Coast Pilots:
Volume 1. Atlantic Coast: Eastport to Cape Cod 42nd Edition 2012
Volume 2. Atlantic Coast: Cape Cod to Sandy Hook 42nd Edition 2013
Volume 3. Atlantic Coast: Sandy Hook to Cape Henry 45th Edition 2012

Other publications
Lloyd's Ports of the World 2010
IHS Fairplay Ports and Terminals Guide 2011-2012
The Statesman's Yearbook 2012
Whitaker's Almanack 2011

Rear Admiral Ian Moncrieff CBE BA
Chief Executive
United Kingdom Hydrographic Office

13th December 2012

PURPOSE OF ADMIRALTY SAILING DIRECTIONS

Sailing Directions are intended for use by vessels of 150 gt or more. They amplify charted detail and contain information needed for safe navigation which is not available from charts or other hydrographic publications. They are written with the assumption that these are to hand and are intended to be read in conjunction with the charts quoted in the text which includes both charted and uncharted information.

They are normally arranged as follows:
- Preface. Includes a list of publications and documents consulted in the writing of the volume.
- Preliminary pages. Includes explanatory notes abbreviations and a glossary.
- Chapter 1. Contains general information on navigation, regulations, countries, ports and natural conditions, pertaining to the whole book.
- Chapter 2. Through-routeing information where appropriate.
- Chapter 3 and subsequent chapters. Geographical chapters containing coastal passage information, directions for waterways, and essential information on ports and anchorages.
- Appendices. Transcripts or extracts of regulations.
- Index.

Each volume has a book index diagram facing Page 1 which indicates the geographical coverage of each chapter. This will assist to identify which chapter contains the information required.

Each chapter has an index diagram facing its first page showing paragraph numbers against arrows or port names, which indicates the start of the appropriate text.

Chapters are divided into sections containing a number of sub-sections. Each sub-section is either a description of a waterway, offshore, coastal or inshore, with suitable cross-references to the texts in which the continuation of routes, or alternative routes, can be found. Otherwise it describes a major port. Smaller ports are described within the waterway sub-section.

General information relating to the whole book is contained in Chapter 1. General information at the start of the chapter is that relating to the chapter as a whole and includes material under the headings of topography, hazards, pilotage, VTS and traffic regulations, natural conditions and other topics. General information at the start of a section or sub-section only relates to that particular section.

Warning. This volume should only be used once fully updated by Section IV Notices to Mariners.

HOW TO REPORT NEW OR SUSPECTED DANGERS TO NAVIGATION OR CHANGES OBSERVED IN AIDS TO NAVIGATION

A Hydrographic Note, Form H.102, with instructions, is contained in the back of the Weekly Edition of Admiralty Notices to Mariners. This form can also be downloaded from the UKHO Website. The form should be used to report all observations, including new or suspected dangers to navigation or changes to aids to navigation.

FEEDBACK

In order to maintain and improve the accuracy of information contained within this volume, The United Kingdom Hydrographic Office welcomes general comments, new, additional or corroborative information and digital images from mariners and other users. Such information should be forwarded by post, fax or e-mail to the address below giving, where possible, the source for the information if this is not based on personal observation.

UKHO CONTACT DETAILS

Customer Services

Admiralty
The United Kingdom Hydrographic Office
Admiralty Way
TAUNTON
Somerset
TA1 2DN
United Kingdom
e-mail: customerservices@ukho.gov.uk
Tel: +44 (0)1823 723366
Fax: +44 (0)1823 330561
Website: www.admiralty.co.uk

Admiralty Sailing Directions

e-mail: sailingdirections@ukho.gov.uk
Tel: +44 (0)1823 337900 extension 3814   (Book Support Unit)
                                       extension 3382   (Head of Sailing Directions)
Fax: +44 (0)1823 351865   (Book Support Unit)

HOW TO OBTAIN ADMIRALTY CHARTS AND PUBLICATIONS

A complete list of Admiralty Charts and Publications (both paper and digital), together with a list of authorised Admiralty Distributors for their purchase, is contained in the "*Catalogue of Admiralty Charts and Publications*", which is published annually. The Admiralty Digital Catalogue is available to download free of charge from the UKHO Website.

Details of authorised Admiralty Distributors can also be obtained from the UKHO Customer Services.

RELATED ADMIRALTY PUBLICATIONS AND THEIR CONTENTS

Admiralty Notices to Mariners (NMs):

Weekly Notices to Mariners
Navigationally significant changes to nautical charts, lights, fog signals, radio signals and Sailing Directions
Reprint of all Radio Navigational Warnings in force for Navarea 1 and a summary of charts and publications being published.

Cumulative List of Notices to Mariners
Published in January and July of each year
A list of all nautical charts available and a complete list of all NMs affecting them during the previous two years.

Annual Summary of Notices to Mariners
Published at the beginning of the year in two parts
Annual Notices to Mariners, Temporary and Preliminary notices
Cumulative summary of updates to Sailing Directions.

For more information, please visit www.ukho.gov.uk/msi

The Mariner's Handbook:
Information on charts and their use
Operational information and regulation
Tides and currents
Characteristics of the sea
Basic meteorology
Navigation in ice
Hazards and restrictions to navigation
IALA Maritime Buoyage System.

Admiralty Sailing Directions (Pilots):
Waterway directions
Port facilities
Directions for port entry
Navigational hazards
Buoyage
Climate Information
National regulations affecting shipping.

Admiralty List of Radio Signals:
Maritime Radio Stations
Radio Aids to Navigation
Time
Maritime Safety Information
Radio weather services
Global Maritime Distress and Safety System (GMDSS)
Pilot services
Vessel Traffic Services
Port operations.

Admiralty List of Lights:
Lighthouses, lightships
Characteristics and intensity
Elevation
Range of light
Description of structure.

Admiralty Tidal Publications:
Tide Tables
  Daily predictions of time and height of high and low water at Standard Ports
  Time and height differences for Secondary Ports
  Harmonic constants where known
  Supplementary Tables including Land Levelling and Chart Datum corrections where known.
Tidal Stream Atlases
  Major tidal streams for selected waters of north-west Europe
  Direction and rate of tidal streams at hourly intervals.

For more information, please visit www.admiralty.co.uk

GENERAL INFORMATION

Remarks on subject matter:

Buoys are generally described in detail only when they have special navigational significance, or where the scale of the chart is too small to show all the details clearly.

Chart references in the text are normally referred to the largest scale Admiralty chart and smaller scale charts have occasionally been quoted where more appropriate. Increasingly, the text now refers back to the relevant ENC cell which may be quoted as the reference chart.

Firing, practice and exercise areas. Submarine exercise areas are mentioned in Sailing Directions. Other firing, practice and exercise areas may be mentioned with limited details. Signals and buoys used in connection with these areas may be mentioned if significant for navigation. Attention is invited to the Annual Notice to Mariners on this subject.

Names have been taken from the most authoritative source. When an obsolete name still appears on the chart, it is given in brackets following the proper name at the principal description of the feature in the text and where the name is first mentioned.

Port plans in this book are intended to assist the mariner in orientation and they are not to be used for navigation. The appropriate scale of chart should always be used.

Tidal information relating the daily vertical movements of the water is not given. For this information *Admiralty Tide Tables* or *Admiralty Total Tide* should be consulted. Changes in water level of an abnormal nature are mentioned.

Time difference used in the text when applied to the time of High Water found from the *Admiralty Tide Tables*, gives the time of the event being described in the Standard Time kept in the area of that event. Due allowance must be made for any seasonal daylight saving time which may be kept.

Wreck information is included where drying or below-water wrecks are relatively permanent features having significance for navigation or anchoring.

Units and terminology used in this volume:

Bands is the word used to indicate horizontal marking.

Bearings and directions are referred to the true compass and when given in degrees are reckoned clockwise from 000° (North) to 359°.

Bearings used for positioning are given from the reference object.

Bearings of objects, alignments and light sectors are given as seen from the vessel.

Courses always refer to the course to be made good over the ground.

Conspicuous objects are natural and artificial marks which are outstanding, easily identifiable and clearly visible to the mariner over a large area of sea in varying conditions of light. If the scale is large enough they will normally be shown on the chart in bold capitals and may be marked "conspic".

Depths are given below chart datum, except where otherwise stated.

Distances are expressed in sea miles of 60 to a degree of latitude and sub-divided into cables of one tenth of a sea mile.

Elevations, as distinct from heights, are given above Mean High Water Springs or Mean Higher High Water whichever is quoted in *Admiralty Tide Tables*, and expressed as, "an elevation of ... m". However the elevation of natural features such as hills may alternatively be expressed as "... m high" since in this case there can be no confusion between elevation and height.

Heights of objects refer to the height of the object above the ground and are invariably expressed as "... m in height".

Latitude and Longitude given in brackets are usually given to two decimal places in order to aid location on an ENC. They are usually established from an ENC which may not be the quoted reference chart. When using paper charts the Latitude and Longitude should only be taken as a guide to aid location.

Metric units are used for all measurements of depths, heights and short distances, but where feet/fathoms charts are referred to, these latter units are given in brackets after the metric values for depths and heights shown on the chart.

Principal marks are marks which qualify for inclusion and are outstanding and clearly visible throughout most of the waterway (or 15 to 20 miles of the waterway for particularly long waterways) as marks by day or lights by night; thereby being associated with the waterway as a whole, rather than being confined to any single set of Directions within it. In particular:

> Landmarks comprise buildings and structures (including lighthouses, whether major lights or not), daymarks and natural features. They may be on the coast or farther inland, provided they are distinctly visible from seaward.
> Major lights is used in Sailing Directions to refer to all lights with a range of 15 miles or over.
> Offshore marks include light vessels, light floats, LANBY, buoyant beacons, and oil production platforms.

Prominent objects are those which are easily identifiable, but do not justify being classified as conspicuous.

Stripes is the word used to indicate markings which are vertical, unless stated to be diagonal.

Tidal streams and currents are described by the direction towards which they flow.

Time is expressed in the four-figure notation beginning at midnight and is given in local time unless otherwise stated. Details of local time kept will be found in *Admiralty List of Radio Signals Volume 2*.

Vertical clearance is given above Highest Astronomical Tide, Mean High Water Springs or Height Datum as defined by the responsible authority. Readers should be guided by the text beneath the reference chart title or as shown on NP5011.

Winds are described by the direction from which they blow.

ABBREVIATIONS

The following abbreviations are used in the text:

AIS	Automatic Identification System	GPS	Global Positioning System
ALC	Articulated loading column	GRP	glass reinforced plastic
ALP	Articulated loading platform	grt	gross register tonnage (obsolete)
AMVER	Automated Mutual Assistance Vessel Rescue System	gt	gross tonnage
ARCS	Admiralty Raster Chart Service	HAT	Highest Astronomical Tide
ASL	Archipelagic Sea Lane	HF	high frequency
ATBA	Area To Be Avoided	hm	hectometre
ATLAS	autonomous temperature line acquisition system	HMS	Her (His) Majesty's Ship
		hp	horse power
AVCS	Admiralty Vector Chart Service	hPa	hectopascal
		HSC	High Speed Craft
°C	degrees Celsius	HW	High Water
CALM	Catenary anchor leg mooring		
CBM	Conventional buoy mooring	IALA	International Association of Lighthouse Authorities
CDC	Certain Dangerous Cargo		
CHA	Competent Harbour Authority	IHO	International Hydrographic Organization
cm	centimetre(s)	IMB	International Maritime Bureau
COTP	Captain of the Port	IMDG	International Maritime Dangerous Goods
CVTS	Co-operative Vessel Traffic System	IMO	International Maritime Organization
		ISPS	International Ship and Port Facility Security Code
DART	Deep-ocean Assessment and Reporting Tsunamis	ITCZ	Intertropical Convergence Zone
DF	direction finding	ITZ	Inshore traffic zone
DG	degaussing		
DGPS	Differential Global Positioning System	JRCC	Joint Rescue Co-ordination Centre
DMA	Dynamic Management Area	kHz	kilohertz
DPG	Dangerous and Polluting Goods	km	kilometre(s)
DSC	Digital Selective Calling	kn	knot(s)
DW	Deep Water	kW	kilowatt(s)
dwt	deadweight tonnage		
DZ	danger zone	LANBY	Large Automatic Navigation Buoy
		LAT	Lowest Astronomical Tide
E	east (easterly, eastward, eastern, easternmost)	LF	low frequency
		LHG	Liquefied Hazardous Gas
ECDIS	Electronic Chart Display and Information System	LMT	Local Mean Time
		LNG	Liquefied Natural Gas
EEZ	exclusive economic zone	LOA	Length overall
ELSBM	Exposed location single buoy mooring	LPG	Liquefied Petroleum Gas
ENC	Electronic Navigational Chart	LW	Low Water
ENE	east-north-east		
EPIRB	Emergency Position Indicating Radio Beacon	m	metre(s)
		m^3	cubic metre(s)
ESE	east-south-east	mb	millibar(s)
ESSA	Environmentally Sensitive Sea Area	MCTS	Marine Communications and Traffic Services Centres
ETA	estimated time of arrival		
ETD	estimated time of departure	MF	medium frequency
EU	European Union	MHz	megahertz
		MHHW	Mean Higher High Water
FAD	fish aggregating device	MHLW	Mean Higher Low Water
feu	forty foot equivalent unit	MHW	Mean High Water
fm	fathom(s)	MHWN	Mean High Water Neaps
FPSO	Floating production storage and offloading vessel	MHWS	Mean High Water Springs
		MLHW	Mean Lower High Water
FPU	Floating production unit	MLLW	Mean Lower Low Water
FSO	Floating storage and offloading vessel	MLW	Mean Low Water
ft	foot (feet)	MLWN	Mean Low Water Neaps
		MLWS	Mean Low Water Springs
		mm	millimetre(s)
g/cm^3	grams per cubic centimetre	MMSI	Maritime Mobile Service Identity
GMDSS	Global Maritime Distress and Safety System	MRCC	Maritime Rescue Co-ordination Centre

ABBREVIATIONS

MRSC	Maritime Rescue Sub-Centre	SBM	Single buoy mooring
m/s	metres per second	SE	south-east
MSI	Maritime Safety Information	SHA	Statutory Harbour Authority
MSL	Mean Sea Level	SMA	Seasonal Management Area
MSR	Mandatory Ship Reporting	SPM	Single point mooring
MV	Motor Vessel	sq	square
MW	megawatt(s)	SRR	Search and Rescue Region
MY	Motor Yacht	SS	Steamship
		SSCC	Ship Sanitation Control Certificate
N	north (northerly, northward, northern, northernmost)	SSCEC	Ship Sanitation Control Exemption Certificate
NATO	North Atlantic Treaty Organization	SSE	south-south-east
Navtex	Navigational Telex System	SSW	south-south-west
NE	north-east	STL	Submerged turret loading
NGA	National Geospatial-Intelligence Agency	STS	ship to ship
NNE	north-north-east	SW	south-west
NNW	north-north-west	SWATH	small waterplane area twin hull ship
No(s)	number(s)		
NOAA	National Oceanic and Atmospheric Administration	teu	twenty foot equivalent unit
		TRITON	Triangle Trans-Ocean Buoy Network
nrt	net register tonnage (obsolete)	TSS	Traffic Separation Scheme
nt	net tonnage		
NW	north-west	UHF	ultra high frequency
		UKC	under-keel clearance
ODAS	Ocean Data Acquisition System	UKHO	United Kingdom Hydrographic Office
OPL	off port limits	ULCC	Ultra Large Crude Carrier
		UN	United Nations
PEC	Pilotage Exemption Certificate	USA	United States of America
PEL	Port Entry Light	UT	Universal Time
PLEM	Pipe line end manifold	UTC	Co-ordinated Universal Time
PMSC	Port Marine Safety Code		
POL	Petrol, Oil & Lubricants	VDR	Voyage Data Recorder
PSSA	Particularly Sensitive Sea Area	VHF	very high frequency
PWC	Personal watercraft	VLCC	Very Large Crude Carrier
		VMRS	Vessel Movement Reporting System
RCC	Rescue Co-ordination Centre	VTC	Vessel Traffic Centre
RMS	Royal Mail Ship	VTMS	Vessel Traffic Management System
RN	Royal Navy	VTS	Vessel Traffic Services
RoRo	Roll-on, Roll-off		
RT	radio telephony	W	west (westerly, westward, western, westernmost)
S	south (southerly, southward, southern, southernmost)	WGS	World Geodetic System
SALM	Single anchor leg mooring system	WMO	World Meteorological Organization
SALS	Single anchored leg storage system	WNW	west-north-west
SAR	Search and Rescue	WSW	west-south-west
Satnav	Satellite navigation	WT	radio (wireless) telegraphy

Chapter Index Diagram

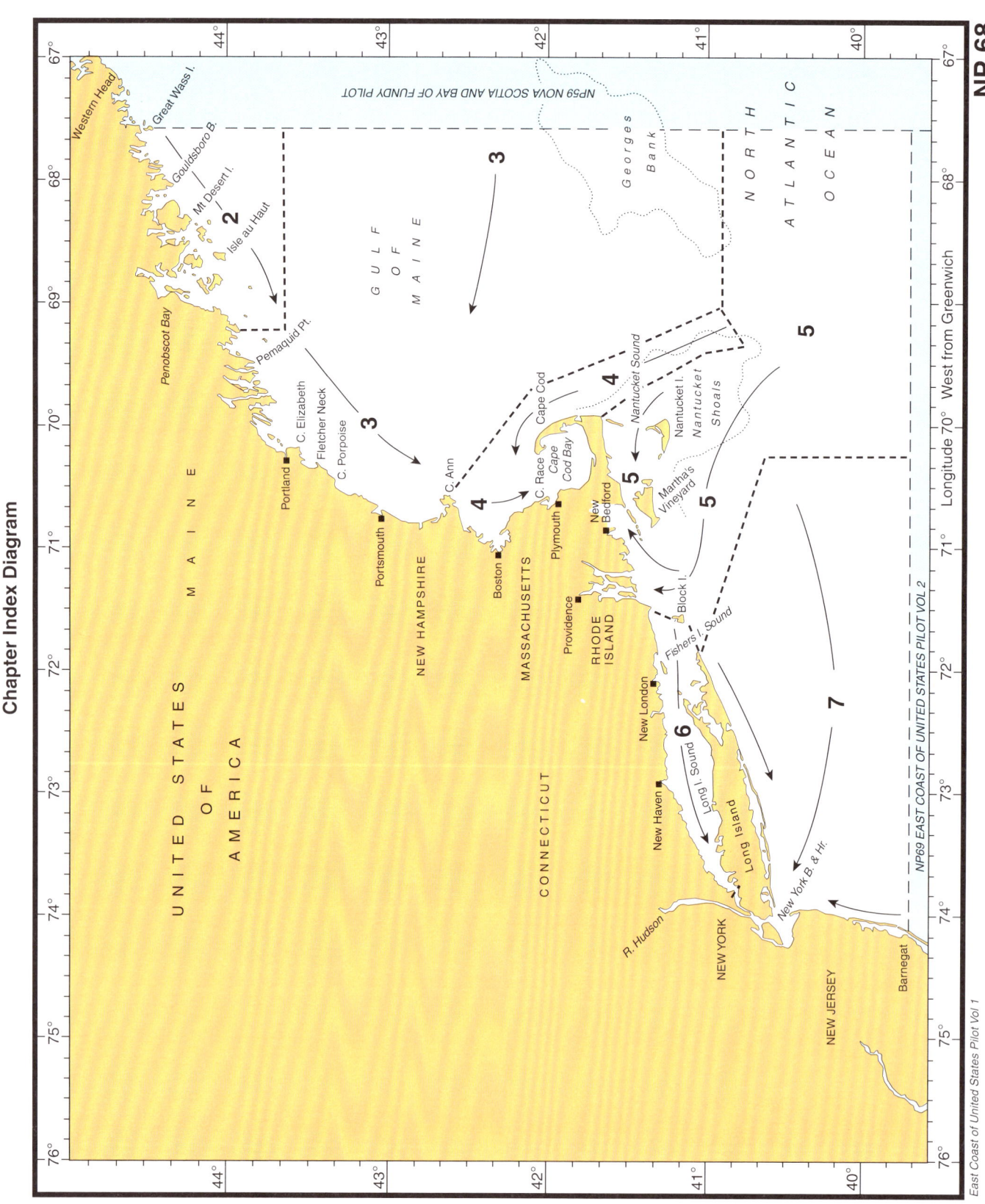

LAWS AND REGULATIONS APPERTAINING TO NAVIGATION

While, in the interests of the safety of shipping, the United Kingdom Hydrographic Office makes every endeavour to include in its hydrographic publications details of the laws and regulations of all countries appertaining to navigation, it must be clearly understood:

(a) that no liability whatever will be accepted for failure to publish details of any particular law or regulation, and

(b) that publication of the details of a law or regulation is solely for the safety and convenience of shipping and implies no recognition of the international validity of the law or regulation.

EAST COAST OF THE UNITED STATES PILOT VOLUME 1

CHAPTER 1

NAVIGATION AND REGULATIONS
COUNTRIES
NATURAL CONDITIONS

NAVIGATION AND REGULATIONS

LIMITS OF THE BOOK

Chart 2670
Area covered
1.1

1   This volume contains Sailing Directions for the NE coast of the United States between Great Wass Island, about 40 miles from the Canadian border and Barnegat Inlet, 60 miles S of New York, and for the sea area contained within the following limits:

	Lat N	Long W
From Great Wass Island	44°27′·00	67°35′·00
Thence S to position	39°45′·00	67°35′·00
Thence W to Barnegat Inlet	39°45′·00	74°06′·00

Thence NE along the coast
of the United States to
Great Wass Island.

NAVIGATIONAL DANGERS AND HAZARDS

Coastal conditions

Outlying dangers
1.2

1   The principal outlying dangers are Georges Bank (3.3) and Nantucket Shoals (5.19). Both these dangers should be entirely avoided.

There are also a number of other shoals in the Gulf of Maine, but only Ammen Rock (3.7) is a danger. There are no outlying dangers in the approaches to New York, to the SW of Nantucket Shoals.

Coastal dangers
1.3

1   In the Gulf of Maine there are a number of dangers lying off the coast. In clear weather the land will be distinguished before these dangers are encountered, but in fog caution is required.

Natural conditions
1.4

1   **Ice.** See 1.108.
   Strong winds. See 1.126.
   Fog. See 1.132.

Former mined areas

1.5

1   The only former mined area in the waters covered by this volume is in the approaches to New York Harbor where mines were laid during the war of 1939-45. Due to the lapse of time this area is considered safe for surface navigation, but a very real risk still exists with regard to anchoring, fishing or any form of submarine or sea-bed activity. See 7.11.

Overhead cables

1.6

1   Overhead cables are mentioned in the text where the clearance beneath them may be a hazard to navigation. Some of these cables carry high voltages and sufficient clearance must be allowed when

passing underneath them. In winter, the published clearance may be varied by ice or snow conditions.

See *The Mariner's Handbook* for information on safety clearances and the radar responses to be expected.

TRAFFIC AND OPERATIONS

Traffic

Ferries
1.7
1 There are numerous ferry routes between the mainland and the islands in Nantucket Sound, Vineyard Sound and Long Island Sound.

Pleasure craft
1.8
1 The coastal and inshore waters covered by this volume, which have many marinas and boatyards, are very popular with yachtsmen.

Fishing

General remarks
1.9
1 Fishing craft are based at most of the ports along the coast covered by this volume. There are numerous lobster and oyster fisheries, and canning factories are established in some harbours.

Fish traps
1.10
1 Lobster pots are set in the inshore waters covered by this volume, especially between Great Wass Island and Portland. The pots are marked by small buoys, the mooring lines of which are liable to foul the propellers of small craft.

Exercise areas

Naval exercises
1.11
1 Naval exercises may take place in the waters covered by this volume. They are mentioned at the appropriate place in the text. Notice of exercises giving limits of the area, nature and duration of the exercise, and specified navigation rules, are promulgated by local *Notices to Mariners* and radio navigation warnings. For signals used by warships, see 1.54.

For general information on such areas see *The Mariner's Handbook.*

Firing practice
1.12
1 Gunnery and bombing practice may take place in the waters covered by this volume. They are mentioned at the appropriate place in the text. Notice of firing practices, giving the limits of the area, nature and duration of the practice, and specified navigation rules, are promulgated by local *Notices to Mariners* and radio navigation warnings. For signals used by warships, see 1.54.

For general information on such areas see *The Mariner's Handbook.*

Submarine exercises

Submarine operating areas
1.13
1 Submarine operating areas are established in Long Island Sound (6.75). As submarines may be operating submerged in these areas, vessels should proceed with caution.

CHARTS

Positions

1.14
1 Geographical positions in this volume are given to two decimal places and are, where possible, based on the WGS 84 datum. Where this is not possible the datum will be quoted alongside the reference chart. These positions are not to be used as an indication of navigational or positional accuracy but are for the purpose of identification and differentiation of named and unnamed topographical, navigational and hydrographic, features, points and marks. Where navigational and/or positional accuracy is required then positions should be obtained direct from the largest scale chart or ENC cell, taking note of the datum.

Admiralty charts

1.15
1 Admiralty charts give full coverage of the offshore waters and most of the coastal waters of the area covered by this volume. They also give plans of all the important harbours and most of the important anchorages.

Admiralty chart coverage is not adequate for entry into some of the minor harbours and bays, especially those lying in the E part of the area between Great Wass Island and Portland.

2 With the exception of one chart which largely covers Canadian waters, there are no current plans to metricate any of the Admiralty charts covering the area of this volume.

Foreign charts

1.16
1 For certain smaller ports and/or navigational areas where coverage by British Admiralty charts is considered inadequate, or it is a requirement to carry foreign government charts of the area, foreign charts are quoted as reference charts. They will normally be of a larger scale and will have been used to write the Sailing Directions on the assumption that mariners wishing to navigate in these areas will have provided themselves with suitable charts on which to do so.

2 US charts and publications of the National Oceanic and Atmospheric Administration (NOAA) and charts of the National Geospatial-Intelligence Agency (NGA) are sold by chart agents in US and some foreign ports. See http://nauticalcharts.noaa.gov for further details of availability.

These charts are not issued by the UKHO nor are they amended by *Admiralty Notices to Mariners.*

Names on charts

1.17
1 Throughout this volume the names of features have been taken from the paper reference chart. It may be noticed on occasions that the name on the ENC may not agree with the paper chart.

Datums

Horizontal
1.18
1 For the area covered by this book, Admiralty and US charts are usually referred to North American Datum 1983 (NAD 83). For practical navigation purposes this equates to World Geodetic System 1984 (WGS84).

On a few Admiralty charts, positions are based on North American Datum (1927) and corrections are shown to align this datum with WGS84. On some smaller scale Admiralty charts, corrections cannot be determined.

2   When transferring positions between charts with different horizontal datums, it is advisable to do so by bearing and distance from a common reference object and not by latitude and longitude.

Vertical
1.19

1   **Depths.** On Admiralty charts for the area covered by this volume the Chart Datum is MLLW.

US charts are reduced to MLLW or MLW as detailed on the chart.

As a consequence, mariners using these charts (see 1.16) should be aware that predicted and actual depths less than those charted may routinely occur. See Table V of *Admiralty Tide Tables* for details.

2   **Drying heights** on Admiralty charts are shown as being above Chart Datum.

Elevations on Admiralty charts are shown as being above MHWS and on US charts are shown against MHW.

Depths

Depth terms used in US waters
1.20

1   **Project depth** is the design dredging depth of a channel. The project depth may or may not be the goal of maintenance dredging after completion of the channel.

Controlling depth is the least depth within the limits of the channel; it restricts the safe use of the channel to draughts of less than that depth.

2   **Centreline controlling depth** of a channel applies only to the centreline; lesser depths may exist in the remainder of the channel.

Mid-channel controlling depth of a channel is the controlling depth of only the middle half of the channel.

3   In this volume project depths are given where available. For the latest controlling depths charts and local harbour and pilotage authorities should be consulted.

Depths alongside wharves are usually those reported by the owner or operator of the wharf. Local authorities should be consulted for the latest controlling depths.

AIDS TO NAVIGATION

Lights
1.21

1   In the US, lights are the responsibility of the Coast Guard. Major lights are those with a nominal range of 15 miles or more.

Light structures only are described in this volume; see *Admiralty List of Lights and Fog Signals* for other details.

Landmarks
1.22

1   Caution is necessary when evaluating the description of some landmarks, such as trees and buildings, that are given in this volume or on some of the older charts. New buildings may have been erected and old trees or houses destroyed, so that such marks, which may at one time have been conspicuous on account of their isolation, shape or colour, may now be difficult to identify or no longer exist.

Beacons
1.23

1   A beacon is a fixed artificial navigation mark which can be recognised by means of its shape, colour, pattern or topmark; it may carry a light, radar reflector or other aid to navigation. In the US unlit aids are known as daybeacons.

Daymarks
1.24

1   The term daymark refers to a large unlit beacon but the term is also used to denote a topmark or other distinguishing mark or shape incorporated into a beacon, light buoy or buoy.

2   Daybeacons in the US are used where navigation at night is negligible or where the conditions are such that it is impractical to operate a light. Reflective material is applied to daybeacons to improve their identification at night with the aid of a searchlight.

The lateral system for fixed artificial aids is based on that used for buoyage.

Buoyage

IALA Maritime Buoyage System
1.25

1   The IALA Maritime Buoyage System Region B (red to starboard) is in use throughout the area covered by this volume, but mariners are cautioned that in minor locations, and where aids to navigation are privately maintained, non-IALA buoys and marks may be encountered.

For full details of the system see *The Mariner's Handbook* and *IALA Maritime Buoyage System*.

Radar reflectors are not charted; it can be assumed that most major buoys are fitted with radar reflectors.

Ocean Data Acquisition System (ODAS)
1.26

1   ODAS buoys (special) may be encountered within the area covered by this volume. These buoy systems, which vary considerably in size, are used for environmental research purposes; they are marked "ODAS" with an identification number. The large systems should be given a clearance of at least 1 mile, and in the case of vessels towing underwater gear this distance should be increased to 2½ miles.

2   As the buoys have no navigational significance, and as they are liable to be moved or withdrawn at short notice, they are not normally mentioned in the text of the book.

See *The Mariner's Handbook* for further details.

Winter buoyage
1.27

1   When threatened by ice, certain lighted buoys may be replaced by lighted ice buoys having reduced candle-power or by unlighted buoys, and certain unlighted buoys may be discontinued.

During winter months buoys may prove unreliable as they may become damaged or break adrift.

PILOTAGE

United States
1.28

1   Pilotage is compulsory for all foreign vessels and, apart from a few exceptions, US registered vessels engaged in foreign trade. It is optional for US vessels in the coastal trade, provided they are under the

control and direction of a pilot duly licensed by Federal Law for the waters that vessel is navigating.

Information on pilotage procedures at individual ports is given in the text at the port concerned.

See *Admiralty List of Radio Signals Volume 6(5)* for details.

RADIO FACILITIES

Position fixing systems

Differential Global Positioning System (DGPS)
1.29

1   Differential Global Positioning System (DGPS) data is broadcast from the following stations providing coverage of the area in this volume:
    Penobscot (44°27′·10N 68°46′·33W).
    Brunswick (43°53′·40N 69°56′·80W).
    Acushnet (41°44′·57N 70°53′·19W).
    Moriches (40°47′·40N 72°44′·83W).
    Sandy Hook (40°28′·29N 74°00′·71W).

For full details of this system see *Admiralty List of Radio Signals Volume 2* and *The Mariner's Handbook*.

Radio aids to navigation

Radar beacons
1.30

1   There are several racons in the area to aid both offshore navigation and entry into harbours. See *Admiralty List of Radio Signals Volume 2* for details.

Radio navigational warnings

Long range warnings
1.31

1   The waters covered by this volume lie in NAVAREA IV of the World-wide Navigational Warning Service. The Area Co-ordinator is the US and navigation warnings are issued by the National Geospatial-Intelligence Agency (NGA). Warnings are broadcast through:
    a) USCG radio station at Boston.
    b) The International SafetyNET Service via an Inmarsat Land Earth Station (LES).

See *Admiralty List of Radio Signals Volume 3(2)* for details.

Local warnings
1.32

1   Local warnings are issued by the USCG for coastal and harbour areas. These warnings are broadcast by the appropriate USCG radio station.

See *Admiralty List of Radio Signals Volume 3(2)* for details.

Radio weather reports

Warnings and bulletins
1.33

1   See *Admiralty List of Radio Signals Volume 3(2)* for full details of all radio weather services and the stations from which they are issued.

Radio medical advice

1.34

1   In US waters the USCG will respond to DH MEDICO messages by providing advice that is immediately available or by referring requests to the International Radio Medical Centre in Rome, Italy. See *Admiralty List of Radio Signals Volume 1(2)* for details.

REGULATIONS

International regulations

Submarine cables
1.35

1   Mariners are advised not to anchor or trawl in the vicinity of submarine cables. See *The Mariner's Handbook* for information on the *International Convention for the Protection of Submarine cables*.

Submarine pipelines
1.36

1   Mariners are advised not to anchor or trawl in the vicinity of pipelines. Pipelines are not always buried and their presence may significantly reduce the charted depth. They may also span seabed undulations and cause fishing gear to become irrecoverably snagged, putting a vessel in severe danger.

Pollution
1.37

1   See *The Mariner's Handbook* for information concerning the *International Convention for the Prevention of Pollution from Ships 1973 (MARPOL 1973)* and the *1978 Protocol to MARPOL 1973*.

Traffic separation schemes
1.38

1   There are a number of TSS's in the area covered by this volume, all of which are IMO adopted. See the IMO publication *Ships' Routeing* and Rule 10 of *International Regulations for Preventing Collisions at Sea (1972)* for further details.

National regulations

United States Coast Guard
1.39

1   The USCG includes amongst its duties:
    Enforcement of the laws of the US, including those of navigation and neutrality, on the high seas and in the coastal and inland waters of the US and its possessions.
    Administration of the Oil Pollution Act.
    Establishment and administration of anchorages.

2   Inspection and documentation of vessels.
    Operation of aids to navigation.
    Operation of AMVER.
    SAR operations.
    Publication of Lights List and Local Notices to Mariners.

3   **Coastguard Sectors**, which combine the missions of a Marine Safety Office (COTP and Marine Inspection Office) with a Coast Guard Group, in the area covered by this volume are situated at:
    Sector Northern New England: 259 High Street, South Portland, ME 04106.
    Sector Boston: 427 Commercial Street, Boston, MA 02109.
    Sector Southeastern New England: 1 Little Harbor Road, Woods Hole, MA 02543-1099.
    Sector Long Island Sound: 120 Woodward Avenue, New Haven, CT 06512.
    Sector New York: 212 Coast Guard Drive, Staten Island, NY 10305.

Code of Federal Regulations
1.40

1   The *US Code of Federal Regulations (CFR)* governs all marine regulatory requirements and should be consulted for detailed information on any of the following summarised regulations, or any other US Federal Regulation. CFR extracts can be found in the relevant edition of the US Coast Pilots.

Selected extracts from Titles 33 and 50 CFR are given in the Appendices to this volume.

Pollution of the sea
1.41

1   **Oil and hazardous substances**. The Federal Water Pollution Control Act, as amended, and the Fishery Conservation and Management Act of 1976, prohibit the discharge of oil or any hazardous substance into any US waters to the limits of the EEZ. Any spillage that does occur must be reported immediately to the nearest USCG station by radio, or by an established nationwide toll free telephone number, 1-800-424-8802. Vessels are required to have on board and available for inspection an International Oil Pollution Prevention Certificate verifying compliance with Marpol 73/78 and that all necessary equipment is fitted and operational, also to maintain an Oil Record Book reporting all oil transfers and discharges.

2   **Garbage and refuse**. The Refuse Act of 1899 prohibits the dumping of any refuse into US waters. Whilst within US waters all garbage and refuse matter must be contained in leak-proof receptacles for supervised off-loading at the next US port visited.
    Area to be avoided. See 5.6.

3   **No-Discharge Zones (NDZ)** have been established at numerous specific locations throughout the United States. These zones, which are shown on US charts, are areas into which the discharge of sewage (whether treated or untreated) from all vessels is completely prohibited. For further details see the US Environmental Protection Agency website at www.epa.gov.

National Marine Sanctuaries
1.42

1   National Marine Sanctuaries are established over large areas of the water and are described in the text. In general terms, the purpose of the sanctuaries is to protect and preserve the ecosystems, including marine birds and mammals and other natural resources, and to ensure the continued availability of the areas as research and recreational resources.

2   Prohibited activities, consistent with international law, include hydrocarbon operations, dumping of certain substances, placing of structures on the seabed, disturbance of marine life, and the removal of historical or cultural resources.
    The principal area, within the limits of this volume, is Stellwagen Bank National Marine Sanctuary (4.3).

Navigation Safety Regulations
1.43

1   The general purpose of the US Navigation Safety regulations is to set a minimum level of navigational practice and equipment, so as to reduce the risk of casualty to vessels, bridges and other structures on or in navigable waters, or any land structure or shore area immediately adjacent to those waters; and to protect the navigable waters and resources therein from environmental harm resulting from damage to a vessel or structure.

2   The regulations require all self-propelled vessels over 1600 gt navigating in US waters to carry up-to-date charts, Sailing Directions, Light Lists, Tide Tables and Tidal Current Tables. US charts and publications are not mandatory, provided up-to-date foreign government charts of an adequate scale and foreign publications containing equivalent information are carried in lieu.

3   In general Admiralty charts and publications, including *Admiralty Tide Tables* which contain Tidal Stream Tables where appropriate, meet these requirements but the chart service does not include cover of all US ports and their approaches.
    The regulations are reproduced in Appendix IV and an up-to-date synopsis of them, with explanatory notes, is published in *Annual Summary of Admiralty Notices to Mariners*.

Navigation Rules for United States Inland Waters
1.44

1   **Inland Navigational Rules Act of 1980** modifies *International Regulations for Preventing Collisions at Sea, 1972,* for use in US Inland Waters, inshore of established lines of demarcation. These rules apply in all inland waters of the US. The COLREG demarcation lines are defined in the general information of each chapter of the text, with reference to the area covered by that chapter.

2   The Navigation Rules, International-Inland (COMDTINST M16672·2 series), are published by the US Coast Guard, obtainable on request from USCG Marine Inspection offices in major US ports, or by writing to:
    Superintendent of Documents,
    US Government Printing Office,
    Washington, DC 20402-9325.

3   Any vessel intending to navigate in US inland waters should obtain a current copy of the document mentioned above.
    See Appendix VII for further information.

Special anchorage areas
1.45

1   Vessels not more than 19·8 m (65 ft) in length, when at anchor in any special anchorage area, shall not be required to carry or exhibit the white anchor lights or shapes required by the navigation rules.

Communication between vessels
1.46

1   For information on the US Bridge-to-Bridge Telephone Act, see Appendix I.

Notification of Arrivals, Hazardous Conditions, and Certain Dangerous Cargoes
1.47

1   For extracts from US regulations concerning Ports and Waterways Safety see Appendix II.

Regulated Navigation Areas
1.48

1   Areas of regulated vessel movement designated as a Regulated Navigation Area, a Safety Zone, or a Security Zone may be established under certain circumstances by the US Coast Guard. For further information see Appendix V and the relevant edition of the US Coast Pilot.
    In such areas described in this volume, special regulations apply and are given in the relevant text.

Danger Zones and Restricted Area Regulations
1.49

1   A number of areas covered by this book are subject to regulations concerning danger zones and restricted areas, and are described in the relevant text. For further details see Appendix VI and the relevant edition of the US Coast Pilot.

National Terrorism Advisory System
1.50

1   The National Terrorism Advisory System (NTAS) has replaced the colour-coded Homeland Security Advisory System (HSAS). NTAS is used throughout the United States to disseminate information about

terrorist threats. Further information is available from the Homeland Security website (http://www.dhs.gov).

The Commandant of the US Coastguard employs a three-tiered system of Maritime Security (MARSEC) threat levels to communicate scalable responses to maritime industry partners. If an NTAS Alert is issued, the US Coastguard will consider whether a MARSEC Level change is appropriate. For further details see the US Coastguard website (http://www.uscg.mil/).

North Atlantic right whale
1.51

1   The North Atlantic right whale is one of the world's most endangered large whale species. They migrate annually along the east coast of North America between the feeding grounds off New England and Canada and the calving grounds off Florida, Georgia and South Carolina. Regulations are in force for the protection of the whale relating to speed restrictions, reporting procedures and an ATBA together with recommended two-way avoidance routes. For details see *Admiralty List of Radio Signals Volume 6(5)* and Appendices VIII and X.

Vessel arrival inspections
1.52

1   Vessels subject to US quarantine, customs, immigration, and agricultural quarantine inspections generally make arrangements in advance through ships' agents. Government officials conducting such inspections are stationed at most major ports. Mariners arriving at ports where officials are not stationed should contact the nearest office providing that service.

Quarantine and customs
1.53

1   **Quarantine.** All vessels arriving in the United States are subject to inspection by the Public Health Service. Vessels subject to routine boarding for quarantine inspection are only those which have had on board, during the last 15 days preceding the date of expected arrival or during the period since departure (whichever period of time is shorter), the occurrence of death or ill person amongst passengers or crew (including those who have disembarked or have been removed). The master of a vessel must report such occurrences immediately by radio to the quarantine station at or nearest the port at which the vessel will arrive. In addition, the master of a vessel carrying 13 or more passengers must report by radio 24 hours before arrival the number of cases (including nil) of diarrhoea in passengers and crew recorded in the ship's medical log during the current voyage. All cases that occur after the 24 hour report must also be reported not less than four hours before arrival.

2   Any death or illness occurring during a vessel's stay in a US port must be reported immediately to the nearest quarantine station.

Specific public health laws, regulations, policies and procedures may be obtained by contacting US Quarantine Stations, US Consulates or the Chief Program Operations, Division of Quarantine, Centers for Disease Control, Atlanta GA 30333.

3   A special signal code has been adopted internationally for the transmission of Radio Pratique messages. The code, which forms part of *The International Code of Signals,* is given in *Admiralty List of Radio Signals Volume 1(2).*

Customs. Vessels may be entered and cleared at any port of entry or customs station so described under an individual port heading. However, entry at a customs station is with prior authorisation only from the Custom Service district director.

4   Yachts of foreign countries having reciprocal agreements with the US may be granted cruising licenses, enabling them to cruise in the designated waters of the US without having to enter and clear formally at each port visited.

SIGNALS
National signals

Naval vessels
1.54

1   Certain types of US Navy vessels that cannot comply fully with the requirements as to the number and positioning of navigation lights, will comply as closely as possible in accordance with Rule 1(e) of *International Regulations for Preventing Collisions at Sea 1972*. They may also exhibit other lights such as coloured recognition lights, special coloured flashing lights, or landing lights for aircraft or helicopters (details are given in US Notices to Mariners annually). When darkened during naval manoeuvres, navigation lights will be temporarily exhibited if possible on the approach of other shipping.

2   US helicopters engaged in mine-sweeping operations exhibit a red or amber rotating beacon; the amber mode is used during towing operations.

Submarine Emergency Identification Signals and Hazard to Submarines.
1.55

1   1. US Navy submarines are equipped with signal ejectors which may be used to launch identification signals, including emergency signals. Two general types of signals may be used: smoke floats and flares or stars. A combination signal which contains both smoke and flare of the same colour may also be used. The smoke floats, which burn on the surface, produce a dense, coloured smoke for a period of fifteen to forty five seconds. The flares or stars are propelled to a height of 300 to 400 ft from which they descend by small parachute. The flares or stars burn for about 25 seconds. The colour of the smoke or flare/star has the following meaning:

2   (a) **Green or black.** Used under training exercise conditions only to indicate that a torpedo has been fired or that the firing of a torpedo has been simulated.

(b) **Yellow.** Indicates that submarine is about to come to periscope depth from below periscope depth. Surface craft terminate anti-submarine counter attack and clear vicinity of submarine. Do not stop propellers.

3   (c) **Red.** Indicates an emergency condition within the submarine and that it will surface immediately, if possible. Surface ships clear the area and stand by to give assistance after the submarine has surfaced. In case of repeated red signals, or if the submarine fails to surface within a reasonable time, she may be assumed to be disabled. Buoy the location, look for submarine buoy and attempt to establish sonar communications. Advise US Naval Authorities immediately.

(d) **White.** Two white flares/smoke in succession indicates that the submarine is about to surface, usually from periscope depth (non-emergency surfacing procedure). Surface craft should clear the vicinity of the submarine.

⁴ 2. **Submarine Marker Buoy** consists of a cylindrically shaped object about 3 feet by 6 feet with connecting structure and is painted international orange. The buoy is a messenger buoy with a wire cable to the submarine; this cable acts as a downhaul line for a rescue chamber. The buoy may be accompanied by an oil slick release to attract attention. A submarine on the bottom in distress and unable to surface will, if possible, release this buoy. If an object of this description is sighted, it should be investigated and US Naval Authorities advised immediately.

⁵ 3. Transmission of the International Distress Signal (SOS) will be made on the submarine's sonar gear independently or in conjunction with the red emergency signal as conditions permit.

⁶ 4. Submarines may employ any or all of the following additional means to attract attention and indicate their position while submerged:
 (a) Release of dye marker.
 (b) Release of air bubble.
 (c) Ejection of oil.
 (d) Pounding on the hull.

⁷ 5. US destroyer-type vessels in international waters engaged in naval manoeuvres will, on occasion, stream a towed underwater object at various speeds. All nations operating submarines are advised that this underwater object in the streamed condition constitutes a possible hazard to submerged submarines.

Survey vessels and buoy tenders
1.56

₁ National Oceanic and Atmospheric Administration (NOAA) vessels engaged in survey operations which limit their ability to manoeuvre, and US Coast Guard vessels handling or servicing aids to navigation, each exhibit the lights and shapes required by Rule 27 of *International Regulations for Preventing Collision at Sea 1972*.

₂ Wire drags, used by the National Ocean Survey in sweeping for dangers to navigation, may be crossed by vessels without danger of fouling at any point along their lengths, except between the towing launches and the large buoys near them. Vessels passing over the drag, when it is in motion, are advised to cross it at right angles, as a diagonal course may cause the propeller to foul the supporting buoys and wires.

₃ No attempt should be made to pass between the wire drag launches while the wire is being streamed or taken in, unless it would endanger a vessel to do otherwise. In streaming or taking up the wire drag, the tension on the bottom wire is released and the floats at each 30 m (100 ft) section may cause the wire to be held near the surface. At the same time, the launches are usually heading either directly towards or away from each other and the operation of taking up or streaming may be clearly seen.

DISTRESS AND RESCUE

General information

Radio monitoring
1.57

₁ For general information concerning distress and rescue, including helicopter assistance, see *Admiralty List of Radio Signals Volume 5* and *The Mariner's Handbook*.

Global Maritime Distress and Safety System
1.58

₁ The GMDSS enables SAR authorities on shore, in addition to shipping in the immediate vicinity of a vessel in distress, to be rapidly alerted to an incident so that assistance can be provided with the minimum of delay.

The sea area covered by this volume lies within the Boston RCC.

See *Admiralty List of Radio Signals Volume 5* for details.

Ship reporting system

Automated Mutual Assistance Vessel Rescue System
1.59

₁ The AMVER system, maintained and administered by the US Coast Guard with the co-operation of coast radio stations of many nations, is a global ship reporting system for SAR which provides important aid to the development and co-ordination of SAR efforts in the offshore areas of the world.

₂ Vessels of all nations on the high seas are encouraged to voluntarily send movement reports and periodic position reports to the AMVER Centre located in Martinsburg, West Virginia through selected radio stations and coast earth stations. US Maritime Administration regulations require certain US flag vessels and foreign flag "War Risk" vessels to report and regularly update their voyages to the AMVER Centre.

See *Admiralty List of Radio Signals Volume 6(5))* for details.

Rescue services

United States Coast Guard
1.60

₁ The US Coast Guard conducts and/or co-ordinates SAR operations for surface vessels and aircraft that are in distress or overdue. Coast Guard Stations have SAR capabilities and may provide lookout, communication, and/or patrol functions for vessels in distress. The National VHF-FM Distress System provides continuous coastal radio coverage out to 20 miles.

Coast Guard District. The area covered by this volume lies within the First Coast Guard District, the office of which is situated in Boston.

Coast Guard Stations
1.61

₁ The following Coast Guard stations are situated in the area covered by this volume:
 Jonesport (44°31'·68N 67°36'·96W) (2.12).
 Southwest Harbor (44°16'·50N 68°18'·72W) (2.47).
 Rockland (44°06'·28N 69°06'·21W) (2.152).
 Boothbay Harbor (43°50'·60N 69°38'·53W) (3.76).
 South Portland (43°38'·73N 70°14'·83W) (3.178).
 Portsmouth (43°04'·28N 70°42'·55W) (3.219).

₂ Merrimack River (42°48'·69N 70°51'·88W) (3.258).
 Gloucester (42°36'·60N 70°39'·59W) (4.14).
 Cape Cod Coast Guard Air Station (41°37'·50N 70°31'·50W)
 Chatham (41°40'·27N 69°57'·07W) (4.61).
 Boston (42°22'·10N 71°03'·10W) (4.77).

₃ Point Allerton (42°18'·16N 70°54'·82W) (4.78).
 Scituate (42°11'·70N 70°43'·43W) (4.126).
 Provincetown (42°02'·70N 70°11'·50W) (4.142).
 Brant Point (41°17'·40N 70°05'·46W) (5.65).
 Woods Hole (41°31'·24N 70°40'·04W) (5.97).

Menemsha (41°21′·02N 70°45′·85W) (5.107).
Cape Cod Canal (41°46′·39N 70°30′·01W) (5.133).
Castle Hill (41°27′·69N 71°21′·47W) (5.203).
Point Judith (41°21′·69N 71°28′·85W) (5.186).
Montauk Point (41°04′·37N 71°56′·08W) (6.9).
Fishers Island (41°15′·41N 72°01′·88W) (6.31).
Eatons Neck (40°57′·26N 73°23′·87W) (6.94).
New London (41°20′·70N 72°05′·68W) (6.97).
New Haven (41°16′·33N 72°54′·25W) (6.118).
Kings Point (40°48′·81N 73°45′·87W) (6.250).

Shinnecock (40°51′·01N 72°30′·23W) (7.23).
Moriches (40°47′·26N 72°44′·98W) (7.24).
Fire Island (40°37′·52N 73°15′·52W) (7.25).
Jones Beach (40°35′·44N 73°33′·38W) (7.26).
Rockaway (40°35′·46N 73°52′·84W) (7.22).
New York (40°36′·73N 74°03′·66W) (7.39).
Bayonne (40°40′·32N 74°05′·38W) (7.115)
Sandy Hook (40°28′·04N 74°00′·61W) (7.58).
Manasquan Inlet (40°06′·16N 74°02′·24W) (7.36).
Shark River (40°11′·29N 74°00′·83W) (7.38).
Barnegat (39°45′·63N 74°06′·53W) (7.35).

CHAPTER 1

COUNTRIES

UNITED STATES OF AMERICA

General description
1.62

1 The United States of America, including Alaska and Hawaii, comprises fifty states and the Federal District of Columbia, and extends across the North American Continent from the Atlantic to the Pacific Ocean for a distance of about 4800 km. Except for Alaska and Hawaii, they are bounded on the N by the Dominion of Canada, and on the S by Gulf of Mexico and the Republic of Mexico. The area of the fifty states and the Federal District cover an area of about 9·2 million sq km.

2 Washington is the capital city, in the Federal District of Columbia; in 2012 the estimated population of the city was 603 860.

States covered in this volume are Maine, New Hampshire, Massachusetts, Rhode Island, Connecticut, New York and New Jersey.

National limits
1.63

1 The US claims a limit of 12 miles for territorial waters and a 200-mile EEZ. See *Annual Summary of Admiralty Notices to Mariners* and *The Mariner's Handbook*.

History
1.64

1 The area which is now the United States was first inhabited by nomadic hunters who it is thought arrived from Asia *c.*30 000 BC. The first (failed) European colony was founded by Sir Walter Raleigh in 1585. By 1733 there were 13 British Colonies, which were made up, largely of religious non–conformists who had left Britain to escape persecution; the French and Spanish had also founded colonies.

2 The War of Independence broke out in 1775 largely because of the colonists' objection to being taxed by, but having no representation in, the British Parliament. The forces of the British government were defeated with French, Spanish and Dutch assistance. The Declaration of Independence which inaugurated the United States of America was signed on 4 July 1776; Britain recognised American sovereignty in 1783. The first federal constitution was drawn up in 1787; ten amendments, termed the Bill of Rights, were added in 1791. The 13 original states of the Union ratified the constitution between 1787 and 1790. Vermont, Kentucky and Tennessee were admitted in the 1790s but most of the states acceded in the nineteenth century as the opening up of the centre and the west led to the creation of new states and European or neighbouring countries ceded or sold their territories to the USA.

3 The Civil War was fought over the issue of slavery, which was integral to the economy of the southern states but was opposed by the northern states. The northern states defeated the confederacy of southern states (South Carolina, Georgia, Alabama, Florida, Mississippi, Louisiana).

The US emerged as a world economic and military superpower in the twentieth century and played a decisive role in the two world wars. Its economic and military (including nuclear) supremacy gave the US a key role in shaping the post–war world.

Government
1.65

1 The constitution is that of a Federal Republic consisting of fifty states and the Federal District of Columbia and of the outside territories. Of the present fifty states, thirteen are original states, seven were admitted without previous organisation as territories, and thirty were admitted as organised territories.

2 By the constitution of 1787, and as subsequently amended, the government of the US is entrusted to three separate authorities; the executive, the legislature, and the judiciary. The President is elected every four years; his tenure is limited to two terms.

Each state manages its own affairs and has a Governor, Senate and House of Representatives, or institutions of corresponding authority.

Population
1.66

1 In 2012 the total population was estimated to be 313 780 673.

Language
1.67

1 The language spoken is English but there is a significant minority who speak Spanish.

Maine

General description
1.68

1 **Area.** The area of Maine, which is bounded on the W, N and E by Canada, is 30 865 sq miles.

Population. In 2012 the estimated population of Maine was 1 334 843.

State capital. Augusta.

History
1.69

1 After several unsuccessful attempts by both the British and the French, a permanent settlement was established by the Plymouth Company in 1623, in the area that became the State of Maine. From 1652 to 1820 this area was part of Massachusetts and was admitted into the Union as a separate state on 15 March 1820.

Natural resources and industry
1.70

1 **Natural resources** consist of minerals, agriculture, forestry and fisheries.

Industry. Paper manufacture, agriculture and tourism are important industries.

New Hampshire

General description
1.71

1 **Area.** The area of New Hampshire is 8993 sq miles. The state has only 15 miles of coastline.

Population. In 2012 the estimated population of New Hampshire was 1 330 344.

State capital. Concord.

History
1.72

1 New Hampshire was first settled in 1623 and was one of the 13 original states of the Union.

Natural resources and industry
1.73

1 **Natural resources** consist of agriculture and forestry.

Industry. Electronic goods, machinery and metal products.

Massachusetts

General description
1.74

1 **Area.** The area of Massachusetts is 7838 sq miles.
Population. In 2012 the estimated population of Massachusetts was 6 571 760.
State capital. Boston.

History
1.75

1 The first permanent settlement within the borders of the present state was made at Plymouth in 1620 and in 1628 a further settlement was made at Salem. In 1630 Boston was settled. During the American War of Independence Massachusetts took a leading part in the war and in February 1788 became the sixth state to ratify the US constitution.

Natural resources
1.76

1 Natural resources consist of minerals, agriculture, forestry and fisheries.

Rhode Island

General description
1.77

1 **Area.** The area of Rhode Island is 1054 sq miles. It is the smallest state in the Union.
Population. In 2012 the estimated population of Rhode Island was 1 051 669.
State capital. Providence.

History
1.78

1 Rhode Island was first settled in 1636 by colonists from Massachusetts who had been driven out by religious disputes. A policy of religious tolerance was followed and by 1663 the area was recognised as a separate colony. In 1790 the state accepted the federal constitution and entered the Union as the last of the 13 original states.

Industry
1.79

1 Manufacturing is the main economic activity.

Connecticut

General description
1.80

1 **Area.** The area of Connecticut is 4844 sq miles.
Population. In 2012 the estimated population of Connecticut was 3 595 417.
State capital. Hartford.

History
1.81

1 Connecticut was first settled in 1634 and has been an organised Commonwealth since 1637. It was one of the original 13 states to ratify the US constitution.

Industry
1.82

1 Manufacturing is the main economic activity.

New York State

General description
1.83

1 **Area.** The area of New York State is 47 224 sq miles.
Population. In 2012 the estimated population of New York State was 19 417 081. It is the third most populous state in the Union.
State capital. Albany.

History
1.84

1 In 1603 the N part of what is now New York State was explored by Samuel de Champlain and a party of French fur traders and in 1609 Henry Hudson, an Englishman in the service of the Dutch, sailed up the river that bears his name as far as the area of present day Albany.

From 1609 to 1664 the region was claimed by the Dutch and the Dutch West India Company made its first permanent settlement in 1624 at what is now the site of New York. In 1664 the area was taken over by the British.

2 In July 1788 New York ratified the constitution of the United States and became one of the 13 original states of the Union.

Natural resources and industry
1.85

1 **Natural resources** consist of minerals and agriculture.
Industry. Service industries, clothing, machinery and metal products, clothing and printing and publishing.

New Jersey

General description
1.86

1 **Area.** The area of New Jersey is 7417 sq miles.
Population. In 2012 the estimated population of New Jersey was 8 850 190.
State capital. Trenton.

History
1.87

1 New Jersey was first settled in the early 1600s and was one of the original 13 states to ratify the US constitution.

Industry
1.88

1 Manufacturing is the most important economic activity.

CHAPTER 1

NATURAL CONDITIONS

MARITIME TOPOGRAPHY

General remarks
1.89

1   The coast of the United States covered by this volume was largely shaped by the pressure of ice during the glacial period and its subsequent retreat; the offshore islands from New York to Cape Cod are disconnected fragments of the coastal plain, the intervening strata having sunk under pressure.

Seabed
1.90

1   The continental shelf bordering this part of the coast extends between 70 and 110 miles offshore to the vicinity of the 180 m (100 fm) depth contour and then drops steeply at a gradient of about 1:7 and then more moderately at about 1:15 to North American Basin which stretches E to Mid Atlantic Ridge. A ridge of seamounts, rising to a least depth of 1400 m (770 fm) extends SE from Georges Bank for nearly 600 miles.

2   The NW part of North American Basin is comprised of mud and sand; on the continental shelf NE of Cape Cod, the bottom is mud, sand and gravel, while SW of that peninsula the bottom is mainly sand.

The continental slope and continental shelf as defined by the 180 m (100 fm) depth contour, is penetrated by deeper water extending into Gulf of Maine to within 20 miles of the shore in places. Farther SW the shelf is indented by numerous submarine canyons. See 5.5 and 7.8.

Seismic and volcanic activity
1.91

1   Earthquakes of shallow depth have been felt on the continental shelf NE of Cape Cod and in the vicinity of Long Island.

There are no known active volcanoes in the area covered by this volume.

CURRENTS, TIDAL STREAMS AND FLOW

General information

General description
1.92

1   The currents in the area covered by this volume are generally neither strong nor constant, and are mainly the result of strong or persistent winds and the SW extension of the Labrador Current. The mean rate of the currents over the whole of the area is between ½ and ¾ kn, with less than 15% of observations reporting 1 kn and only a very few exceeding 2 kn.

Current Diagrams
1.93

1   In the current diagram (1.93), arrows indicate predominant direction, average rate and constancy, the definitions of which will be found in the glossary of *The Mariner's Handbook* under current diagrams.

Labrador Current
1.94

1   The predominant current over the greater part of the area is a SW extension of the Labrador Current which rounds Newfoundland and sets close inshore and parallel to the coasts of Nova Scotia and the NE States of the United States. Within Gulf of Maine there is a weak anti-clockwise set to the current.

In the SE of the area, branches of the Labrador Current successively leave the SE flank of the main flow and set S and then SE to converge, outside the area of this volume, with the NW flank of the Gulf Stream.

Gulf Stream
1.95

1   On some occasions the Labrador Current to the SE of about 40°N 72°W is displaced by branches or eddies from the Gulf Stream. Due to the marked sea temperature gradients that result, currents of 1 to 2 kn setting between NE and SE may be experienced, and may persist for several weeks.

Effects of strong winds
1.96

1   After prolonged periods of strong winds from a constant direction, a wind drift current may be generated, the rate of which varies according to the wind speed and direction. These wind drift currents may reduce or enhance the main underlying current. For further information on how currents are influenced by wind, tropical storms, pressure gradient and topography, see *The Mariner's Handbook*.

2   Rates of 2 kn or over are possible on the relatively infrequent occasions when a hurricane or extra-tropical storm affects the area, and particularly when such a storm nears the coast.

SEA LEVEL AND TIDES

Sea level
1.97

1   Tidal, meteorological and seasonal factors acting individually or in combination, may give rise to abnormally high or low water levels. See *The Mariner's Handbook* for further details.

Tidal ranges
1.98

1   In the N half of the area covered by this volume the spring range is between 3·4 and 4·5 m. This decreases to about 1·5 m in the S half of the area.

SEA AND SWELL

General remarks
1.99

1   For general information on sea and swell see *The Mariner's Handbook*.

Sea conditions
1.100

1   Sea waves are generated locally by the wind and can be very variable in direction, especially when NE-moving mobile depressions move across the area.

In January, the frequency of reported combined sea and swell waves of 3·5 m and over is around 5 to 10% of occasions near the coast, but steadily increases to about 20% in the extreme SE of the area. By July, combined sea and swell heights of 3·5 m and over are uncommon, except when a tropical storm moves towards the area from the S.

Swell conditions
1.101

1   Diagrams 1.101.1 to 1.101.4 give swell roses for February, May, August and November. The roses show the percentage of observations recording swell from a number of directions and for various ranges of wave height.

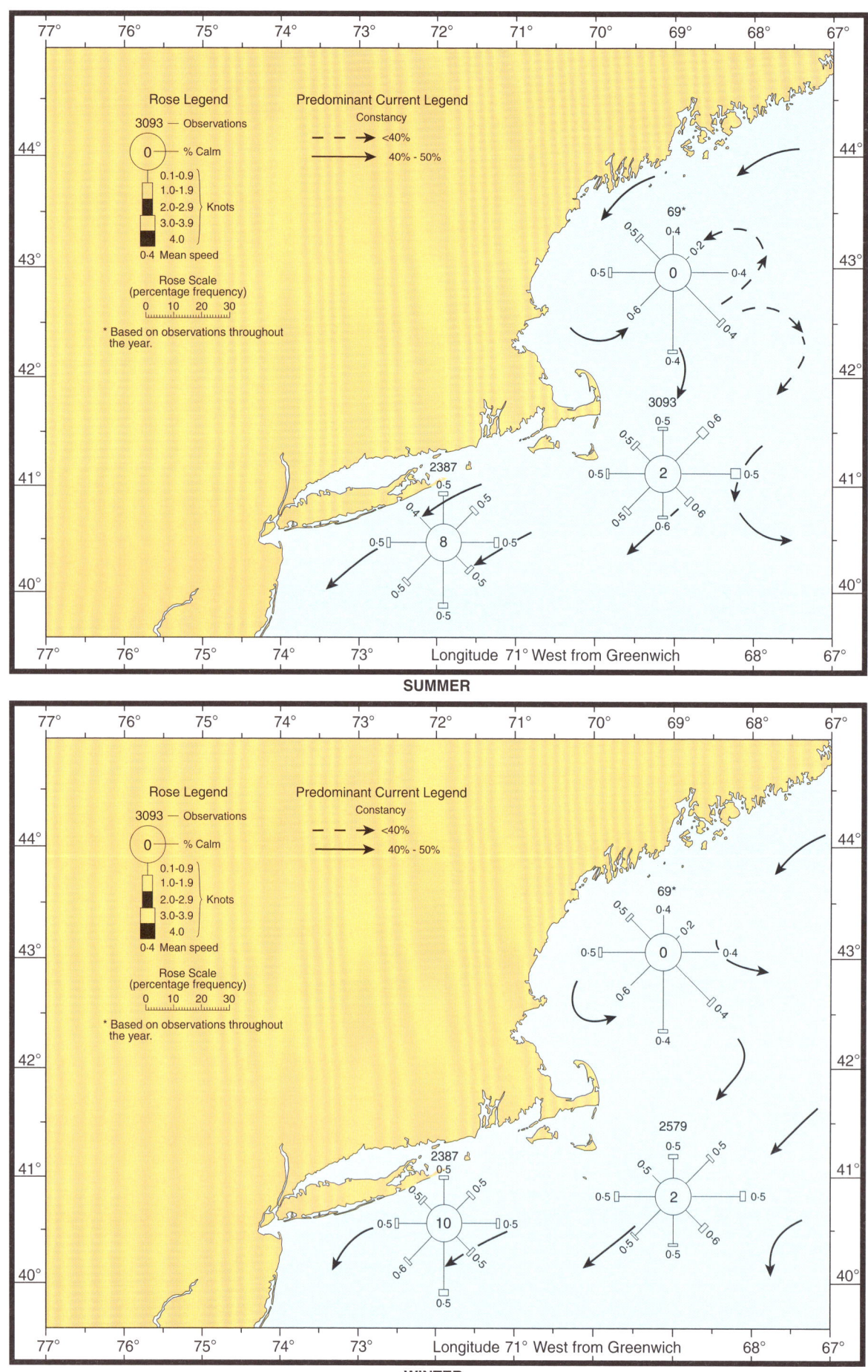

Predominant currents - direction, constancy and variability (1.93)

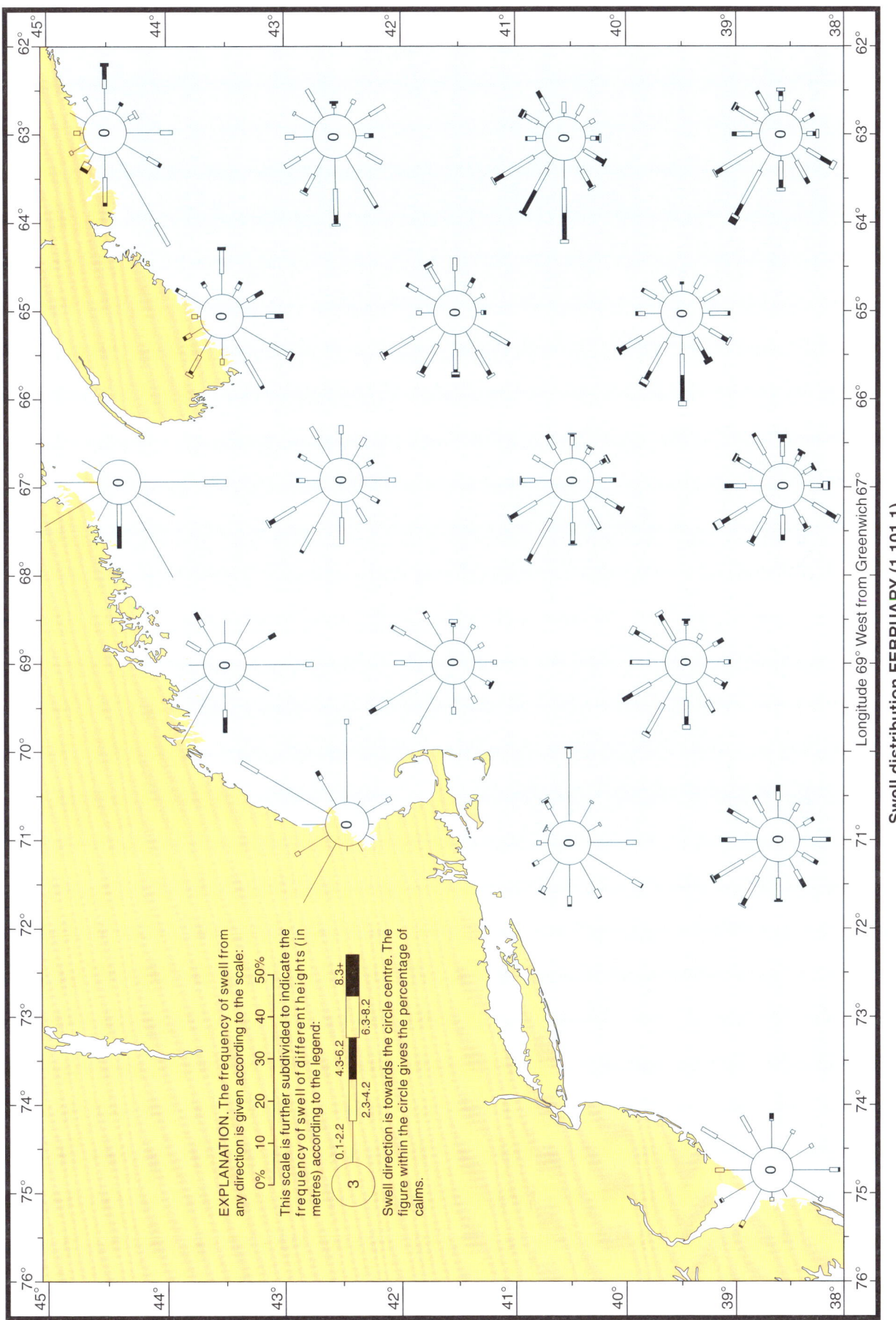

Swell distribution FEBRUARY (1.101.1)

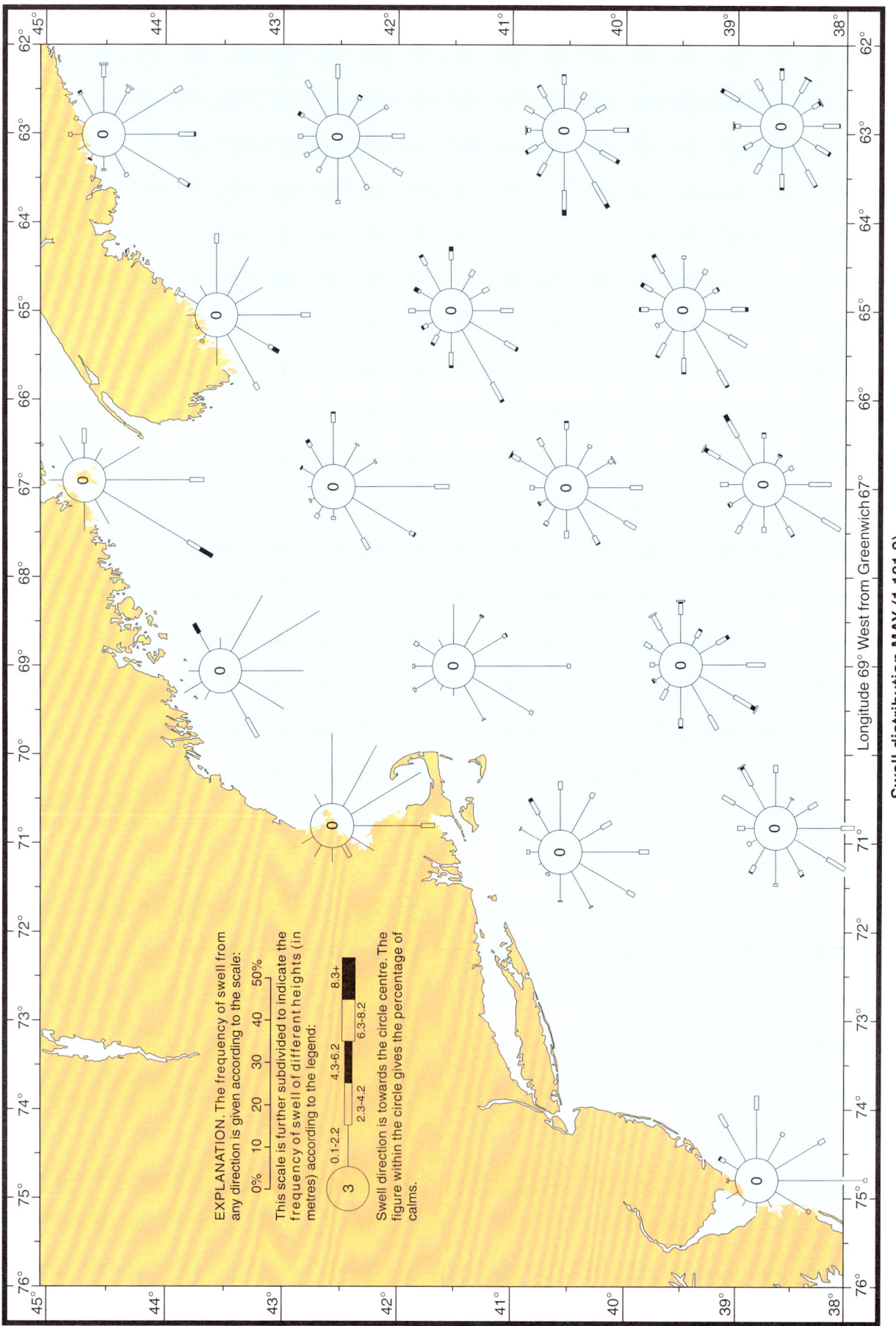
Swell distribution MAY (1.101.2)

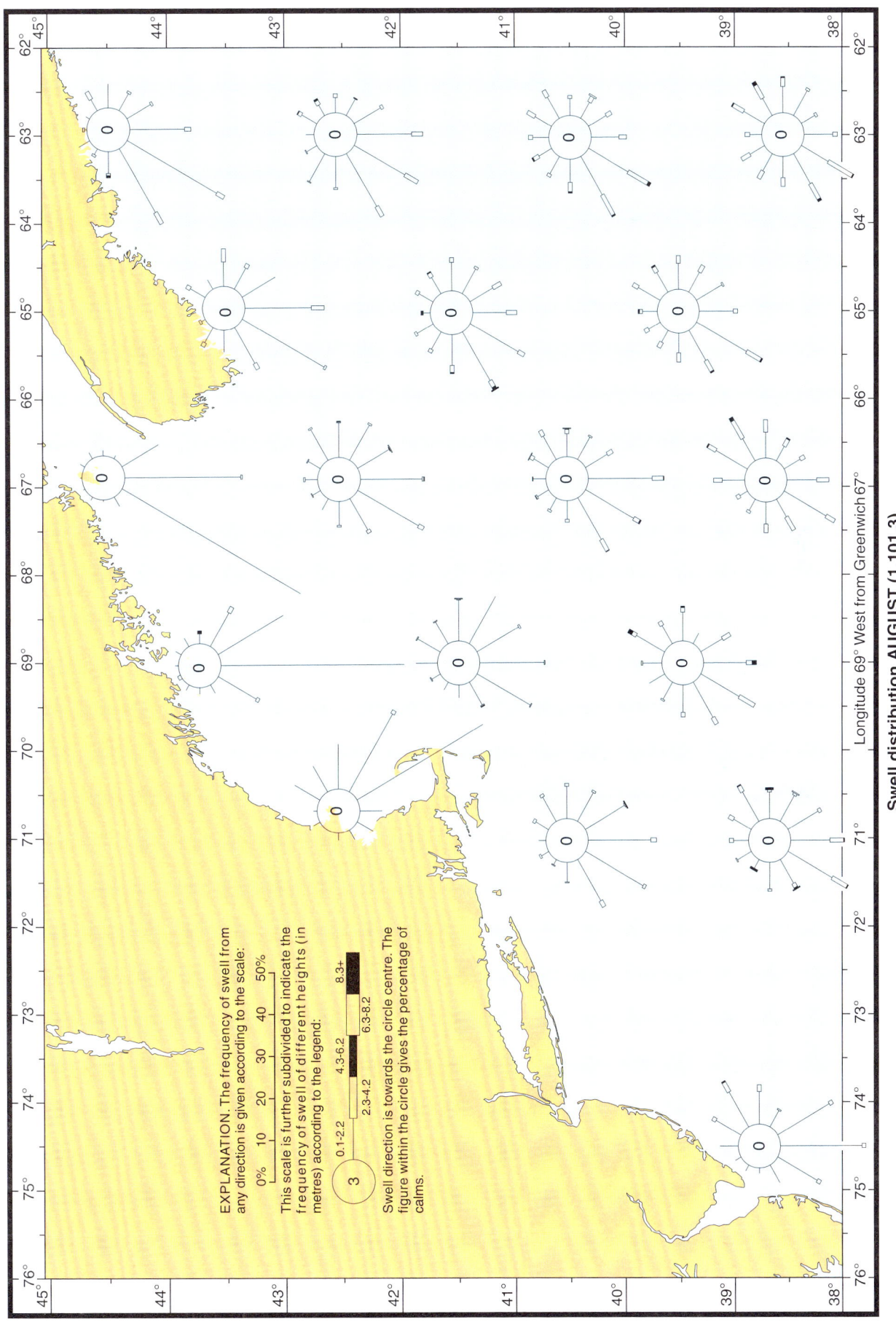

Swell distribution AUGUST (1.101.3)

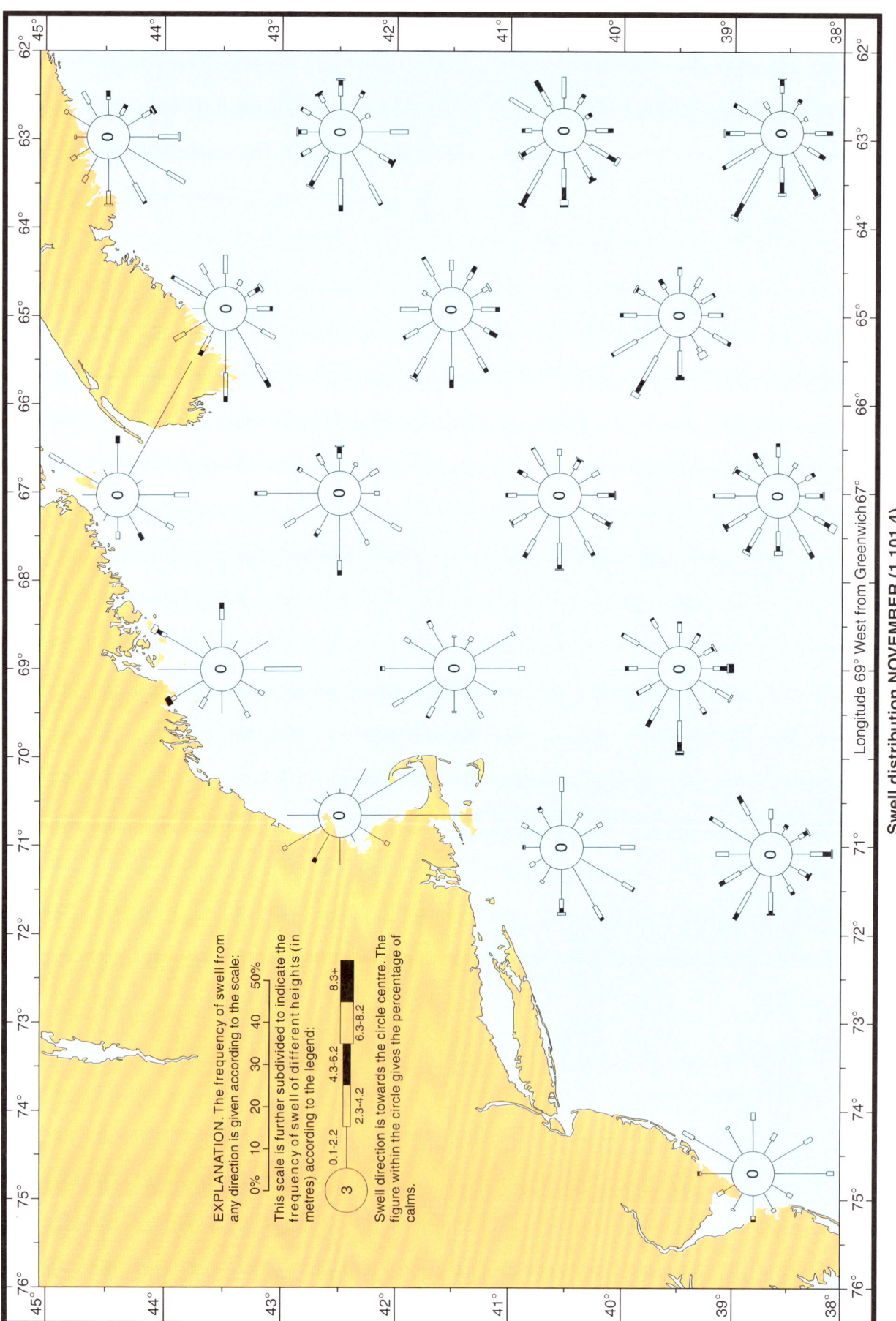

In winter, the swell is predominantly from the NW. Swell heights of 4 m and over are reported on less than 5% of occasions near the coast, but steadily increase to around 14% in the extreme SE of the area. By July, swell heights of 4 m and over are relatively rare, and the swell direction is mainly from between SSE and SW.

Sea and swell waves associated with tropical storms
1.102

1   Mountainous and confused seas are raised by the violent winds associated with tropical storms and hurricanes. Near the centre of a storm, groups of large waves moving in different directions, create very irregular wave heights and can combine together to give exceptionally high waves.

2   Waves travel radially outwards from the storm centre as swell waves, with the highest swell moving ahead of the storm and roughly in the same direction as the storm. High tides may occur as a storm approaches a coastline, caused initially by the addition of the heavy swell and subsequently by the very high seas. These tides may cause severe flooding in low-lying areas.

3   The approach of a tropical storm is often indicated by long period swells whose height increases as the storm gets closer.

Tsunamis
1.103

1   Tsunamis, or seismic waves, have been reported in the coastal region of Penobscot Bay, between Portland and Cape Ann and off Narragansett Bay.

SEA WATER CHARACTERISTICS

Salinity
1.104

1   For an explanation of salinity as applied to sea water, see *The Mariner's Handbook*.

Salinity values for the area covered by this volume vary across the area with isohalines running parallel to the coast due to the Labrador Current setting to the SW and the Gulf Stream setting to the NE. In winter values vary from 32·00 along the coast to 35·00 at the SE limit of the area covered. In summer the values fall to 31·00 along the coast to 34·50 at the SE limit of the area.

Density
1.105

1   For an explanation of density as applied to sea water, see *The Mariner's Handbook*.

Density values for the area covered by this volume vary across the area with isopycnics generally running parallel to the coast due to the Labrador Current setting SW and the Gulf Stream setting NE. However, the isopycnics turn towards the coast in the Gulf of Maine and Bay of Fundy areas. In winter values vary from 1·02550 gm/cm^3 along the coast and in the Bay of Fundy, to 1·02675 gm/cm^3 at the SE limit of the area covered by this volume. In summer the values fall to between 1·02350 gm/cm^3 and 1·02375 gm/cm^3 at the SE limit of the area.

Sea surface temperature
1.106

1   The mean sea surface temperatures for February, May, August and November are shown in diagrams 1.106.1 to 1.106.4. Sea surface temperatures are generally at their lowest in late January and February and highest in August. The steep temperature gradient in the extreme SE of the area is the result of the proximity of the cold Labrador Current setting towards the SW and the warm Gulf Stream setting towards the ENE.

2   In winter mean sea surface temperatures decrease from 10°C in the extreme SE of the area to below 4°C in coastal waters, and in severe winters to below freezing, especially in sheltered inlets and harbours in the N. By August, the mean sea surface temperatures have risen to around 10°C in the N and 22°C in the S.

Variability
1.107

1   Mean sea surface temperatures in coastal waters can be variable in both summer and winter depending on the wind direction. Due to the steep temperature gradient in the SE of the area, day-to-day variability at any one position can be considerable. In the SE of the area, occasional Gulf Stream meanders may result in a vessel passing through alternating areas of warm and cold water that may vary by as much as 4° to 6°C above or below the mean.

ICE CONDITIONS
General information
Sea ice
1.108

1   A complete list of ice terms and their definitions, as agreed by the WMO in 1970, together with photographs of typical ice formations, is given in *The Mariner's Handbook*.

The area in this volume lies outside the main sea ice and iceberg region of the NW Atlantic Ocean, which extends S from Baffin Island to S of Nova Scotia. The extreme limits of this ice and the maximum extent of icebergs are shown, by months, in the *Nova Scotia and Bay of Fundy Pilot*. Drift ice, which in late winter and spring is liable to spread S off Newfoundland and also SW off Nova Scotia, has not been known to extend W of 67°W or S of 42°N.

Icebergs
1.109

1   Except for very isolated cases, icebergs are not encountered W of 67°W. However, at extremely rare intervals, icebergs or their remnants have been reported within the area of this volume. Three such sightings are known to have occurred since 1925.

Inshore ice
1.110

1   The severity of the winters along the coasts covered in this volume varies greatly in different years. In the average winter ice forms in many rivers, estuaries, harbours, bays and other shallow inshore localities but most of the harbours remain open. In severe winters most such locations are affected by ice and only some of the harbours and anchorages are available. An account of the ice conditions of affected areas is given in the appropriate part of the body of the book.

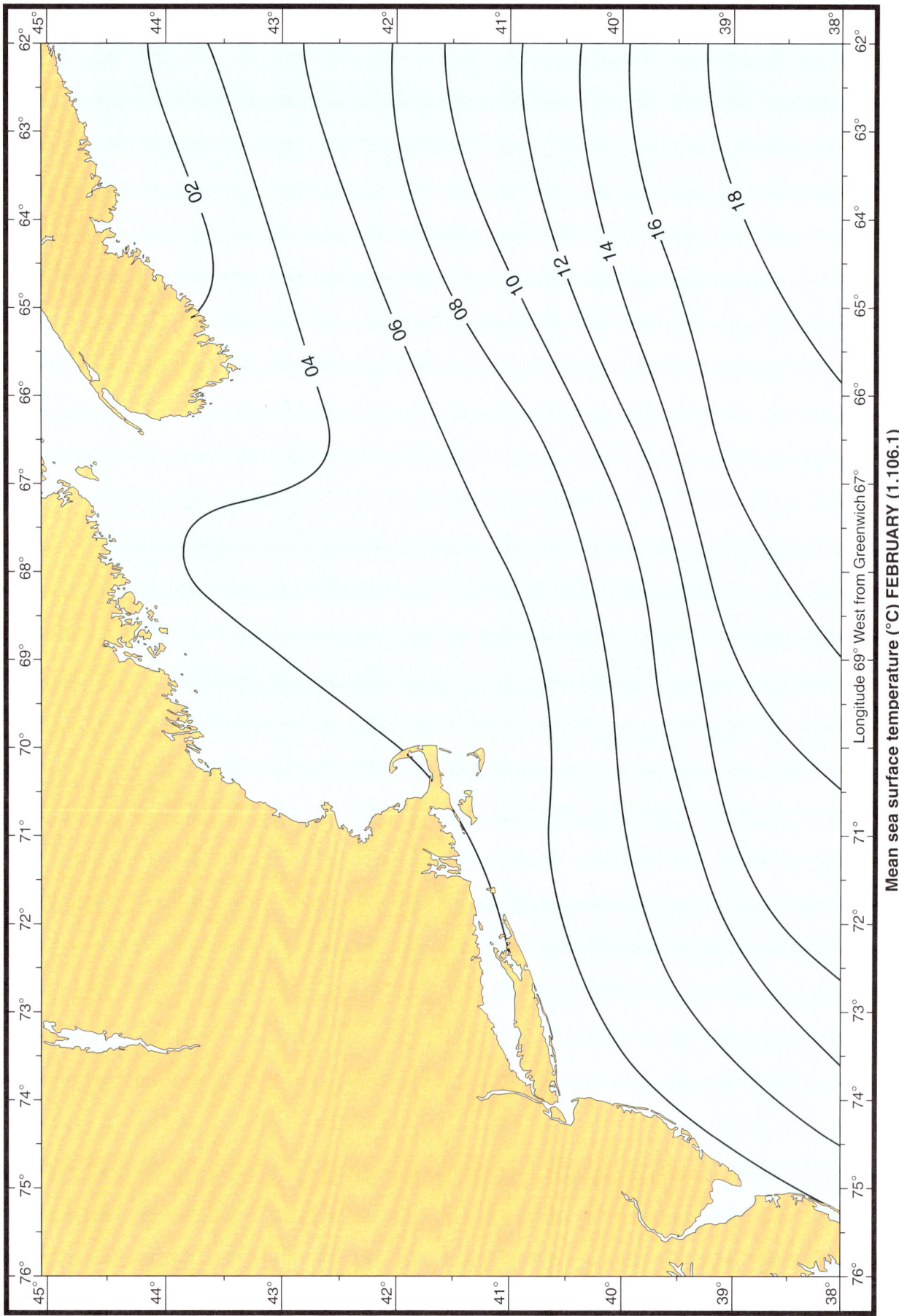

Mean sea surface temperature (°C) FEBRUARY (1.106.1)

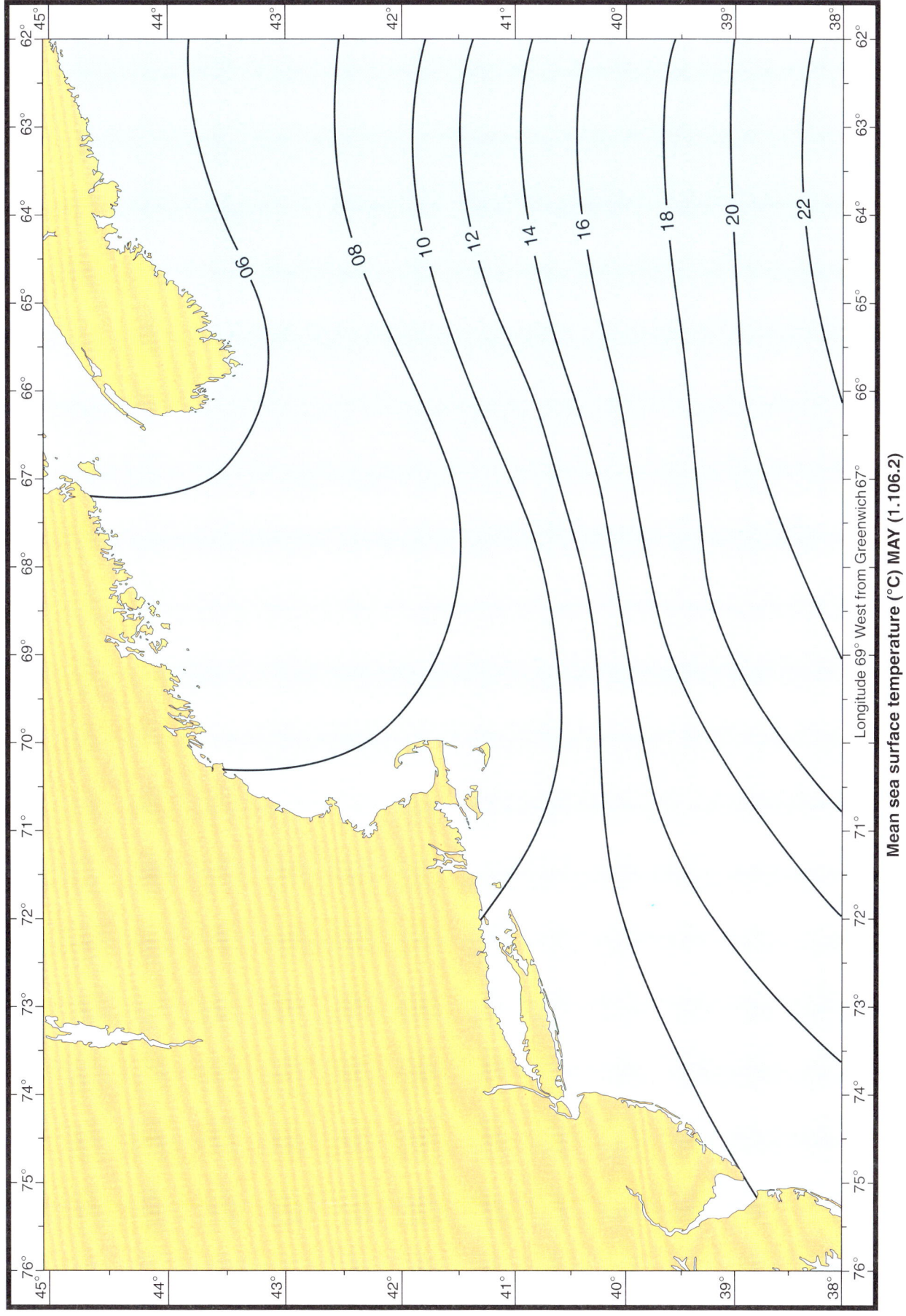

Mean sea surface temperature (°C) MAY (1.106.2)

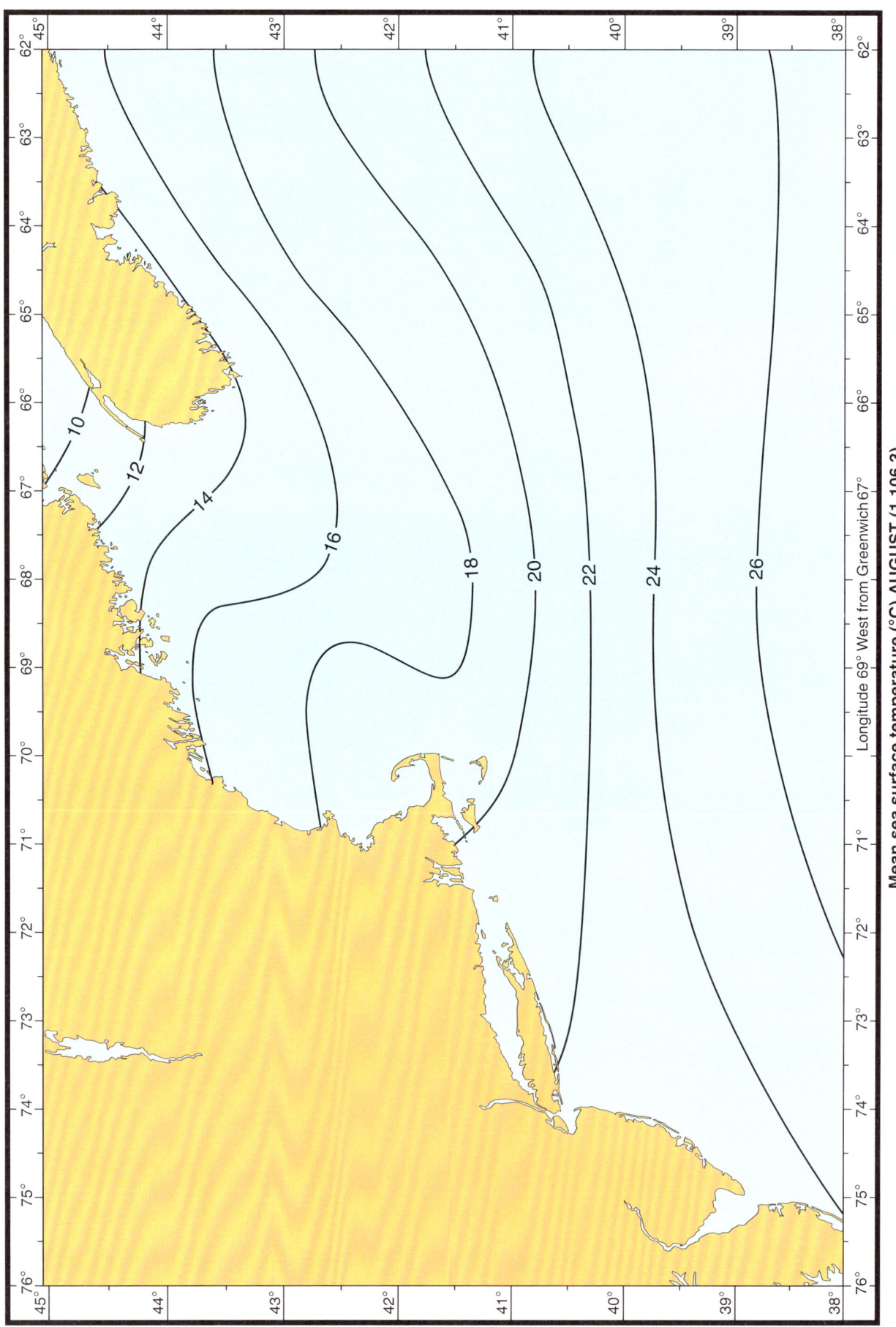

Mean sea surface temperature (°C) AUGUST (1.106.3)

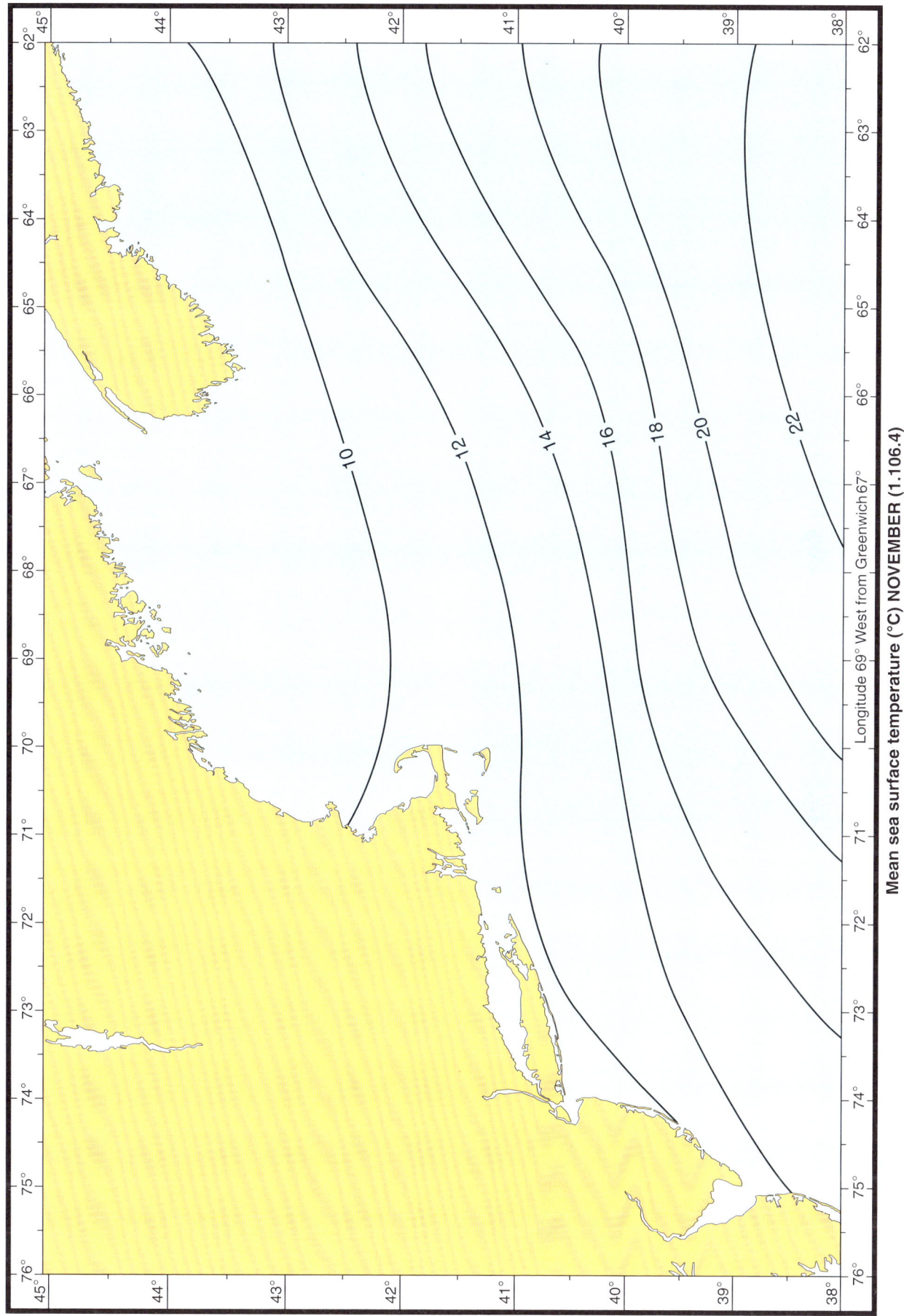

Mean sea surface temperature (°C) NOVEMBER (1.106.4)

Access to ports
1.111
1 Access to the principal ports is not seriously restricted even in severe winters, but many of the smaller, more land-locked ports are liable to be closed at times. For example, Portland Harbor generally preserves an open channel due to the constant traffic. Similarly at Boston, the greater part of the harbour is sometimes frozen during a severe winter, but shipping keeps the main channel open. As an example of a smaller port, Plymouth, in Cape Cod Bay, is usually closed to navigation during a part of each winter.

CLIMATE AND WEATHER

General information
1.112
1 The following information on climate and weather should be read in conjunction with the information contained in *The Mariner's Handbook* which explains in more detail many aspects of meteorology and climatology of importance to the mariner.

Weather reports and forecasts, that cover the area, are regularly broadcast in English; see *Admiralty List of Radio Signals Volume 3(2)* for details.

2 **Ice accumulation.** In certain weather conditions, ice accumulation on hulls and superstructures of ships can be a serious danger. This is a possible hazard, in winter, particularly in the N of the area. See *The Mariner's Handbook* for details on the causes of ice accumulation and the recommended course of action.

General conditions
1.113
1 In the region covered by this volume conditions can be very variable, especially in winter, with marked fluctuations in both temperature and visibility. Mobile depressions tend to move most frequently from SW to NE across the region and are more frequent and violent in winter than summer. These depressions generally give rise to periods of stormy wet weather followed by clear dry spells.

In winter, precipitation is plentiful and is highest in the NE of the area with much of the precipitation in coastal areas falling as snow.

2 Fog is a problem, especially in summer, when warm moist SW air is cooled by the Labrador Current. In settled conditions in autumn and winter, radiation fog often forms over the land and may drift out over coastal sea areas, but usually clears by midday. Land and sea breezes are common in summer.

During the hurricane season, June to November, an occasional tropical storm or hurricane may affect some parts of the area.

Pressure

Average distribution
1.114
1 The average pressure distribution at mean sea level for February, May, August and November is shown in diagrams 1.114.1 to 1.114.4. Seasonal variations in the average pressure distribution are only about 3 to 4 hPa. In winter, the average pressure increases from NE to SW and, in summer, increases from NW to SE.

Variability
1.115
1 It is stressed that the diagrams depict the average pressure distribution and that the actual pressure pattern can be markedly different from the mean due to the numerous NE-moving mobile depressions that frequently parallel the coast. Changes of 20 hPa in 24 hours are common when a series of deep depressions and anticyclones cross the region.

Diurnal variation
1.116
1 The diurnal variation is about 2 hPa. Maxima occur around 1000 and 2000 and minima at 0400 and 1600. This daily variation is often obscured by fast moving mobile depressions.

Anticyclones

Bermuda anticyclone
1.117
1 In summer, a ridge of high pressure normally extends NW from the Azores anticyclone to the vicinity of Bermuda as a semi-permanent feature and is often described as the Bermuda high or anticyclone. As a consequence, mobile depressions are displaced farther N. In winter, the ridge weakens and retreats E.

North American anticyclone
1.118
1 This anticyclone forms over N America in winter as the land mass cools, and, on occasions, a ridge of high pressure may extend E towards Bermuda. Whenever a ridge or high pressure cell moves towards the area covered by this volume in the late autumn or winter, winds turn to the W or NW and bring with them cold, or extremely cold, but relatively dry unstable air to the region. If a high pressure cell becomes slow moving over the area then NE-moving mobile depressions are either blocked or diverted farther N away from the region.

The anticyclone normally weakens in spring as the land warms up and the pressure falls.

Depressions

Frontal depressions
1.119
1 Depressions are most frequent and violent in winter and least frequent and intense in summer. These depressions may move into the area from the SW or develop within, or just to the E, of the area covered by this volume. Part of one of the world's densest concentration of depression tracks is to be found within the area, where the NE track parallels the NE coast of the United States between 150 and 250 miles offshore. Depressions generally move across the area, often at intervals of 2 to 3 days between November and March, and with greater speeds in winter (between 10 and 30 kn) than summer, although deep secondary depressions (see *The Mariner's Handbook* for a full description) may become slow moving within the area. As with all mobile depressions, tracks other than NE are possible.

2 In winter, depressions are most likely to bring with them gale force winds, heavy rain or snow, poor visibility and very low temperatures. Each year about 40 depressions rapidly deepen, occasionally within 24 hours, and produce waves of 7 to 15 m with hurricane force winds in exposed places. These depressions are sometimes referred to as Hatteras storms as they often develop to the S of the area between Cape Hatteras and Delaware Bay, and can extend out over most of the W North Atlantic. Hatteras storms often cause the NE winds to reach storm force or even higher in coastal waters. As the storms move rapidly NE, the winds usually back to the SW.

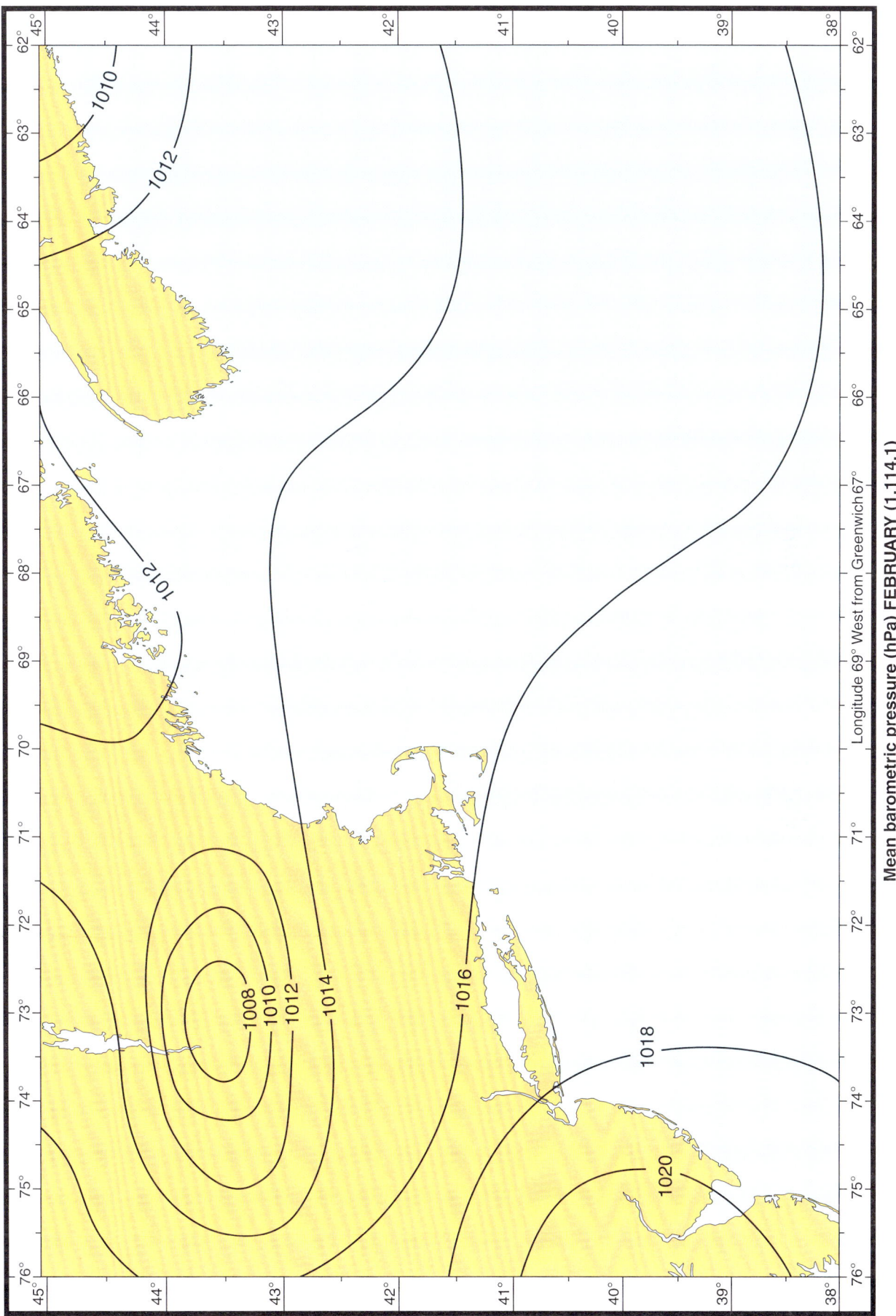

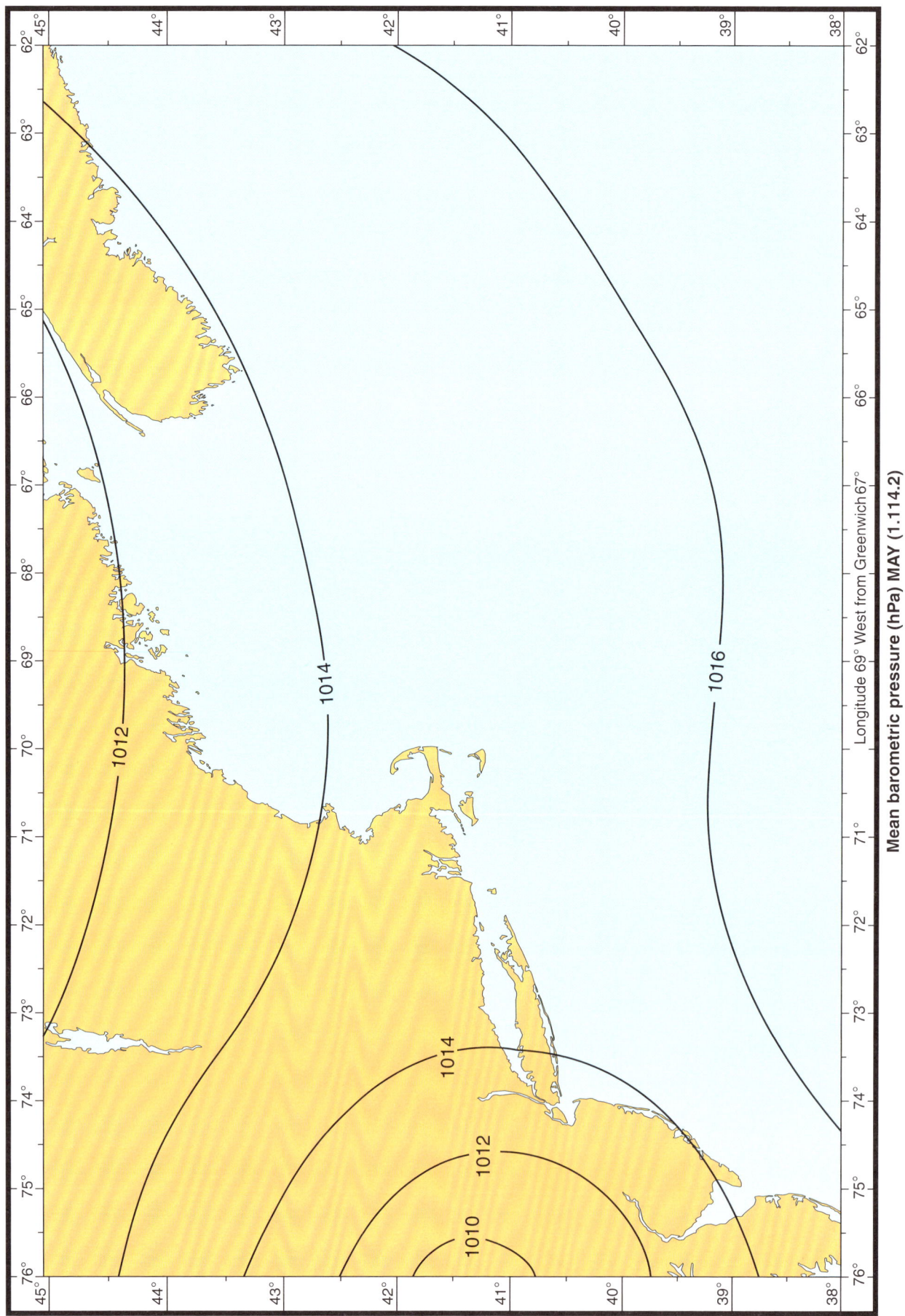

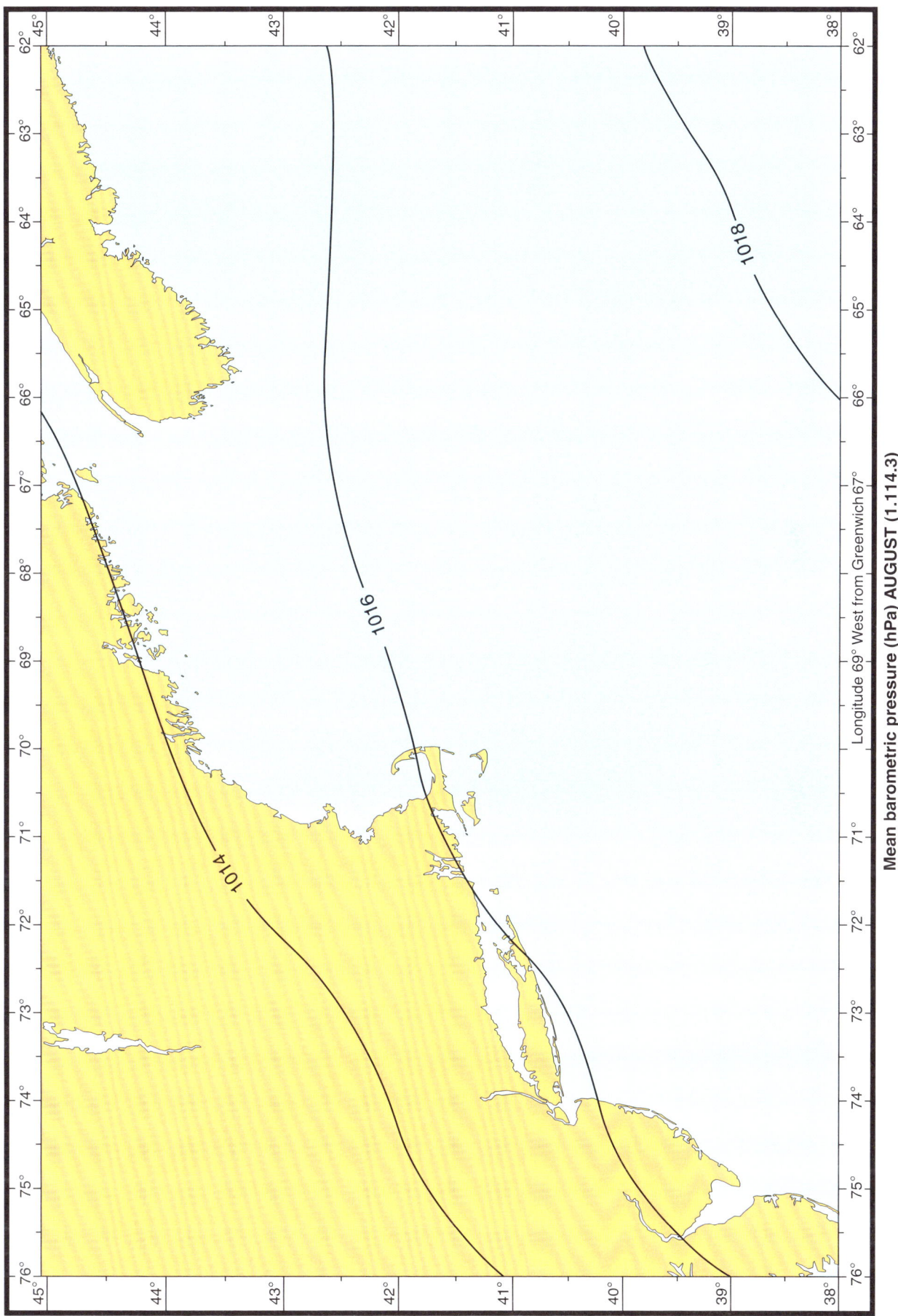

Mean barometric pressure (hPa) AUGUST (1.114.3)

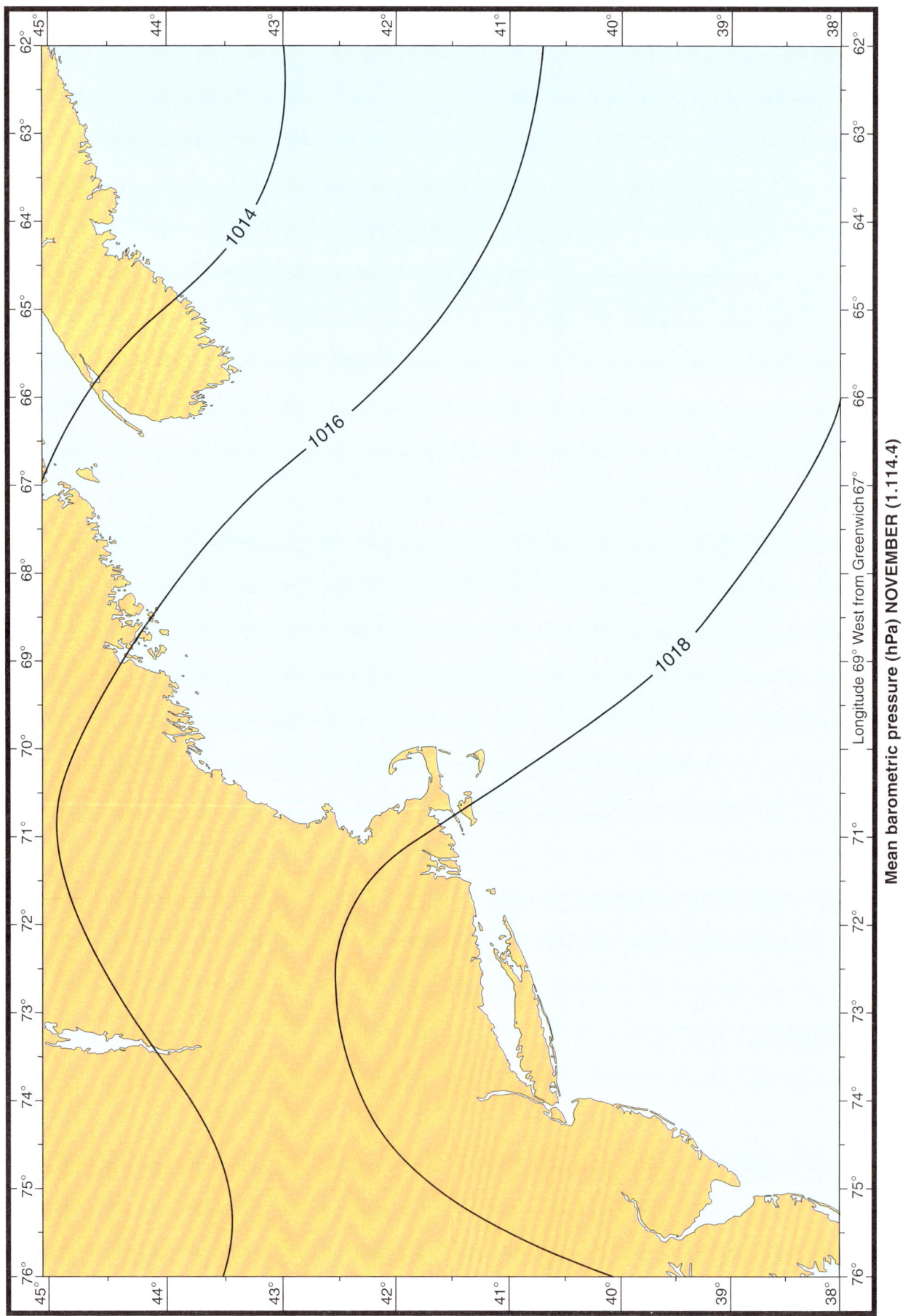

Mean barometric pressure (hPa) NOVEMBER (1.114.4)

Hurricanes and tropical storms

1.120

1   The hurricane season lasts from 1st June to 30th November although a few tropical storms have been recorded at other times throughout the year. The number of tropical storms generally reaches a peak during the period from August to early October. In an average season there are about nine or ten tropical depressions, of which five reach hurricane strength with about two affecting the United States. Tropical storms that recurve N towards the area covered by this volume generally lose much of their strength but occasionally they may retain their original intensity. One such hurricane made landfall near Atlantic City, New Jersey on 29 October 2012. With a diameter of around 1000 nm, Hurricane Sandy was the largest Atlantic hurricane on record and affected 24 states including the entire E seaboard from Florida to Maine. New Jersey and New York City experienced particularly severe damage, exacerbated by a storm surge that exceeded 4·2 m in New York.

The track of any particular tropical storm can be extremely erratic but often they track NE and generally affect a smaller area than mid-latitude depressions. Tropical storms usually increase in speed to around 20 kn or more as they recurve towards the N.

2   See *The Mariner's Handbook* for a detailed description of tropical storms, signs of approach and recommended evasive action.

The Hurricane Havens Handbook for the North Atlantic Ocean gives detailed information on the vulnerability of North Atlantic ports to hurricanes. It is obtainable from The National Technical Information Service, Springmead, Virginia 22161 www.ntis.gov

Fronts

Warm and cold fronts

1.121

1   Most of the mobile depressions, other than tropical storms or hurricanes, have well defined and active warm and cold fronts associated with them. The fronts mark the boundaries between the cool or very cold air of N regions and the mild or warm moist air of the sub-tropical S.

2   Most cold fronts approach from between the W and N. Winds ahead of the front tend to be from the S or SW and squally, veering to the W or NW on frontal passage. Frontal speed varies from 10 to 20 kn in summer up to 40 kn in winter. From spring through to autumn, the fronts are often preceded by dense fog, whilst frontal passage is often marked by a line of thunderstorms which often develop 50 to 300 miles ahead of a fast-moving front. Active fronts may even contain tornados or waterspouts.

3   See *The Mariner's Handbook* for a detailed description of the weather patterns that are usually associated with warm and cold fronts and occlusions.

Winds

Average distribution

1.122

1   Wind roses showing the frequency of winds of various directions and speeds for February, May, August and November are given in diagrams 1.122.1 to 1.122.4.

Open sea

1.123

1   Winds are predominantly from between WSW and NNW between November and March as a result of the North American anticyclone, with the frequency of strong to gale force winds reaching a maximum during this period. Winds of force 5 and above occur on about 45 to 50% of occasions in the SW of the area and between 55 and 60% in the N and E.

2   In summer, the winds are predominantly from between S and WSW as a result of the Bermuda anticyclone, with relatively few occasions with winds of gale force and above. Winds of force 5 and above occur on about 35 to 40% of occasions in the N of the area and around 27 to 32% in the S.

Coastal waters

1.124

1   Topography has a major influence on the strength and direction of the wind. In the more sheltered locations like New York and Providence, offshore winds are usually greatly modified within a relatively short distance of the coast; whereas in Buzzards Bay, SW winds are often double those offshore due to funnelling. Because of this funnelling, winds in Buzzards Bay may remain SW even though the wind offshore may have veered to the W or NW.

2   See *The Mariner's Handbook* for further details on the modification of both wind speed and direction in coastal waters.

Land and sea breezes

1.125

1   Land and sea breezes affect most of the coastline. Summer sea breezes are common, particularly in the areas around New York and Portland. Depending on the prevailing wind, these breezes may reinforce or moderate the strength of the prevailing wind. Sea breezes normally set in by late morning, increase to a maximum of about force 3 to 4 by mid-afternoon and then die away by sunset. The land breeze is generally weaker and blows as a light offshore wind from around midnight to soon after dawn.

Gales

1.126

1   Winds of gale force 8 and above occur within the circulations of tropical storms and hurricanes. These storms normally develop well to the S of the area, or in Gulf of Mexico, and can on occasions move N to affect the area.

Winds of force 7 or more are reported, in January, on 5 to 10% of occasions near the coast and steadily increase to about 20% in the SE of the area covered by this volume. The frequency decreases during the spring and by mid-summer the frequency falls to less than 2% across most of the area (see accompanying diagrams 1.126.1 to 1.126.4).

2   Gales frequently develop as NE-moving mobile depressions, often called "Nor'easters", move across the area, or when slow moving deep vigorous depressions develop in or just to the east of the area, especially during late autumn and winter. The circulations around these deep winter depressions may extend for many hundreds of miles, with winds occasionally increasing to hurricane strength. Gale force winds may blow from any direction. In winter, the most likely direction is from between SW and N and, in summer, strong winds are most frequent from between S and WSW.

---

3   Deep depressions may also give rise to storm surges which can result in unexpectedly high tides, particularly in the N.

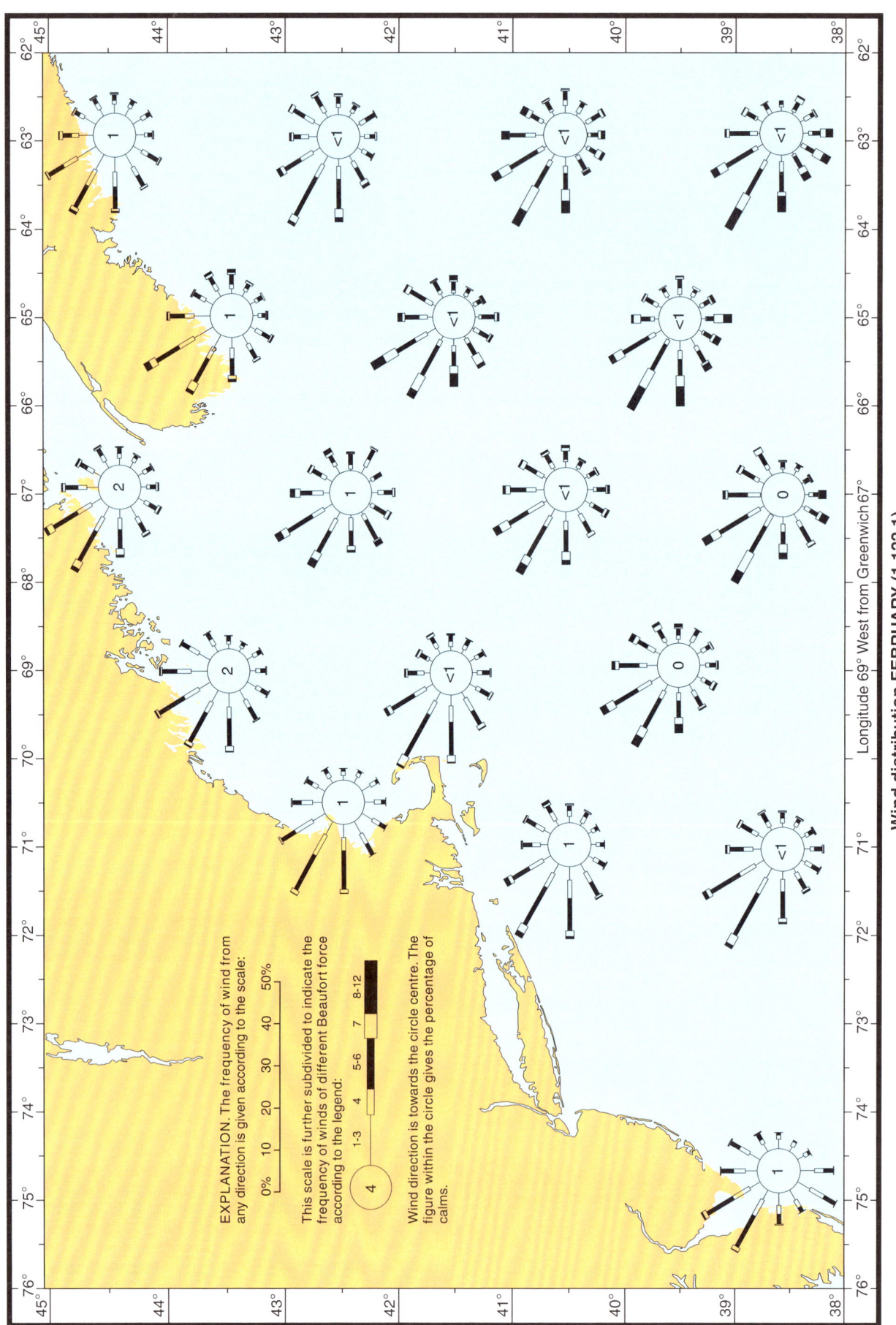
Wind distribution FEBRUARY (1.122.1)

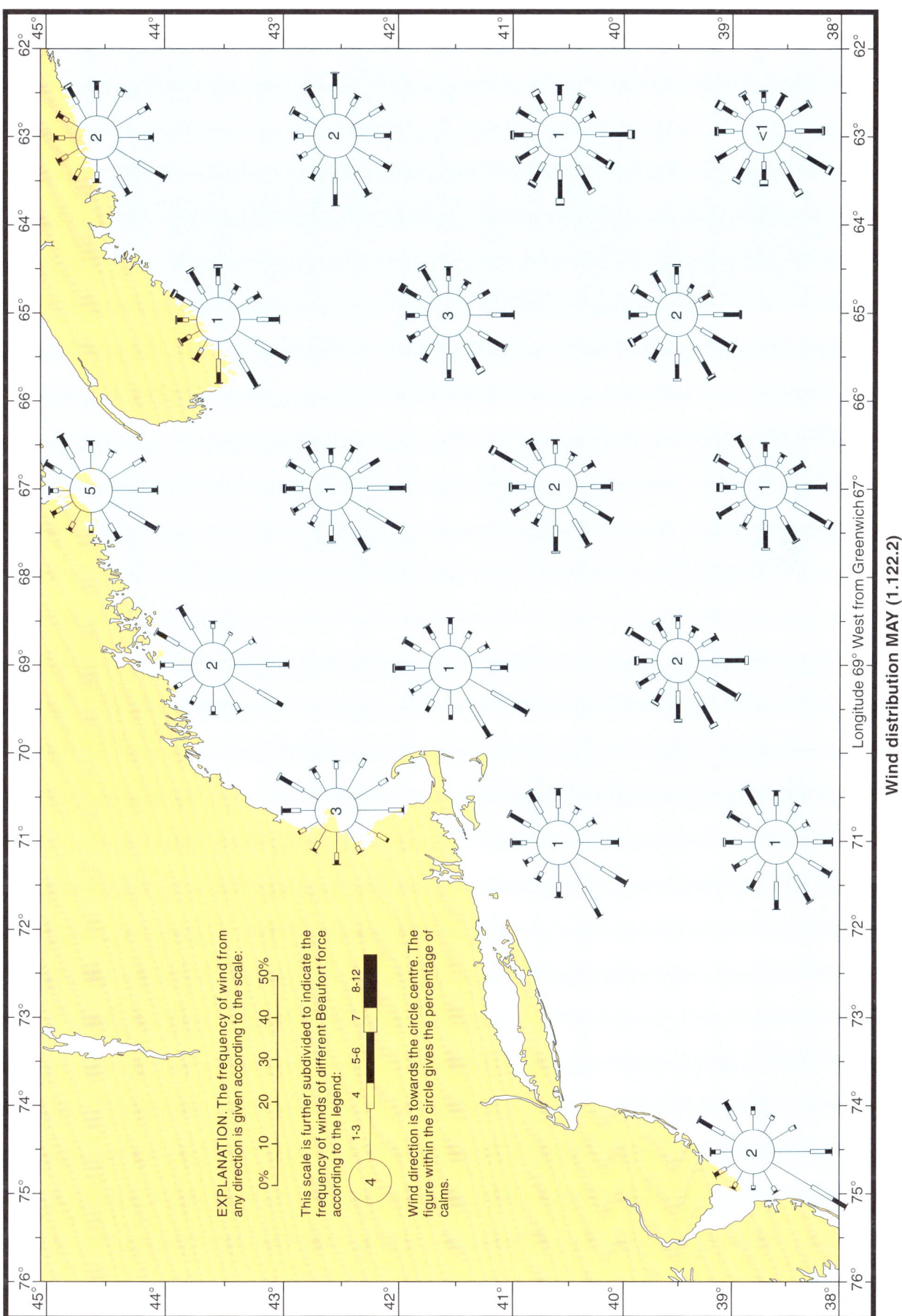

Wind distribution MAY (1.122.2)

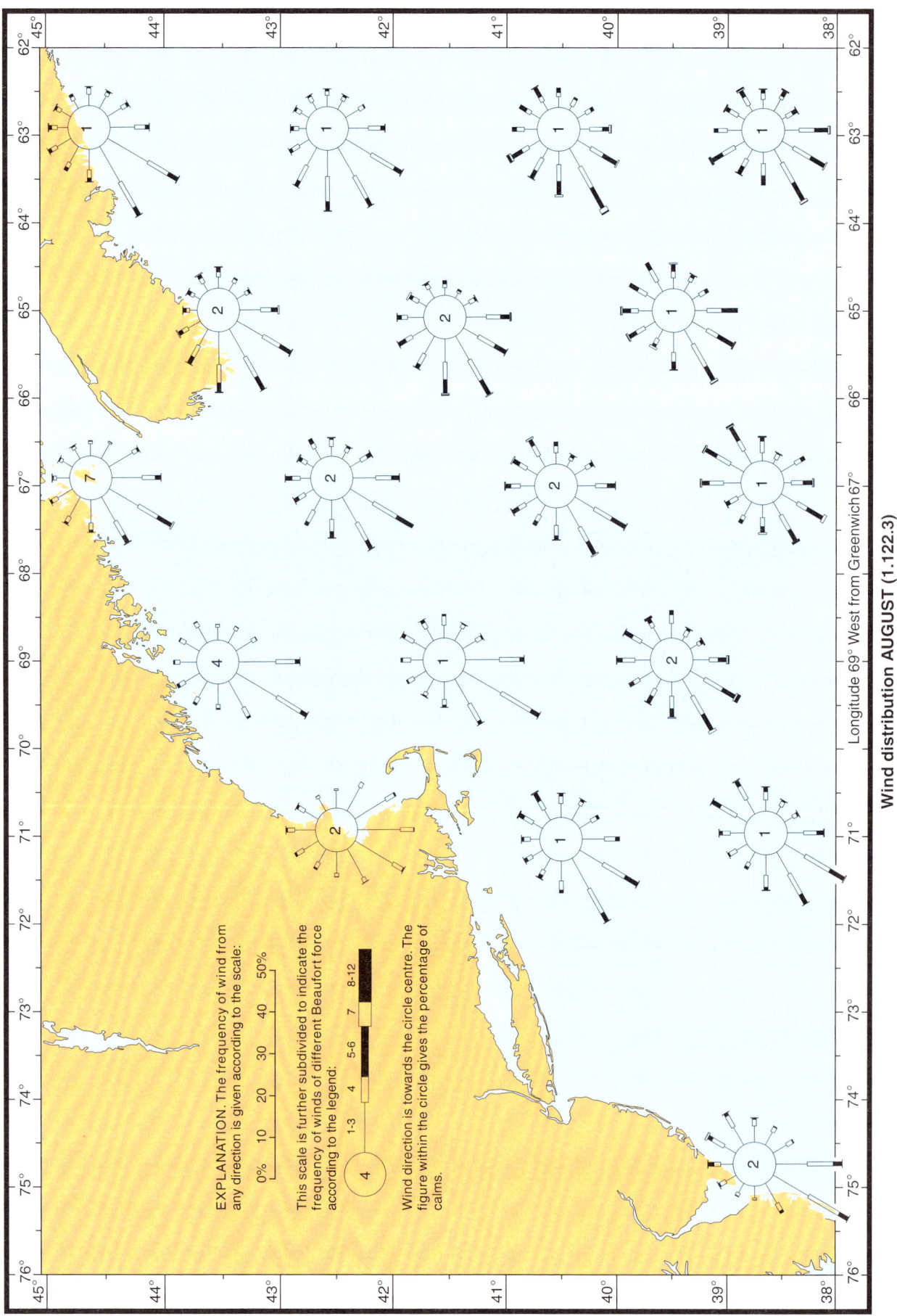

Wind distribution AUGUST (1.122.3)

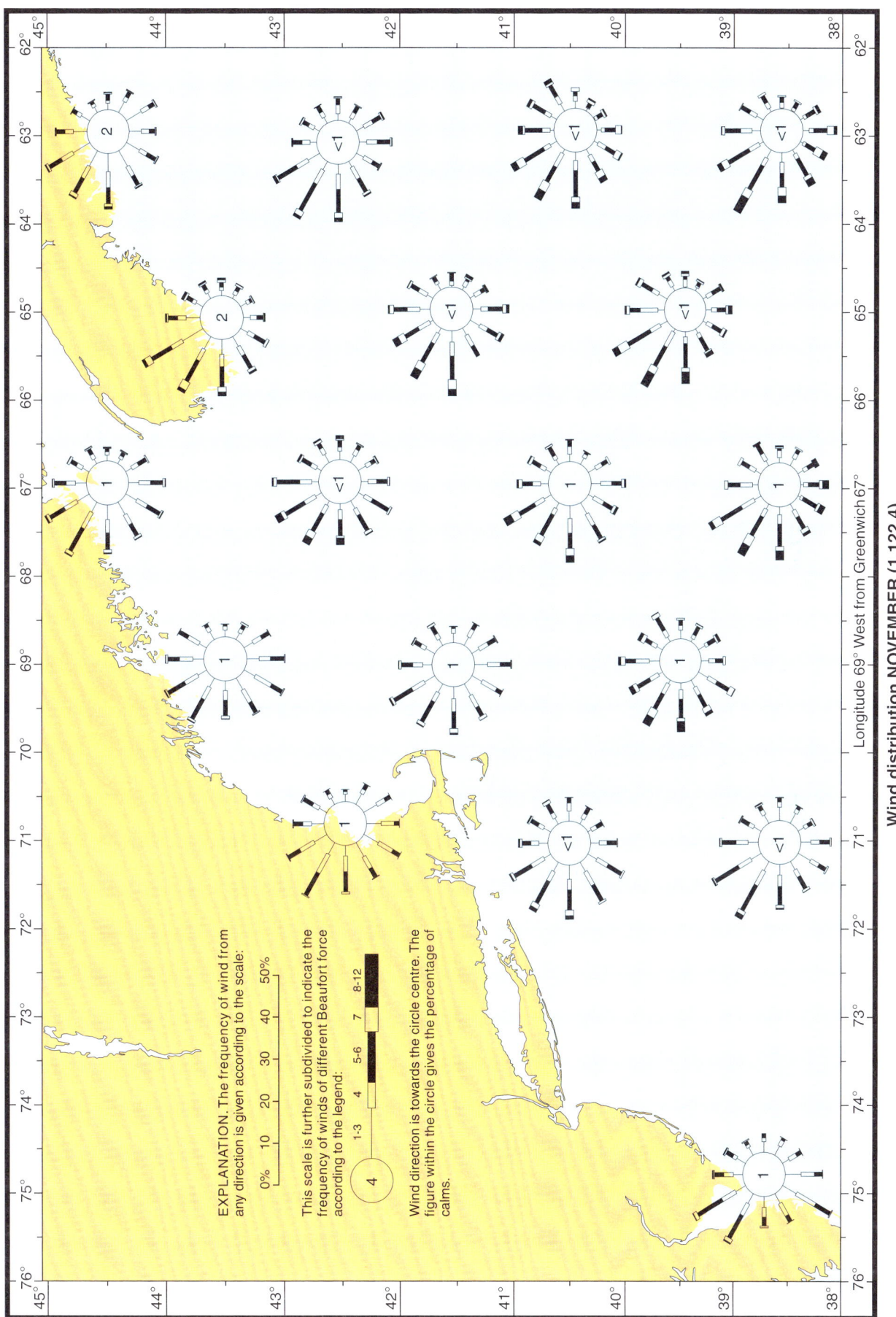

Wind distribution NOVEMBER (1.122.4)

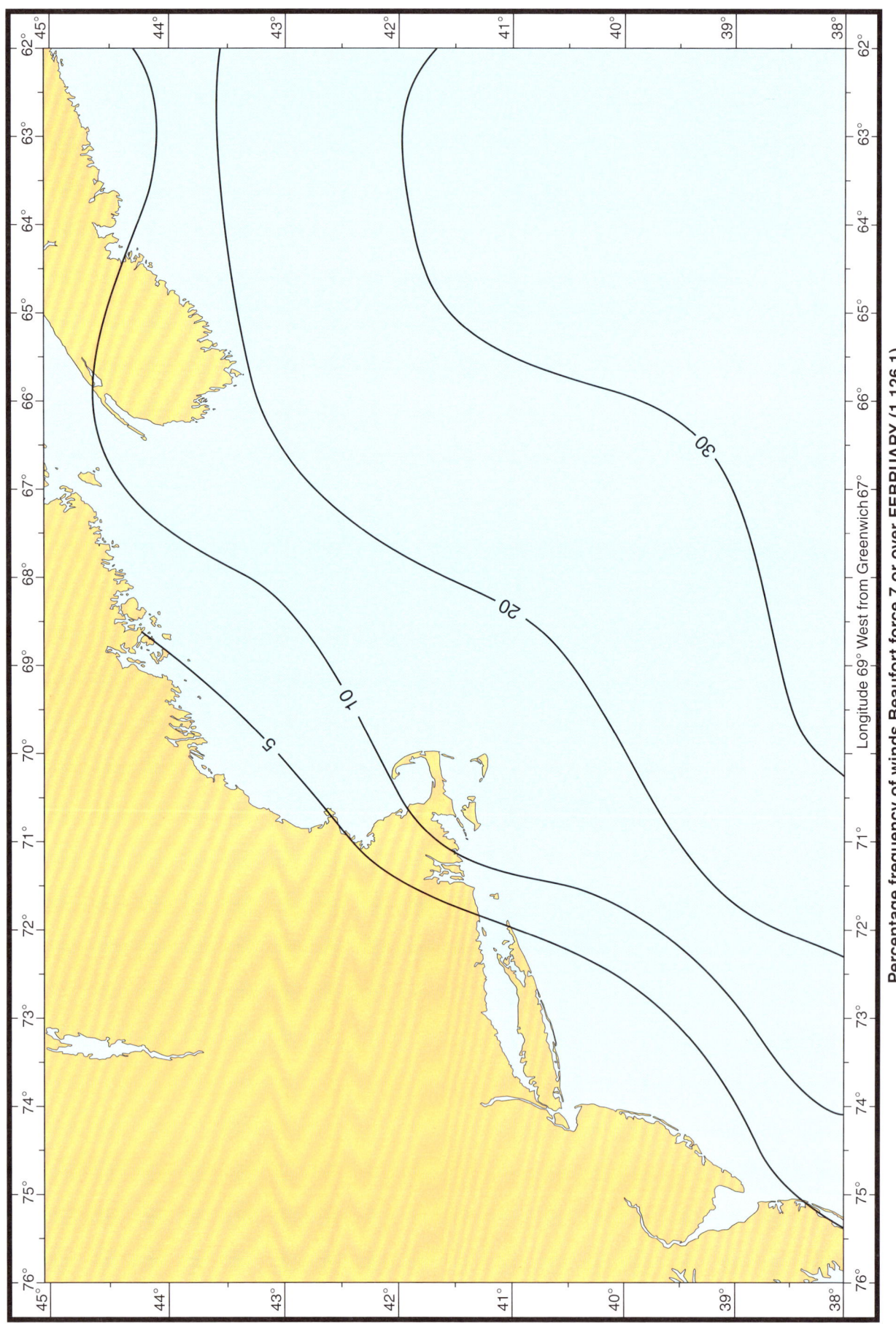

Percentage frequency of winds Beaufort force 7 or over FEBRUARY (1.126.1)

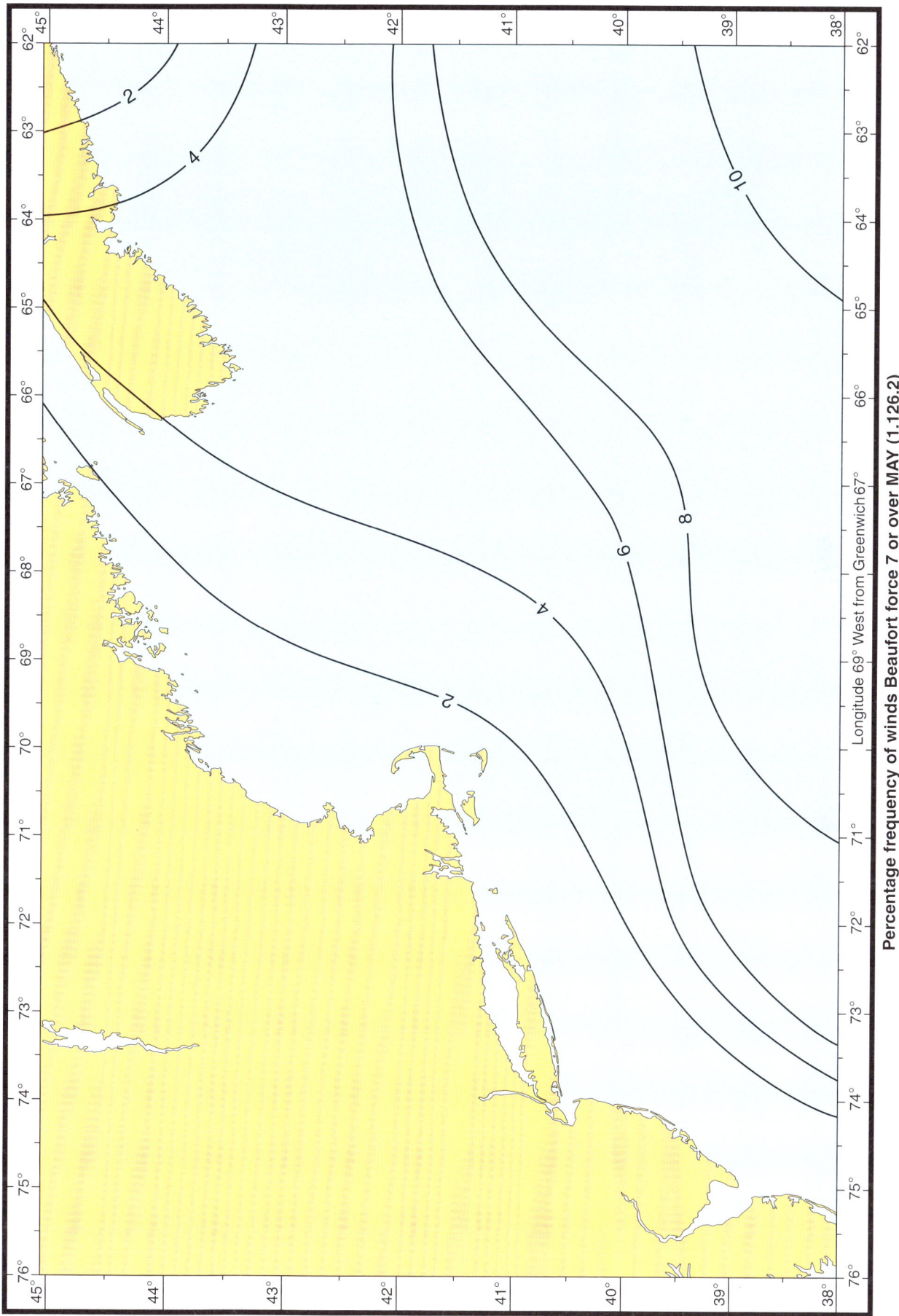

Percentage frequency of winds Beaufort force 7 or over MAY (1.126.2)

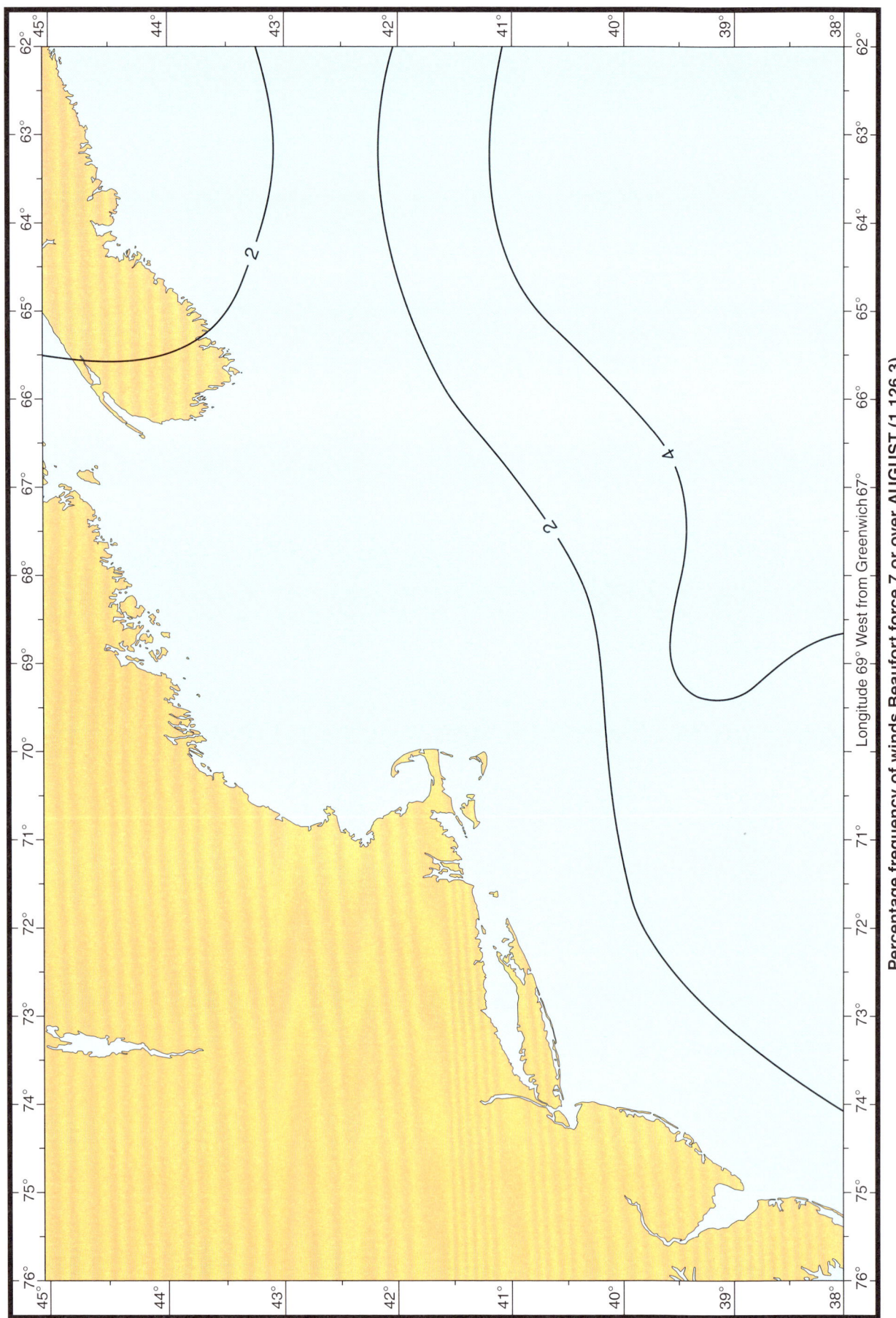

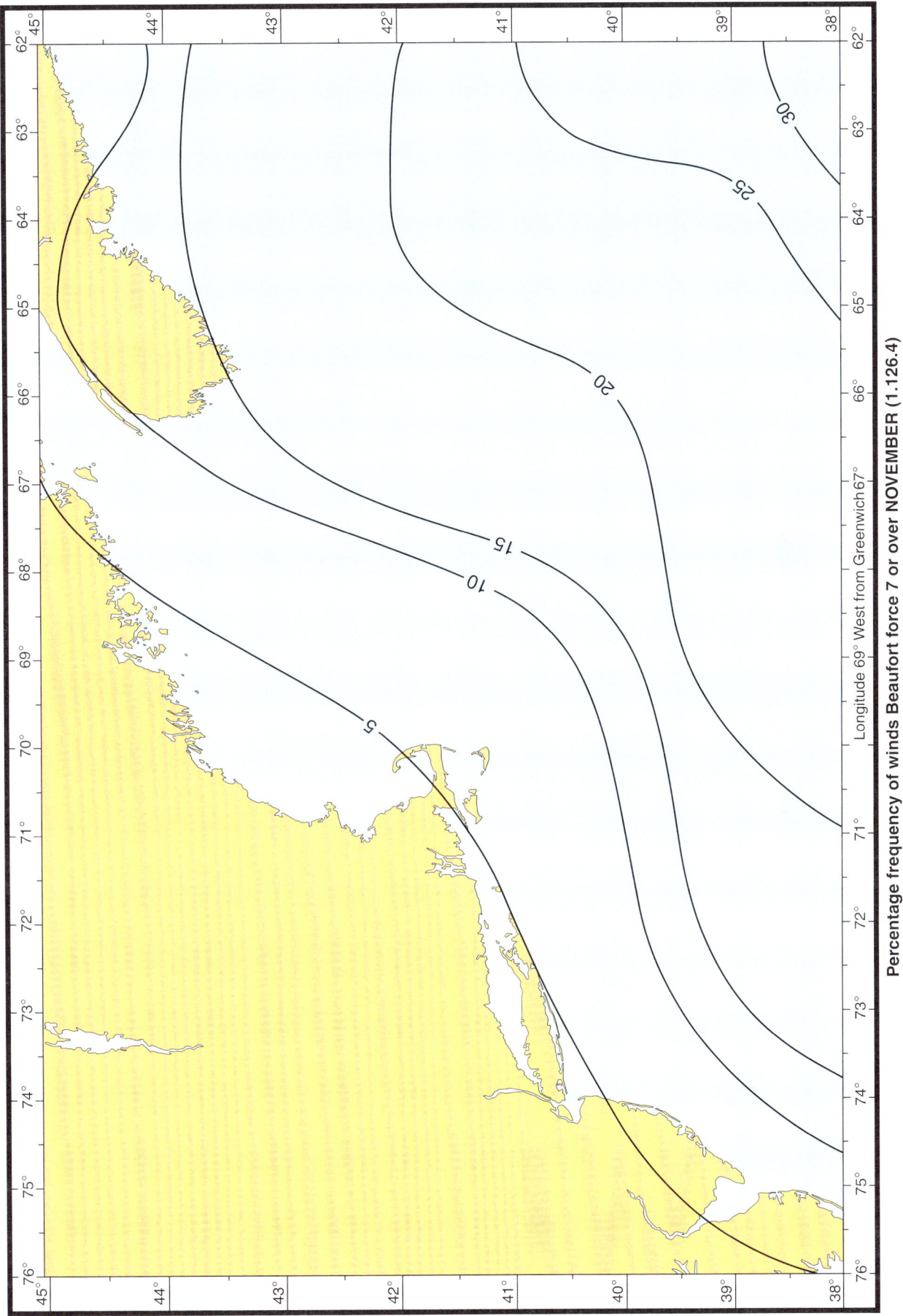

Percentage frequency of winds Beaufort force 7 or over NOVEMBER (1.126.4)

Cloud

1.127

1 Due to the alternating anticyclones and depressions that usually move NE across the area, it is uncommon for either clear or overcast skies to persist for more than a few days, except when the Azores anticyclone extends NW to Bermuda in summer to give a period of settled weather. Even then coasts may be affected by widespread summer fog, especially in the N of the area.

2 In mid-winter, the mean cloud amount in coastal areas is around 4 oktas in the N and 5 oktas in the SW, and increases to 6 oktas over the open waters to the SE. By July, the mean cloud amount is between 4 and 5 oktas in the N and E and decreases slightly to around 4 oktas in the SW.

Precipitation

1.128

1 The climate information (1.139) gives the average amounts of precipitation for each month at a number of coastal stations and the mean number of days in each month when significant precipitation is recorded. In coastal areas, rainfall amounts are generally higher on wind facing coasts, and over high ground, than at sea to windward.

Rain

1.129

1 Rain, which often turns to snow in winter in the N of the area, can be expected in January, on about 10 to 12 days a month in the SW and 13 to 15 days in the extreme NE. In late summer and early autumn, significant rainfall is recorded on about 7 to 9 days per month in the SW and 10 to 12 days in the extreme NE.

2 Annual rainfall averages around 1000 to 1100 mm in most coastal areas and is fairly evenly spread throughout the year, although August tends to be the wettest month in the SW and the driest in the NE. The quantity and duration of any precipitation can vary significantly from one day to another and one year to another.

Snow

1.130

1 Snow mainly occurs between November and April but occasionally as early as October and as late as May, especially in the N. The annual number of days with appreciable falls of snow (25 mm or more) varies from around seven days in the SW to about 15 to 25 days in the extreme NE. Blizzard conditions are not uncommon when an active cold front moves across the area to the rear of a deep depression. The frequency of occurrence of snow over the open waters to the extreme SE of the area is about 50% of that in the SW.

Thunderstorms

1.131

1 Rapidly moving thunderstorms with violent squalls are not uncommon. Around 13 to 16 thunderstorms are reported each year in the N and about 25 in the SW, but with a significantly higher frequency inland. They are relatively rare in mid-winter but steadily increase in frequency to reach a maximum in June and July. Hail is almost entirely confined to the summer months and is generally associated with thunderstorm activity. Severe thunderstorm activity may also give rise to the occasional tornado over land or waterspout over the sea.

Fog and visibility

1.132

1 Radiation fog often forms over low lying land on calm clear winter nights and is generally thickest towards dawn. This fog may drift out over coastal waters, especially on an out-going tide, before dispersing by mid-morning, although on occasions it may be more persistent and extensive. For a full description of the different types of fog see *The Mariner's Handbook*.

2 Sea or advection fog affects nearly all of the area covered by this volume (see diagrams 1.132.1 to 1.132.4) from late May to early September. It is caused by sub-tropical moist S air being cooled by the Labrador Current and is often dense and extensive. In the extreme SW, towards the W half of Long Island and Sandy Hook, the majority of fog occurs in early summer and is less persistent than that to the NE.

3 The frequency of occurrence of fog increases rapidly to the N and E of Nantucket Island in summer and may persist for several days until the arrival of a relatively dry NW wind. Over the central part of Gulf of Maine the frequency of fog is about 20% and decreases to around 3 to 5% in the extreme S of the area. In winter, sea fog is mainly confined to the N of the area with a frequency of occurrence of around 6 to 8%.

4 In settled conditions, offshore sea fog may move inshore on an in-going tide or with a light sea breeze. Fog frequency often increases in summer in the approaches to Long Island Sound and Narragansett Bay; the area around Point Judith is often referred to as "the fog hole".

Visibility is, on occasions, reduced to near fog limits during heavy thunderstorms and on the passage of warm and cold fronts. Good visibility of over 10 miles is frequent with NW winds in both summer and winter.

Air temperature

General information

1.133

1 January and February is generally the coldest time of the year with July and August being the warmest. Notwithstanding this, the numerous frontal depressions that affect the area and the subsequent marked changes of airstream result in the temperatures being extremely variable from one day to the next, especially in winter. This variation between mild S air and the very cold NW winds in winter is more pronounced than in most other areas of the world at similar latitudes.

Open sea

1.134

1 In the extreme N of the area covered by this volume, the mean air temperature over open waters in January is about −1·5°C, and increases to around 4°C in the SW and 6°C in the SE. By July, the mean air temperature is about 8°C in the North and 13 to 14°C in the S. The temperature gradient is most marked in the extreme SE of the area due to the proximity of the Gulf Stream.

Coastal waters

1.135

1 Air temperatures in the coastal waters covered by this volume are much more variable than over the open sea. The temperature is greatly affected by both land and sea breezes with large diurnal, latitudinal and seasonal variations. The climate information (1.140 to 1.147) gives mean temperatures for a number of coastal stations.

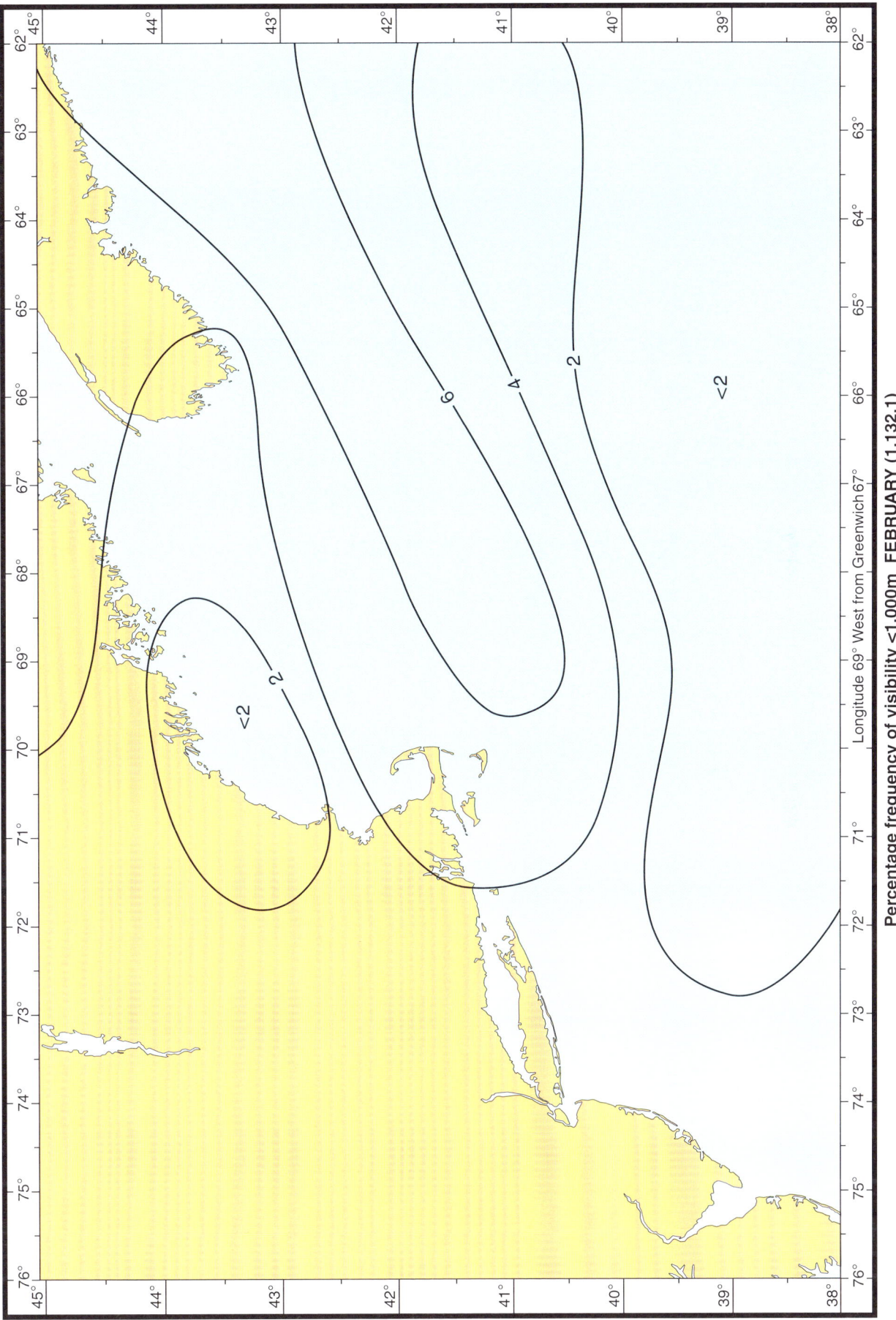

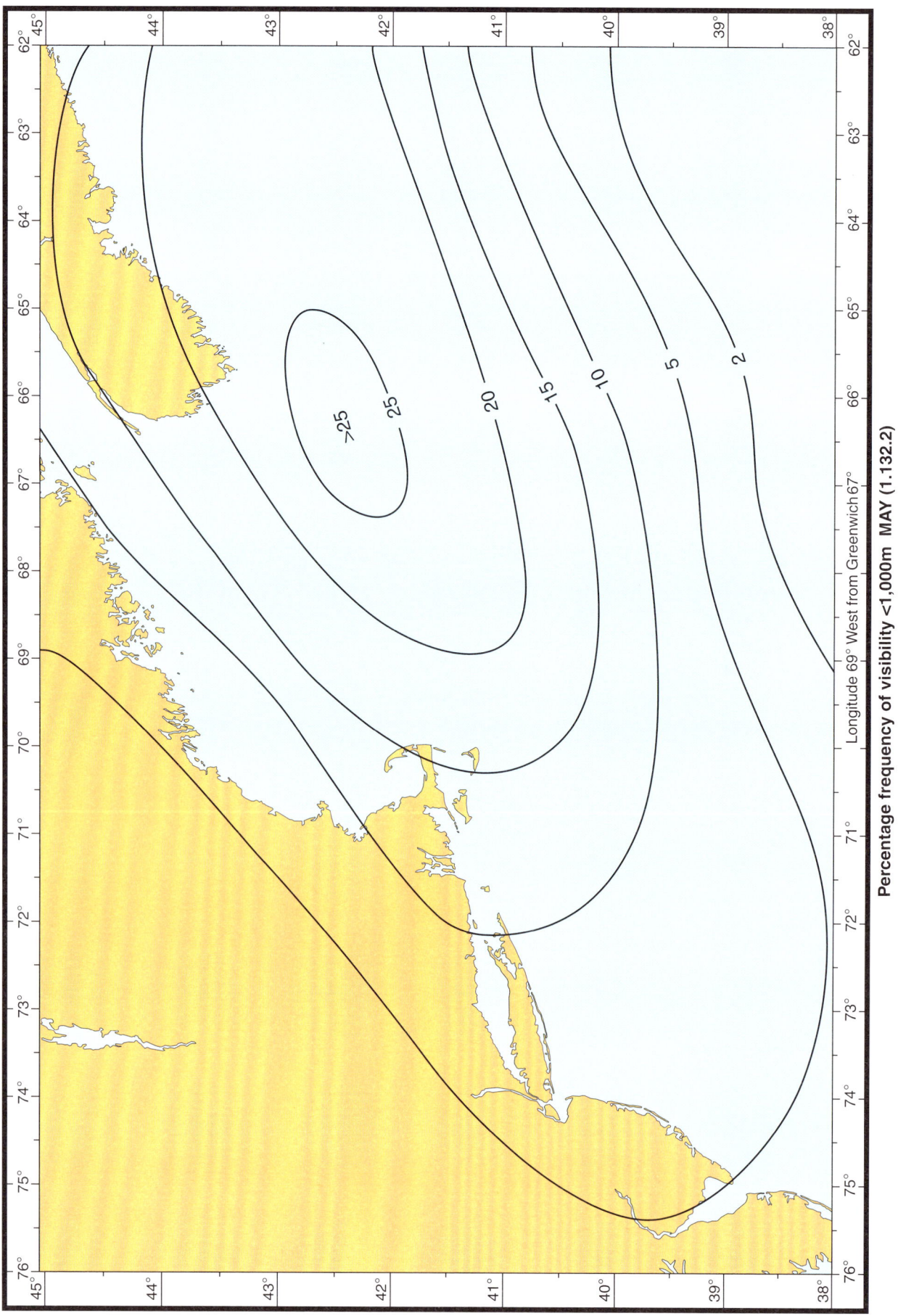

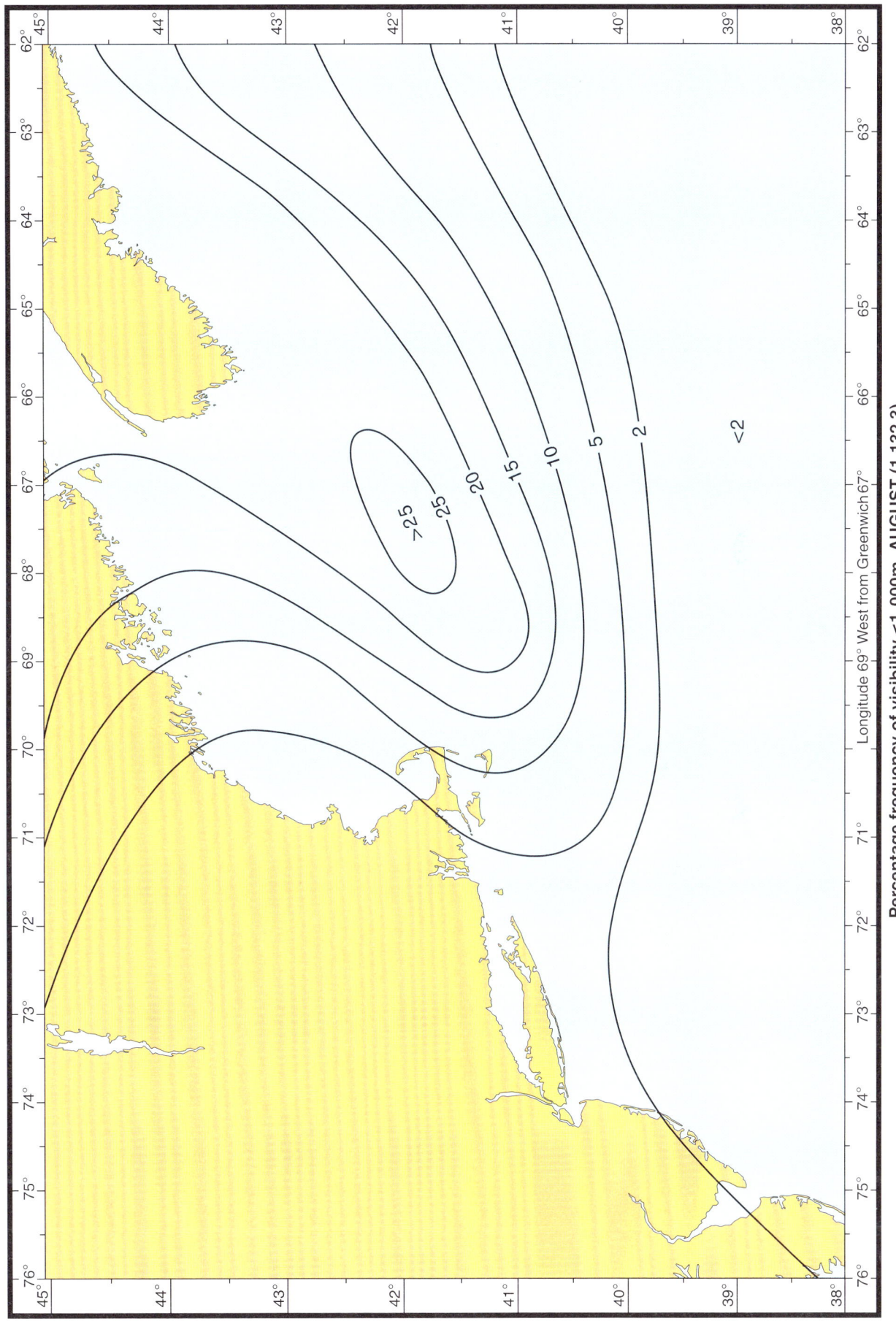
Percentage frequency of visibility <1,000m AUGUST (1.132.3)

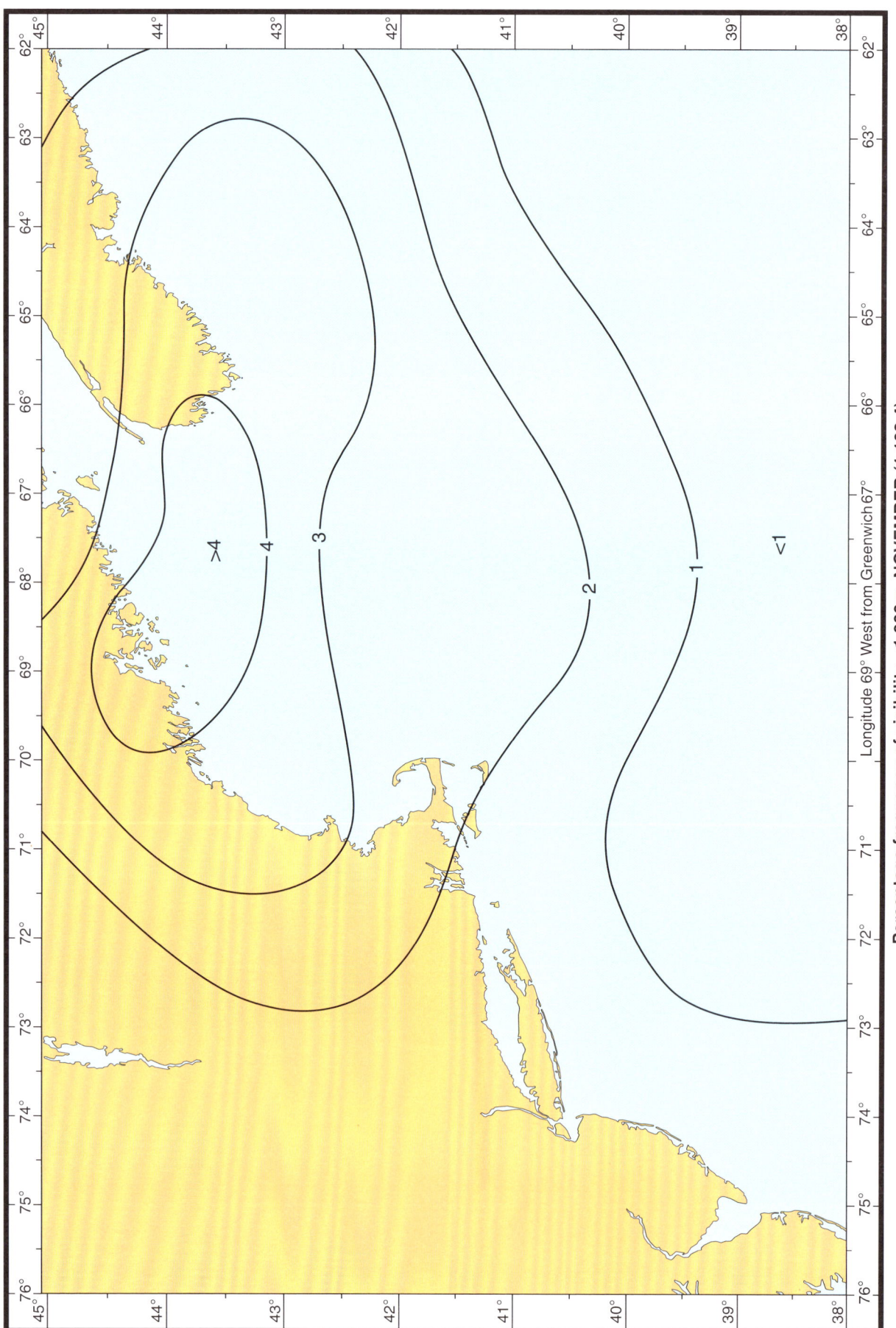

2 Extreme values of 35°C are not uncommon in summer, especially in the S, and -25°C in severe winters in the N. In mid-winter, temperatures normally remain below freezing to the N of Boston.

Relative humidity

General information
1.136
1 Humidity is closely related to air temperature and generally decreases as the temperature increases. During the early morning, when the air temperature is normally at its lowest, the humidity is generally at its highest, and falls to a minimum in the afternoon. In fog, the air is saturated with a humidity of 100%.

Open sea
1.137
1 The mean humidity is about 80% in the N of the area, in winter, and decreases to around 76% in the SW and 78% in the SE. In summer, the figures are 90, 82 and 86% respectively. Actual daily values will, however, be dependant on the wind direction and the distance from land with little or no diurnal variation.

Coastal waters
1.138
1 In coastal waters the mean humidity is around 80% in the early morning and 65 to 70% in the afternoon. However, large changes in humidity along the coast are possible and will depend on latitude, the airstream, exposure to the prevailing wind, distance from the open sea and both land and sea breeze effects.

CLIMATE INFORMATION
1.139
1 The climate information gives data for several coastal stations which regularly undertake weather observations. Some of these stations have been re-sited and the position given is the latest available. The positions of these coastal stations are shown on diagram 1.139.

2 It is emphasised that these data are average conditions and refer to the specific location of the observing station and therefore may not be representative of the conditions over the open sea or in approaches to ports in their vicinity. The following comments briefly list some of the differences to be expected between conditions over open sea and those at the nearest reporting station (see *The Mariner's Handbook* for further details).

3 Wind speeds tend to be higher at sea with more frequent gales than on land, although funnelling in narrow inlets can result in an increase in wind strength.

Precipitation along mountainous wind facing coasts can be considerably higher than at sea to windward. Similarly, precipitation in the lee of high ground is generally less.

4 Air temperature over the sea is less variable than over the land.

Topography has a marked effect on local conditions.

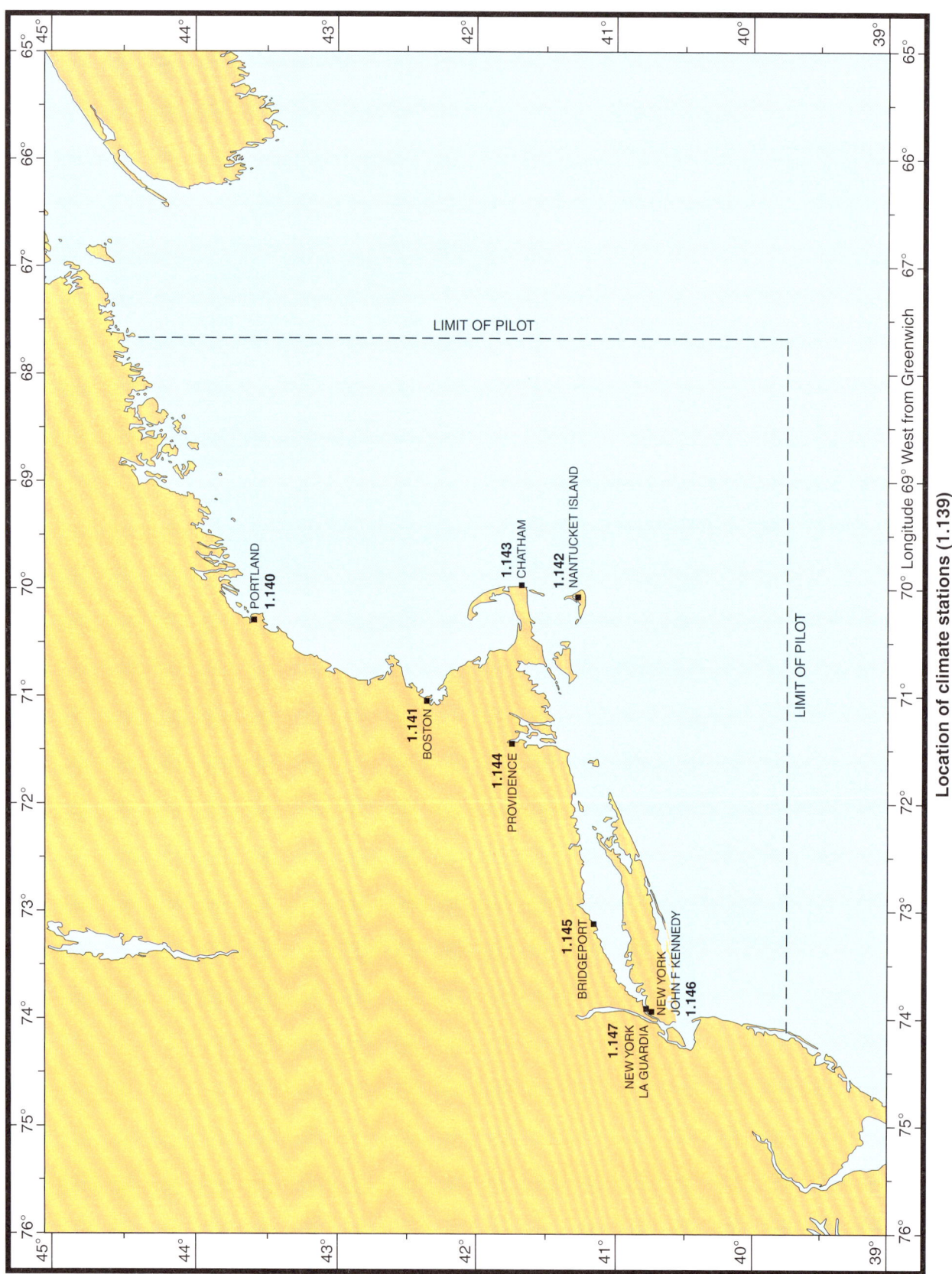

Location of climate stations (1.139)

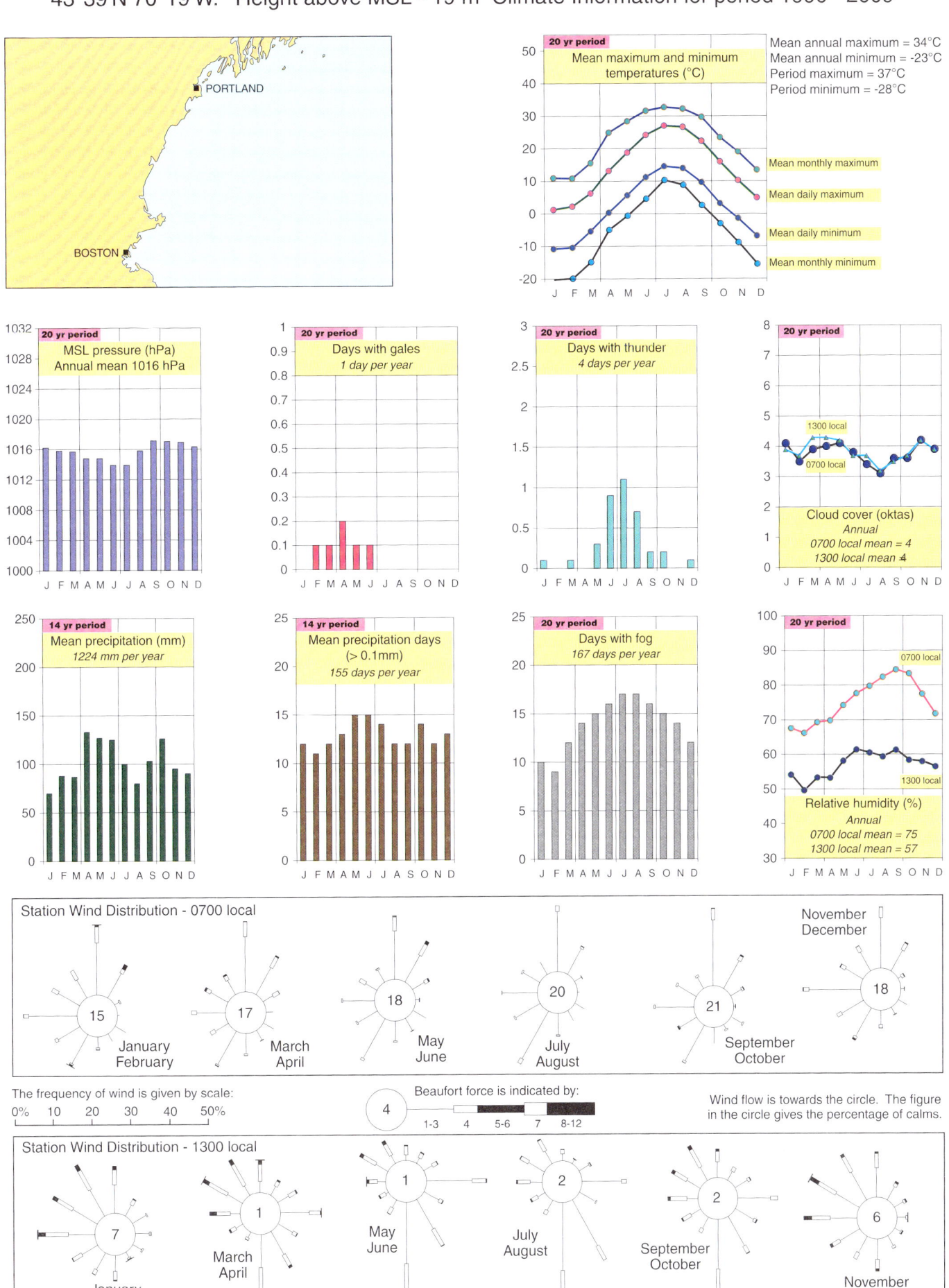

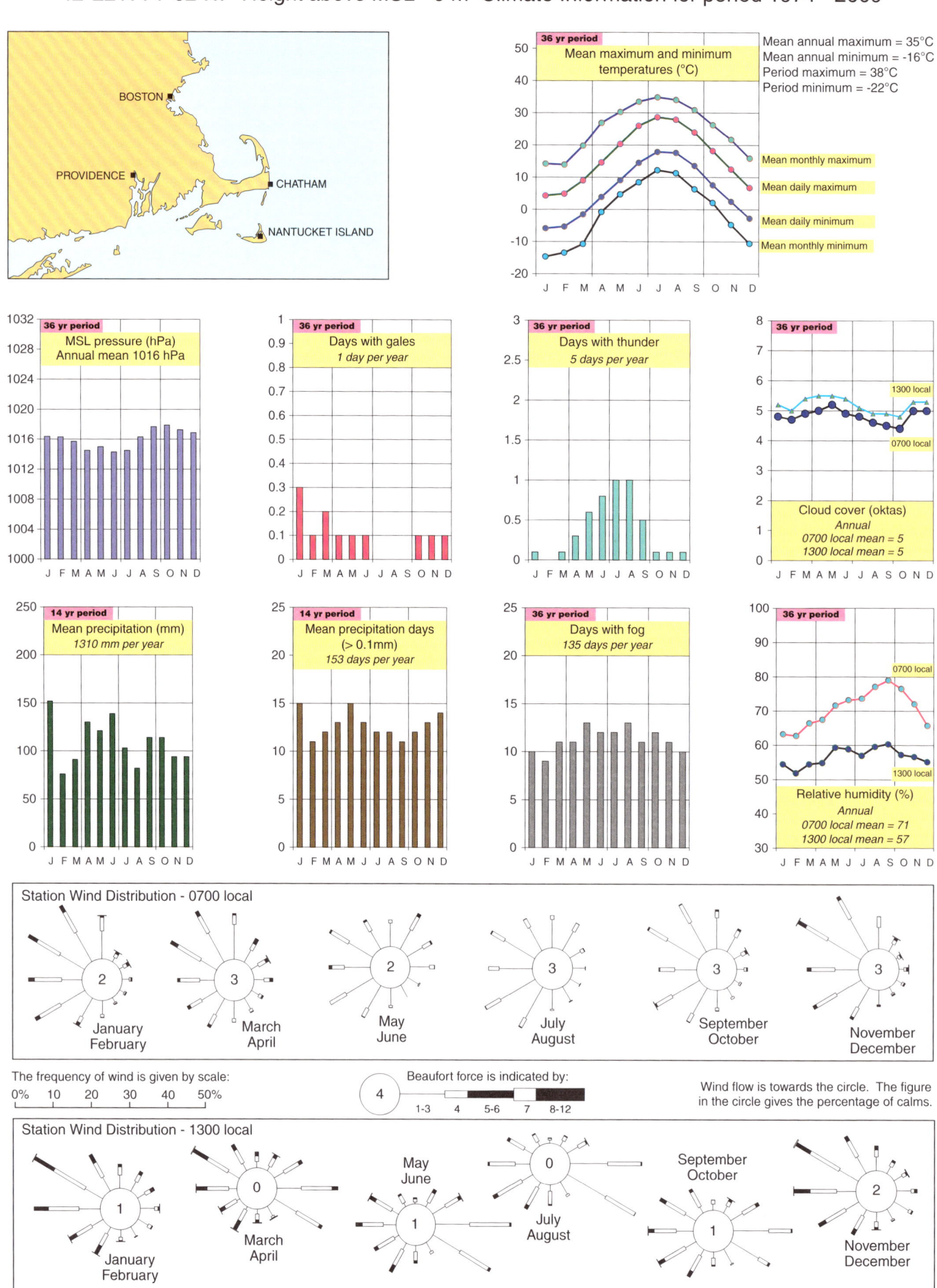

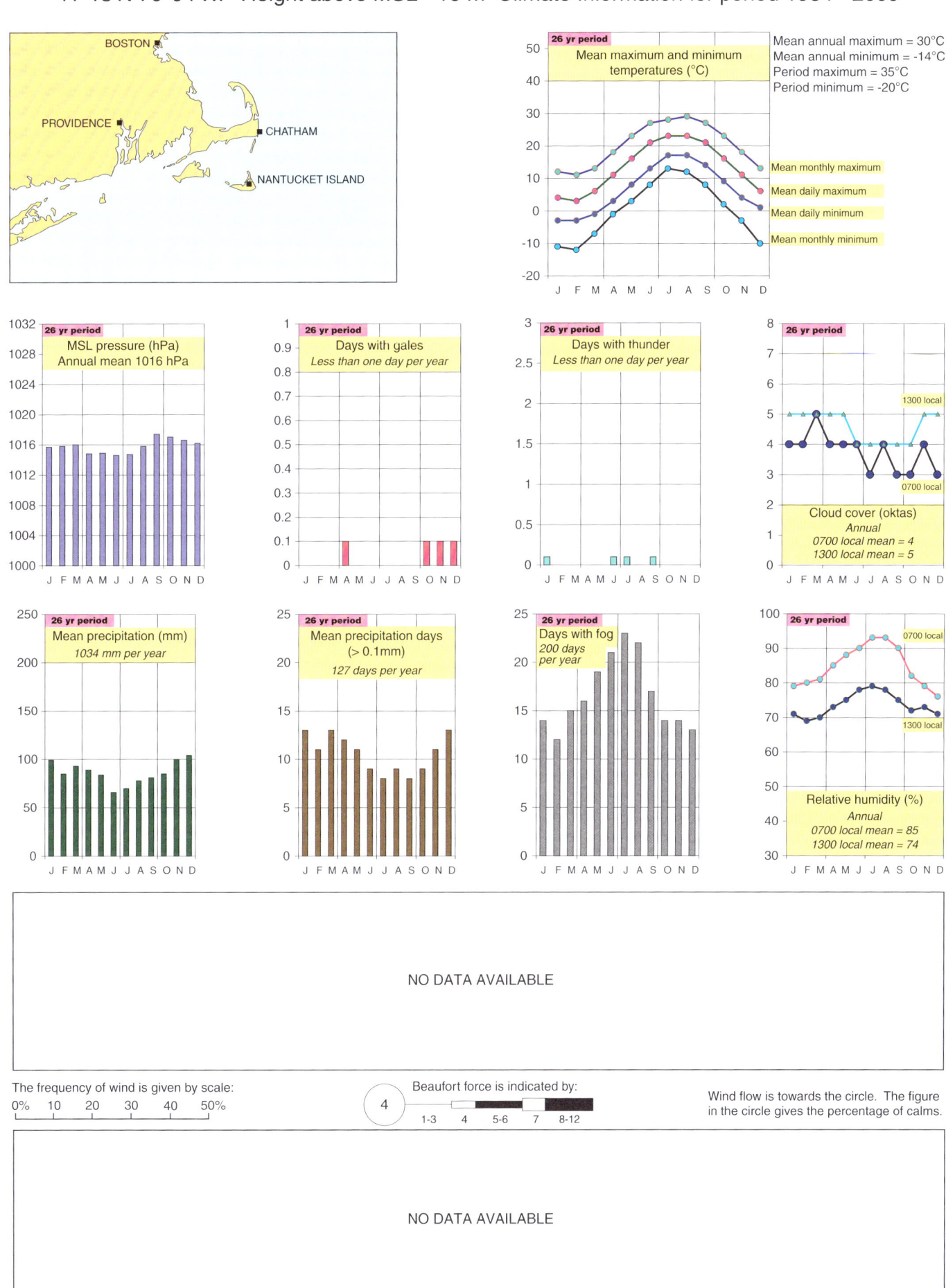

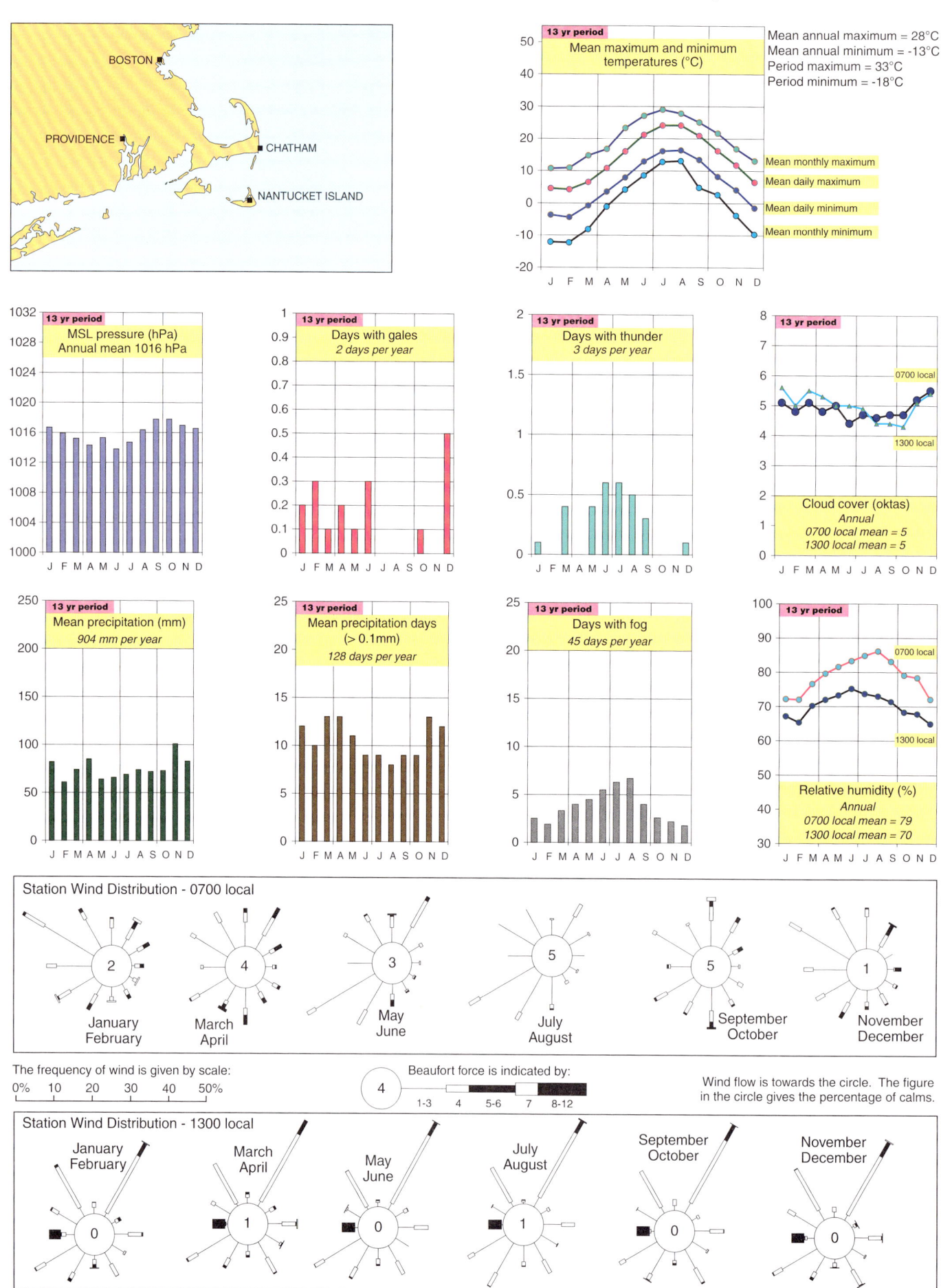

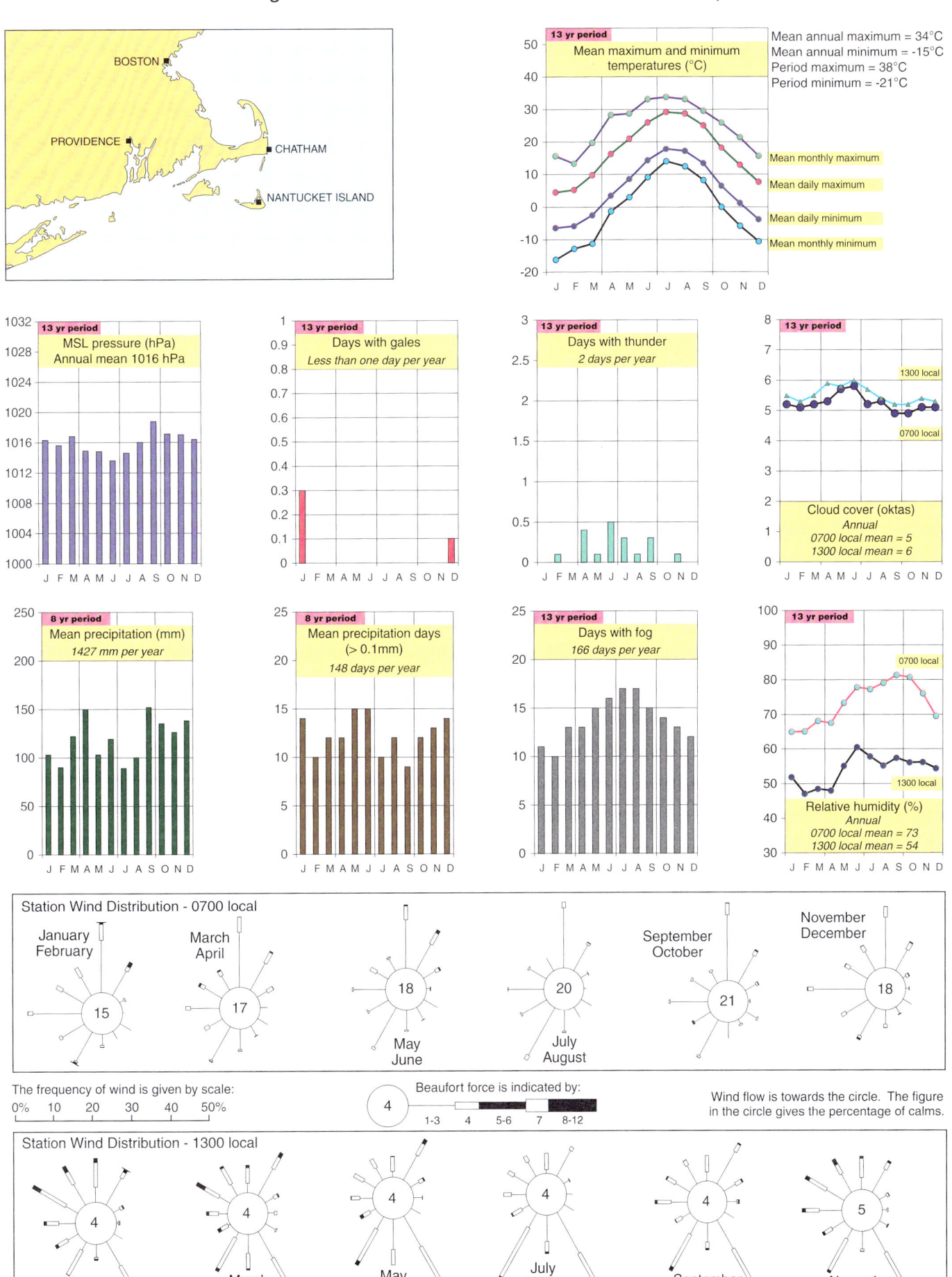

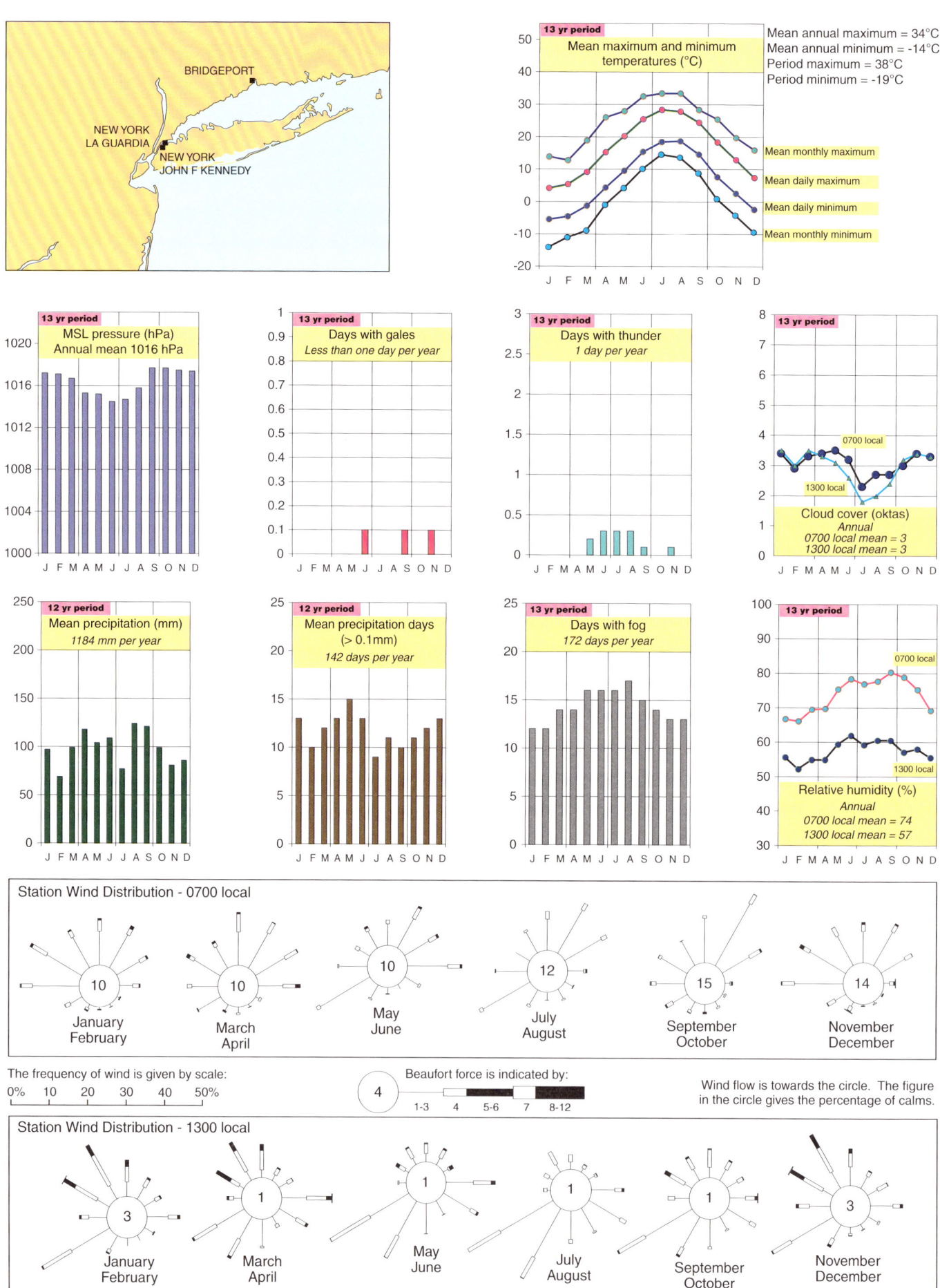

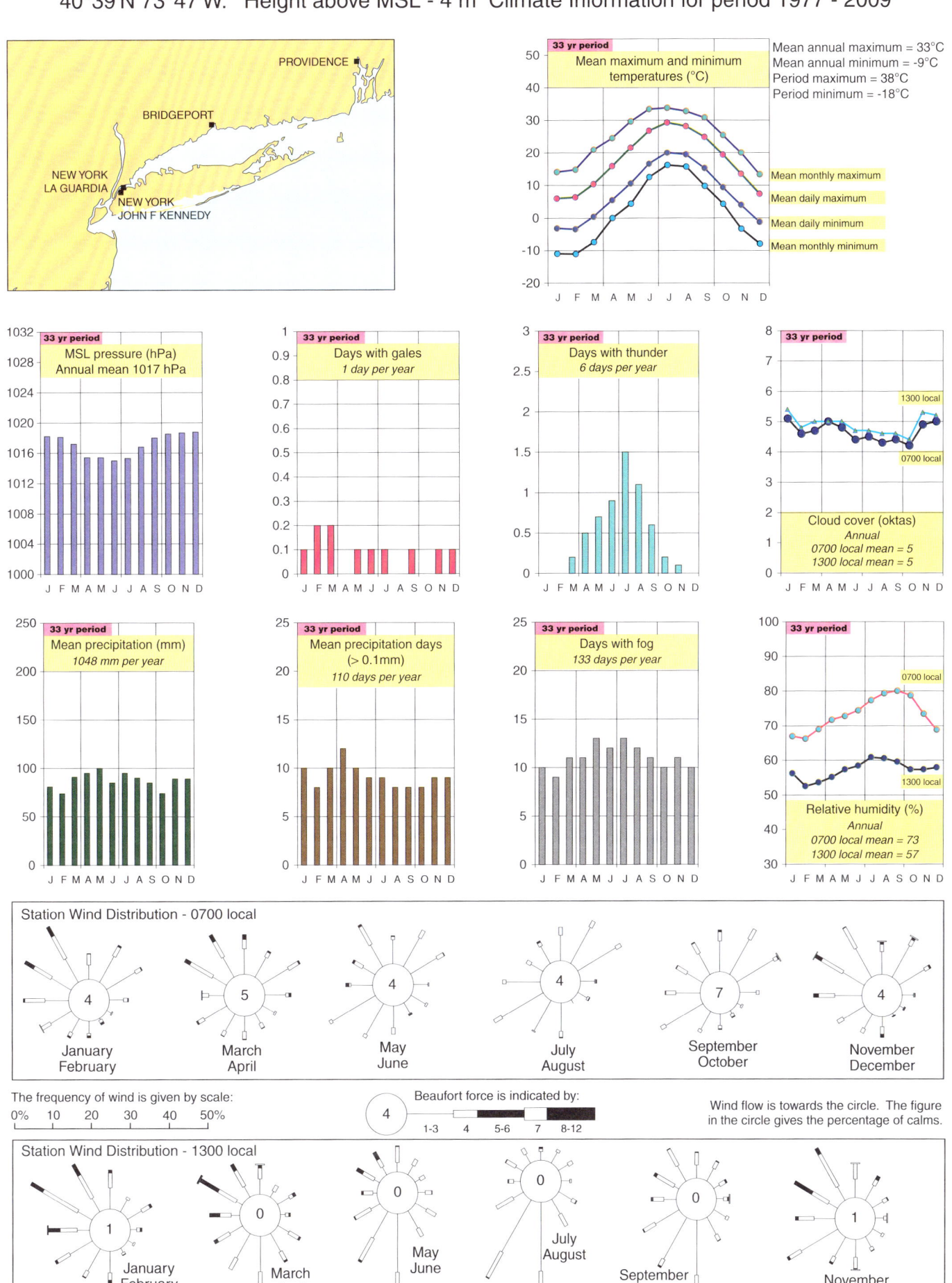

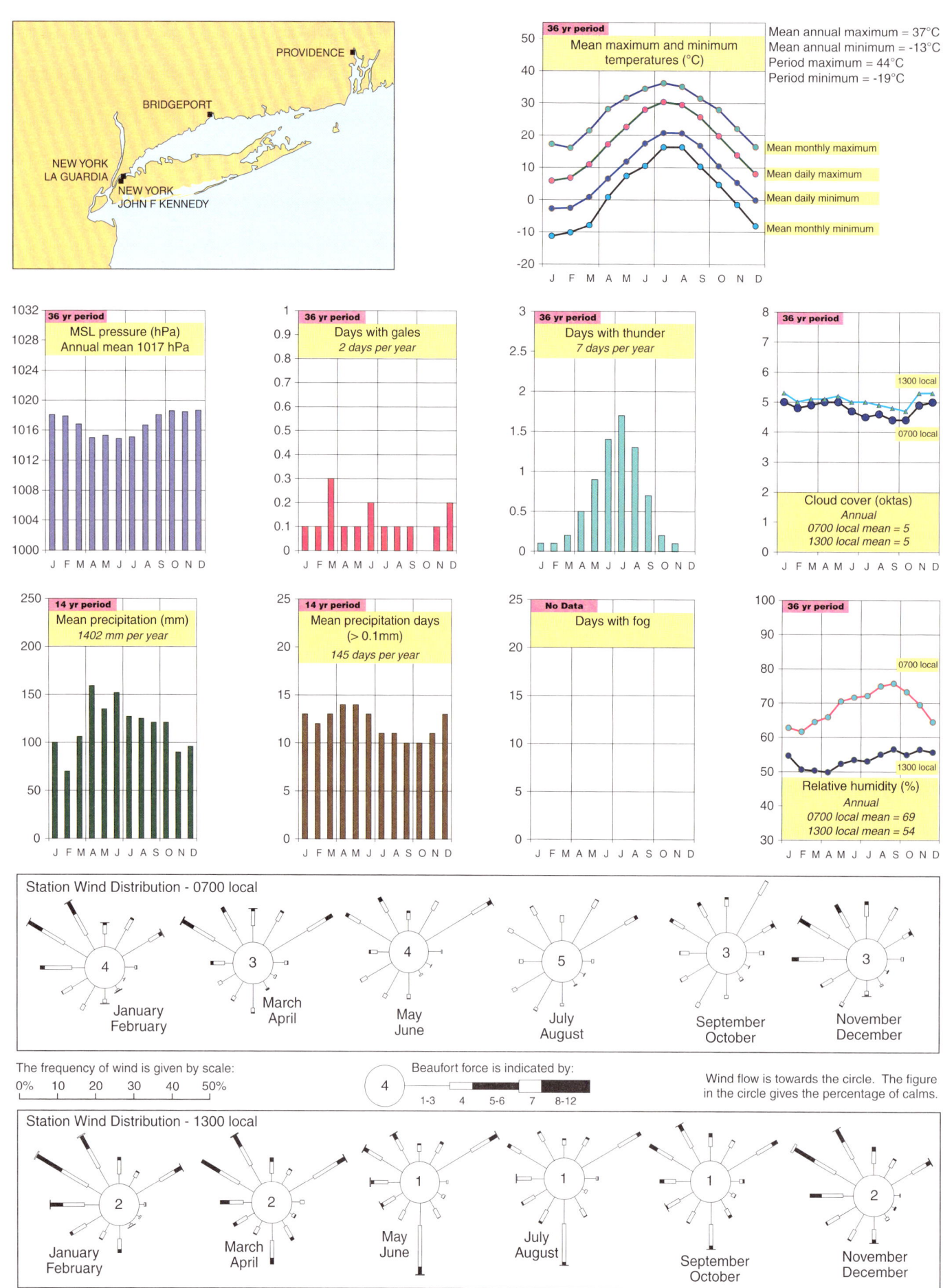

NOTES

Chapter 2 - North part of Gulf of Maine

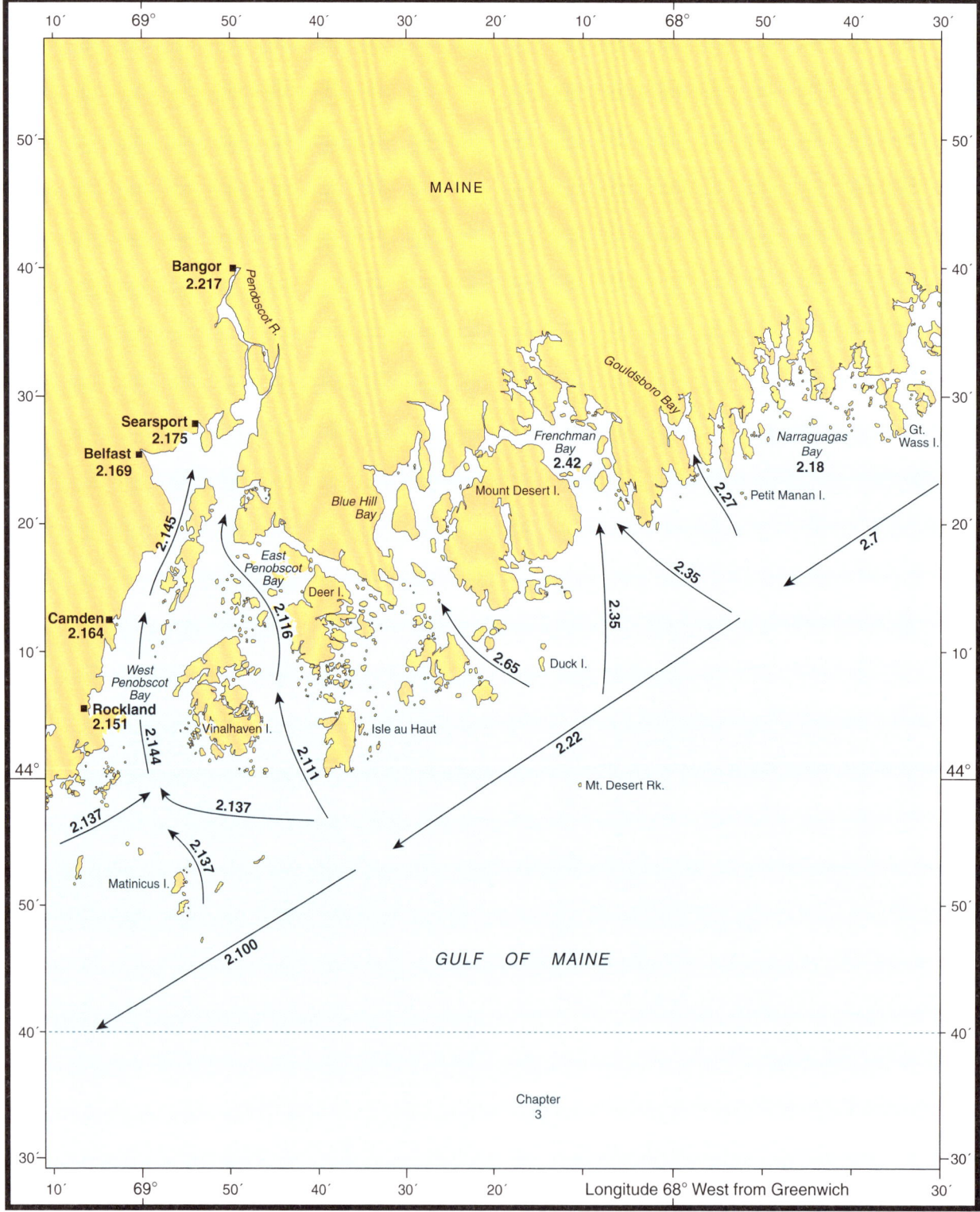

Arrows indicate the waterway described. Numbers refer to paragraphs in the chapter

CHAPTER 2

NORTH PART OF GULF OF MAINE

GENERAL INFORMATION

Chart 2492
Scope of the chapter
2.1

1   The area covered by this chapter comprises the coast of Maine from Great Wass Island (44°29′·00N 67°35′·50W) to Monhegan Island (43°45′·90N 69°18′·80W), 85 miles WSW. The description includes the ports of Bar Harbor (2.52) and Searsport (2.175).
   The chapter is divided into the following sections:
      Great Wass Island to Isle au Haut (2.2).
      Penobscot Bay and approaches (2.93).

GREAT WASS ISLAND TO ISLE AU HAUT

GENERAL INFORMATION

Charts 4746, 2492.
Area covered
2.2

1   This section describes the coastal and offshore route from Great Wass Island (44°29′·00N 67°35′·50W) to Isle au Haut (44°03′·00N 68°37′·50W), 50 miles SW. Also described are the anchorages at Bar Harbor (2.52) used by cruise vessels.
   It is arranged as follows:
      Great Wass Island to Petit Manan Island (2.7).
      Petit Manan Island to Isle au Haut (2.22).
      Frenchman Bay and adjacent waters (2.35).
      Blue Hill Bay and adjacent waters (2.65).

Topography
2.3

1   The coast of Maine between Great Wass Island and Isle au Haut (2.112), 50 miles SW, is generally rocky and indented by bays and broken by numerous islands. Amongst these islands are inshore passages, much used by shallow-draught vessels as they afford shelter and anchorage in adverse weather. Many of the bays make excellent anchorages.

2   In its W part, this coast forms a large bight between Schoodic Head (44°21′·00N 68°03′·20W) and Isle au Haut, the centre being occupied by Mount Desert Island, which divides the bight into Frenchman Bay to the E, and Blue Hill Bay with Jericho Bay, to the W.

3   Mount Desert Island (44°20′·50N 68°18′·00W) is mountainous and the highest feature on the coast of Maine. Its summits are rounded and several are nearly the same height, making it difficult to identify individual summits from a distance. Cadillac Mountain (2.35) is the highest peak.
   Other features that are prominent are Pigeon Hill (2.21), Schoodic Head and Isle au Haut.

Vertical datums and depths
2.4

1   Depths on Chart 4746 are reduced to Chart Datum which is approximately the level of LAT.
   Depths on Chart 2492 are reduced to Chart Datum which is the level of MLLW in US waters.

Dangers
2.5

1   Off-lying dangers extend up to 5 miles offshore from salient points in the E part of the area, and up to 10 miles off in the W part. Mount Desert Rock (2.24), the outermost danger, is isolated and lies 23 miles S of Schoodic Head.
   Caution. Many dangers on this coast rise abruptly from deep water, and sounding does not generally indicate their proximity until it is too late to avoid them.

Tidal streams
2.6

1   Tidal streams E of Mount Desert Rock are stronger than those farther W, and are more regular and conform more exactly to the rise and fall of the tides.

GREAT WASS ISLAND TO PETIT MANAN ISLAND

General information

Chart 4746, US Charts 13326, 13324, (see 1.16)
Description
2.7

1   The following paragraphs describe the coastal passage between Great Wass Island (44°29′·00N 67°35′·50W) and Petit Manan Island (2.9), 13 miles SW, and the inshore waters that lie between these two islands.

Directions
(continued from Nova Scotia and Bay of Fundy Pilot)

Principal marks
2.8

1   Major lights:
      Moose Peak Light (white tower) (44°28′·48N 67°31′·92W). See *Nova Scotia and Bay of Fundy Pilot.*
      Petit Manan Light (grey granite tower, 36 m in height) (44°22′·06N 67°51′·86W).

Great Wass Island to Petit Manan Island
2.9

1   From a position abreast Pond Point (44°26′·90N 67°35′·22W), the SW extremity of Great Wass Island, the coastal passage leads SW, passing:
      SE of Crumple Island (44°26′·60N 67°36′·00W), which is high, bare and rocky with several hummocks, thence:
      SE of Egg Rock (44°26′·09N 67°37′·84W). Seahorse Rock, 3½ cables SW, dries and is marked 2 cables farther SW by 2SR Light Buoy (starboard hand). Thence:

2   SE of a rock (44°22′·48N 67°46′·54W), with a depth of 3·0 m (10 ft), which is marked by

DTS Buoy (isolated danger). Tibbett Rock, marked by DT Buoy (isolated danger), lies 7½ cables farther NNW. Thence:

SE of Southeast Rock (44°19'·95N 67°48'·63W), a rocky shoal marked by 6A Light Buoy (starboard hand). A 12·4 m (40 ft) shoal lies 1¾ miles SW of Southeast Rock. Thence:

3   SE of Petit Manan Island (44°22'·05N 67°51'·94W), which is low and bare, with several buildings on it. Petit Manan Light (2.8) stands on the E extremity of the island. Simms Rock (44°20'·42N 67°51'·14W), with two below-water heads 2 cables apart, lies 1¾ miles SSE of the lighthouse. No 1 Buoy (port hand) is moored close NW of Simms Rock.

(Directions continue for coastal passage at 2.23)

Western Bay and west part of Moosabec Reach

General information
2.10
1   Western Bay, which is entered between Pond Point (44°26'·90N 67°35'·22W) and Nash Island (2.15), 7 miles W, is obstructed with a number of groups of islands and rocks, which lie mainly in a N-S direction. Between these groups are passages, available to mariners with local knowledge, which lead to the W entrance of Moosabec Reach. For details of the E part of Moosabec Reach, E of the bridge, see *Nova Scotia and Bay of Fundy Pilot*.

2   On the E side of the entrance to the bay, Fisherman Island (44°26'·85N 67°36'·60W) and Browney Island (44°27'·72N 67°37'·12W) lie on foul ground extending 2½ miles N from Crumple Island (2.9). A line of above and below-water rocks extends NE from Browney Island to Great Wass Island.

In the central part of the bay Outer Sand Island (44°27'·73N 67°40'·32W), 13 m (44 ft) in height and wooded, lies 2 miles W of Browney Island. Inner Sand Island (44°28'·30N 67°40'·45W), Drisko Island (44°28'·75N 67°40'·38W) and Stevens Island (44°29'·45N 67°40'·14W) form a group of wooded islands that lie on foul ground that extends N from Outer Sand Island in the central part of Western Bay, 3 miles W of Great Wass Island.

3   On the W side of the bay Black Rock (44°26'·25N 67°42'·75W), Flat Island (44°27'·56N 67°42'·39W), Green Island (44°29'·19N 67°42'·43W), both low and grassy, Plummer Island (44°29'·16N 67°41'·85W), wooded, and Ram Island (44°29'·48N 67°42'·35W), not to be confused with a larger island of the same name 3 miles E (2.11), lie in a N-S direction about 1½ miles W of the islands in the centre of the bay. Flat Island is separated from the other islands by a channel and the group is separated from Moose Neck (44°30'·30N 67°42'·80W), on the mainland NW, by Tibbett Narrows (2.12).

Passages
2.11
1   **Ram Island.** The passage that leads between Ram Island (44°29'·47N 67°37'·86W), not to be confused with a smaller island of the same name 3 miles W (2.10), and Stevens Island (2.10), though wide in its S part, is restricted by foul ground in its N part and is consequently only available to mariners with local knowledge.

Directions
2.12
1   **West approach to Moosabec Reach.** The W end of Moosabec Reach can be approached either through the passage that leads between Outer Sand Island, Drisko Island and Stevens Island on the E and Flat Island and Plummer Island on the W, or through Tibbett Narrows (44°29'·60N 67°42'·43W). Tibbett Narrows is a narrow channel, the NE entrance of which is marked by No 27 Light Buoy (port hand) and No 28 Buoy (starboard hand), leading between Tibbett Island and Ram Island (44°29'·48N 67°42'·35W) (2.10). These narrows are ¾ cable wide at the narrowest part with a least depth of 11 m (36 ft).

2   **Caution.** There are patches, with depths of 8·5 and 7·6 m (28 and 25 ft), 1½ cables ESE and 4 cables ENE of the E point of Tibbett Island.

West part of Moosabec Reach. From a position NE of Shabbit Island (44°30'·38N 67°41'·04W) the track through the W part of Moosabec Reach, which is marked by light buoys (lateral), leads ENE, passing:

3   SSE of the entrance to Wohoa Bay (44°31'·50N 67°41'·00W), into which flow West River and Indian River, thence:

NNW of Shabbit Island Ledge (44°30'·70N 67°40'·44W), which dries 3·4 m (11 ft) and is marked by No 23 Buoy (port hand), thence:

4   Between Fessenden Ledge (44°31'·10N 67°39'·97W) and the N point of Hardwood Island. The former dries 0·3 m (1 ft) and is marked by No 22 Light Buoy (starboard hand). The latter is wooded and has a house on its N point. A shoal, marked by No 21 Buoy (port hand), extends 3 cables NE from the island. Thence:

5   Between No 20 Buoy (starboard hand) and Pomp Island (44°31'·10N 67°39'·97W), wooded. No 4 Beacon marks a rock 1½ cables W of the N point of Pomp Island.

Thence to the bridge crossing Moosabec Reach linking Jonesport to Beals. For further details of this area see *Nova Scotia and Bay of Fundy Pilot*.

Anchorage
2.13
1   **Wohoa Bay.** Good anchorage may be obtained in the entrance to Wohoa Bay in 4 to 11 m (13 to 36 ft) between Fessenden Ledge (2.12) and Carrying Place Island, 1¼ miles W.

Anchorages and harbours

Eastern Harbor
2.14
1   **General information.** Eastern Harbor (44°30'·50N 67°43'·60W), on the W side of Moose Neck (2.10), is a secure anchorage for small vessels. A buoyed channel 1 cable wide leads into the harbour, a large part of which dries.

2   **Directions.** From position 44°29'·50N 67°43'·95W, S of the harbour entrance, the track into Eastern Harbor leads midway between Nos 1 and 2 Buoys (lateral), marking the limits of the shoal ground on either side of the harbour entrance, and thence N to the anchorage. This harbour is easily entered by day.

3   **Anchorage**, with the most swinging room, may be obtained in 5 to 7 m (18 to 22 ft), 4 cables inside the W entrance point. Vessels with a draught of 2·7 m (9 ft) can anchor in 3 to 5 m (9 to 15 ft) in Otter Cove on the E side of the harbour 5 cables within the entrance. Good anchorage may also be obtained in 2 to 4 m (8 to 12 ft), 1 cable NW of the fish factory pier.

Berth. A pier at the fish factory, on the E side of the harbour 9 cables from the entrance, has a depth alongside of 1·5 m.

Pleasant Bay
2.15
1   **General information.** Pleasant Bay (44°30′·50N 67°46′·50W), entered between Flint Island (44°28′·60N 67°47′·25W) (2.16) and Nash Island, 1¾ miles ESE, is a secure anchorage. There are numerous islands and reefs in the bay but important dangers are buoyed. A channel, not less than 5 cables wide with a least depth of 11 m (36 ft), leads up the bay to an anchorage.

2   **Navigation at night.** As there are no lighted aids to navigation N of Nash Island, a vessel should not enter the harbour at night. Navigation in the bay should present no difficulty by day in good visibility.

Ice obstructs navigation in the Pleasant River from December to April. In ordinary winters, ice that forms in the bay is swept out by the tide.

2.16
1   **Directions.** From a position SW of Nash Island (44°27′·85N 67°44′·75W) the route to the anchorages in Pleasant Bay leads N, passing:

W of NI Light Buoy (safe water) (44°27′·86N 67°45′·48W). The tower of a disused lighthouse stands on the W end of Nash Island. Thence:

2   W of Pot Rock (44°28′·77N 67°45′·07W), which is 1·8 m (6 ft) in height and bare, and:

E of Coles Ledge (44°28′·74N 67°46′·52W) which is 3 cables E of Flint Island (44°28′·60N 67°47′·25W), a wooded island 23 m (75 ft) in height and wildlife sanctuary. The ledge is marked by C1 Buoy (port hand). Thence:

3   Between Norton Island Ledge (44°29′·67N 67°45′·80W) and the E extremity of Dyer Island (44°29′·92N 67°48′·42W), 1¼ miles W. Dyer Island is separated from Flint Island to the S by Flint Island Narrows (44°28′·84N 67°47′·70W), a deep but narrow passage 1 cable wide, the S side of which is marked by C1 Buoy (port hand). The passage should not be used without local knowledge.

Thence proceed as necessary to the anchorages.

4   **Anchorages.** The best anchorage in 4 to 5 m (14 to 18 ft), which is used most frequently, is situated SE and E of Birch Islands (44°32′·00N 67°45′·80W), 4 miles N of Nash Island.

Anchorage may also be found in 9 to 11 m (30 to 36 ft), W of Nightcap Island (44°31′·19N 67°45′·55W), 3½ miles N of Nash Island.

In an emergency at night, anchorage may be obtained 2¼ miles NNW of Nash Island, close inside the entrance to the bay, in 18 m (60 ft).

Harrington Bay
2.17
1   **General information.** Harrington Bay (44°32′·00N 67°48′·60W), which is entered from the NW side of Pleasant Bay, is separated from the upper part of that bay on the E by Ripley Neck (44°32′·00N 67°47′·50W), and from Narraguagus Bay (2.18) on the W by Foster Island (44°31′·70N 67°49′·85W). The bay extends 2½ miles N from Strout Island (44°30′·96N 67°48′·25W), a wooded island which lies in the middle of its entrance. Harrington River enters the N end of the bay.

Ice very frequently forms in Harrington River and Bay between December and April as far down as Ripley Neck.

2   **Directions.** The main channel leads W of Strout Island through Strout Island Narrows (44°30′·90N 67°48′·43W), and has a depth of 8·2 m (27 ft).

Dyer Island Narrows (44°30′·85N 67°49′·40W), which has a depth of 2·4 m (8 ft), leads N of Dyer Island from Harrington Bay to Narraguagus Bay (2.18). The passage is buoyed but there are numerous dangers near to the fairway and the channel should not be used without local knowledge.

3   **Anchorage** may be obtained in 9 to 14 m (30 to 47 ft) on the E side of the bay, but the bay is seldom used except by local vessels.

Narraguagus Bay
2.18
1   **General information.** Narraguagus Bay (44°30′·20N 67°49′·90W) is entered between Bois Bubert Island (44°26′·20N 67°52′·00W) and Flint Island (2.16), 4 miles SW, which is wooded. It is a well sheltered anchorage, used year-round as a harbour of refuge by vessels up to 5·5 m (18 ft) draught, which anchor in the lower part of the bay.

A number of islands and rocks lie in the entrance to the bay.

2   **Directions.** From a position SSE of Flint Island the route to the anchorages in Narraguagus Bay leads NW, passing:

NE of Black Ledge (44°26′·38N 67°48′·63W), which dries 3·4 m (11 ft). This ledge is the N extremity of Jordans Delight Ledge (44°26′·00N 67°48′·93W), at the S extremity of which is a pipe, marked by No 2 Buoy (starboard hand). Thence:

3   NE of Mackerel Rock (44°26′·91N 67°48′·26W), an unmarked rock with a depth of 3 m (10 ft), thence:

NE of Pond Island (44°27′·50N 67°50′·20W) with a bare conical hill 48 m (158 ft) in height. A disused lighthouse (white tower) 5·5 m (18 ft) in height, stands on its E extremity and is prominent from E and S. No 1 Light Buoy (port hand) is moored off this point. Thence:

4   SW of Shipstern Island (44°28′·40N 67°48′·10W), 29 m (95 ft) in height and, wooded with rocky bluffs on its S side, thence:

Either side of Trafton Island (44°29′·05N 67°49′·80W), 26 m (84 ft) in height and wooded. There is a good channel on either side of the island. The E channel, 5 cables wide, separates Trafton Island from Tommy Island (44°29′·03N 67°48′·90W) and Western Reef (44°28′·66N 67°48′·83W). The S extremity of Western Reef is marked by No 2 Buoy (starboard hand).

5   Thence to the anchorages and the entrance to the Narraguagus River.

Caution. The vicinity of Black Ledge should be avoided as the bottom is very irregular and other dangers may exist.

2.19
1   **Anchorage** for vessels seeking shelter is usually obtained in 6 m (21 ft) between Trafton Island and No 5 Buoy (port hand) marking Lower Middle Ground (44°29′·85N 67°50′·78W), 1 mile NW. Good anchorage may also be obtained 4 cables NE of No 6 Beacon, marking Trafton Halftide Ledge (44°29′·91N 67°50′·10W).

2   Vessels up to 3 m (10 ft) draught sometimes anchor, in 4 to 5 m (14 to 17 ft), between Trafton Island and Trafton Halftide Ledge, 1 mile N.

Vessels bound for Narraguagus River (2.20) anchor, in 4 to 6 m (12 to 16 ft), 7 cables E of Mitchell Point (44°30′·60N 67°51′·35W).

3   Anchorage may also be obtained in 7 to 11 m (24 to 35 ft) in Douglas Island Harbor (44°27′·80N 67°51′·10W), which is formed by Pond Island, Douglas Islands (44°27′·00N 67°51′·00W), the N part of Bois Bubert Island and the mainland NW. It is seldom used as the anchorage above Trafton Island is better and a considerable sea enters the harbour between the Douglas Islands in heavy S weather.

Narraguagus River
2.20

1   **General information.** Narraguagus River flows into the NW corner of Narraguagus Bay.

A dredged channel, marked by buoys, leads for 2¾ miles from a position 5 cables SE of Mitchell Point to the town of Milbridge (44°32′·20N 67°52′·80W).

Ice seldom obstructs navigation except in January and February when the river is normally frozen to the mouth.

2   **Depths.** There are project depths of 3·3 to 6·1 m (11 to 20 ft) to Jordan Pier, thence 2·7 m (9 ft) to No 13 Buoy, thence 1·8 m (6 ft) to the town wharf. In 2004-2006 the anchorages off Mitchell Point and Millbridge had 0·7 to 2·7 m (2·4 to 9 ft) of water.

Berth. The town wharf, with reported depths alongside of 2·4 to 3 m, lies on the E side of the river, 2½ cables E of the bridge.

3   **Caution.** Old fish weirs, only part of which show at LW, are on either side of the channel just above No 1 Buoy at the channel entrance. Care should be taken to pass close to this buoy when heading up for the channel entrance.

Pigeon Hill Bay
2.21

1   **General information.** The entrance to Pigeon Hill Bay (44°25′·50N 67°52′·80W) lies between the S end of Bois Bubert Island (2.18) and Petit Manan Point, 2½ miles SW. The bay is easy of access by day and affords good anchorage.

2   **Directions.** From a position N of Petit Manan Light (44°22′·06N 67°51′·86W) (2.8) the route to the anchorages in Pigeon Hill Bay leads NNW, passing:
WSW of Whale Ledge (44°23′·88N 67°51′·94W), which dries 1·8 m (6 ft) and is marked on its S side by No 4 Buoy (starboard hand), thence:

3   WSW of Egg Rock (44°24′·40N 67°52′·12W), 5 m in height and consisting of a ledge of dark boulders, parts of which are dry. There is a narrow unmarked channel for small vessels between Egg Rock and Bois Bubert Island, the use of which requires local knowledge. Thence:
ENE of Wood Pond Point (44°24′·52N 67°53′·40W), from which a bank with depths of 2·1 to 5·2 m (7 to 17 ft) extends 8½ cables SSE, thence:

4   WSW of Gull Rocks (44°25′·85N 67°52′·55W), which dry 1·8 m (6 ft).
Thence to the anchorage.

Useful mark:
Pigeon Hill (44°27′·30N 67°53′·37W), a bare-topped hill, 97 m (317 ft) in height, standing on the W side of the head of the bay.

5   **Channel.** A narrow channel leads from the head of the bay to Douglas Island Harbor (2.19). Local knowledge is necessary to use this channel.

Anchorage may be obtained in 4 to 7 m (12 to 24 ft), clear of a cable area running through the centre of the bay, but is seldom used except by local fishermen.

Caution. Fish weirs extend from either side of the bay.

PETIT MANAN ISLAND TO ISLE AU HAUT
General information
Charts 4746, 2492, US Charts 13312, 13313, (see 1.16)
Description
2.22

1   The following paragraphs describe the coastal passage between Petit Manan Island (44°22′·05N 67°51′·94W) (2.9) and Isle au Haut (2.112), 40 miles SW.

Directions
(continued from 2.9)

Principal marks
2.23

1   **Major lights:**
Petit Manan Light (44°22′·06N 67°51′·86W) (2.8).
Mount Desert Rock Light (granite conical tower, 23 m in height) (43°58′·11N 68°07′·71W).
Great Duck Island Light (white tower, black lantern) (44°08′·52N 68°14′·75W).

Petit Manan Island to Isle au Haut
2.24

1   From a position SE of Petit Manan Island (44°22′·05N 67°51′·94W) (2.9) the coastal passage leads SW, passing:
SE of Moulton Ledge (44°21′·87N 67°56′·09W). This ledge, awash, is marked on its W side by ML Light Buoy (preferred channel to port). Many rocky patches surround the ledge including 5·5 and 7 m (18 and 23 ft) ones, situated respectively, 6 cables SSE and 3 cables SE. Thence:

2   SE of Schoodic Island (44°19′·90N 68°01′·97W), low and fringed by reefs. Its N end is grassy and S end is wooded; 2S Light Buoy (starboard hand) is moored 4 cables S of the S end of the island. Thence:
SE of Baker Island (44°14′·47N 68°11′·94W) (2.41). This island forms the W entrance point to Frenchman Bay. Thence:

3   Clear of No 1 Light Buoy (special) (44°06′·36N 68°06′·53W), thence:
SE of Great Duck Island, which is partly wooded and appears as two islands from a distance E or W. A light (2.23) stands on the island. Thence:
Clear of Mount Desert Rock (43°58′·11N 68°07′·71W), which is 6 m in height. A light (2.23) and house stand on the rock. Thence:

4   SE of Long Island (44°06′·80N 68°21′·21W), wooded, but with no prominent marks, thence:
SE of Great Spoon Island (44°02′·55N 68°33′·40W), the largest of a group of grassy islands that lie 2 miles off the E coast of Isle du Haut. Colt Ledge (44°01′·23N 68°34′·01W), which has a depth of 2·4 m (8 ft) and is marked by 2A Buoy (starboard hand) on its S side, lies 1½ miles SSW. Thence:

5   SE of Eastern Head (44°00′·80N 68°36′·90W), 39 m (129 ft) in height, the SE extremity of Isle

au Haut (2.112). Eastern Ear Ledge (44°00′·30N 68°35′·80W), awash, lies 7½ cables SE of this headland and is marked on its SE side by No 2 Buoy (starboard hand). Thence:

SE of Roaring Bull Ledge (43°59′·60N 68°37′·95W), which dries 1·2 m (4 ft) and is marked on its S side by No 2 Light Buoy (starboard hand), and:

6 SE of Western Head (44°00′·80N 68°39′·18W), 54 m (176 ft) in height, at the S extremity of Isle au Haut.

Useful mark:
Baker Island Light (white stone tower, 13 m in height) (44°14′·47N 68°11′·94W).

(Directions continue for coastal passage at 2.102, for East Penobscot Bay at 2.114, and for West Penobscot Bay at 2.142)

Anchorages and harbours

Charts 4746, 2492, US Chart 13324, (see 1.16)

Dyer Bay

2.25

1 **General information.** Dyer Bay (44°26′·60N 67°55′·20W) affords good anchorage, but the dangers in it are unmarked and it is seldom used except by small local vessels.

It is entered 3¼ miles NW of Petit Manan Light (2.8) between Petit Manan Point (44°23′·70N 67°53′·98W) and Dyer Point (44°24′·71N 67°55′·93W), 1¾ miles NW. Bonney Chess Ledge (44°24′·39N 67°55′·42W) and The Castle (44°24′·39N 67°55′·17W), groups of rocks with passages between them, lie in the entrance to the bay.

2 **Tidal streams** in the entrance are strong but follow the direction of the channel except near Dyer Point where they set into Gouldsboro Bay (2.27).

2.26

1 **Directions.** Vessels entering the bay should pass about 1½ cables E of The Castle (2.25) and proceed up Dyer Bay in mid-channel.

There should be no difficulty for a vessel to enter by day with good visibility, but no vessel with a draught of over 2·4 m (8 ft) should attempt to enter at LW without local knowledge.

2 The channel through the bay narrows to a width of 1½ cables between shoals which extend from Stanley Point (44°25′·24N 67°55′·64W) on the W side, and Yellow Birch Head (44°25′·07N 67°54′·73W) on the E side of the bay, 1 mile N of the entrance. Then it widens to 5 cables, before reducing to 2 cables abreast Sheep Island (44°27′·63N 67°54′·91W).

3 **Caution** should be exercised as there are several fish weirs, which are covered at or near HW, in the bay.

Anchorage should be selected near the middle of the bay, not less than 1¼ miles above The Castle, in 6 to 13 m (19 to 42 ft), but not more than 2½ cables above Sheep Island (3 miles N of the entrance).

Gouldsboro Bay

2.27

1 **General information.** Gouldsboro Bay (44°25′·40N 67°57′·70W), which provides good anchorage, is entered 4 miles NW of Petit Manan Light (2.8) between Dyer Point (2.25) and Youngs Point (44°23′·97N 67°57′·59W), 1¼ miles SW.

The bay is also the approach route to the villages of Gouldsboro (44°28′·81N 68°02′·62W) and Steuben (44°30′·55N 67°58′·33W), which lie at the NW and NE heads of the bay 6¼ and 6½ miles, respectively, above the entrance. Steuben can be reached at HW by vessels with a draught of 2·1 to 2·4 m (7 to 8 ft).

2 Sally Islands (44°24′·06N 67°56′·77W) are a chain of islands and rocks that lie across the entrance to Gouldsboro Bay. Eastern Way and Western Passage are the two navigable channels leading through the Sally Islands into the bay. These passages are not easy to identify when approaching from the W.

Ice obstructs navigation in Gouldsboro Bay from December to March and in severe winters the bay is completely closed.

2.28

1 **Directions.** Eastern Way (44°24′·18N 67°56′·48W) leads between Eastern Island (44°24′·25N 67°56′·19W) and Bald Rock (44°24′·15N 67°56′·69W), 3 cables W. The passage is 1½ cables wide with depths of over 5·5 m (18 ft) and ¾ cable wide with depths of over 13·7 m (45 ft). Depths of 5·2 m (17 ft) extend up to 1¼ cables from the islands on either side of the channel. Vessels should pass midway between Eastern Island and Bald Rock.

Caution. The tidal streams set strongly across this channel with the flood tide setting NE and the ebb SW.

2 Western Passage leads between Sally Island (44°24′·06N 67°56′·77W) and Sheep Island (44°23′·85N 67°57′·31W), 4 cables W, at the W end of the Sally Islands. The passage has a least depth of 4·9 m (16 ft) and is ½ cable wide. Vessels should pass close along the E side of Sheep Island and W of the drying ledges that extend 2½ cables W of Sally Island.

3 **Tidal streams** follow the channel at a maximum rate of between 2 and 3 kn.

Caution. This passage should not be attempted without local knowledge.

Useful mark:
Point Francis (high and wooded) (44°26′·85N 67°58′·94W). This point, 3¼ miles above Youngs Point, can be clearly seen from the entrance of the bay.

4 **Anchorage** can be obtained anywhere between the entrance and Point Francis, not less than 2½ cables from the shore.

Corea Harbour

2.29

1 **General information.** Corea Harbor (44°23′·85N 67°58′·20W) is a well sheltered cove which lies 4½ cables SW of Youngs Point (2.27) inside Western Island (44°23′·43N 67°58′·03W) and Outer Bar Island (44°23′·43N 67°57′·69W), the W two islands of the Sally Islands (2.27).

Corea, a fishing village, stands at the head of the harbour.

Ice usually obstructs the harbour from December to March, but fishing vessels can continue to operate from the entrance piers during that period.

2.30

1 **Landmark:**
Church spire (44°24′·10N 67°58′·60W), standing NW of the head of the harbour.

Track. From a position S of Western Island (2.29) an unmarked channel leads N and then NE, passing:

2 W of a rock which dries 1·8 m (6 ft) (44°23′·27N 67°57′·81W). No 2 Buoy (starboard hand) is moored 1 cable ESE of the rock. Thence:

W of Western Island (wooded), thence:

NW of a rock awash (reported 1979) (44°23'·55N 67°58'·16W).

Thence NW along the NE side of the entrance into the harbour. Low water is the best time to enter the harbour.

3   **Anchorage** may be obtained in the centre of the harbour. The anchorage has controlling depths of 1·5 to 2·4 m (5 to 8 ft), with lesser depths along the edges.

Berths. Two lobster wharves with pontoons have reported depths alongside of 1·8 to 2·4 m. Other wharves dry at LW.

Supplies. Fuel.

Prospect Harbor
2.31

1   **General information.** Prospect Harbor, 4½ miles NNE of Schoodic Island (2.24), is entered between Cranberry Point (44°23'·12N 67°59'·00W), 1½ miles SW of Youngs Point, and Spruce Point (44°21'·41N 68°01'·65W), 2½ miles farther SW. The outer harbour has ample depth and affords anchorage for large vessels, but is exposed to S and SE winds. It is easily entered through the channels that lead on either side of the dangers off the entrance.

2   Prospect Harbor Point (44°24'·20N 68°00'·75W), 1½ miles NW of Cranberry Point, divides the head of the harbour into two coves, Inner Harbor, to the W, with the village of Prospect Harbor at its head, and Sand Cove, to the NE.

The approaches to Prospect Harbor are obstructed by a group of rocky patches.

Ice seldom obstructs the harbour.

3   **Directions from east.** From a position SE of Cranberry Point the E approach to Prospect Harbor leads NW, within the white sector (317°–323°) of Prospect Harbor Point Light (white conical tower, 12 m in height) (44°24'·20N 68°00'·78W), passing:

   SW of Moulton Ledge (44°21'·87N 67°56'·09W) (2.24), thence:

4   NE of Little Black Ledge (44°22'·09N 67°58'·64W) and Big Black Ledge (4 cables W), which are awash and 1·5 m (5 ft) in height, respectively. 1LB Buoy (port hand) is moored 2 cables E of Little Black Ledge. Thence:

   SW of Cranberry Point. 2CP Buoy (starboard hand) is moored 3 cables S of this point.

Thence into the outer harbour.

5   **Directions from south.** From a position E of Spruce Point the S approach to Prospect Harbor leads N, within the white sector (348°–356°) of Prospect Harbor Point Light, passing:

   E of the entrance to Bunkers Harbor (44°22'·20N 68°01'·65W) (2.33), and:

6   W of Old Woman (44°22'·35N 68°00'·00W), drying 1·5 m (5 ft) and marked on its SW side by No 2 Buoy (starboard hand), thence:

   E of Prospect Point (44°23'·08N 68°01'·00W).

Thence into the outer harbour.

Useful mark:

   Church spire (44°23'·38N 68°02'·48W) at the head of Birch Harbor (2.33).

2.32

1   **Inner Harbor** (44°24'·08N 68°01'·20W), entered between Prospect Harbor Point and Clark Point (44°23'·85N 68°01'·15W), has 3·7 to 11 m (12 to 36 ft) just inside its entrance and is sheltered from all but SE winds. Small local vessels use the harbour.

The head and NE side of the harbour are obstructed by ledges; those extending from Clark Point on the SW shore are marked by No 3 Buoy and No 5 Beacon (both port hand).

2   **Anchorage** may be obtained in 4 to 10 m (13 to 33 ft), soft bottom, in the SW part of the harbour.

Pier with depths alongside of 3 m is situated at the cannery at Clark Point.

Supplies are available at the village of Prospect Harbor, at the head of the inlet.

Sand Cove (44°24'·40N 68°00'·40W), NE of Inner Harbor, with depths of 7·3 to 11 m (24 to 36 ft) in its outer part, is seldom used.

2.33

1   **Bunkers Harbor** (44°22'·21N 68°01'·77W) and Birch Harbor (44°22'·95N 68°01'·50W) are two shallow coves lying on the W side of the harbour between Prospect Point and Spruce Point. Both these coves are obstructed by reefs and their entrance channels are unmarked. Each harbour has a fishing village at its head.

Bunkers Harbor is obstructed by Bunkers Ledge (44°22'·10N 68°01'·28W) on the S side of its entrance. The E end of this ledge is marked by No 1 Buoy (port hand). The harbour has a pier with a pontoon, with a depth alongside of 1·8 m, and a dredged anchorage with a depth of 1·5 m (5 ft).

Schoodic Harbor
2.34

1   Schoodic Harbor (44°21'·10N 68°02'·10W), the entrance to which lies between Spruce Point (2.31) and Schoodic Point (2.41), has ample depth, but is exposed to the sea and is considerably obstructed by reefs. It is rarely used as an anchorage.

FRENCHMAN BAY AND ADJACENT WATERS

General information

Chart 4746, US Chart 13318, (see 1.16)
Description
2.35

1   Frenchman Bay (44°26'·00N 68°11'·50W), lies between Schoodic Peninsula and the E side of Mount Desert Island. From its entrance between Schoodic Point (2.41) and Baker Island (2.41), the bay is 12 miles long and 4 miles wide to its head, which is divided into several arms. It is rocky, but the water is deep and generally free from dangers except near its shores.

2   The bay is divided halfway up by the Porcupine Islands (44°24'·30N 68°10'·65W), a group of islands which extend across the bay and have two good channels leading between them to the upper part of the bay.

Cadillac Mountain (44°21'·08N 68°13'·59W), the summit of Mount Desert Island, is the highest point on the coast of Maine and in clear weather is visible between 35 and 45 miles. However it should be noted that there are several peaks on the island of nearly the same elevation, making it difficult to identify individual peaks.

Recommended routes
2.36

1   Deep-draught vessels, high-speed ferries and other commercial vessels transiting through Frenchman Bay are requested to follow recommended routes as shown on the charts. These routes have been established to provide safe passage for increased commercial traffic and to prevent the loss of fishing gear placed in the approaches to, and within, Frenchman Bay.

Pilotage
2.37

1 Pilotage is compulsory for all foreign vessels and US vessels under register in foreign trade, with a draught of 2·7 m (9 ft) or more. The pilot boards about 1½ miles S or 2 miles SE of FB Light Buoy (2.41). See *Admiralty List of Radio Signals Volume 6(5)* for details.

Natural conditions
2.38

1 **Local magnetic anomaly**. The normal magnetic variation is increased/decreased by 3° in the vicinity of Jordan Island (2.60).

Ice. During mild winters Frenchman Bay is usually clear of ice to Skillings River (2.63), but the bays and rivers opening into the N part of the bay are frozen over. Winter Harbor (2.57) is seldom closed by ice.

Fog. It is reported that during foggy weather Frenchman Bay usually clears of fog during the day, although it may remain thick outside the harbour entrance.

Directions

Principal marks
2.39

1 **Major lights:**
Mount Desert Rock Light (43°58'·11N 68°07'·71W) (2.23).
Great Duck Island Light (44°08'·52N 68°14'·75W) (2.23).
Egg Rock Light (white tower) (44°21'·24N 68°08'·30W).

Other aid to navigation
2.40

1 **Racon:**
FB Light Buoy (44°19'·35N 68°07'·40W).
See *Admiralty List of Radio Signals Volume 2*.

Approach
2.41

1 **South-east approach.** From position 44°15'·00N 67°56'·00W the recommended track leads WNW to FB Light Buoy (44°19'·35N 68°07'·40W), passing:
SW of Schoodic Point (44°19'·90N 68°02'·95W), the S point of Little Moose Island (44°20'·00N 68°03'·00W) which lies 1 mile S of Schoodic Head, the most prominent hill on the E side of Frenchman Bay, thence:

2 SW of Big Moose Island (44°20'·23N 68°03'·74W), on the top of which stands a prominent water tower.
Thence to a position close NE of FB Light Buoy.

South approach. From position 44°03'·00N 68°09'·00W the recommended track leads N to FB Light Buoy (preferred channel to port), passing:

3 E of Baker Island (44°14'·47N 68°11'·94W), mostly wooded but with grass on its NW end and several houses on it. The island is surrounded by above and below-water ledges and should be given a berth of at least 4 cables. A light (2.24) stands on the island. Thence:

4 E of East Bunker Ledge (44°16'·80N 68°13'·39W) (2.44), which lies in the entrance to Southwest Harbor (2.47), thence:
E of Otter Point (44°18'·44N 68°11'·48W). Otter Cliff Ledge (44°18'·52N 68°11'·08W), which dries 1·8 m (6 ft), lies 2 cables E of the point and is marked by No 1 Buoy (port hand).
Thence to a position close W of FB Light Buoy.

Entrance and inner part
2.42

1 From a position in the vicinity of FB Light Buoy the recommended track through the entrance and into the inner part of Frenchman Bay leads generally WNW then NNW, passing:
ENE of Old Whale Ledge (44°20'·10N 68°10'·31W), awash and marked by No 3 Light Buoy (port hand), and:

2 WSW of No 4 Buoy (starboard hand) (44°20'·26N 68°08'·59W), thence:
WSW of Egg Rock (44°21'·24N 68°08'·30W), a low and mostly bare island from which drying ledges extend 1 cable NE and 4 cables SW. A light (2.39) is exhibited from the rock. Thence:

3 ENE of The Thrumcap (44°21'·80N 68°10'·60W), round and rocky with a clump of trees in the centre, thence:
SW of Ironbound Island (44°23'·40N 68°08'·20W), the largest island in Frenchman Bay and thickly wooded with high vertical cliffs, thence:

4 NE of Bald Porcupine Island (44°23'·23N 68°10'·90W), with bare rocky slopes. A breakwater, which dries, extends SW from the island for 1¼ cables, its extremity being marked by a light beacon (white diamond, orange border, marked DANGER SUBMERGED BREAKWATER). The island and the breakwater form the S side of Bar Harbor (2.52). Thence two routes lead W and NW into the anchorages.

5 **West route** leads W between Bald Porcupine Island and Sheep Porcupine Island (44°24'·01N 68°11'·63W) to Anchorage A (2.55), in Bar Harbor.

North-west route leads NW between Sheep Porcupine Island and Burnt Porcupine Island (44°24'·29N 68°10'·70W), 5 cables ENE. This channel, the W side of which is marked by No 7 Buoy (port hand), is deep and clear of dangers, and leads to Anchorage B (2.55).

East route leads NE between Long Porcupine Island (44°24'·40N 68°09'·75W) and Ironbound Island.

Southwest Harbor and adjacent waters
Chart 4746, US Chart 13321, (see 1.16)

General information
2.43

1 The waters on the W side of the approaches to Frenchman Bay, W of a line joining Baker Island (44°14'·47N 68°11'·94W) (2.41) and East Point (44°17'·30N 68°14'·10W), 3 miles NNW, contain a number of harbours and coves, of which the most important is Southwest Harbor (2.47), much used as a harbour of refuge. These waters are the approaches to several important villages and summer resorts, and are frequented by fishing boats and pleasure craft.

2 **Approaches.** Eastern Way (44°16'·85N 68°15'·00W), with a least depth of 12·2 m (40 ft), is the main approach to Southwest Harbor. It is well marked and the recommended route for deep-draught vessels. Small vessels may approach Southwest Harbor through Gilley Thorofare (2.45), the channel S of Sutton Island, or through Western Way (2.46).

3 **No-Discharge Zone (NDZ).** Southwest Harbor and adjacent waters have been designated as a NDZ. See 1.41.

Directions for Southwest Harbor
2.44

1 **Eastern Way**. From a position N of Baker Island the main route to Southwest Harbor leads generally W through a well marked channel, passing:

N of Lewis Rock (44°17'·01N 68°13'·45W), which lies 2 cables NNW of East Bunker Ledge (44°16'·80N 68°13'·39W), which is partly above-water and has a stone beacon standing near its SW end. 3A Buoy (port hand) marks the NW side of Lewis Rock. Thence:

S of No 4 Light Buoy (starboard hand) (44°17'·17N 68°13'·82W), which marks a rocky ledge extending SE from East Point, thence:

S of Bowden Ledge (44°17'·15N 68°14'·60W), with a depth of 0·6 m (2 ft) and marked by No 6 Buoy (starboard hand), thence:

N of Sutton Island (44°16'·40N 68°15'·40W), a wooded island with the summer resort of Sutton standing at its W end. The ferry pier, with a depth alongside of 1·8 m, is on the S shore. And:

S of Long Pond Shoal (44°17'·01N 68°15'·29W), with a least depth of 1·5 m (5 ft) at its W end. No 8 Buoy (starboard hand) marks the S side of the shoal. Thence:

S of Bear Island (44°17'·02N 68°16'·12W), partly wooded. No 10 Light Buoy (starboard hand) is moored ¾ cable S of the island and a light (white tower) is exhibited from the island. Thence:

S of Eastern Point (44°16'·57N 68°17'·50W), the SE extremity of Greening Island (2.47). No 6 Buoy (starboard hand) is moored 1 cable S of the point.

2.45

Passage south of Sutton Island. From a position S of East Bunker Ledge (44°16'·80N 68°13'·39W), Gilley Thorofare, the passage S of Sutton Island, which has a depth of 4·9 m (16 ft), leads WSW, passing:

S of Old Tom (44°16'·49N 68°13'·97W), a patch with a depth of 7·3 m (24 ft), thence:

Between Spurling Rock (44°15'·88N 68°15'·35W), marked by No 2 Light Buoy, and the S side of Sutton Island.

Thence W through waters clear of charted dangers to Southwest Harbor.

2.46

Western Way (44°14'·00N 68°17'·40W), which leads between the W side of Great Cranberry Island and Mount Desert Island, has a least depth of 4 m (13 ft) over the bar at its N end and is marked by light buoys and buoys. Unmarked 3 and 3·6 m (10 and 12 ft) patches lie close to the fairway.

This passage is frequently used by small vessels approaching Southwest Harbor and Frenchman Bay from the W in calm weather, but should not be used by vessels with a draught of more than 3 m (10 ft) without local knowledge.

Southwest Harbor

2.47

Description. Southwest Harbor (44°16'·35N 68°18'·40W) is entered between the SE extremity of Greening Island (44°16'·75N 68°18'·00W), low and wooded, and Kings Point (44°16'·02N 68°17'·98W), 6 cables SSW. It is the most important harbour on the S side of Mount Desert Island, providing well sheltered anchorage in 2 to 15 m (6 to 50 ft). The village of Southwest Harbor lies on the N side of the head of the harbour.

Ice does not usually restrict the harbour. In very severe winters it has been known to extend as far as the Cranberry Islands but is carried out to sea from Somes Sound on the ebb tide.

Anchorage may be obtained in 10 to 15 m (34 to 50 ft) midway between Greening Island and the S shore. Small vessels can anchor farther in and depths decrease gradually to 3·7 m (12 ft) at a distance of ½ cable from the rock, marked by a beacon, at the head of the harbour.

Alongside berths. A number of berths, including the Coast Guard wharf, with depths alongside of 1 to 5 m, are situated on the N and S shores of the harbour.

Repairs. Patent slip available to vessels, of up to 30 m in length, is situated at a boat building yard on the N shore.

Supplies: fuel, water and limited stores.

Other anchorages and harbours

2.48

Seal Harbor (44°17'·52N 68°14'·44W), on the N side of Eastern Way, between East Point and Crowninshield Point (44°17'·30N 68°14'·64W), 3½ cables W, provides anchorage for small vessels in 5 m (15 to 18 ft), but is exposed to SE winds. No 1 Buoy (port hand) marks the E side of a ledge, partly above water, that extends 2 cables E from the W side of the entrance.

The village of Seal Harbor has numerous summer homes. Its main wharf, with a depth alongside of 2·7 m, is situated on the E side of the harbour. Water is available.

Bracy Cove (44°17'·40N 68°15'·22W), 6 cables W of Seal Harbor, is unsuitable for anchoring as the bottom is rocky and the cove is open SE.

2.49

Cranberry Harbor (44°15'·40N 68°14'·50W) is situated between Little Cranberry Island (44°15'·62N 68°13'·54W) and Great Cranberry Island (44°16'·75N 68°18'·00W), both of which are low and wooded, and provides anchorage in 4 to 6 m (14 to 20 ft) in the middle of the harbour SW of Hadlock Cove (44°15'·62N 68°14'·39W).

Caution. An unmarked obstruction, with a swept depth of 1·8 m (6 ft), lies in the approaches.

Piers. Three piers with pontoons are situated at Hadlock Cove. The ferry pier has a depth alongside of 2·7 m.

Repairs. Three patent slips at Hadlock Cove are available for craft of up to 15 m in length.

2.50

Northeast Harbor (44°17'·80N 68°16'·87W), an important yachting centre, is entered W of Bear Island (44°17'·03N 68°16'·10W).

The harbour is reported to be free of ice in the average winter, but to freeze out as far as Bear Island in severe winters.

A rock, which dries 0·9 m (3 ft), lies in the middle of the entrance to the harbour. No 2 Light Buoy (starboard hand) and No 1 Buoy (port hand) are moored close W and E, respectively, of the rock. The best passage into the harbour leads W of the rock.

The head of the harbour is shallow, but there is anchorage for small vessels in 4 to 9 m (14 to 28 ft) in the lower part of the harbour.

Piers, with depths alongside of 3·0 m, are situated on the W shore of the harbour.

Supplies: fuel; water and provisions.

2.51

Somes Sound (44°20'·00N 68°18'·70W), a narrow rocky inlet, is entered to the N of Greening Island, between Manchester Point (44°17'·68N 68°18'·21W) and Fernald Point (44°17'·82N 68°18'·70W). It extends 4½ miles N to Somes Harbor (44°21'·68N 68°19'·60W).

The entrance, where the navigable channel is only ¾ cable wide, has a least depth of 6·1 m (20 ft). Middle Rock (44°17'·60N 68°18'·47W), marked by No 5 Light Buoy (port hand), lies in the W side of the entrance.

2 Anchorage may be obtained within Somes Sound in 16 to 22 m (54 ft to 12 fm). Heavy squalls occasionally blow down from the mountains.

Bar Harbor

Chart 4746, US Chart 13323, (see 1.16)

General information
2.52

Bar Harbor (44°23'·51N 68°11'·48W) is bounded on the W and N by the coast of Mount Desert Island, Bar Island (44°23'·90N 68°12'·40W), wooded, and Sheep Porcupine Island (2.42). On the S it is bounded by Bald Porcupine Island and a breakwater (2.42). Cruise liners use the anchorages.

Port Authority. Maine Port Authority, State House Station, Augusta, ME 04333.

Website. www.maineports.com

Limiting conditions
2.53

1 **Swell.** Although the breakwater affords some shelter, a swell sets into the harbour with SE winds and vessels should not attempt to ride out a gale from that direction.

Ice. Port operations are not affected by ice.

Directions
2.54

1 The harbour is normally entered from the E between Bald Porcupine Island and Sheep Porcupine Island (2.42), through the main entrance, which is clear of dangers.

There is also a channel, ¾ cable wide with a depth of 11·3 m (37 ft), leading into the harbour from the S, between the SW breakwater and the W shore. This channel should be used with caution as in calm weather at HW, there may be no indication of the breakwater except for the light beacon marking its SW end. This channel should only be used with local knowledge.

Berths
2.55

1 **Anchorage A,** with 9 to 31 m (30 ft to 17 fm), is centred 5 cables SE of Bar Island. This is a general anchorage reserved for passenger vessels, small commercial vessels and pleasure craft.

Anchorage B, with 14 to 55 m (46 ft to 30 fm), soft mud, is centred 3½ cables N of Bar Island. This anchorage is a general anchorage reserved primarily for passenger vessels of 61 m (200 ft) or more LOA. A dangerous wreck lies in the W part of the anchorage.

2 **Municipal Pier,** situated on the N side of the town, has a reported depth of 3 m at its head. There are other wharves and landing stages with similar or less water.

Ferry terminal, situated 1 mile NW of the town, is currently (2012) disused.

Port services
2.56

1 **Repairs.** Minor repairs.
Other facility. Hospital.
Supplies: fuel; water; provisions and stores.

Anchorages and harbours

Chart 4746, US Chart 13322, (see 1.16)

Winter Harbor
2.57

1 Winter Harbor (44°22'·40N 68°04'·90W), situated on the E side of Frenchman Bay, is a much frequented harbour of refuge and provides good anchorage and holding in 9 to 16 m (30 to 54 ft). It is comparatively free from dangers, and although open S, a heavy sea never enters.

2 **Entrances.** The main entrance lies 2 miles NW of Schoodic Point, between Turtle Island (44°21'·56N 68°05'·94W) and Mark Island (44°21'·70N 68°05'·28W) on the W and the Schoodic Peninsula on the E. This entrance is deep, and clear of dangers. The harbour can also be entered from N along the W side of Grindstone Neck (44°22'·70N 68°05'·60W), a promontory which forms the W side of the N part of the harbour. This entrance should not be used without local knowledge and only by vessels with a draught of 3 m (10 ft) or less.

Bar Harbor from SW (2.52)
(Original dated 2007)

(Photograph - Cdr S Foster, MV Saga Ruby)

2.58

1 **Directions.** From a position S of Mark Island (44°21'·70N 68°05'·28W) the route through the main entrance leads N, passing:

E of MI Light Buoy (preferred channel to starboard) (44°21'·49N 68°05'·12W), thence:

E of Mark Island, thence:

2 E of Grindstone Ledge (44°22'·17N 68°05'·26W), a drying ledge, marked close SE by GL Light Buoy (preferred channel to starboard). A beacon stands on the ledge. Thence:

E of Grindstone Point (44°22'·31N 68°05'·30W).

Thence the track continues N to the head of the harbour, which is divided into three coves.

3 **Useful marks**:

White tower (disused lighthouse) (44°21'·69N 68°05'·26W) standing on Mark Island.

Cupola (44°23'·01N 68°05'·50W). Grey house with glass roof on the W side of the harbour.

Spire (44°23'·60N 68°05'·22W) in the town of Winter Harbor.

2.59

1 **Winter Harbor**, a small town, stands at the head of Henry Cove, the E cove. Supplies and small repairs are available.

Anchorage. Best anchorage may be obtained in Sand Cove, the W cove.

Chart 4746, US Chart 13318, (see 1.16)

Stave Island Harbor

2.60

1 Stave Island Harbor (44°25'·40N 68°07'·50W), which is on the E side of Frenchman Bay 5 miles within the entrance, is a much frequented excellent harbour of refuge.

The harbour is bounded on the E by the mainland, the S by Jordan Island (44°24'·76N 68°07'·52W) and the W by Stave Island (44°26'·30N 68°08'·13W). Both these islands are linked to the mainland by bars.

2 South Gouldsboro (44°26'·06N 68°07'·02W) is a village on the NE shore of the harbour and Summer Harbor (44°24'·87N 68°06'·61W) is a cove with a settlement on the SE shore.

Ice usually obstructs the harbour from December to March.

3 **Directions.** The route into the harbour leads ENE between Yellow Island (44°25'·03N 68°08'·21W), wooded with yellowish rocks, which lies off the NW point of Jordan Island, and the S end of Stave Island. The entrance is clear of charted dangers.

Anchorage, which is sheltered from all but SW winds, may be found in the harbour in 6 to 11 m (21 to 37 ft), soft bottom.

Pier with depth alongside of 1 m is situated at South Gouldsboro.

Flanders Bay

2.61

1 Flanders Bay (44°28'·00N 68°07'·80W), which is in the NE part of Frenchman Bay, 7 miles within the entrance, is an excellent anchorage, but is seldom used except by small craft.

Sullivan Harbor

2.62

1 **Description.** Sullivan Harbor is situated in the N part of Frenchman Bay, 8 miles within its entrance. It is entered between Bean Point (44°28'·35N 68°11'·60W) and Hancock Point (44°27'·96N 68°13'·45W), the SE extremity of Crabtree Neck, 1½ miles WSW.

The harbour extends 9 miles N and has a least depth of 7·6 m (25 ft) as far as Sullivan Falls (44°31'·25N 68°13'·23W), 3 miles NNW of Bean Point. Navigation above Sullivan Falls should not be attempted without local knowledge.

Ice obstructs navigation in Taunton Bay and Sullivan Harbor from January to March.

Skillings River

2.63

1 **Description.** Skillings River (44°29'·70N 68°16'·00W) is situated in the NW part of Frenchman Bay. It is entered between Hancock Point and Meadow Point (44°27'·60N 68°16'·20W), 1¾ miles W. The river narrows to a width of 2 cables abreast Pecks Point (44°29'·27N 68°16'·62W), 1¾ miles NW of Hancock Point, above which is a narrow, winding, unmarked channel much obstructed by dangers.

Local knowledge is required for navigation beyond Pecks Point.

2 **Anchorage,** for vessels wishing to enter the river, may be obtained in 9 to 13 m (30 to 42 ft), 1½ miles above Hancock Point.

Eastern Bay

2.64

1 **Description.** Eastern Bay (44°26'·50N 68°16'·90W) is situated at the head of Frenchman Bay, 9 miles from the entrance. It is entered between Sand Point (44°26'·32N 68°16'·15W) and Meadow Point, 1 mile N. The bay is generally clear of dangers, except for Googins Ledge (44°26'·73N 68°17'·26W) lying off the N side of the bay. This ledge dries and its S edge is marked by No 14 Buoy (starboard hand).

2 Eastern Bay leads into Mount Desert Narrows (44°25'·80N 68°22'·00W), which in turn leads through a narrow, shallow and unmarked channel into Blue Hill Bay (2.65). This channel, which is crossed by a fixed bridge with a vertical clearance of 7·6 m (25 ft), can be used at HW by craft with a draught of 2·7 m (9 ft).

3 **Anchorage** may be obtained by deep-draught vessels. A good berth is W of Googins Ledge in 11 to 16 m (36 to 54 ft). Another good berth is S of Googins Ledge in 13 to 15 m (42 to 48 ft), 3 cables from the shore off Salsbury (44°25'·94N 68°17'·11W) and Emery Coves (44°25'·96N 68°17'·59W).

BLUE HILL BAY AND ADJACENT WATERS

General information

Charts 4746, 2492, US Charts 13313, 13316, (see 1.16)

Description

2.65

1 The following paragraphs describe Blue Hill Bay and its adjacent waters, including Jericho Bay (2.77).

Blue Hill Bay (44°15'·00N 68°28'·00W) lies between Mount Desert Island on the E, and the mainland with a chain of islands and shoals which extend SE from Naskeag Point (44°13'·73N 68°31'·44W) on the W.

The bay is entered between Bass Harbor Head (44°13'·31N 68°20'·24W), the S end of Mount Desert Island, and North Point (44°11'·42N 68°25'·49W), the N end of Swans Island (44°09'·50N 68°26'·20W), 4 miles SW, and extends 18 miles N.

2 A group of islands lies in the entrance to the bay and other islands lie within the bay. The channels between these islands are mostly deep and clear and important dangers are marked.

The bay is frequented by many fishing vessels and pleasure craft.

Ice
2.66

1 Ice will prevent navigation in bays at the head of Blue Hill Bay during winter months.

Approach and entrance channels
2.67

1 Blue Hill Bay may be entered from E across Bass Harbor Bar (44°12'·88N 68°20'·22W) (2.73), from the S through Eastern Passage (44°10'·54N 68°22'·95W) (2.69), from the SW through Southwest Approach (44°06'·25N 68°23'·30W) (2.74) and the W from Jericho Bay through Casco Passage (44°11'·70N 68°27'·90W) (2.75).

Deep-draught vessels can only enter the bay through Eastern Passage.

Directions

Principal marks
2.68

1 **Landmark:**
Blue Hill (44°26'·04N 68°35'·46W), a rounded peak that appears blue from a distance. A conspicuous lookout tower stands on the summit.

Major light:
Great Duck Island Light (44°08'·52N 68°14'·75W) (2.23).

Eastern Passage
2.69

1 From a position SW of Great Duck Island Light (44°08'·52N 68°14'·75W) the route through Eastern Passage into Blue Hill Bay leads NW, passing:
NE of Richs Head (44°06'·40N 68°20'·15W), the SE extremity of Long Island (2.24), thence:
SW of The Drums (44°08'·69N 68°18'·70W), a dangerous ledge awash, which is marked on its SE side by D Buoy (preferred channel to starboard), thence:

2 NE of Northeast Ledge (44°08'·07N 68°20'·43W), with a depth of 4 m (13 ft). LI Light Buoy (safe water) is moored 3 cables NNW of the ledge. Thence:
SW of Green Islands (44°09'·46N 68°20'·20W), two rocky islets with grassy summits. Otter Ledge (44°08'·78N 68°21'·79W), awash, lies 1 mile SW of the W islet and two patches, each with a depth of 7 m (23 ft), lie 2 and 4 cables E of the ledge. Thence:

3 SW of Black Island (44°10'·60N 68°20'·70W), wooded. Marine farms lie on the NW side of the island. Thence:
NE of East Point (44°09'·34N 68°23'·10W), on Swans Island. This island is the largest of the islands in the approaches to Blue Hill Bay and has permanent inhabitants, who are mainly fishermen. Thence:

4 SW of Placentia Island (44°11'·30N 68°22'·00W), wooded except at its E end, thence:
NE of Staple Ledge (44°11'·20N 68°24'·01W), which dries. This ledge, which lies nearly in mid-channel, is marked on its NE side by No 1 Buoy (port hand).

2.70

1 From a position NE of Staple Ledge the route continues NNW and then NW, passing:
ENE of Ship and Barges Ledge (44°13'·54N 68°25'·87W), which dries 1·8 m (6 ft). The ledge is marked at its S end by SB Beacon, and No 3 Buoy (port hand) is moored off the E side of the ledge. Thence:
NE of Ship Island (44°14'·03N 68°26'·45W) and Trumpet Island (44°14'·54N 68°26'·52W), the S islands of a chain of islands which lie in the centre of Blue Hill Bay. Ship Island is high and Trumpet Island is low. Thence:

2 NE of Bar Island (44°15'·43N 68°27'·44W) and Tinker Island (44°16'·30N 68°28'·80W). Bar Island is high and grassy and Tinker Island is partly wooded. No 5 Buoy (port hand) is moored at the edge of foul ground that extends 3 cables NE from Bar Island, and Nos 6 and 8 Buoys (starboard hand) mark the N and W limits of Cow and Calf Ledge (44°17'·10N 68°29'·72W) which extends from the NW end of Tinker Island. A channel, the centre of which is marked by T1 Buoy (safe water) and with a depth of 3·3 m (11 ft), crosses the shoal ground between Bar Island and Trumpet Island.

3 Thence most vessels proceeding to the N part of the bay follow the route between Tinker Island and Hardwood Island (44°16'·30N 68°28'·80W) and thence between Long Island (44°21'·00N 68°30'·30W) and Bartlett Island (44°21'·00N 68°26'·20W). Small vessels sometimes use the more protected passage between Moose Island (44°17'·40N 68°25'·97W) and Hardwood Island.

2.71

1 **Useful marks:**
Spire in West Tremont (44°15'·80N 68°23'·62W).
Bass Harbor Head Light (white tower and dwelling) (44°13'·31N 68°20'·24W).

Other entrance channels

General
2.72

1 As most of the vessels navigating Blue Hill Bay do not exceed 2·7 m (9 ft) in draught, the bay is usually entered through one of the inshore channels described as follows.

Bass Harbor Bar
2.73

1 The entrance across Bass Harbor Bar (44°12'·90N 68°20'·20W) is used by small vessels entering Blue Hill Bay from the E. Vessels with a draught of not more than 2·7 m (9 ft) frequently use this passage; in smooth seas vessels with a draught of 5·5 m (18 ft) sometimes use this passage at HW.

2 **Directions.** From a position NE of Great Gott Island (44°12'·10N 68°19'·70W), the route across the bar leads 1½ cables S of Bass Harbor Head Light (2.71), through a narrow channel which had a mid-channel controlling depth of 4·3 m (14 ft) (1994). The centre of the channel is marked at each end by a buoy (safe water).

Caution. The channel should be navigated with caution because in heavy weather breakers extend right across it and with strong winds against the tidal stream conditions dangerous to small vessels can build up.

Southwest Approach
2.74

1 Southwest Approach (44°06'·70N 68°23'·40W) may be used by vessels entering Blue Hill Bay from the W.
Directions. From a position SSW of Southwest Point (44°05'·90N 68°22'·04W), the approach leads N between Long Island (44°06'·85N 68°21'·20W) and Johns Island (44°06'·58N 68°24'·30W), passing

between J Buoy (preferred channel to port) marking Johns Island Sunken Ledge and No 2 Buoy (starboard hand) marking Beach Ledge (44°06′·32N 68°22′·86W). It then leads between the W Sister Island (44°08′·51N 68°22′·86W) and Red Point (44°08′·54N 68°23′·59W), the SE point of Swans Island. This part of the route passes over patches with swept depths of 7·3 and 4·6 m (24 and 15 ft). From a position NW of Sister Islands, the route then leads NE to join Eastern Passage (2.69).

Charts 4746, 2492, US Chart 13315, (see 1.16)
Casco Passage
2.75

1   Casco Passage connects Jericho Bay with Blue Hill Bay through a channel, N of Swans Island, between Orono Island (44°11′·22N 68°27′·66W) and Black Island (44°12′·10N 68°27′·64W). This passage divides into two branches in its W part, the N part continuing as Casco Passage and the S part as York Narrows.

Both channels are well marked, and buoyed as for a passage proceeding from E to W.

2   Casco Passage is the straighter and recommended passage with a least width of ½ cable and a depth of 3·7 m (12 ft) in the fairway, but rocks lie on both sides of it.

York Narrows, with a width of ½ cable and a depth of 4 m (13 ft), has dangerous rocks on either side of it and is not recommended.

Tidal streams in Casco Passage set E with a rising tide and W with a falling tide.

Local knowledge is required.

Charts 4746, 2492, US Chart 13316, (see 1.16)
Pond Island Passage
2.76

1   Pond Island Passage leads from Blue Hill Bay into the N part of Jericho Bay, N of Pond Island (44°13′·45N 68°28′·60W).

The passage, which is marked by buoys, has a least depth of 5·8 m (19 ft) in the fairway, but shoal patches lie close by.

Local knowledge is required.

Jericho Bay

Charts 4746, 2492, US Charts 13313, 13316, 13315, (see 1.16)
Description
2.77

1   Jericho Bay comprises the area, 3 miles wide, between Swans Island and Marshall Island (44°06′·80N 68°30′·40W) on the E, and Isle au Haut (2.112) and Deer Isle (44°12′·50N 68°39′·50W) on the W. It is obstructed by numerous islands and shoals.

The upper portion of the bay provides inshore navigation for local vessels between Blue Hill Bay on the E and Penobscot Bay (2.94) on the W. The lower part of the bay is little used except by local fishermen and yachts.

2   Neither the bay nor its approaches should be entered without local knowledge and therefore only an outline description of this area is given.

Passages and channels
2.78

1   **South-east approach** to Jericho Bay leads from S of Johns Island Sunken Ledge (44°05′·89N 68°24′·47W), between Brimstone Island (44°06′·56N 68°28′·02W) and Green Island (44°06′·85N 68°26′·78W) and then between Marshall Island and Swans Island passing through Toothacher Bay (44°07′·50N 68°28′·70W). This passage, which is marked by buoys (lateral) enters Jericho Bay N of Halibut Rocks Light (red and white chequered diamond on framework tower) (44°08′·05N 68°31′·53W).

2   **South approach.** Two entrance channels, for which local knowledge is required, lead into Jericho Bay from S between the dangers which lie between Marshall Island and Isle au Haut. Though these channels are the most direct route to the bay from the S, many dangers are unmarked and consequently the recommended channel is that from the SE through Toothacher Bay.

Passages to Blue Hill Bay. See 2.75 and 2.76.
2.79

1   **Merchant Row** (44°07′·05N 68°39′·00W), the S of the inner channels between Jericho Bay and E Penobscot Bay, leads through the islands and shoals lying between Deer Isle (2.77) and Isle au Haut, 4 miles SSE. The channel is entered between Southern Mark Island (44°07′·21N 68°34′·34W), lying 2¾ miles W of Long Point (44°07′·64N 68°30′·45W), the N extremity of Marshall Island, and Southern Mark Island Ledge (44°07′·94N 68°34′·72W).

2   This channel is used by vessels of moderate draught at all times of the year, and in winter is used by other vessels when Deer Island Thorofare is blocked by ice. Merchant Row is not quite so direct as Deer Island Thorofare, but the channel is wider and deeper. There are numerous dangers on both sides of the channel, but the principal ones are marked by buoys and beacons.

The channel can easily be followed, by day, by those with local knowledge.
2.80

1   **Deer Island Thorofare** (44°07′·21N 68°34′·34W) is a narrow channel along the S side of Deer Isle, between it and the numerous islands S. It is entered from the E, either S of Whaleback Ledge (44°09′·29N 68°33′·26W), thence N of Bold Island (44°09′·32N 68°36′·88W), or between Long Ledge (44°10′·81N 68°32′·82W) and Potato Ledge (44°10′·52N 68°33′·06W), 3 cables SSW.

2   The passage, which connects Jericho Bay and East Penobscot Bay and is used by vessels proceeding coastwise, is marked by buoys and beacons. It has a least width of ½ cable and a least depth of 4·2 m (14 ft) at its W end between Moose Island (44°08′·95N 68°40′·94W) and Crotch Island (44°08′·53N 68°40′·40W).

3   Vessels of up to 5·5 m (18 ft) draught are reported to have used the passage but many unmarked dangers, with depths of 2·7 to 4·3 m (9 to 14 ft), lie close to the channel.

The channel should not be attempted without local knowledge.

This channel is occasionally closed by ice which is soon broken up by icebreakers. During severe winters solid ice has formed between Stonington (2.84) and Isle au Haut.

Charts 4746, 2492, US Charts 13313, 13316, 13309, 13315, (see 1.16)
Eggemoggin Reach
2.81

1   **Description.** Eggemoggin Reach (44°16′·30N 68°38′·00W) is the channel between the Deer Isles and the mainland N, which connects the head of Jericho Bay with Penobscot Bay, near its head. There are several villages along its shores.

The reach is 11 miles long and has a least width of 4 cables near Byard Point (44°17′·83N 68°41′·10W).

The Deer Isle-Sedgwick Bridge, with a vertical clearance of 25·9 m (85 ft) for 30·5 m (100 ft) either side of the centreline, spans the reach near this point, narrowing the channel to 1¾ cables.

2   The main channel through the reach is generally broad and has sufficient depth for deep-draught vessels, however the channel is narrow in places and the bottom irregular and its navigation needs care.

The channel is entered from the E about 1 mile SW of Mahoney Island (44°13'·03N 68°30'·72W), a position 2 miles SW and WNW of the W ends of Pond Island Passage and Casco Passage, respectively.

3   The channel is marked with beacons and buoys (lateral), as for a vessel entering from the E. The principal dangers are buoyed and can easily be avoided by day in clear weather.

Anchorages and harbours

2.82

1   **Burnt Coat Harbor** (44°08'·03N 68°26'·68W), on the S side of Swans Island, is entered from Toothacher Bay (2.78) between Harbor Island (44°07'·70N 68°26'·50W) on the SE and Hockamock Head (44°08'·05N 68°26'·83W) on the NW. The fairway in the entrance has a least width of ¼ cable, with a depth of 6·4 m (21 ft). Burnt Coat Harbor Light stands on Hockamock Head. A prominent tower is situated on the E side of the harbour, 1 mile N of the lighthouse.

2   Anchorage, small but well sheltered, can be obtained E of the lighthouse in an area 2½ cables wide in 6 to 10 m (20 to 33 ft), soft bottom, or in the channel farther N in 4 to 7 m (13 to 23 ft). These anchorages are much used by local fishing vessels and yachts.

2.83

1   **Southeast Harbor** (44°11'·95N 68°38'·00W), lying NW of the E end of Deer Island Thorofare between the W end (44°11'·57N 68°36'·00W) of Stinson Neck (44°11'·95N 68°38'·00W) and the N end (44°11'·80N 68°38'·39W) of Whitmore Neck provides the best anchorage in the vicinity of this thoroughfare.

Anchorage may be obtained in 6 to 12 m (20 to 39 ft). Boat Rock (44°10'·78N 68°35'·28W), marked on its SE side by a buoy (preferred channel to port), lies 9 cables SE of the entrance.

The harbour is seldom closed by ice.

2.84

1   **Stonington** (44°09'·40N 68°40'·00W) is a town on the N shore of Deer Island Thorofare, NE of Crotch Island.

Wharf. There is a cannery wharf, with depths alongside of 2·1 m, extending from Staple Point (44°09'·28N 68°39'·64W) in the centre of the town. There are several wharves with depths alongside of 1·5 to 3·0 m, either side of Staple Point.

Supplies: fuel and provisions.

2   **Allen Cove** (44°08'·98N 68°40'·68W), situated on the E side of Moose Island, 1 mile W of Staple Point, is protected by a breakwater. A shipyard, with several piers and patent slips, for vessels up to 250 tonnes, is situated on the SE side of Moose Island. General hull and engine repairs can be carried out at the shipyard.

2.85

1   **Eggemoggin Reach** (2.81). Vessels can anchor anywhere within the reach, clear of a cable area crossing the reach about 1 mile SE of Byard Point, where the depth is suitable and the bottom soft. Small vessels can anchor in the coves described as follows, all of which are on the N side of the reach:

Benjamin River (44°17'·70N 68°37'·60W) lies close NW of Cape Carter (44°16'·80N 68°37'·54W). The entrance channel has a least depth of 5·8 m (19 ft), but is obstructed by shoals and ledges and is only ½ cable wide.

2   A wharf with a depth alongside of 2·4 m is situated on the W side about 6 cables above the river entrance.

Billings Cove (44°17'·85N 68°40'·75W) entered close E of Byard Point at the N end of the suspension bridge, provides anchorage in about 8 m (25 ft) in the middle of the cove just inside the entrance.

Sargentville, a village on the E shore, has a wharf with a depth alongside of 2·4 m.

2.86

1   **Bucks Harbor** (44°20'·20N 68°44'·55W) is an excellent anchorage often used by small vessels. Harbor Island, in the middle of the harbour, has a channel either side of it. The best anchorage is in 8 to 11 m (28 to 37 ft), W and NW of the island.

South Brooksville, a village at the head of the harbour has two wharves with depths alongside of 3·7 m.

Supplies: fuel, water and provisions.

2   **Orcutt Harbor** (44°20'·20N 68°45'·40W) is entered W of Condon Point (44°19'·85N 68°45'·00W). It has good anchorage in the middle of the harbour in 4 to 16 m (14 to 52 ft), just above a wooded islet on the W side near the entrance. A rock, with a depth of 1·5 m (5 ft) lies 1 cable S of the islet.

Anchorages and harbours

Bass Harbor

2.87

1   **General information.** Bass Harbor (44°14'·00N 68°21'·10W), which is entered between Bass Harbor Head and Lopaus Point (1 mile WNW) on the E side of the entrance to Blue Hill Bay, is an important fishing village and is sometimes used as an anchorage by coastal traffic.

Limiting conditions. The outer anchorage is exposed to the S.

2   **Directions.** The outer harbour can be entered passing either side of Weaver Ledge, which lies 3 cables E of Lopaus Point. This ledge dries 0·9 m (3 ft) and is marked by Nos 1 and 2 Buoys (lateral) at its SE and NW extremities.

The villages of Bass Harbor (E side) and Bernard (W side), in the inner harbour, are reached by a buoyed channel, with a depth (2011) of 3 m (10ft).

3   **Anchorage** may be obtained in 9 to 14 m (30 to 46 ft) in the outer harbour between Weaver Ledge and the entrance to the channel.

Wharves, with depths alongside of 2·1 and 3 m, exist in Bass Harbor. There are also fish wharves, with depths alongside of 1·8 m, at Bernard.

Repairs. Minor repairs.

Supplies: fuel; water and provisions.

Mackerel Cove

2.88

1   **General information.** Mackerel Cove, on the N side of Swans Island, is entered between North Point (44°11'·40N 68°25'·46W) and Crow Island, 6 cables WSW, and is a good anchorage.

The village of Atlantic stands on the SE side of the cove.

2 **Directions.** Although there are several dangers in the cove, it is easy to enter from N during the day. To enter the bay vessels should pass W of No 1 Light Buoy (port hand) that marks the ledge extending NW from North Point, and E of No 2 Buoy (starboard hand) that marks the ledge close E of Crow Island. Care must be taken to avoid a rock with a depth of 2·1 m (7 ft) that lies 7 cables SSW of North Point. This patch is marked by No 3 Buoy (port hand) on its W side. Below-water rocks lie in the approach to the ferry pier 5 cables S of North Point and a reported below-water rock (position approximate) lies mid-way between Nos 2 and 3 Buoys.

3 **Useful mark.** Church tower (44°10′·32N 68°24′·81W), situated in the village of Atlantic.

Anchorage may be obtained, clear of a cable area and the reported below-water rock, between Nos 2 and 3 Buoys, in 7 to 10 m (24 to 32 ft), or between No 3 Buoy and a drying ledge (3 cables SW).

Ferry pier is situated 5 cables S of North Point.

Western Bay
2.89

1 **General information.** Western Bay is entered between North Point, Bartlett Island (44°22′·40N 68°25′·40W) and Oak Point (2.90), 1¼ miles N.

Topography. The bay forms part of the channel which separates Mount Desert Island from the mainland and leads into Mount Desert Narrows (2.64). Alley Island, the largest in the bay, lies 1¾ miles ENE of Oak Point. Foul ground extends 2½ cables SE from the island, which is connected to the NW side of the bay by a drying ridge.

2 **Anchorage** may be obtained by vessels of all sizes in 13 to 19 m (42 to 62 ft) SW of Alley Island, but the broken rocky ground which extends 4 cables SE of Oak Point should be avoided.

There is also anchorage in 6 to 12 m (20 to 39 ft) SE and E of Alley Island, avoiding the foul ground extending from the island.

Union River Bay
2.90

1 **General information.** Union River Bay is entered between Oak Point (44°23′·80N 68°25′·50W) and High Head on Newbury Neck, 1½ miles SW.

Topography. The bay extends 5½ miles N to Weymouth Point (44°29′·00N 68°26′·25W) and is almost free of dangers except near its head where it divides into two arms; Patten Bay, the W arm which leads to the village of Surry, and Union River, the N arm, which leads to the city of Ellsworth, 3½ miles N of Weymouth Point.

2 Tupper Ledge, partly awash and marked on its S side by TL Buoy (preferred channel to starboard) lies 6 cables S of Weymouth Point in the entrance to Union River.

Anchorage. Good anchorage may be obtained in 6 to 12 m (19 to 39 ft) in mid-channel, 1 mile NW of Tupper Ledge.

Landing stage with a depth alongside of 1·5 m is situated in Contention Cove 1¾ miles WNW of Tupper Ledge.

3 **Union River**, which should only be entered with local knowledge, flows into the arm of Union River Bay, E of Weymouth Point. The river is about 1 mile wide at the entrance but reduces to ½ cable in width 1¼ miles above the entrance. In 2008 the controlling depth to Ellsworth was 1·3 m (4·2 to 4·3 ft).

Ice usually closes the river from December to April.

Morgan Bay
2.91

1 **General information.** Morgan Bay is entered between Darling Island, (44°24′·02N 68°31′·20W), wooded, and the SW shore of Newbury Neck, 1¾ miles ESE. The bay extends 3 miles N from its entrance.

Topography. The inner part of Morgan Bay is obstructed by Jed Islands, which lie on a shallow bank which extends 1 mile W from Newbury Neck.

2 **Directions.** From a position E of No 8 Buoy (starboard hand) marking Darling Ledge, awash, and W of No 2 Buoy (starboard hand), which marks a rock 5½ cables SSW of Jed Islands, the route into the bay leads N and NE through a narrow channel. This channel, with a least depth of 7 m (23 ft), passes W of Conary Nub, a rock with a clump of scrub on it, that lies 4½ cables W of Jed Islands and 2 cables from Conary Point, on the W shore. The channel E of Conary Nub should only be used with local knowledge.

3 **Useful mark.** Spire (44°25′·08N 68°31′·34W) in the village of East Blue Hill.

Anchorage. Good anchorage may be obtained in 2 to 11 m (7 to 36 ft) N of Seal Ledge and Black Rock, two dangers that lie 3 and 5 cables, respectively, NE of Conary Nub.

Alongside berths are available on the shore W of Darling Island and in McHeard Cove at East Blue Hill.

Supplies: fuel and water.

Blue Hill Harbor
2.92

1 **General information.** The outer part of Blue Hill Harbor is entered between Woods Point (44°23′·90N 68°31′·90W) and Stills Point, 1¾ miles SSW.

Topography. Blue Hill Harbor consists of an outer and inner harbour. The inner harbour is entered between Sculpin Point, 1¼ miles W of Woods Point, and Parker Point, 2 cables SW, and extends 1¼ miles WNW to the village of Blue Hill. Middle Ground, with rocks awash, lies off the entrance to the inner harbour and No 1 and No 3 Buoys (port hand) mark the E side of the ground.

2 **Directions for entering the inner harbour.** Vessels can enter the inner harbour on either side of Middle Ground, but the N side is easier and safer. After passing along the N side of Middle Ground, the entrance channel, which S of Sculpin Point is only 15 m (49 ft) wide with a depth of 5·8 m (19 ft), leads between Nos 5 and 6 Buoys (lateral) and into the anchorage.

3 **Local knowledge** is necessary to enter the harbour with vessels with a draught of more than 3·7 m (12 ft).

Ice. In severe winters the harbour is usually closed between December and April but during mild winters is relatively free of ice.

4 **Anchorage**, protected from N and W, may be obtained in 7 to 15 m (23 to 49 ft) in the middle of the outer harbour. In the inner harbour secure anchorage may be obtained in 3 to 8 m (10 to 26 ft), 1 to 3 cables above Sculpin Point, and also in 4 to 8 m (13 to 26 ft) about 6 cables WNW of that point.

Facility. Hospital.

Supplies: fuel; water and provisions.

CHAPTER 2

PENOBSCOT BAY AND APPROACHES

GENERAL INFORMATION

Chart 2486
Area covered
2.93

1 This section describes the coastal and offshore route from the SW end (44°01'·00N 68°39'·00W) of Isle au Haut to Monhegan Island, 33 miles WSW. Also described is Penobscot Bay together with the port of Searsport (2.175).

It is arranged as follows:
Isle au Haut to Monhegan Island (2.100).
Approaches to Penobscot Bay (2.104).
East Penobscot Bay (2.111).
West Penobscot Bay and entrances (2.137).
Penobscot River (2.195).

Description
2.94

1 The entrance to Penobscot Bay lies between Western Head (44°00'·80N 68°39'·18W) (2.24), the S point of Isle au Haut, and Whitehead Island, 20 miles W. This bay is the largest of the many indentations on the coast of Maine, and extends 28 miles inland to the mouth of Penobscot River. There are several towns on the bank of Penobscot River and the city of Bangor is situated 20 miles upstream at the head of navigation.

2 A chain of islands, of which the largest are Vinalhaven Island, North Haven Island and Islesboro Island, divides the bay into two parts, East Penobscot Bay (2.111) and West Penobscot Bay (2.137). The S part of East Penobscot Bay is known as Isle au Haut Bay.

A number of islands and dangers lie in the S and SW approaches to Penobscot Bay. These are well marked by lights, buoys and beacons.

Logs
2.95

1 With high tides many logs from the Belfast area are adrift in the bay and are a danger to small vessels.

Pilotage
2.96

1 Pilotage is compulsory for all foreign vessels and US vessels under register in foreign trade, with a draught of 2·7 m (9 ft) or over, entering or leaving any harbour within the waters of Penobscot Bay or River, N of a line joining Western Head, Matinicus Rock Light (2.102) and Marshall Point Light (43°55'·05N 69°15'·68W).

2 **Pilots board as follows:**
Vessels from the E. Three miles E of WP Light Buoy (43°55'·83N 68°53'·13W) (2.143).
Vessels from the W. In the vicinity of 14M Light Buoy, about 2½ miles WSW of Monhegan Island Light (43°45'·89N 69°18'·95W).

See *Admiralty List of Radio Signals Volume 6(5)* for details.

Tugs
2.97

1 Tugs are available at Belfast (2.169) and 24 hours' advance notice is required. Large vessels require the services of a tug for docking at Searsport (2.175) and for the river ports a tug usually accompanies the vessel upriver. Tugs meet vessels bound for Searsport 2 miles SSW of the harbour and for the river ports, off Fort Point (44°28'·03N 68°48'·71W).

Under-keel clearances
2.98

1 The US Coast Guard recommends the following minimum under-keel clearances for vessels navigating in Penobscot Bay and River:
(a) A minimum of 0·9 m (3 ft) when transiting S of Turtle Head (2.146).
(b) A minimum of 0·6 m (2 ft) when transiting Penobscot River N of Turtle Head.
(c) A minimum of 0·3 m (1 ft) at all berthing areas.

Ice
2.99

1 In winter many of the harbours are obstructed by ice, but Penobscot River usually remains open with assistance of ice breakers. The inner channels are only occasionally obstructed by ice.

ISLE AU HAUT TO MONHEGAN ISLAND

General information

Chart 2486,
Description
2.100

1 The following paragraphs describe the coastal passage between Western Head (44°00'·80N 68°39'·18W) (2.24), the S point of Isle au Haut, and Monhegan Island, 32 miles WSW.

Traffic regulations
2.101

1 **Danger and safety zone.** Seal Island (2.103) lies within a danger and safety zone used by naval aircraft as a bombing target area. See Appendix VI for details.

Directions
(continued from 2.24)

Principal marks
2.102

1 **Landmarks:**
Monhegan Island (43°45'·90N 69°18'·80W). The island has a rocky coast with high bluffs in places. A light stands in the centre of the island.
Radio tower (43°45'·80N 69°19'·61W) on Manana Island.

Major lights:
Matinicus Rock Light (27 m in height) (43°47'·01N 68°51'·30W).
Two Bush Island Light (43°57'·85N 69°04'·43W) (2.142).
Monhegan Island Light (white tower, 54 m in height) (43°45'·89N 69°18'·95W).

Isle au Haut to Monhegan Island
2.103

1 From a position SE of Western Head (44°00'·80N 68°39'·18W) the coastal passage leads SW, passing:
SE of Seal Island (43°53'·20N 68°44'·50W), bare and rocky, in the entrance to Penobscot Bay (2.94). Three Fathom Ledge, marked by DTF Light Buoy (isolated danger) close E, lies 1½ miles ENE of the NE end of Seal Island, and Malcolm Ledge lies 1½ miles SW of the SW end of the island. Thence:

2 SE of Wooden Ball Island (43°51'·30N 68°49'·10W), which is rocky with grass on its summit and has a prominent knoll, 19 m in height at its E end. 2WB Light Buoy (starboard

hand) is moored 5 cables SW of the island. Thence:

SE of Matinicus Rock (43°47'·01N 68°51'·30W), which is 17 m in height and is the outermost danger in the S approaches to Penobscot Bay. A light (2.102) stands on the S end of the rock. Thence:

SE of Monhegan Island (43°45'·90N 69°18'·80W) (2.102).

(Directions continue for coastal passage at 3.13, and for West Penobscot Bay at 2.144)

APPROACHES TO PENOBSCOT BAY

General information

Chart 2486, US Chart 13303, (see 1.16)
Description
2.104

1 The outlying islands and dangers in the approaches to Penobscot Bay extend from Three Fathom Ledge (2.103) (43°54'·31N 68°42'·28W) to Monhegan Island (2.102) and its surrounding dangers, 28 miles WSW.

There is no secure harbour in any of these outlying islands.

There are settlements on the E side of Matinicus Island (43°51'·70N 68°53'·76W) (2.109), on the NW side of Ragged Island (43°49'·70N 68°53'·45W) (2.107) and on the W side of Monhegan Island (2.110).

Approach channels
2.105

1 The E part of the bay may be entered between Isle au Haut and Vinalhaven Island. An alternative route (2.143) lies E and NE of Matinicus Island.

The main approach route for entering the W part of the bay from the S is through Two Bush Channel (43°57'·00N 69°03'·90W) (2.138). Muscle Ridge Channel (44°00'·45N 69°05'·06W) (2.147) also leads into the bay, but its use requires local knowledge.

2 There are other channels between the islands, which are mostly deep and have been well surveyed. However they have much broken ground with irregular soundings, and such areas should be avoided.

Deep-draught vessels
2.106

1 There are recommended routes for deep-draught vessels in Penobscot Bay. The route for vessels approaching from the W is described at 2.144, and for vessels approaching from the E at 2.143.

Deep-draught vessels entering and departing Penobscot Bay and River are requested to remain within the recommended routes; two-way traffic is possible within all parts of the routes. Other vessels, while not excluded, should exercise caution in these areas and monitor VHF for information concerning vessels transiting.

Anchorages and harbours

Ragged Island
2.107

1 **Criehaven Harbor** (43°50'·10N 68°53'·51W) is situated on the NW side of Ragged Island, partly wooded. The harbour does not provide shelter in NW winds.

Layout and berths. A breakwater extends N from the S entrance point of the harbour. Fish wharves in the harbour dry out.

Supplies. Limited supply of water.

2.108

1 **Seal Cove** is situated on the E side of the island and is sheltered from NW winds.

Anchorage, clear of the cable area that runs through the cove, may be obtained by small vessels up to 30 m in length in 21 m (69 ft), sand and shell.

Local knowledge is necessary.

Matinicus Island
2.109

1 **Matinicus Harbor** (43°51'·80N 68°52'·90W) is situated on the E side of Matinicus Island.

This island is mostly wooded and has a prominent mast, 30 m (100 ft) in height and visible from all directions, standing near its centre.

2 The harbour is protected by a breakwater which extends ¾ cable from the N side. No 2 Light (red triangle on framework tower) is exhibited from the outer part of the breakwater. Harbor Ledge, with a depth of 1·2 m (4 ft), lies off the entrance to the harbour and is marked on its S side by a buoy (preferred channel to port).

Berths. The village of Matinicus stands at the head of the harbour and has a pier with a depth alongside of 0·3 m.

3 **Anchorage.** Small vessels can anchor in the outer harbour in 2 to 8 m (6 to 26 ft), but this anchorage is exposed to NE winds.

Supplies: fuel; limited supply of water.

Monhegan Island
2.110

1 **Monhegan Harbor** (43°45'·80N 69°19'·40W), used principally by fishermen and yachtsmen, lies on the W side of Monhegan Island (2.102). It is situated in the channel, the N end of which is almost closed by a grass-covered islet, that lies between Monhegan Island and Manana Island.

2 **Berths.** Anchorage may be obtained in 4 to 7 m (13 to 26 ft), but the harbour is narrow, with poor holding ground and is exposed to the S.

The village of Monhegan stands on the E side of the harbour, where there is a pier with 3·7 m alongside.

A ferry sails to Port Clyde (3.18) on the mainland.

Supplies: fuel; limited supply of provisions and water.

EAST PENOBSCOT BAY

General information

Chart 2486, US Charts 13303, 13305, 13309, (see 1.16)
Description
2.111

1 **East Penobscot Bay** is entered from the S between Western Head (44°00'·80N 68°39'·18W) (2.24) and Brimstone Island (5 miles W) and is the part of Penobscot Bay which lies E of Vinalhaven (2.94), North Haven (2.94) and Islesboro Island (2.94). The S part of the bay, known as Isle au Haut Bay, lies between Isle au Haut and Vinalhaven Island. The N part of the bay is separated from the remainder of the bay by a group of islands that stretch NE from North Haven Island to the W entrance of Eggemoggin Reach.

2 The recommended route for deep-draught vessels proceeding to the N part of the bay lies W of Vinalhaven and North Haven Islands and is described at 2.143 and 2.144.

The islands in East Penobscot Bay have numerous coves and small harbours, but few of these are suitable as anchorages, some on account of their depth and others owing to the numerous dangers which obstruct their entrances.

Topography
2.112
1   **Isle au Haut** (44°03'·00N 68°37'·50W), which forms the E shore of Isle au Haut Bay, is a prominent landmark 166 m in height, wooded, and the highest land in the vicinity. The island is surrounded by numerous dangers and should be approached with caution. There are no good anchorages on its coast except Isle au Haut Thorofare (2.118).

Traffic routes
2.113
1   The principal traffic through the S part of East Penobscot Bay is in an E-W direction through the inside passages, but there is a clear channel, in which the principal dangers are marked, through the bay from the sea to its head.

Directions
(continued from 2.24)

Principal mark
2.114
1   **Major light:**
    Fort Point Light (44°28'·03N 68°48'·71W) (2.202).

Isle au Haut Bay
2.115
1   From a position S of Western Head (44°00'·80N 68°39'·18W) the route from sea into Isle au Haut Bay leads NNW with a least depth of 9·1 m (30 ft), passing:
    WSW of Western Ear (44°00'·28N 68°39'·30W), a wooded islet, close S of Western Head. Western Ear Ledge and The Washers, groups of rocks that dry, lie 2 cables S and 8 cables WNW, respectively, of the island. No 2 Buoy (starboard hand) is moored 8 cables W of Western Ear. Thence:
    WSW of a 9·1 m (30 ft) patch (44°01'·04N 68°41'·58W), thence:
2   ENE of Saddleback Ledge Light (grey conical tower) (44°00'·86N 68°43'·59W), standing on a small rocky islet, and:
    WSW of The Brandies (44°01'·50N 68°40'·96W), a group of rocks, the highest of which dries 2·7 m (9 ft). No 4 Buoy (starboard hand) is moored 3 cables W of The Brandies. Thence:
3   WSW of Isle au Haut Light (44°00'·86N 68°43'·59W), which stands on Robinson Point, the S entrance point to Isle au Haut Thorofare (2.118). The red sector (060°-034°) of this light covers The Brandies and the 9·1 m (30 ft) patch 6 cables SW. Thence:
    WSW of Kimball Head (44°04'·50N 68°40'·20W). Kimball Rock and several patches with depths of less than 9·1 m (30 ft) lie between 5 cables and 1¼ miles SW of the headland. And:
4   ENE of Calderwood Point (44°03'·84N 68°46'·52W), the E point of Vinalhaven Island. Thence:
    WSW of The Brown Cow (44°07'·31N 68°43'·61W), which is the westernmost danger at the W entrance of Merchant Row (2.79). 2BC Buoy (starboard hand) is moored 6 cables SSW of the rock.
    Thence into the inner part of East Penobscot Bay.

Inner part of East Penobscot Bay
2.116
1   From the vicinity of The Brown Cow (44°07'·31N 68°43'·61W) the main route through the inner part of East Penobscot Bay leads generally N and then NW, passing:
    W of Stinson Point (44°10'·15N 68°43'·15W). Sellers Rock, which partly dries, lies 3 cables W of the point and a patch with a depth of 5·5 m (18 ft) lies 4 cables farther WSW. No 2 Buoy (starboard hand) is moored 2 cables WSW of the rock. Thence:
2   Between Hardhead Island (44°13'·45N 68°45'·25W), a bare island, and Eagle Island, 45 m in height and wooded, 7 cables SW. Eagle Island Light (white conical tower), with a prominent chimney close SW, stands on the NE point of Eagle Island and 3A Buoy (port hand) is moored 2 cables off the point. Thence:
3   SW of Middle Rock (44°13'·70N 68°45'·77W), which is marked on its W side by No 4 Buoy (starboard hand), thence:
    Between Bradbury Island (44°14'·60N 68°45'·50W) and Butter Island, 1½ miles WSW. The channel between Bradbury Island and Pickering Island, wooded, 1½ miles NNE, is much obstructed and should not be used without local knowledge. Thence:
4   NE of Beach Island (44°15'·60N 68°49'·50W), thence:
    SW of Green Ledge Light No 4 (red triangle on framework tower) (44°17'·41N 68°49'·70W) which stands on Green Ledge, a grassy islet which is the W of a group of islands in the W entrance to Eggemoggin Reach (2.81). No 2 Buoy (starboard hand) is moored 3 cables SW.
    Thence the route leads N into the N part of East Penobscot Bay, which lies between Cape Rosier, an extension of the mainland on the E side of the bay, and Islesboro Island on the W.
5   **Useful mark:**
    Deer Island Thorofare Light (white and black tower) (44°08'·06N 68°42'·20W) which stands on Mark Island (2.120) and lies at the W entrance to Deer Island Thorofare.

East Penobscot Bay deep-draught route
(continued from 2.143 and 2.144)
2.117
1   From a position E of Monroe Island (44°04'·70N 69°02'·30W) the recommended route for deep-draught vessels to the head of Penobscot Bay passing E of Islesboro Island initially leads N, then NE, passing:
    NW of PB Light Buoy (safe water) (44°05'·89N 69°00'·20W), thence:
2   SE of McIntosh Ledge (44°09'·41N 68°57'·76W), a rock awash at LW. No 1 Buoy (port hand) is moored close E.
    The route then continues NNE, passing:
    ESE of No 3 Buoy (port hand) (44°10'·95N 68°56'·44W), thence:
    ESE of Pendleton Point (44°13'·95N 68°55'·80W), the S point of Islesboro Island, thence:
3   ESE of Hewes Point (44°18'·25N 68°53'·30W), thence:
    ESE of No 9 Buoy (port hand) (44°21'·01N 68°51'·37W), which marks the E side of Islesboro Ledge, a rock with a depth of 2·4 m (8 ft).
    Thence the track continues N, passing:

W of Dice Head (44°22'·96N 68°49'·13W) (2.134), thence:

Through an oil transfer area (44°25'·00N 68°50'·70W).

Thence to a position at the entrance to Penobscot River.

Side channels

Isle au Haut Thorofare

2.118

1   Isle au Haut Thorofare, which is entered from the W between Robinson Point (44°03·'89N 68°39'·06W) (2.115) and Marsh Cove Head, 3 cables NW, separates Kimball Island from Isle au Haut.

A dredged channel, marked by buoys, leads across the ledges at the NE end of the passage. This channel is 23 m (75 ft) wide and in 2008 had a mid-channel controlling depth of 1·5 m (4·8 ft).

2   **Local knowledge** is required to navigate this passage.

Useful marks (with positions relative to Robinson Point):

Isle au Haut Light (on Robinson Point) (2.115).
Spire (9 cables NE), in village of Isle au Haut.

West entrance of Merchant Row

2.119

1   The W entrance of Merchant Row (2.79) is entered S of The Brown Cow (44°07'·31N 68°43'·61W) (2.115) between Scraggy Island and Farrel Island, both of which are wooded, on the N, and Sparrow Island, which is grassy, on the S.

West entrance of Deer Island Thorofare

2.120

1   The W entrance of Deer Island Thorofare (2.80) is entered N of The Brown Cow (44°07'·31N 68°43'·61W) between West Mark Island Ledge (44°08'·28N 68°43'·11W), which is marked by No 2 Buoy (starboard hand), and Mark Island (44°08'·06N 68°42'·20W) on which stands Deer Island Thorofare Light.

Chart 2486, US Chart 13302, (see 1.16)

Fox Islands Thorofare

2.121

1   Fox Islands Thorofare, leading from East Penobscot Bay to West Penobscot Bay, between Vinalhaven Island and North Haven Island, is one of the chain of inshore passages that commences at Bass Harbor (2.87) and ends at Whitehead Island (43°58'·80N 69°07'·80W).

The thoroughfare, which is 7 miles long, is entered from East Penobscot Bay between Bluff Head (44°06'·08N 68°47'·77W) and Babbidge Island, 2¼ miles N.

2   The thoroughfare has a least depth of 5·2 m (17 ft) and a least width of ½ cable between Iron Point (44°07'·60N 68°51'·48W) and Zeke Point. These narrows and the principal dangers are marked by buoys and beacons. It is sometimes closed by ice in winter.

At LW the thoroughfare is seldom used by vessels exceeding 4·3 m draught and should not be attempted without local knowledge.

3   **Tidal streams** are usually not strong and meet at Iron Point, the stream setting through either entrance with a rising tide.

Caution is necessary during strong winds from E and W as they may considerably increase the rate of the tide.

Useful mark:

Goose Rocks Light (white conical tower, with black round base) (44°08'·12N 68°49'·84W), standing inside the E entrance.

Chart 2486, US Chart 13305, (see 1.16)

North of North Haven Island

2.122

1   There is a passage for small vessels N of North Haven Island, with a least depth of 7·6 m (25 ft), which is used in winter when Fox Islands Thorofare is closed by ice.

Local knowledge is required.

Directions. From a position 4 cables N of Bald Island (44°11'·35N 68°47'·07W) the route leads W, passing N of Grass Ledge and Oak Island, both grassy, and S of Spoon Ledge, with a grassy summit.

Anchorages and harbours in south part of East Penobscot Bay

Chart 2486, US Chart 13305, (see 1.16)

Moores Harbor

2.123

1   Moores Harbor (44°02'·70N 68°39'·00W), which lies 2½ miles N of Western Head, is obstructed by many dangers, both in the harbour and its approach, and is an unsafe anchorage.

Isle au Haut and Lookout

2.124

1   Isle au Haut and Lookout (44°05'·00N 68°37'·80W) are villages on the SE side and at the NE end of Isle au Haut Thorofare (2.118). Both have wharves, with depths alongside of 1·8 and 2·8 m, respectively, which are approached by buoyed channels.

Supplies. Fuel and limited provisions are available at Isle au Haut.

Carver Cove

2.125

1   Carver Cove (44°07'·20N 68°50'·05W) lies on the S side of the E entrance to Fox Islands Thorofare (2.121) and may be approached from either side of Widow Island (44°07'·80N 68°49'·85W).

Anchorage may be obtained 5 cables from the head of the cove in 5 to 6 m (16 to 20 ft), good holding. The shores of the cove should be given a berth of 1½ cables.

Kent Cove

2.126

1   Kent Cove is entered W of Goose Rocks Light (44°08'·12N 68°49'·84W) (2.121) at the E end of Fox Islands Thorofare.

Good anchorage for small vessels may be obtained in 5 to 7 m (15 to 24 ft), good holding.

Waterman Cove

2.127

1   Waterman Cove, separated from Kent Cove by Fish Point (44°08'·32N 68°51'·10W), and 9 cables W of Goose Rocks Light, is a good anchorage for small vessels in 5 m (18 ft) at its entrance. The cove shoals to 1·2 m (4 ft) near its head.

North Haven

2.128

1   North Haven is a village on the N shore of Fox Islands Thorofare, 7 cables W of Iron Point (44°07'·60N 68°51'·48W) (2.121). It is an important yachting centre.

Depths. 0·6 and 2·4 m (2 and 8 ft) shoals, marked by buoys, lie off the village.

Berths. The town wharf has a depth alongside of 3·7 m. There are several other wharves.
Repairs: patent slip; minor repairs.
Supplies: fuel and provisions.

Southwest Harbor
2.129
1 Southwest Harbor is entered 1½ miles N of Stinson Point (44°10'·15N 68°43'·15W) and lies within Sheephead Island and Sheephead Island Ledges.
Anchorage may be obtained in 5 to 9 m (18 to 28 ft), but is seldom used as it is open S.
The village of Sunset is situated at the head of the harbour.
Useful mark: Church spire in village.

Sylvester Cove
2.130
1 Sylvester Cove is entered 8 cables SE of Dunham Point (44°13'·26N 68°43'·95W). A reef that partly dries lies on the S side of the entrance, and its extremity is marked by No 2 Buoy (starboard hand).
Berth. A wharf, used by ferries, with a depth alongside of 2·7 m, stands on the N side of the harbour.

Northwest Harbor
2.131
1 Northwest Harbor is entered between Heart Island (44°14'·70N 68°42'·12W), partly wooded, and Gull Ledge, 7 cables SW. A rocky spit, which partly dries, extends 2½ cables NW from the S entrance point and is marked at its outer end by No 2 Buoy (starboard hand).
Ice. The harbour is closed by ice during January and February.
2 **Anchorage.** Good anchorage may be obtained by small vessels in mid-channel, in the outer part of the harbour, in 4 to 5 m (13 to 17 ft). There is also good anchorage in 6 to 9 m (19 to 30 ft) between Gull Ledge and Heart Island.
The village of Deer Isle is situated near the head of the harbour, and has two small wharves that dry.

Anchorages and harbours in north part of East Penobscot Bay

Chart 2486, US Chart 13309, (see 1.16)
Islesboro Harbor
2.132
1 Islesboro Harbor is entered N of Hewes Point (44°18'·25N 68°53'·25W). Hewes Ledge, awash, lies 2½ cables N of Hewes Point and is marked on its N end by No 1 Buoy (port hand) and its S end by No 2 Buoy (starboard hand).
Anchorage with good shelter from the W, may be obtained in 9 to 13 m (31 to 42 ft), rocky bottom.
The village of Islesboro stands on the S side of the harbour.

Sabbathday Harbor
2.133
1 Sabbathday Harbor is entered 2 miles N of Hewes Point (44°18'·25N 68°53'·25W). A dangerous rock, with a depth of 1·8 m (6 ft), lies ¾ cable SSE of the W entrance point.
Anchorage may be obtained by small vessels in 2 to 6 m (6 to 20 ft). Local knowledge is necessary.
The village of North Islesboro stands on the W side of the harbour.

Castine Harbor
2.134
1 Castine Harbor is entered between Dice Head (44°22'·96N 68°49'·13W) and Nautilus Island, 7 cables SE, at the mouth of Bagaduce River. The town of Castine, which is an important summer resort, stands on the N bank of the river about 1 mile from its mouth. Small cruise liners occasionally visit.
Ice. Bagaduce River is usually free of ice at Castine and for some distance above but in very severe winters it is entirely closed.
2 **Directions.** From a position S of Dice Head Light (white tower) (44°22'·96N 68°49'·13W), the track into the harbour leads NE passing:
   Clear of CH Buoy (safe water), moored 4 cables SSE of Dice Head, thence:
   SE of No 1 Buoy (port hand) that marks Otter Rock Shoal, an area of foul ground extending from the N side of the entrance.
2.135
1 **Alongside berths.** The wharf of Maine Marine Academy, at the W end of the waterfront, has a depth alongside of 7·9 m. There are other wharves with depths alongside of 3 and 3·7 m.
Repairs. Minor repairs.
Other facility. Hospital.
Supplies: fuel; water and limited stores.

Smith Cove
2.136
1 Smith Cove is entered between Hospital Island and Henry Point (44°23'·04N 68°46'·75W), 1½ miles SE of the town of Castine.
Anchorage may be obtained in 6 to 18 m (19 to 58 ft), soft bottom and well sheltered.

WEST PENOBSCOT BAY AND ENTRANCES

General information

Chart 2490, 2486, US Charts 13301, 13303, 13305, 13309, (see 1.16)
Description
2.137
1 West Penobscot Bay (44°08'·00N 69°00'·00W) is that part of Penobscot Bay that lies W of Vinalhaven Island, North Haven Island and Islesboro Island.

Entrance routes
2.138
1 From E the seaward entrance to West Penobscot Bay is clear of the islands and shoals which front the S and W sides of Vinalhaven Island. This entrance is suitable for deep-draught vessels (see 2.106). An alternative route (2.143) lies E and NE of Matinicus Island.
From W the entrance for deep-draught vessels is through Two Bush Channel, a deep and well marked channel, which is entered E of Two Bush Island (43°57'·85N 69°04'·43W). Muscle Ridge Channel also leads into West Penobscot Bay from W, passing E of Whitehead Island (43°58'·80N 69°07'·80W), but local knowledge is required for its use.
2 For vessels of moderate draught the entrance from East Penobscot Bay is either through Fox Islands Thorofare (2.121), or through the passage between the islands N of North Haven Island (2.122).

Pilotage
2.139
1 See 2.96 for pilotage to ports in West Penobscot Bay.

Oil transfer anchorage areas
2.140

1 Two oil transfer areas have been established at the head of Penobscot Bay, centred off Turtle Head (44°23'·50N 68°52'·85W):
  One centred 2 miles NW, with diameter of 2 miles.
  One centred 2 miles NE, with diameter of 1 mile.

No-discharge zones
2.141

1 A No-Discharge Zone has been established in the waters between Owls Head (2.145) and Camden (2.164), including the harbours of Rockland (2.152) and Rockport (2.160). See 1.41.

Directions
(continued from 2.24)

Principal marks
2.142

1 **Landmark:**
  Monhegan Island (43°45'·90N 69°18'·80W) (2.102).
  Major lights:
  Matinicus Rock Light (43°47'·01N 68°51'·30W) (2.102).
  Monhegan Island Light (43°45'·89N 69°18'·95W) (2.102).
  Two Bush Island Light (white tower) (43°57'·85N 69°04'·43W).
  Owls Head Light (white tower) (44°05'·53N 69°02'·64W).
  Rockland Breakwater Head Light (44°06'·24N 69°04'·65W) (2.155).
  Fort Point Light (44°28'·03N 68°48'·71W) (2.202).

Entering from east
2.143

1 From a position S of Western Head (44°00'·80N 68°39'·18W) the recommended route for deep-draught vessels (2.106) from E into West Penobscot Bay leads initially W, passing:
  Clear of PBA Light Buoy (safe water) (43°55'·61N 68°39'·62W), thence:
  N of Three Fathom Ledge (43°54'·31N 68°42'·28W) (2.103), thence:

2 N of Seal Island (43°53'·20N 68°44'·50W) (2.103), thence;
  S of Snippershan Ledge (43°57'·00N 68°45'·70W), thence:
  S of Bay Ledge (43°58'·07N 68°51'·66W), marked close SW by DBL Buoy (isolated danger), thence:
  S of WP Light Buoy (safe water) (43°55'·83N 68°53'·13W).
  Thence the track leads NW, passing:
  SW of a 9·1 m (30 ft) patch that lies 5 cables SSW of Perry Ledge (44°00'·50N 68°55'·87W), thence:

3 NE of Junken Ledge (43°59'·45N 68°59'·50W), marked by DJ Buoy (isolated danger), thence:
  NE of PA Light Buoy (safe water) (44°01'·16N 69°00'·33W).
  Thence the track leads N to a position E of Monroe Island (44°04'·70N 69°02'·30W).

4 **Alternative route.** An alternative recommended deep-draught route leads initially NE from a position 1 mile SW of Wooden Ball Island (43°51'·30N 68°49'·10W) (2.103), passing:
  NW of 2WB Light Buoy (43°50'·41N 68°49'·95W), thence:
  NW of Wooden Ball Island (43°51'·30N 68°49'·10W), thence:
  SE of Greens Ledge (43°52'·24N 68°50'·84W).

5 The route then leads NW passing:
  NE of Zephyr Rock (43°53'·69N 68°51'·89W), marked on its NE side by No 5 Light Buoy.
  Thence to a position SW of WP Buoy (43°55'·83N 68°53'·13W), where it joins the recommended route described above.
  Useful mark:
  Heron Neck Light (44°01'·51N 68°51'·72W).
  (Directions for West Penobscot Bay continue at 2.145;
  directions for East Penobscot Bay continue at 2.117)

Entering from south and west
(continued from 2.103)
2.144

1 From the vicinity of 14M Light Buoy (starboard hand) (43°45'·31N 69°22'·46W), which is moored 2½ miles WSW of Monhegan Island Light, the main route from S and W leads NE, and then generally ENE through Two Bush Channel (2.138), passing:

2 NW of the dangers lying off the NW side of Monhegan Island (43°45'·90N 69°18'·80W) (2.102). No 5 Light Buoy (port hand) is moored 2 cables NW of Sunken Duck Rock, the outermost of these dangers. Thence:
  SE of Old Man Ledge (43°50'·50N 69°18'·90W), marked by 2 OM Light Buoy (starboard hand). The recommended route for deep-draught vessels (2.106) is entered 1 mile SE of this buoy. Thence:

3 SE of Burnt Island (43°52'·05N 69°17'·45W), wooded and forming part of the Georges Islands. A prominent Coast Guard lookout tower stands on its summit. Thence:
  SE of Old Cilley Ledge (43°53'·22N 69°15'·40W), marked by 2 OC Buoy (starboard hand), and:
  NW of the dangers lying W of Metinic Island (43°53'·00N 69°07'·55W), partly wooded. No 3 Buoy and MI Buoy, respectively, mark Roaring Bull and Metinic Island Ledge, two dangers on the SE side of the channel that lie 3 miles W and 2¼ miles NW, respectively, of the S point of Metinic Island. Thence:

4 SE of Mosquito Island (43°55'·20N 69°13'·20W), wooded. No 2 Buoy (starboard hand) is moored 2 cables S of the island. Thence:
  NW of MP Light Buoy (safe water) (43°55'·30N 69°10'·87W), marking the SW approach to Two Bush Channel, thence:
  NNW of No 4 Buoy (starboard hand) (43°55'·61N 69°08'·87W), marking a rocky shoal with a least depth of 11·9 m (39 ft), thence:

5 Between 5TB Light Buoy (port hand) (1¼ miles SSW) and No 6 Buoy (starboard hand) moored 6 cables ESE, thence:
  SSE of Two Bush Island Light (43°57'·85N 69°04'·43W), thence:
  NNW of a shoal with a least depth of 4·5 m (15 ft) (43°56'·99N 69°02'·00W), marked by DTBS Buoy (isolated danger), thence:
  SSE of No 7 Buoy (port hand) (43°58'·53N 69°01'·36W).
  The route then leads N, passing:
  W of TBI Light Buoy (safe water) (43°58'·28N 69°00'·27W), thence:
  W of Junken Ledge (43°59'·45N 68°59'·50W) (2.143), thence:

Between PA Light Buoy (safe water) (44°01'·16N 69°00'·33W) and No 9 Buoy (port hand), 9 cables NW, marking a 7 m (23 ft) shoal 1 mile SE of Fisherman Island, thence:

W of F Light Buoy (special) (44°03'·32N 68°59'·83W), thence:

To a position E of Monroe Island (44°04'·70N 69°02'·30W). No 11 Light Buoy (port hand) is moored 3 cables E of the island.

Useful mark:
Browns Head Light (44°06'·70N 68°54'·57W) (2.151).

(Directions continue for East Penobscot Bay at 2.117)

To the head of Penobscot Bay
(continued from 2.143)

2.145

Monroe Island to Seven Hundred Acre Island. From a position E of Monroe Island (44°04'·70N 69°02'·30W) the recommended route for deep-draught vessels passing W of Islesboro Island to the head of Penobscot Bay leads N then NNE, through the S part of West Penobscot Bay, passing:

E of Owls Head (44°05'·53N 69°02'·64W), a prominent headland that forms the S entrance point of Rockland Harbor (2.152). A light (2.142) stands on the headland. Thence:

W of PB Light Buoy (safe water) (44°05'·89N 69°00'·20W), thence:

E of Beauchamp Point (44°10'·15N 69°03'·60W), prominent. Indian Island, on which stands a disused lighthouse, and Lowell Rock, on which stands Light No 2 (2.161), lie close S of Beauchamp Point and form the E side of the entrance to Rockport Harbor (2.160). Thence:

W of Mark Island (44°10'·40N 68°58'·90W), high, rounded and prominent. This island lies 7¾ cables N of Robinson Rock, grassy. The limit of the dangers that extend S from Robinson Rock is marked by No 12 Buoy (starboard hand). Thence:

E of The Graves (44°10'·95N 69°02'·11W), a reef partly above water, with a large drying area; No 13 Light Buoy (port hand) is moored close E. Thence:

E of Curtis Island Light (44°12'·08N 69°02'·93W) (2.166), which stands on Curtis Island. The island and light, situated on the S side of the entrance to Camden Harbor (2.164), are prominent. Thence:

ESE of Moxy Reef (44°12'·90N 69°01'·80W), thence:

ESE of Dillingham Ledge (44°13'·65N 69°01'·95W), marked by No 1 Buoy (port hand), thence:

WNW of Seven Hundred Acre Island (44°15'·40N 68°57'·20W).

2.146

Seven Hundred Acre Island to the head of the bay. From a position WNW of the N point of Seven Hundred Acre Island (44°15'·40N 68°57'·20W), the route to the head of West Penobscot Bay leads NNE, passing:

WNW of Grindel Point Light (44°16'·90N 68°56'·57W), standing on the N entrance point of the N entrance of Gilkey Harbor (2.190), and:

ESE of Spruce Head (44°17'·75N 68°58'·80W), the NE entrance point of Ducktrap Harbor (2.191), thence:

ESE of Great Spruce Head (44°19'·44N 68°57'·30W), a bold headland, thence:

WNW of Marshall Point (44°22'·66N 68°54'·10W), which is marked by prominent yellowish bluffs. No 11 Light Buoy (safe water) is moored 7 cables NW of the headland.

The route then leads generally NE passing:

NW of Turtle Head (44°23'·50N 68°52'·85W), a wooded and prominent headland that is joined to Islesboro Island by a low, narrow wooded neck.

Thence as necessary to the ports at the head of West Penobscot Bay or to the mouth of Penobscot River.

(Directions continue for Penobscot River at 2.202; directions for Belfast are given at 2.172)

Other entrance and side channels

Muscle Ridge Channel

2.147

Description. Muscle Ridge Channel leads W of the group of islands and rocks lying on the NW side of Two Bush Channel. It is entered from seaward close S of Whitehead Island (43°58'·80N 69°07'·80W).

The channel is much used in clear weather in daylight as it is sheltered and provides good anchorage.

Depths. The channel has a least depth of 7·9 m (26 ft) in the fairway, but shoal depths of 4 to 6·7 m (13 ft to 22 ft) are close by. Vessels of 9·1 m (30 ft) draught have passed through the channel at HW.

Local knowledge. The channel is narrow in places and should not be used without local knowledge.

2.148

Directions. From a position S of Whitehead Island the channel leads NE for 5 miles, passing between dangers that are well marked by beacons and buoys.

Useful mark:
Whitehead Island Light (grey granite tower) (43°58'·71N 69°07'·46W).

Fisherman Island Passage

2.149

Description. Fisherman Island Passage, with depths of 6·7 to 8·2 m (22 to 27 ft), leads between Fisherman Island (44°02'·50N 69°02'·32W) and Sheep Island, 1¼ miles NNW, from the N end of Muscle Ridge Channel into West Penobscot Bay. The channel, which is about 2½ cables wide between the shoals extending from the two islands, is marked by buoys.

Owls Head Bay

2.150

Description. Owls Head Bay is a channel that leads between Sheep Island (44°03'·90N 69°02'·90W) and Monroe Island on the E, and the mainland on the W. It is an alternative route to Fisherman Island Passage, leading into West Penobscot Bay.

Width and depths. The channel is buoyed but is very narrow off the W side of Sheep Island, being only 76 m (250 ft) wide between the 9·1 m (30 ft) depth contours, and with a depth of 11·6 m (38 ft) in the fairway.

West entrance to Fox Islands Thorofare

2.151

Fox Islands Thorofare is entered from the W between Crockett Point (44°05'·74N 68°54'·60W) and Stand-in Point, 1¼ miles NW. The entrance is considerably restricted by numerous off-lying dangers.

Directions. From the vicinity of FT Light Buoy (safe water) (44°05′·29N 68°57′·28W), the white sector (050-061°) of Browns Head Light (white round tower) (44°06′·70N 68°54′·57W) leads through the dangers in the W entrance to Fox Islands Thorofare. The channel is marked by buoys and beacons.

Useful marks:
Beacon (44°06′·10N 68°56′·38W), a grey stone column standing on Fiddler Ledge.
Sugar Loaves (44°06′·90N 68°54′·88W), a ledge of prominent rocks 9 m (30 ft) in height.

Rockland Harbor

Chart 2486, US Chart 13307, (see 1.16)

General information
2.152

Position and function. Rockland Harbor (44°05′·97N 69°05′·60W), which is situated on the W side of West Penobscot Bay, is entered between Owls Head (2.145) and Jameson Point.

Rockland Harbor is one of the most important harbours in Penobscot Bay and is a port of entry.

The city of Rockland has trade in fish and petroleum products and a number of light industries. Small cruise liners call between June and September.

Limiting conditions
2.153

Controlling depths. In 2008 the main approach channel had a controlling depth of 5·4 m (17·6 ft), the SW channel 4·3 m (12·1 ft) and basin 4·3 m (14 ft), the N channel 3·6 m (13 ft) with 4 m (14 ft) in the basin and the W channel 3·4 m (11 ft) and turning basin.

Tidal levels. Mean spring range about 3·4 m (11·2 ft); mean neap range about 2·4 m (7·9 ft). See information in *Admiralty Tide Tables*.

Local weather. The harbour is exposed to E winds and NE winds raise a heavy sea in the SW part of the harbour.

Arrival information
2.154

Pilotage and tugs. See 2.96 and 2.97.

Principal marks
2.155

Landmarks:
Rockland Breakwater Head Light (red brick tower) (44°06′·24N 69°04′·65W).
Radio tower (44°07′·50N 69°08′·42W).
Knox County Airport Light (44°03′·56N 69°05′·44W).

Major light:
Rockland Breakwater Head Light — as above.

Directions
2.156

From a position N of Owls Head Light the track leads W passing S of Breakwater Head Light, giving the breakwater a berth of at least ½ cable, and thence between anchorage areas A and B towards No 2 Light Buoy (starboard hand), moored 3 cables W of the entrance to the dredged channel.

Berths
2.157

Anchorages (the limits of which are shown on the national chart):
Anchorage A. In the S part of the harbour in 6 to 15 m (20 to 50 ft). A general anchorage for vessels over 20 m in length.
Anchorage B. In the N part of the harbour in 4 to 11 m (13 to 36 ft). A general anchorage for vessels over 20 m in length.
Special anchorage. In the W part of the harbour in 4 to 6 m (13 to 21 ft). For pleasure craft up to 20 m in length.
Prohibited anchorage. A channel, 2½ cables wide, is left between Areas A and B. No vessel may anchor in the channel or within 1½ cables of any wharf without permission.

2.158

Alongside berths:
Ferry terminal. Length 85 m. Reported depth alongside of 3·4 m.
Other wharves. Reported depths alongside of 1·8 to 4·3 m (Main Pier).

Port services
2.159

Repairs to small vessels may be carried out at a shipyard at Atlantic Point in the SW part of the harbour. A slipway can handle vessels up to length 68 m, beam 12·2 m, displacement 1200 tonnes and draught 4·8 m.
Other facility. Hospital.
Supplies: fuel; water; provisions and stores.

Rockport Harbor

General information
2.160

Position. Rockport Harbor is entered between Lowell Rock (44°09′·80N 69°03′·61W) and the coast W. It is a good anchorage for all classes of vessels and is sheltered from all but S winds.

The entrance to the harbour is deep and clear, with the exception of Porterfield Ledge, which lies 6 cables S of Lowell Rock. It is 7 cables wide at the entrance and narrows to 1 cable at its head and is easy of access.

Rockport is a town at the head of the harbour.

Directions
2.161

Vessels may enter Rockport Harbor on either side of Porterfield Ledge Beacon, giving the ledge a berth of at least ¾ cable.

Useful marks:
Porterfield Ledge Beacon (44°09′·24N 69°03′·70W), which stands on a ledge that dries several feet.
Lowell Rock Light No 2 (red triangle on post) (44°09′·24N 69°03′·70W).
Disused lighthouse (44°09′·93N 69°03′·66W), standing on Indian Island.
Clock Tower (44°11′·34N 69°04′·36W).

Anchorage
2.162

Anchorage may be obtained by deep-draught vessels between the entrance and 1 mile from the head of the harbour in 13 to 19 m (42 to 63 ft), soft bottom. Small vessels can anchor nearer the head of the harbour.

Port services
2.163

1   **Repairs.** Boatyard for minor repairs on W side of harbour.

Supplies: fuel; provisions and stores.

Camden Harbor

General information
2.164

1   **Position and function.** Camden Harbor (44°12′·51N 69°03′·15W) is entered between Curtis Island and Northeast Ledge (3 cables NE), which extends 3 cables SSE from Northeast Point.

The town of Camden, situated at the head of the inner harbour in an inlet off the W side of the bay, is a yachting centre and small cruise liners call between June and September.

Limiting conditions
2.165

1   **Ice** sometimes forms in the harbour from January to March, but is not dangerous for vessels in the outer harbour and is usually cleared by W winds.

Directions
2.166

1   From a position N of The Graves (44°10′·95N 69°02′·11W) the track into the harbour leads NW, passing:

    Between Curtis Island (44°12′·12N 69°03′·00W) and Nos 2 and 4 Buoys (starboard hand) which mark the NE side of the channel, thence:

    Between No 7 Buoy (port hand) off Dillingham Point (44°12′·20N 69°03′·32W) and No 6 Buoy (starboard hand), marking the SE side of Inner Ledges.

    Thence to the anchorage in the outer harbour.

2   **Useful marks**:

    Curtis Island Light (44°12′·08N 69°02′·93W).

    Northeast Point Light No 2 (red triangle on white framework tower and small white house) (44°12′·51N 69°02′·79W).

    Mount Battie (44°13′·37N 69°04′·15W). The summit, which is marked by a small stone memorial tower, shows as a long ridge from the offing.

Berths
2.167

1   **Anchorage** may be obtained in the outer harbour clear of the special anchorages shown on the US chart.

Alongside berths. The inner harbour, entered between Eaton Point and the shore 1 cable SW, has two berths with depths alongside of 2·4 m. It is mainly used by small pleasure and fishing craft.

Port services
2.168

1   **Repairs.** Boatyard where minor repairs can be carried out. The largest slip in the inner harbour can accommodate craft up to 33 m in length.

Other facility. Hospital.

Supplies: fuel; water; provisions and stores.

Belfast Harbor

Chart 2486, US Chart 13309 plan of Belfast Harbor, (see 1.16)

General information
2.169

1   **Position and function.** Belfast Harbor (44°25′·75N 69°00′·30W), situated at the head of Belfast Bay, is entered between Browns Head (44°23′·10N 68°58′·66W) and Moose Point, 3 miles NNE. Passagassawakeag River flows into the head of the bay.

The city of Belfast, which by the 2010 census had a population 6668, stands on the SW side of the river.

Belfast is a port of entry. Small cruise liners call between June and September.

Limiting conditions
2.170

1   **Channel depth.** There is a least depth of 4·3 m (14 ft) in the channel to Belfast.

Tidal levels. Mean spring range about 3·5 m (11·5 ft); mean neap range about 2·5 m (8·3 ft). See information in *Admiralty Tide Tables*.

Ice obstructs navigation in the river and bay in severe winters. The bay has been frozen as far as Islesboro Island.

Arrival information
2.171

1   **Pilotage and tugs.** See 2.96 and 2.97.

Directions
2.172

1   From a position NE of Browns Head (2.169), the approach leads NW passing SW of Steets Ledge (44°25′·16N 68°58′·34W), an extensive shoal, with a least depth of 0·3 m (1 ft). No 2 Light Buoy (starboard hand) is moored close S of the ledge and a disused lighthouse stands on the ledge. Thence the approach leads to the anchorage and river mouth.

Berths
2.173

1   **Anchorage.** Good anchorage, but exposed to SE winds, may be obtained in 6 to 9 m (20 to 26 ft) W of Steets Ledge and also in mid-channel in the river 5 cables W of Paterson Point. Small vessels may anchor ½ cable off the wharves, abreast the town, in 3 to 7 m (10 to 22 ft).

2   **Alongside berths.** Deepest berth is Marshall Wharf, owned by a towage company, with a reported depth alongside of 4·6 m. There are two other berths with depths alongside of 2·4 to 3 m.

Port services
2.174

1   **Repairs.** Boatyard with 12 m patent slip for hull repairs.

Other facility. Hospital.

Supplies: fuel; provisions and stores.

Searsport Harbor

Chart 2486, US Chart 13309, (see 1.16)

General information

2.175

1   **Position and function.** Searsport Harbor and Long Cove (2.178) lie at the head of a bay which is entered between Moose Point (44°25'·75N 68°56'·70W) and the S end of Sears Island.

Searsport Harbor provides good anchorage for all classes of vessels. The town of Searsport stands at the head of the harbour.

The port is small but busy, handling mainly petroleum products, general and dry bulk cargoes.

2   The commercial berths are situated on the SE side of Mack Point (44°27'·20N 68°54'·20W) and the W shore of Sears Island at the entrance to Long Cove, 1½ miles ESE of the town.

Port Authority. Maine Port Authority, State House Station, Augusta, ME 04333.

Website. www.maineports.com

Searsport from S (2.175)
(Original dated 2006)

(Photograph - Captain Peter Mosselberger)

Limiting conditions

2.176

1   **Approach channel depth**. In 2009 the controlling depth in the dredged approach channel and turning basin was 10·1 m (33 ft).

Arrival information

2.177

1   **Pilotage and tugs**. See 2.96 and 2.97.

Customs and quarantine officers for Searsport are stationed at Belfast.

Berths

2.178

1   **Anchorage.** Good anchorage may be obtained in Searsport Harbor by all classes of vessels in 14 to 15 m (45 to 50 ft), within 1½ miles SSW of Mack Point.

Long Cove, which is entered E of Mack Point, is mostly shoal but provides good anchorage just inside the entrance, in 7 m (24 ft).

2   **Alongside berths.** Two commercial piers extend SSE from the SE corner of Mack Point.

Maine Port Authority Dry Cargo Pier, 244 m in length, with depths alongside of 12·2 m (E side), 9·7 m (W side) is the largest berth. Vessels of up to 80 000 dwt, 228 m length, 32 m beam can be handled.

Port services

2.179

1   **Facilities:** hospital in Belfast; oily waste disposal.

Supplies: fuel; water and provisions.

Anchorages and harbours in the entrances to West Penobscot Bay

Chart 2486, US Chart 13305 plan of Carvers Harbor and approaches, (see 1.16)

Carvers Harbor

2.180

1   **Description.** Carvers Harbor (44°02'·55N 68°50'·30W), the entrance to which lies on the S side of Vinalhaven Island, 1½ miles NE of Heron Neck Light (2.143), affords secure anchorage for small vessels, but local knowledge is required. The village of Vinalhaven stands at the head of the harbour.

Ice seldom closes the harbour.

Approaches. The harbour may be approached:

2   From the E through the buoyed channel between Vinalhaven Island and the islands S of it.

From the S, in the buoyed channel between Colt Ledge, 1¼ miles SE of Heron Neck Light, and Arey Ledges on the E and The Breakers on the W.

From the SW, in the white sector of Heron Neck Light.

From the NW, through The Reach.

3   **Useful marks**:

Carvers Harbor Light No 2 (red triangle on post) (44°02'·05N 68°50'·62W).

Water tower (44°02'·85N 68°50'·26W).

2.181

1   **Anchorages**. The best anchorage for small vessels lies on the E and SE side of the harbour. The W side is used for commercial craft and fishing vessels. In 2012 the harbour had depths of 2·4 to 4·6 m (8 to 15 ft) in the centre and about 2 to 3 m (8 to 10 ft) along the N and S sides.

Alongside berths. Small wharves in Vinalhaven with depths alongside of 2 to 3 m.

Repairs. Minor repairs only.

Supplies: fuel; water; provisions and some stores.

Chart 2486, US Chart 13301, (see 1.16)

Tenants Harbor

2.182

1   **Description.** Tenants Harbor, which is entered between Southern Island (43°57'·70N 69°11'·20W) and Northern Island, 2½ cables N, is an excellent anchorage, easy of access. It is much used by small vessels as a harbour of refuge.

Ice frequently obstructs the harbour in February and in extremely cold periods it may be frozen as far as Southern Island.

2   The village of Tenants Harbor stands on the N side of the bay. A tower (disused lighthouse) stands on the E end of Southern Island and No 1 Light Buoy (port hand) is moored 1 cable E of the island.

Anchorage. Depths gradually shoal from 10 m (33 ft) in the entrance to 4 m (13 ft) 9 cables farther in. Anchorage may be obtained in 9 to 5 m (30 to 16 ft) between 1 and 6 cables W of a line joining the W ends of Southern and Northern Islands.

3   **Alongside berths.** Landing stages with depths alongside of 1·2 to 2·4 m are situated at the village.

Repairs. Minor repairs only.

Supplies: water and stores.

Chart 2486, US Chart 13305, (see 1.16)
Seal Harbor
2.183

1 **Description.** Seal Harbor (43°59'·60N 69°07'·75W) lies on the NW side of the S part of Muscle Ridge Channel (2.147). It was formerly much used as an anchorage by coasters. The outer part has depths of 5 to 12 m (15 to 39 ft). The principal dangers in the entrance are buoyed. The harbour is easily entered in daytime.

Dix Island Harbor
2.184

1 **Description.** Dix Island Harbor (44°00'·25N 69°04'·00W) is an anchorage off the SE side of Muscle Ridge Channel. The harbour is entered from SW through a narrow channel leading between the ledges N of Hewett Island.

Local knowledge is required to use this anchorage.

Anchorages and harbours in the south part of West Penobscot Bay
Hurricane Sound
2.185

1 **Description.** Hurricane Sound (44°02'·80N 68°53'·00W), between the W coast of Vinalhaven Island and the islands about 1 mile offshore, is deep but little used except by local vessels as there are no good anchorages in it. Several buoyed channels lead into the sound, but are narrow and obstructed and should not be used without local knowledge.

Southern Harbor
2.186

1 **Description.** Southern Harbor, situated at the W end of Fox Islands Thorofare, is entered between Dumpling Islands (44°07'·65N 68°54'·10W) and Amesbury Point, 5 cables WNW.

Good anchorage may be obtained in the middle of the harbour in 6 to 7 m (19 to 23 ft), soft bottom.

Bartlett Harbor
2.187

1 **Description.** Bartlett Harbor, 2 miles NNE of Stand-in Point (44°06'·63N 68°56'·53W), is a small cove that provides good anchorage in 11 to 15 m (36 to 50 ft), sheltered from all but W and N winds.

Caution. A rock with a depth of 2·7 m (9 ft), and steep-to, lies on the S side of the entrance.

Pulpit Harbor
2.188

1 **Description.** Pulpit Harbor (44°09'·30N 68°53'·20W), 2 miles NE of Bartlett Harbor and 2½ miles SW of Webster Head, the partly wooded headland at the N end of North Haven Island, provides secure anchorage to small vessels of up to 4 m (13 ft) draught. Local knowledge is required.

Pulpit Rock, 3 m in height and pointed, stands nearly ½ cable within the outer end of a reef that extends from the W entrance point. The entrance channel, which lies E of Pulpit Rock, is over ½ cable wide.

2 **Caution.** A patch with a depth of 3·4 m (11 ft) lies in mid-channel just within the entrance. It has deeper water on its W side.

Anchorage is obtainable in the widest part of the harbour in 5 to 10 m (18 to 33 ft).

Owls Head Harbor
2.189

1 **Description.** Owls Head Harbor is situated close SW of Dodge Point (44°05'·16N 69°02'·88W) at the N end of Owls Head Bay (2.150).

Anchorage may be obtained by small vessels in the entrance to the harbour in 3 to 7 m (9 to 24 ft).

Local knowledge is required.

Anchorages and harbours in north part of West Penobscot Bay

Chart 2486, US Charts 13305, 13309, (see 1.16)
Gilkey Harbor
2.190

1 **Description.** Gilkey Harbor (44°15'·30N 68°56'·00W) lies between the W side of the S end of Islesboro Island and Seven Hundred Acre Island. The harbour provides secure anchorage and in summer is much frequented by yachts. Local knowledge is required.

Ice frequently closes the harbour in winter.

2 **Entrances.** The main entrance to the harbour is from the SW between Job Island (44°13'·50N 68°56'·70W) and Ensign Islands, 6 cables NW. This entrance, which is partly buoyed, is easy to enter and has a least depth of 8·2 m (27 ft) in mid-channel. The N entrance, between Grindel Point (44°16'·90N 68°56'·57W) to the N and Warren Island and Spruce Island to the S, is narrow and also partly buoyed.

3 **Anchorage**, clear of the charted cable areas, may be obtained in 7 to 18 m (23 to 59 ft), with good holding.

Repairs. Minor repairs in Cradle Cove on the W side.

Supplies. Fuel, water and provisions are available in the village of Dark Harbor on the E side of the anchorage and in Cradle Cove.

Ducktrap Harbor
2.191

1 **Description.** Ducktrap Harbor is an open bay, which is entered between Frohock Point (44°16'·55N 69°00'·35W) and Spruce Head (1½ miles NE).

Haddock Ledge, with a depth of 1 m (3 ft), lies in the middle of the harbour and is the only off-lying danger. It is marked on its S side by No 2 Buoy (starboard hand). Other dangers can be avoided by giving the shores of the bay a berth of 2½ cables.

2 **Anchorage**, sheltered from N and W winds, may be obtained in 9 to 13 m (31 to 43 ft) with soft bottom in places, at a distance of 2½ cables off the N shore.

Berth. A ferry pier and landing stage, with reported depths of 1 m alongside, are situated at the village of Lincolnville.

Seal Harbor
2.192

1 **Description.** Seal Harbor (44°19'·50N 68°54'·50W) on the W side of Islesboro Island, provides good anchorage, sheltered from all but SW winds. The harbour is easy of access and used by vessels as a night anchorage.

Main entrance is from SW between Flat Island, a bird sanctuary which is grassy, and the shore of Islesboro Island. This entrance is deep and clear of dangers. Other entrances should not be used without local knowledge.

2 **Anchorage**, with plenty of swinging room, may be obtained by deep-draught vessels 5 cables E of Flat Island in about 19 m (63 ft). Anchorage may also be obtained in about 15 m (49 ft) in the middle of the harbour 2½ cables off the SE shore. Attention is

drawn to the foul ground that extends 2 cables S from the N shore.

Turtle Head Cove
2.193

1 **Description.** Turtle Head Cove is entered between Marshall Point (44°22′·66N 68°54′·10W) and Turtle Head, 1¼ miles NE.

Dangers. The E and S shores should not be approached within 1½ and 2½ cables respectively, and in the W half of the cove foul ground extends 4 cables from the S shore.

Anchorage. The cove provides good anchorage in 5 to 11 m (18 to 36 ft) sheltered from S and E winds in its E part. The anchorage has a clear width of 3½ cables and is in the E part of the cove.

Stockton Harbor
2.194

1 **Description.** Stockton Harbor is entered between the SE extremity of Sears Island (44°26′·50N 68°52′·80W) and Squaw Point, 1½ miles NE, the S extremity of Cape Jellison.

Entrance channel is marked by buoys (lateral).

Anchorage. It is a secure harbour for vessels up to 6·7 m draught, and is easy of access.

2 **Berth.** An offshore platform with dolphins and mooring buoys is situated off the NE point of Sears Island. It has 61 m of berthing space with a reported depth alongside of 10·1 m and handles chemical cargoes. It was reported (2009) that the platform was no longer being used.

PENOBSCOT RIVER

General information

Chart 2486, US Chart 13309 (see 1.16)
Description
2.195

1 The mouth of Penobscot River, which flows into the head of Penobscot Bay, lies between Fort Point (44°28′·03N 68°48′·71W) and Wilson Point, 1 mile SE.

The river forms the approach to the towns of Bucksport (2.205) and Winterport (2.211), and the cities of Brewer (2.217) and Bangor (2.217), the latter two being situated at the head of navigation, 24 miles from the river mouth.

2 **Local knowledge.** There is considerable trade to Bangor, but the river should not be entered without local knowledge.

Depths
2.196

1 For latest controlling depths, the charts and port authorities should be consulted.

Logs
2.197

1 At HW springs, many logs floating down river may be a hazard to small vessels.

Pilotage
2.198

1 See 2.96.

Arrival anchorages
2.199

1 The usual anchorage for small vessels waiting at the river entrance is N of Fort Point on either side of the channel. Anchorage in the river is not advised because vessels tend to drag anchor on strong ebb tides.

Large vessels usually anchor S of Fort Point or off Searsport (2.178).

An alternative anchorage in 2 to 7 m (5 to 23 ft), often used by small vessels, is in Fort Point Cove.

Vertical clearances
2.200

1 **Bridges.** There are two bridges spanning the Penobscot River between Fort Point and Bangor, which are situated:
    One mile S of Bucksport, vertical clearance of 41·1 m (135 ft).
    One mile S of Bangor, vertical clearance of 22·5 m (74 ft).

2 **Overhead power cables.** Power cables span the river 5 cables NW of Fort Knox (44°33′·97N 68°48′·15W) and 5 cables N of Oak Point (44°40′·20N 68°49′·00W). The vertical clearance of these cables is 44·2 and 48·5 m (145 and 159 ft), respectively.

Natural conditions
2.201

1 **Tidal streams** between Odom Ledge (3 miles N of Fort Point) and Orrington (5 miles below Bangor) often reach a rate of 3 kn during the outgoing ebb stream, which may be occasionally increased to 5 kn at maximum spring tides.

2 **Ice** impedes, but seldom prevents, navigation above Winterport for nearly 5 months of the year, beginning about the end of November. During extreme winters the river may be closed at its mouth. The most difficult place below Winterport is abreast Fort Knox, opposite Bucksport, where ice jams may occur. If this point can be passed, it is normally possible to reach Winterport.

3 The river is kept open by an icebreaker, which prevents much of the damage that might otherwise be caused by ice and freshets.

Freshets occur in the river during March and April and are sometimes dangerous to vessels.

Directions
(continued from 2.146)

Principal mark
2.202

1 **Major light:**
    Fort Point Light (white house) (44°28′·03N 68°48′·71W).

Penobscot Bay to Bucksport
2.203

1 From a position WNW of Turtle Head (2.146) the track leads generally NE for 5 miles, passing:
    SE of No 1 Light Buoy (port hand) (44°25′·06N 68°52′·46W), marking a 6·7 m (22 ft) patch 6 cables S of Sears Island (2.175), thence:
    SE of Squaw Point (44°26′·80N 68°51′·50W) (2.194).

2   Between Fort Point Ledge (44°27′·65N 68°48′·60W) and Fort Point. Fort Point Ledge, which dries 1·5 m (5 ft), has No 2 Light (red triangle on post on stone monument) near its N end. No 1 Buoy (port hand) is moored off Fort Point. Thence:

Thence the channel up river leads generally N for 6 miles, passing:

3   E of Sandy Point (44°29′·85N 68°48′·60W). Buoys (lateral), which mark the main channel, are moored off this point (see Caution). Thence:
    W of Odom Ledge (44°30′·93N 68°48′·05W), which partly dries. No 6A Beacon (red

triangular daymark, stone base) stands on the ledge and No 6 Light Buoy (starboard hand) marks its SW side (see Caution). Thence:

4 Between the towers marking the ends of the road bridge (2.200), 3 cables S of Fort Knox (44°33′·97N 68°48′·15W). See 2.201.

Caution. Deep-draught vessels should proceed with caution between Fort Point and Bucksport as there are mid-channel depths of 9·4 m (31 ft), 5 cables E of Sandy Point, and of 10·1 m (33 ft), 2½ cables SW of Odom Ledge.

Bucksport to Bangor
2.204

1 The river channel from Bucksport to Bangor, which is buoyed as far as 3 miles below Bangor, can best be seen on the chart.

Cautions. The channel is crooked and narrow in places and frequent changes occur.

The most difficult sections are off Lawrence and Luce Coves, 1 mile NW of Bucksport, where depths are liable to change, and off Frankfort Flats, 2 miles farther upstream, where there are sharp bends.

2 Navigation at night is extremely dangerous due to the lack of lighted aids to navigation.

Large vessels require the assistance of a tug to navigate the turns.

At times of maximum out-going tidal stream, buoys are occasionally pulled under.

Bucksport

General information
2.205

1 **Position and function.** Bucksport (44°34′·33N 68°48′·18W), which is situated 6 miles from the mouth of Penobscot River, stands on the E bank of the river.

Bucksport is a railway terminal. Paper production and oil distribution are its main industries. The town has a customs station. The port handles petroleum, paper products and small cruise liners.

Limiting conditions
2.206

1 **Controlling depth.** See 2.196.

Arrival information
2.207

1 **Pilotage and tugs.** See 2.96 and 2.97.

Directions
2.208

1 See 2.203.

Berths
2.209

1 **Tanker berth** 213 m in length, depth alongside of 10·7 m, can accommodate vessels of up to 213 m length and 10·36 m beam.

Paper mill has berths with depths alongside of 1·5 to 7·3 m.

Port services
2.210

1 **Supplies**: fuel; water and provisions.

Winterport

General information
2.211

1 **Position and function.** Winterport (44°37′·89N 68°50′·68W), which is situated about 12 miles above the mouth of Penobscot River, stands on the W side of the river. The port handles fresh and frozen foods.

Limiting conditions
2.212

1 **Controlling depth.** See 2.196.

Arrival information
2.213

1 **Pilotage and tugs.** See 2.96 and 2.97.

Directions
2.214

1 See 2.204.

Berths
2.215

1 A floating barge, 82 m in length, with depths alongside of 7·6 m is moored 90 m offshore, 3 cables S of the town, and can accommodate vessels of up to 150 m in length and 7·45 m draught.

Port services
2.216

1 **Repairs.** Boatyard for minor repairs.
Other facility. Hospital 20 km.
Supplies: fuel; water and provisions.

Bangor

General information
2.217

1 **Position and function.** Bangor (44°47′·73N 68°46′·16W), which is situated at the head of navigation, stands on the W bank of Penobscot River. The city of Brewer stands on the E bank opposite Bangor, and South Brewer is 1 mile S.

Bangor, which by the 2010 census had a population of 33 039, is an important city. The port handles mainly oil cargoes and some small cruise liners. It is a port of entry.

Limiting conditions
2.218

1 **Controlling depth.** See 2.196.
Vertical clearance. See 2.200.
Tidal levels. Mean spring range about 4·5 m (14·8 ft); mean neap range about 3·5 m (11·5 ft). See information in *Admiralty Tide Tables.*

Arrival information
2.219

1 **Pilotage and tugs.** See 2.96 and 2.97.

Directions
2.220

1 See 2.204.

Berths
2.221

1 **East Hampden.** Oil wharf 1½ miles S of Bangor.
South Brewer. Paper mill wharf 1 mile S of Bangor with depths alongside of 3·9 to 4·5 m.
Brewer. Oil wharves for small tankers.
Bangor. Number of wharves with depths alongside of 2·1 to 4·2 m.

Port services
2.222

1 **Facilities:** hospital; oily waste disposal.
Supplies: fuel; water and stores.

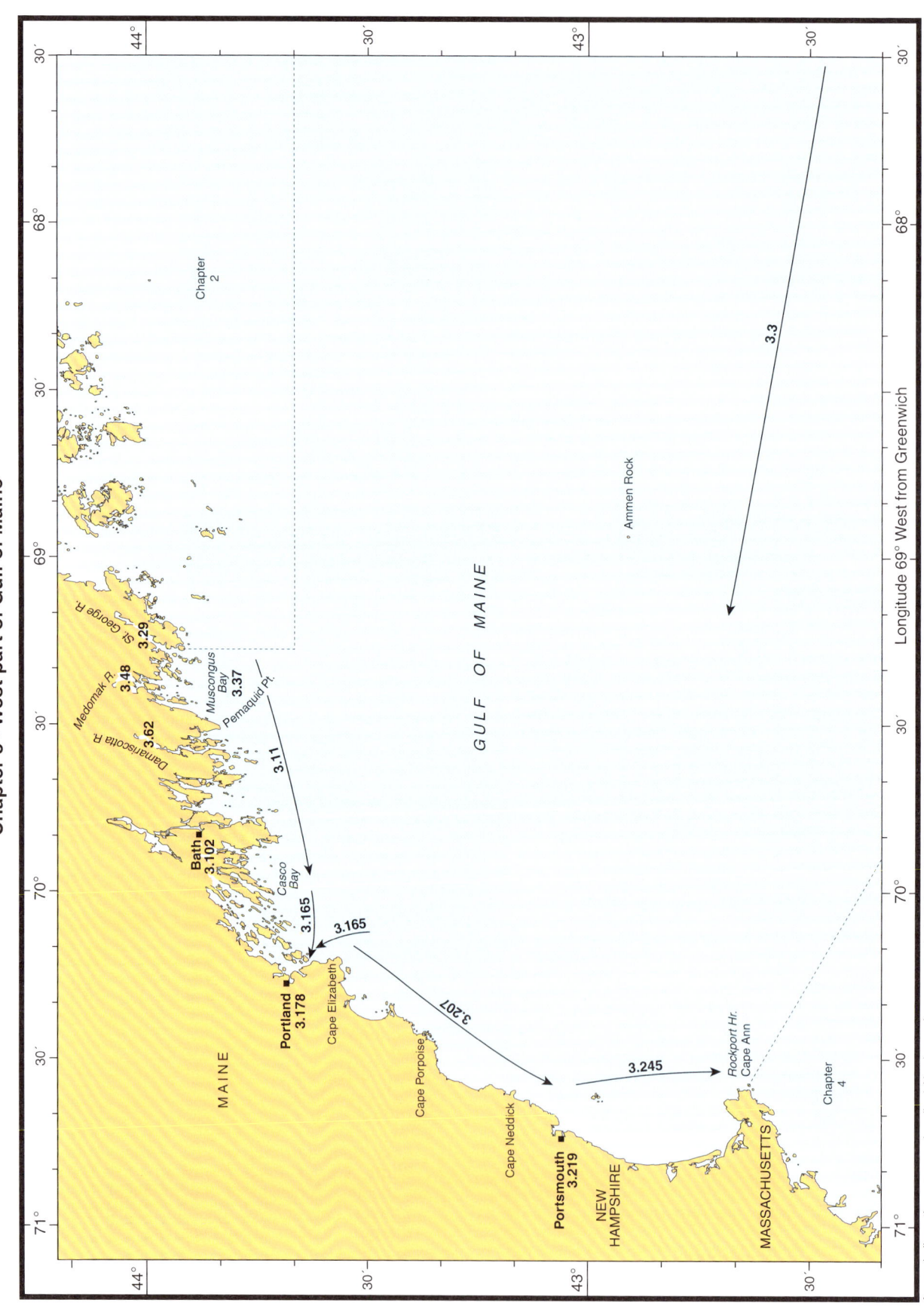

CHAPTER 3

WEST PART OF GULF OF MAINE

GENERAL INFORMATION

Chart 2492
Scope of the chapter
3.1

1 The area covered by this chapter comprises the coast of Maine from Monhegan Island (43°46′·00N 69°18′·80W) to Cape Ann (42°39′·00N 70°38′·00W), about 90 miles SW. The description includes the principal ports of Portland (3.178) and Portsmouth (3.219).

The chapter is divided into the following sections:
Offshore approach to Gulf of Maine (3.2).
Monhegan Island to Cape Elizabeth (3.8).
Cape Elizabeth to Cape Ann (3.202).

OFFSHORE APPROACH TO GULF OF MAINE

General information

Chart 2492
Area covered
3.2

1 This section describes the offshore approach to Gulf of Maine.

Outlying banks
3.3

1 Gulf of Maine is entered between the SW end of Nova Scotia (43°46′·00N 66°07′·00W) (see *Nova Scotia and Bay of Fundy Pilot*) and Cape Cod (4.61), about 200 miles WSW.

Georges Bank. The W part of the entrance to Gulf of Maine is obstructed by Georges Bank (41°17′·00N 67°35′·00W), which extends between 80 miles ESE and 120 miles E of Cape Cod. This bank has depths of less than 90 m (50 fm) and the bottom is sand, with shells and pebbles in places.

2 The two principal dangers on Georges Bank are Georges Shoal (3.7) and Cultivator Shoal (3.7), which lie in the middle part of an area 100 miles in extent, on the NW part of the bank. These shoals have irregular depths of less than 37 m (20 fm) and are dangerous to navigation.

On the NE side of Georges Bank there is a deep channel about 25 miles wide in which there are depths of over 180 m (100 fm).

3 **Other outlying banks.** There are several other outlying banks in the central part of the Gulf of Maine, but of these Ammen Rock on Cashes Ledge is the only danger.

Cashes Ledge (42°53′·50N 68°56′·50W) has several patches of around 25 m (13 fm) and, near its centre, Ammen Rock (3.7).

4 **Fippennies Ledge** (42°48′·00N 69°18′·80W) has a least charted depth of 67 m (36 fm).

Jeffreys Bank (43°21′·50N 68°44′·00W) has a depth of 64 m (35 fm).

Platts Bank (43°11′·60N 69°40′·00W) has a least known depth of 49 m (27 fm).

Unexploded Ordnance
3.4

1 Unexploded ordnance has been reported in several areas in the Gulf of Maine, as shown on the chart.

Mandatory Ship Reporting System (MSR)
3.5

1 A mandatory ship reporting system has been established for the protection of the North Atlantic right whale. See Appendix X and *Admiralty List of Radio Signals Volume 6(5)* for details.

Tidal streams
3.6

1 Tidal streams over Georges Bank and its vicinity are rotary, and there is no slack water. The maximum rate over Georges Bank is 2 kn.

Details of tidal streams in Gulf of Maine are given on the charts.

Directions
3.7

1 From the vicinity of 42°25′·00N 67°35′·00W the offshore approach route to the ports in the W part of Gulf of Maine leads generally W, passing:

2 N of Georges Shoal (41°40′·00N 67°44′·00W). This shoal has a least depth of 2·7 m (9 ft) and the submerged remains of a tower lie on the N part of the shoal. From its centre, shoals and patches, with depths of 18 m (60 ft) or less extend for between 15 and 25 miles. A shoal with a depth of 9·4 m (31 ft) lies 15 miles NE of the shallowest part of Georges Shoal. Thence:

3 N of Cultivator Shoal (41°34′·00N 68°10′·00W). This shoal has a least depth of 5·4 m (18 ft) near its N end, with patches with depths of less than 18 m (60 ft) extending between 4 miles N and 46 miles SSW from the shallowest part. Thence:

S of Ammen Rock with a depth of 8·0 m (25 ft). In heavy weather the sea breaks over this shoal.

Thence proceed as necessary clear of charted dangers to the approaches to the ports of Portland (3.178), Portsmouth (3.219) and Boston (4.77).

4 **Caution.** The whole area covered by Georges Bank, within depths of 37 m (20 fm), has an extremely broken bottom in which all the shoalest spots may not have been found. The S and W sides of Georges Bank should not be approached in depths of less than 55 m (30 fm). On the SE side of the bank depths decrease gradually and soundings can be of considerable value, but on the NW side of the bank depths decrease abruptly. The area should be avoided.

(Directions continue for
approaches to Portland at 3.172,
for Portsmouth at 3.235,
for Boston at 4.66)

MONHEGAN ISLAND TO CAPE ELIZABETH

GENERAL INFORMATION

Chart 2490
Area covered
3.8

1 This section describes the coast between Monhegan Island (43°46'·00N 69°18'·80W) and Cape Elizabeth, 40 miles WSW; this coast is rocky and indented by numerous bays and rivers, many of which are excellent harbours. The approaches to these bays and rivers are obstructed by many islands and dangers.

The W part of this coastline consists of Casco Bay, entered between Cape Small (43°42'·60N 69°50'·60W) and Cape Elizabeth, 18 miles WSW. The principal port of Portland is also included.

2 The section is arranged as follows:
   Coastal passage between Monhegan Island and the approaches to Portland (3.11).
   Inshore waters between Mosquito Island and Georges Islands (3.16).
   Muscongus Bay (3.37).
   Inshore waters between Pemaquid Point and Cape Newagen (3.60).
3 Inshore waters between Cape Newagen and Cape Small (3.80).
   Eastern part of Casco Bay (3.104).
   Western part of Casco Bay (3.123).
   Approaches to Portland (3.165).
   Portland Harbor (3.178).

Inside Passage
3.9

1 Inside Passage from Boothbay Harbor (43°50'·72N 69°38'·08W) to Bath (3.102) is about 11 miles long and leads through the islands between Boothbay Harbor (3.76) and Kennebec River (3.94). The channel is very narrow in places, has strong tidal currents and is obstructed by rocks and shoals. Most dangers are marked.

Local knowledge is required by vessels with a draught of more than 2 m.

2 **Route.** The passage leads through Townsend Gut (3.77), across Sheepscot River, through Goose Rock Passage (3.88), Knubble Bay (3.88), Hockomock Bay (3.88), Sasanoa River (3.88) and thence into Kennebec River opposite the city of Bath.

Regulations
3.10

1 **Navigation Rules for US Inland Waters** apply to the greater part of the inland waters of Casco Bay. The limits of the waters to which these rules apply are given in each section. See 1.44 and Appendix VII for further information.

No-Discharge Zone (NDZ). All the waters of Casco Bay, N of a line from Bald Head (3.107) to Cape Elizabeth Light (3.172), have been designated as a NDZ. See 1.41.

COASTAL PASSAGE BETWEEN MONHEGAN ISLAND AND APPROACHES TO PORTLAND

General information

Chart 2490
Description
3.11

1 The following paragraphs describe the coastal passage between Monhegan Island (43°46'·00N 69°18'·80W) and the approaches to Portland, 30 miles WSW.

Traffic regulations
3.12

1 **Danger zone.** An area SE of Cape Small, centred approximately on 43°40'·60N 69°47'·70W, is used by naval aircraft for mining practice. For details see Appendix VI.

Restricted area. A naval sonobuoy test area, 1 mile in radius, is situated 8 miles SSE of Pemaquid Point (43°50'·10N 69°30'·80W). Vessels are requested to keep clear when sonobuoys are being dropped. The area is connected to the shore by submarine cables. For details see Appendix VI.

Directions
(continued from 2.103)

Principal marks
3.13

1 **Landmark:**
   Monhegan Island (43°46'·00N 69°18'·80W) (2.102).

Major lights:
   Monhegan Island Light (43°45'·89N 69°18'·95W) (2.102).
   Seguin Island Light (white brick conical tower, 16 m in height) (43°42'·45N 69°45'·48W), standing on the summit of Seguin Island, grassy and 44 m (144 ft) in height.
2 Halfway Rock Light (white tower and dwelling, 23 m in height) (43°39'·35N 70°02'·21W).
   Portland Head Light (43°37'·39N 70°12'·47W) (3.172).
   Cape Elizabeth Light (43°33'·96N 70°12'·00W) (3.172).

Other aid to navigation
3.14

1 **Racon:**
   P Light Buoy (43°31'·61N 70°05'·47W).
   See *Admiralty List of Radio Signals Volume 2*.

Track
3.15

1 From a position about 10 miles SE of Monhegan Island (43°46'·00N 69°18'·80W) (2.102) the coastal passage to the approaches to Portland leads W for about 37 miles, passing:
   S of Monhegan Island, thence:
   S of Pemaquid Point (3.39), the W entrance point to Muscongus Bay (3.37), thence:
2 S of Poor Shoal (3.74); Bantam Rock (3.74) lies 6½ cables NW, thence:
   S of Mile Ledge (43°41'·52N 69°45'·30W), marked by 20ML Light Buoy (3.96), thence:
   S of Seguin SSW Ledge (43°39'·95N 69°46'·47W), thence:
   S of Fuller Rock Light (red and white chequered diamond on white framework tower) (43°41'·75N 69°50'·02W), thence:
3 S of Temple Ledge (43°40'·90N 69°52'·97W), thence:
   S of Lumbo Ledge (43°40'·86N 69°55'·91W). 2Q Buoy (starboard hand) marks the SW part of the ledge. Thence:
   S of a shoal with a depth of 10·7 m (35 ft), 3 cables SSW of Halfway Rock Light (3.13). Deep-draught vessels should not pass N of Halfway Rock.

⁴ **Useful marks**:
Pemaquid Point Light (43°50'·21N 69°30'·35W) (3.39).
The Cuckolds Light (43°46'·77N 69°39'·00W) (3.74).

*(Directions continue for
approaches to Portland at 3.172,
and for coastal passage at 3.209)*

INSHORE WATERS BETWEEN MOSQUITO ISLAND AND GEORGES ISLANDS

General information

Charts 2486, 2490, US Charts 13301, 13302, 13288 (see 1.16)

Description
3.16
¹ The inshore waters between Mosquito Island (43°55'·20N 69°13'·20W) (2.144) and Georges Islands, 5 miles SW, consist of Port Clyde and adjacent waters, the approaches to Saint George River, and Saint George River.

Traffic regulations
3.17
¹ **Navigation Rules for US Inland Waters** do not apply to any of the waters described in this sub-section.

Port Clyde and adjacent waters

General information
3.18
¹ **Position and function.** Port Clyde (43°55'·53N 69°15'·62W) is a small but excellent harbour between Marshall Point and the E side of Hupper Island, 2½ cables W. The port is used as a harbour of refuge by fishermen and small vessels, and is the mainland terminal of the ferry service to Monhegan Island. Small cruise liners occasionally visit.
Local knowledge is required.
² **Approaches.** The main approach channel is from the E. See 3.20.
The harbour can also be entered through the N entrance, 7 cables N of Marshall Point. The N entrance is obstructed by a bar and Raspberry Island lies on this bar. There is a narrow passage with a depth of 1·5 m (5 ft) on either side of the island, but both are difficult to navigate and should not be attempted without local knowledge.

Limiting conditions
3.19
¹ **Ice** rarely interferes with navigation except in very severe winters and even then usually only lasts for a short time.

Directions for approach from east
3.20
¹ From a position close S of No 2 Buoy (starboard hand), moored 2 cables S of Mosquito Island (43°55'·20N 69°13'·20W) (2.144), the E approach channel to Port Clyde leads:
clear of Barter Shoal (43°54'·64N 69°13'·51W) and a 5·5 m (19 ft) patch 3 cables NW, thence:
NE of Hay Ledge (43°54'·54N 69°13'·98W), 4·6 m in height, thence:
² N of The Brothers (43°54'·65N 69°14'·40W), 5·6 m in height, thence:
Between Nos 4 and 5 Buoys (starboard and port hand) marking, respectively, the SE side of Mosquito Ledge and the N end of Gunning Rocks, thence:
S of Marshall Ledge, marked on its S side by No 6 Buoy (starboard hand), thence:
³ Close W of a 5·5 m (18 ft) patch situated mid-channel in the harbour entrance, thence:
Through the entrance into the S part of the harbour.
Useful mark:
Marshall Point Light (white round tower) (43°55'·05N 69°15'·68W).

(Directions for approach to Saint George River continue at 3.24)

Berths
3.21
¹ **Anchorage** may be obtained, with good holding with a width of 1 to 1½ cables, in the channel between Marshall Point and the bar, in 7 to 11 m (23 to 35 ft). Attention is drawn to a cable area, shown on the national chart, which extends across the harbour N of the ferry wharf.
In S winds good anchorage may be obtained N of Hupper Island, E of a line between Blubber Island (43°55'·86N 69°16'·40W) and Hupper Point (3 cables N), in 6 to 7 m (20 to 23 ft).
² **Alongside berths.** The ferry wharf lies 5 cables N of Marshall Point on the E shore of the harbour. The town landing stage with depths alongside of 1·5 to 3 m, lies close N of the ferry and there are several other wharves in the harbour with depths alongside of 1·8 to 5·4 m.
Supplies: fuel; water and stores.

Approaches to Saint George River

Description
3.22
¹ The approaches to Saint George River are obstructed by Georges Islands and by numerous dangers, the most important of which are marked by buoys and beacons. Between these islands and dangers several channels lead to the river.
² **Georges Islands** extend 5 miles S from Caldwell Island (43°56'·20N 69°17'·80W) to Allen Island (43°56'·20N 69°17'·80W). The larger islands are generally wooded, the smaller are grassy and rocky. Many dangers fringe these islands and some navigable channels lead between them.

Main approach channels
3.23
¹ There are two main approach channels:
From the east by the E approach to Port Clyde (3.20) and thence between Hupper Island and the Georges Islands to pass E of Caldwell Island.
From the south-west coming from the E part of Muscongus Bay, passing NW of Franklin Island (43°53'·53N 69°22'·48W) (3.39) and thence NW of Caldwell Island.

Directions
(continued from 3.20)
3.24
¹ **East approach.** From a position S of the entrance to Port Clyde the E approach to the entrance to the Saint George River continues SW and then N around the S and W side of Hupper Island, passing:
NW of the dangers extending N from Hart Island, marked on their N edge by No 7 Buoy (port hand), thence:
² S of two shoals, 1·8 m (6 ft) and 3·7 m (12 ft) in depth, that lie off the S side of Hupper Island,

marked by No 8 Buoy (starboard hand), thence:

W of Kelp Ledges (43°55'·14N 69°17'·03W), marked off their SW side by No 2 Buoy (starboard hand). A 2·7 m (9 ft) patch lies 1 cable NW of the N end of the ledge. Thence:

3   Clear of Murray Ledge (43°55'·91N 69°16'·91W), with a depth of 4·5 m (15 ft), thence:

Clear of Channel Rock (43°56'·16N 69°16'·78W), with a depth of 1·5 m (5 ft) and with DCR Buoy (isolated danger) marking its W side, thence:

Into the entrance to Saint George River.

Useful mark:
No 10 Beacon (43°54'·42N 69°17'·45W), standing on Old Horse Ledge.

(Directions continue at 3.33)

3.25

1   **South approach.** See 3.41.

Other channels
3.26

1   **Davis Strait** (43°53'·44N 69°18'·40W), leading between Davis Island, grassy, and the islets extending SE from Thompson Island, is a narrow channel that forms part of the inshore route used by many vessels drawing 3·7 m (12 ft) or less. It is reported that barges with a draught of 4·9 m use the strait.

Griffin Ledge, with a depth of 3 m (10 ft), lies in mid-channel, and is marked on its SE side by No 12 Buoy (starboard hand). The channel SE of the buoy is 68 m wide.

Local knowledge is required.

(Directions for the inshore route continue at 3.45)

3.27

1   **Davis Strait to Hupper Island.** A channel leads NE from Davis Strait to Hupper Island passing NW of Gig Rock and The Sisters. These dangers are marked by Nos 11 and 9 Buoys (port hand), respectively, on their NW sides. The channel then passes SE of Old Horse Ledge Beacon (3.24).

Anchorages
3.28

1   **Caldwell Island.** Anchorage may be obtained by deep-draught vessels E of Caldwell Island (43°56'·20N 69°17'·80W) in 10 to 16 m (33 to 53 ft), soft bottom.

Hupper Island. See 3.21.

Saint George River

Chart 2486, US Chart 13301 (see 1.16)

Description
3.29

1   From its entrance, close N of Caldwell Island, Saint George River extends 10 miles NE to the town of Thomaston, the head of navigation (3.36).

Depths
3.30

1   There are depths of 6·7 to 24 m (22 ft to 13 fm) as far as Broad Cove, 5 miles above the entrance. After this the depth gradually decreases and the channel narrows to pass between extensive flats, which dry. The channel has a least depth of 6·7 m (22 ft) to within 1 mile below Thomaston.

Thence a narrow channel, dredged to a depth of 4·9 m (16 ft), leads toward the wharf. In 1984 the controlling depth to the bend at Thomaston was 3·3 m (11 ft).

Vertical clearance
3.31

1   A fixed bridge with a vertical clearance of 1·5 m (5 ft) crosses the river above the wharf at Thomaston.

Ice
3.32

1   Ice closes the river in severe winters from December to March. In ordinary winters the river is not normally entirely closed for more than a month, though ice sufficient to interfere with navigation may be encountered at any time during this period.

Directions
(continued from 3.24 and 3.41)
3.33

1   From a position NE of Caldwell Island the passage up Saint George River leads NE, passing:

Between Nos 4 and 5 Buoys (starboard and port hand), that are moored off Howard Point (43°56'·90N 69°16'·50W) and Pleasant Point, respectively, thence:

2   SE of Stones Point, the SW entrance point to Maple Juice Cove (3.35). No 7 Buoy (port hand) (2 miles SW), marks the dangers extending E from Stones Point. Thence:

Through the middle of the Narrows (43°58'·90N 69°15'·40W), taking care to avoid two rocks with depths of 6·7 and 7 m (22 and 23 ft), which are situated, respectively, 1¼ miles and 7 cables SSW of Bailey Point, thence:

3   SE of Bailey Ledge (43°59'·91N 69°14'·40W), which has a rock awash near its outer end and is marked by No 9 Buoy (port hand). There is a marine farm in Broad Cove, 4 cables N of the ledge. Thence:

Between Watts Point (44°00'·18N 69°13'·38W) and Bradford Point (5½ cables NW).

4   From NNE of Watts Point the passage leads through a channel between the mud flats, marked by buoys (lateral). The safest time to make this passage is at LW when the flats are uncovered or when the tide is rising.

Anchorages on east side
3.34

1   **Deep Cove** (43°56'·50N 69°16'·30W), just N of Hupper Point, provides good anchorage, with soft bottom, in 6 to 13 m (21 to 43 ft). A rocky patch, with a depth of 3·7 m (12 ft), lies in the N part of the cove.

Turkey Cove, S of Turkey Point (43°57'·65N 69°16'·00W), provides good anchorage in its entrance in 5 to 8 m (15 to 27 ft), soft bottom.

Otis Cove (43°59'·25N 69°14'·60W) provides anchorage off its entrance in 6 to 8 m (20 to 27 ft).

Anchorage on west side
3.35

1   **Maple Juice Cove** (43°58'·60N 69°16'·60W), entered between Henderson Ledge and Burton Point, 3 cables N, provides anchorage in depths of 4 to 7 m (13 to 24 ft). No 7 Buoy (port hand) marks Henderson Ledge.

Thomaston
3.36

1   Thomaston (44°04'·27N 69°10'·90W) is not a commercial port but has a public wharf with a reported depth alongside of 4·6 m.

Repairs. Slipway and two boatyards where hull and engine repairs can be effected.

Supplies: fuel; water and limited stores.

MUSCONGUS BAY

General information

Charts 2490, 2492, 2486, US Chart 13301 (see 1.16)
Description
3.37

1 Muscongus Bay (43°53'·40N 69°23'·50W) lies between Georges Islands (3.22) and Pemaquid Neck (43°51'·50N 69°30'·20W), a wooded peninsula lying 7 miles W. It forms the approach to Meduncook River (3.44), Medomak River (3.48), and Muscongus Sound (3.47).

2 The bay is frequented by many local fishing boats and yachts, but is obstructed by numerous islands and ledges, and is seldom entered by vessels seeking shelter in heavy weather as Tenants Harbor (2.182) and Port Clyde (3.18) to the E, and Boothbay Harbor (3.76) to the W, are easier to enter and more convenient.

Many of the dangers in the bay are marked by buoys.

Traffic regulations
3.38

1 **Navigation Rules for US Inland Waters** do not apply to any of the waters described in this sub-section.

Approach to Muscongus bay

Directions
3.39

1 **Major Light:**
Monhegan Island Light (43°45'·89N 69°18'·95W) (2.102).

South approach. Muscongus Bay is approached from the S between Monhegan Island (43°46'·00N 69°18'·80W) and Pemaquid Point, 10 miles WNW. Moser Ledge, marked on its NW side by DM Buoy (isolated danger), lies in the middle of the entrance, 3¾ miles ESE of Pemaquid Point. Depths are irregular 1 mile S of the ledge.

2 **Useful marks:**
Franklin Island Light (white tower) (43°53'·53N 69°22'·48W), standing on the NW side of Franklin Island.
Pemaquid Point Light (white conical tower) (43°50'·21N 69°30'·35W).

Unexploded ordnance is reported (1961) to lie in an area, 1 mile radius, centred 3 miles SSE of Pemaquid Point. A similar sized area used for the naval testing of sonobuoys lies 5 miles farther S. See 3.12.

Rivers and channels in the east part of Muscongus Bay
3.40

1 There are three deep, but mostly unmarked, channels that lead in a N direction through the E part of Muscongus Bay and into Saint George River.

West of Georges Islands
3.41

1 From a position W of Old Man Ledge (43°50'·50N 69°18'·90W), marked on its S side by 2OM Light Buoy, the E channel leads N and then NE, passing:
Between Allen Island (3.22) and Little Egg Rock (43°51'·28N 69°20'·42W), thence:
E of Seal Ledges (43°51'·28N 69°20'·42W); No 13 Buoy (port hand) is moored on the N side of the ledges, thence:

2 Between Thompson Rock (43°53'·77N 69°19'·59W), with a depth of 3·4 m (11 ft) and The Kegs, 7 cables WSW, awash and marked by TK Beacon, thence:
Between Jenks Ledge (43°55'·43N 69°19'·32W), awash at LW and marked on its W side by 2JL Buoy (starboard hand), and Otter Island, 1 mile WNW. A number of dangers lie off the E side of Otter Island. Thence:

3 Between Goose Rock (43°55'·90N 69°18'·47W) and Goose Rock Ledge, 3 cables NW. The SE side of the ledge is marked by No 1 Buoy (port hand). Thence:
Between the N point of Caldwell Island and Gay Cove Ledge (43°56'·66N 69°17'·97W). The SE side of the ledge is marked by No 3 Buoy (port hand).
Thence to the entrance of Saint George River.
(Directions continue at 3.33)

Old Hump Channel
3.42

1 From a position W of Shark Island (43°50'·70N 69°21'·33W) Old Hump Channel leads generally NNE, passing:
ESE of Eastern Egg Rock (43°51'·65N 69°22'·93W), with No 15 Beacon on its N point and No 14 Buoy (starboard hand) marking Egg Rock N Ledge, 2 cables N; thence:

2 WNW of Old Hump Ledge (43°52'·63N 69°21'·37W), above water. A rock, with a depth of 4·3 m (14 ft), lies 3½ cables S. Thence:
Between The Kegs (3.41) and Gangway Ledge (43°54'·03N 69°21'·38W), a bare above-water rock lying at the N end of the dangers extending N from Eastern Egg Rock.
(Directions continue as in 3.41)

Between Franklin Island and Crane Island
3.43

1 From a position W of Eastern Egg Rock (3.42), the channel between Franklin Island (43°53'·53N 69°22'·48W) and Crane Island leads NNE, to the W of the dangers extending N from Eastern Egg Rock, passing:
Between Franklin Island and Crane Island, 5 cables NW, thence:
Between Gangway Ledge (3.42) and Hall Island, 1 mile NW.
(Directions continue as in 3.41)

Meduncook River
3.44

1 Meduncook River (43°57'·80N 69°19'·10W) is entered 5 cables W of the W entrance to Saint George River, between Gay Island and Morse Island, 3 cables W. The estuary forms an approach to Friendship Harbor (3.51).

The river extends 3 miles NNE from its entrance. It has a narrow channel and is obstructed by numerous unmarked dangers.

Local knowledge is required for its navigation.
Anchorage. See 3.50.

Inshore route
(continued from 3.26)
3.45

1 The inshore route, suitable for vessels with a draught of not more than 3·7 m (12 ft), leads WSW from Davis Strait (3.26), passing:
N of Seal Ledges (3.41), marked on their N side by No 13 Buoy (port hand), thence:

2   S of Old Hump Ledge (3.42). A rock (3.42) lies 3½ cables S. Thence:
   Between Eastern Egg Rock (3.42) and Egg Rock North Ledge (3.42), marked on its SE by No 14 Buoy (starboard hand).
   Thence the route continues WSW to pass S of Pemaquid Point.

Rivers and channels in the west part of Muscongus Bay

Approaches to Friendship Harbor and Medomak River
3.46

1   From a position SW of Eastern Egg Rock (43°51'·65N 69°22'·93W) the approach route to Friendship Harbor (3.51) and Medomak River (3.48) leads generally NNE, passing:
   ESE of Western Egg Rock (43°52'·70N 69°25'·00W), 8 m (25 ft) in height and grassy. A shoal, with a depth of 1·2 m (4 ft), marked by No 1 Buoy (port hand), lies 3 cables ENE. Thence:
2   ESE of Devils Elbow and Devils Back (43°53'·78N 69°24'·19W), two rocks which dry 0·3 m (1 ft) and 2·4 m (8 ft), respectively. No 3 Buoy (port hand) is moored close SE of Devils Back, thence:
   WNW of Harbor Island Rock (43°54'·32N 69°23'·36W) with a depth of 2·4 m (8 ft), thence:
3   SE of the 4·5 m (15 ft) patch lying 3 cables E of Wreck Island (43°54'·60N 69°24'·00W), and SE of a patch with a swept depth of 2·7 m (9 ft), 5 cables ENE of this island. Wreck Island is 15 m (48 ft) in height and wooded. Thence:
   Between Black Island (43°55'·58N 69°22'·40W) and Jones Garden Island, 6 cables WNW, thence:
4   E of Gull Rock (43°57'·44N 69°22'·30W), two rocks close together, if bound for Friendship Harbor (3.51), or:
   W of Gull Rock if bound up Medomak River (3.48).

Muscongus Sound
3.47

1   **Description.** Muscongus Sound (43°56'·40N 69°26'·70W) is situated on the W side of Muscongus Bay between Louds Island and Hog Island on the E and the mainland on the W.
   The S entrance, entered between the S point of Louds Island and Browns Head (43°54'·20N 69°27'·60W), is obstructed by dangers, but the most important of these are marked by buoys.
2   The N entrance to the sound leads through Lower Narrows, a narrow passage between Hog Island and Hockomock Point. There is no safe passage between Louds Island and Hog Island.
   Directions. From a position about 1 mile W of Haddock Island (43°53'·27N 69°26'·38W) the route through Muscongus Sound leads generally N, passing:
3   W of Webber Sunken Ledge (43°53'·41N 69°26'·96W), Browns Head Ledge (5 cables NNW) and Bar Island Ledge (1 mile N), all of which are marked by buoys (starboard hand), thence:
   E of Poland S Ledge (43°55'·46N 69°27'·01W) and Poland N Ledge, 3 cables N. The ledges are marked on their E sides by Nos 7 and 9 Buoys (port hand), respectively. Thence:
4   E of Halftide Ledge (43°58'·32N 69°26'·00W), marked on its S side by No 11 Buoy (port hand), thence:
   Through Lower Narrows (43°58'·74N 69°25'·30W), depth 4 m (13 ft) and marked by Nos 13 and 15 Buoys (port hand).

Medomak River
3.48

1   Medomak River (43°59'·40N 69°22'·60W) flows into Muscongus Bay between Martin Point (43°57'·92N 69°22'·00W) and Hockomock Point, 2½ miles WNW.
   The lower part of the river is divided by islands into two channels. The E entrance channel, 9 cables wide between Martin Point and Cow Island, divides into two passages at its upper end, 2 miles N of Martin Point. One passage leads along the E and N sides of Hungry Island and the other through Flying Passage between Hungry Island and Bremen Long Island. Both passages are very narrow in places and unmarked rocks are situated in the fairway and at its sides.
2   The W entrance channel, Hockomock Channel, with a least depth of 6·1 m (20 ft), leads between Bremen Long Island and the mainland NW. It is the preferred channel, but it is narrow in places and the tidal streams are strong.
   Local knowledge is necessary to enter the river owing to the numerous unmarked dangers, narrow winding channels and the strong tidal streams.
3.49

1   Both entrance channels unite N of Bremen Long Island, from the N end of which a reef extends 4 cables N.
   For 5 miles above the entrance, the channel up the river has a least depth of 6·1 m (20 ft) and some of the dangers are marked, but unmarked dangers lie close to the fairway. For the next 2½ miles, to within 1½ miles of Waldoboro (44°05'·70N 69°22'·10W), the channel leads through flats which are almost dry at LW and depths decrease gradually to 1·5 m (5 ft).
2   **Tidal streams** are reported to be strong in the narrow passage off Locust Island, 4 miles S of Waldoboro.
   Ice closes the river from December to April.

Anchorages and harbours in Muscongus Bay

Estuary of Meduncook River
3.50

1   Good anchorage may be obtained in the entrance in 3 to 9 m (10 to 30 ft).

Friendship Harbor
3.51

1   Friendship Harbor (43°58'·30N 69°20'·06W) lies between Friendship Long Island and Garrison Island on the S and Jameson Point on the N.
   The harbour has two entrances. The E, which is marked by buoys, leads from the estuary of Meduncook River (3.44) between Garrison Island and Friendship Long Island. The W entrance leads NE from between the SW end of Friendship Long Island and Martin Point, 1 mile N.
2   **Useful mark.** Spire (43°59'·14N 69°19'·82W).
   Anchorage, much used by fishing vessels and small craft, may be obtained in 6 to 9 m (21 to 28 ft) clear of the cable area between Jameson Point and Friendship Long Island.
   Ice seldom closes the harbour.

Dangers
Ledges extend from the N and S shore of the harbour. Their outer edges are marked by beacons and buoys.

Friendship
3.52

1   Friendship is a town on the N shore of Friendship Harbor.

Alongside berths. There are several piers and wharves, with depths alongside of 0·6 to 3·7 m, on the N side of the harbour along Jameson Point. Caution is necessary when approaching the town pier in the N part of the harbour due to underwater rocks in the vicinity.

Repairs. Minor repairs.

Supplies: fuel; water and stores.

Hatchet Cove
3.53

1   Hatchet Cove between Martin Point (43°57'·92N 69°22'·00W) and Jameson Point, 1 mile ENE, is shallow and obstructed by islands and rocks. It is not suitable as an anchorage.

Long Cove
3.54

1   Long Cove (43°53'·10N 69°28'·65W) is open S, but provides good anchorage in winds from other directions, in 4 to 16 m (14 to 53 ft).

Round Pond
3.55

1   Round Pond (43°56'·60N 69°27'·30W), a small landlocked harbour, is situated on the W shore of Muscongus Sound, 2¼ miles N of Browns Head. The village of Round Pond stands on the N shore of the harbour.

Anchorage may be obtained by small vessels in 3 to 5 m (10 to 17 ft). The best anchorage is in the middle of the harbour.

2   **Berths** with depths alongside of 0·9 to 1·8 m are situated in the harbour.

Repairs. Patent slip for craft up to 14 m (45 ft) long.

Supplies: fuel and limited supplies.

North of Poland North Ledge
3.56

1   **Anchorage** may be obtained in Muscongus Sound between Poland North Ledge (3.47) and Muscongus Harbor in depths decreasing gradually from 15 to 7 m (48 to 24 ft).

Muscongus Harbor
3.57

1   Muscongus Harbor (43°58'·07N 69°26'·54W) is a small cove on the W side of Muscongus Sound.

Broad Cove
3.58

1   Broad Cove (44°01'·45N 69°23'·75W) on the W side of Medomak River is sometimes used by fishermen. The channel into the cove is unmarked.

Waldoboro
3.59

1   Waldoboro (44°05'·70N 69°22'·10W) is at the head of navigation on Medomak River. There is no commercial water-borne traffic from the town. There are two wharves, both in a poor state of repair and with little water alongside.

Supplies: fuel; provisions and stores.

INSHORE WATERS BETWEEN PEMAQUID POINT AND CAPE NEWAGEN

General information
Chart 2490, US Chart 13293 (see 1.16)

Description
3.60

1   The inshore waters between Pemaquid Point (43°50'·10N 69°30'·80W) and Cape Newagen, 7 miles WSW, consist of Johns Bay and adjacent waters, Damariscotta River and approaches, and Booth Bay and adjacent waters.

Traffic regulations
3.61

1   **Navigation Rules for US Inland Waters** do not apply to any of the waters described in this sub-section.

Johns Bay and adjacent waters
General information
3.62

1   Johns Bay is entered between Pemaquid Point (43°50'·10N 69°30'·80W) and Thrumcap Island, 1½ miles WSW. It extends 2 miles N between Pemaquid Neck and Rutherford Island, to Johns Island. Pemaquid River (43°52'·95N 69°31'·00W) and Johns River (43°53'·80N 69°32'·60W) flow into the head of the bay.

There is no commercial traffic and the bay is only used as an anchorage by fishermen and yachtsmen as, except near the head of the bay and in the coves, the holding is poor. Port Clyde (3.18), and Boothbay Harbor (3.76), are at all times preferable anchorages.

Damariscotta River and approaches
General information
3.63

1   **Damariscotta River** (43°52'·65N 69°35'·00W) is entered between Thrumcap Island (43°49'·05N 69°33'·05W) and the S end of Linekin Neck. The main entrance channel lies W of Inner Heron Island (3.67), situated 7 cables NW of Thrumcap Island. From its entrance the river leads N for 14 miles to the towns of Damariscotta and Newcastle, situated on either side of the river at the head of navigation.

2   **Topography.** A group of islands and dangers, extending 5 miles S from Linekin Neck, lie in the S and W approaches to Damariscotta River.

The channel of the river is narrow and in many places further restricted by islands and shoals.

Depths. There is a least depth of 6·1 m (20 ft) in the channel for a distance of 11 miles. Above this point the depth decreases gradually to 3 m (10 ft).

3   **Pilotage** is compulsory for all foreign vessels and for US vessels under registry with a draught of 2·7 m (9 ft) or more and may be obtained from the fishermen at South Bristol (3.69) or East Boothbay (3.70).

Local knowledge is required to navigate above The Narrows (3.67), 4½ miles above the entrance.

Natural conditions
3.64

1   **Tidal streams** are strong.

Ice. The river is closed by ice for a distance of 4 miles below Damariscotta from January to March.

Directions for south approach
3.65

1   From the vicinity of 43°44'N 69°32'W the S approach to the mouth of Damariscotta River leads generally N, passing:

E of Pumpkin Island (43°45′·20N 69°34′·94W). A shoal, with a swept depth of 3 m (10 ft), lies 5 cables E of the island. Thence:

E of Outer Heron Island Ledge (43°46′·18N 69°33′·84W), marked on its E side by No 1 Buoy (port hand). Outer Heron Island, wooded, lies 1 mile WNW of the ledge. Thence:

E of White Islands Ledge (43°47′·62N 69°33′·38W). White Islands, two high, rounded and prominent landmarks, lie 7½ cables WSW of the ledge.

Directions for west approach
3.66

From a position about 3 cables W of Fisherman Island (43°47′·90N 69°35′·90W) the W approach to Damariscotta River leads NE and ENE through Fisherman Island Passage, passing:

NW of Ram Island, grassy. Ram Island Light (43°48′·23N 69°35′·95W) (white tower) stands on the NW side of the island. Thence:

SE of Gangway Ledge (43°48′·52N 69°36′·14W), marked on its S side by No 4 Buoy (starboard hand), thence:

Between Fisherman Island and Green Island, 5½ cables N. No 3 Buoy (port hand) marks the N limit of a shoal extending N from Fisherman Island. Thence:

NNW of the Hypocrites (43°48′·05N 69°35′·26W), two low, bare, above-water rocks lying on a reef, marked off their N end by No 1 Buoy (port hand), thence:

NNW of HL Light Buoy (safe water) (43°48′·39N 69°34′·79W).

Useful mark:
Large stone house (43°47′·94N 69°35′·86W), standing on the highest part of the N end of Fisherman Island.

Local knowledge is required for this passage, which may only be used by vessels with a draught not exceeding 5·5 m (18 ft).

Directions for river
3.67

From a position SW of Thrumcap Island (43°49′·05N 69°33′·05W) the channel up Damariscotta River leads generally N, passing:

W of Inner Heron Island (43°49′·70N 69°33′·90W), thickly wooded. No 2 Buoy (starboard hand) marks Inner Heron Ledge which lies 3 cables SW of the island. Thence:

W of Foster Point (43°50′·60N 69°33′·85W), the SW point of Rutherford Island. FP Buoy (preferred channel to port) is moored 1¼ cables S of the point at the outer edge of a ledge. Thence:

Between Farnham Point (43°51′·55N 69°34′·40W) and No 6 Buoy (starboard hand), 3 cables ESE, marking a 2·4 m (8 ft) patch off the entrance to South Bristol (3.69), thence:

SW of Jones Point (43°52′·01N 69°34′·36W), opposite the village of East Boothbay (3.70). Shoals with swept depths of 6·4 and 4 m (21 and 13 ft) lie on the W side of the channel 2 cables SW and 4 cables NW of this point. Thence:

E of Western Ledge (43°53′·08N 69°35′·03W), awash. The ledge is marked on its S side by No 11 Buoy (port hand). Thence:

SE of Fort Island (43°53′·50N 69°35′·15W), which restricts The Narrows to ½ cable.

Above The Narrows the channel, though marked by beacons and buoys, should not be attempted without local knowledge. The final 2 miles below Damariscotta are bordered by mudflats.

Inner Heron Island
3.68

Berths with depths alongside of 3·7 m, for pleasure craft only, are situated on the NE side of Inner Heron Island (43°49′·70N 69°33′·90W). Vessels approaching the berths should avoid the reef which extends N from the island and dries 1·5 m (5 ft), the limit of which is marked by No 4 Buoy (starboard hand).

South Bristol
3.69

South Bristol (43°51′·70N 69°33′·57W) is a village on the S side of The Gut, the narrow passage between the mainland and Rutherford Island.

Alongside berth. The town wharf, with a depth alongside of 0·9 m, lies close W of the bridge, and there are several other marina and lobster wharves.

Supplies: fuel; water and stores.

East Boothbay
3.70

East Boothbay (43°51′·90N 69°34′·97W) is a village 5 cables N of Farnham Point (3.67). The large buildings of three boatyards, where small craft are built, are prominent.

Anchorage may be obtained in 2 m (7 ft) close off the village.

Alongside berths. There are three wharves in use with depths alongside of 3 m.

Repairs. Patent slips are available for craft up to 30 m in length. Hull and engine repairs can be effected.

Supplies: fuel; water; provisions and stores.

Meadow Cove
3.71

Anchorage may be obtained in Meadow Cove (43°52′·46N 69°35′·30W), NW of Montgomery Point, in 9 to 15 m (30 to 48 ft). This anchorage is normally used by vessels bound up river above The Narrows, while awaiting favourable weather, the tide or a pilot (3.63).

Above The Narrows
3.72

Anchorage may be obtained anywhere in the channel above The Narrows (43°53′·28N 69°34′·95W) where the depth and bottom are suitable.

Booth Bay and adjacent waters

General information
3.73

Booth Bay lies between Linekin Neck and Fisherman Island (43°47′·90N 69°35′·90W) on the E and Southport Island on the W. Cape Newagen, the SE extremity of Southport Island, lies 3 miles SW of the S point of Linekin Neck.

Squirrel Island (3.74) is situated in the middle of the bay with a deep channel on either side. North of the island the bay divides into Linekin Bay (3.75) to the NE and Boothbay Harbor (3.76) to the NW.

Approaches. Islands and dangerous rocks extend 5½ miles SSW from Linekin Neck. For a description of the islands and dangers forming the E part of this group see 3.65.

No-Discharge Zone (NDZ). Boothbay Harbor (3.76) has been designated as a NDZ. See 1.41.

Directions
3.74

1 **Approach from east.** Booth Bay is approached from the E through Fisherman Island Passage (43°48′·45N 69°36′·80W) (3.66).
Approach from south. From a position SW of Bantam Rock (43°43′·85N 69°37′·38W) the approach route into Booth Bay leads generally NNE, passing:

2 WNW of Bantam Rock, awash; 2BR Light Buoy (starboard hand) marks the SW side of the rock. Poor Shoal lies 6½ cables SE of Bantam Rock. Thence:
WNW of Damariscove Island (43°45′·80N 69°36′·80W), bare and nearly divided in the middle. Shoal patches with depths of 2·7 to 7·3 m (9 to 24 ft) lie up to 5 cables off the W coast of the island. Thence:

3 ESE of The Cuckolds, two bare islets 3 to 4 m in height. Cuckolds Light (white 8-sided tower on dwelling) (43°46′·77N 69°39′·00W) stands on the E islet. 1C Buoy (port hand) is moored 4 cables S of the lighthouse. Thence:
Between Squirrel Island (43°48′·50N 69°37′·80W), wooded with many large houses visible on it, and Wylie Rock, 6 cables SE, thence:
Follow the E coast of Squirrel Island until abreast the N point.

4 Thence NE to the entrance of Linekin Bay or NW to the entrance of Boothbay Harbor (3.76).
Useful marks:
Two towers (the W one 43°45′·29N 69°36′·94W), standing on the S end of Damariscove Island.
Burnt Island Light (white conical tower, 19 m in height) (43°49′·51N 69°38′·41W).

Linekin Bay
3.75

1 **Description.** Linekin Bay, the NE arm of Booth Bay, is entered between Negro Island (43°49′·20N 69°36′·65W), and Spruce Point, 6 cables NW.
The entrance is obstructed by Spruce Point Ledges, awash, the SE and NW extremities of which are marked by Nos 1 and 2 Buoys (port and starboard hand, respectively).

2 **Entrance channels.** The best and deeper channel passes between Negro Island and Spruce Point Ledges.
A narrow passage leads between Spruce Point Ledges and the reef extending S from Spruce Point. Local knowledge is required.

3 **Dangers.** The inner part of the bay is obstructed by Cabbage Island (43°50′·50N 69°36′·36W), wooded with a house in its centre, and a number of dangers. The principal dangers are:
Tibbits Ledge (43°50′·12N 69°35′·91W), which has a depth of 2·4 m (8 ft) and is marked on its SW side by No 2 Buoy (starboard hand).
Holbrook Ledge (43°50′·50N 69°35′·91W), which dries 0·9 m (3 ft), lying nearly in mid-channel, marked on its NW side by No 4 Buoy (starboard hand).

4 Seal Rock (43°50′·93N 69°36′·11W), awash, lying on a shoal, marked on its E side by No 5 Buoy (port hand). The channel between the rock and the shoal extending from the shore W should not be navigated without local knowledge.

Perch Island (43°51′·04N 69°35′·54W), marked by No 6 Buoy (starboard hand), and Fish Hawk Island (4½ cables farther NW), both of which have several trees on them, nearer the head of the bay. There are numerous unmarked rocks at the head of the bay.

5 **Anchorage** may be obtained in 12 to 23 m (40 ft to 13 fm) in the lower part of the bay and in 9 to 11 m (30 to 36 ft) in the upper part of the bay, clear of a cable area extending across the bay E of Cabbage Island.

Boothbay Harbor
3.76

1 **Description.** Boothbay Harbor (43°50′·72N 69°38′·08W), the NW arm of Booth Bay, is one of the best anchorages on the coast of Maine, being well sheltered with good holding. It is entered between Spruce Point (43°49′·65N 69°37′·30W) and Burnt Island, 8 cables WSW, and extends N for 1¾ miles to the town of Boothbay Harbor. Small cruise liners occasionally visit.

2 Mouse Island, wooded, lies on the W side of the harbour, 1½ cables N of Burnt Island.
Tumbler Island, low and wooded with a house and flagstaff on it, lies 7½ cables NW of Spruce Point. The passage between the island and the shore E is obstructed with rocks and should not be attempted without local knowledge.

3 McFarland Island lies close off the town of Boothbay Harbor, 7 cables NNE of Tumbler Island. No 9 Light Buoy (port hand) marks the S end of a shoal that surrounds the island.
Ice sometimes obstructs navigation above Tumbler Island, during severe winters, during February and March. In normal winters the harbour is free of ice as far as the footbridge.

4 **Pilotage** is compulsory and may be obtained at any time; pilots board 1 mile S of Cuckolds Light (3.74).
3.77

1 **Entrance channel from south.** The main entrance channel leads NNW from between Burnt Island and No 6 Buoy (starboard hand) which marks a 2·7 m (9 ft) shoal 2½ cables W of Spruce Point. It then leads NNE passing WNW of No 8 Light Buoy (starboard hand), which lies 1 cable WNW of Tumbler Island, and thence into the inner harbour.

2 **Townsend Gut** (43°50′·70N 69°39′·40W), the SE entrance of which lies 3 cables NW of Mouse Island, is a narrow and winding channel that leads into Boothbay Harbor from Sheepscot River (3.82).
As part of the Inside Passage (3.9), used by small vessels between Boothbay Harbor and Bath (3.102), it leads from Boothbay Harbor between Southport Island and the mainland N, into Ebenecook Harbor (3.89).

3 A swing bridge with an open span 16 m wide crosses the channel 5 cables within the SE entrance.
Local knowledge is necessary.
Useful mark:
Tower, McKown Point (43°50′·65N 69°38′·41W).
3.78

1 **Anchorage** may be obtained between Tumbler Island and the head of the harbour clear of a pipeline area extending NNW from McKown Point to the opposite shore. There are depths of 7 to 13 m (24 to 42 ft), good holding, in the outer harbour between N of Tumbler Island and McKown Point, 5 cables NW, and depths of 2 to 7 m (6 to 24 ft) in the inner harbour SE of McFarland Island (43°50′·85N 69°37′·78W).

2 **Alongside berths** are available as follows:

Two public landings are available: close below the swing footbridge in the NE part of the harbour, and on the W side of the harbour. The E shore has many fishing vessel wharves serving seafood processing plants.

There are various jetties and marinas for small craft around the harbour, with reported depths of 1·2 to 4·6 m alongside.

3.79

1 **Repairs.** There are several small shipyards along the waterfront. Hull and engine repairs are available.
Other facility. Hospital.
Supplies: fuel; water and provisions.

INSHORE WATERS BETWEEN CAPE NEWAGEN AND CAPE SMALL

General information

Chart 2490, US Charts 13293, 13295, 13296 (see 1.16)
Description
3.80

1 The inshore waters between Cape Newagen (43°47'·20N 69°39'·25W) and Cape Small, 10 miles SW, consist of Sheepscot River and approaches, Kennebec River and approaches, and the port of Bath.

Traffic regulations
3.81

1 **Navigation Rules for US Inland Waters.** The Navigation Rules for US Inland Waters do not apply to any of the waters described in this sub-section.
Danger zone. For information on a danger zone SE of Cape Small see 3.12.

Sheepscot River and approaches

Description
3.82

1 **Sheepscot River** (43°49'·00N 69°41'·80W) is the approach to several small villages and the city of Wiscasset (3.93). The river is entered between The Cuckolds (3.74) and Griffith Head, 3 miles W.
Approach. Sheepscot Bay (43°46'·60N 69°41'·50W), lying between the S end of Damariscove Island (3.74) and Salter Island, 6 miles W, forms the approach to Sheepscot River.

2 **Recommended route.** A recommended route, shown on the US chart, has been established for vessels arriving and departing Sheepscot River.
Depths. The channel in Sheepscot River is deep and the principal dangers are marked; however, depths are irregular and many rocks and ledges rise abruptly from deep water.

The channel has a depth of over 9·1 m (30 ft) as far as Wiscasset.

3 **Pilotage** is compulsory and is normally available during daylight hours only. Pilots board in the vicinity of 2SR Light Buoy (3.85). See 3.76 for further details.
Under-keel clearances. The US Coast Guard recommends a minimum under-keel clearance of 0·6 m (2 ft) for vessels transiting Sheepscot River N of 2SR Light Buoy (3.85) and of 0·3 m (1 ft) at all berthing areas.

Measured distance
3.83

1 There is a measured distance in the vicinity of 43°54'·30N 69°41'·10W, off the W side of Barters Island (3.91).
Distance – 1 mile.
Running track – 015¾°/195¾°.

Natural conditions
3.84

1 **Tidal streams** generally follow the direction of the channel, their strength being considerable in the narrow parts.
Ice does not generally interfere with navigation S of Wiscasset, but N of the town the river is usually closed in winter.

Directions
3.85

1 **Sheepscot Bay.** From a position about 3 miles E of Seguin Island Light (43°42'·45N 69°45'·48W) (3.13) the route through Sheepscot Bay leads N to the entrance of Sheepscot River, passing:

E of Tom Rock (43°43'·98N 69°42'·92W), awash, lying at the SE end of a shoal. 2TR Buoy (starboard hand) is moored SW of the rock. Thence:

2 E of The Sisters (43°44'·47N 69°43'·25W), three small above-water rocks lying at the NW end of the same shoal. 4S Buoy (starboard hand) lies 2 cables NW of The Sisters. Thence:

E of The Black Rocks (43°45'·50N 69°43'·25W), a group of rocks of which the two most northerly are 5 m and 3 m in height, and:

3 W of No 2SR Light Buoy (starboard hand) (43°45'·64N 69°41'·15W), which marks the W side of two shoals with swept depths of 12·1 m (40 ft), thence:

W of The Cuckolds (3.74), from which a light is exhibited, and:

E of Griffith Head Ledge (43°47'·03N 69°42'·52W), marked on its SE side by No 3 Buoy (port hand).

3.86

1 **Lower Sheepscot River.** From a position E of Griffith Head Ledge the channel in Sheepscot River leads N, passing:

W of Lower Mark Island (43°47'·58N 69°40'·55W), high, wooded and prominent, thence:

2 W of Cat Ledges (43°48'·20N 69°41'·05W), a group of rocks partly above water. A shoal with a depth of 7 m (23 ft), marked by 4CL Buoy (starboard hand), lies 4 cables SW of the ledges. Thence:

E of a line of shoals extending 2 miles N from 43°47'·84N 69°42'·28W, with depths of 6·1 to 10·7 m (20 to 35 ft), which lie between Griffith Head Ledge and Bull Ledge, 3 miles N, and:

3 W of Hendricks Head Light (white dwelling) (43°49'·36N 69°41'·38W). The dangers on the E side of the channel between Lower Mark Island and Hendricks Head are covered by the red sector of this light. And:

E of Bull Ledge (43°50'·18N 69°41'·91W), marked at its S end by No 9 Buoy (port hand), and:

4 W of Dogfish Head (43°50'·23N 69°41'·07W), rocky and grass-covered with a low neck behind, which forms the S entrance point to Ebenecook Harbor (3.89), thence:

E of Middle Mark Island (43°50'·80N 69°41'·76W), round and bare, lying on a reef that extends 1 cable N and S of it, and:

5 W of Harding Ledge (43°51'·00N 69°41'·18W), which has a depth of 1·5 m (5 ft) and is marked on its S side by No 10 Buoy (starboard hand), and:

E of Middle Ledge (43°51′·20N 69°41′·76W), with a charted depth of 2·4 m (8 ft), although less has been reported. No 13 Buoy (port hand) marks the N end of the ledge and the approach to Goose Rock Passage (3.88).

6   **Caution.** With an out-going tide there is a strong set W near Bull Ledge and a strong set E near Middle Ledge, but the sets are not noticeable on a rising tide.

3.87

1   **Upper Sheepscot River.** From a position E of Middle Ledge (3.86), the channel leads N and then NNE, passing:

Between Clous Ledge (43°51′·47N 69°41′·80W), which dries and is marked by No 15 Beacon (port hand), and Powderhorn Island (3½ cables E), grassy. No 16 Light Buoy (starboard hand) marks Powderhorn Ledge, 1½ cables N of the island. Isle of Springs, a wooded island with a high tank on its summit, lies 1½ cables NE. Thence:

2   W of Ram Islet (43°52′·07N 69°41′·20W). A rocky patch with a depth of 7·3 m (24 ft) lies 1 cable W of Ram Islet. Thence:

Between Upper Mark Island (43°52′·37N 69°41′·76W) and No 18 Buoy (starboard hand) marking a ledge, 5 cables NE, thence:

Between Hodgdon Ledge (43°52′·85N 69°41′·70W), marked on its S end by No 19 Buoy (port hand), and Stover Ledge, marked on its S side by No 20 Buoy (starboard hand), thence:

3   W of the southerly pair (43°53′·71N 69°41′·10W) of beacons marking the measured mile (3.83), thence:

Between Cross Point (43°55′·65N 69°40′·25W) and the shore of Westport Island, close N of Fowle Point. Cross River flows into the E side of Sheepscot River at Cross Point and CP Light Buoy (preferred channel to port) is moored at the junction.

4   Thence the channel leads between the N part of Westport Island and the mainland E to the head of navigation at Wiscasset.

Side channels

3.88

1   **Goose Rock Passage** (43°51′·10N 69°42′·60W), which forms part of the Inside Passage (3.9), is entered between the N side of MacMahan Island and Whittum Island, 3 cables N, wooded.

Clous Ledge and Middle Ledge, which lie in the E approaches, are marked by No 15 Beacon and No 13 Buoy (port hand), respectively, and a shoal which extends from the N point of MacMahan Island is marked by No 1 Beacon (port hand).

2   The passage is marked by No 5 Light (green square on framework tower on caisson) on the S shore of the W end of the passage, and by Nos 3 and 4 Buoys (lateral) at the N entrance to Little Sheepscot River.

Ice usually closes the passage for about 2 months but it has been known for it to remain open in mild winters.

Knubble Bay (43°52′·00N 69°43′·80W), part of the Inside Passage, leads N from the W end of Goose Rock Passage into Hockomock Bay.

3   **Lower Hell Gate** (43°53′·00N 69°44′·13W). The NW entrance to Knubble Bay is narrow, being only 1 cable wide at its narrowest point and its passage should only be attempted at slack water as tidal streams of up to 9 kn have been observed in the vicinity.

Hockomock Bay (43°53′·50N 69°44′·60W). A channel marked by buoys (lateral) leads through Hockomock Bay into Sasanoa River.

4   **Sasanoa River** (43°53′·70N 69°46′·35W) is entered between Mill Point and Hockomock Point, 1 cable N. The channel, marked by buoys (lateral) and beacons, is very narrow. It passes through Upper Hell Gate, ¼ cable wide, 9 cables NW of Mill Point.

A bridge, with a vertical clearance of 15·5 m (51 ft), crosses the W end of the river at its junction with Kennebec River.

Ebenecook Harbor

3.89

1   Ebenecook Harbor (43°50′·40N 69°40′·55W) is situated between Green Islands, Boston Island, high and partly wooded, and Spectacle Islands on the W, and the N part of Southport Island on the E. This is the first large anchorage for vessels entering the river.

Entrances. The harbour is entered from Sheepscot River between Dogfish Head (3.86) and the S point of Green Islands. The W end of Townsend Gut (3.77), part of the Inside Passage (3.9), enters the NE part of the Ebenecook Harbor at Cameron Point.

2   **Anchorage** may be obtained near the middle of the harbour in 7 to 11 m (23 to 36 ft), soft bottom. The S side of the harbour divides into three arms, the entrances of which provide good anchorage in 4 to 7 m (13 to 23 ft). Attention is drawn to a cable area situated in the E arm.

Sawyer Island

3.90

1   **Anchorage** may be obtained in the channel, part of the Inside Passage leading from Ebenecook Harbor between Sawyer Island (43°52′·30N 69°40′·40W) and Isle of Springs (3.87), noting a cable area lying between the islands.

Barters Island

3.91

1   **Anchorage** may be obtained in 22 m (12 fm) or less in the channel off Barters Island above Stover Ledge (43°53′·06N 69°41′·30W).

Colby Cove

3.92

1   **Anchorage** may be obtained in 14 to 18 m (47 to 60 ft) in Colby Cove (43°57′·82N 69°40′·18W), on the W side of the river 2½ miles S of Wiscasset.

Wiscasset

3.93

1   Wiscasset (43°59′·80N 69°39′·90W) is situated on the W side of Sheepscot River, 14 miles above the entrance. The wharves are in ruins and there is virtually no commercial traffic.

Anchorage may be obtained S and SW of the town wharves in 8 to 9 m (25 to 30 ft), mud.

2   **Alongside berths.** Pier at Birch Point, 5 cables SW of Wiscasset with a depth alongside of 10 m for a length of 230 m; but it was reported (2009) that it was closed to traffic.

Town landing, with depth of 4·6 m alongside, is situated S of the ruined wharves.

Supplies: fuel; water; provisions and stores.

Kennebec River and approaches

General information

3.94

1   **Kennebec River** is entered between Salter Island (43°44′·80N 69°45′·25W) and Pond Island (3.98),

7 cables SW. It is the approach to the cities of Bath (3.102), Richmond and Augusta; there is little commercial traffic beyond Bath. Small craft can reach Augusta, the head of navigation on Kennebec River, about 44 miles above the river entrance.

Approaches. There are two entrance channels which lead E and W, respectively, of Seguin Island (3.13). The E channel (3.96) is generally used by vessels of over 5·5 m (18 ft) draught.

2 **Project depth** from the mouth of the river to a point 6 cables above the bridge at Bath is 8·2 m (27 ft), thence 4·9 to 5·5 m (16 to 18 ft) to Gardiner and 3·4 m (11 ft) to Augusta. For the latest controlling depths the charts and port authority should be consulted.

Dangers. The principal dangers in Kennebec River are marked, but the channel is narrow in places.

3 **Caution.** Water-logged boom logs are a constant hazard in the river. They are weighted at one end by parts of mooring chains, with one end down and the other end at the surface or just under, shift position with the tidal or river currents and are hard to detect, especially at night. A sharp lookout should be kept for them.

Pilotage is compulsory; pilots usually board near White Ledge Light Buoy No 1 (43°43'·82N 69°44'·90W). See *Admiralty List of Radio Signals Volume 6(5)* for details.

4 **Local knowledge** is required.
Traffic regulations:
Danger zone. See 3.12.
Restricted area. See 3.102.

3.95

1 **Local magnetic anomaly.** The normal magnetic variation can alter by up to 8° in the vicinity of Ellingwood Rock (3.97), for 1 mile in all directions.

Tidal streams have considerable strength at the entrance to Kennebec River and in the narrow parts of the river. Between the entrance and Bath the average maximum rate is from 2 to 3 kn but a rate of 6 kn may occur on the out-going stream.

2 **Freshets** occur in March and April and also after heavy rains in the autumn, but are not dangerous to shipping unless accompanied by ice.

Ice usually closes the river above Bath from December to April. Below Bath vessels are rarely delayed by ice and icebreakers clear the channel if necessary.

Drift ice coming down the river generally follows the W shore.

Directions
3.96

1 **Landmark:**
Seguin Island Light (43°42'·45N 69°45'·48W) (3.13).
Major Light:
Seguin Island Light — as above.
South-east approach. From a position E of Seguin Island (43°42'·50N 69°45'·50W) the route through the SE approaches to Kennebec River leads NW, passing:
NE of Mile Ledge (43°41'·54N 69°45'·32W), marked on its S side by 20ML Light Buoy (starboard hand), thence:

2 NE of Seguin Island, thence:
SW of Tom Rock (43°43'·98N 69°42'·92W) and The Sisters, 5 cables NNW. 2TR Buoy (starboard hand) marks the SW side of a shoal around Tom Rock and 4S Buoy (starboard hand) lies 2 cables NW of The Sisters. Swept depths of 11·2 and 15·2 m (37 and 50 ft), lie 3 cables WSW and SSW of Tom Rock, respectively. Thence:

3 NE of Seguin Ledges (43°43'·40N 69°45'·25W) and White Ledge, 3 cables NNE, which is marked by No 1 Light Buoy (port hand), thence:
NE of a 4·8 m (16 ft) patch (43°43'·92N 69°45'·28W), marked by KR Buoy (preferred channel to starboard), thence:
SW of Whaleback Rock (43°44'·48N 69°45'·44W), 2 m (8 ft) in height, and bare.

3.97

1 **South-west approach.** From a position SE of Cape Small (43°42'·60N 69°50'·60W) the route through the SW approaches to Kennebec River leads NE, through a danger zone (3.12), passing:
SE of Halibut Rocks (43°41'·80N 69°49'·15W), thence:
NW of Camel Ground (43°41'·75N 69°46'·50W), over which the sea breaks in heavy weather, thence:

2 Between Ellingwood Rock (43°43'·03N 69°45'·58W), 5 m in height and bare, and Jackknife Ledge. No 1 Buoy (port hand) marks the SE side of the ledge. Thence:
Between Seguin Ledges (3.96) and No 3 Buoy (port hand) which is moored on the outer part of Pond Island Shoal, 5 cables NW. Vessels should not pass between this buoy and Pond Island (3.98), which lies 6 cables farther NW. Thence:
NW of White Ledge (43°43'·72N 69°45'·07W) (3.96). Thence as directed for SE approaches.

3.98

1 **Kennebec River.** From a position SE of Pond Island Light (white tower) (43°44'·40N 69°46'·22W), a light intensified up and down the river, the channel to Bath leads generally NW and then N, passing:

2 Between Pond Island, 9 m in height and grassy, and Stage Island (43°44'·85N 69°45'·90W). No 4 Buoy (starboard hand) marks the S limit of a spit extending 3 cables S from Stage island. Thence:
SW of Sugarloaf (43°44'·89N 69°46'·33W), high, rounded, bare and rocky, and North Sugarloaf (4 miles SSE), similar in appearance, 2 cables farther NW. A 4·6 m (15 ft) shoal lies ½ cable NW of North Sugarloaf and is marked on its SW side by No 6 Buoy (starboard hand). The fairway is only ½ cable wide at this point and this is the narrowest part of the channel below Bath. Thence:

3 SW of Gilbert Head (43°45'·41N 69°46'·79W), high and wooded. A prominent large grey house stands on the head and is a good mark in hazy weather. And:
NE of Fort Popham (43°45'·30N 69°47'·00W), a disused stone fort on a rocky peninsula. Fort Popham Light (post), intensified up and down the river, stands on a parapet of the fort. Thence:

4 W of Shag Rock (43°45'·87N 69°46'·94W), which dries. No 8 Light Buoy (starboard hand) lies close W of the rock. And:
E of Cox Head (43°46'·10N 69°47'·20W), 43 m in height and wooded, thence:
Between Dix Island (43°46'·10N 69°47'·20W) and Perkins Island Ledge, which extends 4 cables SSW from Perkins Island. These dangers are marked by Nos 11 and 12 buoys respectively. The white sector (018°-038°) of Perkins Island

Light (white conical tower) leads clear of the ledge. Thence:

5 Between Perkins Island (43°47′·20N 69°47′·07W), bare on the S end and wooded at the N end, and No 13 Buoy (port hand) which lies 1 cable W, marking the SE side of a patch with a depth of 1·5 m (5 ft), thence:

E of Parker Head (43°47′·40N 69°47′·50W), a prominent headland, and Parker Flats, which lie NNW. The white sector, astern, of Perkins Island Light (172°-188°) and the white sector of Squirrel Point Light (321°-324°) lead clear of these flats. No 15 Buoy (port hand) marks the E edge of the flats. Thence:

6 ENE of Seal Rocks (43°48′·53N 69°48′·02W), which dry 1·5 m (5 ft) and are marked by No 17 Buoy (port hand), thence:

W of Squirrel Point (43°48′·99N 69°48′·14W), from which a light (white conical tower) is exhibited.

Useful mark:
Church spire (43°49′·16N 69°48′·58W). A good leading mark for the reach between Bald Head and Squirrel Point.

3.99

1 From a position W of Squirrel Point the channel continues generally N, passing:

E of Goat Island (43°49′·28N 69°48′·38W), wooded, with a ledge extending S marked by No 19 Buoy (port hand), thence:

E of Pettis Rocks (43°49′·85N 69°47′·93W), which are bare at the top and marked by No 23 Light (green square on framework tower) at the S end, thence:

2 E of Ram Island (43°50′·16N 69°47′·87W), low and bushy with a ledge extending N. No 25 Light (green square on framework tower and small white house) stands on the island.

Caution. This is a dangerous part of the river and vessels inbound, after passing the S end of Lee Island (43°49′·90N 69°48′·35W), 39 m in height and wooded, should keep close to the E side of the river to keep clear of the shoals extending from Pettis Rocks and Ram Island.

3.100

1 From a position E of Ram Island the channel continues N, passing W of Bluff Head (43°51′·23N 69°47′·66W), where the river narrows to a width of 1 cable.

Doubling Point Leading Lights:
Front light (white conical tower) (43°52′·97N 69°47′·74W).
Rear light (similar structure) (215 m from front light).

2 From a position W of Bluff Head, the alignment (359°) of these lights leads N through the upper part of the reach between Bluff Head and the turn W into Fiddler Reach (43°52′·82N 69°48′·25W).

After passing through Fiddler Reach and rounding Doubling Point (43°52′·97N 69°48′·37W), the track continues N to the port of Bath.

Useful mark:
Doubling Point Light (conical tower) (43°52′·95N 69°48′·41W).

Side channels

3.101

1 **Sasanoa River**, part of the Inside Passage (3.9), enters Kennebec River opposite Bath. See 3.88.

Bath

3.102

1 **General information.** Bath (43°54′·49N 69°48′·70W), a city which in 2010 had a population of 8514, stands on the W side of Kennebec River, 12 miles above the entrance.

It is a port of entry and shipbuilding facility for the US Navy (Bath Iron Works), but there is little water-borne traffic except for occasional visits by small cruise liners, barges and vessels for repair at the shipyard.

2 **Depths.** Channel is dredged to depth of 8·2 m (27 ft) and vessels with a draught of up to 9·1 m can be accepted at a suitable tide.

Vertical clearance. A combined road and rail drawbridge crosses the river between Bath and Woolwich (3.103). Vertical clearances of 41·1 m (135 ft), when open, and 3 m (10 ft) when closed. A road bridge close N of the drawbridge has a fixed span with a clearance of 21·3 m (70 ft).

3 **Tidal levels.** Mean spring range about 2·1 m (6·9 ft); mean neap range about 1·5 m (4·9 ft). See information in *Admiralty Tide Tables.*

Ice. See 3.95.

Pilotage. See 3.94.

Restricted area surrounds the shipyard. Entry is prohibited without permission from the Supervisor of Shipbuilding, USN Bath, Maine. See Appendix VI for definitions and general regulations covering restricted areas.

4 **Anchorage** may be obtained off Bath more than 1 cable S of the bridge. For precise limits of anchorage, port regulations should be consulted.

Alongside berths. Pier 213 m in length, 4 cables S of the bridge, extends SE from the S end of the repair yard with depths alongside of 7·9 to 15·2 m. Floating dock, 750 ft long, on the S side of the yard. Town landing with depth alongside of 4·6 m is situated on the W side just above the bridge.

5 Berth, 1 mile N of the bridge, used for receipt of fish; 79 m of berthing space with depth alongside of 4·6 m.

Repairs. Shipyard situated on the W side of the river just below the bridge. Shipbuilding and repairs carried out.

Other facilities. Hospitals.

Supplies: fuel; provisions and stores.

Anchorages and harbours

3.103

1 **White Ledge Light Buoy No 1** (43°43′·82N 69°44′·90W). Large vessels awaiting a pilot may anchor in the vicinity of this light buoy in 15 to 20 m (50 to 65 ft).

Perkins Island Ledge (43°46′·65N 69°47′·20W). Anchorage may be obtained in 11 to 15 m (36 to 48 ft) on the E side of the channel S of No 12 Buoy which marks the S edge of this ledge.

2 **Parker Flats** (43°48′·15N 69°47′·50W). Anchorage may be obtained in 6 to 11 m (20 to 36 ft) on the W side of the channel off Parker Flats, clear of the cable area crossing the channel close N of Parker Head.

Above Parker Flats vessels anchor wherever they can find suitable depths and good holding, keeping out of the strength of the tidal streams and clear of the cable area crossing the channel W of Squirrel Point.

3 **Woolwich** (43°54′·98N 69°48′·14W), on the E side of the river above Carlton Lift Bridge, has a pier with a depth alongside of 6·7 m.

EASTERN PART OF CASCO BAY

General information

Chart 2490, US Chart 13290 (see 1.16)

Description
3.104

1   Casco Bay, entered between Cape Small (43°42'·60N 69°50'·60W) and Cape Elizabeth, 18 miles WSW, is divided by Harpswell Neck and Halfway Rock.

The E part of the bay is obstructed with islets and above and below-water rocks, with narrow but deep channels leading up to 10 miles N.

There are a number of anchorages in this area which are suitable for small vessels, but are of little importance. There are several villages, but no towns in this part of Casco Bay.

Traffic regulations
3.105

1   **Navigation Rules for US Inland Waters.** The limit of the waters to which these rules apply is a line joining Bald Head (43°42'·30N 69°51'·25W), SE point of Ragged Island (43°43'·60N 69°56'·30W), S point of Jaquish Island (43°42'·80N 70°00'·20W) and Little Mark Island (43°42'·54N 70°01'·87W). See 1.44 and Appendix VII for further information.

Natural conditions
3.106

1   **Tidal streams** in Casco Bay are not strong, but in the bay and across its entrance, there is a perceptible N set with a rising tide and a S set with a falling tide.

Ice forms in considerable quantities at the heads of the numerous sounds, bays and river in the E part of Casco Bay, but the principal anchorages are usable throughout the year.

Outer approaches to east part of Casco Bay

Topography
3.107

1   The many islands and peninsulae in Casco Bay are mostly oriented NNE to SSW, as are the rivers and coves. Most of the land is densely wooded, and forestry is a major industry.

2   Cape Small, the E entrance point of Casco Bay, is wooded. Small Point (43°42'·20N 69°50'·20W) is its SE extremity and Bald Head, a bare round knob, is at the SW extremity. Fuller Rock, low and bare, lies 3 cables SSE of Small Point; a light (3.15) is exhibited from the rock.

There is much broken ground and many isolated rocks and islets in the E part of the bay.

Approaches to New Meadows River

Description
3.108

1   The approaches to New Meadows River, which lie between Bald Head (43°42'·30N 69°51'·25W) and Ragged Island, 4 miles WNW, are obstructed by numerous islands and dangers, the positions of which are best seen on the national charts.

Local knowledge is required to navigate in the approaches to New Meadows River.

Directions
3.109

1   **From south.** From a position about 5 cables SW of Bald Head (43°42'·30N 69°51'·25W) the approach leads NNW and N, passing:

ENE of East Brown Cow (43°42'·46N 69°53'·48W) and the patches within 7 cables E and NE of it, and:

WSW of Gooseberry Island Ledge (43°43'·11N 69°51'·65W), awash, marked on its NW side by No 2 Buoy (starboard hand), thence:

2   Between Wyman Ledge (43°43'·18N 69°53'·16W), marked by No 3 Buoy (port hand), and Wood Island S Ledge, 8 cables NE, marked by No 4 Light Buoy (starboard hand), extending 2½ cables S of Wood Island, partly wooded; thence:

3   Between Carrying Place Head (43°44'·60N 69°52'·10W) and No 7 Buoy (port hand) marking the S end of Jamison Ledge, 5 cables W, which dries at its S end.

Thence clear of shoals NNW of Jamison Ledge to the mouth of New Meadows River.

3.110

1   **From south-west.** From a position in the vicinity of WB Light Buoy (safe water) (43°42'·81N 69°55'·21W) the approach leads NNE, passing:

Between Mark Island Ledge (43°43'·06N 69°54'·32W), marked on its W side by No 2 Buoy (starboard hand), and White Bull, 8 cables W, a high, bare, rounded island, thence:

2   WNW of Mark Island (43°43'·25N 69°53'·95W), high and thickly wooded, thence:

ESE of Sisters Ground (43°44'·10N 69°55'·10W), a shoal that lies 5 cables SE of The Sisters, two above-water rocks, thence:

Between Flag Island (43°45'·10N 69°53'·45W), high and thickly wooded, and Long Ledge, 4 cables NW, two grassy islets 3 and 4 m (10 and 12 ft) in height, thence:

3   Between Goudy Ledge (43°45'·88N 69°53'·55W), marked by a beacon, and North Jenny Ledge, 5 cables W, marked on its S side by No 2 Buoy (starboard hand), thence:

ESE of No 9 Buoy (port hand) (43°46'·11N 69°53'·75W), moored 1½ cables S of Rogue Island, low with scattered trees.

Thence to the river entrance.

New Meadows River

Description
3.111

1   **New Meadows River** is entered between Bear Island (43°46'·90N 69°52'·90W) and Fort Point, 3 cables W. No 1 Light Buoy (port hand) is moored off Fort Point.

The river extends N for 8½ miles to road and railway bridges and a dam at the head of navigation. There is a deep-water channel from the river entrance for about 5 miles; above this the depths gradually decrease and the channel has a least depth of 3·7 m (12 ft) to within 5 cables of the bridges. The principal dangers are marked.

2   Thence the channel is winding and unmarked and has a depth of 2·1 m (7 ft) to the villages of New Meadows and Harding.

The river is seldom used except by local fishing boats and small pleasure craft.

Local knowledge is required.

Anchorages and harbours
3.112

1   **Cundy Harbor** (43°47'·50N 69°53'·40W) lies on the W side of the river, 1 mile above its entrance. Cedar Ledges, partly above-water, extend S from the N side

of the harbour entrance. No 3 Buoy (port hand) marks the S end of the ledges.

Anchorage may be obtained by small vessels in 7 to 9 m (22 to 31 ft).

2 The village of Cundy Harbor is situated on the W side of the harbour. Wharves, with depths alongside of 2·1 to 3 m, are situated at the fish factories.

3 **Winnegance Bay** (43°49'·50N 69°51'·70W) is entered between Birch Point and Basin Point, 1 mile SSE. Foul ground with Bushy Islet and Hen Islet on it, extends 3 cables from the SE side of the bay. No 6 Beacon (red triangular-shaped daymark) stands on Hen Island Ledge, which dries 0·6 m (2 ft), at the SW end of the foul ground, 3 cables N of Basin Point. A dangerous wreck, position approximate, lies 1½ cables WNW of Hen Island Ledge.

4 Anchorage may be obtained in the NW side of the bay in 5 to 7 m (16 to 23 ft).

Bragdon Rock (43°51'·06N 69°52'·38W), which has No 10 Beacon (starboard hand) on it, marks the entrance to two long narrow inlets separated by the peninsula of Rich Hill.

Quahog Bay and adjacent waters

Description
3.113

1 Quahog Bay (43°48'·50N 69°55'·10W) (3.115) is a narrow cleft on the S side of Sebascodegan Island.

The approaches from S lead between two chains of islands that extend S from either entrance point. The approach from E or W is by the buoyed channel leading across the entrance of the bay, between the waters off the E side of Bailey Island and the entrance to New Meadows River.

Ridley Cove (3.116) and Gun Point Cove (3.117) lie to the E and W of Quahog Bay, respectively.

Directions
3.114

1 From a position SW of Bold Dick (43°42'·78N 69°56'·39W), a S approach route leads NNE, passing:
Between Saddleback Ledge (43°43'·10N 69°56'·80W), which dries 1·5 m (5 ft), and Round Rock, 5 cables W, marked on its S side by No 3 Light Buoy (port hand), thence:
Between Ragged Island (43°43'·60N 69°56'·30W) and Middle Ground Rock, 6 cables W, which dries 0·6 m (2 ft), thence:

2 WNW of Blacksnake Ledge (43°44'·30N 69°56'·45W), which dries. A rock, with a swept depth of 4·6 m (15 ft), lies 3 cables WNW of this ledge. Thence:
Between Yellow Rock (43°44'·80N 69°56'·27W) and Cedar Ledges, 5 cables WNW, bare and partly above water with a height of 0·6 m, thence:

3 WNW of Two Bush Island (43°45'·15N 69°56'·15W), grassy, and Elm Islands, 2 cables NNE, which stand on a reef and are separated by a narrow channel from the S end of Yarmouth Ledges. No 6 Buoy (starboard hand) marks the N side of this channel.

Quahog Bay
3.115

1 Quahog Bay is entered between Yarmouth Ledges (43°46'·27N 69°55'·80W), which extend S from Yarmouth Island, and the S extremity of Sebascodegan Island, 2½ cables NE of Gun Point. It is a narrow arm extending 4 miles NNE.

Good anchorage may be obtained by small vessels. **Local knowledge** is required.

Ridley Cove
3.116

1 Ridley Cove, on the E side of Yarmouth Island, is entered between West Cundy Point (43°46'·33N 69°54'·13W), which has a prominent white house on it, and Flash Island, 4 cables W.

Foul ground extends 5 cables SSW and 1 mile SW from the E and W entrance points of the cove.

2 A narrow obstructed passage leads from the N part of the cove, N of Yarmouth Island into Quahog Bay.

Anchorage, exposed to S and SW winds, may be obtained in 7 to 11 m (23 to 37 ft) in the cove.

Local knowledge is necessary.

Gun Point Cove
3.117

1 Gun Point Cove (43°46'·50N 69°57'·00W) is a narrow and unimportant inlet that extends 2 miles NNE between the S part of Sebascodegan Island and Orrs Island, W of it.

Lowell Cove
3.118

1 Lowell Cove (43°45'·30N 69°58'·60W), used as an anchorage by local fishermen, is situated at the S end of Orrs Island.

Merriconeag Sound and Harpswell Sound

Description
3.119

1 **Merriconeag Sound** (43°43'·70N 70°00'·70W), entered between Jaquish Island (3.105) and Haskell Island, 1 mile W, extends with Harpswell Sound 10 miles NNE. Although of little commercial importance, they afford good anchorage, with good holding, for deep-draught vessels.

Dangers. The principal dangers are marked for the first 4 miles above the entrance, but above this the channel is narrow and flats extend in places to a considerable distance from the shore.

2 **Depths**. The fairway of the approach channel, which lies on the E side of the channel, has been swept to a depth of 12·8 m (42 ft) as far as Stover Point (3.121).

Local knowledge is necessary to proceed beyond Stover Point.

Directions
3.120

1 **Approaches**. From a position NNW of Halfway Rock (43°39'·35N 70°02'·21W), a low, rocky islet, the fairway of the approach channel into Merriconeag Sound leads NNE, passing:
Close WNW of Drunkers Ledges (43°41'·30N 70°01'·70W), two rocky ledges, 3 cables apart. The NW ledge is marked by No 4 Buoy (starboard hand). Eastern Drunkers Ledge, over which the sea breaks in rough weather, is marked by No 2 Buoy (starboard hand). Thence:

2 WNW of Mark Island Ledge (43°42'·05N 70°01'·16W), marked on its N side by No 6 Buoy (starboard hand), and:
ESE of Little Mark Island (43°42'·54N 70°01'·87W), 11 m in height and grassy. A light (black and white square stone pyramid) is exhibited from the island. Thence:

3 WNW of Turnip Island Ledge, which dries 0·6 m (2 ft) and is marked by No 8 Light Buoy (starboard hand). Turnip Island (43°42'·85N

70°00′·51W), grassy with a stone cairn, lies 1 cable NE of the ledge.

Swept depths. Swept depths of shoals and dangers are charted.

4   **Useful Marks:**

Two observation towers and a house (43°43′·05N 70°00′·22W), standing on the S end of Bailey Island.

3.121

1   **Merriconeag Sound.** From a position between Turnip Island and Great Mark Island (43°42′·94N 70°01′·60W), 7 m in height and grassy, the channel through Merriconeag Sound and Harpswell Sound leads NNE, passing:

WNW of Abner Point (43°43′·50N 70°00′·26W), the N entrance point to Mackerel Cove (43°43′·60N 70°00′·00W). No 1 Light Buoy (port hand) is moored off the point. Thence:

2   ESE of Pinkham Island (43°44′·01N 70°01′·01W), grassy with a white house on it. No 2 Buoy (starboard hand) marks the outer end of a reef that extends 3 cables SSW from the island. Thence:

ESE of Interval Shoal (43°44′·50N 70°00′·35W), marked by No 9 Buoy (port hand), thence:

3   ESE of Stover Point (43°45′·47N 69°59′·89W). No 13 Buoy (port hand) is moored at the outer end of a reef that extends 2 cables NE from the point.

Thence into Harpswell Sound.

Anchorages and harbours
3.122

1   **Harpswell Harbor** (43°43′·60N 70°00′·00W) is entered between Stover Point (3.121) and the S end of Merriman Ledges, 1 mile NNE. These ledges dry in the centre and are marked by Nos 17 and 15 Buoys (port hand) at the N and S ends. A rock, with a swept depth of 4 m (13 ft), lies 2½ cables S of No 15 Buoy.

2   Anchorage may be obtained in 5 to 11 m (18 to 36 ft), with depths decreasing gradually to the head of the harbour. Harpswell Harbor is a special anchorage (1.45).

WESTERN PART OF CASCO BAY

General information

Chart 2490, US Chart 13290 (see 1.16)
Description
3.123

1   The W part of Casco Bay, between Harpswell Neck and Halfway Rock (43°39′·35N 70°02′·21W) on the E and the port of Portland on the W, contains numerous sounds, bays and rivers, separated by islands lying in a NE-SW direction.

There are broad channels into this part of the bay, through Broad Sound (3.130), Luckse Sound (3.147) and Hussey Sound (3.154) and secure anchorage can be found for vessels of any draught. The bay is frequented by small inter-island ferries, many small craft and some fishing vessels.

Recommended routes
3.124

1   Recommended two-way routes have been established through Hussey Sound (3.154) to Cousins Island (3.158), Broad Sound 3.130) to the berth (3.143) at Harpswell Neck, and the approaches to Portland Harbor. Deep-draught vessels, tugs and barges are requested to follow the designated routes.

2   The routes were designed to reduce the potential for conflict with pleasure craft, fishing gear and other small craft, and to reduce the potential for grounding or collision. Vessels are responsible for their own safety and are not required to remain inside the routes nor are fishermen required to keep fishing gear outside the routes. Other vessels, while not excluded from these routes, should exercise caution in and around these areas and should monitor VHF channels for information concerning deep-draught commercial vessels, tugs and barges transiting these routes.

Traffic regulations
3.125

1   **Navigation Rules for US Inland Waters.** The limit of the waters to which these rules applies is a line joining Little Mark Island (43°42′·54N 70°01′·87W), NE and SW extremities of Jewell Island (43°40′·80N 70°05′·70W), Outer Green Island (43°39′·00N 70°07′·43W), Ram Island Ledge (43°37′·89N 70°11′·24W) and Portland Head (43°37′·39N 70°12′·47W). See 1.44 and Appendix VII for further information.

Natural conditions
3.126

1   **Tidal streams.** See 3.106 for details of tidal streams in Casco Bay.

Ice forms in considerable quantities at the heads of the numerous sounds, bays and river in the W part of Casco Bay, but the principal anchorages are usable throughout the year.

Special anchorages
3.127

1   Potts Harbor (3.132), Staples Cove (3.142) and Diamond Island Pass (3.156) are designated special anchorages (1.45).

Inshore channel
3.128

1   An inshore channel, used by inter-island ferries, yachts and fishing craft, extends from the S point of Great Chebeague Island (43°42′·60N 70°07′·60W) around either side of Bangs Island (43°43′·60N 70°05′·44W), across Broad Sound and through Potts Harbor (3.132) to Merriconeag Sound (3.119).

Principal marks
3.129

1   **Landmarks:**

Stone tower (43°49′·12N 70°06′·69W).
Water tower (43°47′·60N 70°11′·87W).
Two chimneys (tallest 43°45′·10N 70°09′·36W) stand close to the power plant on Birch Point (3.164), the SW point of Cousins Island.

Broad Sound

Description
3.130

1   **Broad Sound** is entered SW of Eagle Island (43°42′·67N 70°03′·15W) and extends 4½ miles NNW from its entrance and is generally about 5 cables wide. Channels lead from the sound to Potts Harbor, Middle Bay and other waters in the N part of Casco Bay.

Depths. The fairway of the channel is swept to a depth of 12·8 m (42 ft).

Anchorage may be obtained in the upper part of the sound in suitable depths under the lee of islands.

Directions
3.131

1   From a position S of Eagle Island (43°42′·67N 70°03′·15W) the fairway leads generally N, passing:

Clear of BS Buoy (safe water) (43°41'·73N 70°03'·44W), moored 6 cables E of West Brown Cow, a grassy islet 11 m (36 ft) in height. Foul ground extends 5 cables NE from this islet. Thence:

2 Between Nos 1 and 2 Buoys (lateral) that lie SW of Eagle Island, prominent and wooded and with a house on its NE side; they mark the entrance to the sound. Thence:

ENE of the N end of Ministerial Island (43°43'·00N 70°04'·48W), 7 m in height and grassy. This island is opposite the entrance to Potts Harbor (3.132). Thence:

3 W of Whaleboat Island Shoal (43°44'·30N 70°03'·77W), marked by WS Buoy (preferred channel to starboard), thence:

Between the S end of Whaleboat Island (3.135) and the N end of Stockman Island (43°44'·20N 70°04'·80W). A light (red and white chequered diamond on white square framework tower) is exhibited from the S end of Whaleboat Island. Thence:

4 WSW of Whaleboat Ledge (43°45'·04N 70°04'·36W), marked close W by No 6 Buoy (starboard hand), thence:

E of Chebeague Point (43°45'·50N 70°05'·76W). The N entrance to Luckse Sound (3.147) is S of this point. Thence:

E of Upper Green Islets (43°46'·30N 70°04'·94W). Green Island Ledge, marked by No 10 Buoy (starboard hand) on its SW side, lies 2 cables SW of the S islet.

Potts Harbor
3.132

1 Potts Harbor (43°44'·30N 70°01'·90W), which indents the SW end of Harpswell Neck, lies between Potts Point and Basin Point, 9 cables WNW.
Directions

From a position 1 mile SW of Basin Point (43°44'·35N 70°02'·50W) the main entrance channel into the harbour leads ENE and NE, passing:

2 Clear of a rock (43°43'·50N 70°03'·06W) with a depth of 0·9 m (3 ft), marked on its SW side by No 4 Buoy (starboard hand), thence:

Between Upper Flag Island (43°43'·50N 70°02'·70W), grassy, and Little Birch Island, which lies 5 cables NW. No 6 Buoy (starboard hand) marks a ledge extending 1 cable S from Little Birch Island. Thence:

Between Horse Island (43°44'·02N 70°02'·65W), grassy, and Thrumcap, 4 cables E, and thence into the anchorage.

3 The harbour can also be entered from Merriconeag Sound, S of Potts Point.
Anchorage may be obtained in 7 to 10 m (24 to 33 ft). The harbour is designated a special anchorage.
Town wharf, with a reported depth alongside of 1·8 m, is situated near the village of South Harpswell, about 4 cables N of Potts Point on the E shore. There are other landings in the harbour with depths alongside of 1·5 to 1·8 m.

Middle Bay

Description
3.133

1 **Middle Bay** (43°47'·60N 70°01'·10W) is entered on the E side of Broad Sound, between Basin Point (3.132) and Little Whaleboat Island, wooded, which lies 1¾ miles NNW. The bay extends NE for 9 miles, its E shore being formed by Harpswell Neck, and its W side by Lower Goose Island, Upper Goose Island, Birch Island and White Island. Shelter Island lies in mid-channel, abreast Upper Goose Island, 2½ miles NE of Whaleboat Island.

2 Middle Bay affords good anchorage, but is seldom used.
Local knowledge is necessary to proceed above the S end of Birch Island (43°49'·20N 70°00'·40W), where only some of the dangers are buoyed.

Measured distance
3.134

1 Off the W side of Whaleboat Island there is a measured distance.
Marks - Beacons in line bearing 128°.
Distance - 5946 ft.
Running track - 038°/218°.

Entrance
3.135

1 There is a deep channel on either side of Whaleboat Island (43°45'·20N 70°03'·10W). This island is wooded at its N end and grassy at its S end. Both channels are marked by buoys (lateral).

Anchorages and alongside berths
3.136

1 **Anchorage.** An extensive anchorage with depths of 14 to 18 m (46 to 59 ft) lies above Whaleboat Island.
Alongside berths. A disused **T**-shaped pier of a former naval fuel depot, with a reported depth alongside of 11 m, extends from the W side of Harpswell Neck, 2½ miles NNE of Basin Point.

Merepoint Bay and Maquoit Bay

Approaches
3.137

1 Merepoint Bay and Maquoit Bay can be approached from Middle Bay through the passages S or N of Goose Islands. They can also be approached from the head of Broad Sound passing NW of the foul ground extending W from Little Whaleboat Island and then W of Lower Goose Island (43°47'·70N 70°02'·50W) and E of French Island, wooded, and the rocks extending NE from it. This channel has been swept to a depth of 9·1 m (30 ft) in its lower part and 6·7 m (22 ft) in its upper part.

Merepoint Bay
3.138

1 Merepoint Bay is entered between Birch Island (43°49'·20N 70°00'·40W) and Mere Point, the SW point of Merepoint Neck, and extends 2 miles NE between Birch Island and White Island on the SE and Merepoint Neck on the NW. The bay is shallow and obstructed by flats in its N part.
Merepoint is a village on the neck at which there are several landing stages.

Maquoit Bay
3.139

1 Maquoit Bay is entered between Mere Point (43°49'·40N 70°01'·56W) and Sister Island, wooded, 6 cables SW. The bay is obstructed by flats, with depths of less than 1·2 m (4 ft), through which two narrow channels with least depths of 5·8 m (19 ft) lead for 1¼ miles from its entrance.
Ice. The bay can be covered by ice about 50 cm thick.

Harraseeket River

Approach and entrance
3.140

1 Harraseeket River is approached between Bustins Island (43°48′·00N 70°04′·30W), high with numerous cottages on it, and Moshier Island, 1 mile SW.

It is entered between Moore Point and Stockbridge Point, 1¼ miles WNW of Bustins Island. The entrance is narrow, being obstructed by Pound of Tea Islet. Except for a dangerous rock, with a depth of 0·6 m (2 ft) that lies in mid-channel ½ cable S of the islet, the fairway has a depth of 7 m (23 ft).

2 The principal dangers in the approach and entrance are buoyed.

Local knowledge is necessary.

Directions
3.141

1 From a position off the E side of Moshier Island the channel leads generally NW, passing:

NE of Moshier Ledge (43°47′·36N 70°05′·20W), marked by No 1 Buoy (port hand), and:

SW of Little Bustins Island (43°47′·60N 70°04′·82W), 5 m in height with a house and clump of trees in the centre, thence:

2 NE of Crab Island (43°47′·73N 70°05′·70W), thence through the harbour entrance.

Useful mark:
Stone turreted tower (43°49′·12N 70°06′·69W), standing on high ground at South Freeport.

Berths
3.142

1 **Anchorage** may be obtained in Staples Cove (43°48′·80N 70°06′·55W) between Stockbridge Point and South Freeport. This berth is designated a special anchorage.

Alongside berths. Town wharf at South Freeport with a reported depth alongside of 4·6 m.

Approaches to Luckse Sound and Hussey Sound

Description
3.143

1 The approaches to the entrances of Luckse Sound (3.147) and Hussey Sound (3.154) lie between a ridge, on which there is a chain of islets and shoals lying between Jewell Island (3.144) and Outer Green Island (43°39′·00N 70°07′·43W) (3.175) on the E; and Long Island and Peaks Island on the W.

Within 2¼ miles of the entrances of the sounds there are several islands and dangers that are common to the approach of both sounds.

Directions
3.144

1 From a position in the vicinity of No 2 Light Buoy (starboard hand) (43°39′·09N 70°09′·13W) the approach routes to Luckse Sound and Hussey Sound lead NE and N, passing:

WNW of Outer Green Island (43°39′·00N 70°07′·43W). Junk of Pork, a high rock surrounded by above-water rocks, lies 1½ cables SE. Thence:

2 Clear of The Hussey (43°39′·51N 70°08′·77W), a rock marked on its S side by No 4 Buoy (starboard hand).

When proceeding to Luckse Sound:
WNW of Inner Green Island (43°39′·99N 70°06′·36W), grassy, and:
ESE of Vaill Island (43°40′·60N 70°09′·25W).

Useful mark:
Stone tower (43°40′·61N 70°05′·85W) which stands on the S end of Jewell Island, partly wooded.

(Directions continue for Luckse Sound at 3.149, and for Hussey Sound at 3.155)

Green Island Passage
3.145

1 Green Island Passage (43°39′·28N 70°07′·00W) leads between Outer Green Island and Green Island Reef. The passage is marked by Nos 3 and 2 Buoys (lateral) which lie, respectively, off Johnson Rock, at the N end of the bank surrounding Outer Green Island, and off the S side of Green Island Reef.

The passage, used by small vessels, is 2 cables wide and has a depth of 11·3 m (37 ft).

Local knowledge is necessary.

Jewell Island
3.146

1 **Pier** is situated on the W side of the island about 7 cables N of the S end of the island. There are depths of 6·7 m at the head of the pier.

Luckse Sound

Description
3.147

1 Luckse Sound, which extends 4 miles NE from its entrance (43°41′·00N 70°08′·00W) to its junction with Broad Sound (3.130), is entered between the SW point of Cliff Island and Vaill Island, 1½ miles WSW.

The sound is bounded by Cliff Island and Stave Island on the SE and by Long Island and Great Chebeague Island on the NW. The sound is divided by Hope Island, Sand Island, Bangs Island and Stockman Island.

Depths
3.148

1 The channel E of Hope Island and Sand Island has been swept to a depth of 12·8 m (42 ft) as far as the vicinity of Bangs Island, and thence the channel SE of that island has been swept to a depth of 7·6 m (25 ft) and the channel to the N of it to a least depth of 6·1 m (20 ft).

Directions
(continued from 3.144)
3.149

1 From a position ESE of Vaill Island (43°40′·60N 70°09′·25W) the swept channel through Luckse Sound leads NE, passing:

SE of Obeds Rock (43°41′·01N 70°08′·85W), thence:

2 NW of Johns Ledge (43°40′·80N 70°07′·25W), extending SW from Cliff Island and marked at its SW extremity by No 6 Buoy (starboard hand), thence:

SE of Stepping Stones (43°41′·65N 70°08′·20W), two islets, thence:

Clear of a dangerous wreck (43°42′·05N 70°06′·76W), and:

3 SE of Hope Island (43°42′·30N 70°07′·10W), wooded, except at its SW end where there is a large house, chimney and flagstaff. No 2 Light Buoy (starboard hand) is moored 2 cables SW of its S extremity and Rogues Island, 5 m in height and grassy, lies off its NE side. Thence:

SE of Sand Island (43°42′·87N 70°06′·37W), low and grassy.

3.150

1 The swept channel then divides and leads both SE and W of Bangs Island (43°43'·60N 70°05'·44W), grassy.

The channel SE of Bangs Island leads NE, passing:
NW of Stave Island (43°43'·00N 70°05'·15W), sparsely wooded with a house on its N point. No 8 Buoy (starboard hand) marks the NE limit of Stave Island Ledge which extends 3 cables NE from the island. Thence:

2 SE of Stockman Island (43°44'·20N 70°04'·80W). Thence into Broad Sound (3.130).

The channel W of Bangs Island leads N, passing:
E of Crow Island (43°43'·77N 70°06'·20W), 5 m in height, grassy with a house on it. A shoal extending NNE from the island is marked by No 5 Buoy (port hand). Thence:

3 W of Goose Nest (43°44'·28N 70°05'·34W), a grassy islet 1 m in height, thence:
W of Goose Nest Ledge (43°44'·58N 70°05'·29W), marked on its NW side by No 8 Buoy (starboard hand). The ledge dries 2·1 m. Thence into Broad Sound.

Other channels
3.151

1 **North-west of Hope Island and Sand Island.** A channel leads between Hope Island and Sand Island to the SE, and Great Chebeague Island, to the NW.

A shoal, 4 m (13 ft) in depth, obstructs the NE entrance to this channel, leaving only a narrow passage, ½ cable wide, between it and the shore bank of Great Chebeague Island.

Between Hope Island and Sand Island. A narrow passage, marked by Nos 1 and 2 Buoys (lateral), leads between Hope and Sand Island.

Cliff Island
3.152

1 **State Pier** (43°41'·71N 70°06'·60W), with a depth alongside of 6·7 m at its head, and a pontoon berth, are situated on the W side of Cliff Island 7 cables from the S end of the island.

Chandler Cove
3.153

1 Chandler Cove (43°42'·80N 70°08'·10W) is situated between the NE end of Long Island and the S end of Great Chebeague Island. Little Chebeague Island, wooded, forms the W side of the cove and is connected at LW with Indian Point, a sandspit with a house on it.

Approach. Chandler Cove can be entered either from Luckse Sound between Long Island and Deer Point, or from between Long Island and Little Chebeague Island. Both entrances are buoyed but the E entrance is preferred, being less obstructed.

2 **Directions for E entrance.** From a position SSW of Hope Island (3.149) the track leads N, passing:
E of Stepping Stones (43°41'·65N 70°08'·20W) (3.149), thence:
W of No 2 Light Buoy (starboard hand) (43°41'·90N 70°07'·47W), thence:
E of the NE point of Long Island (43°42'·13N 70°08'·10W), thence:

3 W of No 2 Light Buoy (starboard hand) (43°42'·39N 70°07'·87W) marking a rock with a depth of 3·3 m (11 ft), thence:
E of Crow Island (43°42'·48N 70°08'·12W); thence into the cove.

The approach to the W entrance to Chandler Cove is described at 3.161.

Anchorage may be obtained in 9 to 18 m (30 to 60 ft) clear of the charted cable areas.

4 **State pier** and landing stage are situated on the NE side of the cove, 5 cables N of Deer Point. The pier, from which a ferry plies to Portland, has depths alongside of 4·6 m.

Hussey Sound
Chart 2488, US Chart 13292 (see 1.16)
Description
3.154

1 Hussey Sound, which extends 2 miles N from its entrance (43°40'·00N 70°10'·00W) into the W part of Casco Bay, is entered between Overset Island, off Jerry Point, the S point of Long Island, and the E extremity of Peaks Island, 7 cables SSW.

The sound is bounded on the E by Long Island and on the W by Peaks Island, Great Diamond Island and Cow Island (3.155).

2 **Depths.** The channel through the sound is swept to a depth of 12·2 m (40 ft).

Under-keel clearances. For recommended minimum under-keel clearances in Hussey Sound see 3.170.

Directions
(continued from 3.144)
3.155

1 From a position in the vicinity of No 2 Light Buoy (starboard hand) (43°39'·09N 70°09'·13W) the channel through Hussey Sound leads NW, N and NNE, passing:
Between No 3 Light Buoy (port hand) (43°39'·83N 70°10'·06W) off the E point of Peaks Island and No 4 Light Buoy (starboard hand), 3 cables NE, thence:
SW of Soldier Ledge (43°40'·38N 70°10'·52W), marked on its SW side by No 6 Light Buoy (starboard hand), thence:

2 NE of Pumpkin Nob (43°40'·50N 70°10'·95W), an islet, marked 1 cable E by No 7 Light Buoy (port hand), thence:
SW of College Island (43°40'·84N 70°10'·40W), which lies on foul ground extending 2 cables from the SW side of Long Island, thence:
ESE of No 9 Light (green square on framework tower, 4 m in height) (43°41'·18N 70°11'·20W), which stands on the S end of Crow Island, thence:

3 ESE of Cow Island (43°41'·50N 70°11'·10W), 17 m in height, thence:
WNW of No 10 Light Buoy (43°41'·53N 70°10'·23W), which marks the outer end of a ledge that extends 2 cables NNW from Ponce Landing.

Diamond Island Pass
3.156

1 Diamond Island Pass (43°40'·10N 70°12'·00W) separates Peaks Island from Great Diamond Island and Little Diamond Island. It is buoyed at either end and is used by small vessels.

Diamond Cove
3.157

1 Diamond Cove (43°41'·12N 70°11'·40W), on the NE side of Great Diamond Island, can be entered on either side of Crow Island (3.155). It is reported that excellent anchorage may be obtained in 5 m (18 ft), sheltered from all but E winds.

South-west part of Casco Bay

Chart 2488, US Chart 13292 (see 1.16)
Description
3.158

1 Between the N end of Hussey Sound and Cousins Island (43°45'·50N 70°08'·60W), 3½ miles NNE, there is a large area, suitable for anchorage, bounded on the E by Long Island and Chebeague Island, and on the W by Clapboard Island and Sturdivant Island, situated respectively 1¼ and 2½ miles N of Cow Island (43°41'·50N 70°11'·10W).

2 The S half of the area is almost clear of dangers with depths of 13 to 24 m (43 ft to 13 fm); the N half is obstructed by Basket Island and adjacent ledges, but there is still a considerable area with depths of 7 to 14 m (23 to 46 ft).

Transhipment Area
3.159

1 An oil transfer area is situated NE of Cow Island. Transfer of liquid cargo between tankers takes place regularly in this area. Vessels engaged in these operations may be at anchor or otherwise unable to manoeuvre, and should be given a wide berth.

Naval anchorage area
3.160

1 A naval anchorage extends N from Great Diamond Island to the S end of Cousins Island, and between Long Island and Great Chebeague Island on the E and the Brothers and Sturdivant Island on the W.

The positions of berths in this anchorage are shown on the charts.

South-west approach to Chandler Cove
3.161

1 From a position NW of Mariner Ledge (43°41'·78N 70°09'·64W), marked on its N limit by No 9 Buoy (port hand), the SW approach channel to Chandler Cove (3.153), marked by buoys, leads NE into the cove. The channel passes SE of Channel Rocks, which have a depth 3·0 m (10 ft) and are buoyed on their S side.

Other channels
3.162

1 From a position N of Great Diamond Island a channel, marked and swept, leads generally NE, passing:
SE of Cow Island Ledge (43°42'·20N 70°11'·28W). At the S end of the ledge, which dries, is a light (red and white chequered diamond on post on red caisson). The ledge is marked on its NE side by CIL Buoy (preferred channel to starboard). Thence:

2 NW of Little Chebeague Island (43°42'·70N 70°09'·00W). Banks extend 2 cables W of this island, and 5 cables NNW, marked by No 14 Light Buoy (starboard hand). Thence:
SE of Lower Basket Ledge (43°43'·84N 70°09'·50W), marked at its E end by No 15 Beacon (port hand), thence:
SE of Spruce Point (43°44'·85N 70°09'·10W), thence:

3 Between No 18 Light Buoy (starboard hand) (43°45'·27N 70°07'·59W) which lies ½ cable NNW of the end of a shoal spit that extends N from Great Chebeague Island, and the SE shore of Littlejohn Island that lies 1 cable NW. Thence into Broad Sound (3.130).

Another channel leads N from Cow Island Ledge to the vicinity of Birch Point (3.164), passing:

4 Clear of Upper Clapboard Island Ledge (43°43'·92N 70°10'·58W), marked on its E side by No 3 Light Buoy (port hand), thence:
Between Basket Island (43°44'·06N 70°10'·00W), wooded, and Sturdivant Island, 6 cables NW. No 4 Light Buoy (starboard hand) marks the shoal water NW of Basket Island. Thence:
NW of Upper Basket Ledge (43°44'·42N 70°09'·60W), marked by a beacon.

3.163

1 From a position N of Great Diamond Island a channel, marked by buoys and beacons, leads generally N along the W shore of Casco Bay, passing:
W of Lower Clapboard Island Ledge (43°42'·74N 70°11'·97W) and Jones Ledge, 2 cables N, both of which lie on the edge of the foul ground that lies SW of Clapboard Island and are marked by Nos 12 and 14 Buoys (starboard hand), thence:

2 E of Prince Point Ledge (43°43'·21N 70°12'·45W) and York Ledge, both of which lie on the coastal bank and are marked on their E sides by Nos 15 and 17 Buoys (port hand), thence:
Between Underwood Ledge (43°44'·00N 70°11'·77W), marked by No 19 Buoy (port hand), and No 20 Buoy (starboard hand) which marks the edge of the shoal ground SW of Sturdivant Island.

3 Thence the track leads NE, passing:
NW of Sturdivant Island (43°44'·50N 70°10'·90W), partly wooded, thence:
SE of The Nubbin (43°45'·50N 70°10'·56W); foul ground extends 1½ cables SW of the islet. Thence:
NW of Sandy Point Ledges (43°46'·02N 70°09'·20W), marked on their SW edge by No 22 Buoy, and after which the channel becomes shallow, winding and unmarked, and passes beneath a bridge with a vertical clearance of 7·6 m (25 ft).

Berth
3.164

1 **Birch Point** (43°45'·10N 70°09'·36W), the SW point of Cousins Island, has a large green painted power plant, with two prominent chimneys, on its N side. A **T**-shaped pier, situated at the plant, has berthing for vessels of up to 217 m in length and a draught of 10 m. In 1979 depths alongside of 10 m were reported.

Vessels usually secure starboard side to and require the assistance of tugs and pilot, both of which are available at Portland.

APPROACHES TO PORTLAND

General information

Charts 2490, 3676, 2488, US Charts 13290, 13292 (see 1.16)
Description
3.165

1 The approaches to Portland lie S of Halfway Rock (43°39'·35N 70°02'·21W) and E of Cape Elizabeth (9 miles SW).

A line of dangerous shoals lies in the approaches to Portland, extending 7½ miles SW from East Cod Ledge (43°36'·50N 70°02'·10W) to Old Anthony Rock, marked by No 2 Light Buoy (starboard hand), at the SW end of West Cod Ledge. The bottom is very irregular in the vicinity.

Recommended route
3.166
See 3.124.

Pilotage
3.167
See 3.187.

Traffic regulations
3.168
Traffic separation schemes. Two TSSs lead from ESE and SSE to the approaches to Portland. Both schemes are IMO-adopted and Rule 10 of *International Regulations for Preventing Collisions at Sea (1972)* applies.

Precautionary area. A precautionary area has been established at the inshore ends of the TSS. Traffic within the precautionary area may consist of vessels operating between Portland and one of the established lanes. Mariners are advised to exercise extreme care when navigating within this area. The centre of this area is marked by P Light Buoy (43°31'·61N 70°05'·47W).

Unexploded ordnance
3.169
Unexploded depth charges were reported (1982) to lie in an area, 6 miles in diameter, which covers the E part of the precautionary area. The limits of this area are shown on the charts.

Under-keel clearances
3.170
The US Coast Guard recommends the following minimum under-keel clearances for vessels navigating in Port of Portland:
  (a) A minimum of 0·9 m (3 ft) when transiting N of a line drawn between Portland Head Light (3.172) and Ram Island Ledge Light, 1 mile NE, to No 5 Light Buoy (43°39'·46N 70°14'·15W).
  (b) A minimum of 0·6 m (2 ft) when transiting Fore River SW of No 5 Light Buoy.
  (c) A minimum of 0·6 m (2 ft) when transiting via Hussey Sound, NW of a line between Nos 3 and No 4 Light Buoys (3.155).
  (d) A minimum of 0·3 m (1 ft) at all berthing areas.

Natural conditions
3.171
Tidal streams in the vicinity of P Light Buoy average less than ¼ kn at strength. The in-going stream sets 335° and the out-going stream 140°.

Current. Since the tidal streams are weak, currents of 1 kn or more only occur with strong winds. See also tidal stream tables on chart.

Directions
(continued from 3.7 and 3.15)

Principal marks
3.172
Major lights:
  Halfway Rock Light (43°39'·35N 70°02'·21W) (3.13).
  Cape Elizabeth Light (white conical tower) (43°33'·96N 70°12'·00W). A disused lighthouse stands 1½ cables SW.
  Portland Head Light (white tower) (43°37'·39N 70°12'·47W).

Cape Elizabeth from NE (3.172)

(Original dated 2007)

(Photograph - Cdr S Foster, MV Saga Ruby)

Portland Head Light (3.172)
(Original dated 2007)

(Photograph - Cdr S Foster, MV Saga Ruby)

Other aid to navigation
3.173
1   **Racon:**
    P Light Buoy (43°31′·61N 70°05′·47W).
    See *Admiralty List of Radio Signals Volume 2*.

General
3.174
1   If approaching the outer dangers to Portland in foggy weather, comparatively frequent on this coast, vessels need to exercise the utmost caution.
    They should not attempt to close the land if relying on soundings only, owing to the uneven nature of the bottom, and should keep in depths of over 90 m (50 fm) until the fog lifts.

From east
3.175
1   From a position S of Halfway Rock (43°39′·35N 70°02′·21W), the coastal passage continues W in the white sector (274·3°-275·8°) of Portland Head Directional Light, passing:
    N of 1EC Light Buoy (port hand) (43°36′·50N 70°02′·10W), marking the N end of East Cod Ledge (3.165), thence:
    N of Bulwark Shoal (43°36′·05N 70°04′·35W), marked on its SE side by BS Buoy (preferred channel to port), thence:
2   S of a 10·4 m (34 ft) patch (43°37′·54N 70°05′·20W), which lies 2 miles N of Bache Rock, thence:
    S of Junk of Pork (3.144), 1½ cables SE of Outer Green Island (43°39′·00N 70°07′·43W),

grassy, which lies on the E side to the approaches to Luckse Sound (3.147) and Hussey Sound (3.154), thence:
N of No 1 Light Buoy (port hand) (43°37′·09N 70°09′·77W), which marks the outer end of the entrance channel.

From east south-east and south south-east
3.176
1   **Traffic separation schemes.** From the vicinity of positions 43°25′N 69°30′W and 43°08′N 69°53′W at the seaward ends of the TSS in the approaches to Portland, the inbound traffic routes lead WNW and NNW, respectively, through waters clear of charted dangers to the centre of the precautionary area.
3.177
1   **Within precautionary area.** From the vicinity of P Light Buoy (safe water) (43°31′·61N 70°05′·47W) the approach route leads NW and N, passing:
    NE of a dangerous wreck (43°31′·22N 70°06′·34W), position approximate, thence:
    NE of East Hue and Cry Rock (43°31′·95N 70°08′·97W), a shoal that is marked on its E side by No 1 Light Buoy (port hand). West Hue and Cry lies 8 cables WSW. Thence:
2   Through the channel between Corwin Rock (43°33′·44N 70°08′·83W) and West Cod Ledge Rock, the limits of which are marked by Nos 3 and 4 Light Buoys (lateral), respectively. 4WC Buoy (starboard hand) lies at the SW end of West Cod Ledge Rock. Alden Rock, marked by No 4 Buoy (starboard hand), lies 4 cables SW of Corwin Rock.

3 The track then leads N, passing:
E of Mitchell Rock (43°34'·28N 70°10'·20W), thence:
E of No 1 Light Buoy (port hand) (43°37'·09N 70°09'·77W).

(Directions continue for Portland Harbor at 3.191. Directions for approaches to Luckse Sound and Hussey Sound are given at 3.144)

PORTLAND HARBOR

General information

Chart 2488, US Chart 13292 (see 1.16)

Position and function
3.178

1 Portland Harbor (43°39'·37N 70°14'·53W) is situated in the NW part of Gulf of Maine and lies on both sides of the Fore River. The cities of Portland and South Portland stand on the N and S sides, respectively, of the river.

Portland is the most important port on the coast of Maine, and claims to be the busiest in the NE on throughput tonnages. Its population in 2010 was 66 194, and it is a port of entry.

2 It is the Atlantic terminus of pipeline shipments of petroleum products to Canada. The main products handled by the port are petroleum products, paper, wood pulp, scrap metal, coal, salt and containerised goods. Cruise liners frequently visit.

The ice-free harbour offers secure anchorage to deep-draught vessels in all weathers.

Port limits
3.179

1 The harbour consists of the area W of Cushing, Peaks, House and Great and Little Diamonds Islands, from the entrance at Portland Head to the entrance of Fore River at Fish Point (43°39'·97N 70°14'·40W).

Port Authority
3.180

1 City of Portland Department of Ports and Transportation, 389 Congress Street, Portland, ME 04101.
Website: www.portofportlandmaine.org

Limiting conditions

Controlling depths
3.181

1 **Project depths. From the sea to Fort Gorges** (43°39'·78N 70°13'·29W) – 13·7 m (45 ft).
Inner Harbor and Fore River between Fish Point (3.179) and the combined road and rail bridge (43°38'·56N 70°17'·00W) – 10·7 m (35 ft).
For the latest controlling depths the charts and port authority should be consulted.

Vertical clearance
3.182

1 **Casco Bay Bridge** (43°38'·70N 70°15'·48W) has a bascule span with a vertical clearance of 16·8 m (55 ft).
Combined road and rail bridge has a vertical clearance of 3 m (10 ft).

Tidal levels
3.183

1 Mean spring range about 3·1 m (10·2 ft); mean neap range about 2·3 m (7·5 ft). See information in *Admiralty Tide Tables*.

Ice
3.184

1 Ice seldom obstructs navigation and when it does it is only for a limited time. Tugs keep a clear channel to the wharves.

Arrival information

Port operations
3.185

1 Speed limit within Portland Harbor is 5 kn. There are also restrictions on the wake produced by vessels in the harbour. The port authority should be consulted for further details.

Vessel traffic service
3.186

1 A VTS is in operation for the control of shipping. See *Admiralty List of Radio Signals Volume 6(5)* for details.

Pilotage
3.187

1 **Pilotage**, available 24 hours, is compulsory for all foreign vessels, and for US vessels engaged in the foreign trade with a draught of over 2·7 m (9 ft).
Pilots embark within a 2 mile radius of P Light Buoy (43°31'·61N 70°05'·47W).

Traffic regulations
3.188

1 **Navigation Rules for US Inland Waters.** See 3.125.
Safety and security zones extending 1 mile ahead, 5 cables astern and 1000 yards on either side is established around any LPG vessel.
Entry into or movement within these zones is prohibited unless previously authorized by the COTP.

2 **Security zone** of 100 yards radius is established around any passenger vessel at anchor or alongside. A security zone extending 200 yards ahead, 100 yards on either side and 100 yards astern is established around any passenger vessel that is underway.
Entry into or movement within this zone is prohibited unless previously authorized by the COTP.

3 See Appendix V for definitions and general regulations covering safety and security zones.

Harbour

General layout
3.189

1 Portland Harbor has an outer and inner harbour.
Outer harbour comprises the area W of Cushing, Peaks, House, Great Diamond and Little Diamond Islands from the entrance at Portland Head to the entrance of Fore River at Fish Point. The outer harbour includes the three deep water anchorages (3.195) and Portland Pipe Line Pier No 2 (3.197).

2 **Inner harbour** is divided into two sections. The outer part, or main harbour, extends from the entrance of Fore River to Casco Bay Bridge and the inner part, or Fore River, from Casco Bay Bridge to the head of navigation at the combined road and rail bridge (3.181), 1¼ miles farther upstream.

Natural conditions
3.190

1 **Tidal streams** within the harbour have a rate of about ½ kn.
Caution. Strong cross currents tend to set vessels on to the S side of the Casco Bay Bridge.
Climate information. See 1.139 and 1.140.

Directions
(continued from 3.177)

Principal marks
3.191

1 **Landmarks:**
Tower (43°36'·93N 70°12'·68W), constructed of stone.
Tower (43°38'·65N 70°11'·63W), standing on NE part of Cushing Island.
Fort Scammel (43°39'·06N 70°12'·74W), standing on the SW end of House Island.

2 Tower (43°39'·92N 70°14'·89W). An old observatory tower which resembles a lighthouse.

Major Light:
Portland Head Light (43°37'·39N 70°12'·47W) (3.172).

Main entrance channel
3.192

1 From the vicinity of 43°37'·15N 70°09'·05W the track leads W in the white sector of Portland Head Light (274·3°-275·8°), passing:
N of No 1 Light Buoy (port hand) (43°37'·09N 70°09'·77W), thence:
S of No 2 Light Buoy (starboard hand) (43°37'·34N 70°10'·54W), marking the S side of Witch Rock, a 7 m (23 ft) shoal, thence:

2 N of No 3 Light Buoy (port hand) (43°37'·34N 70°09'·77W), which lies 3 cables NNE of Jordan Reef. The W side of this shoal is marked by No 10 Buoy (starboard hand). Thence:
S of Ram Island Ledge Light (light-grey conical granite tower) (43°37'·89N 70°11'·24W), on a ledge, awash in places, extending 2½ cables S from Ram Island, thence:

3 N of a shoal (43°37'·25N 70°11'·93W) with a depth of 10·3 m (34 ft), marked by D Light Buoy (isolated danger).

3.193

1 From a position about 3 cables NE of Portland Head Light (43°37'·39N 70°12'·47W) the track leads NNW for about 1½ miles, in the white sector (331°-337°) of Spring Point Ledge Light, through a marked channel, passing:
WSW of No 12 Light Buoy (starboard hand) (1¼ miles SSE), lying 2 cables off the S end of Cushing Island, mostly grassy, thence:

2 Between Spring Point (43°38'·96N 70°13'·56W), on which are several prominent buildings, and No 2 Light (red triangle on tower), 5 cables E, exhibited from Fort Scammel Point, the S end of House Island. This island has the overgrown fort on its SW part and a flagstaff on its NE part. Thence:

3 SW of Fort Gorges (43°39'·78N 70°13'·29W), a prominent grey stone structure on Diamond Island Ledge. A light (red and white chequered diamond on framework tower) is exhibited from the W edge of this ledge.
Thence to the entrance to the inner harbour.

Other entrance channels
3.194

1 **Whitehead Passage** (43°38'·80N 70°11'·90W), sometimes used by small vessels, is entered N of White Head and leads W with a depth of about 7·3 m (24 ft) between Cushing Island and Peaks Island. The principal dangers are marked, but the channel, obstructed by Trotts Rock (43°38'·96N 70°11'·57W), is narrow and should only be used with local knowledge.

2 **Diamond Island Pass.** See 3.156.
West of Great Diamond Island. From a position SE of The Brothers (43°42'·00N 70°13'·00W) a channel with a least charted depth of 6 m (20 ft) and marked by buoys, leads S passing W of Great Diamond Island and Little Diamond Island and into Diamond Island Roads (3.195).
Local knowledge is necessary.

Fort Scammel from SW (3.191)
(Original dated 2007)

(Photograph - Cdr S Foster, MV Saga Ruby)

Fort Gorges from SW (3.193)
(Original dated 2007)

(Photograph - Cdr S Foster, MV Saga Ruby)

Berths

Anchorages
3.195

1 Secure anchorage for any vessel may be obtained at all times in Portland Harbor. Anchorages, which are shown on the chart, as follows:

A (43°39′·95N 70°13′·85W). General anchorage in depths of 7 to 18 m (24 to 60 ft).

2 B (43°39′·50N 70°12′·85W). Diamond Island Roads. General and quarantine anchorage in depths of 12 to 15 m (40 to 50 ft). These roads are especially intended for tankers and deep-draught vessels entering at night for temporary anchorage before berthing the next day.

C (43°39′·00N 70°12′·30W). Temporary small vessel anchorage in depths of 4 to 15 m (13 to 49 ft).

Alongside berths
3.196

1 Deep-water berths include seven petroleum terminals, one general cargo terminal and one international ferry terminal. The oil terminals are on the S side of the river at South Portland and the general cargo terminal and the ferry terminal are on the N side of Fore River at Portland.

3.197

1 Tanker terminals on the S side of Fore River are as follows:

Portland Pipe Line Pier No 2 (43°39′·25N 70°13′·75W), with a depth alongside of 16·7 m, is the terminal for the crude oil pipeline to Montreal in Canada. It can handle tankers up to 292 m in length, 53 m beam, 15·8 m draught and 170 000 dwt.

2 Gulf Oil Terminal (43°39′·22N 70°14′·44W); 219 m in length with depths alongside of 8·5 to 9·7 m.

Portland Pipe Line Pier No 1 (43°39′·15N 70°14′·55W); two berths, 259 m berthing space with a depth alongside of 10·3 m.

Motiva Terminal (43°38′·46N 70°15′·80W); two berths, 274 m in length with a depth alongside of 11·5 m.

3 Cargill Energy Terminal (43°38′·25N 70°16′·56W); 207 m in length with a depth alongside of 11·5 m.

Mobil Terminal (43°38′·33N 70°16′·89W); 183 m in length with a depth alongside of 10·7 m.

Sprague Energy Terminal (43°38′·46N 70°17′·05W); 183 m in length with a depth alongside of 10·9 m.

3.198

1 Terminals on the N side of Fore River are as follows:

Ocean Gateway Passenger Terminal (43°39′·56N 70°14′·60W); approximately 250 m in length, with dolphins.

Maine State Pier (43°39′·40N 70°14′·80W); 85 m in length with a depth alongside of 10·6 m.

International Marine Terminal (43°38′·83N 70°15′·44W); 237 m in length with depths alongside of 10·3 m.

Merrill Marine Terminal (43°38′·44N 70°16′·76W); 274 m in length with depths alongside of 10·6 m.

Port services

Repairs
3.199

1 Repair yard situated 6 cables SW of Fish Point, including part of State Pier. Two repair berths, with total length of 487 m, with depths alongside of 11·3 m.

Dry dock. Length 257 m width 42 m, depth over sill 14·3 m.

Other facilities
3.200

1 Hospitals; oily waste disposal.

Supplies
3.201

1 Fuel at the tanker berths or by barge; fresh water at most piers; provisions and stores.

CHAPTER 3

CAPE ELIZABETH TO CAPE ANN

GENERAL INFORMATION

Charts 3676, 1227, 2492
Area covered
3.202

1   This section describes the coastal route, anchorages and harbours from Cape Elizabeth (43°33′·96N 70°12′·00W) to Cape Ann, about 60 miles SSW. Also described is Portsmouth Harbor (43°05′·06N 70°45′·52W), the only harbour on this stretch of the coast suitable for deep-draught vessels.
The section is arranged as follows:
Coastal passage between Cape Elizabeth and Portsmouth Harbor (3.207).
Portsmouth Harbor (3.219).
Portsmouth Harbor to Cape Ann (3.245).

Regulations
3.203

1   **Navigation Rules for US Inland Waters** on this stretch of the coast only apply to the harbour waters of Portsmouth and Annisquam (42°39′·30N 70°41′·00W). See 3.231.

Outlying danger and banks
3.204

1   See 3.3.

Tidal streams
3.205

1   On the coast of Maine, E of Portland, the in-going stream sets E and is stronger than the out-going stream, that sets W.

Submarine submerged transit lanes
3.206

1   A lane used by submerged submarines runs SE from off Portsmouth Harbor and thence SSE to the N end of Great South Channel (41°00′N 69°00′W). See 1.13.

COASTAL PASSAGE BETWEEN CAPE ELIZABETH AND PORTSMOUTH HARBOR

General information

Charts 3676, 1227
Description
3.207

1   The coast between Cape Elizabeth (43°33′·96N 70°12′·00W) and Portsmouth, 40 miles SW, is less indented than that farther N and the outlying dangers are fewer. This stretch of the coast is more densely populated and there are many summer resorts marked by prominent buildings.

Traffic regulations
3.208

1   **Safety zone**, with a radius of 5 cables around a wreck (43°06′·26N 70°27′·26W), has been established 7 cables SE of Southeast Shoal. Fishing and anchoring are prohibited within the area. See 3.210 and Appendix V for further details.
Security zone, into which entry is prohibited, lies to the SE of Cape Arundel (43°20′·49N 70°28′·00W). For a general description of security zones see Appendix V.

Directions
(continued from 3.15)

Principal marks
3.209

1   Landmark:
Water tower (43°33′·15N 70°21′·51W), standing on Blue Point Hill.
Major lights:
Cape Elizabeth Light (3.172).
Wood Island Light (white conical tower and dwelling) (43°27′·41N 70°19′·74W).
Boon Island Light (grey conical tower and dwelling) (43°07′·27N 70°28′·59W).

Passage
3.210

1   From the vicinity of P Light Buoy (43°31′·61N 70°05′·47W), 5 miles ESE of Cape Elizabeth, the coastal route leads SSW, passing:
Clear of a dangerous wreck (43°31′·22N 70°06′·34W) (3.177), and ESE of East Hue and Cry and West Hue and Cry (3.177), rocks that lie between 2½ and 3 miles SW of Cape Elizabeth, thence:

2   ESE of Richmond Island (43°32′·60N 70°14′·10W), thence:
ESE of Wood Island (43°27′·40N 70°20′·00W), the S entrance point to Saco Bay (3.212). A light (3.209) is exhibited from the island. Thence:
ESE of Cape Island. Goat Island Light (brick conical tower, 12 m in height) (43°21′·47N 70°25′·50W) stands on the SW side of Goat Island, 4 cables SW. Thence:

3   ESE of a shoal patch (43°15′·90N 70°25′·85W) with a depth of 10·4 m (34 ft). A second patch with a depth of 9·8 m (32 ft) lies 1·3 miles WSW. Thence:
ESE of B Light Buoy (special) (43°10′·83N 70°25′·67W), thence:
ESE of Bald Head Cliff (43°13′·28N 70°34′·60W), a prominent headland on which stand two prominent white buildings, thence:

4   ESE of Boon Island Ledge (43°07′·65N 70°24′·78W), awash. No 22A Light Buoy (starboard hand) is moored SE of the ledge. No attempt should be made to pass between Boon Island Ledge and Boon Island because of the shoal, with a depth of 4·8 m (16 ft), that lies between them. Thence:

5   ESE of Southeast Shoal (43°06′·73N 70°27′·93W), which lies 8 cables SE of Boon Island, a low rocky islet, from which a light (3.209) is exhibited. Several lighted mooring buoys mark the wreck of MV *Empire Knight* which lies 7 cables SE of the shoal (see 3.208). US naval vessels may be operating with submarines in this area. A number of rocks with depths of 5·1 to 8·5 m (17 to 25 ft) lie within 1½ miles SE and SW of Boon Island.

(Directions for the coastal route continue at 3.249)
3.211

1   Thence the track continues WSW to the approaches to Portsmouth, passing:
Clear of an obstruction (43°02′·67N 70°32′·59W), position approximate, and:

2   SSE of 24YL Light Buoy (starboard hand) (43°04′·42N 70°34′·45W). This buoy is moored

106

SE of York Ledge and E of Murray Rock, two dangers marked by YL (preferred channel to port), and 2MR (starboard hand) Buoys, respectively, which lie 2½ miles off the coast. Vessels should pass well to seaward of 24YL Light Buoy to avoid the broken ground lying inshore of it. Thence:

3   Clear of a shoal patch (43°02′·53N 70°35′·56W) with a depth of 10·6 m (35 ft) and a second patch, 2 miles WSW, with a depth of 10·3 m (34 ft), and:
    NNW of Duck Island (3.250).
Thence the track continues WSW to a position W of Duck Island.

Useful marks:

4   Tank (43°26′·34N 70°22′·81W), standing on a high framework tower 2½ miles WSW of Wood Island Light.
    Tank (43°22′·23N 70°26′·66W), standing behind Cape Porpoise.
    Mount Agamenticus (43°13′·42N 70°41′·58W), which has a tower on its summit and is the highest and most southerly of three peaks on a ridge.
    Cape Neddick Light (43°09′·91N 70°35′·46W) standing on Cape Neddick Nubble, a rock close off the E extremity of Cape Neddick.
    (Directions for Portsmouth Harbor continue at 3.235)

Anchorages and harbours

Chart 3676, US Chart 13287 (see 1.16)
Saco Bay
3.212
1   Saco Bay is entered between Prouts Neck (43°32′·00N 70°19′·00W) and Wood Island, 4 miles S. Stratton Island and Bluff Island, grass-covered and surrounded by ledges, lie 1 mile S of Prouts Neck.
    In the N part of the bay, Bar Ledge and Little River Rock lie 1 and 1½ miles WSW, respectively, of Prouts Neck and in the S part Eagle Island lies 2 miles NW of Wood Island.
2   **Old Orchard Beach** (43°30′·80N 70°22′·70W) lies in the central part of Saco Bay between Scarborough River and Saco River. It has several large hotels and a pier.

Saco River
3.213
1   Saco River (43°27′·70N 70°23′·10W), with its entrance in the S part of Saco Bay 2 miles W of Wood Island Light, is the approach to the cities of Biddeford on the S bank and Saco on the N bank. The cities are the head of navigation, but there is no commercial traffic on the river and the wharves are no longer in good repair.
    The channel, marked by beacons and buoys, is narrow and crooked and in 2009 had a controlling depth of 1·6 m (5·2 ft) to Brimstone Point about 1¾ miles above the entrance.
    Ice closes the river from January to April.

Wood Island Harbor
3.214
1   **Description.** Wood Island Harbor (43°27′·20N 70°20′·80W), an anchorage suitable for small and medium-sized vessels, is situated between Wood Island, Negro Island and Stage Island on the N and Fletcher Neck on the S. The village of Biddeford Pool stands on Fletcher Neck.

The islands on the N side of the harbour are low; Wood Island, which has a few trees on it, is the highest. Fletcher Neck may best be distinguished by the many large houses standing on it and the tank standing at the inner end of the neck.

2   **Local knowledge** is necessary.
    Submarine cable area, 2 cables in width, extends SW from the W end of Wood Island to the N part of Fletcher Neck.
3.215
1   **Approaches.** Wood Island Harbor can be approached from the N between Negro Island and Stage Island or from the E between Wood Island and Gooseberry Island.
    Directions for north approach. From the vicinity of SA Buoy (safe water) (43°27′·92N 70°20′·30W) the approach leads SW and SSW, passing:
        Between Negro Island Ledge and Ram Island Ledge, which are marked, respectively, on their N and E side by Nos 1 and 2 Buoys (lateral), thence:
2   Between Negro Island and SI Buoy (preferred channel to starboard), which marks the ledges extending from the NE extremity of Stage Island; thence into the anchorage.
    Directions for east approach. From a position E of Wood Island Light the approach leads SW and W, passing:
        Between the E end of Wood Island and the 3 m (10 ft) shoal that lies 2 cables SE, and thence to the anchorage.
3   Alternatively, from a position SE of Wood Island Light the approach leads NW, passing:
        Between Dansbury Reef (43°26′·96N 70°19′·50W), marked on its S side by No 2 Buoy (starboard hand) and Washman Rock, 2 cables SW, marked by 3A Buoy. An unmarked channel, 2 cables wide, leads between Dansbury Reef and the 3 m (10 ft) shoal lying to the N. Thence:
4   N of Gooseberry Island, thence into the anchorage.
    Useful marks:
        Wood Island Light (E extremity of Wood Island) (3.209).
        Monument (NE side of Stage Island) (43°27′·41N 70°21′·09W).
3.216
1   **Anchorage** may be obtained in the following parts of Wood Island Harbor:
        South of Wood Island, E of the cable area, in 5 to 11 m (16 to 36 ft).
        Between Negro Island and Stage Island, in 5 to 7 m (16 to 23 ft).
        South-west part of the harbour, W of the cable area, in 2 to 5 m (6 to 18 ft).

Cape Porpoise Harbor
3.217
1   Cape Porpoise Harbor (43°21′·70N 70°25′·85W) lies in a group of islands and rocks which extend 1 mile from the coast. Cape Island is the E of this group.
    The harbour is a good anchorage for fishing and pleasure craft, and is often used as a harbour of refuge. There is a wharf 61 m in length with depths alongside of 2·0 to 2·4 m. Fuel, water and limited stores are available.

Kennebunk River
3.218
1   **Description.** Kennebunk River (43°21′·15N 70°28′·50W), the entrance of which is fronted by

several reefs and shoals, is entered 6 cables NW of Cape Arundel (3.208) and is the approach to the popular summer resort and yachting centre of Kennebunkport.

A **No-Discharge Zone (NDZ)** has been established for the Kennebunk River. See 1.41.

PORTSMOUTH HARBOR

General information

Charts 3676, 1227, 2483 plan of Approaches to Portsmouth Harbor and plan of Portsmouth Harbor, US Chart 13285 (see 1.16)

Position and function
3.219

1 Portsmouth Harbor (43°05′·06N 70°45′·52W) is situated on the W side of Gulf of Maine and is formed by the mouth of Piscataqua River.

The city of Portsmouth, which in the 2010 census had a population of 20 779, is a port of entry. It stands on the S bank of Piscataqua River, 3 miles above the entrance. The town of Kittery stands on the N bank opposite Portsmouth.

2 Portsmouth is the only harbour of refuge available for vessels of deep draught between Portland and Gloucester (4.14). The port handles petroleum products, gypsum, frozen fish, fish products and salt.

A US Naval Base (3.232) is situated in the harbour.

Port Authority
3.220

1 New Hampshire State Port Authority, 555 Market Street, Portsmouth, NH 03801.
Website: www.portofnh.org

Limiting conditions

Controlling depth
3.221

1 **From entrance to Memorial Highway Bridge.** Marked channel, 10·7 m (35 ft).

Memorial Highway Bridge to upper turning basin. Controlling depth in 2005-11 was 10·0 m (33 ft) in the dredged channel, thence 10·3 m (34 ft) in the basin 3½ miles above the bridge.

For the latest controlling depths the charts and port authority should be consulted.

Under-keel clearance
3.222

1 The US Coast Guard recommends the following under-keel clearances for vessels at Portsmouth:

For all movement inshore of 2KR Buoy (43°02′·96N 70°41′·46W): a minimum of 0·9 m (3 ft).

At all berthing areas: a minimum of 0·3 m (1 ft).

Vertical clearance
3.223

1 **Memorial Highway Bridge.** A lift span bridge with a vertical clearance of 5·8 m (19 ft) when closed and 45·7 m (150 ft) when open.

Sara Mildred Long Bridge. A lift span bridge with a vertical clearance of 3 m (10 ft) when closed and 41·1 m (135 ft) when open.

2 **Interstate Route 95 Bridge.** A fixed bridge with a vertical clearance of 40·8 m (134 ft).

Span bridge operators monitor VHF.

Horizontal clearance
3.224

1 **Memorial Highway Bridge** - Horizontal clearance 79 m.

Sara Mildred Long Bridge - Horizontal clearance 61 m.

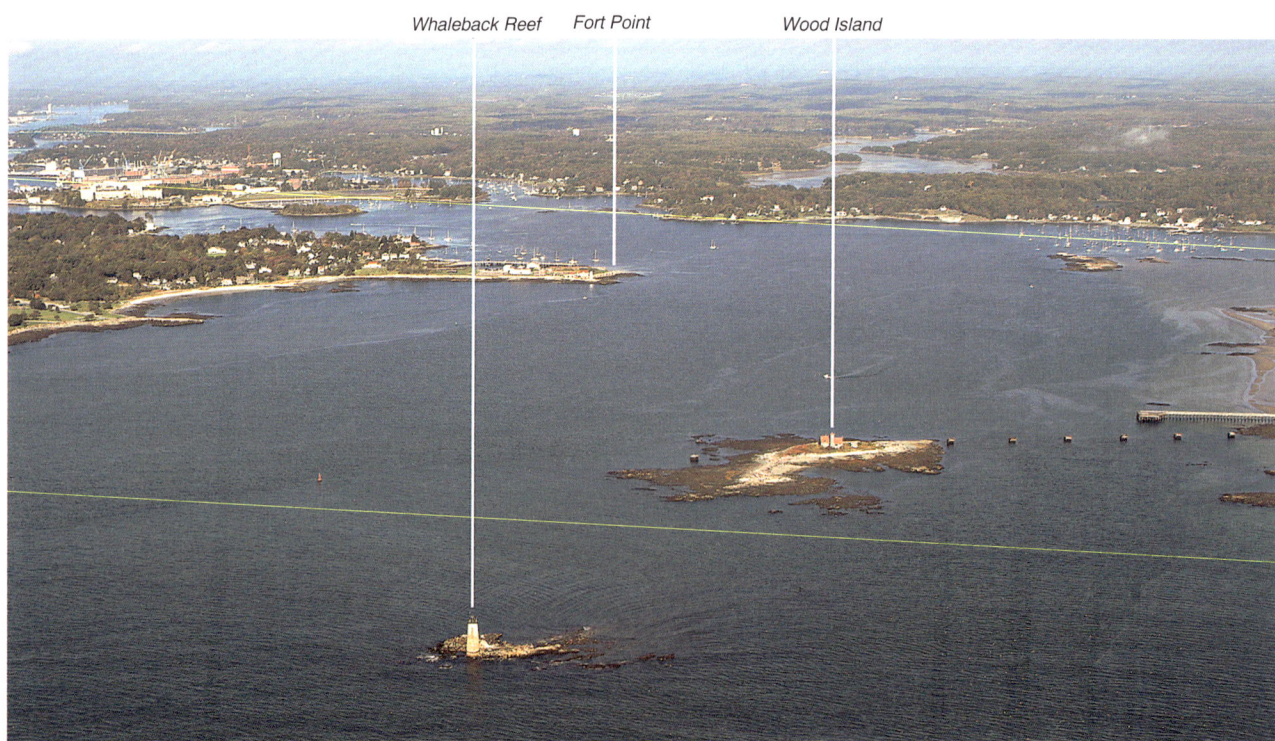

Gulf of Maine - Portsmouth Outer Harbor from SE (3.219)
(Original dated 2005)

(Photograph - David M Walker - Reproduced by permission of Marblehead Sail & Power Squadron. United States Power Squadrons)

Tidal levels
3.225

1   Mean spring range about 2·8 m (9·2 ft); mean neap range about 2 m (6·6 ft). See information in *Admiralty Tide Tables*.

Ice
3.226

1   Portsmouth Harbor has never been frozen over.

Arrival information

Vessel traffic service
3.227

1   A VTS is in operation for the control of shipping. See *Admiralty List of Radio Signals Volume 6(5)* for details. Positions of reporting points are shown on the chart.

Outer anchorages
3.228

1   Anchorage for medium-sized vessels is on the E and N side of the channel between Wood Island (43°03′·83N 70°41′·86W) and Clarks Island, 1½ miles NW, in depths of 5 to 22 m (18 ft to 12 fm), but there is only room for one medium sized vessel N of Fort Point (3.237). With S winds the best anchorage is above Fort Point on the S side of the channel in 15 to 18 m (49 to 58 ft), clay.

2   **Caution.** Deep-draught vessels should not pass N of Kitts Rocks (43°03′·22N 70°41′·51W) without a pilot owing to the strong tidal streams and eddies off Fort Point (43°04′·28N 70°42′·58W). Whilst awaiting a pilot or tide, vessels should anchor between Kitts Rocks and Gunboat Shoal, 2 miles SSW.

     Submarine cable areas, the limits of which are marked on the chart, lie either side of the approaches to Portsmouth.

Pilotage and tugs
3.229

1   **Pilotage**, available 24 hours, is compulsory for all foreign vessels and US vessels engaged in foreign trade.

     Pilots embark 1 mile SSE of 2KR Light Buoy (43°02′·96N 70°41′·46W). See *Admiralty List of Radio Signals Volume 6(5)* for details.

     Tugs, which are also used as pilot boats, are available and two or more are normally required by large vessels.

Mooring master
3.230

1   When the range of tide at HW and LW Boston is 3·66 m (12 ft) or greater, vessels having a draught greater than 9·75 m (32 ft) are recommended to obtain the services of a mooring master when moored on Piscataqua River if LOA meets the following criteria:

       Portsmouth-Schiller terminal - 189·28 m (621 ft).
       Sprague Avery Lane terminal - 197·51 m (648 ft).
       Sprague River Road terminal - 201·47 m (661 ft).

2   Intention to obtain the services of a mooring master must be included in the 24 hour notice of ETA. Vessels meeting the criteria that do not obtain the services of a mooring master must obtain permission from the US Coast Guard COTP, Portsmouth.

Traffic regulations
3.231

1   **Navigation Rules for US Inland Waters** apply within a line drawn SW from the tower (43°04′·03N 70°41′·19W) on the S point of Gerrish Island, to Whaleback Light, thence Jaffrey Point Light 2A and thence Frost Point (43°03′·18N 70°43′·15W). See 1.44 and Appendix VII for further information.

     Regulated navigation area has been established NW of Seavey Island in the vicinity of the Portsmouth Naval Dockyard. A speed limit of 4½ kn is in force in this area.

2   See Appendix V for definitions and general regulations covering regulated navigation areas.

     Safety and security zones extending 1 mile ahead, 5 cables astern and 1000 yards on either side is established around any LPG vessel.

     A safety and security zone, radius 500 yards, is established around any LPG vessel moored at Newington on Piscataqua River.

3   Entry into or movement within these zones is prohibited unless previously authorized by the COTP.

     See Appendix V for definitions and general regulations covering safety and security zones.

     Restricted areas, into which entry is prohibited, have been established at the E end of Seavey Island between Clarks Island and Jamaica Island, 2 cables N, and on the SW and NW sides of Seavey Island. See Appendix VI for definition and details of restricted areas.

Harbour

General layout
3.232

1   Portsmouth Harbor has an outer harbour in the entrance to Piscataqua River, in which are situated the outer anchorages for deep-draught vessels, a number of anchorages for small vessels and a few minor jetties.

     The US Naval Base is situated on Seavey Island (43°04′·80N 70°44′·00W) at the inner end of the outer harbour.

2   The commercial harbour is upstream of Memorial Highway Bridge (43°04′·80N 70°45′·15W), which crosses Badgers Island. The majority of berths lie on the S bank of the river, above the second and third bridges, which lie 5 cables and 1 mile, respectively, above Memorial Highway Bridge. There are two dredged turning basins in this stretch of the river.

Hazards
3.233

1   Owing to the very strong tides on Piscataqua River and its tributaries vessels moving along a berth must only do so during periods of slack water. It is extremely dangerous to attempt to shift a vessel at any other time and it should not be attempted. Masters should be particularly vigilant in tending to their vessel's moorings.

2   The strong tidal streams in the narrow channel make passage through the bridges difficult and large vessels generally require two tugs and pass through at HW.

     See also 3.230 and 3.234.

Tidal streams
3.234

1   Tidal streams in Portsmouth Harbor are strong and require special care. The rates of tidal streams are given in the tables on the chart.

Directions
(continued from 3.7 and 3.211)

Principal marks
3.235

1   **Landmarks:**
       Tower (43°04′·03N 70°41′·19W), standing at the S end of Gerrish Island.

Gangway Rock

Portsmouth Inner Harbor from ESE (3.232)
(Original dated 2005)

(Photograph - David M Walker - Reproduced by permission of Marblehead Sail & Power Squadron. United States Power Squadrons)

Cupola (43°03′·83N 70°41′·86W), on white buildings on Wood Island.

Cupola (43°03′·59N 70°43′·57W), on hotel at the SW end of New Castle Island.

Square tower (43°04′·58N 70°43′·86W) on former prison on the SE part of Seavey Island.

Approach
3.236

1 From a position W of Duck Island (43°00′·30N 70°36′·30W) (3.250) the approach to Portsmouth Harbor leads NW passing NE of No 1 Light Buoy (port hand), which marks the NE side of Gunboat Shoal (43°01′·38N 70°42′·08W).

Vessels approaching from the S should pass at least 5 cables W of Isles of Shoals.

Useful mark:

Round tower (square daymark painted with red and white triangles) (43°02′·00N 70°43′·22W).

Entrance
3.237

1 **Leading lights:**

Front light (red rectangle, white stripe, on framework tower) (43°04′·95N 70°42′·45W).

Rear light (similar structure) (140 m from front light).

From the vicinity of the pilot boarding position, 1 mile SSE of 2KR Light Buoy (43°02′·96N 70°41′·46W), the alignment (352·9°) of these lights leads N, passing:

2 E of Odiornes Point (43°02′·60N 70°42′·80W), thence:

W of Kitts Rocks (43°03′·22N 70°41′·51W), marked on their S side by 2KR Light Buoy (starboard hand), thence:

E of Jaffrey Point (43°03′·40N 70°42′·78W), the SE extremity of New Castle Island and N entrance point to Little Harbor. No 4 Light (red triangle on framework tower) stands on the end of a submerged breakwater that extends SSW from the point. Thence:

3 W of Whaleback Light (grey conical tower) (43°03′·53N 70°41′·78W), standing on Whaleback Reef, thence:

W of Wood Island (43°03′·83N 70°41′·86W) (3.228). No 2 Light Buoy (starboard hand) is moored 2 cables SW. Thence:

E of Stielman Rocks (43°04′·00N 70°42′·51W), which stand on the outer edge of the shore bank. No 3A Beacon (port hand) stands on the W side of the rocks and No 3 Buoy (port hand) marks their outer edge. Thence:

4 E of Fort Point (43°04′·30N 70°42′·55W), the NE point of New Castle Island. Portsmouth Fort Point Light (white conical tower) stands on the SE end of the point. A Coast Guard station and lookout tower also stand on the point.

3.238
1 **Leading lights:**
Front light (red rectangle, white stripe on conical tower) (43°04′·42N 70°44′·42W).
Rear light (similar structure) (78 m from front light).
From a position NNE of Fort Point the alignment (266·6°) of these lights on Pierces Island leads W, passing:
Close N of No 5 Light Buoy (port hand) (43°04′·47N 70°42′·68W), marking Cod Rock ¾ cable SSE, thence:
2 S of No 8 Light (red triangle on sectional post) (43°04′·56N 70°43′·45W), which stands on the S side of Clarks Island, thence:
S of No 10 Light (red triangle on framework tower) (43°04′·49N 70°44′·17W), which stands on Henderson Point.
Thence the track continues upstream, the river channel being marked by buoys and light buoys (lateral).

Berths

Anchorages
3.239
1 There are no anchorages for deep-draught vessels above Clarks Island.

Alongside berths
3.240
1 Deep-water berths include one general cargo and container terminal, two bulk cargo terminals and four petroleum terminals. All deep-water berths are situated on the S side of Piscataqua River between Memorial Highway Bridge and Dover Point, 4 miles farther upstream.
3.241
1 A summary of the main terminals is given as follows:
Granite State Minerals Dock (43°04′·84N 70°45′·53W).
Wharf 91 m in length; depth alongside 9·8 m.
Handles salt, dry bulk cargoes and heavy lift items.
New Hampshire State Port Authority Marine Terminal (43°05′·04N 70°45′·67W).
2 Wharf 176 m in length; depth alongside 10·7 m.
Handles containers, scrap metal and general cargo.
National Gypsum Co Wharf (43°05′·42N 70°45′·90W).
Berth 137 m in length with a depth alongside of 10·4 m.
Bulk handling of gypsum and petroleum products.
Simplex Wire and Cable Co Wharf (43°06′·20N 70°47′·45W).
3 Pier 210 m in length, with dolphins, and a depth alongside of 9·1 m.
Specialist berth for handling wire and cable.
Oil terminals, from 7 cables to 2½ miles above the Interstate 95 bridge (3.223).
76 to 237 m in length, with dolphins, with depths alongside of 9·7 to 11·6 m.
Four terminals, one of which, Newington Dock (43°06′·49N 70°47′·91W), is owned by the US Government.

Port services
Repairs
3.242
1 There are no major repair facilities for commercial vessels.

Other facilities
3.243
1 Hospitals; oily waste disposal.

Supplies
3.244
1 Fuel; water; provisions and stores.

PORTSMOUTH HARBOR TO CAPE ANN

General information
Chart 1227
Route
3.245
1 From the entrance to Portsmouth Harbor the coastal route leads SSE for 25 miles to Cape Ann.
Isles of Shoals (3.251), a group of islands, lie between 5 and 7 miles SE of the entrance to Portsmouth Harbor.

Topography
3.246
1 Between the entrance to Portsmouth Harbor (43°05′·06N 70°45′·52W) and the E extremity of Cape Ann, 25 miles SSE, the coast is composed mainly of sandy beaches.
Merrimack River enters the bay 15 miles SSW of Portsmouth Harbor and N of its mouth the beaches are separated by reefs extending 5 cables offshore.
2 Cape Ann (42°39′·00N 70°38′·00W) is an island separated from the mainland by the Annisquam River. It is rocky and broken, rising to its greatest height at Pool Hill. The E end of the cape is comparatively low and off its NE and E sides are several islands and dangers. The cape is covered with numerous summer residences.
There are a number of summer resorts and small harbours on this stretch of the coast, the latter being used by fishing vessels and small craft.

Traffic regulations
3.247
1 **Mandatory Ship Reporting System (MSR).** A mandatory ship reporting system has been established for the protection of the North Atlantic right whale. See *Admiralty List of Radio Signals Volume 6(5)* for details.
No-Discharge Zone (NDZ). All the coastal waters of New Hampshire, from Portsmouth to Hampton Harbor, extending out 3 miles off shore and including Isle of Shoals, have been designated as a NDZ. See 1.41.

Local magnetic anomaly
3.248
1 The normal magnetic variation varies by as much as 3° in the vicinity of Cape Ann.

Directions
(continued from 3.210)
Principal mark
3.249
1 **Major Light:**
Cape Ann Light (42°38′·21N 70°34′·50W), which stands on the E side of Thacher Island.

Portsmouth Harbor to Cape Ann
3.250

1 From a position ESE of Southeast Shoal (3.210) the coastal passage leads S to Cape Ann, passing:

E of Duck Island (43°00′·30N 70°36′·30W), the N island of Isles of Shoals (3.251). This island is 5 m in height and surrounded by reefs and shoals. Isles of Shoals may be seen from a distance of 10 miles on a clear day, the houses being prominent. Thence:

2 E of Smuttynose Island (42°58′·95N 70°36′·40W), thence:

E of Cedar Island Ledge (42°58′·50N 70°35′·90W) and Anderson Ledge, 8 cables S. Cedar Island Ledge is marked by DC Buoy (isolated danger), and Anderson Ledge is marked by No 2 Buoy (starboard hand). Vessels passing to the E of the islands should give them a berth of 1½ miles, to clear these ledges. Thence:

3 E of The Salvages (42°40′·40N 70°34′·20W), consisting of two reefs connected by a ridge. No 1 Light Buoy (port hand) is moored 5 cables NE of Dry Salvages, the E reef. Thence:

E of Thacher Island (42°38′·25N 70°34′·60W), which lies 5 cables E of Emerson Point, the E point of Cape Ann. Londoner, a shoal marked by a beacon, lies 4 cables ESE of Cape Ann Light.

4 **Caution.** Trawlers and other vessels conducting bottom operations within a 6¾ mile radius seaward of Isle of Shoals Light should exercise caution because of Jet Assist Take-Off racks and other debris on the seabed associated with the naval bombing range centred on Shag Rock (3.252).

Useful marks:

5 Isles of Shoals Light (white conical tower) (42°58′·03N 70°37′·40W), which stands on White Island at the S end of Isles of Shoals.

Plum Island Point Light (white conical tower) (42°49′·00N 70°49′·20W).

Thacher Island North Light, N side (grey stone conical tower) (42°38′·36N 70°34′·50W).

(Directions continue at 4.11)

Isles of Shoals

Chart 1227, US Chart 13283 (see 1.16)

Description
3.251

1 Isles of Shoals (42°59′·00N 70°37′·00W) is a group of seven islands and many rocks and ledges lying 6 miles SE of Portsmouth Harbor. The islands are occupied in summer by fishermen and visitors, but few residents live there in winter. A ferry service operates between Star Island and Portsmouth Harbor.

Approaches to Portsmouth - Isles of Shoals from SSW (3.251)

(Original dated 1990)

(Photograph - Joseph R Melanson of www.skypic.com)

Traffic regulations
3.252
1 **Danger zone.** A naval aircraft bombing practice area of radius 2½ cables is centred on Shag Rock (43°00'·21N 70°36'·17W), E of Duck Island (3.250). For details see Appendix VI.

Channels
3.253
1 **Between Appledore Island and Duck Island.** The channel separating Appledore Island (42°59'·30N 70°36'·80W), 21 m in height and the largest island of the group, from Duck Island (3.250) has irregular depths; rocky patches with depths of 7·6 and 8·2 m (25 and 27 ft) lie in the channel.

Gosport Harbor
3.254
1 Gosport Harbor (42°58'·80N 70°36'·80W) lies between Malaga Island, joined to Smuttynose Island by a breakwater, and the N side of Star Island. It is protected from the E by Cedar Island and the breakwaters that connect this island to Smuttynose Island and Star Island. The harbour offers good protection from all but W winds.

2 **Anchorage** may be obtained by small vessels in 6 to 15 m (20 to 49 ft).

Berth. Stone pier, length 60 m with depths alongside of 3·7 m, extends from the village of Gosport, at the N point of Star Island.

Useful marks
3.255
1 Several useful marks exist in the islands:
   Tower (42°59'·23N 70°36'·91W), standing on Appledore Island.
   Cupola (42°59'·24N 70°36'·81W) of an old Coast Guard station, 1 cable E of the tower.
   White hotel and flagstaff (42°58'·63N 70°36'·88W), on N part of Star Island.
   Monument (42°58'·53N 70°36'·81W), 12 m in height, standing 1 cable SSE of the hotel flagstaff.
   Isles of Shoals Light (3.250).

Sandy Bay
Chart 1227, US Chart 13283 (see 1.16)
Description
3.256
1 Sandy Bay lies between Andrews Point (42°41'·25N 70°37'·25W), 5 cables SE of Halibut Point, and Straitsmouth Island, low and grassy, lying 2 miles SE.

Breakwater. The S part of the bay is protected by a partially completed breakwater, which extends N and NW for 1 mile from Avery Ledge. In 1979 the breakwater was awash except for a length of 1½ cables near the centre, where it was above water, and about 2 cables at either end that are submerged at LW. No 3 Light Buoy (port hand) and No 2 Light Buoy (starboard hand), respectively, mark the NW and S ends of the breakwater.

Arrival information
3.257
1 **Entrance.** The main entrance to the bay, deep and clear, lies between Andrews Point and No 3 Light Buoy. There is a narrow passage, with a least depth of 6·7 m (22 ft) leading into the bay at the S end of the breakwater, but this should not be used without local knowledge.

Dangers. A bank with rocks on it, two of which are awash, lies on the W side of Sandy Bay. The S rock, Dodge Rock (42°40'·07N 70°37'·13W), is marked by No 2 Beacon. A rock with a depth of 2·7 m (9 ft), marked by No 3 Buoy (port hand), lies 3 cables NW of Gap Head, the S entrance point to the bay.

2 **Useful marks** (with positions relative to Andrews Point):
   Chimney (42°40'·66N 70°37'·44W), at the head of Pigeon Cove.
   Tank (42°40'·33N 70°37'·75W), on Pigeon Hill.
   Straitsmouth Island Light (white round tower) (42°39'·74N 70°35'·28W).

Anchorage. The bay has depths from 10 to 26 m (33 ft to 14 fm) and is sometimes used as an anchorage. However, it is exposed to N and NE winds. It has been reported that in good weather vessels up to 46 m in length anchor in the cove S of Sandy Bay Ledge (42°39'·90N 70°37'·20W).

Anchorages and harbours
Chart 1227, US Charts 13282, 13274 (see 1.16)
Merrimack River
3.258
1 Merrimack River is the largest river in the E part of Massachusetts and forms the approach to the cities of Newburyport (42°48'·80N 70°52'·40W) and Haverhill. It is navigable by small vessels with a draught of 3·7 m (12 ft) to Newburyport, but the river is seldom entered for refuge and has virtually no commercial traffic.

Local knowledge is necessary and pilotage is compulsory for all foreign vessels.

2 **Approach and entrance.** The entrance lies 4½ miles S of Hampton Harbor (42°53'·70N 70°48'·80W) and 2¾ miles S of Breaking Rocks, the E side of this shoal being marked by No 2 Buoy (starboard hand).

A breakwater extends from each entrance point, the outer ends being 98 m apart. No 4 Light (red triangle on framework tower) (42°49'·13N 70°48'·23W) stands at the head of the N breakwater and No 2 Light Buoy (starboard hand) is moored 4 cables E of this light.

3 At HW the S breakwater may be difficult to distinguish, particularly at night, as its outer end will be awash.

The entrance is obstructed by a shifting bar dangerous to cross in heavy weather. A bar guide light and visual warning signal, situated at the N end of Plum Island on the S side of the entrance, is operated by the Coast Guard to warn of conditions on the bar.

Tidal streams are strong in the river, with the outgoing stream flowing at a rate of up to 3 kn.

4 **Ice** occasionally obstructs navigation as far as the first bridge at Newburyport. West winds carry drift ice out to sea whilst winds from other directions allow the flood tide to prevent drift ice leaving the river.

Above the bridges at Newburyport the river is normally closed by ice from January to March.
3.259
1 **Channel.** A buoyed channel leads over the bar to Newburyport and thence upstream to Haverhill. It is well marked and easy to follow as far as Newburyport, but is then narrow and winding.

Depths. Merrimack River has a project depth of 4·6 m (15 ft) over the bar at the entrance thence the channel to the road bridge at Newburyport had a controlling depth of 2·7 m (9 ft). For the latest depths the charts and the harbour authorities should be consulted.

Vertical clearance. Road and rail bridges cross the river at Newburyport with a vertical clearance of 10·7 m (35 ft) when open and clearance of 4 m when closed. The channel leads through the N opening span of each bridge.

Alongside berths. There are a number of landings with depths alongside of 2·4 to 5·5 m at the Newburyport waterfront. A town landing is situated on the N bank, E of the bridges.

Facility and supplies: hospital; fuel; water and provisions.

Chart 1227, US Chart 13279 (see 1.16)
Hodgkins Cove
3.260

Hodgkins Cove (42°40'·17N 70°40'·23W) is entered close E of Davis Neck. There are unmarked dangers in the entrance and a channel 21 m wide leads to a long stone pier on the E side, which has a depth alongside of 3·7 m at its outer end.

Folly Cove
3.261

Folly Cove (42°41'·30N 70°38'·50W) is entered E of Folly Point. There is a wharf on the E side with a depth alongside of 4·9 m. A rock with a depth of 0·9 m (3 ft) lies ½ cable W of the wharf.

NOTES

Chapter 4 - Massachusetts Bay, Boston Harbor and approaches

Arrows indicate the waterway described. Numbers refer to paragraphs in the chapter

CHAPTER 4

MASSACHUSETTS BAY, BOSTON HARBOR AND APPROACHES

GENERAL INFORMATION

Chart 2492
Scope of chapter
4.1

1 The area covered by this chapter comprises Massachusetts Bay, including Cape Cod Bay and the entrance to Cape Cod Canal (41°46′·70N 70°29′·40W), the port of Boston and its seaward approach from the S end (40°35′·00N 69°00′·00W) of Nantucket Shoals, and the inshore waters on the E side of Nantucket Sound and Cape Cod.

The chapter is divided into the following sections:
   North part of Massachusetts Bay (4.6).
   Boston Harbor and approaches (4.59).
   South part of Massachusetts Bay (4.116).

Regulations
4.2

1 All the inshore waters within this chapter including the whole of Cape Cod Bay, but excluding the seaward side of Cape Cod extending S from 42°09′·00N 70°10′·00W, are a No-discharge Zone (NDZ). See 1.41.

Stellwagen Bank National Marine Sanctuary
4.3

1 Stellwagen Bank National Marine Sanctuary (42°25′·00N 70°20′·00W) consists of an area of about 638 sq nautical miles situated in the approaches to Massachusetts Bay. The limits of the area surround Stellwagen Bank, Tillies Bank to the NE of Stellwagen Bank, and portions of Jeffreys Ledge to the N of Stellwagen Bank. This area also includes parts of the TSS off Cape Cod.

For information on Marine Sanctuaries see 1.42.

North Atlantic right whale
4.4

1 For Mandatory Ship Reporting Systems, Recommended Two-Way Whale Avoidance Routes, ATBA's and other regulations for the protection of the North Atlantic right whale See 1.51, *Admiralty List of Radio Signals Volume 6(5)* and Appendices VIII and X.

Tidal streams
4.5

1 Tidal streams in Massachusetts Bay are generally weak except in the narrow entrances to the rivers and harbours.

See Tidal Stream tables on the charts.

NORTH PART OF MASSACHUSETTS BAY

GENERAL INFORMATION

Chart 1227
Area covered
4.6

1 This section describes the coastal route, anchorages and harbours between Cape Ann (42°38′·50N 70°36′·40W) and Boston Harbor, 24 miles SW.

The section is arranged as follows:
   Coastal passage between Cape Ann and Boston Harbor (4.8).
   Salem Sound and adjacent waters (4.26).
   Inshore waters between Marblehead Neck and Broad Sound (4.49).

Regulations
4.7

1 No-discharge Zone (NDZ). See 4.2.

COASTAL PASSAGE BETWEEN CAPE ANN AND BOSTON HARBOR

General information

Chart 1227
Description
4.8

1 Between Cape Ann (42°38′·50N 70°36′·40W) and Boston Harbor, 24 miles SW, the coast is rocky and generally bold with many dangers extending up to 3 miles offshore.

Mandatory Ship Reporting System (MSR)
4.9

1 See *Admiralty List of Radio Signals Volume 6(5)* for details.

Local magnetic anomaly
4.10

1 The normal magnetic variation has sometimes been increased by 3° in the vicinity of Cape Ann and Gloucester Harbor.

Directions
(continued from 3.250)

Principal marks
4.11

1 Major lights:
   Cape Ann Light (42°38′·21N 70°34′·50W) (3.249).
   Eastern Point Light (42°34′·81N 70°39′·87W) (4.18).
   Bakers Island Light (42°32′·19N 70°47′·16W) (4.34).

Other aid to navigation
4.12

1 Racon:
   Boston Light Buoy B (safe water) (42°22′·70N 70°46′·97W).
   See *Admiralty List of Radio Signals Volume 2*.

Cape Ann to Boston Harbor
4.13

1 From a position about 2½ miles E of Thacher Island the coastal route to Boston Harbor leads SW, passing:

SE of Thacher Island (42°38′·25N 70°34′·60W) (3.250), thence:

SE of a dangerous wreck (42°37′·01N 70°33′·56W), position approximate, thence:

2 SE of a dangerous wreck (42°34′·30N 70°36′·10W), position approximate. Another dangerous wreck, position approximate, lies 1 mile NW. Thence:

SE of Burnham Rocks (42°32′·41N 70°40′·78W) and Saturday Night Ledge, 4 cables SSW. These rocky patches lie in the approaches to Salem Sound (4.26). Thence:

SE of No 1 Light Buoy (port hand) (42°30′·46N 70°44′·39W), marking the extremity of shoal water that extends 2 miles SE from Bakers Island (4.36), thence:

3 SE of Great Pig Rocks (42°27′·69N 70°50′·49W) (4.51), marked on their E side by No 4 Light Buoy (starboard hand). Foul ground extends between from this shoal to the shore 2 miles NW. Thence:

Clear of B Light Buoy (safe water) (42°22′·72N 70°46′·97W), in the centre of the Boston approaches precautionary area (4.64).

Several light buoys (special) lie off this stretch of the coast.

(Directions for Boston Harbor continue at 4.91)

Gloucester Harbor

Charts 1227, 2483 plan of Gloucester Harbor (see 1.16)
General information
4.14
1 **Position and function.** Gloucester Harbor (42°36′·69N 70°39′·29W) is situated on the S side of Cape Ann. The historic city of Gloucester covers the greater part of Cape Ann.

The harbour is one of the most important fishing ports in the United States. It is also a port of entry and an important harbour of refuge. In 2010 Gloucester had a population of 28 789.

2 Its principal industries are connected with fishing and fish products.

Port limits. Inner Harbor consists of the waters within a line joining Fort Point (42°36′·48N 70°39′·90W) and Black Rock (4.21), 1½ cables SE.

Port Authority. Gloucester Port Authority, 19 Harbor Loop, Gloucester, MA 01930, USA.

Limiting conditions
4.15
1 **Depths.** The main entrance channel to the outer harbour, which leads between shoals extending from Round Rock Shoal (4.18) and Mussel Point, has depths of 10·7 to 15·9 m (35 to 52 ft).

The dredged Entrance Channel to Inner Harbor has a project depth of 6·1 m (20 ft) (2010). Access channels within the harbour have project depths between 4·6 and 5·5 m (15 to 18 ft) (2010).

2 For the latest controlling depths the chart and port authority should be consulted.

Tidal levels. Mean spring range about 2·9 m (9·5 ft); mean neap range about 2·2 m (7·2 ft). See information in *Admiralty Tide Tables*.

Ice seldom extends outside Tenpound Island at the entrance to the Inner Harbor, and boat movements normally keep the Inner Harbor open.

3 **Local weather.** During heavy SE gales the sea at times breaks nearly the whole distance across the entrance.

Arrival information
4.16
1 **Port operations.** A 5 kn speed limit is enforced in Inner Harbor.

Outer anchorages. See 4.22.

Pilotage is compulsory for all foreign vessels over 350 gt or 2·1 m (7 ft) draught, and for US registered vessels over 10 000 gt. Pilots are available 24 hours and board 2 miles SSE of the harbour entrance. The nearest tugs are stationed at Boston.

2 **Traffic regulations.** Navigation Rules for US Inland Waters apply within a line joining the W end of the harbour breakwater and a point on the shore below the stone building with twin towers, 2 cables WSW of Mussel Point. See 1.44 and Appendix VII for further information.

Harbour
4.17
1 **General layout.** Gloucester Harbor consists of an outer harbour and an inner harbour.

The outer harbour, which extends 1½ miles N, is entered between Eastern Point (42°34′·81N 70°39′·87W) and Mussel Point, 1 mile WNW. The harbour is partially protected by a breakwater which extends 4 cables WNW from Eastern Point. There are a number of coves within the harbour.

2 Inner Harbor is entered from the NE part of the outer harbour. Within the harbour, Harbor Cove lies to the NW of the entrance and Smith Cove is entered on the SE side. An anchorage, alongside berths and port facilities are situated in Inner Harbor.

3 **Tidal streams** set directly in and out of the outer harbour and their rates are comparatively small. In the entrance to Inner Harbor the tidal streams are stronger, especially with the out–going stream.

Tidal streams at the entrance to Blynman Canal average over 3 kn in strength.

Directions
4.18
1 **Landmarks:**
Square tower (42°36′·80N 70°40′·57W).
Spire (42°36′·79N 70°39′·97W).
Major light:
Eastern Point Light (white conical tower and dwelling, 11 m in height) (42°34′·81N 70°39′·87W).
Main entrance. From the vicinity of the pilot boarding position (4.16) the route to the entrance of Gloucester Harbor leads NW, passing:

2 SW of Eastern Point Light, keeping clear of a dangerous wreck which lies 5 cables SSW of Eastern Point, thence:

SW of Gloucester Breakwater Light (white tower on brown square framework tower) (42°34′·96N 70°40′·34W), at the head of the breakwater that extends WNW from Eastern Point, thence:

3 Between Round Rock Shoal (42°35′·01N 70°40′·68W), marked by RR Light Buoy (preferred channel to port) and No 3 Buoy (port hand), 6 cables SW, moored 2 cables SE of Normans Woe Rock, a rounded rocky islet 14 m (45 ft) in height.

Thence the track leads NE into the outer harbour.

Useful mark:
4 Twin towers on stone building (42°35′·11N 70°41′·54W).

Gloucester Inner Harbor from SSE (4.17)
(Original dated 2005)

(Photograph - David M. Walker - Reproduced by permission of Marblehead Sail & Power Squadron, United States Power Squadrons)

Caution. Owing to the irregular depths and many dangers in Gloucester Harbor and its approaches, careful navigation is necessary, particularly in foggy weather.

4.19

1 **Dog Bar Channel** (42°35′·00N 70°40′·48W) leads between Dog Bar, on which the breakwater is built, and Round Rock Shoal. It has a least depth of 6·7 m (22 ft) and a width of 160 m. The channel is marked on its E side by 2DB Buoy (starboard hand), and on its W side by 1DB Buoy (port hand) at the NE edge of Round Rock Shoal.

During SE gales the sea at times breaks nearly the whole distance across the entrance and local knowledge is required to navigate this channel.

4.20

1 **Outer harbour.** From the harbour entrance the track through the outer harbour leads NNE, passing:
  ESE of Dolliver Neck (42°35′·55N 70°40′·97W), thence:
  Between Prairie Ledge (42°35′·90N 70°40′·64W), marked on its E side by No 7 Light Buoy (port hand), and a 4·8 m (16 ft) patch, 2½ cables SE, marked by No 6 Buoy (starboard hand); thence:
2 WNW of Tenpound Island Ledge (42°35′·86N 70°40′·21W), thence:
  WNW of Tenpound Island Light (white conical tower) (42°36′·11N 70°39′·93W), which stands on the W end of Tenpound Island. Mayflower Ledge lies 1½ cables SW of the light and is marked by No 8 Buoy (starboard hand).
  Thence the track leads into Inner Harbor.

4.21

1 **Inner Harbor.** The Entrance Channel to the inner harbour leads NE, passing between Fort Point (42°36′·48N 70°39′·90W) and Rocky Neck, high and partly wooded. The entrance is marked by No 10 Light Buoy (starboard hand); Babson Ledge, marked by No 9 Buoy (port hand), lies 1¼ cables WNW of No 10 Light Buoy.

2 Within the entrance the Entrance Channel divides into North Channel and South Channel, which lead either side of Gloucester State Fish Pier, to the head of the harbour. Channels are marked by port and starboard hand buoys.

Leaving harbour. Vessels leaving Inner Harbor on the out–going stream should keep to the NW side of the channel when passing between Fort Point and No 12 Beacon on Black Rock.

Anchorages in the outer harbour
4.22

1 **Southeast Harbor** (42°35′·70N 70°39′·70W), which provides the best anchorage for vessels seeking shelter or bound for Inner Harbor, lies on the E side of the outer harbour between Black Bess Point, 5 cables N of Eastern Point, and Tenpound Island.

This cove, also known locally as Pancake Ground, provides good anchorage in about 7 to 9 m (23 to 30 ft), soft mud and clay.

2 **Western Harbor** (42°36′·42N 70°40′·29W) lies at the S entrance to Blynman Canal between Fort Point and Stage Head. This cove provides good anchorage in 7 to 9 m (23 to 30 ft), soft mud and clay. The shore should be given a berth of 1½ cables, and vessels

Berths in Inner Harbor
4.23

1   **Anchorages.** A dredged anchorage is situated 1½ cables SW of the head of the State Fish Pier. In 2010 it had depths of 4·9 m (16 ft).

4.24

1   **Alongside berths.** There are many wharves within Inner Harbor, most of which are used by the fishing industry. Vessels of up to 152 m in length and 7·3 m draught can be handled. The principal wharves are:

    Gloucester State Fish Pier. NW side (42°36'·88N 70°39'·16W). 305 m in length with a reported depth alongside of 7·3 m.

2   Rogers Street Wharf (42°36'·83N 70°39'·35W). 91 m in length with a reported depth alongside of 7·6 m.

    Rowe Square Wharf, close NE of Rogers Street Wharf. 137 m in length with a reported depth alongside of 6·7 m.

    East Main Street Wharf (42°36'·65N 70°39'·17W). 110 m in length, with reported depth alongside of 6·4 m.

Port services
4.25

1   **Repairs.** There are shipyards on Rocky Neck where repairs can be carried out. Repair berth has a length 82 m; reported depth alongside of 4·6 to 4·9 m.

  Patent slip is available capable of handling craft of up to 44 m in length and 600 tonnes.

2   **Other facilities:** hospital; oily waste disposal.
  Supplies: fuel; water; provisions and stores.

SALEM SOUND AND ADJACENT WATERS

General information

Charts 1227, 2427
Description
4.26

1   Salem Sound and the harbours of Manchester (42°34'·22N 70°46'·40W), Beverly (42°32'·38N 70°53'·00W), Salem (42°31'·31N 70°52'·61W) and Marblehead (42°30'·21N 70°50'·50W) lie in a large irregular indentation in the NW part of Massachusetts Bay. This indentation is entered between Gales Point (42°33'·58N 70°46'·66W) to the N and Marblehead Neck, 4 miles SW. The area is obstructed by numerous islands and rocks, above and below-water, through which several channels lead to the various harbours.

2   Outside this indentation the coast between Gloucester Harbor and Gales Point is indented by several shallow and unimportant coves and is fronted by numerous islands and rocks, above and below–water, which extend up to 1 mile offshore.

Controlling depths
4.27

1   In 2007 the dredged section of Salem Channel, the N most important and deepest channel, had controlling depths of 9·75 m (32 ft) in the channel and 8·2 m (27 ft) (2002) in the turning basin.

  Childrens Island Channel, the middle channel, has a least depth of 7·9 m (26 ft).

  In Marblehead Channel, the SW channel, all dangers in the fairway of less than 5·5 m (18 ft) are marked.

  For the latest controlling depths the charts and port authorities should be consulted.

Pilotage and tugs
4.28

1   **Pilotage** to the ports in this area is compulsory for all foreign vessels, and all US vessels under register in the foreign trade which draw over 2·1 m (7 ft).

  The pilot, provided by Gloucester (4.16), normally embarks in the vicinity of No 2 Light Buoy (42°34'·24N 70°39'·83W) S of Eastern Point (4.17).

  Tugs from Boston, for vessels entering Salem, normally join vessels off No 16 Light Buoy (42°32'·24N 70°51'·14W).

Local knowledge
4.29

1   Local knowledge is required to navigate all channels except for Salem Channel.

Traffic regulations
4.30

1   **Navigation Rules for US Inland Waters** apply inshore of lines joining Gales Point (42°33'·58N 70°46'·66W) to Marblehead Light (42°30'·32N 70°50'·02W), as shown on the chart. See 1.44 and Appendix VII for further information.

  Safety and security zone. A safety and security zone surrounds Salem Terminal Wharf (4.44).

Submarine pipeline
4.31

1   **Gas pipeline.** A gas pipeline extends from Danvers River (4.47) to North Weymouth (42°14'·75N 70°57'·80W) passing through Beverly Channel (4.47), Salem Sound (4.26), Marblehead Channel (4.37), Childrens Island Channel (4.38), Black Rock Channel (4.99), Nantasket Roads (4.104), and Weymouth Fore River (4.112).

  Caution. See 1.36.

Special anchorages
4.32

1   Special anchorages, the positions of which are shown on the chart, are established in Beverly Harbor (4.47), Salem Harbor (4.39) and Marblehead Harbor (4.48). See 1.45.

Natural conditions
4.33

1   **Tidal streams** are weak in Salem and Marblehead Harbors, but have considerable rates in Beverly Harbor, where they set across the channel in places.

  Ice does not seriously effect the harbours in this area except during unusually severe winters when it may extend as far out as Great Haste (42°32'·08N 70°50'·51W) and very occasionally as far as Eagle Island (42°31'·53N 70°48'·78W). Of the ports in the area Marblehead Harbor is the least likely to be obstructed by ice.

CHAPTER 4

Fog presents a problem all the year round, being worst during the late spring and early summer.

Directions

Principal marks
4.34
1   **Landmarks:**
    Tower (42°33'·67N 70°46'·42W), on Gales Point.
    Spire (tallest) (42°32'·90N 70°52'·71W). Rear mark of Salem Channel entrance transit.
    Spire (42°32'·97N 70°52'·65W).
    Radio tower (42°31'·11N 70°51'·66W).
    Chimney (42°31'·10N 70°53'·17W).
    Water tower (42°30'·62N 70°51'·43W).
    Water tower (conical top) (42°30'·05N 70°51'·88W).
2   **Major Lights:**
    Eastern Point Light (42°34'·81N 70°39'·87W) (4.18).
    Bakers Island Light (white conical tower) (42°32'·19N 70°47'·16W).
    Boston Light (42°19'·68N 70°53'·41W) (4.91).
    The Graves Light (42°21'·91N 70°52'·15W) (4.91).

Eastern Point to Salem Channel
4.35
1   From the vicinity of the Gloucester pilot boarding position S of No 2 Light Buoy (42°34'·24N 70°39'·83W), the route to the entrance of Salem Channel leads generally WSW, passing:
    Clear of Middle Ground (42°33'·22N 70°42'·55W) and Kettle Island Ledge, 6 cables SE, and:
    SSE of Kettle Island (42°34'·05N 70°43'·33W), partly wooded, which lies in the entrance to Magnolia Harbor (42°34'·50N 70°43'·20W), and:
2   SSE of Great Egg Rock (42°34'·05N 70°43'·33W), bare, thence:
    N of the foul ground which extends SE from Bakers Island to Newcomb Ledge (42°30'·72N 70°45'·25W), marked on its N side by Nos 3, 5 and 7 Buoys (port hand). In this area are Southeast Breakers, Middle Breakers and Searle Rock, all of which break in heavy weather. No 1 Light Buoy (port hand) lies 5 cables farther SE of this foul ground. And:
3   SSE of a bank on which lie Gales Ledge (42°33'·70N 70°45'·90W) and Pilgrim Ledge, marked on its S edge by No 6 Buoy (starboard hand). A rock with a depth of 11·6 m (38 ft) lies 2 cables SE of this buoy.
4   **Caution.** In view of the irregular depths in the approaches to the harbours of Beverly, Salem and Marblehead and of the islands and rocks, above and below water, on either side of the channels, caution is necessary for their navigation at all times; in foggy weather local knowledge is necessary. Without local knowledge approach should only be made by Salem Channel.

*(Directions continue for
Eagle Island Channel at 4.38)*

Salem Channel
4.36
1   **Leading lights:**
    Front light (white pyramidal tower) (42°32'·79N 70°51'·36W), standing on Hospital Point.
    Rear light (1 mile from front light) (light on tallest of two church spires; see 4.34).
    The alignment (276·3°) of these lights leads W from S of No 6 Buoy, passing:
2   S of Whaleback (42°32'·91N 70°47'·08W), a dangerous rock awash, just outside the entrance to Manchester Bay, on which stands No 8 Beacon (red daymark), thence:
    N of Powers Rock (42°32'·41N 70°47'·21W), at the N end of shoal water extending from Bakers Island, marked by No 9 Light Buoy (port hand). This prominent island, 30 m in height, has numerous houses standing on it. Thence:
3   N of SE Buoy (preferred channel to starboard) (42°32'·36N 70°47'·76W), which lies in the N entrance to Eagle Island Channel (4.38), thence:
    S of Little Misery Island (42°32'·70N 70°47'·85W), lying close S of Great Misery Island. No 10 Light Buoy (starboard hand) (7½ cables WNW), lies at the SW end of the shoal ground extending from the island. A rock with a depth of 10·1 m (33 ft) lies ½ cable WSW of the light buoy. Thence:
4   N of Bowditch Ledge, marked by a beacon (red and white diamond daymark on conical granite monument, 9 m (30 ft) in height) (42°32'·42N 70°48'·69W). No 11 Light Buoy (port hand), 1½ cables NE, lies on the N side of the shoal ground surrounding this ledge. Thence:
    S of John Ledge (42°32'·70N 70°48'·85W), marked on its S side by No 12 Light Buoy (starboard hand).
    Thence into Salem Sound.
    (Directions for Salem Harbor continue at 4.43)

Marblehead Channel
4.37
1   From a position SW of Halfway Rock (42°30'·16N 70°46'·50W), high, bare and resembling a sugar loaf, the route through Marblehead Channel leads WNW, NW and then N, passing:
    NNE of Tinkers Ledge (42°29'·20N 70°48'·20W) and clear of a number of other unmarked shoals with depths of 4·3 to 7·3 m (14 to 24 ft), which extend up to 9 cables E of Marblehead Neck. These shoals break in E gales. Thence:
2   Clear of Fifteen Foot Rock (42°30'·25N 70°49'·11W), marked by FR Light Buoy (preferred channel to port), thence:
    NE of Marblehead Rock (42°30'·19N 70°49'·55W), high and bare, and:
    SW of Childrens Island (42°30'·70N 70°48'·85W), bare with several houses near its centre, thence:
3   NE of Marblehead Light (brown square framework tower, black top) (42°30'·32N 70°50'·02W), standing on the N point of Marblehead Neck. No 1 Buoy and 1MH Buoy (both port hand) mark the shoal ground off this point. Thence:
    W of Archer Rock (42°30'·74N 70°49'·41W), marked by No 2 Buoy (starboard hand), and E of the entrance to Marblehead Harbor (4.48), thence:
4   E of Chappel Ledge (42°31'·15N 70°49'·62W), marked on its E side by No 3 Light Buoy (port hand), which lies on the N side of the entrance to South Channel (4.38), and:

W of No 4 Light Buoy (starboard hand) (42°31′·29N 70°49′·10W), which marks the entrance to Eagle Island Channel (4.38), thence:

5 Between No 5 Buoy (port hand) (42°31′·66N 70°49′·78W) and No 6 Buoy (starboard hand), 4 cables ENE. These mark, respectively, the E side of Coney Ledge, and the W side of Eagle Bar.

Thence into Salem Sound, keeping clear of an obstruction, position approximate, and a wreck, (both 2 miles NNE).

Other Channels
(continued from 4.35)

4.38

1 **Eagle Island Channel** is a buoyed channel that leads SW from the entrance to Salem Channel to Marblehead Channel at the entrance to Marblehead Harbor, passing:

Between Bakers Island and Hardy Rocks (42°32′·18N 70°48′·00W). HR Beacon (red and white daymark) stands on Hardy Rocks. Thence:

2 Between No 5 Buoy (port hand) (42°31′·69N 70°47′·96W), marking Pope Head, a rugged rock, and No 6 Buoy (starboard hand), 2 cables W, which marks Cutthroat Shoal on the NE part of Eagle Bar, thence:

Between Brimbles (42°31′·26N 70°48′·47W), a rock which dries, marked by a beacon, and Eagle Island, a rocky island covered in grass. Thence into Marblehead Channel.

3 **Local knowledge** is required. This channel is used by craft bound for Marblehead Harbor from the NE.

Childrens Island Channel is entered from W of Halfway Rock (4.37) and leads NW between Satan Rock (42°30′·63N 70°48′·03W), above water and marked by No 6 Beacon, and Childrens Island (4.37). The channel then leads between Brimbles and No 7 Buoy (port hand), which marks Martin Rock, into Marblehead Channel SW of Eagle Island. Local knowledge is required.

4 **South Channel**, winding and in places less than ½ cable wide, leads W along the NW side of the peninsula which separates Marblehead Harbor from Salem Harbor. Local knowledge is required.

Salem Harbor

General information
4.39

1 **Position and function.** Salem Harbor (42°31′·31N 70°52′·61W) lies SW of Salem Sound, and is enclosed by Naugus Head at the NW end of Marblehead, and Winter Island, 4 cables NNW, on the E side of Salem Neck. The city of Salem lies on the W side of the harbour.

Salem is a port of entry and a small port, mainly handling coal and petroleum. In 2010 Salem had a population of 41 340.

Port Authority. New England Power Company.

Limiting Conditions
4.40

1 **Controlling depths.** See 4.27.

Tidal levels. Mean spring range about 2·9 m (9·5 ft); mean neap range about 2·1 m (6·9 ft). See information in *Admiralty Tide Tables*.

2 **Ice.** The head of Salem Harbor on the flats is usually closed by ice every winter during January and February, but ice formations rarely extend beyond Salem Terminal Wharf except in very severe winters.

North and NW winds enhance local ice formation; S and SW winds can carry light ice formations out to sea and E winds break up ice within the harbour and its approaches.

Arrival information
4.41

1 **Port operations.** Speed limit of 5 kn within the harbour limits. Berthing is undertaken during daylight hours on a rising tide.

Outer anchorages. Good anchorage may be obtained in 6 to 15 m (20 to 50 ft) in Salem Sound, clear of a gas pipeline, NE of a line drawn between Curtis Point (42°32′·90N 70°50′·75W) and the NE extremity of Eagle Island, 2 miles SE.

2 **Submarine pipeline.** A gas pipeline (4.31) is laid through Salem Sound.

Pilotage and tugs. See 4.28.

Traffic regulations. A safety and security zone surrounds Salem Terminal Wharf (4.44). See Appendix V for general rules covering safety and security zones.

Harbour
4.42

1 **General layout.** Berths are situated on the NW side of the harbour. Large vessels berth at the power station at the end of the dredged channel.

The head of Salem Harbor is shallow.

Natural conditions. See 4.33.

Directions
(continued from 4.36)

4.43

1 From Salem Sound the entrance channel to Salem Harbor leads SW, passing:

NW of Nos 13 and 15 Light Buoys (port hand), the latter marking Haste Shoal (42°32′·42N 70°50′·72W), thence:

SE of No 16 Light Buoy (starboard hand) (42°32′·24N 70°51′·14W), which marks the entrance to the dredged channel, thence:

2 Between two pairs of buoys and light buoys that mark the channel, and into the harbour.

Useful marks:

Fort Pickering Light (white conical tower, concrete base) (42°31′·59N 70°51′·99W), which stands on the SE point of Winter Island.

Chimney (42°31′·53N 70°52′·62W).

Berths
4.44

1 **Alongside berth.** Salem Terminal Wharf (42°31′·35N 70°52′·67W): 250 m in length, with dolphins, with a depth alongside of 10·4 m. Used to receive fuel oil and coal for the power station.

Other wharves are used only by small craft.

Port services
4.45

1 **Facilities:** hospital; oily waste disposal.

Supplies: fuel; water; provisions and stores.

Anchorages and harbours

Manchester Harbor
4.46

1 **General information.** Manchester Harbor (42°34′·22N 70°46′·40W), is principally a yachting centre with a small amount of commercial fishing. It is approached through Manchester Channel, a buoyed

Salem from ENE (4.42)
(Original dated 2005)
(Photograph - Reproduced by permission of Marblehead Sail & Power Squadron, United States Power Squadrons)

and dredged channel, leading from the NE part of Manchester Bay.

Beverly Harbor
4.47

1   **General information.** Beverly Harbor (42°32′·38N 70°53′·00W) is N of Salem Neck and lies at the W end of Salem Sound. It is formed by the confluence of North River, Danvers River and Bass River which flow into the head of the harbour from S, W and N respectively.

The harbour is entered between Juniper Point (42°32′·00N 70°51′·95W), the NE extremity of Salem Neck, and Hospital Point, 8 cables NNE. Beverly Channel, buoyed, leads from the entrance to the inner harbour.

2   A gas pipeline is laid through Danvers River and Beverly Harbor (see 4.31).

The city of Beverly stands on the N side of the harbour.

Local knowledge is required.

Marblehead Harbor
4.48

1   **General information.** Marblehead Harbor (42°30′·21N 70°50′·50W), 1 mile long and 3½ cables wide, lies to the SE of the Marblehead peninsula and is formed by Marblehead Neck, high and rocky, and Back Beach, a narrow ridge with a causeway connecting the neck with the mainland. It is entered between the N end of Marblehead Neck and Fort Sewall, 4 cables WNW.

Marblehead on the W and Marblehead Neck on the E are both important resorts, and the harbour is a very important yachting centre.

2   **Ice** rarely interferes with navigation in the harbour. However the winter of 2004 was the coldest in over 100 years leading to extensive ice formation. The harbour is used as a refuge when Gloucester, Salem or Lynn Harbors are ice-bound.

INSHORE WATERS BETWEEN MARBLEHEAD NECK AND BROAD SOUND

General information

Charts 2427, 1227, US Chart 13275 (see 1.16)
Description
4.49

1   This sub-section describes the foul ground between Marblehead Neck (42°29′·80N 70°50′·35W) and Phillips Point, 3 miles SW; Nahant Bay, and the N part of Broad Sound including Lynn Harbor.

Principal marks
4.50

1   Landmarks:
Water tower (conical top) (42°30′·05N 70°51′·88W).
Water tower (42°28′·67N 70°54′·61W).
Belfry (42°28′·20N 70°54′·62W).
Spire (42°28′·06N 70°54′·95W).
Spire (42°28′·05N 70°56′·45W).

2   Observatory dome (42°28′·08N 70°56′·79W).
Two concrete observation towers (42°25′·03N 70°54′·56W).
Concrete observation tower (42°25′·19N 70°55′·94W).

Major lights:
Bakers Island Light (42°32′·19N 70°47′·16W) (4.34).
Boston Light (42°19′·68N 70°53′·41W) (4.91).
The Graves Light (42°21′·91N 70°52′·15W) (4.91).

Marblehead Neck to Phillips Point

Description
4.51

1   Between Marblehead Neck (4.48) and Phillips Point (4.53) foul ground with islets and rocks, above and

below-water, extends 2½ miles S and SW of Flying Point, the S extremity of Marblehead Neck.

The outer edge of this area is marked by No 4 Light Buoy, which lies on the E side of Outer Breakers and Great Pig Rocks (42°27'·69N 70°50'·49W), which lie 1¾ miles S of Flying Point.

2   Tinkers Island and Ram Island, high and grassy, lie 5 cables SE and 1 mile SW, respectively, of Flying Point; Roaring Bull, Little Pig Rocks and Sammy Rock lie, respectively, 6 cables SSE and 7 cables and 1¼ miles SW of Flying Point. Roaring Bull is marked by No 2 Buoy and Sammy Rock by No 6 Buoy (starboard hand).

Channels
4.52
1   A number of channels lead through the dangers in this area. Some of these dangers are buoyed, but local knowledge is required to navigate in this area.

Nahant Bay

General information
4.53
1   Nahant Bay is entered between Phillips Point (42°27'·70N 70°53'·73W) and East Point (42°25'·15N 70°54'·20W), the E extremity of Nahant, a peninsula 2½ miles S.

Phillips Point is 15 m in height and rocky with houses along its shores. Dread Ledge, a rocky ledge which dries, extends 2½ cables S from Phillips Point and is marked by a beacon (starboard hand).

2   Nahant is a high peninsula about 1½ miles long with bluff seaward faces and on it stands the town of Nahant, a summer resort. Little Nahant, a high grassy head, lies on the E side of Long Beach, a strip of sand that connects it to the mainland. Egg Rock, a bird sanctuary, lies 8 cables NNE of East Point.

Berths
4.54
1   **Anchorage.** The bay, largely clear of dangers, is exposed to S and E winds and is seldom used except for temporary anchorage which may be obtained in 6 to 11 m (18 to 36 ft).

2   The usual anchorage is off Swampscott on the N shore SW or W of Lincoln House Point, a promontory which extends from the N shore 6 cables W of Phillips Point. A dangerous below–water rock, marked by No 2 Buoy (starboard hand) moored close S, lies ½ cable S of Lincoln House Point and rocks, with depths of 4·9 and 5·5 m (16 and 18 ft), lie 2 cables S and 3½ cables SSW, respectively, of the point.

Broad Sound

General information
4.55
1   Broad Sound is entered between East Point (42°25'·15N 70°54'·20W) and Deer Island, 5 miles SSW, and leads to Nahant Harbor on its NE side, to Lynn at its N end, to summer resorts on its W side and the N entrance to Boston Harbor at its S end.

The W side of the sound is very shallow with below–water and drying rocks extending up to 7½ cables offshore in places.

2   **Dangers.** Flip Rock, marked by FR Buoy (preferred channel to port) and Nahant Rock, marked by "1" Buoy (port hand), lie 9 cables SSE and 8 cables SW of Bass Point, the SW point of Nahant.

Safety and security zones. Within Broad Sound a safety and security zone of 500 yards radius has been established around any LNG vessel at anchor in the area.

3   Entry into these zones is prohibited unless previously authorized by the COTP.

See Appendix V for further information, definitions and general rules covering safety and security zones.

Nahant Harbor
4.56
1   Nahant Harbor (42°25'·20N 70°55'·30W) is a cove on the S side of Nahant.

Approaches. Shag Rocks, 4 cables SW of East Point, lie in the E approaches to the cove. No 2 Light Buoy (starboard hand) marks the limit of the shoal that extends S from the rocks.

Directions. From a position SW of Shag Rocks the track into the harbour leads between Joe Beach Ledge and The Spindle, which are marked, respectively, by DJB and DBR Buoys (both isolated danger). Shoal water lies between The Spindle and the W entrance point of the harbour, 3½ cables NW.

2   **Berths.** The town wharf, on the E side of the harbour near its head, has a depth alongside of 1·8 m. The Boston pilot boat lands and picks up pilots at this wharf.

Temporary anchorage in 6 to 7 m (18 to 24 ft) may be obtained off the town wharf.

Lynn Harbor
4.57
1   **General information.** Lynn Harbor is entered between Bass Point (42°25'·00N 70°57'·15W) and Revere Beach, 2 miles W. The harbour is obstructed by shoal ground and drying mud and sand flats, through which a channel leads to the industrial city of Lynn which, in 2010, had a population of 90 329.

Local knowledge is required as the channels in the harbour are narrow and winding.

2   **Controlling depths.** In 2006 the mid–channel controlling depth in the dredged channel to the turning basin was 5 to 5·2 m (16½ to 17 ft), thence depths of 4 to 4·8 m (13 to 16 ft) were available in the basin. For the latest depths the charts and port authority should be consulted.

Pilotage. Pilots may be obtained from the Boston pilot boat (4.86).

3   **Main approach channel,** dredged, is entered 7½ cables WNW of Bass Point, 1 mile N of Nahant Rock (4.55), and leads to a turning basin at the head of Lynn Harbor. The entrance to the channel is marked by No 2 Light Buoy (starboard hand) and thence by beacons, buoys and light buoys.

An extension of the main approach channel leads SW from the turning basin to the power station. In 1985 this channel had a controlling depth of 3 m (10 ft).

4   **Other channels.** Western Channel, entered 1 mile W of Bass Point, leads N from Broad Sound to General Edwards Bridge and Saugus River. Pines River is entered from Saugus River just W of the bridge. In 2006 this channel had a mid-channel controlling depth of 2·2 m (7·3 ft) to the bridge.

4.58
1   **Anchorage** may be obtained W of Bass Point, clear of a pipeline area in 9 to 2 m (30 to 5 ft).

Facilities: hospital; oily waste disposal.

Supplies: fuel; provisions; stores.

CHAPTER 4

BOSTON HARBOR AND APPROACHES

GENERAL INFORMATION

Chart 2492
Area covered
4.59

1 This section describes the outer approaches to Boston Harbor from the S end (40°35′·00N 69°00′·00W) of Nantucket Shoals to the entrance of Massachusetts Bay, N of Race Point (42°03′·74N 70°14′·58W). The inner approaches to Boston Harbor from the entrance of Massachusetts Bay to B Light Buoy (safe water) (42°22′·72N 70°46′·97W) in Boston Bay, and the inshore waters on the E side of Cape Cod, N of Monomoy Island (41°33′·90N 69°59′·63W), but excluding the channels between Nantucket Shoals and leading into Nantucket Sound (41°30′·00N 70°10′·00W) which are described in Chapter 5.

The section is arranged as follows:
 Outer approaches to Boston Harbor (4.61).
 Boston Harbor and inner approaches (4.77).

Regulations
4.60

1 No-discharge Zone (NDZ). See 4.2.

OUTER APPROACHES TO BOSTON HARBOR

General information

Charts 2492, 2489, 3096, 1227
Description
4.61

1 The outer approaches to Boston Harbor lead from SE of Nantucket Island (41°17′·15N 70°05′·62W) between Nantucket Shoals and Georges Bank (3.3), some 45 miles ENE, thence off the E and N side of Cape Cod into Massachusetts Bay.
Nantucket Shoals (5.19) is the name given to the numerous shoals that lie E and S of Nantucket Island.

2 **Cape Cod,** a long peninsula extending 30 miles E and 25 miles N, forms the E extremity of Massachusetts. The S portion of the cape between Cape Cod Canal (41°45′·73N 70°34′·19W) and Chatham (41°40′·80N 69°57′·20W) is known as the Upper Cape. This region is wooded and has numerous towns and villages. The N extension of the peninsula, sometimes called Hook of the Cape, forms the Lower Cape. It is well settled and is composed almost entirely of sand, with high sandhills and low level plains.

Designated Critical Habitat
4.62

1 See Appendix VIII.

Mandatory Ship Reporting System (MSR)
4.63

1 See *Admiralty List of Radio Signals Volume 6(5)* for details.

Traffic regulations
4.64

1 **Navigation Rules for US Inland Waters** do not apply to any of the waters described in this section.
Traffic separation scheme for the approaches to Boston leads NNW and W from the outer precautionary area. This TSS is IMO adopted and Rule 10 of *International Regulations for Preventing Collisions at Sea (1972)* applies. The two traffic lanes are separated by a 1 mile wide separation zone. This zone is marked by light buoys.

2 **Areas To Be Avoided.** An ATBA is established around Nantucket Shoals. See 5.6.
In order to significantly reduce ship strikes of the highly endangered North Atlantic right whale an ATBA, the limits of which are shown on the chart, is established in the Great South Channel, adjoining the NNW bound lane of the TSS, E of Davis Bank (4.68). Vessels of 300 gt or over should avoid the area between 1st April and 31st July.
An ATBA is established surrounding Northeast Gateway Deepwater Ports (4.71).

3 **Precautionary areas.** An outer precautionary area, centred 40°35′·00N 69°00′·00W, has been established SE of Nantucket Island. Traffic separation schemes for New York and Boston originate from the W and N sectors, respectively, of this area.
An inner precautionary area, centred 42°23′·00N 70°47′·00W, marked by B Light Buoy (safe water), and with a radius of 6·17 miles, has been established in the final approaches to Boston Harbor.

4 Mariners should navigate with particular care within these areas.
Safety and security zones extending 2 miles ahead, 1 mile astern and 500 yards on each side have been established around any LNG vessel while underway.
Entry into these zones is prohibited unless previously authorized by the COTP.
Safety zones are established surrounding Northeast Gateway Deepwater Ports (4.71).

5 For information concerning LNG vessels at anchor in Broad Sound see 4.55 and see Appendix V for further information, definitions and general rules covering safety and security zones.
North Atlantic right whale. See 1.51, *Admiralty List of Radio Signals Volume 6(5)* and Appendices VIII and X.

Natural conditions
4.65

1 **Tidal streams** off the N and E side of Cape Cod are comparatively weak, averaging not more than ½ to 1 kn in strength and running approximately parallel to the coast, but the time of strength alters rapidly with position.
Off Nauset Beach Light (41°51′·60N 69°57′·20W) the N-going stream attains its highest rate about 4¼ hours before HW Boston, off Chatham (41°40′·80N 69°57′·20W) the same rate is reached about 5½ hours before HW Boston.

2 Off Race Point (42°03′·74N 70°14′·58W) the tidal streams have a rate of about 2 kn in strength. The in-going stream sets S and the out-going stream N. Overfalls occur during heavy weather when wind and stream are opposed.
See Tidal Stream table on chart 2492 for tidal streams between Georges Bank and Nantucket Shoal.
Ice. See 1.108.

Directions
(continued from 3.7 and 5.8)

Principal marks
4.66

1 **Landmarks:**
 Tower (41°50′·58N 69°56′·85W), ex-Coast Guard station lookout tower.
 Radar dome (white) (42°02′·07N 70°03′·26W).
 Pilgrim Monument (42°03′·14N 70°11′·32W) (4.144).

Race Point Lighthouse (white tower, 12 m in height) (42°03′·74N 70°14′·58W).

2 **Major lights:**
Sankaty Head Light (41°17′·06N 69°57′·97W) (5.22).
Chatham Light (white conical tower, 15 m in height) (41°40′·28N 69°57′·01W).
Nauset Beach Light (white conical tower, red top, 15 m in height) (41°51′·60N 69°57′·20W).
3 Highland Light (white conical tower and dwelling, 20 m in height) (42°02′·37N 70°03′·66W), which stands on a bluff.
Race Point Light — as above.
Boston Light (42°19′·68N 70°53′·41W) (4.91).
The Graves Light (42°21′·91N 70°52′·15W) (4.91).

Other aids to navigation
4.67
1 **Racons:**
B Light Buoy (safe water) (42°22′·72N 70°46′·97W).
NC Light Buoy (safe water) (42°22′·53N 70°54′·30W).
See *Admiralty List of Radio Signals Volume 2*.

From south-east
4.68
1 From the outer precautionary area (4.64) the outer approaches to Boston lead NNW for 100 miles through a TSS, the centre of which is marked by light buoys (special), passing:
ENE of Asia Rip (40°48′·00N 69°20′·50W), Phelps Bank, Middle Rip and Fishing Rip, banks which form the SE part of Nantucket Shoal, thence:
2 ENE of Davis Bank (41°18′·00N 69°29′·20W), the E part of Nantucket Shoal, thence:
ENE of Nauset Beach Light (41°51′·60N 69°57′·20W) (4.66), thence:
ENE of Highland Light (42°02′·37N 70°03′·66W) (4.66). A stone crenellated tower, a red brick chimney and three radar domes stand on a ridge 5 cables S of the light.
Thence to a position N of Highland Light.

From east
4.69
1 From a position N of Highland Light the outer approaches to Boston lead W for 30 miles, through a TSS to the precautionary area in Boston Bay at the entrance to Boston Harbor, passing:
N of Race Point Light (4.66). An aero light stands 1½ miles NE.
Thence into the precautionary area in Boston Bay, marked on its E limit by BF-44013 ODAS Light Buoy (special).

(Directions for Boston Harbor continue at 4.91 and 4.97)

Inshore waters between Chatham and Race Point

Charts 2489, 3096
General information
4.70
1 **Topography.** From Chatham (41°40′·80N 69°57′·20W), at the SE extremity of Cape Cod, to Race Point 30 miles NNW, the shore of the E and N coast of the cape consists of sand dunes which are high in places. The highest stretch of the coast, which has elevations of 45 m (150 ft), lies between Nauset Beach Light (41°51′·60N 69°57′·20W) and Highland Light, 12 miles NNW.
2 There are no sheltered anchorages along this stretch of the coast, but there are breaks in the coast that lead to Chatham Harbor and Nauset Harbor, both of which harbours can only be used by small craft.

Northeast Gateway Deepwater Ports

General information
4.71
1 **Position and function.** Northeast Gateway Deepwater Ports (42°23′·80N 70°36′·30W) are located in an offshore area, 20 miles E of Boston. The ports are offshore terminals, designed to receive gas from dedicated LNG vessels. The gas is transferred ashore through either of two STL Buoys and submarine pipelines.

Limiting conditions
4.72
1 **Local weather and sea state.** Vessels will be required to leave the berth when wave heights exceed 8 m.

Arrival information
4.73
1 **Traffic regulations.** The following routeing measures are based on two overlapping circular areas, centred on 42°23′·94N 70°37′·01W and 42°23′·64N 70°35′·52W:
Area to be Avoided. An oval area, radius 1250 m from the two centre positions, may only be entered by vessels carrying out operations at the port.
Mandatory No Anchoring areas of radius 1000 m from the two centre positions.
2 **Safety zones** of radius 500 m from the two centre positions, may only be entered by vessels calling, or those assisting, at the port.
United States Deepwater Port Operations. Inbound vessels must submit a notice of arrival (NOA) as described in Appendix II.

Offshore moorings
4.74
1 The port consists of two STL Buoys acting as SBMs, in depths of 82 to 88 m (45 to 48 fm) submerged to a depth of about 24·6 m (80 ft) when not in use, that provide discharge facilities for visiting vessels. Multiple submerged moorings radiate to a distance of 6 cables from the buoys, which are connected by a flexible riser to a PLEM located on the seabed.
2 High pressure gas is transferred ashore through submarine pipelines.
A mooring buoy, for use by support vessels, lies about 1 mile W of the westerly STL Buoy.

Port services
4.75
1 **Supplies.** Provisions and stores by launch.

Neptune LNG Deepwater Port

General information
4.76
1 The Neptune LNG Deepwater Port (42°28′·20N 70°36′·20W), is 7 miles SSE of Eastern Point Light (4.18). This offshore terminal is designed to receive gas from dedicated LNG vessels, and pipe it ashore through two STL Buoys and submarine pipelines.

BOSTON HARBOR AND INNER APPROACHES

General information

Charts 1516, 1528
Position and function
4.77

1 Boston Harbor (42°21′·92N 71°02′·75W) lies on the W side of Massachusetts Bay. It is the largest seaport in New England and the busiest port on the US Atlantic coast NE of New York.

The city of Boston is the capital of the state of Massachusetts and is a port of entry. In 2010 it had a population of 617 594.

Port limits
4.78

1 Boston Harbor includes all tidal waters which lie within a line joining the S point of Deer Island (42°20′·70N 70°57′·25W) and Point Allerton, 3¾ miles SE.

Inner approaches and entrance channels
4.79

1 Numerous dangers extend up to 4 miles off the entrance to the harbour. A number of channels lead between these dangers.

Boston North Channel (4.93), entered 2 miles W of The Graves (42°21′·91N 70°52′·15W), is the main entrance channel used by deep–draught vessels visiting the port of Boston.

Boston South Channel (4.94), entered 1½ miles WSW of The Graves, is rarely used by deep–draught vessels.

2 **Hypocrite Channel** (4.95), entered 1¼ miles SW of The Graves, has several unmarked dangers. Local knowledge is required for its navigation and its use by large vessels is not recommended.

A channel (4.97), entered 2¾ miles S of The Graves and used by deep–draught vessels, leads to Nantasket Roads (4.104) and the port facilities in the S part of Boston Harbor.

Port Authority
4.80

1 Massachusetts Port Authority, One Harborside Drive, Suite 200S, East Boston, MA 02128-2909. Website: www.massport.com

Limiting conditions

Controlling depths
4.81

1 Boston North Channel (4.93) has a project depth of 12·2 m (40 ft) in the E part and 10·7 m (35 ft) in the W part.

Boston South Channel (4.94) has a project depth of 9·1 m (30 ft).

Boston Main Channel (4.96) has a project depth of 12·2 m (40 ft). The NE half of the channel from President Roads to Commonwealth Pier No 5 (4.108) and the SW half of the channel just NW of Commonwealth Pier No 5 to the Charles River has a project depth of 10·7 m (35 ft).

2 The channel (4.97), leading to Nantasket Roads (4.104) and the port facilities in the S part of Boston Harbor has a project depth of 10·7 m (35 ft).

For the latest depths the charts and port authority should be consulted.

Vertical clearance
4.82

1 Tobin Memorial Bridge (42°23′·10N 71°02′·85W), a fixed bridge which crosses the entrance to Mystic River, has a vertical clearance of 41·1 m (135 ft).

Two lifting bridges cross the lower part of Chelsea River, Andrew P. McArdle Bridge at the entrance and Chelsea Street Bridge, 8 cables upstream. The former has a vertical clearance of 6·1 m (20 ft) when closed and the latter has a vertical clearance of 2·7 m (9 ft) when closed and 25·3 m (83 ft) when open. A new

Tobin Memorial Bridge from S (4.82)

(Original dated 2009)

(Photograph - Peter Dixon)

lifting bridge at Chelsea Street is under construction (2012).

Tidal levels
4.83

1   Mean spring range about 3·1 m (10·2 ft); mean neap range about 2·3 m (7·5 ft). See information in *Admiralty Tide Tables*.

Ice
4.84

1   The channels of Boston Harbor are navigable throughout the year and ice rarely forms in the main channels. Occasionally during severe winters the greater part of the harbour is frozen, but shipping keeps the main channels open. Charles, Mystic and Chelsea Rivers and the minor passages in the harbour are sometimes frozen during severe winters. When ice is prevalent the buoys may be displaced or even carried away.

Arrival information

Vessel traffic service
4.85

1   A VTS is in operation for the control of shipping; see *Admiralty List of Radio Signals Volume 6(5)* for details. Positions of reporting points are shown on the chart.

Pilotage and tugs
4.86

1   **Pilotage** is compulsory for all foreign vessels and for US vessels under register in the foreign trade. Pilots should be contacted 2 hours in advance.

Pilots for Boston and Quincy board 1½ miles E of BG Light Buoy (safe water) (42°23'·45N 70°51'·48W). The pilot boats have black hulls and orange superstructure with the word "PILOT" on the side.

Tugs are available and normally meet vessels off Anchorage area No 1 (42°21'·30N 71°01'·70W) or No 2 (42°20'·30N 70°58'·30W).

Traffic regulations
4.87

1   **Navigation Rules for US Inland Waters** apply within a line joining the easternmost tower at Nahant (42°25'·41N 70°54'·55W) to B Light Buoy, thence to the E radio tower at Hull (42°16'·74N 70°52'·57W). See 1.44 and Appendix VII for further information.

Safety and security zones. Numerous safety and security zones have been established within Boston Harbor and its approaches. See Appendix V for further information, definitions and general rules covering safety and security zones.

Quarantine
4.88

1   Quarantine is enforced in accordance with the regulations of the US Public Health Service.

Quarantine anchorage. See 4.102.

Harbour

General layout
4.89

1   The main port facilities and berths for deep-draught vessels are situated in the NW part of Boston Harbor on Boston Main Channel (4.96) in South Boston, East Boston and Charlestown, and on Chelsea and Mystic Rivers.

Boston Harbour from SE (4.89)
(Original dated 2001)

(Photograph - Joseph R Melanson of www.skypic.com)

Deep-water berths, which are approached by two marked channels from Nantasket Roads (4.104), are also available on Weymouth Fore River (4.112) and in Town River Bay (4.112) in the SW part of the harbour.

2   Dorchester Bay and Quincy Bay indent the W part of the harbour, and Hingham Bay and Hull Bay indent the SE part of the harbour. These bays are only used by small craft.

Natural conditions
4.90
1   **Tidal streams.** See tables on charts.
Fog is prevalent throughout the year.
Climate information. See 1.139 and 1.141.

Directions for entrance channels
(continued from 4.13 and 4.69)

Principal marks
4.91
1   **Landmarks:**
Water tower (42°22'·07N 70°58'·06W), red, white and blue in colour, standing on Winthrop Head.
Tank (42°21'·29N 70°57'·56W), standing on Deer Island.
Chimney (42°20'·96N 70°57'·55W), standing on Deer Island.
2   Great Brewster (42°19'·95N 70°53'·78W), an island with a bluff at its N end.
Water tower (42°19'·32N 70°57'·91W), standing on Long Island.
Control tower (42°21'·95N 71°01'·11W) of Logan International Airport.
Dome (State House) (42°21'·49N 71°03'·82W).
3   Tower (42°18'·44N 70°53'·10W), turreted, standing on Point Allerton.
Radio towers (42°16'·75N 70°52'·55W), behind central part of Nantasket Beach.
Flagstaff (42°15'·00N 70°56'·52W), standing on Weymouth Great Hill.
Major lights:
4   Boston Light (white conical tower) (42°19'·68N 70°53'·41W).
The Graves Light (light grey conical granite tower) (42°21'·91N 70°52'·15W).

Other aids to navigation
4.92
1   **Racons:**
B Light Buoy (42°22'·72N 70°46'·97W).
NC Light Buoy (42°22'·53N 70°54'·30W).
See *Admiralty List of Radio Signals Volume 2*.

Boston North Channel
4.93
1   From the vicinity of B Light Buoy (safe water) (42°22'·72N 70°46'·97W) the route into Boston Harbor through Boston North Channel leads W and then SW, passing:
Between BG Light Buoy (safe water) (42°23'·45N 70°51'·48W) and No 5 Light Buoy (port hand), 9 cables S. The latter light buoy marks the extremity of shoal water that extends 8 cables NE from The Graves. Thence:
2   N of The Graves (42°21'·91N 70°52'·15W), a group of above and below–water rocks, from which a light (4.91) is exhibited, thence:
Clear of NC Light Buoy (safe water) (42°22'·53N 70°54'·30W), 4½ cables NE of the entrance to Boston North Channel, thence:
Into the dredged channel, marked by light buoys (lateral), thence:
3   Between Deer Island Light (red round tower, black round base) (42°20'·39N 70°57'·27W), standing 3 cables S of the S point of Deer Island, and Long Island Head. Long Island Head Light (white round tower) stands on the N point of Long Island.
Thence into Boston Main Channel (4.96).
(Directions for Boston Main Channel continue at 4.96)

Boston South Channel
4.94
1   From a position E of NC Light Buoy (42°22'·53N 70°54'·30W) the route through Boston South Channel leads SW and WSW, passing:
NW of No 1 Buoy (port hand) (42°21'·88N 70°53'·83W), thence:
NW of Commissioners Ledge, marked by No 3 Buoy (port hand) (42°21'·37N 70°54'·16W), thence:
2   Between No 5 Light Buoy (port hand), marking Devils Back (42°21'·10N 70°54'·38W), and No 6 Light Buoy (starboard hand) (9½ cables W), thence:

Boston Harbor - Approaches to North Channel - Deer Island from NE (4.93)
(Original dated 2012)

(Photograph - HMS Scott)

NW of Aldridge Ledge (42°20′·77N 70°54′·81W), marked by No 7 Buoy (port hand), thence:

Between No 9 Light Buoy (port hand) (42°20′·65N 70°55′·02W) and No 10 Light Buoy (starboard hand), 1½ cables NW. These light buoys mark the bend in the channel and its junction with Hypocrite Channel. Thence:

3   NNW of Nos 11 and No 13 Buoys (port hand), which mark the N side of Ram Head (42°20′·30N 70°55′·60W), a drying reef that extends N from Lovell Island, thence:

SSE of PR Light Buoy (preferred channel to starboard) (42°20′·49N 70°56′·23W) at the S end of Boston North Channel.

Thence into Boston Main Channel.

Hypocrite Channel
4.95

1   From a position S of The Graves (42°21′·91N 70°52′·15W) the track through Hypocrite Channel leads SW into the SW part of Boston South Channel, passing:

SE of Roaring Bulls (42°21′·31N 70°52′·90W), a group of rocks that partly dry, thence:

NW of Outer Brewster (42°20′·50N 70°52′·70W). Another island, Middle Brewster, lies 5 cables WSW. Thence:

2   Between Green Island (42°21′·17N 70°53′·50W) and Little Calf Island, 4 cables S, thence:

SE of Halftide Rock (42°20′·84N 70°54′·04W), marked by No 2 Buoy (starboard hand), thence:

SE and S of Aldridge Ledge (4.94), thence:

Between No 9 Light Buoy (port hand) (4.94), and No 11 Buoy (port hand), 3½ cables WSW, marking Ram Head Flats.

Thence into Boston South Channel.

Boston Main Channel
(continued from 4.93)
4.96

1   From a position S of Deer Island (4.93), Boston Main Channel leads W, NW and then N, to the junction of Chelsea and Mystic Rivers (42°23′·02N 71°02′·70W), passing:

Along the S side of President Roads Anchorage (4.102), thence:

Through a buoyed channel marked with light buoys (lateral) passing N of Spectacle Island (42°19′·60N 70°59′·20W) and SSW of Lower Middle bank (42°20′·35N 70°59′·70W), thence:

2   Between Castle Island (42°20′·30N 71°00′·65W), connected to South Boston by reclaimed land, and Governors Island (42°21′·00N 71°00′·50W) a low-lying peninsula at the S end of Logan International Airport, thence:

Between Boston and Charlestown on the W bank, and East Boston on the E.

Channel to Nantasket Roads
(continued from 4.69)
4.97

1   From a position S of B Light Buoy (safe water) (42°22′·72N 70°46′·97W) a channel leads WSW to Nantasket Roads (4.104), passing:

SE of Three and One–Half Fathoms Ledge (42°21′·23N 70°50′·70W), marked 2 cables SE by No 2 Light Buoy (starboard hand), thence:

NW of Thieves Ledge (42°19′·50N 70°50′·30W), marked on its N side by No 1 Light Buoy (port hand), and:

2   SE of Boston Ledge (42°20′·12N 70°51′·92W), marked by No 6 Buoy (starboard hand), thence:

N of Point Allerton (42°18′·60N 70°53′·00W), a headland backed by a hill with many buildings. No 3 Light Buoy (port hand) lies 5 cables N of the point and 3 cables E of the entrance to the dredged channel.

3   The dredged part of the channel, marked by light buoys and buoys (lateral), leads W, then WSW, for 2 miles, passing:

S of the shoals that lie between Little Brewster Island (42°19′·68N 70°53′·44W) and Georges Island, 1¾ miles WSW. Boston Light (4.91) is exhibited from Little Brewster Island. And:

Boston Inner Harbor - President Roads from ENE (4.97)
(Original dated 2003)

(Photograph - HMS Scott)

Castle Island *Monument*

Boston - Inner Harbor - Fort Independence from ESE (4.97)

(Original dated 2003)

(Photograph - HMS Scott)

Head of Approach Light Lane Jetty *Control tower*

E Boston - Inner Harbor from S (4.97)

(Original dated 2003)

(Photograph - HMS Scott)

4   N of the peninsula running W from Point Allerton to Windmill Point (42°18′·23N 70°55′·30W). Shoals and rocks extend 3 cables N from this coast.

Thence into Nantasket Roads.

Nantasket Roads to Weymouth Fore River
4.98

1   From the E end of Nantasket Roads a channel marked by light beacons, light buoys and buoys, leads S and SE to the port facilities in Weymouth Fore River (42°14′·85N 70°57′·85W), passing:

Through Hull Gut (42°18′·18N 70°55′·46W), which leads between Windmill Point and the NE extremity of Peddocks Island. WP Light (red and white chequered diamond on grey framework tower) stands on Windmill Point. Thence:

2   Between Prince Head (42°17′·14N 70°56′·30W) and Sheep Island. HR Light (red and white chequered diamond on grey framework tower on pile structure), marking the SE side of Harrys Rock, stands 3 cables NE of Prince Head. Thence:

WNW of Grape Island (42°16′·13N 70°55′·40W), thence:

SE of No 16 Light (red triangular framework tower on pile structure) (42°16′·05N 70°56′·11W).

Thence into the entrance of Weymouth Fore River.

Other channels

The Narrows
4.99

1   The Narrows (42°19′·80N 70°56′·10W) is a well marked channel that leads NW to President Roads from the inner end of the entrance channel to Nantasket Roads. It is bounded on the NE by Great Brewster Spit and Lovell Island and on the SW by Georges Island and Gallops Island.

Depths. The channel has a controlling depth of about 7·9 m (26 ft); however there are shoals of considerably lesser depth along the edges.

2   **Directions.** Because of strong currents and sharp turns it is necessary to navigate the ship by eye through the channel and care must be taken to prevent the ship being set off course by cross currents sweeping in and out of Black Rock Channel (42°19′·57N 70°55′·20W) and the channel between Gallops Island and Georges Island.

Nubble Channel
4.100

1   Nubble Channel (42°19′·70N 70°56′·94W), marked by buoys (lateral), leads NNW from Nantasket Roads to President Roads between Gallops Island and Long Island.

Depths. There is a least depth of about 4·3 m (14 ft) in the channel.

Sculpin Ledge Channel
4.101

1   Sculpin Ledge Channel (42°19′·30N 70°58′·45W) leads SW between Long Island and Spectacle Island. Sculpin Ledge lies in the S part of the channel. A fish haven, with a depth of 4·3 m (14 feet), lies in the channel, about 3 cables WNW of the conspicuous water tower on Long Island.

From the S part of Sculpin Ledge Channel a channel leads SE between West Head, the SW extremity of Long Island and Moon Head, passing under Long Island Viaduct, which has a vertical clearance of 15·5 m (51 ft).

2   **Depths.** Channels have sufficient depth to permit the navigation of vessels with a draught of 2·4 m (8 ft).

Directions. When navigating Sculpin Ledge Channel vessels should keep to the Long Island side of the channel, keeping clear of the fish haven described above, and round the SW extremity of this island at a distance of 1½ cables before passing under the channel span of Long Island Viaduct.

A patch with a swept depth of 1·5 m (5 ft) lies on the SE side of the viaduct.

Main anchorages

President Roads
4.102

1   General Anchorage No 2 (42°20′·20N 70°58′·60W) lies on the N side of Boston Main Channel between Deer Island and Governor Island Flats. It is the principal anchorage in Boston Harbor.

Anchorage may be obtained in 8 to 20 m (26 to 64 ft), good holding.

Quarantine anchorage. The N part of the area is used as a quarantine anchorage.

Explosives anchorage. The COTP may authorise this area to be used as an explosives anchorage, in which case vessels may have to move at short notice.

Long Island Anchorage
4.103

1   General Anchorage No 3 (42°19′·20N 70°56′·90W) lies between Gallops Island and Georges Island on the E and Long Island on the W.

Anchorage may be obtained in up to 10 m (34 ft), good holding. The anchorage is sheltered from E winds. Berths in this anchorage are allocated by the COTP.

Nantasket Roads
4.104

1   Explosives anchorage No 5 (42°18′·20N 70°56′·70W) is situated SW of Georges Island (42°19′·20N 70°55′·70W) at the inshore end of the entrance channel to Nantasket Roads.

Good anchorage may be obtained in up to 15 m (49 ft), clear of a submarine gas pipeline (4.31), and SE of a line drawn between the S extremity (42°19′·04N 70°55′·69W) of Georges Island and 4P Light (red triangle on grey framework tower on pile structure) (2 miles SW).

Castle Island Anchorage
4.105

1   General Anchorage No 4 (42°19′·60N 71°00′·80W), for small vessels, lies in the approach to Dorchester Bay.

Anchorage may be obtained in 2 m (7 ft), but there is deeper water in its S part.

Inner Harbor
4.106

1   **Anchorage** in the Inner Harbor is only permitted in anchorage area No 1 on the N side of Boston Main Channel, 1 mile NW of Governors Island (42°21′·00N 71°00′·50W). This anchorage has depths of 7 to 11 m (23 to 35 ft).

Caution. A tunnel crosses Boston Main Channel from a position 1 cable E of Pier 5 (42°20′·98N 71°02′·04W), passing between anchorage areas No 1. Three other tunnels cross the channel about 1 mile farther NW. Mariners should not anchor within an area extending 1 cable each side of the tunnels.

Alongside berths

General
4.107

1   The port of Boston has over 100 piers and wharves. The majority of deep-draught berths are situated on Boston Main Channel in South Boston, East Boston and Charlestown and on Mystic and Chelsea Rivers. There are also deep-draught berths on Weymouth Fore River and Town River Bay in the S part of the harbour.

2   Container traffic is handled at Conley Container Terminal in South Boston and most of the deep-water oil and bulk terminals are on Chelsea and Mystic Rivers.

All of the large general cargo terminals are owned or leased by Massachusetts Port Authority.

A summary of the principal terminals in the various complexes are given as follows.

South Boston
4.108

1   Main berths, from S to N, are:

Conley Marine Terminal (42°20′·53N 71°01′·00W). Container terminal with four berths. Nos 11-12 with a combined length of 622 m with a depth alongside of 13·7 m are the largest.

2   **Boston Marine Industrial Park** (42°20′·70N 71°01′·75W). Nine berths. Berths 1 and 2; length 294 m with a depth alongside of 10·7 m. Berths 1 to 3 handle bulk cement.

Black Falcon Cruise Terminal (42°20′·60N 71°01′·80W), a passenger terminal for cruise vessels, situated at Berths 7 to 9 with a combined length of 640 m with a depth alongside of 10·7 m is the largest.

A safety and security zone surrounds the passenger terminal.

3   **Massport Marine Terminal Wharf** (42°20′·86N 71°01′·48W): 244 m in length with a depth alongside of 10·7 m. US Government vessels only.

Commonwealth Pier No 5 (42°21′·10N 71°02′·40W). SE and NW side; 366 m in length with a depth alongside of 10·1 to 11·6 m. Passenger terminal for cruise vessels.

Charlestown
4.109

1   Only berth still operational:

Mystic Pier No 1 (42°22′·83N 71°02′·84W); S side: length 273 m. N side: 205 m with depths alongside both sides of 10·7 m.

Mystic River
4.110

1   Berths on N bank:

    Chelsea Terminal Wharf (42°23′·10N 71°02′·67W); 171 m in length with a depth alongside of 10·7 m handling petroleum products.

Conley Marine Terminal from NE (4.108)

(Original dated 2009)

(Photograph - Peter Dixon)

2   Everett Terminal Wharf (42°23′·28N 71°03′·50W). Three berths handling petroleum products; Berths 3 and 4 with a combined berthing space of 290 m with depths alongside of 10·7 to 12·2 m are the largest.

   LNG Terminal (42°23′·31N 71°03′·74W); 305 m of berthing space with a depth alongside of 10·9 m. A safety and security zone of 366 m (400 yards) radius surrounds any LNG vessel at this berth.

3   Scrap Metal Wharf (close W of LNG terminal wharf); 250 m of berthing space, with dolphins, with a depth alongside of 12·2 m.

   Berths on S bank:
   Gypsum Wharf (42°23′·03N 71°02′·96W); 150 m in length with a depth alongside of 8·2 m.

4   Boston Autoport (42°23′·07N 71°03′·25W); 335 m in length with a depth alongside of 12·2 m. Vehicle import/export terminal.

   Cement Terminal (42°23′·03N 71°03′·60W); 186 m in length with a depth alongside of 9·4 m.

Chelsea River
4.111

1   Berths on N Bank:
   Coastal Oil New England Terminal (42°23′·15N 71°02′·04W); handling petroleum products, with 192 m of berthing space with depths alongside of 5·5 to 7·3 m.

   Gulf Oil Terminal (42°23′·58N 71°01′·05W); handling petroleum products, with 216 m of berthing space with a depth alongside of 11·0 m.

2   Berths on S Bank:
   Conoco-Phillips Terminal (42°23′·09N 71°01′·48W); handling petroleum products, with 183 m of berthing space with a depth alongside of 11·6 m.

   Three terminals (42°23′·85N 71°00′·70W); handling petroleum products, with berthing lengths 168 to 183 m with depths alongside of 3·0 to 11·3 m.

Weymouth Fore River and Town River Bay
4.112

1   There are two deep–draught facilities on Weymouth Fore River and two on Town River Bay.

   Largest berth on Town River. Sprague Energy Terminal Wharf (42°15′·21N 70°59′·06W), 213 m of berthing space, with dolphins, with a depth alongside of 10·7 m.

   Largest berth on Weymouth Fore River. Citgo Petroleum Corp., Braintree Terminal Wharf (42°14′·17N 70°58′·07W), 213 m of berthing space, with dolphins, with a depth alongside of 11·6 m.

Port services

Repairs
4.113

1   Facilities are available for carrying out all types of hull and engine repair to vessels of all sizes. The largest repair facility is located in South Boston.

   Docking facilities. There are several dry docks and patent slips available in the port. South Boston yard has two dry docks, the largest of which has a length of 358 m, width of 38·7 m and depth over the sill of 10·9 m. A patent slip in the port can handle vessels up to 55 m in length and 1000 tonnes.

Other facilities
4.114

1   Hospitals; oily waste disposal.

Supplies
4.115

1   Fuel; fresh water; provisions and stores.

CHAPTER 4

SOUTH PART OF MASSACHUSETTS BAY

GENERAL INFORMATION

Chart 3096
Area covered
4.116

1 This section describes the coastal waters between Strawberry Point (42°15′·20N 70°46′·10W) and Gurnet Point (42°00′·22N 70°36′·04W), and the waters of Cape Cod Bay.
It is arranged as follows:
Strawberry Point to Gurnet Point (4.122).
West side of Cape Cod Bay (4.127).
East and south side of Cape Cod Bay (4.139).

Routes
4.117

1 Recommended Two-Way Whale Avoidance Routes, as shown on the chart, have been established in Cape Cod Bay to reduce the likelihood of ship strikes of endangered North Atlantic right whales. All vessels are encouraged to use the recommended routes when passing into or out of Cape Cod Bay.

2 A recommended Two-Way Whale Avoidance Route has also been established for vessels passing to and from Provincetown and Cape Cod Canal.

Cape Cod Bay
4.118

1 Cape Cod Bay, which forms the main part of the S part of Massachusetts Bay, is entered between Gurnet Point (42°00′·22N 70°36′·04W) and Race Point (42°03′·74N 70°14′·58W), 16 miles ENE. The bay is bounded on the E and S by the peninsula of Cape Cod (4.61) and on the W by the mainland of Massachusetts.

2 **Ice.** Plymouth, Barnstable and Wellfleet, and other shallow harbours in Cape Cod Bay are usually closed to navigation during a part of every winter. Instances are on record of this ice, and the ice which forms in the shallower parts of the bay in severe winters, being driven by winds out into the bay, where it masses into heavy fields or belts, sometimes 3 m (10 ft) or more in thickness, rendering navigation of parts of the bay unsafe or impracticable at times.

3 The movement of the ice depends largely on the winds, the tidal streams having little or no apparent effect. N winds drive the ice down to the S end of the bay.

North Atlantic right whale
4.119

1 See 1.51, *Admiralty List of Radio Signals Volume 6(5)* and Appendices VIII and X.

Mandatory Ship Reporting System (MSR)
4.120

1 See *Admiralty List of Radio Signals Volume 6(5)* for details.

Regulations
4.121

1 No-discharge Zone (NDZ). See 4.2.

STRAWBERRY POINT TO GURNET POINT

General Information

Charts 1227, 3096 (see 1.16)
Description
4.122

1 Between Strawberry Point (42°15′·20N 70°46′·10W) and Gurnet Point (4.118), 17 miles SSE, the coast is generally low—lying and marshy and the harbours at the mouth of the rivers flowing into this stretch of the coast, are shallow and only available to small craft.

Stellwagen Ledges, which front the coast between Strawberry Point and Cedar Point, consist of numerous rocks and below—water ledges. The outer ledges, mostly unmarked, lie over 1 mile offshore and have depths of 2·1 to 5·5 m (7 to 18 ft), with surrounding deep water.

2 The coast between Scituate Harbor (42°12′·10N 70°43′·25W) and Green Harbor, 8 miles SSE, is fronted by several shoals with depths 9·1 m (30 ft), which extend up to 4½ miles offshore.

NDZ's (No Discharge Zones) have been established in Cohasset Harbor (4.125), Scituate Harbor (4.126) and New Inlet (42°10′·00N 70°42′·50W).

Directions

Principal marks
4.123

1 **Landmark:**
Monument (42°00′·84N 70°40′·94W) (4.133).
Major lights:
Gurnet Point Light (42°00′·22N 70°36′·04W) (4.133).
Race Point Light (42°03′·74N 70°14′·58W) (4.66).

Approaches to Cape Cod Bay
4.124

1 From the inner precautionary area (4.64) the recommended route into Cape Cod Bay (4.117) leads SE to a further precautionary area, then S, passing:
NE of No 21 Light Buoy (port hand) (42°16′·58N 70°42′·36W), which marks a dangerous wreck and a 6·4 m (21 ft) patch at the outer limit of the foul ground that extends 4 miles NE from Strawberry Point, thence:

2 E of No 6 Light Buoy (starboard hand) (42°05′·60N 70°36′·43W), marking Farnham Rock, thence:
W of Race Point (42°03′·74N 70°14′·58W) (4.70), thence:
Clear of a dangerous wreck (42°00′·66N 70°31′·99W), thence:
E of Gurnet Point (42°00′·22N 70°36′·04W) and into Cape Cod Bay.

Useful mark:
Water tower (pointed top) (42°12′·03N 70°45′·32W).

Caution is necessary when navigating in the vicinity of Race Point, especially at night and in low visibility by day, owing to the numerous fishing vessels which operate in the vicinity.

*(Directions for Plymouth Bay continue at 4.133,
and for the N approach to
Cape Cod Canal at 4.130)*

Anchorages and harbours

Cohasset Harbor
4.125

1 **Description.** Cohasset Harbor (42°14′·96N 70°46′·70W), shallow, is situated on the W side of Scituate Neck and is entered between Gull Island, 1½ cables N of Strawberry Point and Brush Islet, 1 mile E. The harbour is used by numerous yachts and fishing craft.

Ice usually closes the harbour for about 2 months in the winter.

Anchorage may be obtained in the outer harbour 5 cables W of Strawberry Point in 2 to 3 m (6 to 10 ft).

Scituate Harbor
4.126

1 Scituate Harbor (42°12'·10N 70°43'·25W) is entered between Cedar Point and First Cliff and is used mostly by yachts and fishing craft.

WEST SIDE OF CAPE COD BAY

General information

Charts 3096, 2891
Description
4.127

1 The W side of Cape Cod Bay lies between Gurnet Point (42°00'·22N 70°36'·04W), the S extremity of Duxbury Beach, a low sandy tongue; and the E entrance to Cape Cod Canal, 14 miles SSE.

The N part of this stretch of coast as far S as Manomet Point (41°55'·57N 70°32'·50W) is indented by Duxbury Bay and Plymouth Bay.

The S part, as far as Peaked Cliff, 7 miles S, consists of a line of bluffs backed by wooded hills.

2 The E entrance to Cape Cod Canal (41°46'·70N 70°29'·40W) is situated in the SW part of Cape Cod Bay. The entrance is protected on its N side by a breakwater, with a light (4.130) at its seaward extremity, which extends 3½ cables ENE from the shore, and on its S side by a short breakwater which extends parallel to the N breakwater.

Vessel traffic service
4.128

1 A VMRS is in operation for the control of shipping. See *Admiralty List of Radio Signals Volume 6(5)*.

Pilotage
4.129

1 Pilotage is compulsory for Cape Cod Canal. Pilots board 5 cables SE of CC Light Buoy (41°48'·88N 70°27'·65W). See *Admiralty List of Radio Signals Volume 6(5)* for details.

Directions
(continued from 4.124)

Principal marks
4.130

1 Landmark:
   Monument (42°00'·84N 70°40'·94W) (4.133).
   Major lights:
   Race Point Light (42°03'·74N 70°14'·59W) (4.66).
   Gurnet Point Light (42°00'·22N 70°36'·04W) (4.133).
   Cape Cod Canal Breakwater Head Light (red round tower) (41°46'·79N 70°29'·39W).

Gurnet Point to Cape Cod Canal
4.131

1 From a position E of Gurnet Point (42°00'·22N 70°36'·04W) in the entrance to Cape Cod Bay, the recommended route to the E entrance of Cape Cod Canal continues S, passing:
   E of a dangerous wreck (41°56'·24N 70°29'·47W), thence:
   E of No 12 Light Buoy (starboard hand) (41°55'·11N 70°30'·37W), marking Mary Ann

Cape Cod Canal - East Entrance (4.131)
(Original dated 2002)

(Photograph - Robert P. David - Reproduced by permission of Cape Cod Sail & Power Squadron, United States Power Squadrons)

Rocks, two rocks which dry about 1·5 m (5 ft) and which are covered by the red sector (323°-352°) of Gurnet Point Light. A dangerous wreck lies about 2 cables S of the buoy. Thence:

2 E of Stellwagen Rock (41°53'·79N 70°31'·03W), thence:

E of a dangerous wreck (41°50'·00N 70°29'·97W), thence:

Clear of CC Light Buoy (safe water) (41°48'·88N 70°27'·65W), thence:

NW of No 1 Light Buoy (port hand) (41°47'·07N 70°28'·07W), which marks the limit of an extension of the shore bank.

Leading lights:

Front light (red rectangle, white stripe on framework tower) (41°46'·29N 70°30'·54W).

3 Rear light (similar structure) (244 m from front light)

The alignment (244·9°) of these lights leads through the canal entrance between the breakwaters, passing:

NNW of No 3 Light Buoy (port hand) (41°46'·81N 70°28'·93W) (3 cables E).

Useful marks:

Manomet Hill (41°55'·60N 70°35'·40W), thickly wooded.

4 Water tower (41°53'·00N 70°32'·04W), standing on Indian Hill.

Water tower (41°47'·84N 70°31'·81W), standing on Sagamore Beach.

Chimney (41°46'·20N 70°30'·59W) of a power station, standing 1 cable SW of Cape Cod Canal front leading light.

(Directions for Cape Cod Canal from W are given at 5.141)

Plymouth Bay

Chart 3096, US Chart 13253 (see 1.16)
General information
4.132

1 **Description.** Plymouth Bay, the approach to Plymouth Harbor (4.136), Duxbury Bay (4.137) and Kingston Bay (4.138), is entered between Gurnet Point (42°00'·22N 70°36'·04W) and Rocky Point (41°57'·00N 70°35'·00W), 3¼ miles S.

2 The bay is bounded on the N by Saquish Neck connecting Gurnet Point to Saquish Head, a bare hill, 18 m in height, which lies 1¾ miles WSW. On the W the bay is bounded by Plymouth Beach, a narrow neck that extends 2½ miles NW from the mainland. The bay is divided by Browns Bank, which partly dries and extends 2½ miles NE from Plymouth Beach.

3 **Depths.** In 2004 the channel through Plymouth Bay had a controlling depth of 3·7 m (12¼ ft) to the SE side of the anchorage basin. For the latest controlling depths the charts and port authority should be consulted.

Traffic regulations. A safety and security zone, close inshore, surrounds the Pilgrim Nuclear Power Plant (41°56'·65N 70°34'·65W). For details see Appendix V.

4 **Tidal streams** between Gurnet Point and Duxbury Pier Light attain a rate of 1½ kn. They generally follow the direction of the channel, but the out–going stream sets S and E across Browns Bank, and the in–going stream sets N and W inside Saquish Head and sweeps strongly round Duxbury Pier Light.

Local knowledge is necessary.

Directions
(continued from 4.124)
4.133

1 **Landmarks:**

Gurnet Point Light, or Plymouth Light (white 8-sided pyramidal tower on dwelling) (42°00'·22N 70°36'·04W).

Standish Monument (89 m in height) (42°00'·84N 70°40'·94W), which stands on Captains Hill, 61 m in height, on the peninsula between Duxbury Bay and Kingston Bay.

2 Tower (41°57'·65N 70°43'·37W), standing on Monks Hill.

Manomet Hill (41°55'·60N 70°35'·40W) (4.131).

Flagstaff (41°56'·22N 70°34'·88W), 8 cables NE of Manomet Hill.

Major light:

Gurnet Point Light — as above.

Track
4.134

1 **Entry.** From a position about 1 mile ESE of Gurnet Point a buoyed channel leads 3 miles in a generally WSW direction through Plymouth Bay, passing between the shoals that front Gurnet Point and Saquish Neck to the N and Browns Bank to the S.

The entrance to the channel, marked by No 2 Buoy (starboard hand) and No 1 Light Buoy (port hand), is 5 cables SE of Gurnet Point.

2 At the W end of the channel the track passes S of Duxbury Pier Light (brown conical tower, white top) (41°59'·25N 70°38'·92W), which stands at the junction of the three channels leading to Duxbury Bay, Kingston Bay and Plymouth Harbor.

Anchorage
4.135

1 Anchorage may be obtained by small vessels, during S winds, in 6 to 10 m (20 to 33 ft), sand, in Warren Cove in the S part of Plymouth Bay.

Anchorage may also be obtained, when waiting for favourable tide or weather, in 7 m (22 ft) on the N side of the approach channel SE of Saquish Head.

Cowyard (41°59'·70N 70°39'·00W) provides the best anchorage in the area. See 4.137.

Plymouth
4.136

1 **General information.** Plymouth Harbor (41°58'·00N 70°39'·20W) is entered between the N end of Plymouth Beach and High Cliff, 1¼ miles W. The port of Plymouth stands on the SW side of the harbour and in 2010 had a population of 7 494. It is a port of entry but is mainly used by fishing vessels and pleasure craft.

Ice often closes Plymouth Harbor from early January to late February. W winds tend to carry the ice out in fields; NW winds sometimes bring in ice, but S winds carry it out.

2 For effect of ice on anchorages, see 4.137.

Directions. From a position W of Duxbury Pier Light (41°59'·25N 70°38'·92W) the white sector (195·5°-199·5°) of No 12 Light (red triangle on red framework tower, black round base) (41°58'·79N 70°39'·40W) leads through the N part of the channel, marked after No 12 Light through to the harbour by buoys and a light beacon.

Anchorage. In 2004 the anchorage basin in Plymouth had depths of 1 to 2 m (5 to 8 ft) in it. See also 4.135 and 4.137.

³ **Berths.** There are two alongside berths, the largest with a depth alongside of 3·6 m.
Facility. Hospital.
Supplies: fuel; water and stores.

Duxbury Bay
4.137

¹ **General information.** Duxbury Bay is bounded on the NE by Duxbury Beach, on the SE by Saquish Neck (42°00'·30N 70°37'·40W) and on the W by the mainland. It is composed of sand and mud flats, mostly drying, through which several channels wind.

The town of Duxbury lies in the NW part of the bay.

² **Anchorage** may be obtained in 6 to 11 m (20 to 36 ft) in Cowyard, a stretch of water that lies between Duxbury Pier Light and Clarks Island, 1 mile N. This is the best anchorage for vessels waiting to enter Plymouth.

Caution. It is not a safe anchorage when there is ice in the harbour and in these conditions vessels should anchor S or E of Saquish Head.

Kingston Bay
4.138

¹ **General information.** Kingston Bay is entered between High Cliff (41°58'·58N 70°40'·97W) and Goose Point, the W point of Duxbury Bay, 1½ miles N. The bay has numerous flats and has little importance as a harbour.

Local knowledge is advised.

EAST AND SOUTH SIDE OF CAPE COD BAY

General information
Chart 3096
Description
4.139

¹ The E and S sides of Cape Cod Bay lie between Race Point (42°03'·74N 70°14'·58W) and the entrance to the Cape Cod Canal, 21 miles SW.

The bay is bounded on its E and S side by the peninsula of Cape Cod, composed almost entirely of sand, with high bare sandhills and low, nearly level plains. The peninsula is well populated.

Route
4.140

¹ A recommended Two-Way Whale Avoidance Route has been established for vessels passing to and from Provincetown (4.142) and Cape Cod Canal (5.133).

Ice
4.141

¹ For general information on ice conditions in Cape Cod Bay, see 4.118.

Provincetown Harbor and approaches

Chart 3096, US Chart 13249 (see 1.16)
General information
4.142

¹ **Provincetown Harbor** (42°02'·52N 70°10'·63W), formed by the bend in the N end of the hook of Cape Cod, lies between Long Point (42°01'·99N 70°10'·12W), the NE end of the hook, and the coast 2 miles NE.

The harbour is one of the best on the Atlantic coast of the United States, having a large anchorage area with excellent holding ground; small vessels and fishing vessels shelter in it from gales from any direction.

² The town of Provincetown, on the NW side of the harbour, is the site of the first landing of the *Mayflower* and is the base of numerous fishing, lobster and pleasure boats.

Ice
4.143

¹ Ice forms in Provincetown Harbor in severe winters only, and then only for short periods. Instances are on record of fields of heavy ice from the shallow harbours of Cape Cod Bay being driven N by the wind into the harbour, closing it to navigation for a few days. Such

Provincetown from SSW (4.142)
(Original dated 2004)

(Photograph - Joseph R Melanson of www.skypic.com)

conditions are rare and usually the harbour is not obstructed by ice.

Principal marks
4.144
1   **Landmarks:**
      Race Point Light (42°03′·74N 70°14′·58W) (4.66).
      Pilgrim Monument (42°03′·14N 70°11′·32W). A stone tower, 77 m in height, from which obstruction lights are exhibited.
      Radar dome (white) (42°02′·07N 70°03′·26W)
      Spire (41°59′·90N 70°03′·28W) of a large church at Truro.
    Major light:
      Race Point Light — as above.

Directions
4.145
1   **Approach from north-west.** From a position about 11 miles WNW of Race Point, in the precautionary area (4.124), the recommended route (4.117) to Provincetown Harbor leads SE, passing:
      SW of Wood End Light (white square tower) (42°01′·28N 70°11′·61W), thence:
      SW of No 1 Light Buoy (port hand) (42°00′·37N 70°11′·56W), moored close SSW of a dangerous wreck, position approximate.
2   Thence the approach leads NE through waters clear of charted dangers, passing:
      SE of No 3 Light Buoy (port hand) (42°02′·04N 70°09′·67W), which marks the limit of a bank extending E from Long Point. A light (white square tower) stands on the point.
      Thence to the anchorages and the inner harbour.
    Caution. See 4.124.

Anchorage
4.146
1   Excellent anchorage may be obtained SE and E of Long Point in depths of up to 18 m (60 ft).
    Anchoring is prohibited in the approach fairway, 90 m (300 ft) wide, which leads NW from a point 3 cables E of Long Point to the piers at Provincetown, and within 90 m (300 ft) of the piers.

Alongside berths
4.147
1   **Town pier,** known as MacMillan Wharf, extends 400 m SE from the waterfront in the NW part of the harbour and has a depth alongside of 4 m at its head.
    Berths at this pier are allocated by the Harbour Master, whose office is at the end of the pier.
    Breakwater, 4 cables long and parallel to the shore, lies 1½ cables off the town pier. Nos 4 and 5 Lights (red triangle and green square, respectively, on framework towers) stand at the W and E ends, respectively, of the breakwater.

Supplies
4.148
1   Provisions and stores can be obtained in the town.

Anchorages and harbours

Chart 3096, US Chart 13250 (see 1.16)
Wellfleet Harbor
4.149
1   **General information.** Wellfleet Harbor (41°54′·00N 70°02′·60W) is entered between Jeremy Point, the S extension of Great Island which forms the W side of Wellfleet Harbor, and the mainland 2½ miles E.
    The harbour is almost filled with shallow flats, between which is a buoyed channel, dredged in its N part, leading into the inner harbour.
    The harbour, protected by a breakwater, is only used by small fishing craft and yachts.
2   The town of Wellfleet stands at the head of the harbour.
    Ice usually closes the harbour for part of each winter.
    Restricted area, around a dangerous wreck (41°49′·88N 70°02′·62W) used as an aerial bombing target, lies to the S of the approaches to Wellfleet. No vessel may enter within a radius of 5 cables of the wreck, which has DJ Light Buoy (isolated danger) moored 70 m W. For details see Appendix VI.
3   **Anchorage** may be obtained in the outer harbour NE of Smalley Bar in 4 to 6 m (12 to 21 ft), but is somewhat exposed to W winds.
    In N gales anchorage is possible on the lee side of Billingsgate Shoal (41°51′·20N 70°07′·80W) in 4 to 13 m (12 to 42 ft).

Chart 3096, US Chart 13251 (see 1.16)
Barnstable Harbor
4.150
1   Barnstable Harbor (41°43′·00N 70°17′·40W) is entered 10½ miles E of the entrance to Cape Cod Canal (5.133), between Beach Point, the E extremity of Sandy Beach, and the coast 1 mile SE. BH Light Buoy (safe water) is moored 1¾ miles N of Beach Point.
    The harbour is the approach to the town of Barnstable, situated 1¾ miles SW of Beach Point, and is used by local fishing craft and yachts.
    Ice generally obstructs the harbour during part of the winter.

NOTES

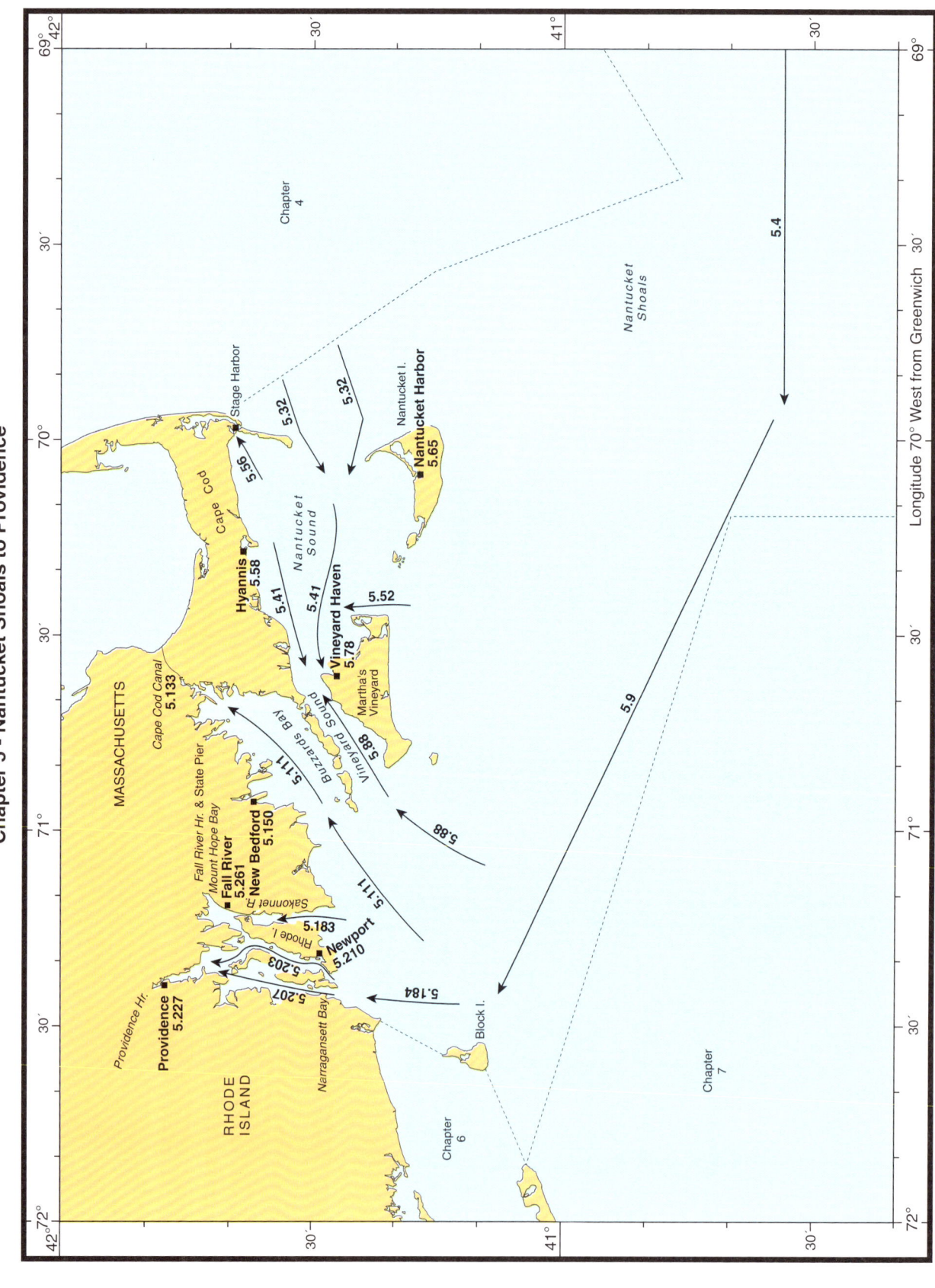

CHAPTER 5

NANTUCKET SHOALS TO PROVIDENCE

GENERAL INFORMATION

Chart 2860
Scope of the chapter
5.1

1　The area covered by this chapter comprises the S side of Cape Cod together with Martha's Vineyard and Nantucket Island, Vineyard and Nantucket Sounds, Buzzards Bay and approaches, and Narragansett Bay. The description includes Cape Cod Canal (5.133) and the ports of New Bedford (5.150) and Providence (5.227).
　　The chapter is arranged as follows:
2　　Nantucket Shoals to Rhode Island Sound (5.3).
　　Nantucket Sound and Vineyard Sound (5.24).
　　Buzzards Bay, Cape Cod Canal and New Bedford Harbor (5.110).
　　Narragansett Bay and adjacent waters (5.172).

Recommended routes
5.2

1　Recommended routes for deep-draught vessels, tugs and barges have been established in Buzzards Bay and Narragansett Bay. Pleasure craft, fishing vessels and other small vessels should exercise caution in and around these routes and should monitor VHF channels for information concerning vessels transiting these routes.

NANTUCKET SHOALS TO RHODE ISLAND SOUND

GENERAL INFORMATION

Chart 2860
Area covered
5.3

1　This section describes Nantucket Shoals (41°02'·00N 69°40'·00W) and the approach to them from seaward; also described is the approach from the Shoals to Rhode Island Sound.
　　The section is arranged as follows:
　　Seaward approach to Nantucket Shoals (5.4).
　　Seaward approach from Nantucket Shoals to Rhode Island Sound (5.9).
　　Nantucket Shoals (5.19).

SEAWARD APPROACH TO NANTUCKET SHOALS

General information

Charts 2670, 2492
Routes
5.4

1　Transatlantic routes from Europe, which terminate in the vicinity of Nantucket Shoals, are described in *Ocean Passages for the World*.

Maritime topography
5.5

1　The edge of the continental shelf, situated 30 to 50 miles seaward of Georges Bank (3.3) and Nantucket Shoals (5.19), is indented by several submarine gorges or canyons.
　　Lydonia Canyon (40°27'·00N 67°40'·00W) lies 75 miles S of Georges Shoal (41°40'·00N 67°44'·00W) and Atlantis Canyon (39°52'·00N 70°14'·00W) lies 85 miles S of Nantucket Island (41°17'·15N 70°05'·62W). Between these two canyons, from E to W, lie Gilbert Canyon (40°22'·00N 67°52'·00W), Oceanographer Canyon (40°23'·00N 68°09'·00W), Welker Canyon (40°12'·00N 68°31'·00W), Hydrographer Canyon (40°08'·00N 69°03'·00W) and Veatch Canyon (39°57'·00N 69°37'·00W).

2　By echo sounding along the charted 180 m (100 fm) depth contour in this area, a vessel's position can be verified with some accuracy when crossing these canyons.

Traffic regulations
5.6

1　**Precautionary area**, centred 40°35'·00N 69°00'·00W, has been established SE of Nantucket Shoals.
　　Traffic separation scheme which forms part of the precautionary area leads W from the W side of this area. Another TSS leads NNW from the N side of the precautionary area. Both schemes are IMO adopted and Rule 10 of *International Regulations for Preventing Collisions at Sea (1972)* applies.

2　**Area To Be Avoided.** Because of the great danger of stranding, and for reasons of environmental protection, all vessels carrying dangerous cargoes of oil or hazardous materials, and all other vessels of more than 1000 gt, should avoid the area of Nantucket Shoals.
　　The limits of the area are shown on the chart.

Tidal streams
5.7

1　See tidal stream tables on charts.

Directions

Seaward approach
5.8

1　From the vicinity of 40°30'·00N 67°35'·00W the seaward approach to Nantucket Shoals leads generally W, passing:
　　S of Little Georges Shoals (41°04'·00N 68°13'·00W), the SW part of Georges Bank (3.3), thence:
　　Through the precautionary area (centred 40°35'·00N 69°00'·00W).
　　Caution. When passing Georges Bank continuous sounding is essential for safety owing to the irregularity of the depths.

*(Directions continue for
approaches to Boston at 4.66,
for Rhode Island Sound at 5.13,
and for New York at 7.13)*

SEAWARD APPROACH FROM NANTUCKET SHOALS TO RHODE ISLAND SOUND

General information

Charts 2860, 2890
Route
5.9

1   The seaward approach to Rhode Island Sound, the area of water lying between Block Island (41°10'·50N 71°35'·00W) (5.184) and Martha's Vineyard, 35 miles ENE, leads through waters clear of charted dangers, between 25 and 40 miles SW of Nantucket Island (5.16) and Martha's Vineyard (5.18).

Traffic regulations
5.10

1   **Precautionary area**, centred 41°06'·00N 71°23'·40W with a radius of 5·4 miles, has been established SE of Block Island. Traffic separation schemes for Narragansett Bay (5.185) and Buzzards Bay (5.115) originate from the N and NE sectors, respectively, of this area.

Mariners are advised to exercise extreme caution when navigating within this area.

North Atlantic right whale. See 1.51, *Admiralty List of Radio Signals Volume 6(5)* and Appendices VIII and X.

Submarine exercise areas and transit lanes
5.11

1   Submarines, both surfaced and dived, exercise frequently in the area between the meridians of 69°30'·00W and 72°15'·00W in the approaches to New York and Rhode Island Sound. See *The Mariner's Handbook*.

Lanes used by submerged submarines run S from Block Island for 80 miles and thence run E. Positions of these lanes are shown on charts of the US Ocean National Survey, and the times that the lanes are used are published in local Notice to Mariners. When the lanes are in use by submarines, ships should not tow submerged objects within the lanes.

Unexploded ordnance
5.12

1   Areas of unexploded ordnance, the positions of which are shown on the chart, exist in this area.

Directions
(continued from 5.8)

Principal marks
5.13

1   **Major lights:**
   Gay Head Light (41°20'·92N 70°50'·10W) (5.93).
   Block Island South–east Light (41°09'·17N 71°33'·07W) (5.186).

Other aid to navigation
5.14

1   **Racon:**
   Light Buoy A in the centre (41°06'·01N 71°23'·37W) of the precautionary area.
   See *Admiralty List of Radio Signals Volume 2*.

East approach to Rhode Island Sound
5.15

1   From the vicinity of the W end (40°33'·00N 70°14'·00W) of the TSS, S of Nantucket Shoals, the approaches to Rhode Island Sound lead NW for about 60 miles to the precautionary area SE of Block Island, passing:
   Clear of a dangerous wreck, position approximate, (40°41'·20N 70°23'·07W), thence:
   NE of a dangerous wreck, position approximate, (40°52'·85N 71°13'·22W).

(Directions continue for Buzzards Bay at 5.118 and for approaches to Narragansett Bay at 5.186 Directions for inshore route off S coast of Long Island are given at 7.20, for Vineyard Sound at 5.93 and for Block Island Sound at 6.14)

South shores of Nantucket Island and Martha's Vineyard

Charts 2489, 2456
Nantucket Island
5.16

1   The S coast of Nantucket Island has no harbours and is only frequented by local fishermen. Old Man Shoal (41°13'·00N 69°59'·00W) extends 6 miles SSW from the SE part of the island and Miacomet Rip (41°14'·00N 70°06'·00W) extends 1¼ miles offshore from midway along the island.

Fishing stakes, which may be submerged, are likely to be met within the areas adjacent to the coast.

2   **Useful marks:**
   Aero Light (41°15'·42N 70°03'·81W) and dome, 2 cables WSW, at Nantucket Memorial Airport.
   Radio tower (41°15'·06N 70°07'·80W).

Muskeget Channel
5.17

1   Muskeget Channel (5.52) leads E of Wasque Point (5.18) into Nantucket Sound.

Martha's Vineyard
5.18

1   The S coast of Martha's Vineyard, for 13 miles W from Wasque Point (41°21'·00N 70°27'·30W), is low and backed by ponds.
   Useful marks:
   Water tower (41°22'·69N 70°31'·15W), at Edgartown.
   Wasque Shoal Light (metal tripod with mast) (41°19'·50N 70°34'·00W), S of Edgartown Great Pond.
   Aero Light (41°23'·39N 70°36'·67W), at Martha's Vineyard Airport.

NANTUCKET SHOALS

General information

Chart 2489
Description
5.19

1   Nantucket Shoals (41°02'·00N 69°40'·00W) is the name given to the numerous shoals which lie E and S of Nantucket Island. The shoals extend 24 miles E, 41 miles SE and 29 miles S from Sankaty Head Light (41°17'·06N 69°57'·97W).

The shoals are liable to shift and their depths vary from 0·9 to 9 m (3 to 30 ft), with channels of depths of 18 m (60 ft) or more between those farthest offshore.

Area To Be Avoided
5.20

1 An ATBA (5.6) has been established encompassing Nantucket Shoals.

Tidal streams
5.21

1 Tidal streams over Nantucket Shoals and their vicinity are rotary, and there is no slack water. They have a maximum rate of 2½ kn, but vary from place to place and can reach a velocity of 5 kn around the sides of shoals.

Principal mark
5.22

1 **Major light:**
   Sankaty Head Light (white tower, red band, 21 m in height) (41°17'·06N 69°57'·97W), standing on Sankaty Head, a high bluff.

Caution
5.23

1 Nantucket Shoals should be entirely avoided by deep–draught vessels on account of the treacherous currents.

Local knowledge is necessary for shallow–draught vessels to navigate the channels which pass through the various shoals.

NANTUCKET SOUND AND VINEYARD SOUND

GENERAL INFORMATION

Charts 2489, 2456
Area covered
5.24

1 This section describes Nantucket Sound (41°27'·00N 70°10'·00W) and Vineyard Sound (41°27'·00N 70°44'·60W) (5.88), which lie between the S coast of Cape Cod and Elizabeth Islands (5.88) on the N, and Nantucket Island and Martha's Vineyard, with their off–lying islands and shoals, to the S.

The section is arranged as follows:
East approaches to Nantucket Sound (5.32).
Nantucket Sound (5.41).
Vineyard Sound and SW approaches (5.88).

Route
5.25

1 The sounds are a thoroughfare for numerous medium-draught coastwise vessels and pleasure craft, this route being more direct for vessels bound along the coast than the route outside Nantucket Shoals.

Depths
5.26

1 Vessels of 7·3 m (24 ft) draught can pass through the sounds, and with good local knowledge a depth of 9 m (30 ft) can be obtained through them.

Hazards
5.27

1 **Concentration of traffic.** Caution is necessary in the navigation of Nantucket and Vineyard Sounds owing to the large number of vessels which are often encountered in the narrow parts of the channels.

Natural conditions. Caution is necessary when navigating Nantucket and Vineyard Sounds owing to the numerous shoals, and thick fog at certain seasons. The tidal streams are strong, in some places set directly on the shoals, and their times and rates vary considerably from place to place. Most of the shoals are steep–to and the depths are very irregular, so soundings alone cannot be depended upon for warning of too close an approach to danger.

Pilotage
5.28

1 Pilotage is compulsory in Nantucket Sound and Vineyard Sound for all vessels of 350 gt or more and tows with barges carrying 6000 barrels or more of petroleum cargoes.

Pilots board in the vicinity of 41°23'·30N 71°21'·20W, 4 miles SSE of the entrance to Narragansett Bay (5.172), or 5 cables SE of CC Light Buoy (41°48'·88N 70°27'·65W), off the E entrance to Cape Cod Canal.

Traffic regulations
5.29

1 **North Atlantic right whale.** See 1.51, *Admiralty List of Radio Signals Volume 6(5)* and Appendices VIII and X.

Natural conditions
5.30

1 **Tidal streams.** See Tidal Stream tables on the charts and 5.27.

Ice interferes little with navigation in the sounds in mild winters. In severe winters pack ice accumulates, but powered vessels can normally force their way through it. During NW winds, which prevail in winter, the passage along the N shore of Nantucket Sound will be clear when other parts of the sound are unsafe.

2 **Local weather.** Fog is liable to occur in the sounds at any time but is more frequent from April to October than during the remainder of the year. It occurs more frequently with E and S winds; NW winds clears it away, SW winds are usually accompanied by haze.

Aids to navigation
5.31

1 The direction of aids to navigation is as if proceeding from E to W.

EAST APPROACHES TO NANTUCKET SOUND

General information

Chart 2489, US Chart 13244 (see 1.16)
Description
5.32

1 Nantucket Sound is entered from the E between Monomoy Point (41°32'·90N 70°00'·20W), the S extremity of Monomoy Island, and Great Point (41°23'·56N 70°02'·97W), the low, sandy tip of a long beach extending N from Nantucket Island.

Route
5.33

1 The E entrance to Nantucket Sound passes through Monomoy Shoals (41°30'·00N 69°55'·00W), numerous and detached, which extend 6 miles E and 10 miles SE from Monomoy Point. These shoals are subject to change in depth and position.

Two principal channels lead into Nantucket Sound from E.

2 **Pollock Rip Channel** (41°33′·00N 69°56′·60W) (5.38) and Butler Hole (41°31′·20N 70°00′·80W) (5.38), which lead through the N part of Monomoy Shoals, form the most direct route for vessels from N of Cape Cod to Nantucket Sound.

Great Round Shoal Channel (41°25′·80N 69°45′·90W) (5.39) is entered 10 miles SE of Pollock Rip Channel and passes between Monomoy Shoals and Nantucket Shoals. It is used by many large fishing vessels.

Depths
5.34
1 **Pollock Rip Channel** has a least charted depth of 6·7 m (22 ft).

Great Round Shoal Channel. The buoyed channel has a controlling depth of about 8·2 m (27 ft), but is subject to change.

Local knowledge
5.35
1 Due to the numerous shoals existing in the channel, mariners should seek local knowledge before entering Pollock Rip Channel or Butler Hole.

Tidal streams
5.36
1 **Pollock Rip Channel.** At its E entrance the NE–going stream sets about 055° and the SW–going stream 225°, or at an angle of about 20° to the axis of the channel, at a rate of 2 kn at springs and 1¼ kn at neaps. See also Tidal Stream table on chart.

At No 8 Light Buoy (41°32′·72N 69°58′·93W) the strength of the NE and SW streams set, respectively, in an 035° and 225° direction, with average rates of 2 and 1¾ kn. The strength of the NE stream occurs about 5 hours before, and that of the SW stream about 1 hour after, HW at Boston.

2 Off the S end of Handkerchief Shoal (5.38), the strength of the E and W streams set, respectively, about 080° and 250°, at an average rate of about 2¼ kn. The strength of the E stream occurs about 4¼ hours before, and that of the W stream about 2 hours after, HW at Boston.

Great Round Shoal Channel. See Tidal Streams table on chart.

Directions

Principal marks
5.37
1 **Landmark:**
Disused lighthouse (41°33′·55N 69°59′·62W), standing 1 mile NNE of Monomoy Point.
Major lights:
Chatham Light (41°40′·28N 69°57′·01W) (4.66).
Sankaty Head Light (41°17′·06N 69°57′·97W) (5.22).

Pollock Rip Channel and Butler Hole
5.38
1 From the vicinity of 41°33′·00N 69°51′·00W, Pollock Rip Channel and the channel through Butler Hole lead W and WSW, passing:
S of a dangerous wreck (41°35′·43N 69°52′·51W), position approximate, thence:
2 S of No 4 Light Buoy (starboard hand) (41°33′·24N 69°54′·57W), moored between the NW end of Broken Part of Pollock Rip and the SE end of Bearse Shoal, thence:
NNW of Pollock Rip (41°32′·47N 69°55′·55W), marked on its N side by No 5 Buoy (port hand), thence:
SSE of Bearse Shoal (41°33′·20N 69°57′·64W), marked on its S side by No 6 Light Buoy (starboard hand).

3 Thence the track leads SW through Butler Hole, passing:
NW of No 9 Light Buoy (port hand) (41°32′·11N 69°59′·45W), thence:
SE of No 10 Light Buoy (starboard hand) (41°31′·85N 70°00′·51W), which marks the SE side of Shovelful Shoal. An obstruction and a dangerous wreck, position approximate, lie between this shoal and Monomoy Point. Thence:

4 NW of the W end of Stone Horse Shoal, marked by No 11 Buoy (port hand) (41°30′·30N 69°58′·80W), thence:
SE of Handkerchief Shoal (41°30′·85N 69°03′·64W), marked on its SE side by Nos 12 and 14 Buoys (starboard hand). An isolated shoal patch, with a depth of 4·3 m (14 ft), lies about 7 cables W of No 14 Buoy.
Thence into Nantucket Sound.

5 **Cautions.** Small craft and fishing vessels should avoid the area during foggy weather, since large vessels may be encountered in this channel.

Owing to the distance of Monomoy Shoals from land and the strong tidal streams that set over them, navigation through them in foggy weather is hazardous.

6 Attention is drawn to the dangerous wrecks which are in the vicinity of the channel.

The channel is liable to change frequently and the buoys are moved as necessary.

(Directions continue at 5.48)

Great Round Shoal Channel
5.39
1 From the vicinity of 41°26′·00N 69°43′·00W, Great Round Shoal Channel leads WSW, passing:
Between Orion Shoal (41°27′·00N 69°49′·00W) and Great Round Shoal on the N side of the channel, and McBlair Shoal, on the S. The channel is marked by light buoys (lateral). Thence:

2 N of a dangerous wreck (41°24′·00N 69°53′·99W) position approximate, lying on the S side of the channel, thence:
Between No 10 Light Buoy (starboard hand) (41°24′·83N 69°54′·44W) and No 9 Buoy (port hand), 1 mile SSW; a dangerous wreck lies 4 cables W of No 9 Buoy.
Thence the track leads NW, passing:

3 NE of Point Rip shoal (41°24′·75N 70°00′·00W), marked on its NE end by No 13 Light Buoy (port hand).
Thence the track leads W to the vicinity of No 17 Light Buoy (41°26′·58N 70°11′·19W) and into Nantucket Sound, passing:
N of No 15 Light Buoy (port hand) (41°26′·20N 70°05′·08W).

4 **Caution.** Great Round Shoal and Great Round Shoal Channel are subject to continual change.
Useful mark:
Great Point Light (white tower) (41°23′·41N 70°02′·90W).

(Directions continue at 5.48)

Anchorages

Anchorages
5.40

1   Anchoring is permitted in the following areas:

Anchorage K. East of Monomoy Island out to 3 miles from the coast, between Chatham (41°40'·77N 69°57'·22W) and the SE part of Monomoy Island.

Anchorage J. East of the charted pecked line running from about 41°41'N 69°48'W to No 17 Light Buoy, 22 miles SW, and thence SSE to the shore.

2   **Prohibited anchorage.** Anchoring is prohibited in or near the fairways of Pollock Rip Channel and Butler Hole and also near any of the aids to navigation, as local vessels navigate from buoy to buoy in poor visibility.

NANTUCKET SOUND

General information

Charts 2489, 2456, US Charts 13237, 13229 (see 1.16)

Description
5.41

1   Nantucket Sound (41°27'·00N 70°10'·00W) lies between the S coast of Cape Cod to the N and Nantucket Island and part of Martha's Vineyard to the S. It has a length of 28 miles between its E entrances on the N side of Nantucket Shoals and its W entrance at the NE entrance to Vineyard Sound. The sound is between 6 and 22 miles wide.

Shoals. There are numerous shoals in the sound with well marked channels between. Unlike the shoals in the E approach and entrance, those in the sound are stable.

Routes
5.42

1   Two well marked channels lead from E between the shoals in Nantucket Sound to the NE end of Vineyard Sound. Both channels unite N of West Chop (41°28'·85N 70°35'·99W).

Main Channel leads through the centre of the sound S of Horseshoe Shoal (41°30'·50N 70°21'·50W). This channel is used by most vessels passing through the sound.

2   **North Channel** leads along the N side of the sound and is entered either side of Bishop and Clerks (41°34'·45N 70°15'·01W) and passes N of Horseshoe Shoal (5.49) and L'Hommedieu Shoal (5.51). This channel is used mostly by vessels bound to places on the N side of Nantucket Sound and by vessels passing through that sound during N winds or in winter, when the prevailing NW winds keep the N shore clear of ice.

Caution. Passage of this channel should not be attempted at night or without local knowledge.

Depths
5.43

1   **Main Channel** has a least depth of 9·4 m (31 ft), but the draught of vessels using this channel seldom exceeds 7·3 m (24 ft).

North Channel has a least depth of about 4·9 m (16 ft).

Pilotage
5.44

1   See 5.28.

No-discharge Zones
5.45

1   Numerous No-discharge Zones (NDZs) have been established throughout Nantucket Sound. See 1.41.

Anchorages
5.46

1   Anchoring is permitted in the following areas:

Anchorage I. In the N part of Nantucket Sound N of the Main Channel and extending from Monomoy Point (41°32'·90N 70°00'·20W) to Nobska Point (41°30'·95N 70°39'·31W).

2   **Anchorage G.** In the S part of Nantucket Sound W of the Nantucket Harbor entrance channel, and S of a line joining No 21 Light Buoy (5.49) to Oak Bluffs (41°27'·59N 70°33'·58W).

Anchorage H. In a triangular area centred 2 miles N of Cape Poge (41°25'·17N 70°27'·14W). Squash Meadow, a shoal marked by buoys, lies at the W end of this area.

3   **Prohibited anchorage.** Anchoring is prohibited in or near the fairway of Main Channel and also near any of the aids to navigation, as local vessels navigate from buoy to buoy in poor visibility.

Fish traps
5.47

1   Numerous fish traps are located in Nantucket Sound, particularly along the S shore of Cape Cod. These areas may be marked by private lights.

Directions
(continued from 5.38 and 5.39)

Principal marks
5.48

1   **Landmarks:**

Tower (41°36'·58N 70°15'·98W). A disused lighthouse standing on the S extremity of Point Gammon, wooded.

Water tank (41°37'·38N 70°26'·42W), on W side of Cotuit Bay. A second prominent water tank stands 4 cables N.

2   Spire (41°16'·94N 70°05'·94W), in Nantucket (5.65).

Church tower (41°23'·43N 70°30'·91W), in Edgartown.

Dome (41°27'·34N 70°33'·61W), in Oak Bluffs.

Major lights:

Chatham Light (41°40'·28N 69°57'·01W) (4.66).

Barnstable Airport Light (41°39'·98N 70°17'·12W).

Main Channel
5.49

1   From the vicinity of No 17 Light Buoy (41°26'·58N 70°11'·19W), Main Channel is entered between Halfmoon Shoal and Tuckernuck Shoal and leads W, passing:

S of Halfmoon Shoal (41°27'·90N 70°13'·90W), marked on its S side by No 18 Light Buoy (starboard hand), thence:

2   Between No 20 Light Buoy (starboard hand) (41°27'·55N 70°16'·93W), marking the S side of Horseshoe Shoal, and No 21 Light Buoy (port hand), 8 cables SSW, marking the N side of Cross Rip Shoal, thence:

Clear of a wreck (41°27'·14N 70°18'·09W), thence:

S of MT Light (monopole metal tower on pile supported platform marked MT) (41°28'·33N 70°18'·88W), thence:

N of No 21A Light Buoy (port hand) (41°26'·91N 70°25'·20W), thence:

Clear of a wreck (41°27'·66N 70°26'·06W), noting the shoal patch 7 cables N with a least depth of 8·8 m (29 ft), and another wreck 1 mile NW, and:

3   N of Cape Poge, a bare precipitous bluff at the N extremity of Chappaquiddick Island. Cape Poge Light (white conical tower) (41°25'·17N 70°27'·14W) stands on this headland.

Thence the track leads WNW, passing:

SSW of No 22 Light Buoy (starboard hand) (41°28'·36N 70°29'·01W), moored SE of Hedge Fence shoal; a wreck lies close SSW. The red sector of Nobska Point Light (263°-289°) (5.86) covers Hedge Fence and the patches W of it bordering the N side of the channel. Thence:

4   NNE of East Chop (41°28'·22N 70°34'·05W) and West Chop, 1½ miles WNW, the entrance points to Vineyard Haven (5.78). Both of these headlands terminate in a high wooded bluff and are prominent from the sound. Lights stand on each headland. And:

Useful marks:

East Chop Light (41°28'·22N 70°34'·05W) (5.82).
West Chop Light (41°28'·85N 70°35'·99W) (5.82).

North Channel
5.50

1   North Channel is entered from E, either S or N of Bishop and Clerks, a shoal awash in the middle, the central part marked by a light (white and red round tower) (41°34'·45N 70°15'·01W).

South entrance. From a position SSE of Bishop and Clerks the S entrance channel leads NW then W, passing:

2   Between No 2 Light Buoy (starboard hand) (41°33'·36N 70°14'·62W) and Broken Ground, 1 mile W, thence:

SW of Bishop and Clerks Light, thence:
S of No 4 Buoy (starboard hand) (41°34'·47N 70°15'·97W), which marks the W side of Bishop and Clerks.

North entrance. From a position E of Bishop and Clerks the N entrance channel leads W, passing:

3   N of No 1 Light Buoy (port hand) (41°34'·73N 70°14'·12W), marking the NE side of Bishop and Clerks, thence:

N of Bishop and Clerks Light, thence:
S of Hallets Rock (41°35'·52N 70°15'·76W). A 3·9 m patch lies 2½ cables ESE of this rock. Thence:

4   S of HH Light Buoy (safe water) (41°35'·96N 70°17'·37W), which marks the approach to Hyannis Harbor (5.58), thence:

Across West Southwest Ledge (41°35'·50N 70°17'·65W), thence:
SE of No 2 Buoy (starboard hand) (41°35'·38N 70°18'·98W), then joining the S entrance channel.

5.51

1   From a position W of Broken Ground (5.50) North Channel continues W, passing:

N of Horseshoe Shoal (41°31'·70N 70°23'·00W), marked on its N side by No 5 Light Buoy (port hand), thence:

Between No 7 Buoy (port hand) (41°32'·31N 70°23'·11W) and No 8 Light Buoy (starboard hand), 7 cables W, which mark, respectively, the NW side of Horseshoe Shoal and the E end of Wreck Shoal, thence:

2   NNW of Eldridge Shoal (41°31'·70N 70°25'·30W), marked on its N side by No 9 Buoy (port hand), thence:

S of No 10 Light Buoy (starboard hand) (41°31'·96N 70°26'·40W), S of Succonnesset Shoal, thence:

S of a 4·5 m (15 ft) shoal (41°31'·90N 70°27'·12W), thence:

3   N of a patch with a depth of 2·7 m (9 ft) (41°31'·67N 70°28'·09W) off the NE extremity of L'Hommedieu Shoal, marked on its N side by a buoy (preferred channel to starboard). The red sector (263°-289°) of Nobska Point Light (5.86) covers L'Hommedieu Shoal with the exception of the N extremity of a shoal spit that extends from the middle of the N side of the shoal. Thence:

4   S of the coastal bank which extends up to 6 cables offshore between Succonnesset Point and Falmouth Harbor (41°32'·70N 70°36'·30W) (5.86). The limits of the bank are marked by Nos 12 and 2 Light Buoys and No 14 Buoy (starboard hand). Thence:

N of the shoal spit (41°31'·80N 70°31'·05W) that extends N from the middle of the N side of L'Hommedieu Shoal. No 13 Buoy is moored 4 cables S. Thence:

Clear of a dangerous wreck (41°31'·66N 70°34'·00W), thence:

5   N of No 15 Buoy (port hand) (41°31'·27N 70°34'·46W), marking the W end of L'Hommedieu Shoal, thence:

N of No 17 Buoy (port hand) (41°31'·08N 70°36'·69W), which marks the W end of a ridge that extends W from L'Hommedieu Shoal.

Vineyard Sound can be entered W of No 15 Buoy or No 17 Buoy, or clear of a detached shoal (41°31'·20N 70°38'·15W), which has a least depth of 4 m (13 ft) and is marked on its N side by FW Buoy (preferred channel to port).

Muskeget Channel

Chart 2456, US Chart 13233 (see 1.16)

Description
5.52

1   Muskeget Channel is an opening 6 miles wide that leads into the S part of Nantucket Sound between the dangerous shoals that extend SW, W and NW of Muskeget Island (41°20'·20N 70°18'·20W), and Chappaquiddick Island.

Buoyage. The channel is marked by buoys and a light buoy.

Local knowledge is required to navigate this channel due to the very strong tidal streams and shifting shoals that make navigation dangerous.

Tidal streams
5.53

1   Tidal streams are strong, with an average rate of 3¾ kn on the in–going stream and 3¼ kn on the out–going stream. A rate of 5 kn is reached in the channel at times. See tide table on chart.

Directions
5.54

1   From the vicinity of MC Light Buoy (safe water) (41°15'·01N 70°26'·17W) the channel leads N, passing:

Clear of a dangerous wreck (41°16'·25N 70°26'·28W), thence:

E of No 1 Buoy (port hand) (41°17'·52N 70°26'·74W), thence:

W of Mutton Shoal (41°19'·60N 70°24'·40W), marked by No 2 Light Buoy (starboard hand), and:

E of Wasque Shoal (41°19'·80N 70°26'·50W), steep–to, marked on its E side by No 3 Buoy (port hand) thence:

E of No 5 Buoy (port hand) (41°22'·33N 70°26'·26W), which marks the coastal bank that extends from the E side of Chappaquiddick Island, thence:

W of the S extremity of Hawes Shoal (41°24'·80N 70°24'·20W), marked by No 4 Buoy (starboard hand), thence:

W of No 6 Buoy (starboard hand) (41°26'·02N 70°25'·26W), which marks the NW extremity of Hawes Shoal and the N end of the channel.

Thence into Nantucket Sound.

(Directions for Main Channel are given at 5.48)

Chatham Roads

Chart 2489, US Chart 13229 (see 1.16)
General information
5.55

Chatham Roads (41°39'·00N 70°01'·20W) are situated at the NE end of Nantucket Sound between Common Flat, which extends 1½ miles NW from the N part of Monomoy Island, and the shoal ground extending S from the N shore at Harwich Port, 2½ miles NW.

The roads are the approach to Stage Harbor and the summer resort of Chatham.

Ice closes the harbour for short periods each winter.

Climate information. For Chatham see 1.143.

Directions
5.56

Landmarks:
Stage Harbor Light (tower) (41°39'·50N 69°59'·07W), at SE end of Harding Beach.
Dome (41°39'·41N 69°57'·53W), of National Weather Service installation on Morris Island.
Chatham Light (41°40'·28N 69°57'·01W) (4.66).

Major light:
Chatham Light — as above.

Entry. From a position S of Kill Pond Bar (41°37'·80N 70°07'·30W), the alignment (063°) of Stage Harbor Light and Chatham Light leads to SH Light Buoy (safe water), 8 cables WSW of Stage Harbor Light.

Anchorage
5.57

Anchorage may be obtained in Chatham Roads for vessels up 5·5 m (18 ft) draught in 6 to 9 m (21 to 30 ft), soft bottom.

Caution. In SW gales this anchorage is insecure for small vessels.

Hyannis Harbor and adjacent waters

Charts 2489, 2456, US Chart 13229 (see 1.16)
General information
5.58

Hyannis Harbor (41°37'·81N 70°17'·22W), on the N side of Nantucket Sound, is entered between Point Gammon (5.48) and Hyannis Point, 2½ miles WNW. Lewis Bay, with depths of 0·6 to 3·6 m (2 to 12 ft), extends NE from Hyannis Harbor and has the summer resort of Hyannis in its NW corner. A dredged channel leads from Hyannis Harbor to Lewis Bay.

Hyannis Harbor, protected by a breakwater extending 5 cables SE from Hyannis Port on the W side of the harbour, is used as a harbour of refuge by coasters and pleasure craft drawing less than 4·3 m (14 ft).

Limiting conditions
5.59

Depths in the approach channel to Hyannis Harbor are 4 to 4·9 m (13 to 16 ft).

Controlling depths (2011) of the dredged channel leading from Hyannis Harbor to Lewis Bay and thence to the anchorage basin (5.63) N of Harbor Bluff, were 1·8 m (6 ft) to the anchorage basin, 2·4 to 4 m (8 to 13 ft) in the basin and 2·1 m (7 ft) to the town wharf.

Ice seldom interferes with the movement of vessels in Hyannis Harbor during normal winters. During severe winters or persistent SW winds the harbour may be temporarily closed to navigation and during very severe winters it has been closed by ice for up to 3 months.

Arrival information
5.60

Port operations. Speed limit of 5 kn is in force in the channel leading to Hyannis Port Yacht Club and in Lewis Bay, N of Harbor Bluff (5.62).

Directions
5.61

Landmarks:
No 4A Beacon (starboard hand) (41°37'·06N 70°17'·15W), standing on Great Rock.
Lighthouse (disused) on Point Gammon (41°36'·58N 70°15'·98W) (5.48).
Tower (41°37'·99N 70°17'·96W).
Tower (41°37'·86N 70°18'·43W).

Major light:
Barnstable Airport Light (41°39'·98N 70°17'·12W).

Hyannis Harbor. From a position S of Point Gammon the approach to Hyannis Harbor leads S and W of that point, passing:
S of Gazelle Rock (41°36'·14N 70°15'·70W), marked by No 2 Light Buoy (starboard hand). Hallets Rock and a dangerous wreck lie 6 and 8½ cables, respectively, S of Gazelle Rock. Thence:

Clear of HH Light Buoy (safe water) (41°35'·96N 70°17'·37W), thence:

W of No 4 Light Buoy (starboard hand), 2 cables W of No 4A Beacon, marking a rock, thence:

E of Hyannis Harbor Breakwater Light (black and white chequered diamond on black framework tower) (41°37'·45N 70°17'·55W).

Thence into Hyannis Harbor.

5.62

Lewis Bay. From a position SSE of Hyannis Harbor Breakwater Light the entrance channel, dredged and marked by light buoys and buoys, leads:
NW of No 6 Light Buoy (starboard hand) (41°37'·20N 70°17'·32W), which marks the entrance to the channel, thence:

Between Dunbar Point (41°38'·00N 70°16'·37W) and the W extremity of Egg Island, 1½ cables E, the entrance points of Lewis Bay; thence:
NE of Harbor Bluff (41°38'·68N 70°16'·43W).

Thence to the town wharf at Hyannis.

Berths
5.63
1   **Anchorage** may be obtained in Hyannis Harbor N of the breakwater in 5 to 6 m (15 to 20 ft). A dangerous wreck lies 3½ cables N of the Breakwater Light.

Port services
5.64
1   **Facility.** Hospital at Hyannis.
    Supplies: fuel; water and stores.

Nantucket Harbor

Chart 2489, US Chart 13242 (see 1.16)
General information
5.65
1   **Position and function.** Nantucket Harbor (41°17′·15N 70°05′·62W) is situated on the N side of Nantucket Island, in the SE part of Nantucket Sound.
    Nantucket, situated on the W side of the harbour, is the main town on the island and its principal industry is fishing. Small coastal tankers carry fuel to Nantucket and it is also the terminal for the car ferry service to Hyannis on the mainland.
    The harbour is protected by Brant Point (41°17′·40N 70°05′·45W), extending from the W shore, and Coatue Point, the SW end of Coatue Beach, 4 cables N.

Limiting conditions
5.66
1   **Project depth** is 4·6 m (15 ft). For the latest controlling depths the charts and port authority should be consulted.
    Ice. Except in severe winters, ice of local formation seldom closes the harbour, however the harbour is frequently closed by drift ice from the sound during N winds.
    Fog is frequent, particularly in the spring and summer.

Arrival information
5.67
1   **Port operations.** Speed limit of 5 kn is in force in the harbour.
    Local knowledge is required to enter the harbour.

Directions
5.68
1   **Landmarks:**
        Spire (41°16′·94N 70°05′·94W).
        Water tower (41°17′·31N 70°07′·98W).
    Leading lights:
        Front light (red rectangle, white stripe, on white framework tower) (41°17′·39N 70°05′·53W).
        Rear light (similar structure) (81 m from front light).
2   From the vicinity of NB Light Buoy (safe water) (41°19′·02N 70°06′·22W) the alignment (162°) of these lights leads SSE to the harbour entrance, passing between pairs of buoys and light buoys (lateral) which mark the edge of the dredged channel. The channel leads between two breakwaters extending across shallow flats that extend 1 mile offshore. At half tide the E breakwater is almost entirely below water and the W breakwater partially so.
    Useful marks:
        East Breakwater Head No 3 Light (green square on framework tower) (41°18′·61N 70°05′·99W).
        Brant Point Light (white round tower) (41°17′·40N 70°05′·42W).

Berths
5.69
1   **Anchorage** may be obtained in 2 to 5 m (6 to 17 ft) off the S and SW sides of Brant Point or in 4 to 5 m (12 to 17 ft) in the general anchorage S of Brant Point.
    In general the bottom is good holding. In NE winds anchorage may be dangerous off the wharves and safer anchorage may be obtained in Head of the Harbor, 4 miles NE of Brant Point (5.65), in 2 to 8 m (6 to 23 ft).
2   **Alongside berths.** Ferry pier with depths alongside of 4·3 m extends from the W shore 3½ cables SW of Brant Point.

Port services
5.70
1   **Facility.** Hospital.
    Supplies: fuel; water and stores.

Edgartown Harbor and adjacent waters

Chart 2456, US Chart 13238 (see 1.16)
General information
5.71
1   **Position and function.** Edgartown Harbor (41°23′·39N 70°30′·30W) is formed by the channel between Chappaquiddick Island and Martha's Vineyard. It is divided into an outer and inner harbour.
    The outer harbour is used primarily as a harbour of refuge in winds from E and S, and as a night anchorage. The inner harbour provides a good anchorage for small vessels.
    Edgartown, on the W side of the inner harbour, is a fishing town and summer resort and is much frequented by small craft during the summer.
2   **Cape Poge Bay**, a shallow lagoon in the N part of Chappaquiddick Island, is entered from the E side of Edgartown outer harbour. The unmarked entrance is mainly used by local pleasure and fishing craft.

Limiting conditions
5.72
1   **Controlling depths.** In 2011 there was a controlling depth of 4·6 m (15 ft) in the channel from the outer harbour to off the town.

Arrival information
5.73
1   **Pilotage and tugs.** There are no pilots; fishing vessels will assist as tugs in an emergency.

Harbour
5.74
1   **Tidal streams.** The in–going and out–going tidal streams in the narrow part of the channel have a double period. Near the middle of each period there is a slack period preceded and followed by a period of maximum rate. The average rate is about 1 kn and a maximum rate of 3 kn has been reported.
    Fog is prevalent in the summer and at times appears without warning.
2   **Ice.** It is reported that the harbour is normally closed by ice during January and February, except for the ferry channel that is kept open. Strong tidal streams normally keep the inner harbour open.

Directions
5.75
1   **Landmarks:**
        Edgartown Light (white conical tower) (41°23′·45N 70°30′·18W).
        Church tower (41°23′·43N 70°30′·91W) standing in Edgartown.
        Water tower (41°22′·69N 70°31′·15W).

2 **Entry.** From the vicinity of 41°26'·00N 70°29'·00W the buoyed channel through the outer harbour leads S through waters free from dangers, and has depths of 6·1 to 11·3 m (20 to 37 ft) until No 8 Buoy is reached at the S end of the harbour. The channel then leads W to the wharves at the town.

Berths
5.76

1 **Outer harbour anchorage.** Anchorage may be obtained in E gales W of Cape Poge on the E side of the harbour, and in W and S gales in the S part of the harbour 4 cables E or ESE of Edgartown Light.

Inner harbour anchorage. Anchorage may be obtained 5 cables SE of the town, S of Middle Ground Shoal, in 7 to 9 m (24 to 30 ft), clay.

2 Vessels should not anchor in the channel abreast the town where the bottom is hard, the channel narrow, the tidal stream strong and where there are cable areas and a ferry route.

Alongside berth. Town wharf has a depth alongside of 7·6 m. Other wharves have general depths alongside of 3·4 m.

Port services
5.77

1 **Facility.** Health clinic.
Supplies: fuel; water and stores.

Vineyard Haven and adjacent waters

General information
5.78

1 **Position and function.** Vineyard Haven (41°28'·33N 70°35'·15W) is situated on the N side of Martha's Vineyard. This haven, easy of access, is the most important harbour of refuge for small vessels between Provincetown (4.142) and Narragansett Bay (5.172). It is exposed to NE gales, but vessels with good tackle can ride out most gales.

2 The village of Vineyard Haven is situated on the W side of the head of the haven. It is the ferry terminal for services to the mainland. The ferry slip is protected by a detached breakwater which extends SE from the shore N of the town.

Lagoon Pond, only used by local and fishing craft, extends 2 miles SSW from the SE part of Vineyard Haven.

Limiting conditions
5.79

1 **Depths** in the haven are sufficient for the largest vessels passing through Nantucket and Vineyard Sound, ranging from 12·2 to 4·6 m (40 to 15 ft) between the entrance and the head of the harbour.

The dredged channel from SE of the breakwater to the ferry wharf has a controlling depth of 4·9 m (16 ft).

Arrival information
5.80

1 **Pilotage and tugs.** Pilots are not available; a tug equipped for salvage is stationed in the harbour.

Harbour
5.81

1 **Tidal streams** in Vineyard Haven are weak.

Ice. Both fast ice and pack ice obstruct and, at times, entirely close the harbour during severe winters. Strong N winds drive pack ice into the harbour and endanger vessels at anchor.

Directions
5.82

1 **Landmarks:**
Water tower (41°26'·39N 70°34'·84W).
Tank (41°26'·73N 70°36'·81W).

Entry. From Main Channel in approximate position 41°29'·50N 70°34'·50W the track leads SSW into Vineyard Haven passing between East Chop Light (white tower) (41°28'·22N 70°34'·05W) and West Chop Light (white conical tower), 1½ miles WNW, which stand, respectively, on East Chop and West Chop (5.49).

2 Vessels proceeding to the head of the haven pass between No 7 Light (green square on post) and No 6 Buoy (starboard hand) which mark the edge of the shoal water on either side of the haven.

Caution. Care should be taken during the W–going stream not to approach West Chop too closely, as this stream sets onto the shoal ground extending N and E from the point.

3 **Useful marks:**
Breakwater Head Light No 10 (red triangle on post) (41°27'·45N 70°35'·78W).
Ferry slip light (on roof of shed) (41°27'·35N 70°35'·96W).

Berths
5.83

1 **Anchorage** may be obtained anywhere according to draught clear of the cable area, shown on the chart, shallow-draught vessels favouring the W shore. A good berth is NE of No 6 Buoy in 6 to 7 m (20 to 23 ft). The anchorage is very crowded in bad weather and the principal danger in NE gales is from vessels with poor ground tackle that are liable to drag.

2 **Ferry wharf** at the head of the channel has a reported depth alongside of 7·3 m at its outer face.
Town wharf lies 1 cable N of the ferry wharf.

Port services
5.84

1 **Facility.** Hospital.
Supplies: fuel; water and stores.

Anchorages and harbours

Chart 2456, US Chart 13229 (see 1.16)
Centerville Harbor
5.85

1 **Description.** Centerville Harbor (41°37'·50N 70°20'·60W), which lies between Hyannis Point (5.58) and Osterville Point, 3 miles WSW, is an open bay the approach to which is obstructed by numerous rocks and shoals which extend nearly 2½ miles offshore.

Although good anchorage can be obtained, it is seldom used for shelter as it is exposed to the S and the shoals off the harbour do not break the sea sufficiently to make it a safe anchorage.

2 **Depths** of 3 m (10 ft) can be found in the natural channel leading to the anchorage.

Ice sometimes closes the anchorage in winter.

Local knowledge is required to enter the anchorage, except in clear weather during daylight.

3 **Directions.** From a position S of Hodges Rock (41°35'·43N 70°18'·94W), a buoyed channel leads NW into Centerville Harbor, passing:
SW of Hodges Rock, marked on its S side by No 2 Buoy (starboard hand), thence:
NE of Gallatin Rock (41°35'·80N 70°20'·07W), marked by No 3 Buoy (port hand) on its E side, thence:

⁴ Between Bearse Rock (41°36′·15N 70°19′·76W) and Channel Rock, 3½ cables W, which are marked, respectively, by No 4 Buoy (starboard hand) and a buoy (preferred channel to starboard); thence:

SW of Gannet Ledge (41°36′·93N 70°20′·25W), marked by No 6 Buoy (starboard hand).

Thence into Centerville Harbor.

⁵ **Useful marks:**
Church spire (41°38′·74N 70°20′·79W).
Water tower (41°39′·51N 70°21′·16W).

Anchorage, with depths of 5 to 6 m (15 to 21 ft), may be obtained about 5 cables offshore, taking care to avoid Spindle Rock (41°37′·90N 70°20′·27W), marked on its S side by No 8 Buoy (starboard hand).

Chart 2456, US Chart 13229 (see 1.16)
Falmouth Harbor
5.86
¹ **Description.** Falmouth Harbor is the open roadstead extending from 1 to 3 miles ENE of Nobska Point (41°30′·95N 70°39′·31W), a bluff headland, on which stands a light (white tower). It affords a lee in N winds and in S winds the sea is partly broken by L'Hommedieu Shoal.

This anchorage is frequently used by vessels with good ground tackle which can ride out a gale here in comparative safety, without the crowded conditions that prevail in Vineyard Haven at such times.

² **Directions.** The anchorage can be entered either between No 18 Buoy (starboard hand), which lies 3 cables ENE of Nobska Point, and West Shoal, 3½ cables farther E; or between West Shoal and No 17 Buoy (port hand) (41°31′·08N 70°36′·69W), which marks the NW side of East Shoal.

³ **Useful mark:**
High green water tower (41°33′·11N 70°38′·42W).

Anchorage may be obtained about 8 cables offshore in 7 to 11 m (24 to 36 ft). Smaller vessels can anchor closer inshore in 5 to 6 m (15 to 18 ft). Holding is good and depths decrease gradually towards the shore.

Oak Bluffs Harbor
5.87
¹ Oak Bluffs Harbor (41°27′·59N 70°33′·58W) is a landlocked basin entered between two breakwaters. It is frequented by pleasure craft, some fishing vessels and ferries connecting to Woods Hole, Falmouth, New Bedford and Hyannis.

VINEYARD SOUND AND SOUTH-WEST APPROACHES

General information

Charts 2890, 2456
Description
5.88
¹ Vineyard Sound (41°27′·00N 70°44′·60W) is bounded on the NW by Elizabeth Islands extending 14 miles SW from the SW end of Cape Cod. The principal of these islands are Cuttyhunk Island, Nashawena Island (41°25′·90N 70°52′·30W), Pasque Island (41°27′·00N 70°49′·40W), Naushon Island (41°29′·10N 70°45′·00W) and Nonamesset Island (5.97). The islands are from 30 to 50 m high and their coasts are generally low bluffs separated by narrow passages forming harbours and means of communication between Vineyard Sound and Buzzards Bay (5.111).

² The SE side of Vineyard Sound is bounded by the NW shore of Martha's Vineyard. This coast is rugged and generally inaccessible.

To the W, Vineyard Sound joins Rhode Island Sound on a line joining Cuttyhunk Island (41°25′·20N 70°56′·10W) and Gay Head, 5½ miles SE; and to the E it joins Nantucket Sound on a line joining Nobska Point (41°30′·95N 70°39′·31W) (5.86) and West Chop (3 miles SE).

³ The channel through the sound is well marked and generally free of dangers.

South-west approach to Vineyard Sound is made from the E part of Rhode Island Sound. Nomans Land (41°15′·40N 70°49′·00W), an island 5 miles S of Gay Head, lies on the E side of these approaches. The island is prominent and rocky with many hills, the highest being over 30 m high. The shore is mainly clay and gravel cliffs.

Scientific Test Area
5.89
¹ A Scientific Test Area (41°16′·00N 71°02′·00W), marked by four light buoys (special), lies 10 miles WSW of Gay Head. Numerous surface and subsurface buoys may lie within this area.

Pilotage
5.90
¹ See 5.28.

Traffic regulations
5.91
¹ **Navigation Rules for US Inland Waters** apply to the waters that lie inshore of lines joining:
The S entrance to the Canapitsit Channel (41°25′·28N 70°54′·40W).
Fox Point (41°26′·00N 70°50′·93W), the E point of Nashawena Island, and the SE tangent of Naushon Island, 2¾ miles ENE.
Tarpaulin Cove Light (41°28′·13N 70°45′·45W) and Nobska Point Light, 5½ miles NE.

² See 1.44 and Appendix VII for further information.
Prohibited area. A danger area surrounds Nomans Land. Vessels should not enter this area. For details see Appendix VI.

Prohibited anchorage. Anchoring is prohibited in the fairway. The limits of the general areas where anchoring is permitted are shown on the chart.

North Atlantic right whale. See 1.51, *Admiralty List of Radio Signals Volume 6(5)* and Appendices VIII and X.

Tidal streams
5.92
¹ See Tidal Stream tables on the chart.

Directions

Principal marks
5.93
¹ **Landmarks:**
Buzzards Bay Entrance Light (41°23′·82N 71°02′·08W) (5.118).
Monument (41°24′·85N 70°56′·89W), 15 m in height, standing at the W end of Cuttyhunk Island.
Major lights:
Gay Head Light (red brick tower) (41°20′·92N 70°50′·10W).
Buzzards Bay Entrance Light — as above.

Other aid to navigation
5.94
1   **Racon**:
    Buzzards Bay Entrance Light (41°23′·82N 71°02′·08W).
    See *Admiralty List of Radio Signals Volume 2*.

South-west approaches
5.95
1   From the vicinity of 41°10′·00N 71°00′·00W, in the W part of Rhode Island Sound, the SW approach to Vineyard Sound leads generally NNE, passing:
    WNW of a dangerous wreck (41°08′·38N 70°51′·07W), position approximate, thence:
2   WNW of Southwest Shoal (41°12′·90N 70°51′·90W), which lies on the SW side of the prohibited area surrounding Nomans Land. The S limit of this area is marked by No 2 Light Buoy (starboard hand). And:
    ESE of the Scientific Testing Area (41°15′·87N 71°02′·05W) (5.89).
3   Thence to the entrance to Vineyard Sound, which lies between Gay Head and Cuttyhunk Island, 6 miles NW. Deep–draught vessels should steer to pass at least 3½ miles S of the SW end of Cuttyhunk Island.

Vineyard Sound
5.96
1   From a position about 5 miles WSW of Gay Head Light (5.93), in the entrance to Vineyard Sound, the track leads generally NE through the sound, passing:
    SE of No 32 Light Buoy (starboard hand) (41°22′·08N 70°57′·42W), which marks the S limit of the shoals with a least depth of 6·1 m (20 ft) that extend SW from Cuttyhunk Island and S of Sow and Pigs Reef (41°24′·00N 70°58′·20W). The S and SW sides of Sow and Pigs are marked by No 34 Buoy and No 36 Light Buoy (both starboard hand), respectively. And:
2   NW of Devils Bridge (41°21′·50N 70°51′·10W), which extends 1 mile NW from Gay Head and is marked by No 31 Light Buoy (port hand), thence:
    SE of No 30 Light Buoy (starboard hand) (41°24′·00N 70°50′·18W), moored 8 cables S of an 8·5 m (28 ft) patch, thence:
3   NW of Lucas Shoal (41°25′·05N 70°46′·95W), a narrow shifting ridge which lies on the SE side of the channel, whose W extremity is marked by No 29 Light Buoy (port hand), thence:
    NW of Middle Ground (41°28′·75N 70°38′·50W), the NE part of the ridge. The SW end of Middle Ground is marked by No 27 Light Buoy (port hand).
4   Thence the channel leads E into the W part of Nantucket Sound.
    Useful mark:
    Tarpaulin Cove Light (white tower with small white building) (41°28′·13N 70°45′·45W).
    (Directions for Main Channel through Nantucket Sound are given at 5.48, and for North Channel at 5.50)

Woods Hole
Chart 2456, US Chart 13235 (see 1.16)
General information
5.97
1   **Position and function.** Woods Hole (41°31′·10N 70°40′·35W) lies between the SW end of Cape Cod and Nonamesset Island (41°30′·57N 70°41′·16W) and provides a narrow and intricate passage between Vineyard Sound and Buzzards Bay.
2   The town of Woods Hole is a busy commercial centre and ferry terminal for traffic to Nantucket Island

Woods Hole from NW (5.97)
(Original dated 2003)

(Photograph - Joseph R Melanson of www.skypic.com)

and Martha's Vineyard. During the summer it is a busy holiday resort.

No-discharge Zones (NDZs) have been established in the vicinity of Woods Hole. See 1.41.

Limiting conditions
5.98

1   **Project depths** for The Strait (5.100), Broadway and Branch are 3·9 m (13 ft). For the latest controlling depths the charts and port authority should be consulted.

Arrival information
5.99

1   **Local knowledge** is necessary to navigate this channel except at slack water.

Navigation Rules for US Inland Waters. See 5.91.

Harbour
5.100

1   **General layout.** Woods Hole includes Great Harbor (5.103) and Little Harbor (5.104) in the E part, and Hadley Harbor in the W part. The two parts of Woods Hole are connected by Woods Hole Passage, which has a dredged section. Its E part also forms the approach to the town of Woods Hole on the NE shore of Great Harbor.

The main E–W part of Woods Hole Passage, known as The Strait, has two spur channels at either end. The S spur at the E end is known as Broadway, and the N spur at the W end is known as Branch.

2   **Tidal streams** through Woods Hole are so strong that passage is difficult and dangerous. Buoys marking the channel are sometimes towed under by the strong tidal stream.

Tidal streams in the passage turn W at about ½ hour before HW Boston and to the E about 4¾ hours after HW Boston. At the E entrance the maximum rate of the streams is about 1½ kn and at the W entrance 1 kn, but at the narrowest part of the passage the rate is about 4 kn at springs. Both the rate of the streams and the time of slack water are affected by strong winds.

3   **Ice.** Strong tidal streams normally keep Great Harbor clear of ice. Drift ice is brought through from Buzzards Bay, but seldom interferes with navigation, except in unusually severe winters, when it may close the W entrance to Woods Hole.

Directions
5.101

1   **Landmarks:**
    Nobska Point (41°30'·95N 70°39'·31W) (5.86).
    Water tower (41°31'·54N 70°39'·68W).
    Dome (41°31'·46N 70°40'·28W), of Woods Hole Oceanographic Institution.
    Great Harbor Directional Light (tower) (41°31'·65N 70°40'·55W)

2   From a position SW of Nobska Point in the vicinity of No 2 Light Buoy (starboard hand), the white sector (343·25° - 344·75°) of Great Harbor Directional Light (41°31'·65N 70°40'·55W) leads NNW through the S entrance to Woods Hole, passing:
    ENE of Nonamesset Shoal (41°30'·62N 70°40'·37W), marked by No 1 Buoy (port hand), and:

3   WSW of Great Ledge (41°30'·73N 70°40'·06W), marked by No 4 Buoy (starboard hand), thence:

  Between No 5 Light Buoy (port hand) and Juniper Point Light No 6A (red triangle on framework tower, concrete base) (41°31'·04N 70°40'·09W), on the tip of Juniper Point. No 6 Buoy (starboard hand) marks foul ground to the S of this point.
  Thence into Great Harbor (5.103).

5.102

1   **Woods Hole Passage.** From a position W of Juniper Point the dredged channel, marked by buoys (lateral), leads WNW through Broadway, WSW through The Strait and WNW through Branch, passing:
    NE of Mink Point (41°31'·00N 70°40'·63W), on Nonamesset Island, which lies 1 cable SW of the entrance to Broadway, thence:

2   SSE of Penzance Point (41°31'·25N 70°40'·95W), the S extremity of Penzance, a peninsula forming the NW side of Great Harbor, thence:
    SSW of No 10 Light Buoy (starboard hand) (41°31'·25N 70°41'·40W), at the W end of the dredged channel.
  Thence the passage leads N into Buzzards Bay.

3   **Useful mark:**
    Woods Hole Passage Directional Light (red and white chequered diamond on dolphin) (41°31'·29N 70°40'·28W), a directional light exhibited along the 077°/257° axis of The Strait.

Great Harbor
5.103

1   Great Harbor lies on the NE side of Woods Hole N of the entrance from Vineyard Sound. There are several wharves and piers on the E side of the harbour.

Anchorage may be obtained in the N part of the harbour in 6 to 19 m (19 to 62 ft). The holding at the head of the harbour is poor, but good anchorage can be obtained in 9 to 11 m (29 to 36 ft) about 1 cable NW of the National Marine Fisheries Service wharf.

2   **Alongside berths.** Depths alongside the various berths vary from 3·4 to 9·1 m. The principal berths are:
    Ferry Pier (41°31'·41N 70°40'·26W).
    Oceanographic Institute wharf (41°31'·47N 70°40'·31W).
    Marine Biology Laboratory wharf (41°31'·49N 70°40'·46W).
    National Marine Fisheries Service wharf (41°31'·54N 70°40'·49W).
    Town Pier (41°31'·59N 70°40'·51W).

Little Harbor
5.104

1   Little Harbor is the E cove in Woods Hole and is separated from Great Harbor by Juniper Point. Woods Hole Coast Guard station is on the W side of the harbour.

Entrance. The harbour is entered from Vineyard Sound by a narrow dredged channel, entered E of No 1 Light Buoy (port hand), 5½ cables SE of Juniper Point.

2   **Controlling depth.** The project depth is 3·7 m (12 ft) from Vineyard Sound to the turning basin off the Coast Guard Wharf. For the latest controlling depths, the charts and port authorities should be consulted.

Speed limit of 5½ kn is enforced in the harbour.

Other channels

Chart 2456, US Chart 13233 (see 1.16)
Between Nomans Land and Martha's Vineyard
5.105

1 The passage between Nomans Land (41°15′·40N 70°49′·00W) and Squibnocket Point (41°18′·20N 70°46′·70W), the S point of Martha's Vineyard, is obstructed by below–water rocks of which Old Man and Lone Rock lie in mid–channel.

Channel. A buoyed channel, suitable for small vessels by day, leads through this passage N of these rocks and S of the shoal ground extending S and SW from Squibnocket Point. No 1 Light Buoy (port hand) marks the SE end of the channel.

Chart 2456, US Chart 13233 (see 1.16)
Quicks Hole
5.106

1 Quicks Hole (41°26′·50N 70°50′·95W) leads between Nashawena Island and Pasque Island (5.88).

It is the only passage from Vineyard Sound to Buzzards Bay, through the Elizabeth Islands, that does not require local knowledge and is available to vessels with a draught of more than 3 m (10 ft). The passage is much used by vessels in tow, especially with W and S winds, to avoid the heavy sea in the entrance to Vineyard Sound.

2 The channel through this passage is nearly straight and has a width of 2 cables. It is marked by light buoys and buoys as for vessels proceeding N.

Depths are generally 9 m (30 ft) or more, but there are several shoaler spots. Rocks with depths of 8·2 to 11·3 m (27 to 37 ft) lie near the centre of the channel.

Local knowledge. Owing to the irregular depths the passage should not be attempted by vessels drawing more than 6·4 m (21 ft) unless local knowledge is available.

3 **Tidal streams** attain a rate of about 2½ kn and set N with the W–going stream in Vineyard Sound and S with the E–going stream. Strong winds affect the regularity of the tidal streams.

Directions. From a position NE of No 1 Light Buoy (41°25′·81N 70°50′·37W), which marks the S entrance, the channel leads generally N, passing:

4 W of No 2 Light Buoy (starboard hand) (41°26′·67N 70°50′·67W), marking shoal ground that extends 2½ cables W from Pasque Island, thence:

E of Felix Ledge (41°26′·82N 70°51′·07W), a patch with a depth of 4·5 m (15 ft) at its outer edge, marked by No 3 Buoy (port hand), thence:

E of Lone Rock (41°27′·70N 70°51′·25W), marked on its E side by LR Light Buoy (preferred channel to starboard).

Thence into Buzzards Bay.

Other anchorages and harbours

Menemsha Bight
5.107

1 Menemsha Bight (41°21′·30N 70°47′·00W) is situated near the W end of Martha's Vineyard.

Anchorage may be obtained, which provides shelter for vessels of any size from S and E winds, in 8 to 18 m (25 to 60 ft) with good holding. The shores of the bight should be given a berth of 3 cables.

Menemsha Creek
5.108

1 Menemsha Creek (41°21′·21N 70°46′·08W) is entered on the E side of Menemsha Bight through a dredged channel leading into a basin just inside the entrance. The village of Menemsha stands on the E side of the basin.

Entrance to the creek is protected by two stone jetties. No 1 Buoy (port hand) lies in the approach to the entrance and the outer end of the E jetty is marked by No 3 Light (green square on framework tower).

2 **Tidal streams** through the entrance have a rate of 3 kn or more. Slack water is reported to occur 45 minutes after local HW and LW.

Depths. In 1992 the controlling depth was 3 m (10 ft) to Menemsha Basin. There are depths of 1·7 to 3 m (5·5 to 10 ft) in the NW part of the basin and 1·1 to 1·5 m (3·5 to 5 ft) in the SE part. For the latest controlling depths the national charts should be consulted.

3 **Berths.** Moorings and alongside berths are available in the basin.

Tarpaulin Cove
5.109

1 Tarpaulin Cove (41°28′·50N 70°45′·30W) lies on the NW side of Vineyard Sound. It provides shelter from N and W winds and is frequently used. Tarpaulin Cove Light (5.96) stands on the S entrance point.

Marks and dangers. No 1 Buoy (port hand) is moored 2 cables NE of the light off a shoal bank, and a buoy (special purpose), moored 3 cables N of the light, marks a rock with a depth of 2·4 m (8 ft). The N shore of the cove should be given a berth of 1 cable and the W and SW shores a berth of more than 1½ cables.

2 **Navigation Rules for US Inland Waters.** See 5.91.

Anchorage may be obtained in the cove in 4 to 6 m (14 to 18 ft), good holding, with Tarpaulin Cove Light bearing between 189° and 212°. Large vessels should anchor farther out in 11 m (36 ft) or more.

BUZZARDS BAY, CAPE COD CANAL AND NEW BEDFORD HARBOR

GENERAL INFORMATION

Charts 2890, 2456
Area covered
5.110

1 This section describes Buzzards Bay and its approaches, Cape Cod Canal and adjacent waters, and New Bedford and its approaches.

It is arranged as follows:
Buzzards Bay and approaches (5.111).
Cape Cod Canal and adjacent waters (5.133).
New Bedford and approaches (5.150).

BUZZARDS BAY AND APPROACHES

General Information

Charts 2890, 2456
Description
5.111

1 **Buzzards Bay**, entered between Cuttyhunk Island (41°25′·20N 70°56′·10W) and Gooseberry Neck

(41°29′·11N 71°02′·30W), 5½ miles NW, extends 24 miles NE. Besides this main entrance the bay may also be entered from Vineyard Sound through Woods Hole (5.97) and Quicks Hole (5.106). The bay forms the approach to the port of New Bedford and the W entrance of the Cape Cod Canal.

2 The shores are generally low, rocky and indented by many bays and rivers. Large boulders are a prominent feature and in some places they extend a considerable distance offshore rendering a close approach to the land dangerous.

Approach. The main entrance to the bay is approached from Rhode Island Sound.

3 **Entrance.** The main entrance has a clear width of 4¼ miles between Sow and Pigs Reef, which extends SW from Cuttyhunk Island, and Hen and Chickens which lies S of Gooseberry Neck.

Recommended routes for deep-draught vessels, tugs and barges have been established in Buzzards Bay. See 5.2.

No-discharge Zone (NDZ). The whole of Buzzards Bay has been designated as a NDZ. See 1.41.

Depths
5.112
1 Depths in Buzzards Bay, especially in its entrance and approach, are irregular with boulder reefs in places. There are shoals in the entrance, with depths of 5·2 to 10·7 m (17 to 35 ft), over which the sea breaks in heavy SW gales.

The recommended route (5.2), which leads up the bay to the entrance of the dredged channel leading to Cape Cod Canal, has a least depth of 9·1 m (30 ft). The head of the bay is obstructed by shoals.

Caution. See 5.123.

Vessel traffic service
5.113
1 A VMRS with full radar surveillance is maintained for the control of shipping. For details and list of reporting points see *Admiralty List of Radio Signals Volume 6(5).*

Pilotage
5.114
1 Pilotage is compulsory in Buzzards Bay for all vessels of 350 gt or more and tows with barges carrying 5000 barrels or more of petroleum cargoes.
Pilots board:
In the vicinity of 41°23′·20N 71°21′·40W, 4 miles SSE of the entrance to Narragansett Bay (5.172), or:

2 In the vicinity of 41°17′·20N 71°30′·40W, 4 miles E of the NE entrance to Block Island Sound (6.7), or:
About 1 mile NW of Buzzards Bay Entrance Light (41°23′·82N 71°02′·08W) (5.118), or:
5 cables SE of CC Light Buoy (41°48′·88N 70°27′·65W), off the E entrance to Cape Cod Canal.

Traffic regulations
5.115
1 **Navigation Rules for US Inland Waters** apply to all waters lying within a line joining the extremity of Cuttyhunk Island (41°25′·20N 70°56′·10W) and the tower on Gooseberry Neck, 5¾ miles NW. See 1.44 and Appendix VII for further information.

Precautionary area. See 5.10.

2 **Traffic separation scheme** for the approaches to Buzzards Bay leads NE from the precautionary area. This TSS is IMO–adopted and Rule 10 of *International Regulations for Preventing Collisions at Sea (1972)* applies. The two traffic lanes are separated by a 1 mile wide separation zone. This TSS is not marked by buoys.

Speed limits. A speed limit of 4½ kn is enforced in many of the small harbours within Buzzards Bay.

Anchorages
5.116
1 General anchorage areas L and M lie in the central part of Buzzards Bay, SE and NW, respectively, of the recommended route (5.2).

Natural conditions
5.117
1 **Ice**. The head of Buzzards Bay and the harbours in its vicinity are generally closed to navigation during the winter months.

The approaches to the harbours on the E side are rendered dangerous by drift ice which, in exceptionally severe winters, extends across the bay and joins local ice on the W shore, thus forming an impassable barrier for short periods. Ice forms more rapidly with the wind from between N and W. Under ordinary circumstances a NE wind, lasting for 2 days, will clear the bay of ice. South and especially SE winds diminish the extent and weaken the strength of the pack ice.

2 **Tidal streams** are strong in the passages between Vineyard Sound and Buzzards Bay.
At a position about 2 miles SSE of the S extremity of Gooseberry Neck, the tidal stream is rotary, turning clockwise. The maximum stream sets 065° and 215° at an average rate of ½ kn at about 4¾ hours before and ½ hour after HW at Boston.

The average rate of tidal streams in Buzzards Bay is less than ½ kn.

Directions
(continued from 5.15)

Principal marks
5.118
1 **Landmarks:**
Buzzards Bay Entrance Light (tower on red square on three red piles with large tube, marked BUZZARDS on sides) (41°23′·82N 71°02′·08W).
Monument (41°24′·85N 70°56′·89W) (5.93).
Watch tower (41°29′·11N 71°02′·29W), standing on Gooseberry Neck.
Twin cupolas (41°34′·18N 70°38′·87W), on a hotel standing on Hamlin Point.
Bird Island Light (white tower) (41°40′·17N 70°43′·04W).

2 **Major lights:**
Buzzards Bay Entrance Light — as above.
Gay Head Light (41°20′·92N 70°50′·10W) (5.93).
Cleveland East Ledge Light (white round tower and dwelling, red caisson) (41°37′·86N 70°41′·65W).

Other aids to navigation
5.119
1 **Racons**:
Buzzards Bay Entrance Light (41°23′·82N 71°02′·08W).
Cleveland East Ledge Light (41°37′·86N 70°41′·65W).
See *Admiralty List of Radio Signals Volume 2.*

Approaches
5.120
1 From within the precautionary area off Block Island, centred 41°06′·00N 71°23′·40W, the approach to the

main entrance to Buzzards Bay leads NE for 20 miles through a TSS, passing:

NW of Browns Ledge (41°19′·80N 71°06′·00W) and an unnamed bank, with a depth of 9·8 m (32 ft), which lies 2 miles farther NE.

Entrance
5.121

1 From the NE end of the TSS the route to the entrance to Buzzards Bay leads NE, passing:

NW of Buzzards Bay Entrance Light (5.118), thence:

SE of a 6·7 m (22 ft) shoal (41°25′·96N 71°02′·36W), marked by No 1 Light Buoy (port hand), thence:

2 NW of No 2 Light Buoy (starboard hand) (41°26′·14N 71°00′·66W), thence:

SE of No 3 Light Buoy (port hand) (41°27′·25N 71°00′·57W).

Thence the track leads through the entrance to Buzzards Bay.

5.122

1 An alternative route, suitable for vessels with a draught not exceeding 4·9 m (16 ft), leads ENE from the vicinity of 41°27′·00N 71°05′·00W, passing:

Between Old Cock (41°27′·75N 71°02′·00W), marked by No 1 Buoy (port hand) moored close S, and No 3 Light Buoy (port hand), 1¼ miles SE, thence:

Between Nos 5 and 6 Light Buoys (5.124).

5.123

1 **Caution.** Owing to the irregular depths, vessels should proceed with caution in areas where their maximum draught is within 1·8 m (6 ft) of the charted depth. Those that draw more than 4·9 m (16 ft) should avoid the irregular depths in the approach and entrance.

Within Buzzards Bay
5.124

1 From the entrance to Buzzards Bay (41°27′·00N 71°00′·00W) the route leads 18 miles ENE, NE and NNE, passing:

NNW of Coxens Ledge (41°27′·05N 70°59′·00W), marked at its W extremity by No 4 Light Buoy (starboard hand), thence:

2 Between Mishaum Ledge (41°29′·40N 70°57′·98W) and a 7 m (23 ft) shoal (4½ miles S), which are marked, respectively, by No 5 Light Buoy (port hand) and No 6 Light Buoy (starboard hand), thence:

Between Wilkes Ledge (41°30′·75N 70°54′·60W), marked on its SE side by No 7 Light Buoy (port hand), and a shoal with a depth of 8·8 m (29 ft), 2 miles SE, marked on its NW side by No 8 Light Buoy (starboard hand). Thence:

3 Clear of BB Light Buoy (safe water) (41°30′·55N 70°49′·90W), which lies at the entrance to the buoyed channel leading to New Bedford (5.150), thence:

SE of a shoal with a depth of 9·1 m (30 ft) (41°33′·03N 70°46′·56W), marked on its SE side by No 9 Light Buoy (port hand), thence:

NW of a shoal with a depth of 8·2 m (27 ft) (41°34′·19N 70°43′·18W) marked on its N side by No 10 Light Buoy (port hand), thence:

4 WNW of No 2 Light Buoy (41°36′·64N 70°42′·18W), thence:

WNW of Cleveland East Ledge Light (41°37′·86N 70°41′·65W) (5.118), at the W entrance to Cape Cod Canal (5.133).

(Directions continue for Cape Cod Canal at 5.141. Directions for New Bedford Harbor are given at 5.164)

Anchorages and harbours

Chart 2456, US Chart 13230 (see 1.16)
Cuttyhunk Harbor
5.125

1 **Position and function.** Cuttyhunk Harbor (41°25′·80N 70°54′·70W) is formed by the bay between the E end of Cuttyhunk Island and the W end of Nashawena Island and is protected from the N by Penikese Island (41°27′·10N 70°55′·25W), grassy and hilly, and Gull Island (41°26′·77N 70°54′·41W), together with the shoal ground surrounding them. It is exposed to NE winds.

The harbour, sometimes used for shelter by small vessels and fishing vessels, forms the approach to Cuttyhunk Pond (5.126) and the village of Cuttyhunk (5.126).

2 **Approach and depths.** The harbour is normally entered from Buzzards Bay. Vessels approaching from NW should not have a draught of more than 3 m (10 ft). The approach from NE is deeper. The principal dangers are buoyed.

Local knowledge. The harbour is foul round its shores and entry should not be attempted without local knowledge except in daytime with clear weather.

Ice is carried into the harbour with N winds and closes it for short periods in severe winters.

Anchorage in 3 to 7 m (10 to 24 ft), with reported poor holding, can be obtained clear of the cable area and the foul ground that extends up to 2½ cables offshore.

Cuttyhunk Pond
5.126

1 Cuttyhunk Pond (41°25′·50N 70°55′·60W) is entered on the SW side of Cuttyhunk Harbor through a narrow dredged channel. The village of Cuttyhunk lies on the SW side of Cuttyhunk Pond. The entrance is protected by two jetties, the N, above water, being marked at its end by No 8 Light (red triangle on grey framework tower, concrete base) (41°25′·51N 70°55′·02W) and the S, which dries, being marked by No 9 Buoy (port hand) (41°25′·50N 70°54′·96W).

2 **Depths.** There is a project depth of 3 m (10 ft) from Cuttyhunk Harbor to Cuttyhunk Pond thence to the turning basin and anchorage.

Chart 2455, US Chart 13230 (see 1.16)
Apponagansett Bay
5.127

1 Apponagansett Bay (41°34′·76N 70°56′·74W), 2 miles SW of New Bedford, is entered SW of Padanaram Breakwater (41°34′·45N 70°56′·36W). No 8 Light (red triangle on grey framework tower) stands at the head of the breakwater.

The bay is used by pleasure craft and a few fishing vessels in summer, but is not safe in SE gales.

2 **Local knowledge** is required to enter Apponagansett Bay at night or during thick weather owing to the dangers in the approach.

Anchorage may be obtained in the bay in 4 to 6 m (13 to 20 ft), sticky bottom, between the entrance and 3½ cables NW of the breakwater light. Care should be taken to avoid Dartmouth Rock (41°34′·71N 70°56′·59W) which lies on the E side of the bay.

Clarks Cove

5.128

1 Clarks Cove (41°35′·92N 70°55′·25W) is entered between Ricketsons Point (41°34′·65N 70°56′·28W), to the W, and Clarks Point (5.151), the W entrance point to New Bedford Harbor (5.150), to the E. It provides anchorage in 4 to 7 m (13 to 23 ft), but is exposed to S winds and seldom used.

Charts 2456, 2455, 2891, US Chart 13232 (see 1.16)
Mattapoisett Harbor

5.129

1 Mattapoisett Harbor (41°38′·70N 70°47′·74W), 6 miles E of New Bedford, is entered between the SE extremity of Mattapoisett Neck (41°37′·75N 70°48′·25W) on the W, and Strawberry Point (41°38′·49N 70°46′·17W) and Angelica Point (41°38′·48N 70°45′·90W) on the E. The harbour is the approach to the town of Mattapoisett and is much frequented by yachts in the summer.

Anchorage may be obtained 3 cables W of Ned Point (41°39′·05N 70°47′·74W) in 5·1 m (17 ft).

Chart 2891
Wild Harbor

5.130

1 Wild Harbor (41°38′·30N 70°38′·80W), a cove on the E side of Buzzards Bay, is entered between the W end of Nyes Neck (41°38′·64N 70°38′·64W), on which stands a prominent tower, and Crow Point (41°38′·12N 70°38′·80W), 3 cables SE. No 1 Light Buoy (port hand) marks the N side of the entrance.

The shores of the harbour are foul and its E part is shoal.

Anchorage, sheltered from N and E winds, may be obtained just inside the entrance in 4 to 6 m (13 to 20 ft).

Megansett Harbor

5.131

1 Megansett Harbor (41°39′·30N 70°38′·30W), on the E side of Buzzards Bay, is entered between Nyes Neck and Scraggy Neck (41°40′·00N 70°38′·70W) and leads to the towns of North Falmouth, Megansett and Cataumet, situated respectively, on the SE, E and NE shores of the harbour. Cataumet Rock (41°39′·12N 70°38′·78W), marked by No 4 Buoy (starboard hand), lies on the S side of the entrance.

2 A channel, marked by buoys and with a least depth of 2·4 m (8 ft), leads into the harbour.

Anchorage in 3 to 7 m (10 to 22 ft) may be obtained between 2 and 5 cables W of the breakwater at Megansett.

Pocasset Harbor and Red Brook Harbor

5.132

1 **General information.** Pocasset Harbor (41°41′·70N 70°37′·17W) and Red Brook Harbor (41°40′·53N 70°36′·95W), on the E side of Buzzards Bay, are only used by small craft.

2 **Entrance.** Irregular depths of 5·2 to 5·8 m (17 to 19 ft) extend across the entrance, and Eustis Rock (41°40′·49N 70°38′·70W), marked by ER Buoy (preferred channel to port), lies about 2 cables off the N side of Scraggy Neck.

Anchorage may be obtained, by vessels drawing up to 4·3 m (14 ft), in the entrance in 6 to 9 m (20 to 30 ft) about 2½ cables W of Eustis Rock.

CAPE COD CANAL AND ADJACENT WATERS

General information

Chart 2891
Description
5.133

1 Cape Cod Canal is a sea–level waterway connecting Buzzards Bay and Cape Cod Bay. The waterway is 15 miles long from its W entrance at Cleveland East Ledge Light (41°37′·86N 70°41′·65W) to deep water in Cape Cod Bay.

The canal shortens the distance between points N and S of Cape Cod by 50 to 150 miles and provides an inside passage to avoid Nantucket Shoals.

2 Vessels of up to 251·6 m (825 ft) in length, 38·1 m (125 ft) beam and 9·76 m (32 ft) draught may transit the canal.

The canal is maintained by the Federal Government as a free waterway.

Depths
5.134

1 The project depth for the canal is 9·76 m (32 ft). For the latest controlling depths the charts and port authority should be consulted.

Vessel traffic service
5.135

1 See 4.128.

Tidal levels
5.136

1 **Tidal levels.** At the Buzzards Bay entrance to Cape Cod Canal, mean spring range is about 1·1 m (3·8 ft), and mean neap range about 0·8 m (2·7 ft). At the Cape Cod Bay entrance the mean spring range is about 2·7 m (8·9 ft); mean neap range about 2·1 m (6·9 ft). See information in *Admiralty Tide Tables*.

Pilotage and tugs
5.137

1 **Pilotage.** See 5.114.

Traffic regulations
5.138

1 For regulations governing the use, administration and navigation of Cape Cod Canal, see Appendix IX.

Navigation Rules for US Inland Waters apply W of a line drawn from Canal Breakwater Light 4 (41°46′·82N 70°29′·30W) S to the shoreline. See 5.115, 1.44 and Appendix VII for further information.

Traffic signals, red, green and yellow in colour, are situated:

2 At the SW end of Wings Neck (41°40′·82N 70°39′·68W) governing the W entrance of Hog Island Channel.

On the S side of the E canal entrance (41°46′·49N 70°29′·77W).

At the Canal Electric Terminal Basin (41°46′·32N 70°30′·35W) on the S side of the canal at Sandwich.

Traffic signals apply to all vessels over 20 m (65 ft) in length wishing to transit the canal. For detailed information of signals see Appendix IX.

Vertical clearance
5.139

1 Bridges cross the Cape Cod Canal as follows:
Rail bridge at Buzzards Bay (41°44′·52N 70°36′·81W) with vertical lift span. Vertical clearance when opened 41 m (135 ft). Span is normally in raised position.

Cape Cod Canal - West Entrance (5.133)

(Original dated 2002)

(Photograph - Robert P. David - Reproduced by permission of Cape Cod Sail & Power Squadron, United States Power Squadrons)

State Route 25/28 road bridge at Bourne (41°44′·86N 70°35′·37W). Fixed span with vertical clearance of 41 m (135 ft).

2   US 6/State Route 3 road bridge at Sagamore (41°46′·57N 70°32′·60W). Fixed span with vertical clearance of 41 m (135 ft).

Overhead power cables crossing the canal have a least safe vertical clearance of 48·7 m (160 ft).

Natural conditions
5.140

1   **Tidal streams.** The large differences in range and timing of the tide between Buzzards Bay and Cape Cod Bay cause strong tidal streams in the canal. Tides may lower the canal level 0·6 m below MLW or even more if attended by heavy offshore winds. Under ordinary conditions the E–going tidal stream has a rate of 4 kn and the W–going tidal stream a rate of 4½ kn.

2   **Ice.** The canal itself has never been closed by ice, but occasionally Buzzards Bay and Cape Cod Bay become so congested with ice that navigation through the canal is prevented.

Fog is said to be less dense over Cape Cod Canal than outside, but at times a water vapour rises from the canal to such an extent that traffic has to be suspended.

Directions
(continued from 5.124)

Principal marks
5.141

1   **Landmarks:**
Cleveland East Ledge Light (41°37′·86N 70°41′·65W) (5.118).
Rail and road bridges crossing canal. See 5.139.
Major lights:
Cleveland East Ledge Light — as above.
Cape Cod Canal Breakwater Head Light (41°46′·79N 70°29′·39W) (4.130).

Other aid to navigation
5.142

1   **Racon:**
Cleveland East Ledge Light (41°37′·86N 70°41′·65W).
See *Admiralty List of Radio Signals Volume 2.*

Cleveland Ledge Channel
5.143

1   **Leading lights:**
Front light (red rectangle, white stripe, on white tower) (41°41′·55N 70°40′·46W).
Rear light (red rectangle, white stripe, on white framework tower) (1·6 miles from front light).

From a position WNW of Cleveland East Ledge Light (5.118) the alignment (015°) of these lights leads NNE for 3 miles through Cleveland Ledge Channel, passing:

2   Between Nos 7 and 8 Light Buoys (lateral) (41°39′·11N 70°41′·38W), thence:
ESE of Bird Island (41°40′·17N 70°43′·04W) (5.118), from which a light (white tower) is exhibited.

Hog Island Channel
5.144

1   From the vicinity of No 1 Light Buoy (port hand) (41°40′·92N 70°40′·78W) at the N end of Cleveland Ledge Channel, Hog Island Channel leads NE for about 4 miles between pairs of light buoys (lateral) and light beacons, passing:
SE of Stony Point Dike (41°42′·20N 70°39′·80W), 1½ m high, thence:

2   Between Cedar Island Point (41°43′·09N 70°39′·00W) and the W extremity of Mashnee Island (41°43′·03N 70°38′·13W), 4½ cables E, thence:
Between Hog Neck (41°43′·44N 70°38′·55W) and Hog Island, 2½ cables E.
Thence into Canal Land Cut.

Canal Land Cut
5.145

1 From the vicinity of Taylor Point (41°44'·37N 70°37'·50W) Canal Land Cut leads generally ENE for 7 miles through the isthmus connecting Cape Cod to the mainland, to Cape Cod Bay.

(Directions for E entrance to Cape Cod Canal are given at 4.130)

Basins and berths

Basins
5.146

1 Mooring basins, with mooring dolphins, are situated at both ends of Canal Land Cut. The basin at the W end, where shoaling was reported (1979), is on the E side of Hog Island Channel abreast Hog Island (41°43'·44N 70°38'·00W). The basin at the E end is on the N side of the canal, 5 cables within the entrance.

Anchorages
5.147

1 Anchorage areas C and D have been established on the W and E side, respectively, of the N part of Cleveland Ledge Channel (5.143). The limits of these areas are shown on the chart.

Alongside berths
5.148

1 **State Pier** at Taylor Point (41°44'·37N 70°37'·50W), site of Massachusetts Maritime Academy, 182 m in length with a depth alongside of 7·6 m. In 1981 shoaling to 3 m (10 ft) was reported off the W end of the pier. Vessels should not attempt to go alongside except at slack water. Passing vessels should proceed slowly.

2 **Tanker berth** (41°46'·30N 70°30'·84W), 1 mile inside the E entrance. Mooring platform 228 m in length with a depth alongside of 12·2 m. Vessels over 50 000 tonnes or 9·76 m (32 ft) draught moor at HW slack during daylight hours only. Vessels under 50 000 tonnes moor at slack water day or night.

Adjacent waters

Onset Bay
5.149

1 Onset Bay (41°44'·14N 70°39'·00W) lies on the NW side of Hog Island Channel W of Sias Point (41°44'·09N 70°38'·15W). It forms the approach to the village of Onset.

Approach. Onset Bay is entered between Hog Neck, the E extremity of Great Neck, and Sias Point, 7 cables NNE. A dredged channel, marked by buoys, leads from between Hog Neck and No 21 Light (green square on framework tower) along the S side of the bay to a turning basin off the village.

2 **Depths.** In 1995 depths were 4·2 m (14 ft) in the channel and 3·9 to 4·6 m (13 to 15 ft) in the basin.

Anchorage, special, with depths of 2 to 4 m (7 to 13 ft) is situated in the N part of Onset Bay between Wickets Island, high and wooded, and the mainland NE. There are additional anchorages at the head of the channel with depths of 2 m (6 to 8 ft).

Wharf. The public wharf at Onset has a depth alongside of 4·3 m.

NEW BEDFORD AND APPROACHES

General information

Chart 2455

Position and function
5.150

1 New Bedford (41°38'·00N 70°55'·00W), which in 2010 had a population of 95 072, is a manufacturing city and a major fishing port standing on the W bank of the Acushnet River at the head of New Bedford Harbor. Fairhaven stands on the opposite bank of the river.

2 The port handles bulk, break-bulk, container, project and RoRo cargoes and is one of the largest fishing ports on the E coast of the US. It is a port of entry.

Ferries link New Bedford with Cuttyhunk (5.125) and Vineyard Haven (5.78).

Port limits
5.151

1 New Bedford Harbor, the tidal estuary of Acushnet River, includes all the tidal waters N of a line joining Clarks Point (41°35'·60N 70°54'·10W) and Wilbur Point (41°34'·95N 70°51'·24W), the S extremity of Sconticut Neck (41°36'·50N 70°51'·50W), 2 miles ESE.

Port Authority
5.152

1 Address: Harbor Development Commission, 52 Fisherman's Wharf, P.O. Box 50899, New Bedford, Massachusetts 02745.

Website: www.portofnewbedford.org

Limiting conditions

Controlling depth
5.153

1 The project depth is 9·1 m (30 ft) in the main channel leading from Buzzards Bay to the turning basin above the New Bedford - Fairhaven Bridge. For the latest controlling depths the charts and port authority should be consulted.

Vertical clearance
5.154

1 Swing Bridge connects Fish Island and Popes Island providing a double opening, each with a vertical clearance of 1·8 m (6 ft) when closed.

Two road bridges with fixed spans, about 1 mile above the swing bridge, have vertical clearances of 2·4 m (8 ft).

Navigable width
5.155

1 A hurricane barrier extends from the W shore, over Palmer Island to Fort Phoenix on the E.

Hurricane barrier traffic lights are displayed on a house on the W side of the entrance and adjacent to the old fort at Clarks Point (5.151).

2 The 45·7 m (150 ft) opening is kept in the open position during fair weather but is closed during periods of high winds, high tides or when a hurricane is expected.

Lights mark the E and W side of the opening.

Horizontal clearance
5.156

1 The swing bridge connecting Fish Island and Popes Island has a horizontal clearance of 28·9 m (95 ft).

Tidal levels
5.157

1 Mean spring range about 1·3 m (4·3 ft); mean neap range about 0·8 m (2·6 ft). See information in *Admiralty Tide Tables*.

Ice
5.158

1 The channels and anchorage area are usually navigable throughout the year, although in prolonged periods of extreme cold weather the harbour as well as all of Buzzards Bay may be closed to navigation because of ice. Such conditions are infrequent and of short duration.

Arrival information

Outer anchorages
5.159

1 Anchorage may be obtained in 6 to 9 m (20 to 30 ft) in a position 7 cables S of Clarks Point.

Pilotage and tugs
5.160

1 **Pilotage.** See 5.114.

Traffic regulations
5.161

1 **Navigation Rules for US Inland Waters.** See 5.115.

Regulated navigation area has been established close S of the hurricane barrier (5.155).

For definition and general regulations concerning regulated navigation areas see Appendix V.

Harbour

General layout
5.162

1 New Bedford Harbor is divided into an outer and inner harbour. The outer harbour consists of the area S of the hurricane barrier at Palmer Island (41°37′·50N 70°54′·60W) and the inner harbour consists of the area N of the barrier to a short distance above New Bedford–Fairhaven Bridge.

The inner harbour is divided by Fish Island (41°38′·33N 70°55′·16W) and Popes Island (41°38′·44N 70°54′·86W), which are connected by causeways to the W and E shore, respectively, 1 mile above the barrier. A swing bridge (5.154) connects the two islands.

Natural conditions
5.163

1 **Wind.** The prevailing winds during the winter are from N to W, and during the summer from S to SW.

Fog. Thick fog is reported to close in quickly with little warning in New Bedford Harbor.

Directions

Outer harbour
5.164

1 **Main channel.** From the vicinity of BB Light Buoy (41°31′·55N 70°49′·90W) the approach channel leads NNW for about 4 miles, passing:

Between No 1 Light Buoy (port hand) (41°31′·73N 70°50′·77W) and No 2 Light Buoy (starboard hand), 1¾ cables E, thence:

ENE of Negro Ledge (41°32′·82N 70°51′·90W), marked on its E side by No 3 Buoy (port hand). Thence:

2 Between No 4 Light Buoy (starboard hand) (41°33′·60N 70°51′·70W), marking an obstruction 3 cables SW of Mosher Ledge (41°33′·90N 70°51′·30W), and No 5 Light Buoy (port hand), 2 cables SW; thence:

Between Brooklyn Rock (41°34′·16N 70°52′·57W) and Henrietta Rock (41°34′·32N 70°52′·20W), 3¼ cables ENE, marked, respectively, by No 7 Light Buoy (port hand) and No 6 Light Buoy (starboard hand).

Thence through the dredged channel, marked by pairs of light buoys, to the hurricane barrier.

3 **Useful marks:**

Fort Rodman (41°35′·59N 70°54′·08W), standing on Clarks Point.

Fort Phoenix (41°37′·45N 70°54′·14W), on the point at the E end of the hurricane barrier.

Radio tower (41°38′·45N 70°55′·01W), on W side of Popes Island.

Charts 2456, 2455
5.165

1 **Alternative routes.** There are a number of alternative routes with least depths of 6·7 m (21 ft) that lead from Buzzards Bay to New Bedford Harbor W of the main channel. However, they are not as well marked as the main channel and unmarked shoals with depths of 2·7 to 5·5 m (9 to 18 ft) lie near the track.

2 **From south-west.** From a position S of No 5 Light Buoy, moored to the SE of Mishaum Ledge (5.124), a route leads NNE, passing:

ESE of Salters Point Rock (41°31′·53N 70°56′·27W), marked on its SE side by No 1 Buoy (port hand), thence:

WNW of No 2 Buoy (starboard hand) (41°31′·63N 70°55′·38W), marking a 4·8 m (16 ft) patch, thence:

3 WNW of The Sandspit (41°31′·88N 70°54′·80W), marked on its W end by No 4 Light Buoy (starboard hand), and:

ESE of the shoal water that extends S from Dumpling Rocks (41°32′·30N 70°55′·29W). The outer limit of the shoal is marked by No 5 Buoy (port hand). Thence:

WNW of a 5·4 m (18 ft) patch (41°32′·32N 70°54′·35W), marked by No 8 Light Buoy (starboard hand), thence:

4 ESE of Middle Ledge (41°33′·44N 70°54′·58W). AB Light Buoy (preferred channel to port) is moored 3 cables SSW of this ledge, thence:

ESE of Inez Rock (41°33′·77N 70°54′·47W), marked by No 11 Buoy (port hand), thence:

WNW of Decatur Rock (41°33′·78N 70°53′·41W), marked by No 10 Buoy (starboard hand), thence:

5 WNW of North Ledge (41°34′·38N 70°53′·45W), marked on its NW side by No 12 Buoy (starboard hand), thence:

ESE of Clarks Point (5.151).

Thence the track continues NNE to join the main route SE of Butler Flats, marked by a light (white conical tower, black round base) (41°36′·23N 70°53′·67W).

6 **From south.** From a position SE of Wilkes Ledge (41°30′·75N 70°54′·60W), marked on its SE side by No 7 Light Buoy (port hand), a route leads N passing W of Great Ledge, marked on its W side by No 8A Buoy (starboard hand) and E of the 5·5 m (18 ft) patch, marked by No 8 Light Buoy. The route then joins the approach from the SW in the vicinity of Decatur Rock.

Cautions
5.166

1 Vessels should not attempt to enter New Bedford except in clear weather when aids to navigation are visible, unless local knowledge is available.

Vessels should proceed with caution where the under-keel depth is less than 1·8 to 2·4 m (6 to 8 ft), because of the broken nature of the bottom.

Berths

Anchorages
5.167

1 **Outer harbour.** General anchorage areas A and B lie E and W, respectively, of the dredged channel S and SE of the hurricane barrier. No vessel should anchor outside these areas except in cases of great emergency.

Inner harbour. Vessels may anchor in the two dredged anchorage areas on either side of the channel in 7 to 9 m (23 to 30 ft).

Alongside berths
5.168

1 The main alongside berths, which lie on the W side of the inner harbour, are given as follows:

South Terminal Wharf (41°37′·57N 70°54′·90W): 487 m in length with a depth alongside of 9·1 m. Refrigerated storage and seafood products.

Oil Terminal (41°37′·86N 70°55′·09W): N side 225 m in length, with dolphins, with a depth alongside of 9·1 m. Petroleum products.

2 **State Pier** (41°38′·10N 70°55′·15W): N side 183 m in length, S side 236 m in length, face 137 m in length, with depths alongside of 9·1 m. General cargo, ferry and cruise ship terminal.

Maritime Terminal Wharf (41°38′·45N 70°55′·28W): 183 m in length with a depth alongside of 9·4 m. General cargo, frozen food and fish.

Bridge Terminal Wharf (NE side of Fish Island (41°38′·37N 70°55′·13W): 137 m in length with a depth alongside of 8·5 m. Receipt of frozen food.

3 **Two wharves** (N of Maritime Terminal): 177 and 305 m in length with depths alongside of 7·6 to 9·1 m. Frozen fish and foods, and general cargo.

Port services

Repairs
5.169

1 Largest patent slip in area is capable of handling vessels of up to 64 m in length.

Other facilities
5.170

Hospitals; oily waste disposal.

Supplies
5.171

1 Fuel; water ex wharf and by barge to vessels at anchor; provisions and stores.

NARRAGANSETT BAY AND ADJACENT WATERS

GENERAL INFORMATION

Chart 2890
Area covered
5.172

1 This section describes Narragansett Bay (41°36′·00N 71°22′·00W) and the adjacent waters on the N side of Rhode Island Sound between Buzzards Bay and Block Island Sound. Also described are the ports of Newport (5.210), Providence (5.227) and Fall River (5.261).

2 The section is arranged as follows:
   Buzzards Bay to Narragansett Bay (5.178).
   Approaches to Narragansett Bay (5.184).
   Narragansett Bay (5.193).
   Providence (5.227).
   Mount Hope Bay, Fall River Harbor and Taunton River (5.247).

Pilotage
5.173

1 Pilotage is compulsory for all foreign vessels and US vessels under register when entering and departing from Narragansett Bay and all ports in State of Rhode Island.

Pilots embark in the vicinity of 41°23′·20N 71°21′·40W, S of a line extending from Point Judith (41°21′·66N 71°28′·88W) to Sakonnet Point, 14 miles ENE.

Pilot boats have either black or grey hulls with white superstructures and the word "PILOT" on the side.

Pilot services are normally arranged 24 hours in advance through ship's agents or directly by shipping companies.

2 Pilots for US registered vessels in coastwise trade board off Point Judith. The pilot boats have a blue hull with white superstructure and maintain a listening watch on VHF 2 hours before a vessel's ETA.

Traffic regulations
5.174

1 **North Atlantic right whale.** See 1.51, *Admiralty List of Radio Signals Volume 6(5)* and Appendices VIII and X.

Recommended routes
5.175

1 Recommended routes for deep-draught vessels, tugs and barges, as shown on the charts, have been established in Narragansett Bay. See 5.2.

Security Broadcast System
5.176

1 A compulsory system is in force, to be used by vessels to report movements within Narragansett Bay. See *Admiralty List of Radio Signals Volume 6(5)* for details.

No-discharge Zones
5.177

1 Numerous No-discharge Zones (NDZs) have been established throughout Narragansett Bay. See 1.41.

BUZZARDS BAY TO NARRAGANSETT BAY

General information

Chart 2890, US Charts 13228, 13221 (see 1.16)
Description
5.178

1 Between Gooseberry Neck (41°29′·11N 71°02′·30W) and Brenton Point, the E entrance point to Narragansett Bay, 14½ miles W, lie the entrances to Westport Harbor (5.182) and Sakonnet River (5.183). Foul ground extends up to 1½ miles offshore in places along this stretch of the coast.

Fish traps
5.179

1   The limits of areas where fish traps may be found in the coastal waters between Gooseberry Neck and Brenton Point are shown on the chart.

Directions

Principal marks
5.180

1   **Landmarks:**
   Buzzards Bay Entrance Light (41°23'·82N 71°02'·08W) (5.118).
   Tower (41°29'·11N 71°02'·29W) standing on Gooseberry Neck.
   Church tower (41°29'·49N 71°16'·39W) (NW pinnacle of four), on school 7 cables N of Easton Point on the S side of Rhode Island.

2   **Major lights:**
   Buzzards Bay Entrance Light — as above.
   Beavertail Light (41°26'·96N 71°23'·97W) (5.186).

Other aids to navigation
5.181

1   **Racons:**
   Buzzards Bay Entrance Light (41°23'·82N 71°02'·08W).
   NB Light Buoy (41°23'·00N 71°23'·36W).
   See *Admiralty List of Radio Signals Volume 2*.

Anchorages and harbours

Westport River
5.182

1   **General information.** Westport River, with Westport Harbor (41°31'·00N 71°05'·10W) close within its entrance, flows into the head of a bight which extends from Gooseberry Neck to Warren Point (41°27'·70N 71°10'·20W). The river is used by fishing and pleasure craft.

2   Numerous dangers obstruct the bight, of which Pinetree Ground (41°28'·52N 71°04'·10W), Kibby Ground (41°28'·87N 71°05'·49W), Twomile Ledge (41°29'·37N 71°05'·13W) and Twomile Rock (41°29'·52N 71°04'·59W), marked by No 3 Beacon (port hand), lie in the approaches to Westport River. Foul ground also extends 7 cables SW and W from Gooseberry Neck and is marked by No 6 Buoy (starboard hand).
   Local knowledge is required to enter the harbour.

Sakonnet River
5.183

1   **General information.** Sakonnet River lies between the mainland and the E shore of Rhode Island and is entered between Sakonnet Point (41°27'·28N 71°11'·71W) and Sachuest Point (41°28'·42N 71°14'·80W), 2½ miles WNW.
   The river, little used except by fishing vessels and small local craft, extends 12 miles N to Mount Hope Bay (5.247).

2   **Navigation Rules for US Inland Waters** apply to all waters within a line joining Sakonnet Harbor Breakwater Light No 2 (red triangle on framework tower, concrete base) (41°27'·99N 71°11'·70W) and a position on the southernmost part of Sachuest Point. See 1.44 and Appendix VII for further information.
   Ice. The river N of Fogland Point (41°33'·65N 71°13'·15W) is normally closed by ice for short periods each winter.

3   **Anchorage** for vessels drawing up to 5·2 m (17 ft) can be obtained in mid-river just below High Hill Point (41°32'·85N 71°12'·92W), clear of the pipeline areas shown on the chart, in 6 to 8 m (20 to 26 ft). Although open S, a heavy sea seldom reaches as far as this anchorage.
   Local knowledge is required to navigate the river during darkness.

APPROACHES TO NARRAGANSETT BAY

General information
Charts 2890, 2730

Description
5.184

1   Narragansett Bay is approached between Block Island (41°10'·50N 71°35'·00W) and Sakonnet Point, 22 miles NE.
   Block Island is hilly, the highest point being Beacon Hill (41°10'·54N 71°35'·38W), 61 m (200 ft) high. The island is nearly divided in two in its central part by Great Salt Pond (6.22); Old Harbor (5.189) lies on the E coast opposite Great Salt Pond.
   The coast of Block Island is mostly fringed with boulders and should be given a berth of at least 5 cables.

Traffic regulations
5.185

1   **Navigation Rules for US Inland Waters** apply to all waters in Narragansett Bay lying within an E-W line drawn from Brenton Point (41°26'·97N 71°21'·31W) through Beavertail Point (41°26'·96N 71°23'·97W) to Boston Neck (41°27'·00N 71°26'·40W). See 1.44 and Appendix VII for further information.

2   **Traffic separation scheme** leads N from the precautionary area (5.10) in Rhode Island Sound. This TSS is IMO-adopted and Rule 10 of *International Regulations for Preventing Collisions at Sea (1972)* applies. The two traffic lanes are separated by a 2 mile wide zone. This zone is a restricted area (see below).

3   **Safety zones.** All waters of Rhode Island Sound within a ½ mile radius of any high interest vessel while the vessel is anchored within ½ mile of the point 41°25'·00N 71°23'·00W in the Narragansett Bay Precautionary Area. High interest vessels include barges or ships carrying LNG, LPG, chlorine, anhydrous ammonia or any other cargo deemed to be of high interest.
   A moving safety zone has been established 2 miles ahead, 1 mile astern and 1000 yards either side of high interest vessels transiting Narragansett Bay or the Providence and Taunton Rivers.
   For definition and general regulations concerning safety zones see Appendix V.

4   **Restricted area,** situated between the traffic lanes of the TSS, is a Torpedo Range and is closed to shipping during torpedo firing. See Appendix VI.
   North Atlantic right whale. See 1.51, *Admiralty List of Radio Signals Volume 6(5)* and Appendices VIII and X.

Directions
(continued from 5.15)

Principal marks
5.186

1   **Landmark:**
   House (white) (41°12'·83N 71°33'·56W), on Block Island.

Major lights:
Block Island South–east Light (red brick 8-sided pyramidal tower on dwelling) (41°09'·17N 71°33'·07W), standing on Southeast Point.
Point Judith Light (white 8–sided tower, brown top, 16 m in height) (41°21'·66N 71°28'·88W).
Beavertail Light (square granite tower beside white dwelling) (41°26'·96N 71°23'·97W).

Other aids to navigation
5.187

1 **Racons:**
A Light Buoy (41°06'·01N 71°23'·37W).
NB Light Buoy (41°23'·00N 71°23'·36W).
See *Admiralty List of Radio Signals Volume 2.*

Directions
5.188

1 From within the precautionary area centred on 41°06'·00N 71°23'·40W, the approach route to Narragansett Bay leads N through the TSS to the vicinity of the pilot boarding position, passing E of NB Light Buoy, at the N end of the TSS.
(Directions continue at 5.201 and 5.207)

Old Harbor

General information
5.189

1 Old Harbor (41°10'·60N 71°33'·30W) on the E side of Block Island, often used as a harbour of refuge, is situated 1 mile NW of Old Harbor Point (41°09'·88N 71°32'·70W) and is formed by two breakwaters. No 3 Light (green square on white framework tower on base) stands at the head of the E breakwater.

Limiting conditions
5.190

1 **Project depth** in the entrance channel, basin and inner harbour anchorage area is 4·6 m (15 ft).
5.191

1 **Anchorage** may be obtained in the inner harbour, but the E side of the harbour is kept clear for the ferry.
Berth. The ferry wharf is situated in the SE part of the harbour.

Port services
5.192

1 **Supplies.** Fuel.

NARRAGANSETT BAY

General information
Charts 2890, 2730, 2731, 2732
Description
5.193

1 Narragansett Bay is entered between Brenton Point (41°26'·97N 71°21'·31W), the SW extremity of Rhode Island, and Boston Neck, 3½ miles W. From the entrance the bay extends 18 miles N to the mouth of the Providence River (5.227).

2 Rhode Island forms the E shore of the bay. Conanicut Island (41°31'·00N 71°22'·50W) and Prudence Island (41°37'·30N 71°19'·00W), together with several smaller islands, lie in the bay and divide the entrance and the lower part of the bay into East Passage and West Passage, which unite 3 miles below the entrance to Providence River. Bristol Neck (5.221), extending 5 miles S from the head of the bay, divides the head into two arms: Mount Hope Bay (5.247), the NE arm into which Taunton River (5.247) flows; and the NW arm, the approach to Providence River.

Entrances
5.194

1 **East Passage**, the principal passage into Narragansett Bay, is entered between Brenton Point and Beavertail Point (41°26'·96N 71°23'·97W), the S extremity of Beaver Neck. The passage is the deeper and most direct route to the ports of Newport, Bristol, Fall River and Providence.
West Passage is entered between Beavertail Point and Boston Neck, 2 miles W. This passage is the approach to Dutch Island Harbor (5.224) and Greenwich Bay (5.226). Vessels may also go to Providence by West Passage, but the route through East Passage is generally used.

Depths
5.195

1 **East Passage** has depths of 18·3 m (60 ft) in the buoyed channel, for 10 miles from the entrance to where the channel divides E of Prudence Island. For depths beyond this point see 5.230 and 5.249.
West Passage has depths suitable for vessels drawing over 4·9 m (16 ft) as far as Dutch Island Harbor (5.224), and for vessels drawing up to 4·9 m (16 ft) as far as Providence River by way of a narrow channel NW of Patience Island (41°39'·40N 71°21'·60W).

Fish traps
5.196

1 Fish trap areas, in which below–water piling may exist, fringe some of the shores of Narragansett Bay.

Pilotage
5.197

1 See 5.173.

Traffic regulations
5.198

1 **Navigation Rules for US Inland Waters.** See 5.185.
Security Broadcast System. See 5.176. Reporting positions are shown on the chart.
Regulated navigation area. A regulated navigation area has been established between NB Light Buoy (41°23'·00N 71°23'·36W) and Fox Point (41°48'·90N 71°23'·98W). CFR Title 33 §165.122 gives reporting requirements in this area, restrictions on draught and minimum visibility. For definition and general regulations concerning regulated navigation areas see Appendix V.

2 **Safety zones.** See 5.185.
Restricted areas. A restricted area about 6 miles in length is situated between Gould Island (41°32'·00N 71°20'·67W) and a position NE of Hope Island (41°36'·10N 71°22'·10W). See Appendix VI.
Restricted areas surround Coasters Harbor Island (41°30'·60N 71°19'·65W) and Coddington Cove (41°31'·50N 71°19'·10W) (5.219). See Appendix VI.

Vertical clearances
5.199

1 **Newport Bridge** spans East Passage, 4 miles above its entrance, between Taylor Point (41°30′·57N 71°21′·57W) on Conanicut Island and Rhode Island, ESE. The central span has a vertical clearance of 59·1 m (194 ft).

Jamestown Bridge spans West Passage, 5 miles above its entrance, between Conanicut Island and the mainland W. Vertical clearance 41·1 m (135 ft) over the central 91·4 m (300 ft).

Natural conditions
5.200

1 **Tidal streams**. Over the greater part of Narragansett Bay, the maximum rate of flood and ebb streams is about ½ kn in the wider channels and 1½ kn in the narrower parts. For further details see Tidal Stream tables.

Ice. Navigation in Narragansett Bay is sometimes impeded by floating ice, and in severe winters by packs of field ice. The ice breaking up in Providence River and Mount Hope Bay is set by N and NE winds down the bay through East Passage. If there is much ice, a gorge is sometimes formed at Fort Adams but it is of short duration. The passages are rarely closed for any length of time below Gould Island (41°32′·00N 71°20′·67W) in East Passage, and Dutch Island (41°30′·20N 71°24′·00W) in West Passage.

Directions
(continued from 5.188)

Principal marks
5.201

1 **Landmarks for East Passage:**
Hog Island Shoal Lighthouse (white conical tower, black round base) (41°37′·94N 71°16′·39W).
Old Light House (white tower and dwelling) (41°43′·51N 71°20′·34W), standing on Nayatt Point.

2 **Landmark for West Passage:**
Plum Beach Light (white tower, black top) (41°31′·82N 71°24′·31W), close N of the Jamestown Bridge.
Major light:
Beavertail Light (41°26′·96N 71°23′·97W) (5.186).

Other aids to navigation
5.202

1 **Racons:**
NB Light Buoy (41°23′·00N 71°23′·36W).
Newport Bridge tower (41°30′·30N 71°20′·92W).
See *Admiralty List of Radio Signals Volume 2*.

East Passage
5.203

1 **Entrance.** From the vicinity of the pilot boarding position (41°23′·20N 71°21′·40W) the track leads initially NNW, to a position:
ESE of Beavertail Light (41°26′·96N 71°23′·97W) (5.186), standing on Beavertail Point, the S extremity of Beaver Neck.
The track then leads N between Butter Ball Rock (41°27′·50N 71°21′·81W), marked 1¼ cables WSW by No 6 Light Buoy (starboard hand) and Lion Head (41°27′·28N 71°23′·44W) thence NE, passing:

2 NW of Castle Hill Light (conical granite tower, white top) (41°27′·73N 71°21′·78W) standing on Castle Hill, the W point of Rhode Island, and:
SE of Kettle Bottom Rock (41°28′·35N 71°22′·33W), marked on its SE side by No 7 Light Buoy (port hand), thence:
SE of Bull Point (41°28′·82N 71°21′·32W), a rugged headland fronted by above and below–water rocks. No 9 Light Buoy (port hand) is moored 2 cables SE. Thence:

3 SE of The Dumplings (41°28′·97N 71°21′·18W), a group of rocks that extend NE from Bull Point. No 11 Light Buoy (port hand) is moored 2 cables NE. Thence:
W of Fort Adams (41°28′·70N 71°20′·28W) on the N point of Newport Neck, the S entrance point to Newport Harbor. No 2 Light (red triangle on white framework tower) stands at the entrance to a boat camber on the N side of the point.
Useful marks:
Radar tower (41°27′·29N 71°23′·82W).
Cupola (41°28′·54N 71°22′·49W).
(Directions for Newport Harbor continue at 5.214)

5.204

1 **Fort Adams to Halfway Rock.** From a position W of Fort Adams, East Passage continues N through the outer harbour of Newport (5.210) to Newport Bridge, passing:
W of Rose Island (41°29′·80N 71°20′·50W), in the central part of the outer harbour of Newport (5.210). Rose Island Light (white dwelling) stands on the SW point of the island and No 12 Light Buoy (starboard hand) lies 1 cable SW of this point. Thence:

2 Beneath the central span of Newport Bridge (41°30′·33N 71°21′·00W), see 5.199.
The track then leads NNE, passing:
WNW of Bishop Rock Shoal (41°31′·01N 71°20′·02W), marked on its W side by No 14 Light Buoy (starboard hand), thence:
ESE of Gould Island (41°32′·00N 71°20′·67W), a US naval reservation, flat and sparsely wooded. A light (red and white chequered diamond on framework tower) stands at the S end of the island. A small boat harbour at the N end of the island is protected by a mole. Thence:

3 WNW of No 18 Breakwater Light (red triangle on red framework tower) (41°31′·95N 71°19′·47W), at the head of the breakwater protecting Coddington Cove (5.219), thence:
ESE of Halfway Rock (41°33′·82N 71°19′·93W), marked by a beacon (red and white).
Useful marks:
Spire (41°29′·24N 71°18′·80W) (white), in Newport.
Church tower (41°29′·63N 71°19′·24W), in Newport.
Cupola (41°30′·45N 71°19′·77W), on Naval War College, Coasters Harbor Island.

5.205

1 **Halfway Rock to Hog Island.** From a position ESE of Halfway Rock, East Passage continues NNE between Prudence Island and Rhode Island to the vicinity of Hog Island (41°38′·55N 71°16′·84W) (5.221), passing:

Rose Island and Newport Bridge from SE (5.204)
(Original dated 2007)
(Photograph - Cdr S Foster, MV Saga Ruby)

ESE of Fiske Rock (41°34′·03N 71°19′·78W), marked on its N end by a buoy (preferred channel to starboard), thence:

2   ESE of WR 21 Light Buoy (port hand) (41°34′·54N 71°18′·98W), marking a wreck, thence:

WNW of a bank (41°35′·35N 71°18′·09W), with swept depths of 4·9 m (16 ft), extending 3 cables N of Dyer Island and marked by No 24 Light Buoy (port hand). Thence:

Between No 25 Light Buoy (starboard hand) (41°36′·01N 71°18′·14W) and No 26 Light Buoy (starboard hand), 1 cable ESE. These mark the start of the entrance channel leading to Providence River. Thence:

3   ESE of Sandy Point (41°36′·35N 71°18′·21W), on which stands a light (white 8–sided tower), thence:

W of SP Light Buoy (preferred channel to port) (41°36′·93N 71°17′·59W), which marks the division of the routes to Providence River to the NNW and Mount Hope Bay to the NE.

(Directions for Mount Hope Bay continue at 5.256)

Hog Island to Providence River entrance
5.206

1   From the vicinity of SP Light Buoy (41°36′·93N 71°17′·59W) the entrance channel to the mouth of Providence River, marked by light buoys (lateral), leads generally NNW, passing:

WSW of Southwest Point (41°38′·27N 71°17′·10W), the SW extremity of Hog Island (5.221). Shoal water extends 5 cables SW from this point. Thence:

2   WSW of Popasquash Point (41°39′·00N 71°18′·00W), which forms the N entrance point to the SW approach to Bristol Harbor (5.221), thence:

E of Ohio Ledge (41°40′·97N 71°19′·42W), the SE part of a larger shoal area, marked on its SE side by OL buoy (preferred channel to starboard), thence:

Through Rumstick Neck Reach, the final leg of the entrance channel, and thence into Providence River.

(Directions for Providence River continue at 5.239)

West Passage
(continued from 5.188)
5.207

1   **Entrance.** From the vicinity of the pilot boarding position (41°23′·20N 71°21′·40W) the track leads initially NNW, to a position clear of the safety zone in the precautionary area (see appendix V). The mariner must then use caution as the track then leads across the SSW bound recommended route to a position ESE of Whale Rock (41°26′·67N 71°25′·42W). The track then leads N, passing:

Between Whale Rock, marked by No 3 Light Buoy (port hand) off its E side, and a dangerous wreck (41°26′·70N 71°25′·67W), position approximate, marked SE by NR Buoy (preferred channel to starboard) thence:

2   E of Jones Ledge (41°27′·73N 71°25′·19W). No 5 Buoy (port hand) lies 1½ cables E of the ledge. Thence:

W of a dangerous wreck (41°28′·55N 71°24′·30W) (reported 2004), position approximate, thence:

Between South Ferry (41°29′·52N 71°25′·16W), a point with a pier and several dolphins and piles nearby, and Beaverhead (41°29′·53N 71°23′·91W), 1 mile E, a rocky bluff with a disused pier at the S entrance to Dutch Island Harbor, thence:

3   W of Dutch Island (41°30′·20N 71°24′·00W), thence:
      Beneath Jamestown Bridge (41°31′·65N 71°23′·85W). See 5.199.

   Useful marks:
      Radar tower (41°27′·29N 71°23′·82W).
      Church spire (41°29′·56N 71°25′·53W).
      Dutch Island Light (white square tower, black cupola) (41°29′·81N 71°24′·26W).

5.208

1   **Jamestown Bridge to abreast Pine Hill Point**
From a position N of the bridge West Passage continues N, passing:
      W of Fowler Rock (41°32′·11N 71°23′·59W), marked by No 10 Buoy (starboard hand), thence:
      E of Halfway Ledge (41°33′·24N 71°24′·44W) lying 5 cables E of Fox Island (41°33′·26N 71°25′·11W), low lying with a few trees on it, thence:
      Between Conanicut Point (41°34′·40N 71°22′·30W) and a 3·9 m (13 ft) (10 ft on BA2730) shoal (41°34′·76N 71°23′·92W), marked by a buoy (preferred channel to port), thence:

2   W of a shoal with a boiler awash (41°35′·59N 71°22′·66W), lying 4 cables SW of Hope Island on which are low grassy hills with a few trees. No 2 Light Buoy (starboard hand) marks the SW side of the shoal.
      Thence to a position abreast Pine Hill Point (41°37′·92N 71°20′·87W).

5.209

1   **Head of West Passage.** From N of a line joining Pine Hill Point to Calf Pasture Point (41°37′·57N 71°24′·21W), 2½ miles W, the channel leads N and then NE through the shoals that obstruct the head of West Passage to Providence River, passing:
      E of No 5 Buoy (port hand) (41°37′·98N 71°22′·24W), at the entrance to the channel, thence:

2   W of No 6 Buoy (starboard hand) (41°38′·24N 71°22′·16W), marking the E side of the channel, thence:
      Between Warwick Point, on which stands a light (white conical tower) (41°40′·03N 71°22′·70W) and Northwest Point (41°39′·63N 71°22′·00W) on Patience Island, 6½ cables SE. Southeast Ledge (41°39′·90N 71°22′·60W) extends 1½ cables SE from Warwick Point, and No 8 Light Buoy (starboard hand) marks the W limit of shoal water extending from Northwest Point.

3   Thence the track leads NE, passing:
      NW of Providence Point (41°39′·98N 71°20′·70W), the N extremity of Prudence Island, thence:
      NW of Fork Rock Buoy (preferred channel to port) (41°40′·56N 71°20′·85W), which marks the shoals extending N from Providence Point.
      Thence the track leads SE and then E, passing about 6 cables S of Ohio Ledge, to join the entrance channel leading to Providence River.

Newport Harbor

Chart 2730
General information
5.210

1   **Position and function.** Newport Harbor (41°29′·00N 71°20′·00W) situated in the N side of Newport Neck, the SW part of Rhode Island, is an important harbour of refuge, much used by small vessels and yachts. It is a port of entry.
      The town of Newport, which in 2010 had a population of 24 672, lies on the E side of the harbour and is one of the principal summer resorts on the US Atlantic coast. It is a minor port and a naval base.

Limiting conditions
5.211

1   **Depths.** Outer harbour: see 5.195. Inner harbour: 4 to 5·5 m (13 to 18 ft).
      Vertical clearance. A bridge, with a vertical clearance of 4·2 m (14 ft), joins Goat Island to the mainland across the N entrance to the inner harbour.
      Tidal levels. Mean spring range about 1·2 m (3·9 ft); mean neap range about 0·8 m (2·6 ft). See information in *Admiralty Tide Tables*.

2   **Ice** may interfere with navigation for short periods during severe winters. Vessels and tugs keep ice well broken up in the main channel through the inner harbour.

Arrival information
5.212

1   **Port operations.** A speed limit of 4½ kn is in force in the inner harbour.
      Outer anchorages. See 5.215.
      Pilotage. See 5.173.

Harbour
5.213

1   **General layout.** Newport Harbor, divided into an inner and outer harbour, lies between Fort Adams (41°28′·73N 71°20′·28W) and Gould Island, 3 miles N.
      The outer harbour consists of that part of East Passage between The Dumplings (5.203) and Gould Island. It includes the passage, obstructed by Gull Rocks (41°30′·11N 71°19′·98W) and Tracey Ledge (41°29′·91N 71°20′·02W), that passes between Rose Island and Coasters Harbor Island. The outer harbour contains a number of anchorages.

2   The inner harbour, which lies between the E side of Goat Island (41°29′·31N 71°19′·65W) and the waterfront of Newport has two entrances. The S entrance is between the S end of Goat Island and Ida Lewis Rock (41°28′·64N 71°19′·55W), 3 cables S, and the N entrance leads between Goat Island and Rose Island. The inner harbour contains anchorages for small craft and a number of alongside berths.

3   **Natural conditions.** In the S entrance off Bull Point (41°28′·82N 71°21′·32W) the tidal streams are irregular; at strength the in–going stream may reach 1¼ kn and the out–going stream 1½ kn. N of Bull Point rates seldom exceed 1 kn and in the inner harbour are usually less than ½ kn.
      Prevailing winds are SW in the summer and NW in the winter. The heaviest gales are usually from the NW and NE.

Directions
(continued from 5.203)
5.214

1   **Outer harbour.** See 5.204.
      Inner harbour. The two entrances, N and S of Goat Island, are well marked. The harbour is easy to enter by day or night and the chart is the best guide. The bridge (5.211) across the N entrance limits the size of vessels that can enter the harbour from that direction.

2   **Useful marks:**
      Church tower (41°29′·63N 71°19′·24W), in Newport.

Newport Harbor from SSW (5.213)
(Original dated 1990)

(Photograph - Joseph R Melanson of www.skypic.com)

Spire (41°29′·24N 71°18′·80W) (white), in Newport.
Cupola (41°30′·45N 71°19′·77W), on Naval War College, Coasters Harbor Island.

Berths
5.215

1 **Anchorages.** The following anchorage areas are established in Newport. No vessel, except in emergency, may anchor outside these areas.

Outer harbour:
Anchorage A (41°31′·00N 71°21′·20W). West side of East Passage between Bull Point and NW of Gould Island. The part of this area N of Jamestown approach is for US Naval vessels only. US Naval requirements take precedence in the area S of this approach.

2 **Anchorage C** (41°30′·50N 71°20′·30W). Five cables W of Coasters Harbor Island (41°30′·61N 71°19′·63W) US Naval requirements take precedence.
Anchorage D (41°29′·25N 71°20′·20W). Four cables W of Goat Island. US Naval requirements take precedence between 1 May and 1 October.
Anchorage E (41°30′·05N 71°19′·50W). Two cables S of Coasters Harbor Island. US Naval requirements take precedence between 1 May and 1 October.

3 **Inner harbour:**
Anchorage No 1 in Brenton Cove (41°28′·60N 71°19′·80W), in the S part of the inner harbour.
Anchorage No 2 (41°29′·12N 71°19′·30W), in the inner harbour E of Goat Island.
Anchorage No 3 (41°29′·65N 71°19′·45W), in the N entrance to the inner harbour N of the bridge connecting Goat Island to the mainland.
Nos 1, 2 and 3 are special anchorages; see 1.45.

4 **Alongside berths** in the inner harbour consist of a city wharf and numerous private piers. The depths alongside the principal piers range between 2·1 and 5·5 m.

Port services
5.216

1 **Repairs.** Newport has a commercial shipyard specialising in repair, construction and conversion.
The largest patent slip can handle vessels up to 100 m in length and 6·5 m draught.
Other facilities. Hospitals.
Supplies: fuel; water; provisions and stores.

Jamestown
5.217

1 Jamestown (41°29′·92N 71°21′·63W), on the E side of Conanicut Island, is situated at the head of an open bay which forms part of the outer harbour and lies between Bull Point and Taylor Point, 1¾ miles N. A marina lies within the bight.

East Passage — Other anchorages and harbours

Anchorage areas
5.218

1 The following anchorage areas are established in the East Passage N of Newport. No vessels, except in emergency, may anchor outside these areas:

Anchorage B. Naval and General Anchorage (41°34'·00N 71°18'·40W) between Coddington Cove and 1½ miles N of Coggeshall Point (41°35'·54N 71°17'·17W) on the E side of East Passage.

Anchorage B-1. Naval and General Anchorage (41°34'·35N 71°19'·50W). Naval requirements have priority.

Coddington Cove
5.219

1 Coddington Cove (41°31'·40N 71°19'·10W) is entered between Coddington Point (41°31'·38N 71°19'·42W), close N of Newport, and the head of a breakwater on which stands No 18 Light (5.204). The cove lies within a restricted area. See Appendix VI.

Berths. Two piers extend from the shore. The N side of the N pier is used by the US Navy, the S pier is used by a shipyard. There are numerous mooring buoys in the harbour.

Depths of 9·1 m are reported alongside both piers.

Melville
5.220

1 Melville (41°35'·09N 71°17'·41W) stands close S of Coggeshall Point. Weaver Cove (41°34'·70N 71°17'·32W) lies S of Melville between Dyer Island and the shore.

2 **Approach** from the NW is through waters clear of charted dangers. The shoal water N and NE of Dyer Island (41°35'·00N 71°17'·98W) is marked by No 24 Light Buoy (starboard hand) and Nos 7 and 5 Buoys (port hand). The shoal water S of Dyer Island is connected to Rhode Island by a bar with depths of 2·7 to 5·2 m (9 to 17 ft).

Berth. A US Navy fuelling depot with depths alongside of 9·1 to 10·7 m.

Chart 2731
Bristol Harbor
5.221

1 Bristol Harbor (41°40'·00N 71°17'·00W) lies between the S end of Bristol Neck (41°41'·60N 71°16'·35W) and Popasquash Neck (41°40'·00N 71°18'·00W). The town of Bristol stands on the E side of the harbour.

Bristol Harbor is entered between Bristol Point (41°38'·60N 71°15'·65W) and Popasquash Point, 1¾ miles W. Hog Island, low and wooded, lies in the entrance, with a natural channel on either side of it.

2 **Depths.** Both channels have depths of 5·8 to 7·6 m (19 to 25 ft). Bristol Harbor, in the N part of the cove, has depths of 4·6 to 5·2 m (15 to 17 ft).

Landmarks:
Hog Island Shoal Lighthouse (41°37'·94N 71°16'·39W) (5.201).
Tank (41°40'·86N 71°15'·74W).

3 **Directions for west channel.** From the vicinity of No 2 Light Buoy (starboard hand), 8 cables W of Southwest Point (41°38'·27N 71°17'·10W), the W channel leads NNE, passing:

Clear of the shoal patches 5 cables SW and W of Southwest Point, thence:

ESE of Popasquash Point (41°39'·00N 71°18'·00W). A light buoy (preferred channel to port) marks the S limit of shoal water off the point. Thence:

4 WNW of Castle Island (41°39'·23N 71°17'·17W), on which stands No 2 Light (red triangle on framework tower), thence:

ESE of Usher Rocks (41°39'·55N 71°17'·50W), which lie 2 cables SE of Usher Point (41°39'·65N 71°17'·62W). No 3 Buoy (port hand) lies 1 cable E of the rocks.

Thence into Bristol Harbor.

5 **Directions for the east channel.** The chart is the best guide.

Anchorage area O extends from the W shore of Bristol Harbor. This area provides excellent anchorage in 5 m (15 to 17 ft), soft bottom.

Wharves. There are depths alongside of 2·7 to 4 m at the wharves and piers at Bristol.

Chart 2731, US Chart 13224 (see 1.16)
Warren River
5.222

1 Warren River flows into the NE part of Narragansett Bay between Rumstick Point (41°42'·44N 71°18'·13W) and the shore of Bristol Neck, 5 cables E. The river is the approach to the towns of Warren and Barrington, and the Barrington River which flows into Warren River opposite Warren.

2 **Depths.** Warren River, narrow and winding, has depths of about 2·7 m (9 ft) in the well buoyed channel to the lower wharves at Warren, and the same depth is in Barrington River as far as the fixed bridge about 5 cables above the entrance.

Anchorage. Excellent anchorage may be found at the mouth of Warren River in 4 to 5 m (14 to 15 ft), mud, about 2 cables from the E shore.

3 **Useful mark.** Allen Rock Light (green square on framework tower), standing on Allen Rock (41°42'·81N 71°17'·59W).

Alongside berths with depths of 2·1 to 6·1 m are reported at the major wharves at Warren.

Repairs. There is a shipyard on the E side of the Warren River.

Supplies: fuel; water; provisions and stores.

West Passage - Other anchorages and harbours

Chart 2730
Anchorage areas
5.223

1 The following anchorage areas are established in the S part of the West Passage. No vessels, except in emergency, may anchor outside these areas:

Anchorage H (41°28'·70N 71°24'·80W). General anchorage on W side of entrance.

Anchorage I (41°28'·60N 71°24'·10W). General anchorage on E side of entrance. A dangerous wreck (5.207) lies in this anchorage.

2 **Anchorage J** (41°30'·20N 71°24'·90W). General anchorage W of Dutch Island.

Anchorage K (41°29'·85N 71°23'·60W). General anchorage in S part of Dutch Island Harbor (5.224).

Anchorage L (41°32'·60N 71°24'·60W). General anchorage on the W side of West Passage between N side of Dutch Island and Wickford (41°34'·20N 71°27'·10W) (Chart 2890).

3 **Anchorage M** (41°30'·70N 71°23'·70W). General anchorage in N part of Dutch Island Harbor and N of Dutch Island.

Anchorage N (41°34′·00N 71°23′·10W). General anchorage SW of Conanicut Point.

Dutch Island Harbor
5.224

1   Dutch Island Harbor (41°30′·00N 71°23′·40W) lies off the W side of Conanicut Island, E of Dutch Island.
   Approach. The harbour may be entered either S or N of Dutch Island. The S and principal entrance lies between Beaverhead and a light (brick building) on the S end of Dutch Island.

2   A light buoy (preferred channel to port) marks the limit of a drying reef extending from the S point of Dutch Island, and No 2 Buoy (starboard hand) marks the limit of the shoal water extending N from Beaverhead.
   Depths. The S entrance may be used by vessels with a draught of up to 8·5 m (28 ft) and the N entrance by those drawing not more than 4·6 m (15 ft).

3   **Anchorage.** Area K and the S part of Area M (5.223) are situated in Dutch Island Harbor. Excellent anchorage in 4 to 15 m (12 to 48 ft), sticky bottom, may be obtained, but vessels with a draught of more than 5·5 m (18 ft) should give the E shore a berth of more than 4 cables.

Quonset Point and Davisville Depot
5.225

1   Quonset Point (41°35′·15N 71°24′·40W) is marked by the conspicuous buildings of the Industrial Park and Quonset State Airport. Davisville (41°36′·69N 71°24′·08W) lying 1½ miles N is a ferry terminal and major vehicle handling port.
   Depths:
      Channel to turning basin off Quonset Point. 10·4 to 13·7 m (34 to 45 ft).

2   Basin off Quonset Point: 9·8 to 10·7 m (32 to 35 ft) except for patches of 8·2 m (27 ft) and 9·1 m (30 ft).
      Channel to Davisville Depot: 9·8 m (32 ft).

3   **Approach.** Both terminals are usually approached from East Passage, until N of Conanicut Point, thence through a buoyed dredged channel to a turning basin off Quonset Point from which a channel leads N to Davisville Depot.
   Useful marks:
      Quonset State Airport Control Tower (41°35′·61N 71°24′·73W).
      Water tower (white) (41°36′·06N 71°25′·74W).

4   **Berths.** Pier at Quonset Point with a reported depth alongside of 9·1 m.
   Davisville Depot. Depths alongside of 8·8 m on the SW side of Pier 1 and in the basin between Pier 1 and 2.

Greenwich Bay
5.226

1   Greenwich Bay (41°40′·60N 71°25′·00W) is entered from the N part of West Passage between Sandy Point (41°39′·77N 71°24′·60W) and Warwick Point, 1½ miles ENE. Round Rock lies in the entrance 8 cables SW of Warwick Point and is marked on its E side by No 1 Light Buoy (port hand).
   There are general depths of 3 m (10 ft) and over within the bay.
   Approach. The bay is entered through a natural channel from a position S of Warwick Point.
   Useful mark:
      Warwick Point Light (5.209).
   Local knowledge is necessary to enter the bay.

PROVIDENCE

General information

Chart 2731
Position and function
5.227

1   Providence River, which flows into the N arm of Narragansett Bay between Nayatt Point (41°43′·51N 71°20′·34W) and Conimicut Point (41°43′·07N 71°21′·43W), 1 mile WSW, is the approach to the city of Providence and Seekonk River. The city of Providence lies at the head of navigation, 7 miles above the entrance and at the junction with Seekonk River.

2   The port's chief waterborne trade is in petroleum products, cement, lumber, scrap metal, general cargo and automobiles. It is a port of entry and in 2010 had a population of 178 042.

Port limits
5.228

1   The port area of Providence includes both sides of the navigable channel of Providence River above Pomham Rocks (5.240), which lie 4 miles above the entrance.

Port Authority
5.229

1   **Address.** Providence Port Authority, 35 Terminal Road, Suite 200, Providence, RI 02905.
   Website. www.provport.com

Limiting conditions

Depths
5.230

1   Project depth is 12·2 m (40 ft) in the main channel leading from just below Sandy Point Light (41°36′·35N 71°18′·21W) (5.205) to Fox Point (41°48′·90N 71°23′·98W) at the junction of Providence and Seekonk Rivers. For the latest controlling depths the charts and port authority should be consulted.

Tidal levels
5.231

1   Mean spring range about 1·6 m (5·2 ft); mean neap range about 1·1 m (3·6 ft). See information in *Admiralty Tide Tables*. Maximum range due to the effects of wind and other causes is 2·4 m.

Ice
5.232

1   The approach channel and the harbour are generally free of ice and navigable throughout the year. During severe winters, the harbour and lower part of Providence River are frozen over, but ice is usually broken up in the channels to the principal wharves by traffic in the harbour.

Arrival information

Port operations
5.233

1   Security Broadcast System (5.176). A speed limit of 5 kn is in force in the harbour.

Outer anchorages
5.234

1   See 5.218.

Pilotage and tugs
5.235

1   **Pilotage.** See 5.173.

Traffic regulations
5.236

1   **Regulated navigation area.** The deep-draught channel between Conimicut Light (41°43'·02N 71°20'·70W) and Fuller Rock Light (5.241) is part of Providence River, Providence, Rhode Island regulated navigation area.

For definition and general regulations concerning regulated navigation areas see Appendix V.

Harbour

General layout
5.237

1   The piers and wharves of the port of Providence are along both sides of the Providence River between Pomham Rocks Light (41°46'·65N 71°22'·17W) (5.240) and Fox Point (2½ miles NNW). The majority of berths are situated on the W bank.

Natural conditions
5.238

1   **Tidal streams** are weak in the approach channel and in the harbour except for the constricted part of Seekonk River.

Climate information. See 1.139 and 1.144.

Directions
(continued from 5.206)

Principal marks
5.239

1   **Landmarks:**
Lighthouse (disused) (41°43'·51N 71°20'·34W), on Nayatt Point (5.201).
Spire (41°45'·98N 71°23'·48W), at Pawtuxet.

Approach channel
5.240

1   From the mouth of Providence River (41°43'·40N 71°20'·90W) the approach channel, marked by light buoys (lateral), leads generally NNW through Conimicut Point Reach, Bullock Point Reach and Sabin Point Reach to the port of Providence, passing:
WSW of BP Light (red and white chequered diamond on framework tower) (41°44'·26N 71°21'·85W), standing on a rock at the edge of a shoal extending SW from Bullock Point (41°44'·71N 71°21'·55W), thence:

2   Between Gaspee Point (41°44'·65N 71°22'·65W) and Bullock Point, thence:
Between Pawtuxet Neck (41°45'·86N 71°23'·20W) and Sabin Point (41°45'·95N 71°22'·10W). SP Beacon marks the extremity of the shoal extending SW from Sabin Point. Thence:
W of Pomham Rocks Light (white 8-sided tower with dwelling) (41°46'·65N 71°22'·17W), standing on the W side of Pomham Rocks.

Entrance channel
5.241

1   From a position W of Pomham Rocks Light the channel in the port area leads generally NNW through Fuller Rock Reach and Fox Point Reach to the junction of Providence River and Seekonk River at Fox Point, passing:
ENE of Fields Point (41°47'·19N 71°22'·80W), thence:

2   WSW of Fuller Rock Light (red triangle on framework tower, granite base) (41°47'·65N 71°22'·78W), thence:
WSW of Kettle Point (41°47'·77N 71°22'·77W). Thence to the vicinity of Fox Point.

Berths

Anchorages
5.242

1   Vessels anchor as directed by the Harbour Master on the edge of the channel between Fields Point and Fox Point. A few vessels may anchor E of Fox Point in an area where part of Green Jacket Shoal has been removed.

Alongside berths
5.243

1   The principal alongside berths are as follows.
East side of Providence River:
Mobil Oil Co. Wharf (41°46'·95N 71°22'·30W): 213 m berthing face with depths alongside of 6·1 to 11·6 m.
West side of Providence River:
Municipal wharf (41°47'·50N 71°22'·92W): Berths 1 to 6. Overall length 1058 m with depths alongside of 10·7 to 12·2 m. Berths 5 and 6: general and containerised cargo. Berths 1 to 4: general cargo and petroleum products including LPG.

2   New England Bituminous Wharf (41°47'·86N 71°23'·33W): 117 m in length with a depth alongside of 9·1 m.
Lehigh Portland Cement and Lone Star Industries Wharves (41°47'·96N 71°23'·45W): 107 and 64 m in length, respectively, with depths alongside of 6·1 and 8·5 to 9·1 m, respectively.
Algonquin LNG Wharf (41°48'·10N 71°23'·75W): 137 m in length, depth alongside 7·6 m.

3   Texaco Harbor Junction Wharf (41°48'·01N 71°23'·50W): S side 220 m berthing space with a depth alongside of 9·8 m; N side 183 m berthing space with a depth alongside of 7·6 m. Petroleum products.

4   Promet Marine Services (State Pier) (41°48'·47N 71°24'·00W): 36 m face with depths alongside of 9·4 to 11·3 m; N and S sides 182 m in length with depths alongside of 6·7 to 11·3 m. Bulk and general cargo; repair berth.
Northeast Petroleum Corp. Pier (41°48'·57N 71°24'·06W): 183 m in length with a depth alongside of 9·1 m.
C H Sprague & Son Co. Pier (41°48'·65N 71°24'·10W): 158 m in length, with platforms, with a depth alongside of 11·3 m. Petroleum products.

Port services

Repairs
5.244

1   There are no facilities for dry docking large vessels; the nearest such facilities are at Boston. Minor hull, machinery and electrical repairs can be carried out at Providence.

Other facilities
5.245

1   Hospitals; oily waste disposal.

Supplies
5.246

1   Fuel by barge or at tanker berths; water; provisions and stores.

MOUNT HOPE BAY, FALL RIVER HARBOR AND TAUNTON RIVER

General information

Charts 2731, 2732 plans of Sandy Point to Fall River, Fall River Harbor, and State Pier

Description
5.247

1   Mount Hope Bay (41°41'·70N 71°12'·70W), off the NE part of Narragansett Bay, is the approach to the city of Fall River (5.261) and Taunton River, which flows into its NE corner. Fall River Harbor (5.261) is situated at the mouth of Taunton River. The bay is generally shallow with channels dredged through it.

Approaches
5.248

1   Mount Hope Bay can be approached from East Passage and entered between Bristol Point (41°38'·60N 71°15'·65W) and Musselbed Shoals Light (5.258), 4 cables S, or from Sakonnet River (5.183). The main approach is from East Passage (5.194) and the approach from Sakonnet River is little used.

Depths
5.249

1   The project depth in the main channel through Mount Hope Bay to about 9 cables above Brightman Street Bridge (5.252) is 10·7 m (35 ft).

Controlling depth (2004) in side channel to N entrance of Sakonnet River is 9·1 m (30 ft) and to North Tiverton (2004) (5.264) is 10·0 m (33 ft).

For the latest controlling depths the charts and port authority should be consulted.

Pilotage
5.250

1   See 5.173.

Traffic regulations
5.251

1   See 5.176. Vessels bound for Fall River Harbor should call Brightman Street Bridge (5.252) when entering Mount Hope Bay, if they need it opened.

Vertical clearance
5.252

1   **Mount Hope Bridge** crosses the entrance to Mount Hope Bay between Bristol Point and Rhode Island. It is a high level suspension bridge with a vertical clearance of 41·1 m (135 ft).
    Charles M. Braga Junior. Memorial Bridge, a fixed bridge at the mouth of Taunton River at Fall River, has a vertical clearance of 41·1 m (135 ft).

2   **Brightman Street Bridge** crosses Taunton River 1 mile upstream from Charles M. Braga Junior. Memorial Bridge. The bascule span has a vertical clearance of 8·2 m (27 ft) when closed. The bridge operator can be contacted on VHF.
    Veterans Memorial Bridge, a bascule bridge, with a design clearance of 18·3 m (60 ft), lies about 2 cables upstream of the Brightman Street Bridge.

3   **Between Fall River and Taunton** the river is crossed by three bridges. The swing road bridge at Berkley, 5 miles above Fall River, has a vertical clearance of 2·1 m (7 ft) when closed. At Taunton, 10 miles above Fall River, a fixed road bridge has a vertical clearance of 3·0 m (10 ft), and a rail bridge 2 cables farther upstream has a vertical clearance of 2·7 m (9 ft).

4   **Overhead power cables,** with a safe vertical clearance of 44·2 m (145 ft), span the river 2½ cables below Brightman Street Bridge. Overhead power cables, with a least safe vertical clearance of 19·8 m (65 ft), span the river 7 cables below Taunton.

Horizontal clearance
5.253

1   Brightman Street Bridge (5.252) has a horizontal clearance of 29·9 m (98 ft).

Fish traps
5.254

1   The limits of areas where fish traps may be found in the coastal waters of Mount Hope Bay are shown on the chart.

Natural conditions
5.255

1   **Tidal streams.** In Taunton River the tidal streams generally follow the direction of the channel and, except at bridges, do not hinder navigation. The out–going stream is normally stronger than the in–going.

2   **Ice.** The approach channels through Mount Hope Bay and the harbour are generally free from ice and navigable throughout the year. Taunton River is commonly closed from December to March. In severe winters the harbour and Mount Hope Bay are occasionally frozen over, but the channels to the principal wharves are kept open by vessels and tugs operating in the harbour.
    Local weather. The prevailing winds are NE except during the summer months when they are SW. The strongest gales are usually NW.

Directions
(continued from 5.205)

Principal mark
5.256

1   Landmark:
    Towers of Mount Hope Bridge (41°38'·39N 71°15'·48W).

Other aid to navigation
5.257

1   Racon:
    Mount Hope Bridge (41°38'·39N 71°15'·48W).
    See *Admiralty List of Radio Signals Volume 2.*

South-west approach to Mount Hope Bay
5.258

1   From a position S of Hog Island the main approach to Mount Hope Bay leads NE, passing:
    NW of Arnold Point (41°37'·42N 71°16'·29W), thence:
    SE of Hog Island Shoal Light (41°37'·94N 71°16'·39W) (5.201), standing on the SE part of a bank extending S from Hog Island. The SE limit of this bank is marked by No 3 Light Buoy (port hand). Thence:

2   NW of Musselbed Shoals Light No 6A (red triangle on framework tower, granite base) (41°38'·18N 71°15'·93W) at the outer end of Musselbed Shoals, extending NW from Rhode Island. The white sector (049·2°-052·7°) of this light leads between the banks extending from Hog Island Shoal and Arnold Point. No 6 Buoy (starboard hand) lies ½ cable NW of the light.

Thence beneath Mount Hope Bridge (5.252) and into Mount Hope Bay.

Mount Hope Bay

5.259

1 **Main channel.** The main channel through Mount Hope Bay, marked by light buoys and buoys (lateral), leads NE, passing:

SE of Mount Hope Point (41°39'·97N 71°14'·39W). Mount Hope, a prominent hill, stands 5 cables N of the point. Thence:

2 SE of Spar Island (41°41'·30N 71°13'·20W), small, low and in two parts, thence:

SE of Borden Flats (41°42'·35N 71°10'·72W), on the outer part of which stands a light (white conical tower, brown round base) (41°42'·27N 71°10'·46W).

Thence beneath Charles M. Braga Junior. Memorial Bridge (5.252) and into Fall River Harbor (5.261).

5.260

1 **Side channels.** From the vicinity of MH Light Buoy (preferred channel to port), 5 cables SSE of Mount Hope Point, a dredged side channel, marked with light buoys and buoys, leads E for 1 mile passing N of Common Fence Point (41°39'·32N 71°13'·22W). The channel then divides, one branch leading S to the Sakonnet River (5.183) and the other N to North Tiverton (5.264).

2 From a position in the main channel 3¼ miles NE of Mount Hope Point, the alignment (325·3°) of a pair of lights (piles) on the E side of Brayton Point leads through a dredged channel, marked by light buoys, to a power station wharf. In 1998 this channel had a reported controlling depth of 10·4 m (34 ft).

Fall River Harbor

General information

5.261

1 **Position and function.** The city of Fall River (41°42'·35N 71°09'·98W) is situated on the E shore of the mouth of Taunton River and the head of Mount Hope Bay. In 2010 it had a population of 88 857. The port facilities of Fall River Harbor are along Taunton and Sakonnet Rivers and in Mount Hope Bay.

2 Fall River is a port of entry. It has a considerable coasting trade, and is an important manufacturing centre and distribution centre for oil products.

Port Authority. Fall River Port Authority, State Pier. Water Street, Fall River, MA 02721.

Limiting conditions

5.262

1 **Depths.** See 5.249.
Largest berths. See 5.265.
Ice. See 5.255.

Arrival information

5.263

1 **Port operations.** A speed limit of 5 kn is in force in the channel off the piers and wharves.

Anchorage may be obtained either side of the dredged approach channel or anywhere in Mount Hope Bay where depth or bottom are suitable. The chart is the best guide. However, care should be taken not to anchor near the submarine cable area extending across Borden Flats (5.259) and into the main channel of the river.

2 **Pilotage.** See 5.173.
Traffic regulations. See 5.251.

Harbour

5.264

1 **General layout.** The piers and wharves of Fall River Harbor are situated at:

North Tiverton (41°42'·35N 71°09'·98W) between the N entrance to Sakonnet River and the E side of Mount Hope Bay, 2 miles NNE.

East side of Taunton River. Between Charles M. Braga Junior. Memorial Bridge and the turning basin, 2 miles NE.

2 West side of Taunton River. At Brayton Point (41°42'·56N 71°11'·28W) and on W bank of river abreast the turning basin.

Local weather. See 5.255.

Alongside berths

5.265

1 The principal alongside berths are as follows:
North Tiverton:

Tiverton Terminal Pier (41°40'·42N 71°12'·02W): 242 m in length, with dolphins, with a depth alongside of 10·7 m. Petroleum products.

East side of Taunton River:

Borden and Remington Corp. Wharf (41°42'·24N 71°10'·07W): 116 m in length with a depth alongside of 8·5 m. Latex and caustic soda.

2 State Pier (41°42'·34N 71°09'·92W). NW face: 121 m in length with depths alongside of 5·5 to 10·7 m. SW side: 189 m in length with a depth alongside of 10·7 m. General and RoRo cargo. Battleship *USS Massachusetts* and three other USN vessels are berthed close NE of State Pier.

Shell Oil Co. Wharf (41°44'·02N 71°08'·58W): 213 m in length, with dolphins, with a depth alongside of 9·1 m.

3 **West side of Taunton River:**

Brayton Point Station (41°42'·57N 71°11'·30W): 310 m in length with a depth alongside of 10·4 m. Receipt of coal and fuel oil for power station.

Montaup Electric Co. Wharf (41°44'·15N 71°08'·75W); 197 m in length with a depth alongside of 10·4 m. Receipt of coal and fuel oil for power station.

Port services

5.266

1 **Repairs.** Fall River has no dry docking or major repair facilities for deep-draught vessels. The nearest such facilities are at Boston (4.113).

The Gladding-Hearn shipyard at Somerset, 6 cables above Charles M. Braga Junior. Memorial Bridge on the W side of the river, is a modern yard that builds vessels up to 50 m in length and has good repair facilities.

Other facility. Oily waste disposal.
Supplies: fuel; water; provisions and stores.

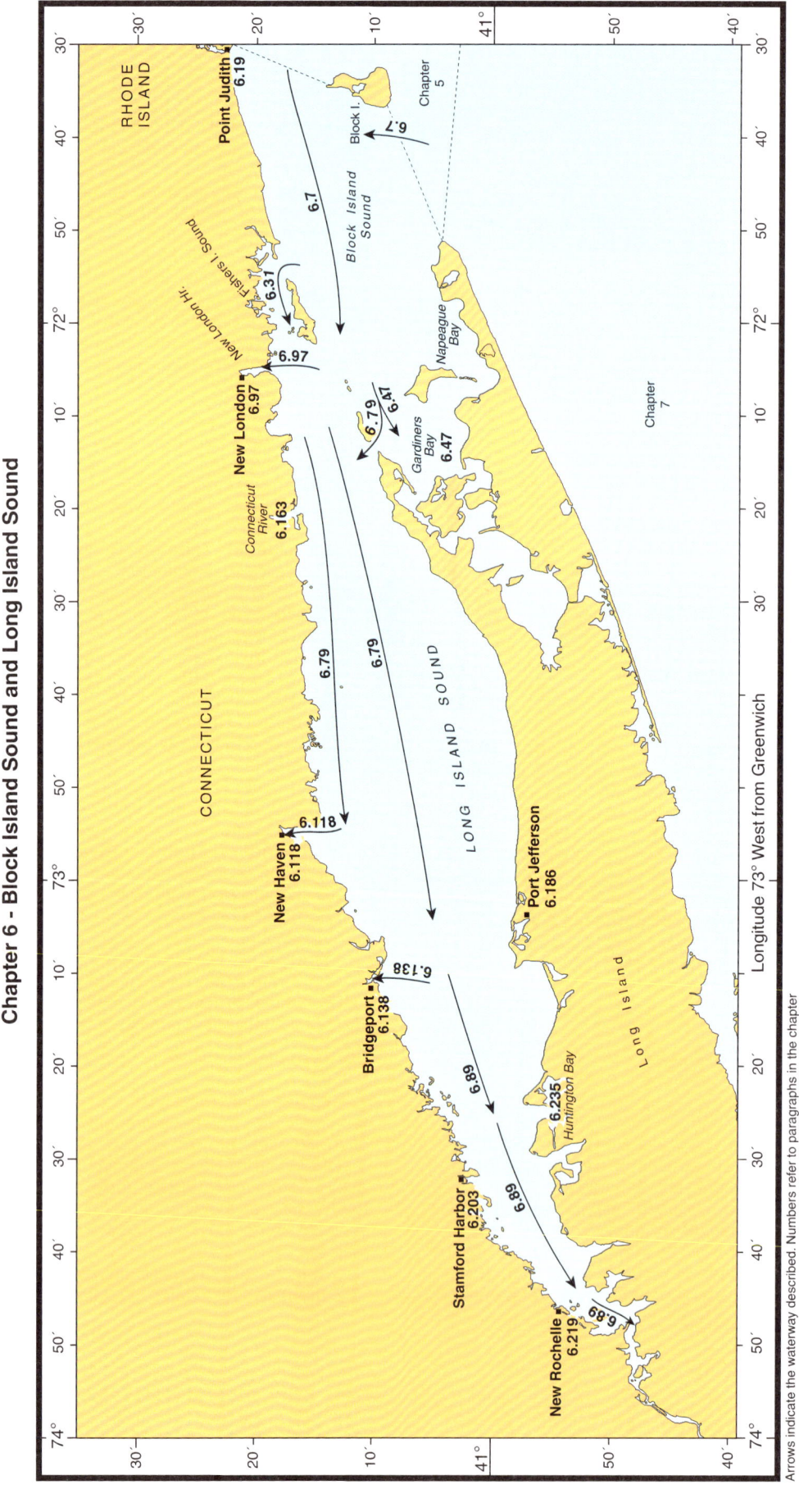

Chapter 6 - Block Island Sound and Long Island Sound

CHAPTER 6

BLOCK ISLAND SOUND AND LONG ISLAND SOUND

GENERAL INFORMATION

Charts 2754, 2580
Scope of the chapter
6.1

1   The area covered by this chapter comprises Block Island Sound (41°12'·00N 71°51'·00W) and Long Island Sound (41°05'·00N 72°45'·00W). The description includes the principal industrial and commercial ports of New London (6.97), New Haven (6.118) and Bridgeport (6.138).
  The chapter is divided into the following sections:
   Block Island Sound and adjacent waters (6.6).
   Long Island Sound (6.71).

Route
6.2

1   The waters of this chapter form a route that connects New York Harbor with Vineyard and Nantucket Sounds or Cape Cod Canal. This route is used extensively by coasting vessels drawing up to about 6 m (20 ft).

Hazards
6.3

1   **Small craft**, including commercial, fishing and pleasure boats, may be found in large numbers nearly all the year round in Block Island Sound and Long Island Sound.
  Tugs and barges on a long tow may also be encountered in these waters.
  Fish traps. The limits of areas where fish traps may be found in the coastal waters of Block Island Sound and Long Island Sound are shown on the chart.

Pilotage
6.4

1   Pilotage is compulsory for all foreign vessels and US vessels under register in the waters covered by this chapter. Vessels bound from E for ports in Long Island Sound, may embark pilots in the following positions in and around Block Island Sound:
   Vicinity of 41°17'·20N 71°30'·40W.
   About 7 miles S of Watch Hill Point (41°18'·23N 71°51'·51W).
   About 3 miles E of MP Light Buoy (41°01'·80N 71°45'·67W).
  Vessels entering Long Island Sound from East River may embark pilots in a position 6 cables E of Execution Rocks (40°52'·69N 73°44'·27W) (6.95). See *Admiralty List of Radio Signals Volume 6(5)* for further information.

Traffic regulations
6.5

1   **Navigation Rules for US Inland Waters** apply to all waters in Long Island Sound and to some of the inshore waters of Block Island Sound, Napeague Bay (41°03'·10N 72°02'·50W) and Gardiners Bay (41°06'·20N 72°12'·30W). See 1.44 and Appendix VII for further information.
  Regulated navigation area. The whole of Block Island Sound and Long Island Sound lie within a regulated navigation area. For details, and definition and general regulations concerning regulated navigation areas see Appendix V.

BLOCK ISLAND SOUND AND ADJACENT WATERS

GENERAL INFORMATION

Chart 2754
Area covered
6.6

1   This section describes Block Island Sound and adjacent waters and is arranged as follows:
   Block Island Sound (6.7).
   Fishers Island Sound (6.31).
   Gardiners Bay and adjacent bays SW (6.47).

BLOCK ISLAND SOUND

General information

Charts 2890, 2754
Description
6.7

1   **Block Island Sound** is a deep navigable waterway forming the E approach to Long Island Sound (6.71), Fishers Island Sound (6.31) and Gardiners Bay (6.47).
  Its E and S limits are defined by Point Judith (41°21'·66N 71°28'·88W), Block Island and the E end of Long Island; its N side by the mainland coast between Point Judith and Watch Hill Point, 17 miles W and thence by Fishers Island and a chain of islands leading WSW for 19 miles from Watch Hill Point to Orient Point (41°09'·60N 72°14'·05W); and its W side by Gardiners Island (41°05'·80N 72°06'·50W).

2   **No-discharge Zone (NDZ).** All the waters W of a line joining Montauk Point (41°04'·26N 71°51'·43W) and Orient Point, 18 miles WNW, have been designated as a NDZ. See 1.41.

Recommended routes
6.8

1   Recommended routes for deep-draught vessels, tugs and barges have been established in Block Island Sound. Pleasure craft, fishing vessels and other small vessels should exercise caution in and around these routes and should monitor VHF channels for information concerning vessels transiting these routes.

Entrances
6.9

1   Block Island Sound has two entrances from the Atlantic. The S entrance leads between Block Island and Montauk Point, a high sandy bluff, 12 miles WSW. The deepest passage in this entrance is just W of Southwest Ledge (41°07'·10N 71°39'·80W) and is 2 miles wide. The E entrance from Rhode Island Sound lies between the N part of Block Island and Point Judith, 9 miles NNE, and is used by vessels with a draught in excess of 11·5 m (38 ft) and those

CHAPTER 6

coming from the bays and sounds E of Block Island Sound. The Race (41°14'·20N 72°03'·50W) is the main entrance to Long Island Sound from Block Island Sound.

Tidal levels
6.10

1   At Point Judith mean spring range is about 1·1 m (3·6 ft); mean neap range about 0·7 m (2·3 ft). At Montauk Point mean spring range is about 0·7 m (2·3 ft); mean neap range about 0·4 m (1·3 ft). See information in *Admiralty Tide Tables*.

Pilotage
6.11

1   See 6.4.

Traffic regulations
6.12

1   **Montauk Channel.** Vessels with a draught in excess of 11·5 m (38 ft) are advised not to use the S entrance (6.17), known locally as Montauk Channel. This channel should also not be used during periods of unfavourable weather, strong tidal streams, poor visibility, reduced under-keel clearance and heavy traffic.

Restricted anchorage, for the use of US submarines is situated 3 miles E of Gardiners Island (41°05'·80N 72°06'·50W).

2   **Danger area.** The area within 1½ cables of the ruin standing on Gardiners Point (41°08'·50N 72°08'·76W) (6.49) is dangerous due to the presence of unexploded ordnance. Anchoring, fishing and trawling should not be carried out in this area.

The ruin itself, a former bombing target known as Fort Tyler, is prohibited to the public.

North Atlantic right whale. See 1.51, *Admiralty List of Radio Signals Volume 6(5)* and Appendices VIII and X.

Natural conditions
6.13

1   **Tidal streams.** See Tidal Stream tables on the chart for the strength of tidal streams in the entrances to Block Island Sound.

2   **Ice.** Large quantities of ice usually pass through The Race during the out-going tide, especially with W winds, and during severe winters may cause some obstruction in Block Island Sound and around Montauk Point especially in February.

Fog is generally thickest with SE winds and its duration is usually from 4 to 12 hours. Periods of fog have been known to last for 4 to 6 days, with very short clear intervals.

Directions
Principal marks
6.14

1   **Landmark:**
Tower (41°12'·11N 72°07'·15W), on Great Gull Island.

Major lights:
Point Judith Light (41°21'·66N 71°28'·88W) (5.186).
Block Island South-east Light (41°09'·17N 71°33'·07W) (5.186).
Montauk Point Light (white conical tower, red band) (41°04'·26N 71°51'·43W).

2   Watch Hill Light (grey square granite tower, white building) (41°18'·23N 71°51'·51W).
Race Rock Light (granite tower and dwelling) (41°14'·61N 72°02'·83W).

Montauk Point Light (6.14)
(Original dated 1999)

(Photograph - US Army Corps of Engineers)

Little Gull Island Light (grey granite tower, red dwelling) (41°12'·38N 72°06'·41W).
Oyster Pond Reef Light (black conical tower, white band) (41°09'·81N 72°13'·42W), also known as Orient Point Light.

Other aids to navigation
6.15
1 Racons:
Southwest Ledge No 2 Light Buoy (41°06'·38N 71°40'·23W).
No 11 Light Buoy (41°13'·76N 72°03'·96W), N of Valiant Rock.
See *Admiralty List of Radio Signals Volume 2.*

East entrance
6.16
1 From a position SSE of Point Judith the route into Block Island Sound leads generally W, passing:
S of No 2 Light Buoy (starboard hand) (41°18'·46N 71°28'·35W), which marks shoal ground consisting of numerous large boulders, extending S from Point Judith. A dangerous wreck lies 4 cables NE of the buoy. Thence:
2 N of Block Island North Reef (41°14'·83N 71°34'·33W) which extends 2 miles NNE from Sandy Point, the N point of Block Island. No 1BI Light Buoy (port hand) lies off the NW side of the reef. Thence:
S of Watch Hill Point (41°18'·23N 71°51'·51W), low and backed by Watch Hill, a high bare bluff, thence:
3 N of Cerberus Shoal (41°10'·35N 71°57'·30W), on which the sea sometimes breaks. The NE side of this shoal is marked by No 9 Light Buoy (port hand).
Thence to the entrance of Long Island Sound or Gardiners Bay.
Useful mark:
Sandy Point Light (framework tower, 18 m in height) (41°13'·66N 71°34'·55W), standing on the N end of Block Island.
(Directions continue, for Gardiners Bay at 6.49 and for Long Island Sound at 6.82)

South entrance
6.17
1 From a position about 9·7 m ESE of Montauk Point Light (41°04'·26N 71°51'·43W) (6.14) the track leads NNW, passing:
WSW of Southwest Ledge (41°07'·10N 71°39'·80W). This ledge, which breaks in heavy weather, is marked on its SW side by No 2 Light Buoy (starboard hand). Thence:
2 ENE of BIS Light Buoy (preferred channel to starboard) (41°06'·95N 71°43'·10W). A depth of 11·2 m (37 ft) lies close NE of the buoy.
Thence into the central part of Block Island Sound.
Caution. See 6.12.

6.18
1 **Side channels.** A channel 1¼ miles wide with a least depth of 9·4 m (31 ft), rounds the SW end of Block Island at a distance of 1½ miles. The E side of this channel is marked by No 4 Light Buoy (starboard hand). It is inadvisable to use this passage in heavy weather.
Another channel leads between BIS Light Buoy and the broken shoal ground that extends from Montauk Point (41°04'·26N 71°51'·43W) (6.9). From a position E of Montauk Point this passage leads across the outer part of Endeavor Shoals, passing:

2 ENE of No 1 Light Buoy (port hand) (41°06'·05N 71°46'·24W), thence:
ENE of Shagwong Rock (41°05'·50N 71°54'·18W), marked on its E side by SR Light Buoy (preferred channel to starboard), thence:
ENE of Shagwong Reef (41°06'·91N 71°54'·91W), marked by 7SR Light Buoy (port hand). Washington Shoal lies between Shagwong Reef and Shagwong Rock. Thence:
3 Clear of Cerberus Shoal (41°10'·35N 71°57'·30W) (6.16).
Caution. Due to the presence of sandwaves, and as the area is subject to continual change, extra caution should be observed where the depths are less than 3 m (10 ft) greater than the draught of the vessel.

Point Judith Harbor of Refuge and Point Judith Pond
Chart 2890
General information
6.19
1 **Point Judith Harbor of Refuge** (41°21'·90N 71°30'·20W) lies on the W side of Point Judith.
The harbour is formed by a detached breakwater, which lies with its knuckle 1¼ miles WSW of Point Judith Light, and two shorter breakwaters extending from the coast. These breakwaters leave two entrances facing S on the E side and W on the W side, known locally as East Gap and West Gap, respectively. The harbour is easy of access for most vessels except with a heavy S sea.
2 **Lights** mark both entrances and the knuckle of the detached breakwater.
Point Judith Pond is a shallow tidal inlet used extensively by small fishing vessels and pleasure craft.

Limiting conditions
6.20
1 **Depths.** In 1981 the controlling depths in East Gap and West Gap were 7·3 m (24 ft) and 5·5 m (18 ft), respectively.
Two shoals are situated in the central part of the Harbor of Refuge. The N shoal has depths of 4·3 to 5·5 m (14 to 18 ft) and the S shoal, marked by a buoy, has depths of 4·3 to 4·9 m (14 to 16 ft).
2 **Tidal stream** in the East Gap has a rate of ¾ kn. The tidal stream off the West Gap is rotary with a rate of ½ kn. Considerably stronger rates have been reported with the out-going tidal stream.

Berths
6.21
1 **Anchorage** may be obtained in the area within the V-shaped detached breakwater, soft bottom. A good berth with depths of 7 to 9 m (22 to 30 ft) is on a line joining the two heads of this detached breakwater, keeping clear of an obstruction 1½ cables SE of the W head and a dangerous wreck, marked on its N side by No 5 Light Buoy (port hand), 2½ cables WSW of the E head. The breakwater should be given a berth of 1 cable to avoid broken and hard bottom.

Great Salt Pond
General information
6.22
1 Great Salt Pond (41°11'·50N 71°34'·90W) is entered on the W side of Block Island, 2 miles SSW of Sandy Point Light (6.16). It is the best harbour in Block Island Sound for vessels of 4·6 m (15 ft) draught or less.

Entrance. The entrance channel is dredged through a narrow strip of beach which forms the W side of Great Salt Pond.

2   **Local knowledge** is required to enter the harbour as the channel is subject to shoaling.

No-discharge Zone (NDZ). The whole of Great Salt Pond has been designated as a NDZ. See 1.41.

Limiting conditions
6.23

1   **Project depth** in the entrance channel is 5·5 m (18 ft).

Tidal streams in the entrance have a maximum rate of less than ½ kn.

Directions
6.24

1   From the vicinity of No 2 Buoy (starboard hand), off the harbour entrance, the track leads through the entrance channel, which is buoyed. No 4 Light Beacon (red triangle on white round tower, red top) stands at the head of the breakwater which forms the SW side of the entrance.

Berths
6.25

1   **Anchorage.** The usual anchorage is near the SE end of the harbour off the ferry pier in 5 to 15 m (15 to 48 ft), taking care to leave a fairway to the ferry pier. Anchorage is prohibited in the N and E part of the harbour, and cable and pipeline areas are situated in the W side of the harbour.

Alongside berths. The main pier, which is also the ferry pier, is reported to have depths of 6 m at its head.

A jetty with dolphins at its head lies 1 cable W of the main pier.

Fort Pond Bay

Chart 2754
General information
6.26

1   Fort Pond Bay lies between Culloden Point (41°04'·26N 71°57'·50W) and Rocky Point, 1¾ miles SW. The bay is free of dangers, but flats with depths of 2·4 to 3·6 m (8 to 12 ft) extend from its E shore and shoaling is abrupt on its E and S sides.

The village of Montauk, the terminus of the Long Island Railroad, lies on the SE side of the bay.

Anchorage may be obtained in 12 to 15 m (40 to 50 ft), soft mud. It is exposed to N winds.

Napeague Bay

General information
6.27

1   Napeague Bay (41°03'·10N 72°02'·50W) is entered between Rocky Point and the S extremity of Gardiners Island. It is shallow in its W and SW part.

The bay forms the approach to Promised Land Channel, a buoyed passage that passes S of Gardiners Island and Cartwright Island, which lies 1¾ miles S of the S extremity of Gardiners Island, and thence into Gardiners Bay (6.47). The channel is marked by S Light Buoy (safe water) at its E entrance.

2   Napeague Harbor (41°00'·60N 72°02'·80W) and Promised Land (41°00'·20N 72°04'·93W) are used by small craft.

Local knowledge. It is not advisable for vessels drawing more than 3 m to attempt Promised Land Channel unless local knowledge is available, and then only if the buoys are visible.

Limiting conditions
6.28

1   **Depths.** Promised Land Channel has a centreline depth of about 4·3 m (14 ft), however the depth is continually changing due to the shifting shoals.

Tidal streams have a rate of about 1½ kn through all the channels between the shoals.

Harbours

Charts 2890, 2754
General information
6.29

1   The coast between Point Judith (41°21'·66N 71°28'·88W) and Watch Hill Point, 17½ miles WSW, is low and consists mainly of sandy beaches separated by rocky points with several summer resorts along this stretch of the coast.

Close behind it are a number of lagoons, the outlets of which may be closed at times.

2   Ninigret Pond entered through Charlestown Breachway, 7 miles W of Judith Point, Quonochontaug Pond entered through Quonochontaug Breachway, 10½ miles WSW of Point Judith, and Winnapaug Pond entered through Weekapaug Breachway, 12½ miles W of Point Judith, are only used by small local craft.

Montauk Harbor
6.30

1   Montauk Harbor (41°04'·30N 71°56'·20W), in the N part of Montauk Lake, is entered nearly 4 miles W of Montauk Point. It provides a good harbour for small craft, but local knowledge is required.

Star Island is situated just inside the entrance and is connected to the mainland by a causeway on its SW side.

FISHERS ISLAND SOUND
General information

Charts 2754, 2732, US Chart 13214 (see 1.16)
Description
6.31

1   Fishers Island Sound is entered from E between Watch Hill Point (41°18'·23N 71°51'·51W) and East Point, 3 miles WSW and lies between Fishers Island (41°16'·00N 71°59'·50W) and the mainland. It is used by shallow-draught vessels but is obstructed by numerous shoals, which are steep-to, and lobster trap buoys. The principal dangers are marked, but the entire area is obstructed by boulder patches.

2   The principal anchorages are on the N side of the sound, the harbours on the S side being suitable only for small craft.

No-discharge Zone (NDZ). Large areas of Fishers Island Sound have been designated as a NDZ. See 1.41.

Entrances
6.32

1   There are five passages between the reefs extending from Watch Hill Point to East Point, of which the most easterly, Watch Hill Passage (6.37), is the only recommended passage.

The other passages, which are only partially buoyed and less frequently used are (with positions relative to Watch Hill Point):

2   Sugar Reef Passage (8 cables SW),
Catumb Passage (1¼ miles SW),
Lords Passage (2 miles WSW), and
Wicopesset Passage (2¾ miles WSW).

Depth. Watch Hill Passage has a least depth of 5·2 m (17 ft) between the reef that extends S from Watch Hill Point and a patch 1½ cables SW.

Local knowledge
6.33

1   Local knowledge is required for the navigation of the sound and harbours connected with it.

Traffic regulations
6.34

1   **Navigation Rules for US Inland Waters** apply inshore of a line joining Watch Hill Point Light and East Point on Fishers Island, 3 miles WSW.
Regulated navigation area. See 6.5.

Natural conditions
6.35

1   **Tidal streams.** In the main channel through Fishers Island Sound slack water before the E-going and W-going stream, respectively, occurs 3 hours before and 4 hours after HW at Sandy Hook. The maximum strength of the stream occurs about HW and LW at Sandy Hook.

2   In the main channel the maximum rate of the stream is about 2½ kn and in Watch Hill Passage is strong enough to tow spar buoys under water.

Ice. The tidal streams are of sufficient strength to prevent the formation of heavy local ice except in the shallow tributaries. The only ice likely to hinder navigation is that set in from Long Island Sound by wind and tidal stream.

Directions for through route

Principal mark
6.36

1   **Major light:**
Watch Hill Light (41°18′·23N 71°51′·51W) (6.14).

Watch Hill Passage to Latimer Reef
6.37

1   From a position 5 cables SE of Watch Hill Point the route through Fishers Island Sound leads NW through Watch Hill Passage and thence W to the vicinity of Latimer Reef, passing:

    Between WH Light Buoy (preferred channel to starboard) (41°17′·89N 71°51′·67W) and No 2 Light Buoy (starboard hand), 1 cable NE. A dangerous wreck, position approximate, lies ½ cable E of No 2 Light Buoy. Thence:

2   N of Sugar Reef (41°17′·71N 71°52′·60W), the N side of which is marked by No 5 Buoy (port hand), thence:

    S of a dangerous wreck (41°18′·01N 71°52′·97W), position approximate, thence:

    S of Napatree Point Ledge (41°18′·04N 71°53′·31W), marked by No 6 Light Buoy (starboard hand), thence:

    N of Wicopesset Island (41°17′·69N 71°54′·82W); Nos 9 and 11 Buoys (port hand) mark the edge of the shoal ground that extends N from this island. Thence:

3   Between No 12 Buoy (starboard hand) (41°18′·27N 71°55′·55W) marking the E side of Latimer Reef, and No 13 Buoy (port hand), 3 cables S, marking a 3·3 m rock; thence:

    S of Latimer Reef Light (white conical tower, brown band on brown column) (41°18′·27N 71°56′·00W), which stands on the W end of Latimer Reef.

Latimer Reef to Seaflower Reef
6.38

1   From a position S of Latimer Reef Light the route through Fishers Island Sound continues W for 4½ miles to the W end of Fishers Island Sound, passing:

    N of Youngs Rock (41°17′·73N 71°56′·22W), marked on its NW side by No 17 Buoy (port hand), thence:

    N of East Clump (41°17′·80N 71°57′·63W), marked on its N side by No 19 Buoy (port hand), thence:

2   S of Ram Island Reef (41°18′·25N 71°58′·39W), marked on its S side by No 20 Light Buoy (starboard hand), thence:

    N of Middle Clump (41°17′·66N 71°58′·61W), marked on its N side by No 21 Buoy (port hand), thence:

    S of Intrepid Rock (41°17′·95N 72°00′·28W); DIR Buoy (isolated danger) marks the SE side of this rock. Thence:

3   N of North Dumpling, a grassy islet, on which stands a light (41°17′·28N 72°01′·16W). The red sector of the light covers East Clump and the dangers W of it, except for the outer 4·6 m (15ft) patch, N of Middle Clump. Thence:

4   S of Seaflower Reef (41°17′·76N 72°01′·99W), on which stands a light (green and white chequered diamond on framework tower).

Thence through the approaches to New London Harbor.

(Directions are given for
New London Harbor at 6.109
and for Long Island Sound at 6.82)

Stonington Harbor

General information
6.39

1   **Position.** Stonington Harbor (41°20′·18N 71°54′·80W) lies 3 miles NW of Watch Hill Point and is entered between Stonington Point and Wamphassuc Point. The town of Stonington lies on the E side of the inner harbour. The port is mainly used by fishing and pleasure craft.

Stonington Harbor can be approached from SE or W. The SE approach is best, with fewer dangers.

2   **Breakwaters.** The entrance is protected by an outer detached breakwater with its NE end on Bartlett Reef, and a W detached breakwater that extends SE from close off Wamphassuc Point.

No-discharge zone (NDZ). Stonington Harbor has been designated as a NDZ. See 1.41.

Depths
6.40

1   **Depths.** The controlling depth to the inner harbour is about 3·4 m (11 ft).

Directions
6.41

1   **South-east approach.** From a position E of Latimer Reef (6.37) the SE approach to Stonington Harbor leads N, passing:

    W of Middle Ground (41°18′·60N 71°54′·30W), marked on its W side by No 2 Buoy (starboard hand), thence:

    E of Noyes Shoal (41°19′·00N 71°55′·33W), the E end of which is marked by No 3 Buoy (port hand), thence:

2   W of No 4 Light (red triangle on framework tower, hut, concrete base) (41°19′·00N 71°54′·48W), at the SW head of the outer breakwater, thence:

    Between the W breakwater head (41°19′·52N 71°54′·79W) and Stonington Point. No 5 Light (green square on framework tower, concrete base) stands at the head of the breakwater. Thence into the inner harbour.

6.42
1   **West approach.** From a position S of Ram Island Reef (41°18′·25N 71°58′·39W) the W approach to Stonington Harbor leads NE and E, passing:

    Between Ellis Reef (41°19′·01N 71°57′·32W), on which stands ER Beacon, and Eel Grass Ground, 3 cables SSE. No 18 Buoy (starboard hand) is moored on the SW side of Eel Grass Ground. Thence:

2   S of White Rock (41°19′·37N 71°56′·27W), above water, thence:

    N of Noyes Rock (41°19′·28N 71°55′·35W). Thence into the inner harbour.

Berths
6.43
1   **Alongside berths.** The wharves have depths alongside of 2·1 to 3·6 m.

Anchorages and harbours
Little Narragansett Bay
6.44
1   **General information.** Little Narragansett Bay (41°19′·60N 71°52′·60W), at the E end of Fishers Island Sound, is a shallow area enclosed by Napatree Beach on the S, and by a long strip of sand, much of which is above water, extending SSE from Sandy Point (41°19′·90N 71°53′·84W).

2   The bay forms the approach to Pawcatuck River, which flows into the SE part of the bay, and Wequetequock Cove and Watch Hill Cove which lie on the N and S side of the bay, respectively. Pawcatuck River, Wequetequock Cove and Watch Hill Cove are only used by small craft.

Ice generally closes the Pawcatuck River from January to March. Ice formations in Little Narragansett Bay are sometimes heavy enough to destroy structures exposed to them.

Local knowledge is essential.

Mystic Harbor
6.45
1   **General information.** Mystic Harbor (41°20′·65N 71°58′·20W) is situated between Mason Island and the mainland. The harbour lies 2 miles W of Stonington Harbor. The town of Noank lies on the W side of the harbour and the town of Mystic lies on the E side of Mystic River, which flows into the head of the harbour.

The harbour is used by local fishing and pleasure craft.

Ice usually closes the river during January and February.

West Harbor
6.46
1   West Harbor (41°16′·00N 72°00′·40W) on the N side of Fishers Island, SE of North Dumpling Light (6.38), affords shelter from S winds.

GARDINERS BAY AND ADJACENT BAYS SOUTH-WEST

General information
Chart 2754, US Chart 13209 (see 1.16)
Description
6.47
1   Gardiners Bay lies at the W end of Block Island Sound, from which it is separated by Gardiners Island. It is formed by the forked E end of Long Island between Orient Point (41°09′·60N 72°14′·05W) and Hog Creek Point, 7 miles SSE, with Gardiners Island on its E side and Shelter Island (6.57) across its head.

The bay affords excellent anchorage and is easily accessible, either by day or by night.

2   It is the approach to Shelter Island Sound (6.57), the name given to the waters on the N, W and S sides of Shelter Island and to Little Peconic Bay (6.57) and Great Peconic Bay (6.70), which extend SW from that island.

No-discharge Zone (NDZ). See 6.7.

Entrances
6.48
1   **Main entrance** from Block Island Sound to Gardiners Bay lies between Gardiners Point (41°08′·50N 72°08′·76W) (6.49) and Pine Point (6.85), 2¾ miles WNW. The bay can also be entered through the narrow passage that leads through Promised Land Channel (6.27), S of Gardiners Island.

Entrance from Long Island Sound is through Plum Gut (6.85) between Orient Point and Plum Island.

Directions
(continued from 6.16)
Main entrance
6.49
1   From a position NNE of Gardiners Island the track through the main entrance to Gardiners Bay leads WSW, passing:

    SSE of Constellation Rock (41°10′·52N 72°06′·60W), marked by No 2 Buoy (starboard hand), thence:

2   NNW of Gardiners Point (41°08′·50N 72°08′·76W) on which stand the ruins of a former bombing target (6.12). No 1Gl Light Buoy (port hand) is moored 5 cables NNW of Gardiners Point.

Thence into Gardiners Bay.

Other entrances
6.50
1   **South entrance.** See 6.27.

Plum Gut. See 6.85.

Anchorages and harbours in Gardiners Bay
General
6.51
1   There is anchorage anywhere in Gardiners Bay according to draught.

Bostwick Bay
6.52
1   Bostwick Bay (41°06′·70N 72°08′·00W) is entered between Bostwick Point, the N extremity of Gardiners Island and Cherry Hill Point.

Anchorage may be obtained in about 8 m (25 ft). This anchorage is excellent in E winds, but is exposed to W winds.

Cherry Harbor
6.53
1   Cherry Harbor (41°04′·80N 72°06′·90W) is entered between the S extremity of Gardiners Island and Crow Shoal, 3 miles WNW.

Anchorage, clear of a cable area extending between Gardiners Island and Hog Creek Point, 3 miles SW, may be obtained in 7 to 8 m (24 to 27 ft), mud. The anchorage is sheltered from NE winds.

Acabonack Harbor
6.54
1   Acabonack Harbor (41°01′·50N 72°08′·40W), 2 miles SSE of Hog Creek Point, is only used by small craft.

Threemile Harbor
6.55

1 Threemile Harbor (41°01′·20N 72°11′·30W), on the S side of Gardiners Bay, is only used by small craft.

Coecles Harbor
6.56

1 Coecles Harbor (41°04′·20N 72°17′·50W), on the W side of Gardiners Bay, is only used by small craft.

Shelter Island Sound and Peconic Bays

US Chart 12358 (see 1.16)
General information
6.57

1 Shelter Island Sound is entered from the W side of Gardiners Bay through channels that run N and S of Shelter Island (41°04′·30N 72°20′·00W), and leads into Little Peconic Bay and Great Peconic Bay (6.70). Little Peconic Bay and Great Peconic Bay extend for about 15 miles to Riverhead at the head of navigation on Peconic River.

2 The town of Greenport (6.60) is situated on the NW side of the N channel, and the town of Sag Harbor (6.61) on the S side of the S channel.

There are many summer resorts in the area which are much frequented by small craft in summer. Shelter Island Sound and Little Peconic Bay are suitable for medium-draught vessels but Great Peconic Bay is only suitable for shallow-draught vessels.

3 **Local knowledge** is necessary.
Navigation Rules for US Inland Waters apply to all the waters within this section. See 1.44 and Appendix VII for details.

Limiting conditions
6.58

1 **Depths.** There is a least charted depth of 6·0 m (20 ft) (41°06′·75N 72°19′·61W) through the channel N of Shelter Island Sound and thence through Little Peconic Bay to Robins Island (40°58′·20N 72°27′·70W), and about 4 m (13 ft) through the channel S of Shelter Island.

Between Little and Great Peconic Bay there is a controlling depth of 4 m (13 ft) across the bar S of Robins Island.

2 **Ice** obstructs navigation in coves and shallow harbours during January and February. In severe winters drift ice is reported to interfere with navigation for short periods and in the S arm of Shelter Island Sound the ice is heavy enough at times to destroy structures exposed to it.

Tidal streams
6.59

1 Tidal streams have a rate of up to 1¾ kn in places where the channel is narrowed.

Greenport Harbor
6.60

1 **General information.** Greenport Harbor (41°06′·01N 72°21′·36W) lies in the N channel of Shelter Island Sound. Greenport, an important town, lies on the W side of the harbour.

The NE side of the harbour is formed by a breakwater which extends 2½ cables SE from the shore. No 8A Light Beacon (red triangle on framework tower) stands at the head of the breakwater.

2 **Wharves** with depths alongside of 1·5 to 6·1 m are situated between the entrance to Stirling Basin and Fanning Point, 1 mile SSW.

Repairs. There are several shipyards and patent slips at Greenport and repairs can be carried out.
Supplies: fuel; water; provisions and stores.

Sag Harbor
6.61

1 **General information.** Sag Harbor (41°00′·30N 72°17′·60W) lies on the S side of the S channel of Shelter Sound, 2½ miles SW of Cedar Point. The town of Sag Harbor lies on the S side of the harbour.

The harbour is formed on the NE by a breakwater extending 5 cables NW from the shore. 3SH Light (green square on framework tower) stands at the head of the breakwater.

The approach to the harbour is obstructed by several dangers, but is well buoyed.

2 **Depths.** In 1974 the dredged channel into Sag Harbor had a controlling depth of 3 m (10 ft) in mid-channel through the entrance into the turning basin. In 1991 this channel was no longer being maintained.

Anchorage may be obtained in 2 m (7 ft) in the main anchorage area in the E part of the harbour.
Repairs. Repairs to hull and engines are available.
Supplies: fuel; water; provisions and stores.

6.62

1 **Sag Harbor Cove** is entered at the SW corner of the harbour through a channel with a depth of 2·4 m (8 ft).

The entrance is crossed by a fixed bridge with a vertical clearance of 6·4 m.

Other anchorages and harbours in the north part of Shelter Island Sound
6.63

1 **Orient Harbor** (41°07′·90N 72°18′·70W) lies on the N side of the entrance to the N channel to Shelter Island Sound. It is entered between Long Beach Point and Cleaves Point, 1½ miles W.

Excellent anchorage may be obtained in 6 m (20 ft) in the S part of the harbour and 5 m (16 ft) in its N end clear of the marine farms shown on the chart.

The village of Orient lies at the NE end of the harbour, where there is a pier with a depth of 2·6 m at its head.

6.64

1 **Dering Harbor** (41°05′·30N 72°20′·90W), on the NW side of Shelter Island opposite Greenport, is a favourite anchorage for small craft. The central part of the harbour has depths of 3 to 4·3 m (10 to 14 ft) with much lesser depths around the edges.

6.65

1 **Southold Bay** (41°03′·50N 72°24′·30W) lies at the S end of the N channel. The town of Southold stands at the head of the bay.

Anchorage can be obtained in 4 to 5 m (12 to 18 ft) between 2 and 4 cables ESE of the jetty at Southold clear of the marine farms shown on the US chart.

Other anchorages and harbours in the south part of Shelter Island Sound
6.66

1 **Northwest Harbor** (41°01′·50N 72°15′·10W) lies on the E side of the entrance to the S part of Shelter Island Sound.

The harbour is strewn with boulders, over many of which there are depths of only 1·2 to 1·8 m (4 to 6 ft).

6.67

1 **Smith Cove** (41°03′·00N 72°18′·60W), a small bight on the S side of Shelter Island, is a good anchorage for small vessels in N winds.

Anchorage may be obtained in 3 to 9 m (11 to 30 ft).

A ferry operates between South Ferry, on the SW side of the cove, and North Haven Peninsula opposite.

6.68

1   **Noyack Bay** (41°00′·70N 72°20′·80W) lies between North Haven Peninsula and Jessup Neck, high and wooded, 2 miles WSW.

Anchorages and harbours in Little Peconic Bay
6.69

1   **Cutchogue Harbor** (41°00′·00N 72°27′·70W), at the NW end of Little Peconic Bay, is mainly used by local craft drawing up to 3 m (10 ft).

The town of New Suffolk stands on the W side of the harbour and has a small basin with a depth of 2·8 m (8 ft).

Great Peconic Bay
6.70

1   Great Peconic Bay (40°56′·40N 72°30′·00W) is used mainly by local small craft. The bay is mainly clear, but shoals extend up to 2 miles from its shores except on the S side. The bay can also be entered from the S through the Shinnecock Canal (7.23).

LONG ISLAND SOUND

GENERAL INFORMATION

Charts 2754, 2580

Area covered
6.71

1   This section describes Long Island Sound, a deep navigable waterway lying between the shores of Connecticut and New York and the N coast of Long Island. It extends from Fishers Island (41°16′·00N 71°59′·50W) to Throgs Neck (7.135), 84 miles WSW. Also described are the principal industrial and commercial ports of New London (6.97), New Haven (6.118) and Bridgeport (6.138).

2   The section is arranged as follows:
   Main and inshore passage through E part of Long Island Sound (6.79).
   Main passage through W part of Long Island Sound (6.89).
   New London Harbor and approaches (6.97).
   New Haven Harbor and approaches (6.118).
   Bridgeport Harbor and approaches (6.138).

3   Harbours in the NE part of Long Island Sound (6.158).
   Harbours in the SE part of Long Island Sound (6.181).
   Harbours in the NW part of Long Island Sound (6.193).
   Anchorages and harbours in the SW part of Long Island Sound (6.231).

Topography
6.72

1   The N shore of Long Island Sound is generally low and marshy on the coast, but rises to elevations of over 120 m at a distance of 3 miles inland. It is indented by numerous bays and rivers. The N coast of Long Island is generally bluff and rocky.

Hazards
6.73

1   **Oyster grounds** exist in shoal water in places in Long Island Sound and are usually marked by stakes and flags. Broken stakes, below-water, may exist in places; these may be dangerous to small craft.

Pilotage
6.74

1   See 6.4.

Submarine operating areas
6.75

1   Submarines operate in the approaches to New London Harbor and Connecticut River, and off the N shore of Long Island. As submarines may be operating submerged in these areas, vessels should proceed with caution. See 1.13.

Traffic regulations
6.76

1   **Navigation Rules for US Inland Waters.** See 6.5.
   Regulated navigation area. See 6.5.

No-discharge Zone (NDZ)
6.77

1   All the waters on the N side of Long Island Sound between Eastern Point (41°19′·20N 72°04′·48W) and Byram Point (40°59′·23N 73°39′·44W) including the navigable reaches of the Hammonasset River, Menunketesuck River, Niantic River, Thames River and Connecticut River have been designated as a NDZ. See 1.41.

The area includes Branford Harbor, New Haven Harbor, Housatonic River, Black Rock Harbor, Bridgeport Harbor, Norwalk Harbor, Stamford Harbor, Captain Harbor and Greenwich Harbor.

Natural conditions
6.78

1   **Tidal levels.** The time of tide is nearly simultaneous throughout Long Island Sound, but the range varies between about 1·0 m (3·3 ft) at the E end and about 2·6 m (8·5 ft) at the W end.

Ice. In ordinary winters the floating and pack ice in Long Island Sound, while impeding navigation, does not render it absolutely unsafe except in exceptionally severe winters, when only the most powerful vessels are able to proceed.

2   Pack ice, formed principally along the N shore, is forced under the influence of the prevailing N winds across to the S side where it accumulates, massing into large fields, and remains until removed by S winds when it drifts back to the N shore.

In ordinary winters ice forms in the W end of the Sound as far E as Eatons Neck (40°57′·10N 73°23′·70W) and in exceptionally severe winters may extend to Falkner Island (41°12′·72N 72°39′·22W), 38 miles ENE and beyond. NE winds force the ice W, causing formations heavy enough to prevent the passage of all vessels until removed by W winds. These W winds, if of long enough duration, drive the ice through The Race into Block Island Sound and thence seaward.

3   **Fog.** Both the N and S shores are equally subject to fog, except that on spring and summer mornings, when there is little or no wind, fog will often hang along the Connecticut shore when it is clear offshore and to the S.

MAIN AND INSHORE PASSAGE THROUGH EAST PART OF LONG ISLAND SOUND

General information

Charts 2732, 2754

Description
6.79

1 **Main route.** A deep, well-marked channel leads through the E part of Long Island Sound.
Inshore route. A well-marked inshore route leads along the N side of the E part of Long Island Sound between Hatchett Point (41°16'·96N 72°15'·71W) and Branford Reef (6.88), 25 miles W.

2 **East entrances.** The main entrance from the E is The Race (41°14'·20N 72°03'·50W) (6.84). The sound can also be entered through Plum Gut (6.85), 9 miles SW, and Fishers Island Sound (6.31).

Dangers
6.80

1 Several shoals of boulders exist in Long Island Sound but all dangers are well marked by light structures, light buoys and buoys.
Caution. Vessels should navigate with caution where depths are irregular and less than 1·8 to 2·4 m (6 to 8 ft) greater than the draught.

Tidal streams
6.81

1 **The Race.** There are always strong rips and swirls in the wake of all broken ground except for ½ hour at slack water. The rips are exceptionally pronounced during heavy weather, especially when a strong wind opposes the tidal stream. See Tidal Stream table (chart 2732) for further details.
Plum Gut. The maximum rate of the in-going stream is 3½ kn and of the out-going stream 4¼ kn. It has been reported that a counter-current develops during the in-going stream along the N shore of Plum Island.

Directions
(continued from 6.16)

Principal marks
6.82

1 **Landmark:**
Tower (41°12'·11N 72°07'·15W), standing on Great Gull Island.
Major lights:
Race Rock Light (41°14'·61N 72°02'·83W) (6.14).
Little Gull Island Light (41°12'·38N 72°06'·41W) (6.14).
Oyster Pond Reef Light (41°09'·81N 72°13'·42W) (6.14).

2 New London Entrance Light, charted as Harbor Light (41°19'·00N 72°05'·39W) (6.109).
Stratford Point Light (41°09'·12N 73°06'·20W) (6.147).
Penfield Reef Light (41°07'·03N 73°13'·33W) (6.92).
Eatons Neck Light (40°57'·24N 73°23'·73W) (6.92).

Other aids to navigation
6.83

1 **Racons:**
No 11 Light Buoy (41°13'·76N 72°03'·96W), N of Valiant Rock.
TE Light Buoy (41°09'·28N 72°30'·40W).
See *Admiralty List of Radio Signals Volume 2*.

East entrances
6.84

1 **The Race.** From a position SE of Race Point the main route into Long Island Sound used by deep-draught vessels leads NW, passing:
Between Race Rock (41°14'·61N 72°02'·83W), on which stands Race Rock Light (6.14), and Valiant Rock (2 miles SW). No 11 Light Buoy (port hand) is moored on the N side of Valiant Rock, which is surrounded by heavy overfalls.
Thence into Long Island Sound.
(Directions for New London continue at 6.109)

6.85

1 **Plum Gut.** From a position ESE of Pine Point (41°09'·95N 72°11'·91W) the route through Plum Gut leads WNW, passing:
SSW of Pine Point, the S point of Plum Island, thence:
NNE of Midway Shoal (41°09'·75N 72°12'·72W), marked on its N side by MS Light Buoy (preferred channel to starboard), thence:

2 SSW of Middle Ground (41°10'·22N 72°12'·90W), thence:
SSW of 2PG Light Buoy (starboard hand) (41°10'·57N 72°13'·10W).
NNE of Oyster Pond Reef (41°09'·80N 72°13'·50W), which extends 6 cables NE from Orient Point. Oyster Pond Reef Light (6.14) stands 2½ cables short of the extremity of the reef. Thence:

3 Thence into Long Island Sound.
Local knowledge is required to navigate Plum Gut because of the rocks in the passage and the strong tidal streams that may be encountered.

Main route from east entrances to Stratford Shoal Middle Ground
6.86

1 From the vicinity of Pl Light Buoy (safe water) (41°13'·29N 72°10'·81W) the main route for deep-draught vessels leads WSW for about 43 miles to the vicinity of Stratford Shoal Middle Ground, passing:
Clear of Cornfield Light Buoy CF (safe water) (41°11'·30N 72°22'·28W), thence:
NNW of Rocky Point (41°08'·34N 72°21'·15W). The lookout tower of a disused coastguard station stands on the point. Thence:

2 SSE of Sixmile Reef (41°11'·00N 72°30'·10W), marked on its S side by No 8C Light Buoy (starboard hand), thence:
NNW of Horton Point, from which a light (white square tower, with dwelling) (41°05'·10N 72°26'·73W) is exhibited, thence:
SSE of TE Light Buoy (preferred channel to port) (41°09'·28N 72°30'·40W), moored on Twenty-Eight Foot Shoal, thence:

3 SSE of Falkner Island (41°12'·72N 72°39'·22W), from which a light (white 8-sided tower) is exhibited, thence:
SSE of a light buoy (special) (41°07'·71N 72°39'·30W), the southernmost of five, thence:
NNW of United Riverhead Terminal (41°00'·01N 72°38'·80W) (6.182), thence:

4 Clear of Stratford Shoal Middle Ground (30 miles W), on which stands Stratford Shoal Middle Ground Light (grey 8-sided granite tower on dwelling) (41°03'·59N 73°06'·08W). It is marked on its N side by No 3 Buoy (port hand) and on its S side by No 2 Light Buoy

(starboard hand). There is deep water N and S of Stratford Shoal, but deep-draught vessels normally use the channel S of the shoal. Thence into the W part of Long Island Sound.

(Directions continue for W part of Long Island Sound at 6.92, and are given for approaches to Bridgeport at 6.147)

Inshore route
6.87

1 From a position S of Hatchett Point (41°16'·96N 72°15'·71W) an inshore route leads W between Long Sand Shoal, Sixmile Reef and Falkner Island, and the N shore of Long Island Sound, passing:

S of Hatchett Reef (41°16'·10N 72°15'·96W), marked on its S side by No 6 Buoy (starboard hand), thence:

2 Between No 8 Light Buoy (starboard hand) (41°14'·85N 72°18'·84W) (6.166) and 'E' Buoy (preferred channel to port), which lie in the approaches to Connecticut River (6.163), thence:

N of Long Sand Shoal (41°13'·80N 72°22'·70W), which extends WSW for 6 miles from E Buoy, and:

S of Cornfield Point Shoal (41°15'·23N 72°23'·16W), which lies 5 cables SSE of Cornfield Point and is marked by No 2 Light Buoy (starboard hand), and:

3 S of Hen and Chickens (41°15'·21N 72°24'·27W), awash in places and buoyed at its E end, and:

S of Crane Reef (41°15'·06N 72°25'·38W), marked on its S side by No 4 Buoy (starboard hand), thence:

N of 'W' Light Buoy (41°13'·58N 72°27'·59W), at the W end of Long Sand Shoal, thence:

Clear of SW Reef (41°14'·10N 72°29'·40W), lying 1 mile SSE from the head of Kelsey Point Breakwater (6.175), thence:

6.88

1 S of Kelsey Point Breakwater Light (41°14'·61N 72°30'·48W). Shoal ground extending S from the light is marked on its S limit by No 8 Buoy (starboard hand). Thence:

S of Hammonasset Point (41°15'·00N 72°32'·66W), low and marshy with several wooded knolls, thence:

N of Kimberly Reef (41°13'·05N 72°37'·40W), marked on its S side by KR Light Buoy (preferred channel to port), and:

2 S of Charles Reef (41°14'·95N 72°37'·50W), marked on its S side by No 14 Buoy (starboard hand). Madison Reef (6.177) lies 1 mile ENE. Thence:

N of the reef extending 4 cables N from Falkner Island (41°12'·72N 72°39'·22W), marked on its N side by No 15 Light Buoy (port hand), thence:

S of Chimney Corner Reef and Goose Rocks Shoals which lie off Sachem Head (41°14'·70N 72°42'·50W) (6.177). These dangers are marked by No 20 Buoy and No 22 Light Buoy (both starboard hand). Thence:

3 S of Browns Reef (41°14'·70N 72°42'·50W), one of several shoals about 7 cables SW of The Thimbles (6.178), a group of islands and shoals that extend 1½ miles SW from Hoadley Point. Browns Reef is marked by No 26 Light Buoy (starboard hand). Thence:

S of Branford Reef (41°13'·28N 72°48'·32W), from which a light (red and white chequered diamond on framework tower) is exhibited, thence:

4 S of Townshend Ledge (41°12'·62N 72°51'·73W), marked on its S limit by No 10A Light Buoy (starboard hand).

Thence to the approaches to New Haven and the W part of Long Island Sound.

(Directions continue for approaches to New Haven at 6.130)

MAIN PASSAGE THROUGH WEST PART OF LONG ISLAND SOUND

General information

Charts 2754, 2580
Description
6.89

1 **Main route.** A deep, well marked route leads through the W part of Long Island Sound from Stratford Shoal Middle Ground (41°03'·59N 73°06'·08W) to Throgs Neck.

Dangers
6.90

1 See 6.80.

Tidal streams
6.91

1 See Tidal Stream tables on chart.

Directions
(continued from 6.86)

Principal marks
6.92

1 **Major lights:**

Stratford Point Light (41°09'·12N 73°06'·20W) (6.147).

Penfield Reef Light (white tower on granite dwelling) (41°07'·03N 73°13'·33W).

Greens Ledge Light (brown conical tower, white top, black base) (41°02'·50N 73°26'·63W).

2 Eatons Neck Light (white stone tower) (40°57'·24N 73°23'·73W).

Great Captain Island Light (red and white chequered diamond on framework tower) (40°58'·95N 73°37'·39W).

Execution Rocks Light (white stone tower, brown band, granite dwelling) (40°52'·69N 73°44'·27W).

Other aid to navigation
6.93

1 **Racon:**

Execution Rocks Light — as above.
See *Admiralty List of Radio Signals Volume 2*.

Stratford Shoal Middle Ground to Cable and Anchor Reef
6.94

1 From the vicinity of Stratford Shoal Middle Ground (41°03'·59N 73°06'·08W) the route continues W for 15 miles to the vicinity of Cable and Anchor Reef, passing:

N of Old Field Point, from where a light (black tower on granite house) (40°58'·62N 73°07'·11W) is exhibited, thence:

2 N of No 11B Light Buoy (port hand) (41°00'·02N 73°23'·70W), which marks the limit of shoal water that extends 3 miles N from Eatons Neck, wooded and 30 m high. Eatons Neck

Light (6.92) stands on Eatons Neck Point (6.231). Thence:

S of Cable and Anchor Reef (41°00′·65N 73°25′·25W), marked on its S part by No 28C Light Buoy (starboard hand).

Cable and Anchor Reef to Execution Rocks
6.95

1 From the vicinity of Cable and Anchor Reef the route through the W part of Long Island Sound continues WSW for 16 miles to the vicinity of Execution Rocks, passing:

Clear of WDA Light Buoy (special) (40°59′·99N 73°28′·25W), moored on the N limit of a spoil ground, thence:

2 NNW of Lloyd Point (40°56′·77N 73°29′·10W), the N extremity of Lloyd Neck. Lloyd Neck is high and wooded. Shoal water, marked on its N limit by No 15 Light Buoy (port hand), extends 1 mile N from this headland. Thence:

SSE of a shoal patch (40°58′·23N 73°32′·81W) with a depth of 7·9 m (26 ft), marked on its S side by No 32A Light Buoy (starboard hand) (3½ miles ESE), thence:

SSE of a light buoy (special) (40°57′·33N 73°34′·80W), thence:

3 NNW of Matinecock Point (40°54′·12N 73°37′·95W). Shoal ground extending 5 cables NNW from this point is marked by No 21 Light Buoy (port hand). A fish haven is established 5 cables NE of Matinecock Point. Thence:

4 SSE of Execution Rocks (40°52′·69N 73°44′·27W), passing between these rocks and Sands Point, 8 cables SSE. The channel is marked on the SE side by Nos 23 and 25 Light Buoys (both port hand), which mark the shoal waters that extend from Manhasset Neck, and on the NW side by No 44A Light Buoy (starboard hand).

Execution Rocks to Throgs Neck
6.96

1 From a position S of Execution Rocks the main route through the W part of Long Island Sound continues SSW for 5 miles to Throgs Neck (7.135), at the E entrance of East River, passing:

WNW of No 27A Light (green square on framework tower) (40°51′·48N 73°44′·76W), standing on Gangway Rock, which with No 27 Buoy (port hand) marks the limit of shoal water extending NW from Barker Point. Thence:

2 Between Hewlett Point (40°50′·28N 73°45′·19W) and the S extremity of Hart Island (6.220), 8 cables WNW. The shoal ground off Hewlett Point is marked by No 29 Light Buoy (port hand); No 46 Light (red triangle on framework tower, concrete base) stands on a rock lying off the S end of Hart Island. Thence:

3 WNW of Stepping Stones Light (red brick building, granite base, white band on SW side) (40°49′·47N 73°46′·48W), which marks the NW end of reefs extending NW from the shore, thence:

ESE of a dangerous wreck (40°49′·20N 73°47′·20W), position approximate, reported (2009).

Thence to the E entrance of East River (7.135) between Willets Point and Throgs Neck.

(Directions for East River are given in reverse at 7.144)

NEW LONDON HARBOR AND APPROACHES

General information

Chart 2732
Position and function
6.97

1 New London Harbor (41°20′·41N 72°05′·03W) is formed by the entrance to Thames River which flows into the E end of Long Island Sound between Avery Point (41°18′·92N 72°03′·81W) and Goshen Point (chart 2754), 2¼ miles SW.

New London is a city situated on the W bank of the River, 2½ miles above its mouth, and is a port of entry. In 2010 the population of the city was 27 620. Groton, on the E bank, is the home of General Dynamics' Electric Boat shipyard, and of a US Navy submarine base 2 miles further upriver.

2 New London Harbor is a medium-sized port and an important harbour of refuge where deep draught vessels can find shelter in any weather and at all seasons. Waterborne commerce is chiefly in petroleum products, coal, sand, chemicals and general cargo.

Port Authority
6.98

1 State of Connecticut Department of Transportation, Bureau of Aviation and Ports, State Pier, New London, CT 06320.

Limiting conditions

Controlling depths
6.99

1 **US Navy project depths:**
Main channel entrance to Fort Trumbull (41°20′·62N 72°05′·60W): 12·2 m (40 ft).
Thence for 1 mile to State Pier No 1: 11·6 m (38 ft).
Thence to US Navy Submarine Base: 11 m (36 ft).

Federal project depth:
To waterfront channels N of Fort Trumbull and in Winthrop Cove: 7 m (23 ft).

For the latest controlling depths the charts and port authority should be consulted.

Vertical clearance
6.100

1 Three bridges cross the river between New London and Groton at Winthrop Point (41°21′·74N 72°05′·37W):
A bascule rail bridge with a vertical clearance of 8·8 m (29 ft) when closed.
Two fixed road bridges, with a vertical clearance of 41·1 m (135 ft), cross the river close N of the rail bridge.

2 A fixed road bridge, with a vertical clearance of 22·9 m (75 ft), crosses the river about 8 miles above New London.

Power cables, with a vertical clearance of 48·8 m (160 ft), span the river about 5 miles above New London.

Horizontal clearance
6.101

1 The bascule rail bridge (6.100) has a horizontal clearance of 45 m (150 ft). The double road bridge (6.100) has a horizontal clearance of 152·4 m (500 ft).

The fixed road bridge about 8 miles above New London has a horizontal clearance of 61 m (200 ft).

Tidal levels
6.102

1 Mean spring range about 0·9 m (3·0 ft); mean neap range about 0·6 m (2·0 ft). See information in *Admiralty Tide Tables*.

Arrival information

Port operations
6.103

1 Berthing and unberthing at Allyn Point (6.114) is in daylight hours only.

Outer anchorages
6.104

1 The following anchorages are established in the approaches to New London Harbor:
   Anchorage C (41°18′·55N 72°05′·22W). General anchorage.
   Anchorage D (41°17′·20N 72°07′·30W). General anchorage.

2 **Anchorage E** (41°17′·10N 72°03′·80W). General anchorage.
   Anchorage F (41°16′·30N 72°03′·40W). Naval anchorage. Except in case of emergency, no other vessel may anchor without permission of the COTP.
   The limits of Areas C, E and F are shown on the chart.

Pilotage
6.105

1 Pilots board about 2 miles S of New London Ledge Light (6.111). See also 6.4.

Traffic regulations
6.106

1 **Security zones.** Zone A encloses the area around the Electric Boat Corporation Shipyard on the E side of the river 1 mile below the bridges. Zone B, as shown on the national chart, extends from 1½ to 2½ miles above the bridges and encloses the US Navy Base.
   For definition and general regulations concerning security zones see Appendix V.

2 **Restricted area.** The area off the US Navy Submarine Base (6.107) is a restricted area. Passage through the area is normally allowed, subject to US Navy requirements.
   For definition and general regulations concerning restricted areas see Appendix VI.
   No-discharge Zone (NDZ) see 1.41.

Harbour

General layout
6.107

1 The main harbour comprises the lower 3 miles of Thames River from Long Island Sound to the bridges at Winthrop Point (6.100) joining New London and Groton.
   The piers and wharves of New London Harbor are situated along both sides of Thames River between a position 1¾ miles N of New London Ledge Light and the bridges 1¾ miles farther N.

2 The upper harbour extends from the bridges to Norwich, the head of navigation, 11 miles N.
   The US Navy Submarine Base is situated on the E side of the river, 1½ to 2½ miles above the bridges.

Natural conditions
6.108

1 **Tidal streams** follow the general direction of the channel and are usually not strong. During freshets, which usually occur in the spring, and when the river is high and the wind is from the N, a strong surface current sets out of the harbour even during the in-going stream.
   See also Tidal Stream tables on chart.

2 **Ice** seldom forms below the Navy base, 5 miles above the entrance. In extremely severe winters, however, pack ice from the sound, driven in by winds, has been known to extend about 1¾ miles above the entrance. Above the Navy base ice obstructs navigation for about 2 months every winter.
   Drift ice sometimes forms a dangerous obstruction in the approaches through Long Island Sound during severe winters, especially during February and March.

Directions
(continued from 6.38 and 6.84)

Principal marks
6.109

1 **Landmarks:**
   Lighthouse (41°18′·92N 72°03′·81W) (octagonal grey stone tower, white lantern), standing on Avery Point.
   Chimney (41°19′·91N 72°04′·72W), N-most of four.
   Major light:
   New London Entrance Light (white 8-sided pyramidal tower) (41°19′·00N 72°05′·39W). Charted as New London Harbor Light.

Other aid to navigation
6.110

1 **Racon:**
   Main channel span of road bridge (41°21′·83N 72°05′·30W).
   See *Admiralty List of Radio Signals Volume 2*.

Approaches
6.111

1 From the vicinity of 41°16′·00N 72°05′·00W, NW of The Race, the track into New London Harbor leads N through the main entrance channel, passing:
   Between No 1 Light Buoy (port hand) (41°17′·62N 72°04′·78W) and No 2 Light Buoy (starboard hand), 1 cable E, which mark the start of the main entrance channel, thence:

2 W of New London Ledge Light, which stands on the NW corner of New London Ledge and 3 cables W of Black Ledge, thence:
   E of New London Entrance Light (41°19′·00N 72°05′·39W) (6.109), thence:
   W of Eastern Point (41°19′·17N 72°04′·50W).
   Thence into New London Harbor.

3 **Caution.** Uncharted fishing and hunting devices and structures, some submerged, may exist in New London Harbor and its approaches. Mariners should proceed with caution.

New London Harbor
6.112

1 From a position abreast Eastern Point the track leads N through the main entrance channel within the harbour to the bridges, 2½ miles N. The channel is marked by light buoys (lateral). A direction light (354·5°) is exhibited from the SE pier of the railway bridge (6.100).
   From the bridges the channel continues N to the US Navy Submarine Base.

2 From the Navy base a channel, with mid-channel controlling depths (2006) of 4·5 m (15 ft), leads past Allyn Point (6.114) to the turning basin at Norwich, which has a depth of 3·7 m (12 ft). The channel is marked by light beacons, light buoys and buoys.

Caution. In 1998 it was reported that cross-currents of 1 to 2 kn may be encountered in the vicinity of the rail bridge.

Berths

Anchorages
6.113

1 The following anchorages are established in New London Harbor (with positions relative to Fort Trumbull (41°20′·62N 72°05′·60W):

Anchorage A (41°20′·95N 72°05′·40W). For barges and small vessels drawing less than 3·6 m (12 feet).

Anchorage B (41°19′·85N 72°05′·20W). General anchorage.

Alongside berths
6.114

1 There are more than 30 wharves and piers. Most of these facilities are used as repair berths, and for mooring recreational craft, fishing vessels, barges, ferries and government vessels. Depths alongside these facilities range from 3 to 12 m.

Deep-draught facilities are as follows:

2 Amerada Hess Corp. Wharf (41°20′·15N 72°04′·92W): T-head pier 292 m in length, with dolphins, depth alongside 12·1 m. Receipt and shipment of petroleum products and receipt of molasses.

State Pier No 1 (41°21′·50N 72°05′·40W) E side: 311 m in length, depth alongside 10·4 to 11·6 m. W side: 305 m in length, depth alongside 7·0 to 8·2 m. General cargo.

Dow Chemicals Allyn Point Wharf (41°26′·50N 72°05′·09W): 228 m in length, depth alongside 9·1 m. Chemicals.

Port services

Repairs
6.115

1 A number of firms in New London carry out repair and salvage work.

Floating docks. The largest is situated 9 cables N of the bridges. Lift 10 000 tonnes; length 91 m, width 33·5 m.

Other facilities
6.116

1 Degaussing range. A degaussing range is situated in the main entrance channel 1½ miles within the entrance, 5 cables SE of Fort Trumbull (41°20′·62N 72°05′·60W).

Hospitals; oily waste disposal.

Supplies
6.117

1 Supplies of all kinds are available. Fuel can be obtained by road tanker from oil companies at 48 hours' notice. Water may be obtained at most of the piers and wharves.

NEW HAVEN HARBOR AND APPROACHES

General information

Chart 2728
Position and function
6.118

1 New Haven Harbor (41°17′·47N 72°54′·60W) is formed by a bay situated on the N side of Long Island Sound about 70 miles NE of New York and 45 miles from the E entrance of Long Island Sound.

New Haven city stands at the head of the harbour at the junction of Mill River and Quinnipiac River. It is an important manufacturing city and a port of entry, and in 2010 had a population of 129 779.

2 The port of New Haven is the busiest port between New York and Boston and the largest deep-water port in the State of Connecticut. It is also an important harbour of refuge. Waterborne commerce consists largely of petroleum products, chemicals, scrap metal, lumber, steel products, mineral; products and general cargo.

Port limits
6.119

1 The harbour comprises all the tidal waters lying N of the breakwaters constructed across the mouth of the bay and the navigable portions of West River, on the W side of the bay, and Mill River and Quinnipiac River, at the head of the bay.

Port authority
6.120

1 New Haven Port Authority, 200 Orange Street, Room G3, New Haven, CT06510 USA.

Websites: www.cityofnewhaven.com/PortAuthority

Limiting conditions

Controlling depths
6.121

1 Project depths:

From the entrance to about 150 m (500 ft) below Tomlinson Bridge - 10·7 m (35 ft), thence:

Through East Haven Reach to the bridge - 5·5 m (18 ft), thence:

Through Mill River for 5½ cables through Entrance Channel, East Fork and West Fork - 3·7 m (12 ft), and:

2 Through Quinnipiac River for 6 cables to Ferry Street Bridge - 5·5 m (18 ft), and:

From Ferry Street bridge for 5 cables to Grand Avenue Bridge - 3·6 to 4·9 m (12 to 16 ft).

For the latest controlling depths the charts and port authority should be consulted.

Vertical clearance
6.122

1 Two bridges cross the harbour above the principal port facilities, at the confluence of Mill River and Quinnipiac River:

Tomlinson Bridge (41°17′·90N 72°54′·32W) has a double bascule span with a vertical clearance of 4·0 m (13 ft) when closed and 18·9 m (62 ft) when open.

A fixed road bridge, close N of Tomlinson Bridge, has a vertical clearance of 18·3 m (60 ft).

2 A bascule bridge with a vertical clearance of 7·6 m (25 ft) crosses the Quinnipiac River and a swing bridge with a vertical clearance of 2·4 m (8 ft) crosses the Mill River.

A power cable, with a safe vertical clearance of 27·7 m (91 ft), spans the channel just above the fixed road bridge.

Horizontal clearance
6.123

1 Tomlinson Bridge has a horizontal clearance of 73·4 m (241 ft).

Fixed road bridge, close N of Tomlinson Bridge, has a horizontal clearance of 86·2 m (283 ft).

Tidal levels
6.124

1 Mean spring range about 2 m (6·6 ft); mean neap range about 1·5 m (4·9 ft). See information in *Admiralty Tide Tables*.

Arrival information

Outer anchorages
6.125

1 Deep-draught vessels awaiting a berth can anchor about 1 mile S of NH Light Buoy (41°12′·13N 72°53′·79W), good holding, clear of the charted cable area.

Pilotage
6.126

1 Pilots board in the vicinity, or 1 mile S, of NH Light Buoy. See also 6.4.

See *Admiralty List of Radio Signals Volume 6(5)* for details.

Traffic regulations
6.127

1 **Regulated navigation area.** There is a regulated navigation area in which the movements of tugs and barges are restricted in the waters surrounding the Tomlinson Bridge (6.122).

For definition and general regulations concerning regulated navigation areas see Appendix V.

No-discharge Zone (NDZ) see 1.41.

Harbour

General layout
6.128

1 The outer harbour extends from the entrance to a line joining Fort Hale (41°16′·23N 72°54′·31W) and Sandy Point, an indistinct spit 8 cables E. The main or inner harbour extends 2 miles farther N.

The deep-draught facilities lie along the N and E sides of the inner part of the harbour.

Natural conditions
6.129

1 **Tidal streams.** See Tidal Stream tables on chart.

Ice generally obstructs navigation to some extent for low-powered vessels from December to March and sometimes extends to the mouth of the harbour. South winds force drift ice in from the sound and prevent local ice from leaving the harbour. Except in severe weather, powered vessels can always enter and leave the harbour without much difficulty.

Directions
(continued from 6.88)

Principal marks
6.130

1 **Landmarks:**
Tower (disused lighthouse) (41°14′·94N 72°54′·23W), on Lighthouse Point.
Monument (41°19′·64N 72°54′·28W).
Chimney (41°17′·03N 72°54′·22W).
Tower (41°18′·20N 72°54′·37W).
Tower (41°18′·50N 72°55′·43W).

Entrance
6.131

1 **Leading lights:**
Front light (white framework tower, concrete base) (41°15′·64N 72°56′·08W).
Rear light (similar structure) (767 m from front light).

From the vicinity of NH Light Buoy (safe water) (41°12′·13N 72°53′·79W) the alignment (333·6°) of these lights leads NNW through the dredged channel, marked by buoys and light buoys (lateral), to the harbour entrance, passing:

2 WSW of Southwest Ledge Light (white 8-sided dwelling, brown round base) (41°14′·06N 72°54′·73W), at the SW head of East Breakwater, and:
ENE of Luddington Rock Light (green and white chequered diamond on framework tower) (41°13′·89N 72°55′·39W), on the NE head of Middle Breakwater.

Thence into the outer harbour.

Harbour
6.132

1 From the breakwater entrance the dredged channel, marked by buoys and light buoys (lateral), leads N through the outer harbour to the main harbour at the head of the bay.

Useful mark:
Sandy Point Breakwater Light (green and white chequered diamond on framework tower) (41°15′·74N 72°55′·08W).

Berths

Anchorages
6.133

1 There are no regulations prescribing the limits within which vessels may not anchor, except that the dredged channels must be kept clear.

Anchorage may be obtained, for vessels with a draught of up to 5·8 m (19 ft), within the outer harbour inside the West Breakwater and the SW part of Middle Breakwater.

2 Anchorage may also be obtained N of Southwest Ledge Light in 6 m (18 to 20 ft), soft bottom. Care should be taken to avoid the ledges N of the E Breakwater.

Caution. Mariners should be aware that water levels may drop significantly following a prolonged NW wind and should also avoid fish stakes in the area.

Alongside Berths
6.134

1 The main deep-draught berths are as follows:
Exxon Co. Terminal Wharf (41°17′·27N 72°54′·50W): 213 m in length, with dolphins, depth alongside 10·7 m, handling petroleum products.

2 New Haven Terminal (41°17′·37N 72°54′·44W) (three berths): Scrap metal dock 195 m in length, depth alongside 10·7 m, handling scrap metal and lumber, and pier 198 m in length on each side, depths alongside 10·7 m on the N side and 11·9 m on the S side, handling general cargo, petroleum products, chemicals and metals.

3 ARCO Petroleum Products Co. Wharf (41°17′·55N 72°54′·46W): 232 m in length, with dolphins, depth alongside 10·7 m, handling petroleum products.
Gateway Terminal Pier (41°17′·67N 72°54′·35W) (three berths): 229 m in length and handles 40 000 dwt tankers and 68 000 dwt dry cargo vessels with 11 m draught.

4 Gulf Refining and Marketing Co. Terminal (41°17′·75N 72°54′·33W): 224 m in length, with dolphins, depth alongside 10·7 m, handling petroleum products.

Wyatt Terminal (41°17'·87N 72°54'·56W) (two berths): 218 and 146 m in length, depths alongside 11·6 and 9·1 m, handling petroleum products.

Port services

Repairs
6.135
1   New Haven has no facilities for major repairs or for dry docking deep-draught vessels. Minor repair facilities are available.

Other facilities
6.136
1   Hospitals.

Supplies
6.137
1   Fuel alongside and by barge; water; provisions and stores.

BRIDGEPORT HARBOR AND APPROACHES

General information

Chart 2726
Position and function
6.138
1   Bridgeport Harbor (41°10'·05N 73°10'·51W) is situated on the N side of Long Island Sound, 52 miles E of New York. It lies at the head of the bight between Stratford Point (6.147) and Penfield Reef (6.156), 6 miles WSW.
    Bridgeport, which in 2010 had a population of 144 229, is a port of entry.
2   The harbour consists of two widely separated areas. The main harbour and its branches serve the E and central parts of the city of Bridgeport, and Black Rock Harbor (6.154), 1½ miles W, serves the W part of the city.
    Waterborne commerce consists largely of petroleum products, lumber, sand and gravel, building materials and scrap iron.

Port authority
6.139
1   Bridgeport Port Authority, 330 Water Street, Bridgeport, CT 06604-4920

Limiting conditions

Controlling depths
6.140
1   **Project depth** in the main entrance channel is 10·7 m (35 ft). For the latest controlling depths the charts and port authority should be consulted.

Vertical clearance
6.141
1   Connecticut Turnpike Bridge, a fixed bridge with a vertical clearance of 18·2m (60 ft), crosses the river 7 cables above Tongue Point.
    Five other bridges cross the upper reach of Pequonnock River, the first four of which are bascule bridges.
    A swing bridge crosses the entrance to Johnsons Creek. A bascule bridge and Connecticut Turnpike Bridge, with a vertical clearance of 11·9 m (39 ft), cross Yellow Mill Channel.

Tidal levels
6.142
1   Mean spring range about 2·2 m (7·2 ft); mean neap range about 1·6 m (5·2 ft). See information in *Admiralty Tide Tables*.

Arrival information

Outer anchorages
6.143
1   Anchorage, which provides shelter from strong N winds, may be obtained off the entrance. The holding is good.

Pilotage
6.144
1   Pilots board in the vicinity, or about 1 mile S, of BH Light Buoy (41°06'·24N 73°11'·74W). See also 6.4.
    See *Admiralty List of Radio Signals Volume 6(5)* for details.

Harbour

General layout
6.145
1   Bridgeport Harbor, protected by two breakwaters that extend from the entrance points of the mouth of Pequonnock River, is formed by the lower part of Pequonnock River and its tributaries, Johnsons Creek and Yellow Mill Channel.
    The deep-draught facilities are S of Tongue Point (41°10'·00N 73°10'·65W) and on the E side of the harbour opposite Tongue Point.
    No-discharge Zone (NDZ), see 1.41.

Natural conditions
6.146
1   **Tidal streams.** See Tidal Stream table on chart.
    Ice does not interfere seriously with navigation in the main harbour, although its branch channels are closed at times. Winds from N and NW clear the harbour of drift ice and winds from SE through S to SW, force ice into the harbour. The ice, in severe weather, may cause the outer buoys to drift.
    Climate information. See 1.139 and 1.145.

Directions

Principal marks
6.147
1   **Landmarks:**
      Radio tower (41°09'·55N 73°09'·84W) (southerly of two), standing on Pleasure Beach, the E entrance point to the harbour.
      Chimney (41°10'·24N 73°11'·05W), with red and white bands.
      White spire (41°10'·42N 73°11'·89W).
2   Tallest spire (41°10'·81N 73°11'·73W).
    Major light:
      Stratford Point Light (white conical tower, brown band) (41°09'·12N 73°06'·20W).
      Penfield Reef Light (white tower on granite dwelling) (41°07'·03N 73°13'·33W).

Entrance channel
6.148
1   From the vicinity of BH Light Buoy (safe water) (41°06'·24N 73°11'·74W) the entrance channel leads NNE for 3 miles between pairs of buoys and light buoys (lateral) to the harbour entrance, passing:
      Between East Breakwater Head Light (red triangle and green square on framework tower) (41°09'·29N 73°10'·61W) and Bridgeport Harbor Light (green square on framework tower), 2 cables NW; thence:

ESE of Tongue Point Light (black conical tower) (41°10′·00N 73°10′·65W).

Thence the track leads NW into Bridgeport Reach.

Berths

Anchorages
6.149

1 Anchorage may be obtained in two areas within the breakwaters:

On the E side of the main channel, NW of Pleasure Beach (41°09′·65N 73°10′·00W), in 7 to 12 m (23 to 40 ft).

On the W side of the channel, NW of Tongue Point, in 5 to 8 m (15 to 25 ft). A rock with a depth of 3 m (10 ft) lies in the inshore part of this anchorage, 3½ cables NW of Tongue Point.

Alongside berths
6.150

1 The main deep-draught berths are as follows:

United Illuminating Co. Fuel Oil Dock (41°09′·90N 73°10′·80W): an offshore wharf 274 m in length, with dolphins, depths alongside 9·5 to 11·3 m, handling petroleum products.

2 Shell Oil Co. Dock (41°10′·02N 73°10′·18W): 58 m face and 213 m in length with shore moorings, depth alongside 10·7 m, handling petroleum products.

Cilco Terminal Co. Wharf (41°10′·18N 73°10′·47W): 283 m in length, depth alongside 10 m, handling general cargo, lumber and steel products.

City recreational pier (41°09′·87N 73°10′·20W), at the NW end of Pleasure Beach, has depths of 6 m at the end of the pier, but is seldom used for mooring vessels.

Port services

Repairs
6.151

1 Bridgeport has no facilities for making major repairs or dry docking deep-draught vessels, but minor repairs are available.

Other facilities
6.152

1 Hospitals.

Supplies
6.153

1 Fuel; water; provisions and stores.

Black Rock Harbor

General information
6.154

1 **Description.** Black Rock Harbor (41°09′·32N 73°12′·91W) is situated on the W side of Bridgeport, 2 miles SW of the entrance to Bridgeport Harbor.

The harbour is approached by a dredged channel entered S of Fayerweather Island (6.156) and leads N through Black Rock Harbor into Cedar Creek. At its head Cedar Creek divides into East Branch and West Branch. Ash Creek, approached by a dredged channel, is entered 8 cables W of Fayerweather Island.

No-discharge Zone (NDZ) see 1.41.

Limiting conditions
6.155

1 **Depths.** The project depth in the dredged channel is 5·5 m (18 ft) from the entrance to the head of the project. For the latest controlling depths the charts and port authority should be consulted.

Ice usually closes the harbour during part of the winter.

Directions
6.156

1 From the vicinity of BH Light Buoy (safe water) (41°06′·24N 73°11′·74W) the outer approach to Black Rock Harbor leads NNW to the entrance of the dredged channel, passing:

ENE of Black Rock (41°07′·21N 73°13′·05W), marked by a beacon, and The Little Cows, 1½ cables N, the outermost dangers of Penfield Reef, marked by LC Light Buoy (port hand). Penfield Reef Light (6.92) stands on the reef 4 cables SSW of these dangers. Thence:

2 WSW of No 2A Light Beacon (red triangle on framework tower) (41°08′·23N 73°13′·04W), which marks the entrance to the dredged channel. This light beacon stands 3 cables S of the S extremity of Fayerweather Island, on which stands a disused lighthouse.

Thence the dredged channel, marked by No 7 Light Beacon (green square on framework tower) and buoys (lateral), leads N and NE to the head of Cedar Creek.

Berths
6.157

1 **Anchorage** in 5 to 7 m (16 to 23 ft), exposed to SE and NE winds, may be found N of the bar which extends E to Black Rock (6.156).

Berths situated in East and West Branch have reported depths alongside of 2·4 to 5·5 m.

HARBOURS IN THE NORTH-EAST PART OF LONG ISLAND SOUND

General information

Chart 2754, US Chart 12354 (see 1.16)

Description
6.158

1 This sub-section describes the smaller harbours and anchorages on the N side of the E part of Long Island Sound.

No-discharge Zone (NDZ), see 1.41.

Niantic Bay and River

General information
6.159

1 **Position and function.** Niantic Bay (41°18′·60N 72°11′·30W) is entered between Millstone Point (41°18′·30N 72°09′·90W) and Black Point, 4¼ miles WSW. The bay affords good anchorage, sheltered from E, N and W winds.

Arrival information
6.160

1 **Outer anchorages.** D Anchorage, 5 cables square, is centred 1 mile NE of Bartlett Reef Light (6.161) between Little Goshen Reef (41°17′·55N 72°06′·85W) and Bartlett Reef, 1 mile WSW.

Traffic regulations. A safety and security zone, close inshore, surrounds Dominion Millstone Nuclear Power Plant (41°18′·57N 72°10′·06W).

For definition and general regulations concerning safety and security zones see Appendix V.

Directions

6.161

1 **Landmark:**

Red and white chimney (41°18′·58N 72°09′·95W), 118 m (389 ft) in height, part of the nuclear power station standing on Millstone Point.

Entry. The main approach is direct from Long Island Sound. The bay can also be approached from the E, through Twotree Island Channel which passes between Bartlett Reef and Twotree Island, and the coast. This channel should not be entered without local knowledge.

2 From a position about 2½ miles SE of Black Point (41°17′·20N 72°12′·35W) the track into Niantic Bay leads generally NNW, passing:

WSW of Bartlett Reef, on the S end of which stands Bartlett Reef Light (red and white chequered diamond on framework tower) (41°16′·48N 72°08′·23W). No 1 Buoy (starboard hand) marks the N end of the reef and No 4 Light Buoy (starboard hand) is moored 1 mile S of the light. Thence:

3 WSW of Twotree Island (41°17′·67N 72°09′·17W), small and bare, thence:

WSW of White Rock (41°18′·18N 72°10′·57W), an islet. No 6 Light Buoy (starboard hand) is moored 2 cables SSE of the rock. Thence:

Between Black Rock (41°18′·59N 72°10′·67W) and Threefoot Rock (9 cables WSW) marked, respectively, by No 8 Buoy (starboard hand) and No 7 Buoy (port hand).

Thence into Niantic Bay.

Anchorage

6.162

1 Anchorage may be obtained in 5 to 6 m (17 to 21 ft). Depths decrease gradually to the head of the bay.

Connecticut River

Chart 2754, US Chart 12375 (see 1.16)

General information

6.163

1 **Position and function.** Connecticut River flows into Long Island Sound between Lynde Point (41°16′·29N 72°20′·58W) and a low, marshy point 8 cables NE.

The river is one of the largest and most important in New England. It is navigable as far as Hartford, the capital of Connecticut, 45 miles above the river entrance. Waterborne commerce on the river is limited to occasional traffic in petroleum products, asphalt and coal.

No-discharge Zone (NDZ), see 1.41.

Limiting conditions

6.164

1 **Project depths** for the Connecticut River are 4·6 m (15 ft) in the entrance channel and in the cuts across the bars to Hartford. For the latest controlling depths the charts and port authority should be consulted.

Vertical clearances. A number of fixed and opening bridges cross the river between the river entrance and the port facilities at Hartford. Vertical clearances and distances above the river entrance are as follows:

2 Bascule rail bridge; 5·8 m (19 ft); (3 miles).

Fixed road bridge; 24·7 m (81 ft); (3½ miles).

Swing road bridge at East Haddam; 6·7 m (22 ft); (14½ miles).

Swing rail bridge at Middletown; 7·6 m (25 ft); (27¾ miles).

Fixed road bridge at Middletown; 27·1 m (89 ft); (28 miles).

3 Fixed road bridge at Wethersfield; 24·4 m (80 ft); (41¼ miles).

Charter Oak Bridge at Hartford, a fixed bridge; 21 m (69 ft); (44 miles).

Power cables spanning the river have a least safe vertical clearance of 19·8 m (65 ft).

Ice closes the river to navigation by wooden hulled boats for about 2 months every winter.

Arrival information

6.165

1 **Pilotage.** River pilot boards off Saybrook Point (41°17′·12N 72°21′·02W); 24 hours advance notice is requested.

Tidal streams. See Tidal Stream tables on chart.

Directions

6.166

1 **Entrance.** Long Sand Shoal (6.87) lies in the approaches to Connecticut River and the entrance is obstructed by Saybrook Outer Bar, which is of a shifting nature.

From the vicinity of 41°14′·00N 72°18′·00W the route leads NW, passing:

Between the S extremity of Saybrook Outer Bar (41°14′·94N 72°18′·81W), marked by No 8 Light Buoy (starboard hand), and the E end of Long Sand Shoal, 5 cables WSW, marked by 'E' Buoy (preferred channel to port), thence:

2 Through the entrance channel between the breakwaters. Saybrook Breakwater Head Light (white conical tower, brown round base) (41°15′·79N 72°20′·56W) stands at the head of the W breakwater and No 2 Light Buoy (starboard hand) marks the E edge of the channel. Thence:

3 E of Lynde Point Light (white stone tower) (41°16′·29N 72°20′·58W). No 5 Light Buoy (port hand) marks the edge of the channel. Thence:

Through the buoyed channel to Saybrook Point (6.165) (8 cables NNW).

Connecticut River. For the passage from Saybrook Point to Hartford, local knowledge is required.

Berths

6.167

1 **Anchorage.** There is a secure anchorage in 5 to 9 m (16 to 30 ft) in the channel E and NE of Lynde Point Lighthouse. Farther up river, anchorage can be obtained in the wider parts of the river.

Wharves. Connecticut River has more than twenty commercial piers and wharves, with depths alongside of 3·4 to 4·6 m, which are mainly used for the discharge of petroleum products from coastal tankers and barges.

2 The only commercial wharf at Hartford is the one used for supplying fuel to the electric power company on the W bank, 2 cables below Charter Oak Bridge.

Housatonic River

Charts 2754, 2726, US Chart 12370 (see 1.16)

General information

6.168

1 **Position and function.** Housatonic River flows into Long Island Sound between Milford Point (41°10′·35N 73°06′·40W) and Stratford Point, 1 mile S. It is navigable for 11½ miles above its entrance, and forms the approaches to the towns of Stratford, on the W bank, and Devon on the E bank. Waterborne commerce is principally in shipments of aggregate,

fuel oil to the power plant at Devon and seasonal commercial shell fishing.

Local knowledge is required.

No-discharge Zone (NDZ) see 1.41.

Limiting conditions
6.169
1 **Project depths** for Housatonic River are 5·5 m (18 ft) from Long Island Sound to Culver Bar, 4½ miles upstream. Above this point the controlling depth (2005) is 0·7 m (2·2 ft). For the latest controlling depths the national charts and port authority should be consulted.

Vertical clearance. Three bridges cross the river between the entrance and the town of Devon, 3½ miles upstream. They are listed as follows (with distances upstream from the river entrance):

2 Bascule road bridge; vertical clearance 9·7 m (32 ft); (3¼ miles).
Fixed road bridge; vertical clearance 19·8 m (65 ft); (3½ miles).
Bascule rail bridge; vertical clearance 5·8 m (19 ft); (3½ miles).

3 **Tidal streams** are strong, the out-going stream especially so when the river is high during freshets. At the entrance to the river there is a strong W set during the in-going stream and off Milford Point the tidal streams attain a rate of 1¼ kn.

Ice closes the river above Stratford during the winter, and it sometimes extends to the entrance.

Pilotage
6.170
1 Pilots can be obtained at New Haven.

Directions
6.171
1 **Entrance**. From a position SE of Stratford Point (41°09′·20N 73°06′·20W) the route into Housatonic River leads NW to the entrance channel, which is narrow and crooked with little depth on either side, passing:

NE of No 1 Light Buoy (port hand) (41°09′·40N 73°05′·43W), which marks the beginning of the Entrance Channel, thence:

2 SW of No 2A Light Beacon (red triangle on framework tower) (41°09′·65N 73°05′·58W), which stands at the end of Outer Breakwater that extends 1 mile SE from Milford Point. The inner end of the breakwater is submerged at HW. Thence:

Through the dredged channel that is marked by No 3 Light Buoy (port hand) and buoys (lateral), and light beacons.

Berths
6.172
1 A berth at Stratford has a depth alongside of 2·7 m at its end.

Anchorages and harbours

Chart 2754, US Charts 12373, 2374 (see 1.16)

Between Black Point and Hatchett Point
6.173
1 The bay between Black Point (41°17′·20N 72°12′·35W) and Hatchett Point, 2½ miles W, is foul. The outer dangers consist of Blackboys, two drying rocks situated 7 cables W of Black Point, and Hatchett Reef, 1 mile S of Hatchett Point. These dangers are marked on their S sides by, respectively, Nos 2 and 6 Buoys (both starboard hand).

Westbrook Harbor
6.174
1 **Description.** Westbrook Harbor (41°16′·10N 72°27′·20W) is the W part of the bight between Cornfield Point and Menunketesuck Island, 3½ miles W. The bight is obstructed by boulders and has not been properly examined.

Westbrook is at the head of the bight. A conspicuous tank stands on the E side of the town.

2 **Anchorage**, entered between Crane Reef (6.87) and Menunketesuck Island, is seldom used, as the anchorage in Duck Island Roads (6.175) is better.

Duck Island Roads
6.175
1 **Description.** Duck Island Roads (41°15′·80N 72°29′·00W), a harbour of refuge, is entered between Menunketesuck Island and Kelsey Point, 2 miles W. Patchogue River flows into the NE part of the harbour.

Depths. Depths in the roads are between 2·4 and 8·2 m (8 and 27 ft). Patchogue River has a project depth of 2·4 m (8 ft) to the head of the project.

2 **General layout.** The harbour is formed by two breakwaters which extend 1¾ cables N and 4½ cables W from Duck Island (41°15′·39N 72°28′·52W), a small islet with a chimney on it, that lies 1½ miles E of Kelsey Point. Further protection is provided by Kelsey Point Breakwater that extends 6½ cables S from Stone Island (41°15′·22N 72°30′·79W), situated 3 cables SW of Kelsey Point.

Anchorage may be obtained:

3 In the dredged anchorage enclosed by the breakwaters extending N and W from Duck Island in 1 to 2 m (3 to 8 ft) in the protected area and 1 to 5 m (4 to 16 ft) in the W end.

In a small area N and NE of Duck Island North Breakwater Light (red and white chequered diamond on framework tower) (41°15′·61N 72°28′·50W); this anchorage can be used in SW weather.

4 Between Duck Island West Breakwater Light (red triangle on framework tower) and the rocky patches, marked by No 8 Buoy (starboard hand), that lie 4 cables SSW of Kelsey Point Breakwater Light (green and white chequered diamond on framework tower) in 6 to 7 m (18 to 24 ft), sticky bottom, exposed to winds S of E and W.

Clinton Harbor
6.176
1 **Description.** Clinton Harbor (41°15′·55N 72°31′·65W), the bight W of Kelsey Point Breakwater (6.175), is entered between Kelsey Point (6.175) and Hammonasset Point and forms the entrance to Hammonasset River, used mainly by fishing and recreational craft.

No-discharge Zone (NDZ) see 1.41.

Hammonasset Point to Sachem Head
6.177
1 **Description.** Between Hammonasset Point (41°15′·00N 72°32′·66W) and Sachem Head, 7½ miles W, there is a broad bight sometimes used as an anchorage, sheltered from N and NE winds. This anchorage has little to recommend it as there are boulders in the bight and it has not been thoroughly examined.

Madison Reef obstructs the central part of the bight.

2 **Guilford Harbor** (41°16′·00N 72°40′·55W) is entered in the NW end of the bight, 2 miles NE of Sachem Head. It is only frequented by small craft.

Sachem Head to Branford Harbor
6.178

1 **Description.** Between Sachem Head and the entrance to Branford Harbor (6.179), 5½ miles W, is a bight obstructed by numerous islands and rocks above and below-water.

Joshua Cove (41°15′·20N 72°42′·80W) is situated N of Uncas Point, the W extremity of Sachem Head. Though little used, it affords good anchorage in its entrance for small vessels in 2 to 3 m (6 to 10 ft). The approach from SW is clear between Goose Rocks Shoals, which extend SW from Uncas Point, and Leetes Rocks, 6 cables NW.

2 **The Thimbles** are a group of islands extending over 2 miles SW from Hoadley Point (41°15′·42N 72°44′·17W) to East Reef. A buoyed passage with a depth of 4 m (13 ft) leads through the N part of The Thimbles.

The whole area is suitable only for small pleasure craft.

Branford Harbor
6.179

1 **Description.** Branford Harbor (41°15′·40N 72°49′·60W) is a shallow cove mainly frequented by pleasure craft and the small local lobster fleet.

Anchorage, sheltered from all but S or SW winds, may be obtained in 3 to 4 m (10 to 14 ft) S of the Mermaids.

No-discharge Zone (NDZ), see 1.41.

Milford Harbor
6.180

1 Milford Harbor (41°12′·75N 73°03′·10W) is principally used by pleasure craft and occasionally by fishing craft.

HARBOURS IN THE SOUTH-EAST PART OF LONG ISLAND SOUND

General information

Chart 2754, US Chart 12354 (see 1.16)
Description
6.181

1 Between Orient Point (41°09′·60N 72°14′·05W) and Old Field Point, 42 miles WSW, are situated United Riverhead Terminal at Jacobs Point, and Port Jefferson Harbor. There are also a number of other small harbours used by pleasure craft.

United Riverhead Terminal

General information
6.182

1 **United Riverhead Terminal** (41°00′·01N 72°38′·80W) is situated 1 mile N of Jacobs Point. The terminal, used for the delivery and receipt of petroleum products, consists of a 30 m by 14 m steel platform with breasting and mooring dolphins.

Port Authority. United Riverhead Terminal, Inc, 212 Sound Shore Road, Riverhead, NY 11901. www.urtny.com

Arrival information
6.183

1 **Port operations**. See *Admiralty List of Radio Signals Volume 6(5)* for details.

Pilotage is compulsory. The pilot serves as docking master and remains on board at standby while the vessel is at the platform. See 6.4.

Quarantine and customs. New York City is the port of entry for the terminal.

Useful marks. Numerous light green oil tanks on Jacobs Point are prominent.

Berths
6.184

1 **Anchorage.** Vessels awaiting a berth at the platform normally anchor N of the platform; vessels of greater than 15 m draught may anchor in deeper water NW of the platform.

Platform. Vessels of up to 225 000 dwt, 350 m in length and 18·9 m draught can be accommodated:
  NE side - depth alongside 19·5 m.
  SW side - depth alongside 15·2 m.

2 **Wharf,** close E of Jacobs Point:
Barge pier: 243 m in length, depth alongside 3·9 m. Vessels with a draught greater than 3·6 m should exercise caution when approaching the pier and should try to arrive or depart at HW.

Port services
6.185

1 **Facilities:** hospital 11 km from the terminal; launch service available to ships at anchor and at the platform.

Supplies: fuel can be obtained from barges at the anchorage, fuelling of a vessel alongside the platform is not permitted; no fresh water at the terminal; supplies by launch.

Port Jefferson Harbor

General information
6.186

1 **Description.** Port Jefferson Harbor (40°57′·05N 73°04′·49W) is entered through a dredged channel between two breakwaters 6 cables W of Mount Misery Point and 1¼ miles ESE of Old Field Point.

Port Jefferson is a town at the S end of the harbour. The principal industries of the port are the shipping of sand and gravel and the distribution of petroleum products.

2 **No-discharge Zone (NDZ).** The whole of Port Jefferson has been designated as a NDZ. See 1.41.

Limiting conditions
6.187

1 **Depths.** The project depth is 7·9 m (26 ft) to the berthing area off an oil wharf at the S end of the harbour. For the latest controlling depths the national charts and port authority should be consulted.

Ice forms over the entire harbour and interrupts navigation in very cold weather, but does not endanger shipping in the harbour.

Arrival information
6.188

1 **Port operations.** Speed limits of 10 and 4 kn are enforced in the channel and off the berths, respectively.

Outer anchorage. Anchorage may be obtained in depths of 25 to 30 m (14 to 16 fm) N of Mount Misery Shoal. Lighters from New York can be arranged.

2 **Pilotage** is compulsory. The pilot boards near PJ Light Buoy (40°59′·27N 73°06′·45W). See also 6.4.

Tugs are available from New Haven, Providence, Brooklyn or Staten Island. Normally two tugs are used for docking and one for undocking.

Port Jefferson from SE (6.189)
(Original dated 1993)

(Photograph - Joseph R Melanson of www.skypic.com)

Harbour
6.189
1   **Measured distance.** Off Old Field Beach on the W side of the harbour entrance there is a measured distance.

    Limit marks - Two pairs of beacons; the front markers are orange posts and the rear markers are rectangles painted red with a black vertical stripe in the middle.
    Length - 1 mile.
    Running track - 121°-301°.

2   **Tidal streams**. In the channel between the jetties the in-going tidal stream has a rate of about 2½ kn.

Directions
6.190
1   **Landmarks:**
    Chimneys at power station (40°57′·02N 73°04′·70W) (NE of three).
    Entry. From the vicinity of PJ Light Buoy (safe water) (6.188) the track leads SE through a dredged channel, marked by light buoys and buoys (lateral), to the head of the harbour, passing:
    SW of Mount Misery Shoal (40°59′·06N 73°05′·10W), marked on its N side by No 11 Buoy (port hand), thence:
    Between No 1 Light Buoy (port hand) (40°58′·41N 73°05′·64W) and No 2 Light Buoy (starboard hand), ½ cable SW, which mark the limits of the channel, thence:

2   Between E Breakwater Light (green and white chequered diamond on framework tower) (40°58′·34N 73°05′·50W), standing at the root of the E breakwater, and No 2A Light (red triangle on framework tower) standing at the head of the W breakwater, 1½ cables SW.
    Thence into the harbour.
    Useful mark:
    Old Field Point Light (40°58′·62N 73°07′·11W) (6.94).

Berths
6.191
1   **Anchorage** may be obtained in the NE part of the harbour in 5 m (16 ft), which provides excellent shelter from the N. Care must be taken to avoid shoal patches at the sides of this area.

    Alongside berths:
    Oil wharf, 2 cables from the head of the harbour on the W side, depth alongside 8·8 m.
    Power plant wharf, 1 cable NW of Oil wharf, depth alongside 8·8 m.
    Commercial wharves and piers at the head of the harbour, depths alongside up to 8·8 m.

Port services
6.192
1   **Repairs.** Available.
    Other facilities. Hospitals.
    Supplies: fuel; water.

HARBOURS IN THE NORTH-WEST PART OF LONG ISLAND SOUND

Norwalk Islands
Charts 2754, 2580, US Chart 12364 (see 1.16)
Description
6.193
1   Norwalk Islands, a group of islands, rocks and shoals, lie between 1 and 2 miles off the N coast of Long Island Sound in the approaches to Norwalk Harbor (6.196). The islands extend between Georges Rock (41°05′·06N 73°19′·72W), 1¼ miles E of Cockenoe Island, and Greens Ledge Light (6.92), 1 mile WSW of Sheffield Island (41°03′·15N 73°24′·90W).

2   **Caution.** The bottom is very irregular in the vicinity of the islands and vessels should proceed with caution when crossing shoal areas. The area is much obstructed by oyster stakes and spars which sometimes tow under and are a danger, especially to small vessels.

Cockenoe Harbor
6.194

1 **Description.** Cockenoe Harbor, W of Cockenoe Island and N of Goose Island, is entered between Peck Ledge Light (white conical tower, brown band, black round base) (41°04'·64N 73°22'·18W) and No 4 Buoy (starboard hand). It is also an approach to Norwalk River (6.196).

Local knowledge is required to enter the harbour.

2 **Anchorage** may be obtained by vessels of up to 2·7 m (9 ft) draught. The best berth is in the deeper part of the harbour in 4 to 7 m (12 to 25 ft), N and NW of Peck Ledge Light. There are depths of only about 4 m (13 ft) in the entrance of the harbour.

Sheffield Island Harbor
6.195

1 **Description.** Sheffield Island Harbor (41°03'·30N 73°25'·20W) lies between Sheffield Island and Shea Island, and the mainland NW. The harbour forms the main approach to Norwalk Harbor and River and is entered between Greens Ledge Light (6.92) and Long Neck Point, 1½ miles WSW.

Anchorage in 4 to 6 m (12 to 20 ft) may be obtained NW of Sheffield Island.

Norwalk Harbor and River

Chart 2754, US Chart 12368 (see 1.16)

General information
6.196

1 **Description.** Norwalk Harbor (41°05'·40N 73°24'·30W) is formed by the lower part of Norwalk River, which flows into the N side of Long Island Sound between Calf Pasture Point (41°04'·97N 73°23'·75W) and Manresa Island, 7½ cables SW. A dredged channel leads from Sheffield Island Harbor in to Norwalk Harbor.

The towns of East Norwalk and South Norwalk lie on the E and W side of the river, 1 and 1½ miles within the entrance, respectively. Norwalk, at the head of navigation, lies 2½ miles within the entrance.

2 South Norwalk is an important commercial and manufacturing city. Commercial traffic on the river is mainly in building materials, petroleum products and shell fishing.

No-discharge Zone (NDZ) see 1.41.

Limiting conditions
6.197

1 **Depths.** The project depth is 3·6 m (12 ft) from Sheffield Island Harbor to the bascule road bridge at South Norwalk, thence 3 m (10 ft) to a basin at Norwalk.

Federal project provides for a depth of 1·8 m (6 ft) in the dredged channel leading W of Fitch Point, to the anchorage basin in East Norwalk.

East of Fitch Point a privately maintained channel, which in 1987 had a controlling depth of 2·4 m (8 ft), leads into Norwalk Cove.

2 For the latest controlling depths the national charts and port authority should be consulted.

Vertical clearance. Three bridges and a power cable span the river between South Norwalk and Norwalk:

Road bascule bridge, with vertical clearance of 2·4 m (8 ft), 6 cables NW of Fitch Point.

Rail swing bridge, with a vertical clearance of 4·9 m (16 ft), close N of the road bridge.

3 Power cable, with a safe vertical clearance of 61·9 m (203 ft), close N of the rail bridge.

Fixed road bridge at Oyster Shell Point, 5 cables N of rail bridge, with a vertical clearance of 18·3 m (60 ft).

Ice. The channel to South Norwalk is navigable throughout the year, but above that the channel is normally closed for about 6 weeks each winter; the channel to East Norwalk is also closed for part of the winter.

Arrival information
6.198

1 **Pilotage.** Pilots who serve New London and New Haven also serve Norwalk.

Directions
6.199

1 **Landmark:**

Chimney (41°04'·35N 73°24'·66W), standing on Manresa Island close NE of Keyser Point.

Major light:

Greens Ledge Light (41°02'·50N 73°26'·63W) (6.92).

Entry. From a position close NW of Greens Ledge Light the approaches to Norwalk Harbor and River lead NE through Sheffield Harbor, passing:

2 NW of No 2A Light Buoy (starboard hand) (41°02'·78N 73°26'·07W). A group of drying rocks lies on the inner part of Greens Ledge, 4 cables E of this buoy. Thence:

SE of a shoal (41°02'·96N 73°26'·16W), with a depth of 3·4 m (11 ft), marked on its SE side by No 1A Buoy (port hand), thence:

3 Between Noroton Point (41°03'·34N 73°26'·00W) and the SW extremity of Sheffield Island, 6½ cables SE. A flagstaff and house with a cupola stand on Noroton Point and a disused lighthouse stands near the SW end of Sheffield Island. Thence:

Between No 2 Light Buoy (starboard hand) (41°03'·51N 73°25'·07W) and No 3 Buoy (port hand), which mark the entrance to the channel.

Thence through the channel marked by light buoys, light beacons and buoys (lateral).

Berths
6.200

1 **Anchorages.** Apart from Cockenoe Harbor (6.194) and Sheffield Island Harbor (6.195), small vessels can anchor in 2 to 3 m (8 to 9 ft) in South Anchorage Basin. This basin lies on the E side of the channel, extending 2½ cables either side of the entrance to East Norwalk, 7 cables NW of Calf Pasture Point.

Alongside berths are available at wharves at South Norwalk, depths alongside 1·5 to 3 m, and at Norwalk, depths alongside 2·1 m.

Supplies
6.201

1 Fuel and stores.

Between Sheffield Island Harbor and Stamford Harbor

Chart 2580

General information
6.202

1 Between Noroton Point (41°03'·34N 73°26'·00W) and Shippan Point, 5 miles SW, the coast is foul with many off-lying dangers up to 1 mile offshore. The coast is much indented by inlets and coves which provide shelter for small craft, but their approaches are obstructed by dangers and they should not be entered without local knowledge.

Stamford Harbor

Chart 2580

General information
6.203

1 **Description.** Stamford Harbor (41°01'·77N 73°32'·24W), close W of Shippan Point and 33 miles E of New York, comprises the bay N of a line from Shippan Point on the E, through Stamford Harbor Ledge Light, to the shore N of Greenwich Point, 2 miles WSW of Shippan Point. The entrance to the bay is protected by two detached breakwaters.

Stamford is a manufacturing city at the head of the harbour. Petroleum products, scrap metal, sand, gravel and crushed rock are the principal shipments handled.

2 The harbour is shoal and obstructed by ledges and rocks. It is entered through a dredged channel that leads N from between the two breakwaters, to a point about 1 mile above the entrance, where it divides into channels leading into East Branch and West Branch.

No-discharge Zone (NDZ) see 1.41.

Limiting conditions
6.204

1 **Depths.** Project depths are as follows:
To a point 5 cables below the junction of the two branches - 5·5 m (18 ft), thence:
To the junction - 4·6 m (15 ft), thence:
In the West Branch to the turning basin, 7 cables above the junction - 4·6 m (15 ft), and:
2 In the East Branch to No 1 Light, 3½ cables above the junction - 4·6 m (15 ft), thence:
To the head of the project, 7 cables above No 1 Light, - 3·6 m (12 ft).

For the latest controlling depths the charts and port authority should be consulted.

3 **Navigable width.** A hurricane barrier which constricts the East Branch to 27 m (90 ft), is situated 4½ cables above the junction with West Branch. The barrier is kept open during fair weather, but will be closed on the approach of a storm or unusually high tides.

4 **Ice** forms in the harbour most winters, but traffic usually keeps the channels clear. West Branch is usually navigable all the year, but East Branch is closed by ice for several weeks in severe winters.

Harbour
6.205

1 **Tidal streams** in the harbour are weak and follow the direction of the channels.

Directions
6.206

1 **Leading lights:**
Front Light (red rectangle, white stripe, on framework tower) (41°01'·82N 73°32'·25W).
Rear light (similar structure) (183 m from front light).

From a position about 1 mile SSW of Shippan Point the alignment (358°) of these lights leads N to the entrance and thence through the dredged channel, marked by buoys, to the junction of East and West Branch, passing:

2 Clear of a dangerous wreck (41°00'·10N 73°32'·00W), position approximate, thence:
W of The Cows (41°00'·46N 73°31'·42W), marked on its S side by No 32 Light Buoy (starboard hand), thence:

Between No 1 Buoy (port hand) (41°00'·69N 73°32'·38W) and No 2 Buoy (starboard hand), 2 cables ENE, which mark shoals either side of the entrance, thence:
3 E of Harbor Ledge (41°00'·82N 73°32'·55W), from which a light (white conical tower, red round base) is exhibited, thence:
Between the ends of the detached breakwaters (3 cables WSW). No 3 Light (green square on tower) (41°00'·90N 73°32'·29W) stands at the E end of the W breakwater, and No 4 Light (red triangle on framework tower) stands off the W end of the E breakwater.

Berths
6.207

1 **Anchorage.** A dredged anchorage with depths of 3 to 5 m (10 to 18 ft) is situated 2½ cables N of the E end of the W breakwater just W of the alignment of the leading lights.

Commercial wharves, with depths alongside of 1·8 to 5·8 m, are situated along the East and West Branch.

Captain Harbor and adjacent waters

General information
6.208

1 **Description.** Captain Harbor lies between Greenwich Point (41°00'·14N 73°34'·30W) and Manursing Island, 4½ miles WSW, and N of Great Captain, Little Captain and Wee Captain Islands.

The harbour provides shelter for vessels drawing up to 3·6 m (12 ft), from all winds. Captain Harbor also forms the approach to Greenwich Cove (6.226), Cos Cob Harbor (6.227), Indian Harbor, Greenwich Harbor (6.228) and Port Chester Harbor (6.213).

No-discharge Zone (NDZ) see 1.41.

Limiting conditions
6.209

1 **Ice** forms in the winter in all the coves and over the greater part of Captain Harbor. It sometimes extends outside Little and Great Captain Islands.

Harbour
6.210

1 **Tidal streams** in the E entrance reach a rate ¾ kn.

Directions
6.211

1 **Major Light:**
Great Captain Island Light (40°58'·95N 73°37'·39W) (6.92), standing at the E end of the island.

East entrance. The harbour is entered from the E between Flat Neck Point (41°00'·09N 73°35'·06W) and Hen and Chickens, a group of rocks 1 mile WSW that extend NE from the Captain Islands. This entrance, marked by No 1 Light Buoy and No 1A Buoy (port hand), and No 2 Buoy (starboard hand), is the clearer and better one for those without local knowledge.

2 **West entrance.** From a position SW of Great Captain Island the entrance route leads NNE, passing:
ESE of Bluefish Shoal (40°58'·31N 73°38'·69W), marked on its S side by No 36 Buoy (starboard hand), thence:
WNW of a dangerous rock (40°58'·61N 73°38'·02W), marked on its E side by No 2 Buoy (starboard hand), and:
3 ESE of Fourfoot Rocks (40°58'·76N 73°38'·55W), marked on their S side by F Buoy (preferred channel to starboard), thence:

WNW of the W end of Great Captain Island (40°58′·86N 73°37′·82W), thence:

ESE of Jones Rocks (40°59′·30N 73°38′·09W), on which stands No 3 Light Beacon (green square on framework tower). No 1 Buoy (port hand) marks a reef 1½ cables SW. And:

4 WNW of Cormorant Reef (40°59′·35N 73°37′·77W), marked on its NW extremity by No 4 Buoy (starboard hand).

Caution. The harbour and its entrances are strewn with boulders. Mariners without local knowledge should proceed with caution, especially in shoaler water.

Anchorage
6.212
1 Anchorage may be obtained in the deeper part of the harbour, 5 cables N of Great and Little Captain Islands, in 5 to 9 m (15 to 30 ft), soft bottom. Vessels with a draught of 2·1 m (7 ft) or less may anchor on the flats.

Port Chester Harbor
6.213
1 **Description.** Port Chester Harbor (40°59′·33N 73°39′·59W) lies at the mouth of Byram River, the lower part of which forms the boundary between the states of Connecticut and New York. The river leads to Port Chester and Byram, 1 mile upstream. Principal commerce is in building materials and petroleum products.

2 **Entrance.** The harbour is entered between the breakwater extending S from Byram Point, and the N part of Manursing Island. A dredged entrance channel, marked for 3 cables above the entrance, leads N through the harbour.

Project depths are 3·7 m (12 ft) in the anchorage area and channel to the Fox Island Yacht Club, thence 3·0 m (10 ft) to the turning basin, thence 0·9 m (3 ft) to the head of the project. For the latest controlling depths the national charts and port authority should be consulted.

3 **Vertical clearance.** A fixed road bridge with a vertical clearance of 18·3 m (60 ft) crosses the river 8 cables above the entrance.

6.214
1 **Directions.** From a position SE of Byram Point (40°59′·23N 73°39′·44W) the approach to Port Chester leads NW through waters obstructed by rocks, passing:

NE of Bluefish Shoal (40°58′·31N 73°38′·69W), thence:

SW of Fourfoot Rocks (40°58′·76N 73°38′·55W), marked on their S side by 'F' Buoy, thence:

2 SW of Great Captain Rocks (40°59′·00N 73°39′·07W), marked on their S side by No 2 Light Buoy (starboard hand), thence:

NE of Manursing Island Reef (40°58′·97N 73°39′·33W), marked on its NE side by No 3 Buoy (port hand), thence:

SW of Byram Point Breakwater Light (red triangle on framework tower) (40°59′·07N 73°39′·39W), thence:

3 NE of No 5 Channel Light Beacon (green square on framework tower) (40°59′·16N 73°39′·59W).

Caution. The channel in Byram River is fairly well defined at LW, but those without local knowledge should take it on a rising tide and proceed with caution.

Wharf. There is an oil terminal with a reported depth alongside of 3·7 m at Fox Island, 6 cables above the entrance.

Supplies: fuel; water and stores.

Between Captain Harbor and Throgs Neck

General information
6.215
1 **Description.** The N shore of Long Island Sound between Captain Harbor (40°59′·70N 73°37′·20W) and Throgs Neck (7.135), 11 miles SW, is similar in character to that farther E, fringed by foul ground, islets and rocks, and there are numerous indentations in the coastline providing anchorage for small vessels.

Local knowledge is required for some of these harbours.

Speed limits of between 4 and 5 kn are in force in the harbours described as follows.

Mamaroneck Harbor
6.216
1 **Description.** Mamaroneck Harbor (40°56′·30N 73°42′·85W) is an open bay, exposed to S winds, between Hen Island and Delancey Point, 1¼ miles SW. The important dangers in the bay are buoyed; these include Outer Steamboat Rock, near the channel entrance and Ship Rock, 5 cables SE.

The town of Mamaroneck stands on both sides of the inner part of the harbour.

2 Commercial traffic in the harbour is mainly barges carrying petroleum products.

No-discharge Zone (NDZ). A NDZ has been established in Mamaroneck Harbor. See 1.41.

Channel. A dredged channel leads from the outer harbour in the bay to the inner harbour.

3 **Depths.** In 2007 the controlling depths in the dredged channel were 3·0 m (9·7 ft) in the entrance channel to the junction with the branch channels and thence 2·6 m (8·4 ft) in the N branch channel.

Anchorage. Depths in the outer harbour range from 2 to 4 m (7 to 12 ft).

Supplies: fuel; water and stores.

Larchmont Harbor
6.217
1 **Description.** Larchmont Harbor (40°55′·35N 73°44′·35W) is entered between Edgewater Point and Umbrella Point, 5 cables SW. A breakwater, with No 2 Light (red triangle on framework tower) at its head, extends 2 cables SSE from Edgewater Point. In summer the harbour is full of mooring buoys for small craft.

2 **Entrance.** The entrance to the harbour is obstructed by Hen and Chickens Reef, Dauntless Rock and Umbrella Rock. Hen and Chickens Reef is marked by No 1 Light Buoy (port hand) and the limits of the other dangers are marked by buoys (lateral).

Channel. A buoyed channel leads into the harbour on either side of Hen and Chickens Reef.

3 **Depths.** Depths in the harbour range from 3·6 m (12 ft) in the entrance to 1·5 m (5 ft) near the islet in the middle of the harbour.

Anchorage may be obtained in 4 to 6 m (13 to 21 ft) in the entrance to the harbour.

Echo Bay
6.218
1 **Description.** Echo Bay (40°54′·35N 73°45′·85W), entered between Premium Point and Davenport Neck, 3 cables SW, is the principal approach to New Rochelle on the W shore of the bay.

Approach. Hicks Ledge, marked on its S side by HL Buoy (preferred channel to starboard), lies in the approaches to Echo Bay, 5 cables SE of its entrance. The entrance is marked by No 3BR Light Buoy (port hand), off the S entrance point and No 4 Buoy (starboard hand), off Premium Point.

2 **Channel.** A dredged channel, marked by buoys, leads from the NW side of Echo Bay to a municipal wharf and turning basin at Beaufort Point, 3 cables within the entrance.

Depths. In 1985 the controlling depth was 2·6 m (8·5 ft) in mid-channel with 2·0 to 2·1 m (6·5 to 7 ft) in the basin.

Anchorage may be obtained either side of the entrance, clear of a sewer outfall, in 6 to 7 m (20 to 24 ft).

Supplies: fuel and water.

New Rochelle Harbor
6.219
1 **Description.** New Rochelle Harbor (40°53′·60N 73°46′·76W) is a narrow channel situated between Davenport Neck and the mainland NW. The harbour leads to the S part of New Rochelle.

Approach channels. Two well marked channels lead to the harbour. From the N, the deeper channel leads between Davids Island and Davenport Neck. From the S a channel leads across the flats SW of Davids Island and thence between that island and Glen Island. The harbour is entered between Glen Island and Davenport Neck.

2 **Depths.** The S channel has a depth of about 4 m (13 ft) and in 1990 the dredged channel in the harbour had a mid-channel controlling depth of 1·8 m (6 ft).

Anchorage is not recommended owing to the restricted nature of the channel.

City Island Harbor
6.220
1 **Description.** City Island Harbor, also known as Hart Island Roads (40°50′·80N 73°46′·60W), lies between Hart Island and City Island, 5 cables W.

The harbour is well sheltered from E and W winds. It is an important anchorage as a harbour of refuge for coasting vessels, and is also frequently used as a temporary anchorage.

2 **City Island** is largely built over and there are shipyards and marinas on its E side. The island is connected to Rodman Neck, NW, by a bridge which has a vertical clearance of 3·6 m (12 ft).

Pilotage. Pilots for New York are based at City Island. They board vessels off Execution Rocks (6.95).

Ice seldom interferes with navigation of powered vessels.

6.221
1 **Useful marks:**
Chimney (40°51′·06N 73°46′·15W), on the S part of Hart Island.
No 46 Light (40°50′·69N 73°46′·00W), on the reef extending from the S end of Hart Island.
Spire (40°51′·26N 73°47′·43W), on N part of City Island.
Spire (40°50′·88N 73°47′·22W), in the centre of City Island.

2 **Anchorages.** The usual anchorage for deep-draught vessels is SE of City Island, S of a line joining the S parts of City Island and Hart Island. Other general anchorages are situated between the W side of Hart Island and Rat Island, in the NW part of the harbour, and SW of Belden Point, the S end of City Island.

Other anchorages and harbours
Chart 2726
Southport Harbor
6.222
1 Southport Harbor (41°07′·90N 73°17′·00W) is the lower part of Mill River, at the head of a bay between Pine Creek Point and Frost Point, 2 miles W. It is used mainly by pleasure craft.

Chart 2754, US Chart 12368 (see 1.16)
Saugatuck River
6.223
1 **Description.** Saugatuck River lies with its entrance between Cedar Point (41°06′·17N 73°21′·20W) and Seymour Point, 8 cables WSW. The river is shallow, full of ledges and boulders and is used by barges carrying petroleum products, sand and gravel. It is also used by pleasure craft.

2 In 2001 it was reported that a depth of about 1·2 m (4 ft) could be carried to Saugatuck, 1½ miles above the entrance on the W side of the river.

Anchorage may be obtained, exposed to SE winds, in 3 to 7 m (12 to 22 ft), 4 cables S of Cedar Point.

Chart 2580, US Chart 12368 (see 1.16)
Fivemile River
6.224
1 Fivemile River is a narrow inlet entered 5 cables W of Noroton Point (41°03′·34N 73°26′·01W). It is chiefly used by pleasure craft and in 2010 had a project depth of 2·4 m (8 ft).

Scott Cove
6.225
1 Scott Cove (41°03′·25N 73°27′·90W), entered W of the Fish Islands, is only used by small craft drawing up to 1·8 m (6 ft). Local knowledge is required.

Chart 2580, US Chart 12367 (see 1.16)
Greenwich Cove
6.226
1 Greenwich Cove (41°00′·85N 73°34′·75W) opens into Captain Harbor N of Flat Neck Point. The cove is used by small local craft. Depths decrease from 2·4 m (8 ft) in the outer part to less than 0·9 m (3 ft) in the E part.

Cos Cob Harbor
6.227
1 Cos Cob Harbor (41°01′·20N 73°35′·80W), on the NE side of Captain Harbor, is entered through a dredged channel which leads N through Mianus River for 1½ miles to the head of navigation at Mianus. It is used by small craft.

Greenwich Harbor
6.228
1 **Description.** Greenwich Harbor (41°00′·70N 73°37′·45W) is situated 1½ miles N of Great Captain Island Light. Greenwich is at the head of the harbour.

No-discharge Zone (NDZ) see 1.41.

Entrance. The harbour is entered through a dredged and marked entrance channel, 1¼ miles in length. This channel leads across the flats to two turning basins, one at the head of the harbour and the other a short distance S, off the W side of the channel.

2 **Depths.** In 2007 the controlling depth in the channel was 2·2 m (7·2 ft) with shoaling to 1·7 m (5·7 ft) at the head of the channel and the depths in the basins were between 0·3 and 2·1 m (1·1 and 7·0 ft).

Berths. Wharves lie on the E side of the harbour.

Rye Beach
6.229

1 Playland (40°57'·70N 73°40'·50W), a recreational centre at Rye Beach, is situated in the N part of a foul bight that lies between Manursing Island and Parsonage Point, 1½ miles SW. There is a small harbour, used by small craft, protected by breakwaters.

Chart 2580
Eastchester Bay and Hutchinson River
6.230

1 Eastchester Bay (40°50'·30N 73°48'·10W) is situated between City Island and the mainland 1½ miles SW. Hutchinson River, flows into the N end of the bay. The river should not be approached without local knowledge.

There are irregular depths in Eastchester Bay and the shores of the bay are fringed with boulders; there are many shoals and several wrecks. The shoals include Cuban Ledge in the centre of the bay, marked by a beacon, and on its SW side by No 2 Light Buoy (starboard hand). Caution is essential.

ANCHORAGES AND HARBOURS IN THE SOUTH-WEST PART OF LONG ISLAND SOUND

Old Field Point to Eatons Neck Point

Chart 2754, US Chart 12364 (see 1.16)
General information
6.231

1 Between Old Field Point (40°58'·62N 73°07'·11W) and Eatons Neck Point, a prominent wooded headland, 12½ miles W, there are a number of small harbours and anchorages.

Speed limit of 4½ kn is enforced in the harbours.

Smithtown Bay
6.232

1 **Description.** Smithtown Bay (40°56'·70N 73°11'·50W) is an open bight extending 7 miles WSW from Crane Neck Point. Rocky shoals extend 1 mile from the shore in places.

Stony Brook Harbor, a narrow shallow inlet in the SE part of Smithtown Bay is entered 2½ miles S of Crane Neck Point and is only used by small craft.

2 **Nissequogue River** (40°54'·40N 73°13'·90W), shoal and winding, is entered 5 miles SW of Crane Neck Point through a dredged channel marked by light buoys, and is only used by small craft.

Anchorage may be obtained in summer in 9 to 15 m (30 to 50 ft), sheltered from E winds, 1 mile S of Crane Neck Point.

Northport Offshore Terminal
6.233

1 **Description.** Northport Offshore Terminal (40°57'·28N 73°20'·48W) for the receipt of oil, owned and operated by LILCO, is situated 2½ miles E of Eatons Neck Point (6.231). The terminal consists of a platform with off-lying mooring buoys. Lights are exhibited from each corner.

2 **Pilotage** is compulsory. The pilot serves as docking master and remains on board at standby while the vessel is at the platform. See 6.4.

Northport Basin
6.234

1 **Description.** Northport Basin (40°55'·50N 73°20'·70W) is a private harbour situated 3 miles SE of Eatons Neck Point. It is entered through a dredged channel between submerged breakwaters. No 1 Light Buoy (port hand) is moored close N of the entrance.

The four chimneys of the power station on the E side of the basin are prominent.

Depths. In 1977 the privately dredged channel had a controlling depth of 3·6 m (12 ft).

Huntington Bay and adjacent waters

Chart 2580
General information
6.235

1 **Description.** Huntington Bay (40°55'·80N 73°25'·00W) lies between Eatons Neck Point (6.231) and East Fort Point at the E end of Lloyd Neck (6.95), 2 miles SW. The bay is the approach to Northport Bay (6.236), Huntington Harbor (6.237) and Lloyd Harbor (6.238).

2 **Anchorage.** The bay is an excellent anchorage for large vessels, with shelter from all but N winds, in 11 to 8 m (36 to 25 ft) for about 1 mile above its entrance. There is also anchorage for small vessels in 11 to 5 m (36 to 18 ft), with shelter from NW winds, in the SW part of the bay.

Measured distance. Off the W side of Eatons Neck in the E part of the bay there is a measured distance.

3 **Limit marks** - Two triangular orange beacons situated 1¾ and 2¼ miles S of Eatons Neck Point.

Length - 5 cables.

Running track - 018°-198°.

No-discharge Zone (NDZ). All the waters inside of a line joining East Beach (40°54'·88N 73°26'·08W) and West Beach (1¼ miles E) have been designated as a NDZ. See 1.41.

Northport Bay
6.236

1 **Description.** Northport Bay (40°55'·10N 73°22'·80W) is entered from the SE part of Huntington Bay close S of the narrow tongue extending 1 mile S from the SW corner of Eatons Neck.

Centerport Harbor and Duck Island Harbor, shallow coves, are situated on the SW and N sides, respectively, of Northport Bay. Northport Harbor is situated on the E side of Little Neck at the SE end of Northport Bay. The village of Northport lies on the E side of the harbour.

2 **Ice** may close Northport Harbor for about two months during severe winters.

Channels and depths. A dredged channel with a depth of 3·6 m (12 ft) leads through the entrance to Northport Bay. No 1 Light Buoy (port hand) is moored at the outer end of the channel marked by buoys and a light buoy.

Anchorage, well sheltered, can be obtained in the W part of Northport Bay in 6 to 15 m (20 to 50 ft), and the E part of the bay in 2 to 3 m (8 to 11 ft).

Huntington Harbor
6.237

1 **Description.** Huntington Harbor (40°53'·93N 73°26'·00W) is entered from the S part of Huntington Bay through a narrow entrance which leads between East Neck and West Neck. The village of Huntington is at the head of the harbour.

2 **Channel,** marked by buoys and light buoys, leads from outside the harbour entrance to the head of the harbour. The outer end of the channel is marked by Huntington Harbor Light (square concrete tower and dwelling) (40°54'·65N 73°25'·87W) and No 1 Light Buoy (port hand), 1 cable E. In 1991 a dangerous

wreck was reported close to the channel 6 cables within the entrance.

3 **Depths.** There is a controlling depth of 2·4 m (8 ft) in the channel.

Tidal stream. The tidal stream in the entrance has an estimated rate of 2 kn.

Wharf at the head of the harbour is used by sand and gravel barges.

Lloyd Harbor
6.238

1 **Description.** Lloyd Harbor (40°54′·80N 73°27′·50W), which lies between West Neck and Lloyd Neck, is a narrow arm extending W that is almost connected to Oyster Bay (6.239). The entrance is marked by Huntington Harbor Light (6.237) on the S side and by buoys.

Anchorage. Vessels can anchor close within the entrance in 2 to 3 m (7 to 11 ft).

Oyster Bay and adjacent waters

General information and limiting conditions
6.239

1 The entrance to Oyster Bay (40°54′·70N 73°30′·00W) lies between NW Bluff on the W side of Lloyd Neck and Rocky Point, the N point of Centre Island. The bay is the approach to Cold Spring Harbor (6.240) and Oyster Bay Harbor (6.241) which are separated by Cove Neck.

Boulder reefs and shallow banks extend from the shores of the bay, especially at the entrance, where a bank extends almost across from the N part of Centre Island. The E end of this bank is marked by Cold Spring Harbor Light (red and white chequered diamond on framework tower on caisson) (40°54′·85N 73°29′·59W).

2 **Largest vessel.** The bay S of Cold Spring Harbor Light offers a secure anchorage to vessels drawing up to 5·5 m (18 ft).

Ice in severe winters may extend over the whole bay during part of January and February.

Cold Spring Harbor
6.240

1 **Description.** Cold Spring Harbor (40°53′·50N 73°29′·00W), at the SE end of Oyster Bay, is entered between Cooper Bluff and the W shore of West Neck, 1 mile E. The village of Cold Spring Harbor is on the E shore near the head of the harbour.

Anchorage may be obtained in the bay, which has general depths of 4·3 to 5·2 m (14 to 17 ft), nearly to its head.

Alongside berth. A tanker jetty, with a depth alongside of 4 m, is situated at the village.

Supplies: fuel; water and limited stores.

Oyster Bay Harbor
6.241

1 **Description.** Oyster Bay Harbor (40°52′·90N 73°31′·10W), the long winding arm that extends SW from Oyster Bay, is entered between Plum Point and No 5 Light Buoy (port hand), marking the limit of the bank that extends N from Cove Point. The village of Oyster Bay is situated on the S side of Oyster Bay Harbor.

2 **Depths and channels.** The harbour has depths of 18 m (60 ft) at the entrance, decreasing to 9 m (30 ft) off Moses Point, 1 mile SSW of Plum Point, where the channel narrows and is only suitable for vessels drawing less than 3 m (10 ft). The channel S of Centre Island between Moses Point and Brickyard Point, 6 cables W, is marked by buoys. Two channels, with depths of 2·7 m (9 ft) and 1·8 m (6 ft), lead SW and S, respectively, from the main channel to the wharves at Oyster Bay.

3 **Anchorages.** Good anchorage can be obtained SE and S of Moses Point in 8 to 11 m (26 to 36 ft). Vessels of less than 2·1 m (7 ft) draught can anchor in West Harbor, W of Centre Island, in about 2 m (6 to 8 ft). Anchorage is also available in Mill Neck Creek, situated on the S side of Oak Neck at the NW end of Oyster Bay Harbor, in 1 to 5 m (3 to 16 ft). This berth is approached through a bascule bridge with a vertical clearance of 2·7 m (9 ft).

4 **Wharves.** A wharf used by fishing vessels with reported depths alongside of about 3 m is situated at the village. There is a tanker berth about 1 cable farther S.

Supplies: fuel; water; provisions and stores.

Hempstead Harbor

General information
6.242

1 **Description.** Hempstead Harbor (40°52′·00N 73°40′·30W) is entered on the NE side of Manhasset Neck (6.95) between Matinecock Point (40°54′·10N 73°37′·94W) and Prospect Point, 4 miles SW. The harbour entrance then narrows to about 1 mile between the shore S of Weeks Point, 1¾ miles SW of Matinecock Point, and Mott Point, 1¾ miles SW. The entrance is free of dangers as long as the shore is given a berth of 3 cables.

2 The harbour is divided into two by Bar Beach, a narrow tongue of land which extends nearly across the harbour, 2 miles SSE of Mott Point. Roslyn is a village at the head of the inner harbour.

The harbour is much used by vessels seeking shelter in any but strong N winds and provides excellent anchorage. Waterborne trade in the harbour is principally in sand, gravel, building materials and petroleum products, usually shipped in vessels with draughts of 1 to 3·7 m.

3 **Ice** may stop navigation in severe winters for about 6 weeks during January and February.

Useful marks:
  Eight chimneys (40°49′·64N 73°38′·87W), at the power station at Glenwood Landing.

Anchorages
6.243

1 **Main anchorage.** Vessels drawing over 6 m (20 ft) should anchor in 7 to 9 m (23 to 30 ft) between the entrance and a line joining Mott Point and Glen Cove Landing (6.244), 8 cables ENE. Vessels drawing 6 m (20 ft) or less will find good anchorage just inside that line in 6 to 7 m (20 to 23 ft). Attention is drawn to the large submarine cable area that runs through Hempstead Harbor.

2 **Glen Cove Harbor**, S of the breakwater extending from the E shore 1 mile S of Weeks Point (40°52′·69N 73°39′·24W), provides anchorage in 5 to 7 m (18 to 22 ft) in its outer half and 2 to 3 m (7 to 9 ft), closer inshore.

Landings
6.244

1 **Glen Cove Landing**, 1 mile S of Weeks Point, is protected by a breakwater extending 2½ cables from the shore. No 5 Light (green square on framework tower) stands at the head of the breakwater.

Glenwood Landing is a village abreast Bar Beach. There are depths alongside of 2·4 to 3 m at the Glenwood Landing wharves.

Manhasset Bay

General information
6.245

1 **Description.** Manhasset Bay (40°49′·60N 73°43′·00W) is entered on the SW side of Manhasset Neck between Barker Point (6.96) and Hewlett Point, 1 mile farther SW.

Port Washington is a village on the E side of the bay, 2 miles SE of Barker Point.

2 The bay affords excellent shelter for vessels drawing up to 3·7 m (12 ft) and is often used by small craft in the summer. Waterborne trade in the harbour is principally in petroleum products carried in vessels drawing 1·8 to 3 m (6 to 10 ft).

Approach. The bay is approached from SW of No 27A Light (40°51′·48N 73°44′·76W) (6.96).

3 **Depths** in the outer part of the bay range from 3·6 to 5·2 m (12 to 17 ft) and in the inner part, inside Plum Point, there are depths of 2·1 to 3·7 m (7 to 12 ft).

Anchorages
6.246

1 General anchorage, with good holding, is situated S of Barker Point and E of Hewlett Point.

Seaplane restricted area
6.247

1 A seaplane restricted area (40°50′·10N 73°43′·00W) is established 5 cables E of Plum Point. Anchoring or mooring are prohibited and vessels traversing the area must pass directly through without unnecessary delay, and must always give seaplanes the right of way.

Channel
6.248

1 A buoyed channel, with a depth of 2·4 m (8 ft), leads E from No 1 Light Buoy (port hand), moored off Plum Point, to the wharves at Port Washington. Thence an unmarked channel leads along the E side of the bay to its N end, NE of Toms Point.

Wharves
6.249

1 Depths alongside the wharves are from 0·6 to 2·7 m.

Little Neck Bay

General information
6.250

1 **Description.** Little Neck Bay (40°47′·80N 73°45′·90W) is entered SW of Great Neck, between Elm Point and Willets Point, 1½ miles SSW.

A small basin is situated at Kings Point, 3 cables SW of Elm Point. The US Merchant Marine Academy is situated on this headland.

2 **Depths.** The bay is shallow with depths of 3 to 3·7 m (10 to 12 ft) at its entrance, decreasing gradually to its head.

Anchorages
6.251

1 General anchorage No 5 is situated at the entrance of the bay.

Alongside berths
6.252

1 In 1991 the basin at Kings Point had reported depths alongside of 3·6 to 4·3 m.

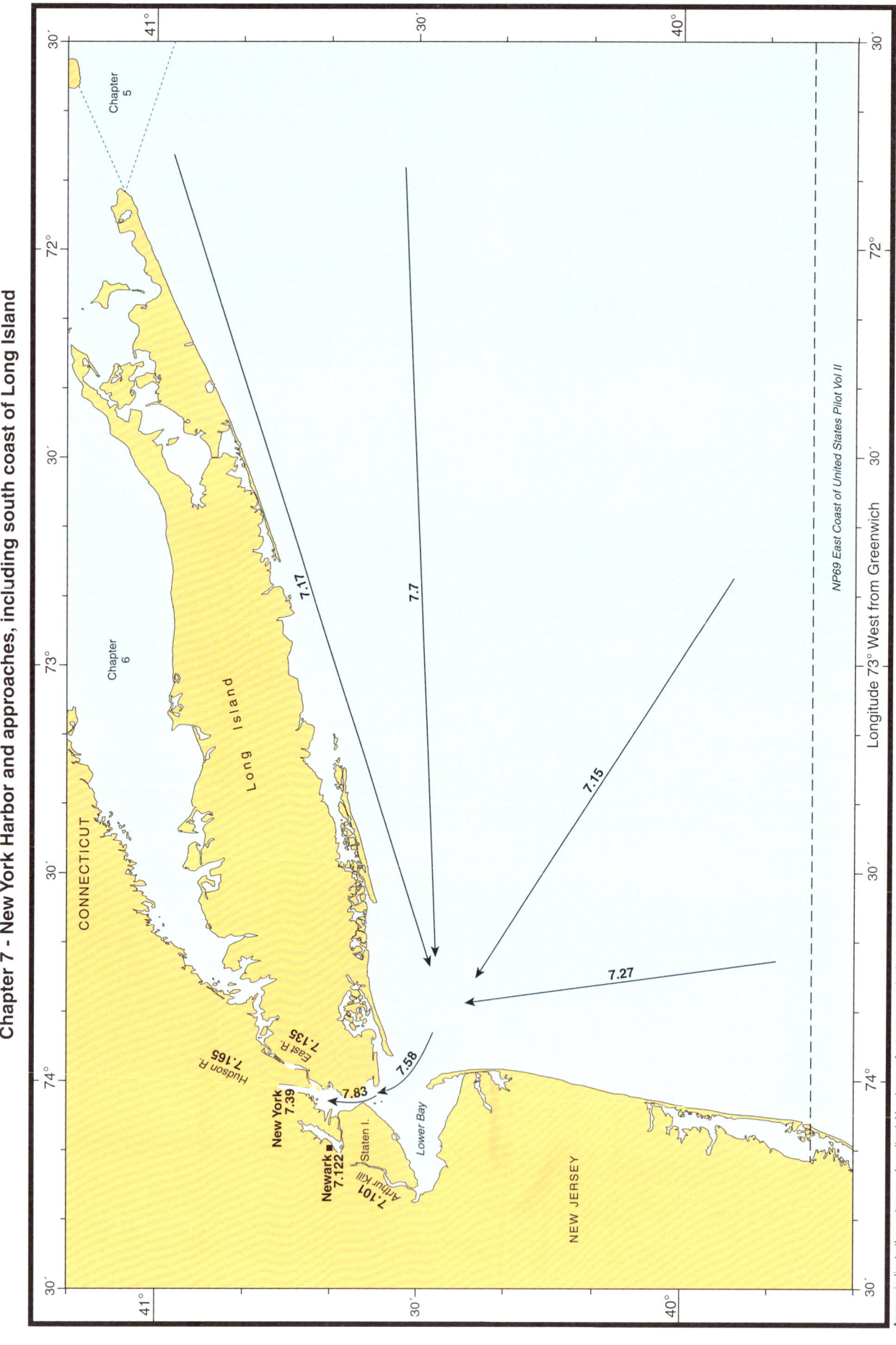
Chapter 7 - New York Harbor and approaches, including south coast of Long Island

CHAPTER 7

NEW YORK HARBOR AND APPROACHES, INCLUDING SOUTH COAST OF LONG ISLAND

GENERAL INFORMATION

Charts 2860, 2754, 2755
Scope of the chapter
7.1

1   The area covered by this chapter comprises the outer approaches to New York Harbor from SW of Nantucket Shoals (40°33′·00N 70°15′·00W) including the S coast of Long Island; the final approaches to New York Harbor including New Jersey coastal waters N of Barnegat Inlet (39°45′·30N 74°05′·00W); and New York Harbor (40°41′·00N 74°02′·00W), including East River.

The chapter is divided into the following sections:
Approaches to New York Harbor (7.2).
New York Harbor and adjacent waters (7.39).

APPROACHES TO NEW YORK HARBOR

GENERAL INFORMATION

Charts 2860, 2754, 2755, 3204
Area covered
7.2

1   This section describes the approaches to New York Harbor from seaward generally along the S coast of Long Island or the E coast of New Jersey, although the harbour is easily approached from any direction between E and S.

It is arranged as follows:
East approach to New York Harbor (7.7).
South coast of Long Island (7.16).
South approach to New York Harbor (7.27).

Topography
7.3

1   During the approach the S shore of Long Island will be seen to the N and the sandy beaches of New Jersey will be observed to the W. The Long Island shore is readily identified by sandy hillocks and thickly settled beach communities backed in places by low dark woods, and the New Jersey shore is characterised by long sandy stretches and many summer resort settlements.

Outer anchorages
7.4

1   It was reported (2006) that the Port of New York and New Jersey had recommended that vessels awaiting a berth should anchor offshore; in 2008 it was reported that anchorage may be obtained ENE and NE of the pilot boarding area clear of charted dangers and hazards.

2   All vessels must limit the use of Stapleton Bay Ridge (7.98) and Gravesend Bay (7.76) anchorages to lightering or loading, bunkering, receiving stores or parts, repairs, Coast Guard inspections, crew changes, or emergencies only.

On completion of these operations vessels must leave these anchorages and anchor offshore to await a berth.

Pilotage
7.5

1   Pilotage is compulsory for all foreign vessels and US vessels under register. Vessels entering Port of New York and New Jersey through Lower Bay are boarded 1½ miles ESE of 'A' Light Buoy (40°27′·47N 73°50′·20N).

The pilot boats have a black hull and white superstructure, with the name "PILOT No 1" or "PILOT No 2" in yellow on each side. Boarding is made from a smaller boat.

2   Pilots are arranged in advance by ship's agents. A 24 hour advance notice of ETA is requested, with a 3 hour update.

Pilots for US registered vessels in coastwise trade board in the same area. The pilot boats have a blue hull and white superstructure, with the word "PILOT" on each side. They maintain a listening watch on VHF 1½ hours before a vessel's ETA.

For vessels entering New York Harbor from Long Island Sound through East River, see 7.139.

Traffic regulations
7.6

1   **Traffic separation schemes.** Vessels approaching New York from E, SE and S use different TSSs during the final approach. These schemes are IMO-adopted and Rule 10 of *International Regulations for Preventing Collisions at Sea (1972)* applies.

Shipping Safety Fairway. A Shipping Safety Fairway has been established between the W end of the TSS S of Nantucket Shoals and the E end of the TSS approaching New York from the E. For details see Appendix XI.

2   **Regulated navigation area.** All the coastal waters off the S shore of Long Island lie within a regulated navigation area that extends 12 miles offshore. For details, definition and general regulations concerning regulated navigation areas see Appendix V.

Safety and security zones. The following areas are safety and security zones:

All waters within 100 yards of each moored or anchored US Coast Guard Cutter.

3   All waters within 25 yards of each commercial waterfront facility that is capable of accepting barge, ferry or other commercial vessels.

All waters of the New York Marine Inspection Zone and COTP Zone within a 200-yard radius of any LHG vessel or LHG facility.

All waters within 25 yards of any bridge pier or abutments, overhead power cable tower, pier or tunnel ventilator south of the Troy, New York locks.

4   **Security zone.** An area between the Ambrose to Hudson Canyon Traffic Lane and the Barnegat to Ambrose Traffic Lane, extending 6 miles SSE from the precautionary area, is a security zone.

For definition and general regulations concerning safety and security zones see Appendix V.

Former mined area is established in the S and SE part of the precautionary area. See 7.11.

5 **Precautionary area.** The TSSs converge on a precautionary area, with a radius of 7 miles, centred on 40°28′·00N 73°50′·00W.

Area To Be Avoided. An ATBA has been established 6¾ miles ESE of Sandy Hook Light (40°27′·70N 74°00′·12W). To avoid the risk of pollution and damage to the environment, all vessels carrying petroleum, dangerous or toxic cargoes, or any other vessel exceeding 1000 gt should avoid this area.

North Atlantic right whale. See 1.51, *Admiralty List of Radio Signals Volume 6(5)* and Appendices VIII and X.

EAST APPROACH TO NEW YORK HARBOR

General information

Charts 2860, 2755, 3204

Route
7.7
1 The E approach to New York Harbor leads for about 160 miles from SW of Nantucket Shoals, along the S side of Long Island.

Maritime topography
7.8
1 Block Canyon and Hudson Canyon, 120 miles ESE and 90 miles SE of New York Harbor entrance, indent the edge of the continental shelf and can be of assistance in determining a vessel's position when approaching New York Harbor from the E or SE. See also 5.5.

Exercise area
7.9
1 Submarines exercise at times between the meridians of 69°30′W and 72°15′W. A good lookout should be kept for them when passing through these waters. For details of submarine distress signals see 1.55.

Pilotage
7.10
1 See 7.5.

Traffic regulations
7.11
1 **Regulated navigation area.** See 7.6.
Security zone. See 7.6.
Former mined area, charted as a danger area, is centred 11½ miles ESE of Romer Shoal Light (40°30′·78N 74°00′·81W). The area is open to unrestricted surface navigation, but all vessels are cautioned not to anchor, dredge, trawl, lay cables or to carry out similar types of operation owing to the residual danger of mines on the bottom. For definition and general regulations concerning danger areas see Appendix V.
North Atlantic right whale. See 1.51, *Admiralty List of Radio Signals Volume 6(5)* and Appendices VIII and X.

Currents
7.12
1 The predominant current between Nantucket Shoals and New York is a branch of the Labrador Current, which flows SW and is strongest in winter.

Directions
(continued from 5.8)

Principal marks
7.13
1 Landmarks:
Fire Island Light (40°37′·95N 73°13′·12W).
Water tower (40°35′·79N 73°30′·49W).
Tank (40°35′·54N 73°35′·63W).
Major lights:
Fire Island Light — as above.
Sandy Hook Light (40°27′·70N 74°00′·12W) (7.63).

Other aids to navigation
7.14
1 Racons:
NA Light Buoy (40°25′·71N 73°11′·47W).
A Light Buoy (40°27′·47N 73°50′·20N).
S Light Buoy (40°26′·55N 73°55′·01W) (7.66).
Sandy Hook Channel Common Front Light (40°29′·25N 73°59′·59W) (7.66).
See *Admiralty List of Radio Signals Volume 2*.

Approaches
7.15
1 **Approach from E.** From the vicinity of 40°33′·00N 70°15′·00W at the E end of the TSS to the S of Nantucket Shoals, the approach to New York Harbor leads 150 miles W through the Shipping Safety Fairway (7.6) to the precautionary area in the entrance of New York Harbor, passing:
2 S of a dangerous wreck (40°34′·13N 72°06′·89W), reported (1994), position approximate, thence:
N of NA Light Buoy (special) (40°25′·71N 73°11′·47W), which lies 5 miles inside the separation zone between the two traffic lanes of the E TSS, thence:
3 S of a dangerous wreck (40°30′·01N 73°29′·95W), position approximate, thence:
S of a dangerous wreck (40°28′·10N 73°39′·04W), position approximate, and:
Thence into the precautionary area.
4 **Approach from SE.** From the vicinity of 40°07′·00N 73°13′·00W the track leads 28 miles NW, through the SE TSS, into the precautionary area.

(Directions continue for New York Harbor at 7.63)

SOUTH COAST OF LONG ISLAND

General information

Charts 2754, 2755

Description
7.16
1 The S coast of Long Island extends from Montauk Point (41°04′·26N 71°51′·43W) to Rockaway Point, at the entrance to New York Harbor, 100 miles WSW. From seaward this coast presents few prominent features.

Routes
7.17
1 **Inshore route.** A route, keeping clear of charted obstructions, leads about 2 to 3 miles offshore in depths of not less than 11 m (36 ft).

Traffic regulations
7.18
1 **Regulated navigation area.** See 7.6.
North Atlantic right whale. See 1.51, *Admiralty List of Radio Signals Volume 6(5)* and Appendices VIII and X.

Fish traps and fish havens
7.19

1   **Fish traps** extend up to 1½ miles from the coast in places and the outer limits to the areas in which they are to be found are shown on the charts.

Fish havens, obstructions artificially placed to attract fish and usually marked by buoys, are situated near the mouths of inlets and their positions are shown on the charts. The least depth ranges between 12·2 and 15·2 m (40 and 50 ft), with the exception of one haven 4½ miles E of Rockaway Point, which has a least depth of 7·0 m (23 ft).

Directions

Principal marks
7.20

1   **Landmarks:**
    Fire Island Light (40°37'·95N 73°13'·12W).
    Water tower (40°35'·79N 73°30'·49W).
    Tank (40°35'·54N 73°35'·63W).
    Major lights:
    Montauk Point Light (41°04'·26N 71°51'·43W) (6.14).
    Fire Island Light — as above.
    Sandy Hook Light (40°27'·70N 74°00'·12W) (7.63).
    See *Admiralty List of Radio Signals Volume 2*.

Montauk Point to Rockaway Point
7.21

1   From a position 5 m ESE of Montauk Point Light (41°04'·26N 71°51'·43W) (6.14) the inshore route along the S shore of Long Island leads WSW, passing:
    SSE of Montauk Shoal (41°01'·88N 71°50'·37W), which lies 2½ miles SSE of Montauk Point, thence:

2   SSE of Shinnecock Light (red framework tower) (40°50'·52N 72°28'·69W) marking the entrance to Shinnecock Bay (7.23) and the approaches to Shinnecock Canal, which leads into Great Peconic Bay (6.70). SH Light Buoy (safe water) is moored 1½ miles S of the entrance. Thence:

3   SSE of a beacon (40°47'·49N 72°37'·33W), thence:
    SSE of E Breakwater Head No 2 Light (framework tower) (40°45'·80N 72°45'·19W), which marks the entrance to Moriches Inlet (7.24); M Light Buoy (safe water) is moored about 1½ miles S of the entrance.

4   The route continues WSW, passing:
    SSE of Fire Island Light (40°37'·95N 73°13'·12W) (7.20), thence:
    SSE of Democrat Point (40°37'·40N 73°18'·25W), which forms the S side of the entrance to Fire Island Inlet (7.25), thence:
    SSE of JI Light Buoy (safe water) (40°33'·62N 73°35'·22W), moored 1½ miles S of the entrance to Jones Inlet (7.26), thence:

5   S of ER Light Buoy (safe water) (40°34'·28N 73°45'·82W), close NNE of the outer limit of the precautionary area. This light buoy is moored 1 mile SW of East Rockaway Inlet. Thence into the precautionary area.

6   **Caution.** A number of dangerous wrecks, as shown on the chart, lie between 1 and 6 miles offshore along this coast.

(Directions continue at 7.63)

Jamaica Bay and Rockaway Inlet

Charts 2755, 3204
General information
7.22

1   **Description.** Jamaica Bay (40°37'·10N 73°50'·80W) is on the S shore of Long Island and lies between Rockaway Beach on the S and Barren Island on the W. It is entered through Rockaway Inlet which is obstructed by a shifting sand-bar, over which there is a channel marked by buoys and light buoys (lateral). There are a number of wrecks and obstructions in the approaches to the inlet, the positions of which can best be seen on the chart.

2   The bay is much obstructed by numerous marshy islands and shoals, with narrow channels between them. Commercial traffic in the bay consists of tankers, tugs and barges. The bay is extensively used by pleasure craft.
    Depths. Rockaway Inlet entrance channel has mid-channel depths of about 5·5 m (18 ft) or more. Channels and basins in the bay have been dredged to project depths of 3·7 to 6·1 m (12 to 20 ft).

3   **Traffic regulations.** Safety and security zones have been established within approximately 100 and 200 yards of John F. Kennedy Airport. For definition and general regulations concerning safety and security zones see Appendix V.
    Vertical clearance. A road bridge with a vertical lift span crosses Rockaway Inlet. The bridge has a vertical clearance of 17 m (55 ft) with the span down and 46·3 m (152 ft) when raised.

4   **Ice** is a problem, mainly in the tributaries and basins, from early January to the middle of March.
    Tidal streams. The rate of the in-going stream is 2¼ kn whilst the rate of the out-going stream probably exceeds 3 kn at times.

Anchorages and harbours

Chart 2754, US Chart 12352 (see 1.16)
Shinnecock Bay
7.23

1   **General information.** Shinnecock Bay (40°51'·30N 72°29'·00W) is situated 30 miles WSW of Montauk Point and lies at the E end of the Long Island Intracoastal Waterway.
    Entrances. The bay is entered from the Atlantic through Shinnecock Inlet and from Great Peconic Bay (6.70) through Shinnecock Canal. Shinnecock Light (7.21) stands on the W side of the inlet.

2   **Caution.** Tidal streams through Shinnecock Inlet and Shinnecock Canal can be dangerous and the area is only used by small craft. Passage through the inlet should not be attempted without local knowledge because of the frequent changes in channel depths.

Moriches Bay
7.24

1   **General information.** Moriches Bay (40°47'·10N 72°44'·00W) is entered through Moriches Inlet, which lies 13 miles WSW of Shinnecock Inlet. Moriches Bay is connected to Shinnecock Bay by Quogue Canal and Quantuck Canal which form part of the Long Island Intracoastal Canal.
    Caution. Due to rapidly changing shoaling conditions and existing dangers in Moriches Inlet, it is considered unsafe for mariners to navigate this inlet at any time.

CHAPTER 7

Charts 2754, 2755, US Chart 12352 (see 1.16)
Great South Bay
7.25

1   **General information.** Great South Bay extends from Bellport Bay (40°44'·50N 72°55'·00W) on the E to South Oyster Bay on the W and is about 20 miles long and 4 miles across at its widest part. The bay is separated from the Atlantic by Fire Island (40°41'·20N 73°00'·00W). Great South Beach, on which stands a number of resorts, forms the S shore of this island.

     Entrances. The bay is entered from the Atlantic through Fire Island Inlet (40°37'·90N 73°18'·40W) and is connected to Moriches Bay by Narrow Bay, which forms part of the Long Island Intracoastal Waterway. It can also be entered from the W through Hempstead Bay (7.26).

2   **Caution.** Fire Island Inlet is subject to frequent shoaling and has been moving W for many years. Mariners are warned to be beware of extreme tidal turbulence especially during times of tidal change and should seek local knowledge of the latest conditions before entering. Navigation of the inlet is difficult even with relatively calm seas, and for small craft it can be extremely dangerous. During heavy weather the entrance is usually obstructed by breakers.

3   **Ice** restricts navigation in the bay from early January to the middle of March, but endeavours are made to keep some of the channels clear.

Chart 2755, US Chart 12352 (see 1.16)
Hempstead Bay
7.26

1   **General information.** Hempstead Bay is the shallow area between the W end of Great South Bay and East Rockaway Inlet (40°35'·35N 73°45'·10W) and is separated from the Atlantic by Jones Beach and Long Beach. The bay has many marshy patches and low-lying islands, separated by channels and inlets, many of which are marked by aids to navigation.

     Jones Inlet (40°35'·40N 73°34'·30W) is the principal entrance to the inside passages and towns of Hempstead Bay. It is mainly used by fishing and pleasure craft, but buoys and soundings are not charted and passage should not be attempted without local knowledge.

SOUTH APPROACH TO NEW YORK HARBOR

General information

Chart 2755
Route
7.27

1   The final approach to New York Harbor from the S leads for about 40 miles along the New Jersey coast from the S end of the TSS, E of Barnegat Inlet (39°45'·30N 74°05'·00W) (7.35), into the precautionary area in the entrance of New York Harbor.

Topography
7.28

1   The coast between Barnegat Inlet and Sandy Hook (7.58), 40 miles N, is low and sandy. For 20 miles N of Barnegat Inlet to Bay Head, the coast is formed by Island Beach which separates Barnegat Bay from the Atlantic. There is an almost continuous line of summer resorts between Bay Head (40°04'·11N 74°02'·88W) and Highlands Light, 20 miles N, the most prominent of which are Asbury Park and Long Branch, 11 and 6 miles S of Highlands Light, respectively.

Fish traps
7.29

1   Fish trap areas extend up to 1½ miles offshore between Sandy Hook and Barnegat Inlet.

Traffic regulations
7.30

1   **Traffic separation scheme.** See 7.6.
     Security zone. See 7.6.
     Area To Be Avoided. See 7.6.
     North Atlantic right whale. See 1.51, *Admiralty List of Radio Signals Volume 6(5)* and Appendix VIII.

Ice
7.31

1   Navigation is rarely hindered by ice along the New Jersey coast, but the inner waters are completely closed in severe winters.

Directions
(continued from East Coast of the United States Pilot Volume 2)

Principal marks
7.32

1   **Landmarks:**
     Barnegat Lighthouse (red and white brick tower) (39°45'·86N 74°06'·37W), standing on the S side of the entrance to Barnegat Inlet.
     Water tower (40°04'·11N 74°02'·71W), at Bay Head.
     Highlands of Navesink (40°24'·00N 74°00'·00W), a high wooded ridge. A disused lighthouse with twin brown towers stands in a cleared space at the SE end of the ridge.

2   Radio tower (40°24'·18N 74°02'·61W).
     Major lights:
     Barnegat Light — as above.
     Sandy Hook Light (40°27'·70N 74°00'·12W).
     Sandy Hook Point Light (40°28'·25N 74°01'·12W) (7.63) (chart 3204).

Other aids to navigation
7.33

1   **Racons:**
     B Light Buoy (39°45'·81N 73°46'·07W).
     A Light Buoy (40°27'·47N 73°50'·20N).
     S Light Buoy (40°26'·55N 73°55'·01W).
     See *Admiralty List of Radio Signals Volume 2*.

South approach
7.34

1   From the vicinity of B Light Buoy (special) (39°45'·81N 73°46'·07W) which marks the S end of the separation zone of the S TSS, the coastal route leads N to the precautionary area centred roughly on A Light Buoy, through waters clear of charted dangers.

2   **Caution.** A number of dangerous wrecks, as shown on the chart, lie within the separation zone between the N and S bound lanes of the TSS.

Inlets and inshore waters between Barnegat Inlet and Sandy Hook

Barnegat Inlet
7.35

1   **General information.** Barnegat Inlet (39°45'·30N 74°05'·00W) leads into Barnegat Bay and to the New Jersey Intracoastal Waterway (7.37). It is only used by small craft.

     Approaches. No 2 Light Buoy (starboard hand) lies 4½ miles E and Bl Light Buoy (safe water) lies 1½ miles SE of the entrance. A number of wrecks and obstructions, the positions of which are charted, lie in the approaches to the inlet.

Manasquan Inlet
7.36
1 **General information.** Manasquan Inlet (40°06′·30N 74°02′·40W) is the entrance to Manasquan River and is the N entrance to the New Jersey Intracoastal Waterway (7.37). Manasquan River is connected to Metedeconk River at the N end of Barnegat Bay by Point Pleasant Canal, which forms part of the Intracoastal Waterway.

Approaches. 2M Light Buoy (starboard hand) lies 1 mile ESE of the entrance.

2 **Pilotage** is compulsory for foreign vessels and US vessels under register. It is available from the Sandy Hook Pilot Association; see *Admiralty List of Radio Signals Volume 6(5)* for details.

New Jersey Intracoastal Waterway
7.37
1 **General information.** New Jersey Intracoastal Waterway is a toll free passage for small craft, which leads from Manasquan Inlet, through Barnegat Bay and other bays, lagoons and thoroughfares for 118 statute miles to the entrance to Delaware Bay. It is described in *East Coast of the United States Pilot Volume 2*.

Ice. See 7.31.

Shark River Inlet
7.38
1 **General information.** Shark River Inlet (40°11′·25N 74°00′·70W) is the entrance to Shark River and lies 15 miles S of Sandy Hook. It is only used by small craft.

Approaches. SI Light Buoy (safe water) lies 3 cables ESE of the entrance.

NEW YORK HARBOR AND ADJACENT WATERS

GENERAL INFORMATION

Charts 2860, 2755
Area covered
7.39
1 This section describes the waterways, anchorages and principal port facilities of New York Harbor and adjacent waters.

The section is arranged as follows:
New York Harbor (7.40)
Entrance channels and Lower Bay (7.58).
The Narrows, Upper Bay, and lower part of Hudson River (7.83).

2 Arthur Kill (7.101).
Kill Van Kull (7.115).
Newark Bay and adjacent waters (7.122).
East River (7.135).
Hudson River (7.165).

NEW YORK HARBOR

General Information

Position and function
7.40
1 New York Harbor (40°41′·00N 74°02′·00W) is situated at the mouth of Hudson River between the W end of Long Island and the coast of New Jersey. It is a spacious, landlocked harbour. It is a port of entry, and the site of the Port of New York and New Jersey, which is the busiest seaport on the E coast of the United States.

New York City, which in 2010 had a population of 8 175 133, is the largest city in the United States.

2 The city comprises five boroughs, each of which is also a separate county: Manhattan on Manhattan Island; Bronx, lying NE of Manhattan and fronting Hudson River and East River; Brooklyn and Queens on Long Island and Richmond, which embraces the whole of Staten Island.

Port Authority
7.41
1 The Port Authority of New York and New Jersey serves as the joint state port development, operations and maintenance organisation. The Port Authority administers piers in Manhattan, Brooklyn, Hoboken, Port Newark and Port Elizabeth.

Address: 225 Park Avenue South, New York, NY 10003.
Website: www.panynj.gov

The New York City Department of Ports and Terminals administers the piers along the New York waterfront within the city limits.

Limiting conditions

Controlling depth
7.42
1 The main channel from the sea to the deep-water terminals in Hudson River has a project depth of 13·7 m (45 ft). The depths of other channels are given in the appropriate section.

Tidal levels
7.43
1 At Sandy Hook and also at The Battery mean spring range about 1·6 m (5 ft); mean neap range about 1·1 m (3·6 ft). See information in *Admiralty Tide Tables*.

Ice
7.44
1 Navigation in New York Harbor is not restricted by ice. The main channels do not freeze over and any ice in the smaller waterways is well broken up by tugs and general traffic.

Fresh water ice in large floes is brought down Hudson River during periods of thaw and occasionally there are large accumulations of ice at Spuyten Duyvil where the Harlem River joins Hudson River. These conditions may obstruct low-powered vessels and tows.

Arrival information

Vessel traffic service
7.45
1 Vessel traffic service scheme with full radar surveillance is maintained for the control of shipping. For details, and list of reporting points, see *Admiralty List of Radio Signals Volume 6(5)* and Appendix III.

Anchorage areas and regulations
7.46

1   The waters of New York Harbor, outside the channels, have been divided into a number of general anchorage areas, the limits of which are shown on the charts.

2   The following general regulations apply to the anchorages within New York Harbor:

No vessel in excess of 244 m (800 ft) in length overall or 12·2 m (40 ft) draught may anchor unless it informs the COTP at least 48 hours prior to entering Ambrose Channel.

3   Except in cases of great emergency, no vessel shall be anchored in the navigable waters of the Port of New York outside the anchorage areas established, nor anchor in a cable or pipeline area shown on the chart.

No vessel shall occupy for a longer period than 30 days, unless a permit is obtained from the COTP for that purpose, any anchorage for which the time of occupancy is not otherwise prescribed.

4   Whenever, in the opinion of the COTP, such action may be necessary, that officer may require any or all vessels in any designated anchorage area to moor with two or more anchors.

Every vessel whose crew may be reduced to such number that it will not have sufficient men on board to weigh anchor at any time shall be anchored with two anchors, with mooring swivel put on before the crew shall be reduced or released, unless the COTP shall waive the requirement of a mooring swivel.

5   Anchors of all vessels must be placed well within the anchorage areas so that no portion of the hull or rigging shall extend outside the boundaries of the anchorage area.

Any vessel anchoring under circumstances of great emergency outside the anchorage areas must be placed near the edge of the channel in such a position as not to interfere with the navigation of the channel.

6   No vessel shall be navigated within the limits of an anchorage at a speed exceeding 6 kn when in the vicinity of an anchored vessel.

Any vessel prohibited by these rules from anchoring in a specific anchorage because of the vessel's length or draught may anchor in the anchorage with permission from the COTP.

Further specific details concerning these anchorage areas are given in the relevant sections. See also 7.4 for outer anchorages.

Pilotage
7.47

1   See 7.5.

Traffic regulations
7.48

1   **Navigation Rules for US Inland Waters** apply to all waters within a line joining East Rockaway Inlet Light (40°34′·94N 73°45′·30W) and Sandy Hook Light (40°27′·70N 74°00′·12W), 13 miles SW. See 1.44 and Appendix VII for further information.

North Atlantic right whale. See 1.51, *Admiralty List of Radio Signals Volume 6(5)* and Appendices VIII and X.

Times of entry
7.49

1   The following are recommended times of entry for starting from the pilot boarding area in normal weather conditions.

Draught of vessel	Time after HW Sandy Hook
14·2 m (46½ ft)	½ hour
14 m (46 ft)	½ to 1 hour
13·9 m (45½ ft)	½ to 1½ hours
13·6 m (44½ ft)	½ to 2½ hours
13·3 m (43½ ft)	½ to 3½ hours
13 m (42½ ft)	½ to 5 hours
12·2 m (40 ft)	½ to 5 hours

2   All vessels in the above categories should pass through The Narrows before LW slack at The Narrows.

The recommended times listed above are guidelines only. Weather conditions, tides, and ship's capabilities must also be taken into consideration.

Harbour

Charts 3456, 3457, 3459, 3458, 3455
General layout
7.50

1   The main harbour is divided into Lower Bay (7.58) and Upper Bay (7.83) by The Narrows (7.83), a passage 6 cables wide. The entrance to Lower Bay is obstructed by an extensive bar, intersected by several channels, the principal being Ambrose Channel (7.65). From the inshore end of Ambrose Channel, the main channel leads through Lower Bay and The Narrows into Upper Bay and the mouth of Hudson River.

2   Two channels, Arthur Kill (7.101) and Kill Van Kull (7.115) which separate Staten Island from the New Jersey mainland, lead N from the W part of Lower Bay and W from Upper Bay, respectively, to Newark Bay (7.122).

East River (7.135), a channel leading to Long Island Sound, is entered from the NE part of Upper Bay.

Tidal streams
7.51

1   **Lower Bay.** The rate of the in-going stream is about 2 kn and generally sets parallel to the lower straight section of Ambrose Channel and tends to continue in that direction where the channel turns towards The Narrows, setting more or less diagonally across the upper straight section of Ambrose Channel.

2   **Upper Bay.** In the channel N of Governors Island the action of the tidal stream is very erratic and great care is necessary when navigating a large vessel. It is reported that the most dangerous conditions occur near the end of the in-going stream about 2 hours after HW at The Battery. At this time the tidal stream is setting N in Hudson River and W from East River.

3   The effect of the meeting of these two streams, known locally as *The Spider*, on a large vessel coming from S and turning E into East River, is to make her sheer to starboard towards the shoal ground off the N end of Governors Island. Coming from N in Hudson River the same effect tends to prevent a ship from turning and to cause her to overrun her course.

For detailed information see Tidal Stream tables on the charts.

Climate information
7.52
1 See 1.139, 1.146 and 1.147.

Berths

Waterfront facilities
7.53
1 The Port of New York and New Jersey has over 1100 waterfront facilities which are grouped into a number of terminals. Many of these facilities are privately owned and operated, and the remainder are owned or operated by railways serving the port, the Port Authority of New York and New Jersey, the city of New York, the States of New York and New Jersey, the Federal Government or other municipalities.

Terminals
7.54
1 **Passenger terminals** are situated on the W side of Upper Bay, Brooklyn and Manhattan.
Container terminals are situated throughout the port, but principally at Elizabeth, Newark, Jersey City and Weehawken on the W side of Hudson River. Other terminals are at Howland Hook, Staten Island and Brooklyn.

2 **General cargo terminals** are situated throughout the port, but principally along the E side of Upper Bay, on East River and at Port Newark.
Oil terminals and other liquid cargo facilities are situated along Arthur Kill, on Passaic and Hackensack Rivers and along Newtown Creek, Brooklyn.
Further details of the various terminals are given in the appropriate sections that follow.

Port services

Repairs
7.55
1 The Port of New York and New Jersey has extensive facilities for making all types of repairs to vessels.
Dry dock facilities. The main facilities are:
Brooklyn. Graving dock: length 332·8 m; width 43·6 m.
Brooklyn. Largest floating dock: lift 16 000 tonnes; length 176·8 m; width 30·5 m.
Staten Island. Largest floating dock: lift 8 000 tonnes; length 147·8 m; width 35·6 m.
Salvage. Several salvage companies perform all types of salvage work.

Other facilities
7.56
1 Oily waste. Facilities for the disposal of oily waste are available at many of the terminals in the Port of New York and New Jersey.
Hospitals.

Supplies
7.57
1 Fuel alongside or by barge; fresh water; provisions and stores.

ENTRANCE CHANNELS AND LOWER BAY

General information
Charts 3204, 3459, 3458

Description
7.58
1 Lower Bay is the part of New York Harbor entered between the N end of Sandy Hook and Rockaway Point, 5¼ miles NE and extends W to Raritan River (7.73) and N to The Narrows (7.83).
Much of Lower Bay is shoal, with depths of less than 5·5 m (18 ft). A number of buoyed channels lead through the bay.

Main channel depths
7.59
1 **Main entrance channels.** Lower Bay is entered from the sea through two main channels:
Ambrose Channel (7.65) is the most important channel. This channel, which leads NW, then N, towards The Narrows and Upper Bay, has a project depth of 13·7 m (45 ft).
Sandy Hook Channel (7.66) is a secondary channel which connects with Raritan Bay Channel and other channels within the bay. It has a project depth of 10·7 m (35 ft).

2 **Other main channels:**
Raritan Bay Channel (7.67), which leads from the inshore end of Sandy Hook Channel to the W part of Lower Bay, has a project depth of 10·7 m (35 ft).
Chapel Hill Channel (7.68), which leads N from the E end of Raritan Bay Channel, has a project depth of 9·1 m (30 ft).
For the latest controlling depths the charts and port authority should be consulted.

Traffic regulations
7.60
1 **Area To Be Avoided.** See 7.6.
Recommended tracks passing W of the ATBA (7.6) have been established for coastwise tug and barge vessels approaching from or leaving to the S and transiting to New York Harbor through Ambrose Channel. Whilst not mandatory, tugs and barges are requested to follow these tracks.

Fish trap areas
7.61
1 Several fish trap areas, the limits of which are shown on the chart, are situated in Lower Bay. Mariners are warned that numerous uncharted stakes and fishing structures, some submerged, may be found in these areas.

Natural conditions
7.62
1 **Local magnetic anomaly.** Differences of as much as 5° from the normal variation have been reported in Lower Bay in the vicinity of 40°29'·60N 74°04'·20W on the N side of Raritan Bay Channel.
Tidal streams. See 7.51.

Directions for main channels
(continued from 7.15 and 7.21)

Principal marks
7.63
1 **Landmarks:**
Highlands of Navesink (40°24'·00N 74°00'·00W) (7.32).
Microwave tower (40°24'·18N 74°02'·61W), at Navesink.

Tower (40°30′·46N 74°12′·80W) on Staten Island.
Major lights:
Sandy Hook Light (40°27′·70N 74°00′·12W).
Sandy Hook Point Light (black and white chequered diamond on framework tower) (40°28′·25N 74°01′·12W).

2 Romer Shoal Light (white conical tower, brown top, black round base) (40°30′·78N 74°00′·81W).
West Bank Light (brown conical tower, black round base) (40°32′·28N 74°02′·57W).
Coney Island Light (white square framework tower) (40°34′·60N 74°00′·71W).
Staten Island Light (8-sided brick tower, grey base) (40°34′·56N 74°08′·48W).

Other aids to navigation
7.64
1 **Racons:**
A Light Buoy (40°27′·47N 73°50′·20N).
S Light Buoy (40°26′·55N 73°55′·01W).
Sandy Hook Channel Common Front Light (40°29′·25N 73°59′·59W).
See *Admiralty List of Radio Signals Volume 2*.

Ambrose Channel
7.65
1 **Leading lights:**
Front light: West Bank Light (40°32′·28N 74°02′·57W) (7.63).
Rear light: Staten Island Light (7.63) (5 miles from front light).
From the vicinity of 'A' Light Buoy (40°27′·47N 73°50′·20W) the alignment (297°) of these lights leads WNW through the outer reach of Ambrose Channel, between East Bank and Romer Shoal, passing:
2 Between light buoys (lateral) which mark the limits of the channel, and:

NNE of Romer Shoal (40°30′·60N 74°00′·00W) (7.63).
Thence the channel leads NNW passing:
ENE of West Bank (40°32′·28N 74°02′·57W), thence:
ENE of Swinburne Island (40°33′·96N 74°03′·00W) and Hoffman Island, 8 cables NNW, which lie on West Bank. Hoffman Island is wooded and Swinburne Island has a few derelict buildings. And:
3 WSW of Norton Point (40°34′·68N 74°00′·75W), the W extremity of Coney Island, from which a light (7.63) is exhibited.
Thence through The Narrows (7.83).
Caution. Numerous wrecks and obstructions lie in the approaches to Ambrose Channel; the chart is the best guide.

(Directions continue at 7.89)

Sandy Hook Channel
7.66
1 **East Leading Lights:**
Common front light (green rectangle, black stripe on SE face of framework tower, concrete base) (40°29′·25N 73°59′·59W).
Rear light (similar structure) (8½ cables from front light).
2 From the vicinity of S Light Buoy (safe water) (40°26′·55N 73°55′·01W) the alignment (308°) of these lights leads NW for 3 miles through the E section of Sandy Hook Channel, marked by light buoys (lateral), to a position between Nos 7 and 8 Light Buoys (port and starboard hand, respectively) where the channel turns WNW to a position SW of the common front leading light.

Swinburne Island from ENE (7.65)
(Original dated 2007)

(Photograph - Cdr S Foster, MV Saga Ruby)

Hoffman Island from E (7.65)
(Original dated 2007)

(Photograph - Cdr S Foster, MV Saga Ruby)

Sandy Hook from NE (7.66)
(Original dated 2002)

(Photograph - Airphoto - Jim Wark)

3   **Main Section Leading Lights:**
Common front light (red rectangle, white stripe on SW face of framework tower, concrete base) (40°29′·25N 73°59′·59W).
Rear light (similar structure) (282 m from front light).

From a position NE of the N point of Sandy Hook the alignment (067·5°), astern, of these lights leads WSW through the W reach of Sandy Hook Channel into Lower Bay, passing between Flynns Knoll (40°29′·20N 74°01′·60W) and the N shore of Sandy Hook. This reach is marked by light buoys (lateral).

Caution. The tip of Sandy Hook is changeable, and the area around it is subject to severe shoaling; caution should be exercised in the area.

Raritan Bay Channel
7.67

1 Raritan Bay Channel, dredged and marked by lights, light buoys and buoys (lateral), consists of a number of reaches and bends that lead from the inshore end of Sandy Hook Channel to the S end of Arthur Kill (7.101), 11 miles W.

Raritan Bay East Reach and West Reach. From the vicinity of 40°28′·50N 74°02′·00W at the inshore end of Sandy Hook Channel, the E and W reaches of Raritan Bay Channel lead WNW to a position off Seguine Point (40°30′·65N 74°11′·75W) on the S shore of Staten Island.

2 **Useful marks:**
Old Orchard Shoal Light (brown conical tower, white top, black round base) (40°30′·74N 74°05′·92W), exhibited from the S part of Old Orchard Shoal (7.76).
No 20 Light (red triangle on framework tower) (40°30′·21N 74°09′·74W), standing on the N side of the channel.

3 **Seguine Point Bend.** Princes Bay Leading Lights:
Front light (red rectangle, white stripe, on white framework tower) (40°30′·46N 74°12′·74W).
Rear light (similar structure) (58 m from front light).

From the W end of Raritan Bay West Reach the alignment (266·8°) of these lights leads W through Seguine Point Bend.

Red Bank Reach and Ward Point Bend lead SW, W and then NNW round the SW part of Staten Island, passing E of Anchorage No 44 (7.76), to the S end of Arthur Kill.

4 **Useful marks:**
No 42 Light (red triangle on square framework tower) (40°29′·79N 74°13′·46W), standing on the NW side of Red Bank Reach.
No 52 Light (red triangle on framework tower with base) (40°29′·43N 74°14′·42W).
No 58 Light (red triangle on framework tower, red base) (40°29′·74N 74°15′·10W).

(Directions continue for Arthur Kill at 7.105)

Chapel Hill Channel
7.68

1 Chapel Hill Channel, marked by light buoys and buoys (lateral), leads from the inshore end of Sandy Hook Channel to the N part of Ambrose Channel, passing to the W of Flynns Knoll and Romer Shoal.

Useful mark:
West Bank Light (40°32′·28N 74°02′·57W) (7.63).

Other channels
False Hook Channel
7.69

1 False Hook Channel (40°28′·00N 73°59′·35W), not marked, leads close up the E side of Sandy Hook and joins Sandy Hook Channel close E of the N point of that promontory.

Local knowledge is necessary. See also caution at 7.66.

Swash Channel
7.70

1 Swash Channel (40°30′·50N 74°01′·10W) is a natural buoyed passage between Ambrose Channel and Sandy Hook Channel. Numerous rocks and obstructions are in the entrance to and within the channel; mariners are advised to use the chart as a guide.

Depths. The channel has a controlling depth of 5·5 m (18 ft) but care must be taken to avoid patches with least depths of 4 m (13 ft) near the edge of the channel, and charted obstructions within the channel.

2 **Directions.** The alignment (305°) of Swash Channel Front Leading Light (white tower) (40°33′·48N 74°06′·44W), on the shore of Staten Island, and Staten Island Light (7.63) leads WNW through the channel.

Fourteen Foot Channel
7.71

1 Fourteen Foot Channel (40°31′·80N 73°58′·95W) enters Lower Bay SW of Rockaway Inlet.

The channel has a depth of about 4·9 m (16 ft) and is not marked.

Coney Island Channel
7.72

1 Coney Island Channel (40°34′·00N 73°59′·50W), marked by buoys and light buoys (lateral), passes S of Coney Island from Ambrose Channel to Rockaway Inlet. A shoal area with at least depth of 1·8 m (6 ft) lies about 1 cable west of No 3 Buoy.

It is mainly used by traffic going to Jamaica Bay and Coney Island.

Charts 3458, 2860, US Chart 12332 (see 1.16)
Raritan River
7.73

1 Raritan River flows into the W end of Raritan Bay between South Amboy (40°28′·85N 74°17′·10W) (7.80) and Ferry Point. The mouth of the river is approached from E through Great Beds Reach and South Amboy Reach, and from the N through Raritan River Cutoff.

The river channel, well marked but very winding, extends 11 miles W from South Amboy to the city of New Brunswick. The principal commerce on the river is in coal, ore and petroleum products.

2 **Depths.** There is a project depth of 7·6 m (25 ft) from Raritan Bay to a point about 3 miles above the river entrance; thence 4·6 m (15 ft) for the next 2 miles to the junction with the Washington Canal; thence a controlling depth (1962) of about 2·7 m (9 ft) in mid-channel to New Brunswick.

Vertical clearance (with distances upstream from Ferry Point, on the N side of the entrance):

3 Swing rail bridge (5 cables). Vertical clearance 2·4 m (8 ft) when closed.
Fixed road bridge (1 mile). Vertical clearance 33·5 m (110 ft).
Fixed road bridges (1½ miles). Least vertical clearance 33·5 m (110 ft).

Ice. See 7.104.

US Naval Ammunition Depot — Leonardo

Charts 3204, 3459
General information
7.74

1 Leonardo US Naval Ammunition Depot (40°25′·60N 74°04′·05W) is situated on the S shore of Sandy Hook Bay.

Approach. The depot is approached from the inshore end of Sandy Hook Channel through Terminal Channel and a turning basin, which are marked by buoys and light buoys (lateral). The alignment (207·5°) of two lights (red rectangle, white stripe, on pile) on the pier leads SSW through the centre of the channel.

2 **Depths.** The channel and turning basin have a project depth of 13·7 m (45 ft) except for 10·7 m (35 ft)

around Nos 2 and 3 Piers. For the latest controlling depths the charts and port authority should be consulted.

Traffic regulations. The installations of the depot are surrounded by a restricted area and security zone, the limits of which are shown on the chart. In that section of the security zone comprising Terminal Channel, the following exceptional rules apply:

3   (1) No vessel shall anchor, stop, remain or drift without power at any time in the security zone.
     (2) No vessel shall enter, cross, or otherwise navigate in the security zone when a public vessel, or any other vessel, that cannot safely navigate outside the Terminal Channel, is approaching or leaving the Naval Ammunition Depot Piers at Leonardo, New Jersey.
     (3) Vessels may enter or cross the security zone, except as provided in paragraph 2 (above).

See Appendix V for definitions and general rules covering security zones and Appendix VI for definitions of restricted areas.

Berths
7.75

1 Piers 2 to 4, deep-water berths, are situated at the head of a jetty extending 1½ miles NNE from the shore. A dredged side channel, with a least depth of about 3·4 m (11 ft), leads along the E side of the jetty to Pier No 1, a berth halfway between the jetty head and the shore; this berth is used to load barges.

Anchorage areas

Charts 3204, 3459, 3458
General anchorages
7.76

1 The following general anchorage areas are established in Lower Bay. For recommendations and general regulations, see 7.4 and 7.46.

In addition to the general regulations the following specific regulations apply to Anchorage Nos 20A-G (7.98), 21A-C (7.98), 23A-B (7.98), 24 (7.98) and 25:

2   No vessel may anchor unless it notifies the COTP when it anchors, of the vessel's name, length, draught and position in the anchorage.
    Each vessel anchored must notify the COTP when it weighs anchor.
    No vessel may conduct lightering operations unless it notifies the COTP before it begins lightering operations.

3   Each vessel lightering must notify the COTP at the termination of lightering.
    No vessel may anchor unless it maintains a bridge watch, guards and answers Channel 16 FM, and maintains an accurate position plot.
    If any vessel is so close to another that a collision is probable, each vessel must communicate with the other vessel and the COTP on Channel 16 FM and shall act to terminate the close proximity situation.

4   No vessel may anchor unless it maintains the capability to get underway within 30 minutes, except with the prior approval of the COTP.
    No vessel may anchor in a "dead ship" status (propulsion or control unavailable for normal operations) without the prior approval of the COTP.

5   Each vessel in a "dead ship" status must engage an adequate number of tugs alongside during tide changes. A tug alongside may assume the Channel 16 FM radio guard for the vessel after it notifies the COTP.
    No vessel may lighter in a "dead ship" status without prior approval from the COTP.

6 **Anchorage No 25** is in Gravesend Bay (40°35'·45N 74°01'·20W) (7.82) on the E side of the channel approaching The Narrows. Good anchorage may be obtained in 3 to 15 m (10 to 49 ft), clear of two wrecks, the positions of which are shown on the chart. When this anchorage is required by naval vessels, any commercial vessels therein must move when directed by the COTP.

7 **Anchorage No 26** is situated in Sandy Hook Bay, in the SE part of Lower Bay, S of a line joining Sandy Hook Point (40°28'·25N 74°01'·12W) and Point Comfort, 5 miles WSW. Sandy Hook Bay provides excellent anchorage in depths ranging from 9 m (30 ft) just inside Sandy Hook to 5 m (15 ft) in its S part. A dangerous wreck lies 1¼ miles SSW of Sandy Hook Light (40°27'·70N 74°00'·12W).

8 Pleasure or commercial craft may not navigate or anchor within 750 yards of the Naval Ammunition Depot Pier at Leonardo (7.74).

See 7.77 and 7.74 for details of explosives anchorages, security zone and restricted area that lie within this general anchorage.

Anchorage No 27 is divided into three parts. The E part, with depths of 2 to 20 m (6 to 65 ft), lies E of Sandy Hook; the other two parts, with depths of 2 to 21 m (5 ft to 12 fm), lie on either side of the Swash Channel, and include Flynns Knoll and Romer Shoal.

9 A pipeline area crosses this anchorage S of Romer Shoal and Flynns Knoll, and two submarine power cable areas cross the anchorage N of Sandy Hook. For further information on submarine pipelines and cables see 1.35 and 1.36.

Anchorage No 28, with depths of up to 18 m (61 ft), lies in the central part of Lower Bay between the N side of No 26 Anchorage Area and Chapel Hill Channel, and the NW shore of the bay. Its W boundary leads NNW from Point Comfort (40°27'·37N 74°08'·20W). Old Orchard Shoal (40°31'·13N 74°07'·10W) and West Bank lie within this anchorage.

10 A pipeline area crosses the S part of the anchorage.

Anchorage No 44, with depths of about 11 m (36 ft), lies in the W part of Raritan Bay outside the S entrance to Arthur Kill (7.101). The anchorage is restricted to deep-draught vessels, except that barges may anchor in the S part of the anchorage. No vessel must occupy the deep-draught part of the anchorage for more than 48 hours without the permission of the COTP.

11 **Anchorage No 45**, with depths of 2 to 10 m (6 to 32 ft), adjoins the S and W sides of Anchorage No 44.

Anchorage No 46, with depths of 2 to 10 m (7 to 33 ft), lies on the W side of Anchorage No 28 and N of Raritan Bay Channel.

Anchorage No 47, with depths of up to 7 m (24 ft), lies on the W side of Anchorage No 28 and on the S side of Raritan Channel. Raritan Bay lies within the anchorage. This bay is full of shoals with depths of 2·1 to 5·5 m (7 to 18 ft).

Explosives anchorages
7.77

1 Anchorages 49F, an emergency naval anchorage, with depths of 5 to 7 m (16 to 22 ft), and 49G, a naval anchorage, with depths of 7 to 10 m (24 to 33 ft), are within and adjacent to Anchorage No 26. They are

reserved for vessels carrying explosives and may not be used as general anchorages.

No pleasure or commercial craft are permitted to navigate or anchor within these areas when naval vessels, which are anchored in the area, display a red flag by day or a red light by night.

Other anchorages and harbours

Chart 3459
Horseshoe Cove
7.78

1 Horseshoe Cove (40°26′·75N 73°59′·90W), on the E side of Sandy Hook Bay, is reported to provide satisfactory anchorage for small craft.

Chart 3204, US Chart 12325 (see 1.16)
Shrewsbury River and Navesink River
7.79

1 **Description.** Shrewsbury River and Navesink River empty through a common entrance (40°24′·60N 73°59′·50W) into the SE part of Sandy Hook Bay, and may be entered by small craft.

No-discharge Zone (NDZ). All the waters of the Shrewsbury and Navesink Rivers have been designated as a NDZ. See 1.41.

Ice. Navigation is generally suspended because of ice between December and March inclusive.

Chart 2860, US Chart 12331 (see 1.16)
South Amboy
7.80

1 South Amboy (40°29′·40N 74°16′·45W) is a city on the S side of the entrance to Raritan River (7.73). Main waterborne commerce at the port is the shipment of coal, petroleum products and building materials.

Berths. Depths alongside the wharves and piers are reported to range from 1·8 to 9·1 m.

Chart 3458
Great Kills Harbor
7.81

1 Great Kills Harbor (40°32′·50N 74°08′·10W), a shallow bight on the S side of Staten Island, is used as an anchorage by small craft.

Chart 3459
Gravesend Bay
7.82

1 Gravesend Bay (40°35′·60N 74°00′·70W) is situated at the N end of Lower Bay. It is entered N of Norton Point, the W end of Coney Island.

Approach. A buoyed channel, with a least depth of 3 m (10 ft), leads from deep water N of Coney Island to the docks in the E part of the bay.

THE NARROWS, UPPER BAY AND LOWER PART OF HUDSON RIVER

General information

Charts 3456, 3455, 3454
Description
7.83

1 **The Narrows**, connecting Lower Bay and Upper Bay, has a width of 6 cables at its narrowest part between the flats which extend from Fort Hamilton (40°36′·52N 74°01′·95W) on Long Island, and Fort Wadsworth on Staten Island.

Upper Bay is the part of New York Harbor situated between The Narrows and The Battery (7.135), 6 miles NNE. On the E side of the bay is the borough of Brooklyn and on the W side the city of Bayonne. Kill Van Kull (7.115) is a waterway leading W from the N side of Staten Island. Hudson River flows into the head of the bay and East River is entered S of the Battery.

2 **Lower part of Hudson River** is the part of the river which lies between New York City waterfront as

New York Harbor from SSW (7.83)
(Original dated 2004)

(Photograph - Airphoto - Jim Wark)

far as 7 miles above The Battery on the E side and the waterfronts of Jersey City, Hoboken, Weehawken and Edgewater on the New Jersey side of the river.

3 **No-discharge Zone (NDZ).** All the waters of the Hudson River from The Battery to Troy, 134 miles N, have been designated as a NDZ. See 1.41.

Depths
7.84
1 **Anchorage Channel** (7.91), an extension of Ambrose Channel, the main channel through Upper Bay to The Battery, has a project depth of 13·7 m (45 ft).

Hudson River Channel (7.92), which continues N from The Battery for 5 miles to the limit of New York's major wharves at 59th Street, has a project depth of 13·7 m (45 ft).

2 **Hudson River Channel to Albany** (7.173). Except for a short stretch along the Weehawken-Edgemont waterfront, where it is 9·1 m (30 ft), the project depth is 9·8 m (32 ft) above Hudson River Channel. See also 7.166.

For the latest controlling depths the charts and port authority should be consulted.

Traffic regulations
7.85
1 **Safety and security zones** have been established as follows:

> The area between Global Marine Terminal (7.100) and Military Ocean Terminal (1 cable SW), and the area surrounding Manhattan Cruise Terminal (7.100).

> All waters within 150 yards of Liberty and Ellis Islands (7.91) and the bridge between Liberty State Park and Ellis Island.

For definition and general regulations concerning safety and security zones see Appendix V.

2 **Restricted area.** An area where navigation is restricted (40°37'·70N 74°04'·10W) lies to the E of Stapleton Naval Station. Navigation is prohibited out to 1 cable E of the pierhead and E of this, is restricted to vessels transiting. Vessels at anchor in 23A and 23B anchorages (7.98) may swing into the seaward part of the restricted area. See Appendix VI.

Vertical clearance
7.86
1 Verrazano Narrows Bridge is a fixed suspension bridge that spans The Narrows. The bridge has a vertical clearance of 65·5 m (215 ft) for the central 610 m, but a travelling maintenance platform, when in operation, reduces the vertical clearance by 4·6 m (15 ft).

Fish traps
7.87
1 Fish traps are placed in the lower part of Hudson River each spring, usually between the middle of March and the middle of May, in mid-channel between Manhattan and the Weehawken-Edgewater waterfront. The limits of these areas are shown on the chart.

Outer limits of the nets are usually marked by flags during the day and by lights at night.

Caution is advised when navigating in a fish trap area because broken off poles from previous traps may remain under the surface.

Hudson River - Verrazano-Narrows Bridge from SE (7.86)

(Original dated 2002)

(Photograph - Airphoto - Jim Wark)

Tidal streams
7.88
1   See 7.51.

Directions
(continued from 7.65)

Principal mark
7.89
1   Landmark:
    Statue of Liberty (Torch) (40°41'·35N 74°02'·67W).

Other aid to navigation
7.90
1   Racon:
    KV Light Buoy (40°39'·04N 74°03'·85W).
    See *Admiralty List of Radio Signals Volume 2*.

Anchorage Channel
7.91
1   From a position S of Verrazano Narrows Bridge (40°36'·39N 74°02'·70W) Anchorage Channel leads NNW and then NNE from The Narrows to The Battery, 6 miles N, passing:
      Between Fort Hamilton (7.83) and Fort Wadsworth (40°36'·10N 74°03'·40W) on either side of The Narrows, thence:
      ENE of the anchorages lying off the coast of Staten Island between Fort Wadsworth and Saint George (40°38'·75N 74°04'·80W), thence:
2   Between the anchorages lying off Bay Ridge Flats (40°39'·70N 74°01'·80W) on the E side of the channel and Jersey Flats (40°40'·00N 74°03'·50W) on the W side of the channel. The W limit of the anchorages lying off Bay Ridge Flats is marked by light buoys (starboard hand). Robbins Reef Light (brown conical tower, white top, white base) (40°39'·44N 74°03'·92W) stands on the S part of Jersey Flats. Thence:
3   Between Governors Island (40°41'·30N 74°01'·20W) and Liberty Island, on which stands the Statue of Liberty (7.89). A light (red framework tower, white central column, on white hut) stands on the SW corner of Governors Island.
    Thence to a position at the entrance of Hudson River between Governors Island and Ellis Island.
    (Directions continue for East River at 7.144)

Chart 3455, 3454
Hudson River Channel
7.92
1   From a position between Governors Island and Ellis Island, Hudson River Channel leads up Hudson River for about 4½ miles to the vicinity of Manhattan Cruise Terminal on the E side and the Weehawken waterfront on the W side.

Other channels
Bay Ridge Channel
7.93
1   Bay Ridge Channel (40°39'·00N 74°02'·00W) leads between Bay Ridge Flats and the wharves and piers of Bush Terminal in Brooklyn. The channel, the W side marked by a buoy and light buoys (port hand),

Statue of Liberty from SE (7.89)
(Original dated 2007)

(Photograph - Cdr S Foster, MV Saga Ruby)

has mid-channel depths generally of 10·7 to 12·2 m (35 to 40 ft), with lesser depths at the sides, and leads to Gowanus Bay (7.100) and the S end of Red Hook Channel.

Red Hook Channel
7.94

1 Red Hook Channel (40°40'·20N 74°01'·30W) leads between Gowanus Flats, the N part of Bay Ridge Flats, and the wharves and berths on the N side of Gowanus Bay. The channel, the W side marked by light buoys (port hand), has mid-channel depths generally of 10·7 to 12·2 m (35 to 40 ft), with lesser depths at the sides, and leads to the S end of Buttermilk Channel.

Buttermilk Channel
7.95

1 Buttermilk Channel (40°41'·20N 74°00'·70W) leads between Governors Island and the wharves on the Brooklyn waterfront. The channel, which has mid-channel depths generally of 10·7 to 12·2 m (35 to 40 ft), with lesser depths at the sides, leads to the W end of East River (7.135).

No 1 Light Buoy (port hand) marks a shoal extending from the SW end of Governors Island, and Nos 5 and 7 Buoys (port hand) mark shallow water off the E side of the island.

Pierhead Channel
7.96

1 Pierhead Channel (40°40'·10N 74°03'·80N) leads NE, within Jersey Flats (7.91), from the E entrance to Kill Van Kull (40°39'·06N 74°04'·70W) along the line of the terminals extending from the New Jersey shore, to a position 6 cables S of Liberty Island. Pierhead Channel has a project depth of 6·1 m (20 ft)

2 A number of connecting channels lead from Pierhead Channel across Jersey Flats and to the terminals. All channels are marked by buoys and light buoys.

Anchorage areas

Regulations
7.97

1 For recommendations and general regulations applying to all anchorages, see 7.4 and 7.46. For additional regulations applying to anchorages Nos 20A-G, 21A-C, 23A-B and 24, see 7.76.

General anchorages
7.98

1 The following general anchorage areas are established in Upper Bay and the lower part of the Hudson River. Where letters are used, 'A' is generally the most northerly:

Anchorage No 24 with depths of 13 to 25 m (42 ft to 14 fm), is situated on the W side of Anchorage Channel close N of the Verrazano Narrows Bridge.

Anchorages No 23A and B with depths of 10 to 17 m (33 to 58 ft), are situated on the W side of Anchorage Channel N of Anchorage No 24.

2 **Anchorages No 21A** with depths of 3 to 5 m (9 to 16 ft), **21B** with depths of 8 to 13 m (27 to 45 ft), and **21C** with depths of 12 m (38 to 52 ft), are situated on the E side of Anchorage Channel on Bay Ridge Flats and W and SW of this shoal.

Anchorages No 20A to 20G, with depths of 2 to 15 m (5 to 45 ft), are situated on the W side of Anchorage Channel between the E entrance to Kill Van Kull (40°39'·06N 74°04'·70W) and Ellis Island, 3 miles NNW.

3 **Anchorage No 19**, with depths of 9 to 21 m (30 ft to 11 fm), is situated on the W side of Hudson River between 1 and 4 miles above Manhattan Cruise Terminal (7.100). See also 7.178.

Additional regulations
7.99

1 Unless otherwise authorised by the COTP the following regulations apply to particular anchorages:

Anchorage No 24
No vessel may occupy this anchorage for more than 48 hours.
No vessel with a draught of more than 12·2 m (40 ft) may occupy this anchorage unless it anchors within 5 hours after the out-going current begins in The Narrows.

2 No vessel with a length overall of less than 243·8 m (800 ft), or with a draught of less than 12·2 m (40 ft), may occupy this anchorage.

Anchorage No 23B
No vessel may occupy this anchorage for more than 48 hours.
No vessel with a length of 204 m (670 ft) or less may occupy this anchorage.

3 No vessel with a draught of 12·2 m (40 ft) or more may occupy this anchorage unless it anchors within 5 hours after the out-going current begins in The Narrows.
See 7.85 for adjacent restricted area details.

Anchorage No 23A
No vessel may occupy this anchorage for more than 48 hours.

4 No vessel with a length of more than 204 m (670 ft) may occupy this anchorage.
No vessel with a draught of more than 12·2 m (40 ft) may occupy this anchorage unless it anchors within 5 hours after the out-going current begins in The Narrows.
See 7.85 for adjacent restricted area details.

Anchorage No 21C

5 No vessel with a draught of 10 m (33 ft) or less may occupy this anchorage.
No vessel may occupy this anchorage for a period of time in excess of 96 hours without prior approval of the COTP.

Anchorage No 21B
No vessel with a draught of 3 m (10 ft) or less may occupy this anchorage.

6 No vessel may occupy this anchorage for a period of time in excess of 96 hours without prior approval of the COTP.

Anchorage No 21A
No vessel may occupy this anchorage for a period of time in excess of 96 hours without prior approval of the COTP.

Anchorage No 20G

7 Although this anchorage is designated a naval anchorage, commercial vessels may be permitted to occupy this anchorage temporarily, for about 24 hours. Upon notification of an anticipated naval arrival, any commercial vessel so anchored must leave the anchorage at its own expense.

Anchorages Nos 20A to 20F
No vessel may occupy these anchorages for more than 72 hours.

8 **Anchorage No 19**
No vessel may anchor in this anchorage without the permission of the COTP.

Each vessel shall report its position to the COTP immediately after anchoring.

No vessel may conduct lightering operations in this anchorage without the permission of the COTP.

9 When the use of this anchorage is required for naval vessels, the vessels anchored therein must move when the COTP directs them.

No vessel in excess of 244 m (800 ft) in overall length or 12·2 m (40 ft) draught may anchor unless it informs the COTP at least 48 hours prior to entering Ambrose Channel.

No vessel may occupy this anchorage for a period of time in excess of 96 hours without prior approval of the COTP.

Terminals

Upper Bay and Lower Hudson River
7.100
1 A brief description of the principal terminals is given as follows:

South Brooklyn Marine Terminal, on the S side of Gowanus Bay (40°39′·70N 74°00′·90W), handles RoRo and breakbulk cargo. Seven berths with depths alongside of up to 9·5 m.

Brooklyn Cruise Terminal (40°40′·98N 74°00′·85W), on Pier 12 at the S end of Red Hook Container Terminal, is 263 m in length with a least depth alongside of 12·4 m.

2 Red Hook Container Terminal, at the S end of Buttermilk Channel (40°41′·13N 74°00′·60W) handles container, RoRo and breakbulk cargoes. Eight berths with depths alongside of 12·8 m.

Brooklyn Marine Terminal, between Brooklyn Bridge and the N end of Buttermilk Channel, extends for 3 km along the Brooklyn waterfront and handles general cargo. Most used berths are at Piers 6 to 8 (40°41′·50N 74°00′·20W) with depths alongside of 10·3 to 10·9 m.

3 Cape Liberty Cruise Terminal (40°39′·90N 74°04′·25W) on the NE corner of the former Military Ocean Terminal, opposite the NE Auto Terminal. The terminal, which in 2009 is estimated to handle 310 000 passengers, is 365 m in length with depths alongside of 11·2 m.

4 Global Marine Terminal on the W side of Upper Bay (40°40′·30N 74°04′·88W), which handles containers, heavy lift and RoRo cargoes, has 548 m of berthing space with a least depth alongside of 12·2 m.

Port Authority NE Auto Terminal (NEAT) (40°40′·30N 74°04′·88W), close SE of Global Marine Terminal, for the import and export of motor vehicles, has 548 m of berthing space and a depth alongside of 9·8 m.

5 Manhattan Cruise Terminal (40°46′·05N 74°00′·00W) is situated on the E shore of Hudson River on Manhattan Island, 4 miles above The Battery. The terminal, which in 2009 is estimated to handle 625 000 passengers, has five berths on Piers 87 to 92 with depths alongside of 11 m.

ARTHUR KILL
General information
Charts 3458, 3457
Description
7.101
1 Arthur Kill is a narrow, winding waterway which separates Staten Island from the mainland of New Jersey, and leads in a general NNE direction for about 10 miles from its S entrance, at the W end of Lower Bay (40°29′·80N 74°15′·60W), to Elizabethport (7.114) at the W entrance of Newark Bay.

2 There is considerable traffic through Arthur Kill; the cities of Perth Amboy (7.108) and Tottenville stand either side of its S entrance. There are many oil terminals, oil refineries, large factories and storage facilities situated on its shores.

Depths
7.102
1 Project depth in Arthur Kill is 10·7 m (35 ft). For the latest controlling depths the charts and port authority should be consulted.

Vertical clearances
7.103
1 Outerbridge Crossing Bridge, a fixed bridge 1¾ miles above the S entrance with a vertical clearance of 43·6 m (143 ft), connects Tottenville and Perth Amboy.

Goethals Bridge, a fixed road bridge with a vertical clearance of 41·8 m (137 ft) is at Elizabethport 1 mile from the N entrance.

A lift rail bridge, 1 cable above Goethals Bridge, has a vertical clearance of 9·5 m (31 ft) when closed and 41·1 m (135 ft) when open.

Ice
7.104
1 In ordinary winters ice does not seriously interfere with navigation in Raritan River or Arthur Kill, but in severe winters the ice sometimes prevents the movements of vessels for two weeks at a time when drift ice collects in Raritan Bay.

Directions
(continued from 7.67)
Other aid to navigation
7.105
1 **Racon:**
Outerbridge Crossing Bridge (40°31′·48N 74°14′·88W).
See *Admiralty List of Radio Signals Volume 2*.

Passage
7.106
1 From the vicinity of Anchorage No 44 (7.76) a dredged channel leads N through Arthur Kill. This channel, entered between Ward Point (40°29′·80N 74°14′·85W) and Ferry Point, is marked by leading lights, light beacons, light buoys and buoys.

Caution. Numerous sunken and visible wrecks are adjacent to both sides of the channel and caution is advised.

Anchorages
General Anchorages
7.107
1 **Anchorage No 42**, with depths up to 4·9 m (16 ft), lies on the E side of Arthur Kill between Tottenville (40°30′·75N 74°14′·80W) and Port Socony, 1½ miles N, and between Port Socony and a point 1¼ miles NE, over Story Flats.

A pipeline area passes through Story Flats. For further information on submarine pipelines see 1.36.

2   **Anchorage No 41**, with depths up to 5·2 m (17 ft), lies on the E side of Arthur Kill, in the passage between Pralls Island (40°36'·60N 74°12'·10W) and Staten Island.

Harbours and terminals

Perth Amboy
7.108
1   Perth Amboy (40°30'·65N 74°15'·55W), a port of entry, is situated at the junction of Raritan River and Arthur Kill.
Anchorage. Good anchorage in 9 m (30 ft) may be obtained abreast some of the wharves.
Berths. The principal wharves have depths alongside of 4·3 to 9·1 m. One tanker berth has a depth of 7·9 m.
Repairs. Several ship and boat repair yards are available.
Supplies: fuel; water and stores.

Port Socony
7.109
1   Port Socony (40°32'·67N 74°14'·80W), on the E side of Arthur Kill, is a bulk oil storage terminal.
Berths. In 2008 there were reported depths of 6·7 m (22 ft) alongside the S half of the dock, and from 3·7 to 8·5 m (12 to 28 ft) alongside the N half.

Port Reading
7.110
1   Port Reading (40°33'·50N 74°14'·30W), 4½ miles above Ward Point on the W side of Arthur Kill, has several oil storage facilities.
Berths. There are reported depths alongside of 5·5 to 11 m.

Fresh Kills
7.111
1   Fresh Kills (40°34'·45N 74°12'·00W) enters Arthur Kill from E, 5 miles N of Ward Point. It is being used as a landfill site and is closed to navigation.

Oil terminals between Fresh Kills and Goethals Bridge
7.112
1   There are a number of oil terminals between Fresh Kills and Goethals Bridge. The majority of them lie on the W side of Arthur Kill.
Berths at these terminals have depths alongside of 7·6 to 10·7 m.

Howland Hook Container Terminal
7.113
1   Howland Hook Container Terminal (40°38'·45N 74°11'·40W), situated on Staten Island close N of Goethals Bridge, handles containers, breakbulk and general cargo.
Berths. There is 914 m of berthing space with depths alongside of 10·7 to 12·8 m.

Elizabethport
7.114
1   Elizabethport (40°39'·00N 74°11'·30W), about 11 miles N of Ward Point, is the E part of the city of Elizabeth. It is at the N end of Arthur Kill at its junction with Newark Bay. The principal trade of the port is in petroleum products, building materials, chemicals and animal and vegetable oils.
Berths. Depths alongside the wharves range from 0·9 to 9·8 m.

KILL VAN KULL

General information

Charts 3457, 3456
Description
7.115
1   Kill Van Kull (40°38'·80N 74°06'·80W) separates the S part of the city of Bayonne on the New Jersey mainland from the N part of Staten Island. It leads W from the W part of Upper Bay for about 3 miles to the entrance of Newark Bay and the N end of Arthur Kill.
Kill Van Kull is a major channel for petroleum and bulk cargo and has extensive through traffic and many factories on its shores. It forms the main approach to Newark Bay.

Depths
7.116
1   Project depth in Kill Van Kull is 13·7 m (45 ft) except for the N of Shooters Island Reach (40°38'·80N 74°09'·97W) which has a project depth of 10·7 m (35 ft). The channel S of Shooters Island has a project depth of 9·1 m (30 ft). For the latest controlling depths the charts and port authority should be consulted.

Vertical clearance
7.117
1   Bayonne Bridge (40°38'·50N 74°08'·55W), a fixed span bridge, crosses Kill Van Kull from close E of Bergen Point, the SW end of the city of Bayonne, to the N shore of Staten Island. The bridge has a minimum vertical clearance of 42·1 m (138 ft) (46·0 m (151 ft) at the centre).

Tidal streams
7.118
1   The in-going tidal stream flows W and the out-going stream flows E. In 1991, tidal streams in Kill Van Kull were reported to deviate significantly from the official predictions.

Directions
7.119
1   **Constable Hook Leading Lights:**
   Front light (red rectangle, white stripe on framework tower) (40°39'·20N 74°05'·28W).
   Rear Light (similar structure) (120 m from front light).
2   From a position in Upper Bay, E of Saint George at the NE end of Staten Island and S of KV Light Buoy (preferred channel to port) (40°39'·04N 74°03'·85W), the alignment (289·6°) of these lights leads WNW through Constable Hook Reach to the entrance of the dredged channel which passes through Kill Van Kull. This channel, entered between Constable Hook at the SW end of Bayonne and Saint George, is marked by light buoys (lateral) and leads to the entrance to Newark Bay.
3   **Caution.** Shoals, obstructions and numerous wrecks are on both sides of the channel. Numerous sunken and visible wrecks are in the channel S of Shooters Island.

(Directions for Newark Bay continue at 7.128)

Terminals and harbours

Oil terminals
7.120
1   Two oil terminals are situated on the N shore of Kill Van Kull.

Kill van Kull and Newark Bay from S (7.115) & (7.122)
(Original dated 2001)

(Photograph - Joseph R Melanson of www.skypic.com

Exxon Bayonne Terminal, situated 1½ miles E of Bayonne Bridge, consists of a concrete pier 213 m in length. Vessels should arrive off the berth at slack water.

Belcher Bayonne Terminal, situated 1 mile E of Bayonne Bridge, consists of two concrete mooring islands protecting a wooden pier. Vessels should approach the terminal at HW.

Harbours
7.121

1 **Port Johnson** is situated on the N shore of Kill Van Kull, 1¼ miles E of Bayonne Bridge, between the two oil terminals (7.120). This port handles shipments of petroleum and other products.

New Brighton and **Port Richmond** are situated on the S shore of Kill Van Kull, 2 miles E and close E, respectively, of Bayonne Bridge. All types of repairs can be carried out on vessels of up to 6400 tonnes at shipyards and floating docks on the S shore of Kill Van Kull.

NEWARK BAY AND ADJACENT WATERS

General information

Chart 3457
Description
7.122

1 **Newark Bay** lies N of the junction of Kill Van Kull and Arthur Kill and is entered between Bergen Point (40°38′·70N 74°08′·70W) and Shooters Island, 5 cables W. The bay extends 4 miles NNE to Kearny Point, where the Passaic River (7.129) flows into the NW side of the bay, and the Hackensack River (7.130) flows into the NE side.

2 The greater part of the bay is very shallow, but a dredged channel leads through the bay to these rivers and branch channels lead to the terminals on the W side of the bay.

Depths
7.123

1 The project depth in the main channel through Newark Bay is 13·7 m (45 ft) to about 3 cables N of the branch channel to Port Elizabeth Marine Terminal, thence 12·2 m (40 ft) to Port Newark and 10·7 m (35 ft) to the Passaic and Hackensack Rivers. For the latest controlling depths the charts and port authority should be consulted.

Tidal levels
7.124

1 Mean tidal range in Newark Bay is about 1·5 m (5 ft).

Traffic regulations
7.125

1 **Safety and security zones.** The waters of Newark Bay, enclosing Port Elizabeth and Port Newark, from the South Elizabeth Channel to the New Jersey Turnpike Bridge (7.126) are a safety and security zone.

For definition and general regulations concerning safety and security zones see Appendix V.

Vertical clearances
7.126

1 New Jersey Turnpike Bridge (40°41′·69N 74°07′·00W), a fixed bridge with a vertical clearance of 41·1 m (135 ft), is 3½ miles above the entrance to Newark Bay and 7½ cables above Port Newark.

A railway lift bridge, 2 cables above New Jersey Turnpike Bridge, has a vertical clearance of 10·7 m (35 ft) when down and 41·1 m (135 ft) when open.

Ice
7.127

1 Ice sometimes closes Newark Bay during a part of January and February.

Directions
(continued from 7.119)

Newark Bay
7.128

1   From a position off Bergen Point (40°38′·70N 74°08′·70W) the main channel through Newark Bay, well marked with light buoys and buoys (lateral), leads NNE for nearly 4 miles to a turning basin at the head of the bay, passing:

   ESE of Port Elizabeth Marine Terminal (7.133) (40°41′·00N 74°09′·10W), thence:
   ESE of Port Newark Terminal (7.134) (40°41′·68N 74°08′·40W).

Side channels

Passaic River
7.129

1   Passaic River, which flows into the NW end of Newark Bay, is used as far as Passaic, at the head of navigation, 13 miles above the mouth.

   Depths. The project depth is 9·1 m (30 ft) from Newark Bay to a point 5 cables above Lincoln Highway Bridge, which crosses the river 1½ miles above the turning basin at the channel entrance. Above this point the project depth reduces in stages and is 3 m (10 ft) at Passaic. For the latest controlling depths the national charts and port authority should be consulted.

2   **Vertical clearance.** There are more than 20 opening and fixed bridges between the mouth of the river and Passaic. The minimum vertical clearance of the fixed bridges is 4·6 m (15 ft) at Union Avenue Bridge, 13¼ miles above the mouth. The least vertical clearance of overhead cables spanning the river is 41·1 m (135 ft).

Hackensack River
7.130

1   Hackensack River, which flows into the NE end of Newark Bay, is navigable for about 18 miles to the dams at New Milford.

   Depths. The project depth is 9·1 m (30 ft) from Newark Bay to a 7·6 m (25 ft) turning basin about 3 miles above the river mouth. Above this point depths of 3·4 m (11 ft) were reported in 1971. For the latest controlling depths the national charts and port authority should be consulted.

2   **Vertical clearance.** There are more than 15 opening and fixed bridges, with a least vertical clearance of 10·7 m (35 ft), between the river mouth and Hackensack, 14 miles above the mouth. The least vertical clearance of overhead cables spanning the river is 27·1 m (89 ft).

Anchorages

Newark Bay
7.131

1   **Anchorage No 34** (40°39′·20N 74°09′·10W) lies on the W side of the entrance to Newark Bay. The W part of this anchorage is designated as a special anchorage. See 1.45.

   Anchorage No 36 (40°40′·90N 74°08′·20W) lies between the main channel and Port Newark Terminal.

2   **Anchorage No 37** (40°40′·80N 74°07′·40W) is situated on the E side of Newark Bay below New Jersey Turnpike Bridge. The S part of this anchorage is designated as a special anchorage.

   Anchorage No 38 (40°42′·30N 74°06′·60W) is situated on the E side of the junction of the Passaic and Hackensack entrance channels.

   Anchorage No 39 (40°42′·90N 74°07′·00W) lies between the entrance channels, S of Kearny Point.

Terminals

General information
7.132

1   Two major terminals, Port Elizabeth Marine Terminal and Port Newark Terminal, consisting of a number of smaller terminals are situated on the W side of Newark Bay. Both terminals are operated by the Port Authority of New York and New Jersey.

Port Elizabeth Marine Terminal
7.133

1   Port Elizabeth Marine Terminal (40°40′·01N 74°08′·54W) is situated 1½ miles above the entrance to the bay.

   Channels. Port Elizabeth South Reach leads to the berths on the SW side of the terminal, Elizabeth Pierhead Channel fronts the berths on the SE side of the terminal and Port Elizabeth Channel Reach fronts the berths on the NE side of the terminal.

2   South Elizabeth and Elizabeth Pierhead Channels have project depths of 10·7 m (35 ft); Port Elizabeth Channel Reach has a project depth of 13·7 m (45 ft). For the latest controlling depths the charts and port authority should be consulted.

   Berths. There are 25 deep-draught berths at the terminal with depths alongside of 7·8 to 9·9 m.

Port Newark Terminal
7.134

1   Port Newark Terminal (40°41′·68N 74°08′·40W) is situated 2½ miles above the entrance.

   Channels. Port Elizabeth Channel Reach which lies between the two terminals, and has a project depth of 13·7 m (45 ft), fronts the berths on the SW side of Port Newark Terminal and Port Newark Pierhead Channel fronts the berths on the SE side. Port Newark Channel fronts the berths on the NW side and its E part links the terminal to the main channel in Newark Bay. These channels have a project depth of 12·2 m (40 ft). For the latest controlling depths the charts and port authority should be consulted.

2   **Berths.** There are 37 deep-draught berths at the terminal with reported depths alongside of 9·8 to 10·7 m.

   Port Newark Container Terminal lies on the N side of Port Elizabeth Channel Reach.

   Several RoRo berths, used mainly for the import of motor vehicles, are located on the N side of Port Newark Channel.

EAST RIVER

General information

Charts 3455, 3451, 2580
Description
7.135

1   East River is a 14 mile long tidal strait that connects Upper Bay (7.83) with Long Island Sound and separates the New York mainland from the W end of Long Island. Its W entrance is between The Battery (40°42′·10N 74°00′·90W), at the S end of Manhattan Island, and Governors Island. Its E

Governors Island from SW (7.135)
(Original dated 2004)

(Photograph - Airphoto - Jim Wark)

entrance is between Throgs Neck (40°48′·30N 73°47′·50W) and Willets Point, 7 cables SE.

Depths
7.136
1   The project depth for the main channel is 12·2 m (40 ft) from deep water in Upper Bay to the former New York Naval Shipyard, 2 miles from the W entrance, thence 10·7 m (35 ft) to Throgs Neck. For the latest controlling depths the charts and port authority should be consulted.

Vessel traffic service
7.137
1   See 7.45.

Tidal levels
7.138
1   **The Battery.** See 7.43.
Horns Hook. Mean spring range about 1·6 m (8 ft); mean neap range about 1·1 m (3·6 ft).
Willets Point. Mean spring range about 2·6 m (8·5 ft); mean neap range about 1·8 m (5·9 ft).

Pilotage
7.139
1   **Pilotage** is compulsory for all foreign vessels and US vessels under register. Vessels entering the Port of New York and New Jersey through Long Island Sound are boarded by the pilot for East River off Execution Rocks (40°52′·69N 73°44′·27W) (6.95).

Arrangements are made 24 hours in advance through ship's agents and 12 and 6 hour ETA updates are requested; 24 hour pilotage service is available on request.

Traffic regulations
7.140
1   **Navigation Rules for US Inland Waters** apply to all waters covered in this section. See 1.44 and Appendix VII for further information.
Safety and security zones have been established within approximately 100 and 200 yards of La Guardia Airport.
Security zones are established in East River during the arrival or departure of dignitaries.
For definition and general regulations concerning safety and security zones see Appendix V.

Submarine pipelines
7.141
1   A gas pipeline is laid through East River and Long Island Sound from a position 2 cables NE of Hunts Point (7.161) to Northport Basin (6.234).
Caution. See 1.36.

Vertical clearance
7.142
1   The following bridges cross the W part of East River:
Brooklyn Bridge (40°42′·35N 73°59′·80W), with a vertical clearance of 38·7 m (127 ft) and 33·5 m (110 ft) under moving platforms.

2   Manhattan Bridge (40°42′·40N 73°59′·42W), with a vertical clearance of 40·8 m (134 ft) and 35·1 m (115 ft) under a moving platform.

Williamsburg Bridge (40°42′·80N 73°58′·30W), with a vertical clearance of 40·5 m (133 ft).

The following fixed bridges cross the middle part of East River:

3   Queensboro Bridge (40°45′·45N 73°57′·36W), with a vertical clearance of 39·9 m (131 ft) under the W span crossing the main channel.

Triborough Bridge (40°46′·77N 73°55′·60W), with a vertical clearance of 42·1 m (138 ft).

Hell Gate Bridge (40°46′·95N 73°55′·32W), with a vertical clearance of 40·8 m (134 ft).

4   The following fixed bridges cross the E part of East River:

Bronx-Whitestone Bridge (40°48′·10N 73°49′·77W), with a vertical clearance of 41·1 m (135 ft).

Throgs Neck Bridge (40°48′·00N 73°47′·62W), with a vertical clearance of 46·3 m (152 ft) at the centre of the main span.

Tidal streams
7.143
1   **Tidal streams.** In East River the tidal streams set E on a rising tide and W on a falling tide, the opposite direction to the tidal streams in Long Island Sound. The tidal streams generally follow the direction of the channel, but there are heavy swirls in Hell Gate and in the channels either side of Roosevelt Island (7.144 and 7.150).

See Tidal Stream tables on charts.

Directions
(continued from 7.91)

Governors Island to Queensboro Bridge
7.144
1   From a position between Governors Island and Ellis Island the channel through East River leads 6 miles ENE then NE to Queensboro Bridge, passing:

Between Governors Island (40°41′·30N 74°01′·20W) and The Battery (40°42′·10N 74°00′·90W on the alignment (079·4°) of East River Deepwater Range Front Light (white framework tower) (40°41′·97N 73°59′·99W), thence:

Beneath Brooklyn Bridge (7.142), Manhattan Bridge (3 cables E) and Williamsburg Bridge (1¼ miles E), thence:

2   On the alignment (160·4°), astern, of Poorhouse Flats Leading Lights (green rectangle, red stripe, on framework towers) (40°43′·47N 73°57′·77W front light), NNW through the deepest water (see caution below).

Thence the track continues NE, passing:

NW of B Light Buoy (preferred channel to starboard) (40°44′·33N 73°57′·74W), moored 3 cables SW of Belmont Island, and NW of the entrance to Newtown Creek (7.149). At this position the main channel of East River crosses from the E side of the river to the W side. Thence:

3   NW of Belmont Island (40°44′·80N 73°57′·86W), which lies 2 cables SW of Roosevelt Island. No 17 Light (green square on framework tower, white base) stands on the S side of the island. Thence:

Beneath the NW span of Queensboro Bridge (7.142), which joins Roosevelt Island to Manhattan Island.

4   **Caution.** Between Brooklyn Bridge and Hunters Point (40°44′·33N 73°57′·74W) shallow-draught vessels normally keep to the W side of the channel whether N or S-bound, thereby reserving the E side of the channel for deep-draught vessels. Vessels transiting East River should be aware of this practice and anticipate N-bound shallow-draught vessels crossing from E to W in the vicinity of Corlears Hook (40°42′·70N 73°58′·60W) and from W to E in the vicinity of Newtown Creek.

Queensboro Bridge to College Point
7.145
1   From Queensboro Bridge the channel through East River leads 6 miles generally NE and E to College Point, passing:

Between Horns Hook (40°46′·58N 73°56′·54W) and the grey stone tower, 2 cables SSE, standing at the NE extremity of Roosevelt Island, thence:

2   Into Hell Gate, passing between Mill Rock (40°46′·84N 73°56′·30W), marked at its N and S ends by Nos 1 and 16 Lights (green square and red triangle, respectively on framework towers, white bases), and Hallets Point. No 15 Light (green square on pile) is exhibited from the point. Thence:

3   S of Hog Back and Holmes Rock (2½ cables NE), on a reef close W of Negro Point, the S end of Wards Island. No 14 Light (red triangle on framework tower) (40°46′·85N 73°55′·92W) marks the SW edge of the reef. Thence:

Beneath Triborough Bridge (7.142) and Hell Gate Bridge, 2½ cables ENE.

Caution. The crooked channel, the strong tidal streams and the heavy traffic in Hell Gate require the mariner to exercise particular caution when navigating this part of East River.

7.146
1   From Hell Gate Bridge the channel continues NE and E, passing:

NW of LP Light (red and white chequered diamond on framework tower) (40°47′·59N 73°54′·24W), marking Lawrence Point Ledge. Lawrence Point, on which stands a power station, lies 3 cables WSW. Thence:

N of North Brother Island (40°48′·05N 73°53′·90W), marked on its N side by No 9 Light (green square on tower), thence:

2   Between the N end of Rikers Island (40°47′·89N 73°53′·27W) and Barretto Point on the N side of the river, thence:

S of Hunts Point (40°48′·10N 73°52′·36W) (7.161), thence:

N of No 5 Light Buoy (port hand) (40°47′·79N 73°51′·95W). Vessels with a masthead height of more than 38·1 m (125 ft) must keep more than ½ cable N of this buoy so as not to interfere with the glide path of La Guardia Airport (7.159).

Thence to a position N of College Point (40°47′·64N 73°51′·20W).

College Point to Throgs Neck
7.147
1   From College Point the channel through East River leads 3¼ miles generally E to a position between Throgs Neck (40°48′·30N 73°47′·50W) and Willets Point, on which stands Fort Totten, passing:

N of College Point Reef (40°47′·86N 73°51′·06W), which extends 2 cables NNE of College Point (7.160). CP Light (green and white chequered diamond on framework tower) stands on the reef and No 3 Buoy (port hand) is moored ½ cable N of it. Thence:

2 Beneath Bronx-Whitestone Bridge (7.142), which extends SSE from Old Ferry Point to Whitestone on Long Island, thence:

N of Whitestone Point Light (green square on black framework tower) (40°48'·11N 73°49'·18W), on the edge of a ledge extending N from the point. No 1A Buoy (port hand) is moored ½ cable N of the light. Thence:

3 Beneath Throgs Neck Bridge (7.142), passing at least 2 cables S of Throgs Neck Light (black and white chequered diamond on framework tower), which stands at the head of Throgs Neck. No 48 Light Buoy (starboard hand) marks the shoal water off Throgs Neck.

(Directions for the main passage through the W part of Long Island Sound are given at 6.92)

Side channels

Charts 3451, 2580
Harlem River
7.148

1 **Description.** Harlem River, which joins East River in Hell Gate (40°46'·80N 73°56'·20W), extends about 7 miles N and connects with Hudson River through Spuyten Duyvil Creek. The channel through Harlem River is narrow and tortuous, and traffic is heavy.

2 **Depths.** In general there is a minimum depth of 4·3 m (14 ft) as far as Hudson River, but care must be taken to avoid several isolated 3·4 to 4 m (11 to 13 ft) spots.

Vertical clearance. There are more than a dozen fixed and opening bridges over Harlem River. The minimum vertical clearance under closed bridges is 7·3 m (24 ft) except for the rail swing bridge over the entrance from Hudson River, where the clearance is only 1·5 m (5 ft). This rail bridge is kept open except for the passage of trains.

3 Vessels with heights too great to pass under the closed bridges should make the passage against the tidal stream. Clearance under raised vertical lift spans and fixed bridges exceeds 30 m (100 ft).

4 **Tidal streams** in Harlem River run S from Hudson River to East River while the E going current is running in Hell Gate. The velocity of the current is 2 kn or more in the narrower parts of the river.

Newtown Creek
7.149

1 Newtown Creek is entered on the E side of East River close S of Hunters Point (7.144). The creek extends 3¼ miles E and S and has several short tributaries or basins. English Kills forms the final 8 cables of the creek.

Traffic is fairly heavy and consists mainly of petroleum products, sand, gravel and crushed rock.

2 **Depths.** The project depth is 7 m (23 ft) to Maspeth Creek, 2¼ miles from East River, then 6·1 m (20 ft) for the next 7½ cables and then 3·6 m (12 ft) to the head of the project. For the latest controlling depths the charts and port authority should be consulted.

Vertical clearance. A number of fixed and bascule bridges, with a minimum vertical clearance of 25·3 m (83 ft) with the bascule bridges open, cross Newtown Creek and its tributaries.

Channel east of Roosevelt Island
7.150

1 The channel E of Roosevelt Island is narrower than the main channel, which passes W of the island, and has a controlling depth of about 5·8 m (19 ft). The currents in this channel are strong (7.143).

Vertical clearance. Two bridges cross this channel: Queensboro Bridge, E span; a fixed bridge with a vertical clearance of 40·5 m (133 ft).

36th Avenue Lift Bridge (40°45'·80N 73°56'·74W); vertical clearance of 12·2 m (40 ft) when closed and 30·2 m (99 ft) when open.

Channel between North Brother Island and South Brother Island
7.151

1 The channel between North Brother Island (40°48'·05N 73°53'·90W) and South Brother Island, 1 cable S, has a controlling depth of about 7·6 m (25 ft). It is marked on the N side by Nos 6 and 8 Buoys (starboard hand), and on the S side by two buoys (port hand) and SB Light (green and white chequered diamond on framework tower). The channel is narrow and subject to strong currents, and should not be used by vessels of limited manoeuvrability.

South Brother Island Channel and adjacent waters
7.152

1 **South Brother Island Channel**, with a project depth 10·7 m (35 ft), leads from deep water E of North Brother Island (7.146), and along the W side of Rikers Island to a turning basin NE of Steinway Creek. The channel is marked by buoys and light beacons.

2 **Vessel Mast Heights.** Vessels using South Brother Island Channel and the turning basin at its S end should ballast prior to entry and are cautioned that mast heights in excess of 38 m (125 ft) may penetrate the glide path of the NW-SE runway of La Guardia Airport. If mast heights cannot be lowered below this height, La Guardia Air Traffic Control Tower should be contacted before entry into the channel or departure from the terminal.

7.153

1 **Rikers Island Channel** leads E from the turning basin along the S side of Rikers Island. Its E end is closed by a runway of La Guardia Airport and its lighted approach.

2 **Bowery Bay** is a shallow bay lying to the S of Rikers Island Channel. It may be approached from the NW by a channel that passes between South Brother Island (40°47'·78N 73°53'·88W) and Lawrence Point Ledge, 3 cables SW. The channel has a controlling depth of about 5·8 m (19 ft) and is marked by No 2 Buoy (starboard hand) and No 3 Light (green square on framework tower) which stands on South Brother Island Ledge.

3 **Vertical clearance.** A fixed bridge crosses Rikers Island Channel and Bowery Bay joining Rikers Island to the Borough of Queens, New York. The bridge has a vertical clearance over the channel of 15·8 m (52 ft) for a width of 38 m (125 ft).

Bronx River
7.154

1 Bronx River (40°48'·70N 73°52'·20W), on the N side of the East River, is entered through a dredged channel 1½ miles W of Old Ferry Point. The channel leads 2¼ miles NW to the head of navigation at East 172nd Street. Waterborne traffic on the river consists mainly of sand, gravel and crushed rock.

Depths. The river has a project depth of 3 m (10 ft) but is subject to shoaling throughout. For the latest controlling depths the charts and port authority should be consulted.

2 **Vertical clearance.** Four bridges cross the river. The least vertical clearances are 5·5 m (18 ft) at the lower end and 2·4 m (8 ft) at the upper end.

Westchester Creek
7.155

1 Westchester Creek (40°48′·70N 73°50′·60W), on the N side of the East River, is entered through a dredged channel between Clason Point and Old Ferry Point, 7 cables E. The channel leads N for 2¼ miles to the town of Westchester and is buoyed for 1 mile above the entrance. Waterborne traffic is mainly in petroleum products and mineral products.

2 **Depths.** In 2010 there were mid-channel controlling depths of 0·3 m (1 ft) to 1·5 m (5 ft). For the latest controlling depths the charts and port authority should be consulted.

Vertical clearance. Three fixed bridges and one bascule bridge cross the creek at Unionport, 1½ miles above the entrance. The fixed bridges have a least vertical clearance of 15·9 m (52 ft) and the bascule bridge a clearance of 4·3 m (14 ft).

Anchorages and harbours

Hallets Cove
7.156

1 No 14 Anchorage, with depths up to 12 m (39 ft), lies in Hallets Cove (40°46′·25N 73°56′·20W), E of the NE end of Roosevelt Island (7.145) and is the only recommended anchorage in East River, W of Rikers Island.

Port Morris
7.157

1 Oil terminals are situated in Port Morris (40°48′·10N 73°54′·40W), on the N shore of East River.

Rikers Island Anchorage
7.158

1 No 11 Anchorage (40°47′·70N 73°52′·50W), much used, with depths of 5·5 to 12·2 m (18 to 40 ft), lies between the S side of the main channel and the flats off the N side of Rikers Island.

Flushing Bay
7.159

1 Flushing Bay is entered between College Point (40°47′·64N 73°51′·20W) and La Guardia Airport, 8 cables SW. Flushing Creek enters the head of the bay 2 miles SSE of its entrance.

Channel. A dredged channel, marked by buoys and light buoys, leads SSE for 1¾ miles from within the entrance of the bay to a turning basin at the entrance to Flushing Creek.

2 **Traffic regulations.** Safety and security zones have been established within approximately 100 and 200 yards of La Guardia Airport.

For definition and general regulations concerning safety and security zones see Appendix V.

Restricted area. Part of the channel, 1¼ miles from the entrance and lying 91 m (300 ft) either side of the extension of the NW-SE runway of La Guardia Airport, is a restricted area in which vessels with a height of more than 10·7 m (35 ft) are prohibited when visibility is less than one mile.

3 **Ice** generally obstructs Flushing Bay and Flushing Creek during part of January and February.

Depths. There is a project depth of 4·5 m (15 ft) from East River through the bay to the railway bridge (40°45′·42N 73°50′·32W) in Flushing Creek. A turning basin with a project depth of 3·6 m (12 ft) lies W of the entrance to the creek.

4 **Anchorages.** No 10 Anchorage and a number of special anchorages are situated in Flushing Bay, the positions and limits of which are shown on the chart. See 1.45.

College Point
7.160

1 The town of College Point lies to the S of the point (40°47′·64N 73°51′·20W) of the same name. The wharves on the W side of the town have depths alongside of up to 3 m.

Hunts Point
7.161

1 Hunts Point (40°48′·10N 73°52′·36W) is on the N side of East River opposite Flushing Bay.

A wharf, with reported depths alongside of 5·2 to 7·3 m, extends 3 cables NE from the point.

Caution. The gas pipeline laid through East River passes through No 8 Anchorage close E of Hunts Point and mariners should bear this in mind when selecting an anchorage position. See 1.36.

Between Throgs Neck and Old Ferry Point
7.162

1 No 6 Anchorage, in the bight on the N side of East River between Throgs Neck and Old Ferry Point (40°48′·32N 73°49′·95W) affords anchorage, with good holding, in 4·6 to 10·7 m (15 to 35 ft). The water shoals abruptly from depths of 5·5 m (18 ft) to depths of 1·2 to 1·5 m (4 to 5 ft), 3 cables from the shore.

Caution. The gas pipeline (7.141) laid through East River passes very close to the S limit of this anchorage and mariners should bear this in mind when selecting an anchorage position. See 1.36.

Fort Schuyler
7.163

1 Fort Schuyler (40°48′·31N 73°47′·50W), used as a base for a nautical school, stands on the outer end of Throgs Neck. A wharf on the SW side of the fort has reported depths alongside of 7·6 m.

Little Bay
7.164

1 No 7 Anchorage, in Little Bay on the S side of East River close E of Throgs Neck Bridge (7.142), is used as a small craft anchorage.

HUDSON RIVER

General information

Chart 3455, 3454, US Charts 12343, 12347 (see 1.16)

Description
7.165

1 Hudson River, sometimes called North River in New York City, rises in the Adirondack Mountains in the NE part of New York State, and flows in a S direction for 275 miles to its junction with East River at The Battery (7.135). The tidal part of the river extends 134 miles to Troy Lock and Troy Dam from where traffic may join the New York State canal system.

2 This canal system leads W to The Great Lakes through Erie Canal and Oswego Canal, and N to Lake Champlain through Champlain Canal.

New York City extends along the E bank for about 14 miles above The Battery.

The river water is usually fresh as far S as Poughkeepsie, midway between Troy Dam and The Battery.

3 Navigation of the river is easy as far N as Kingston, 79 miles above the Battery, then becoming

more difficult because of numerous steep-to shoals and middle banks.

No-discharge Zone (NDZ). All the waters of Hudson River from the Battery to Troy, 134 miles N, have been designated as a NDZ. See 1.41.

Depths
7.166

Project depth from the inner end of Hudson River Channel (7.92) to Albany is 9·8 m (32 ft), except for the section along the New Jersey Weehawken-Edgewater waterfront where the project depth is 9·1 m (30 ft). For the latest controlling depths the charts and port authority should be consulted.

Tidal levels
7.167

Between The Battery and Albany the tidal range varies between about 1 and 1·5 m (3 and 5 ft). See information in *Admiralty Tide Tables.*

Pilotage
7.168

Hudson River Pilots embark N of Yonkers (40°56'·50N 73°54'·00W) about 17 miles N of The Battery (7.135). Pilotage is compulsory.

Largest vessel
7.169

Hudson River. Maximum permissible size for navigation to Albany: length 229 m (750 ft); width 33·5 m (110 ft); draught 9·4 m (31 ft). Vessels with a draught of more than 8·5 m (28 ft) will be required to transit the river on a favourable tide as directed by the pilot.

Erie Canal. The controlling dimensions of the locks in this canal are length 91 m (300 ft), width 13·2 m (43·5 ft), 3·7 m (12 ft) over the sill; vertical clearance under bridges and cables of 4·6 m (15 ft).

Champlain Canal. The size of vessels is limited by a controlling depth of 3·7 m (12 ft) and a least vertical clearance of 5·2 m (17 ft).

Vertical clearance
7.170

The bridges between New York and Albany, which have a least vertical clearance of 40·8 m (134 ft), have either fixed or suspension spans. Overhead cables spanning the river have a least vertical clearance of 44·2 m (145 ft).

Buoyage
7.171

The lighted buoys marking Hudson River are replaced during the winter by smaller lighted buoys or unlighted buoys.

Natural conditions
7.172

Tidal streams:
- George Washington Bridge. In-going 1½ kn; out-going 2¼ kn.
- Kingston. In-going 1¼ kn; out-going 1½ kn.
- Albany. In-going ¼ kn; out-going ¾ kn.

The above figures will be affected by freshets, droughts and winds.

Ice. Even in extremely severe winters Coast Guard icebreakers and continuous river traffic maintain an open channel to Albany. The ice season usually starts in early January and ends in the middle of March. Normally shipping is affected between Tappan Zee and Albany. Aids to navigation are often covered or dragged off station by moving ice.

Albany
General information
7.173

Position and function. Albany (42°38'·93N 73°44'·71W) is situated on the W bank of the Hudson River, 125 miles above New York Harbor (7.135).

The port of Albany is the terminus for deep-draught vessels on Hudson River and serves as a transhipping point for the immediate vicinity and large areas of New England. Waterborne commerce at the port is mainly in petroleum products, but many other products are also handled.

Albany, which in 2010 had a population of 97 856, is the capital of New York State. It is a minor port and a port of entry.

Port Authority. Albany Port District Commission, 106 Smith Boulevard, Albany, NY 12202-1089.
Website: www.portofalbany.com

Limiting conditions
7.174

Depths. See 7.166.
Vertical clearance. See 7.170.

Arrival information
7.175

Anchorage. The restricted width of the river is not sufficient to allow vessels to swing at anchor except in emergency. See 7.178.
Natural conditions. See 7.172.

Berths
7.176

There are 1280 m of wharves on the Albany (W) side of the river, and 335 m on the Rensselaer (E) side. The major facilities have depths alongside of 8·5 to 10 m.

Port services
7.177

Repairs. All types of repairs can be carried out other than those that require docking, for which there are no facilities.

Other facilities: hospitals; oily waste disposal.

Supplies. Bunkering services are not available for deep-draught vessels. Diesel is available for small vessels. Water, stores and provisions are available.

Anchorages and harbours
Anchorages
7.178

General anchorages begin 5 miles above The Battery (7.135) and extend upriver for about 10 miles.

Vessels proceeding from New York to Albany occasionally anchor overnight in the vicinity of Kingston, 79 miles above The Battery and 47 miles below Albany, to await daylight hours before passing through the constricted part of the river.

A buoyed anchorage 122 m wide and 732 m long is situated on the E side of the channel just above Stuyvesant, 15 miles below Albany. The anchorage has depths of 9·8 m (32 ft).

Special anchorages. There are numerous special anchorages on the river between New York and Albany. Their positions are best seen on the national charts of the river. See 1.45.

Newburgh
7.179

Newburgh (41°30'·30N 74°00'·50W) is situated on the W bank of the river 53 miles above The Battery. It is a major petroleum distribution centre.

Berths. Most of the piers of the major oil companies are at the S end of the waterfront. Depths alongside range from 4·2 m at the N end of the waterfront to 10·6 m at the S end.

Poughkeepsie
7.180
1 Poughkeepsie (41°42'·40N 73°56'·30W) is situated on the E bank of the river 66 miles above The Battery. It is an important industrial centre.

Berths. Tanker berths, with reported depths alongside of 3·9 to 6 m, are situated 1 mile S of the town.

Kingston
7.181
1 Kingston (41°55'·66N 73°57'·48W) is situated on the W side of the river 80 miles above The Battery. Waterborne traffic consists mainly of building materials and oil products.

Berths. There is an oil terminal at Kingston Point from which tugs and barges transport oil products up and down the river.

Hudson
7.182
1 Hudson (40°56'·50N 73°54'·00W) is situated on the E bank of the river 102 miles above The Battery. Waterborne commerce is in oil products.

Berths. The bulk petroleum pier has reported depths alongside of about 3 m.

APPENDIX I

CODE OF FEDERAL REGULATIONS TITLE 33 — NAVIGATION AND NAVIGABLE WATERS

PART 26 — VESSEL BRIDGE-TO-BRIDGE RADIOTELEPHONE REGULATIONS

Appendix I contains extracts from the United States Bridge-to-Bridge Telephone Act. For a complete description of this part see 33 CFR 26.

§26.01 Purpose. (See 33 CFR 26)

§26.02 Definitions. (See 33 CFR 26)

§26.03 Radiotelephone required.
(a) Unless an exemption is granted under §26.09 (waters not applicable to this volume) and except as provided in paragraph (a)(4) of this section, this part applies to:
  (1) Every power-driven vessel of 20 m or over in length while navigating;
  (2) Every vessel of 100 gross tons and upward carrying one or more passengers for hire while navigating;
  (3) Every towing vessel of 26 ft (7·9 m) or over in length while navigating; and
  (4) Every dredge and floating plant engaged in or near a channel or fairway in operations likely to restrict or affect navigation of other vessels except for an unmanned or intermittently manned floating plant under the control of a dredge.
(b) Every vessel, dredge or floating plant described in paragraph (a) of this section must have a radiotelephone on board capable of operation from its navigational bridge, or in the case of a dredge from its main control station, and capable of transmitting and receiving on the frequency or frequencies within the 156-162 MHz band using the classes of emissions designated by the Federal Communications Commission for the exchange of navigational information.
(c) The radiotelephone required by paragraph (b) of this section must be carried on board the described vessels, dredges and floating plants upon the navigable waters of the United States.
(d) The radiotelephone required by paragraph (b) of this section must be capable of transmitting and receiving on VHF FM channel 22A (157.1 MHz).
(f) In addition to the radiotelephone required by paragraph (b) of this section each vessel described in paragraph (a) of this section, while transiting any waters within a Vessel Traffic Service Area, must have on board a radiotelephone capable of transmitting and receiving on the VTS designated frequency in Table 161.12 (c) (VTS and VMRS Centers, Call Signs/MMSI, Designated Frequencies and Monitoring Areas).

Note. A single VHF-FM radio, capable of scanning or sequential monitoring, (often referred to as dual watch capability) will not meet the requirements for two radios.

§26.04 Use of the designated frequency.
(d) On the navigable waters of the United States channel 13 (156.65 MHz) is the designated frequency required to be monitored in accordance with §26.05 (a), except that in the area prescribed in §26.03 (e) (not listed - waters not applicable to this volume) channel 67 (156.375 MHz) is the designated frequency.
(e) On those navigable waters of the United States within a VTS area, the designated VTS frequency is an additional designated frequency required to be monitored in accordance with §26.05.

Note: As stated in 47 CFR 80.148 (b) a VHF watch on channel 16 (156.800 MHz) is not required on vessels subject to the Vessel Bridge-to-Bridge Radiotelephone Act and participating in a Vessel Traffic Service (VTS) system when the watch is maintained on both the vessel bridge-to-bridge frequency and a designated VTS frequency.

§26.05 Use of radiotelephone.
Section 5 of the Act states that the radio telephone required by this Act is for the exclusive use of the Master or person in charge of the vessel, or the person designated by the Master or person in charge to pilot or direct the movement of the vessel, who shall maintain a listening watch on the designated frequency. Nothing herein shall be interpreted as precluding the use of portable radiotelephone equipment to satisfy the requirements of this act.

§26.06 Maintenance of radiotelephone; failure of radiotelephone. (See 33 CFR 26)

§26.07 Communications.
No person may use the service of, and no person may serve as, a person required to maintain a listening watch under Section 5 of the Act, 33 U.S.C 1204 unless that person can communicate in the English language.

§26.08 Exemption procedures. (See 33 CFR 26)

§26.09 List of exemptions. (See 33 CFR 26)

APPENDIX II

CODE OF FEDERAL REGULATIONS TITLE 33 — NAVIGATION AND NAVIGABLE WATERS

PART 160 — PORTS AND WATERWAYS SAFETY — GENERAL

Appendix II contains extracts from Subpart C of the above regulations issued by the United States Department of Commerce. For a complete description of this part see 33 CFR 160.

Subpart C — Notification of Arrival, Hazardous Conditions, and Certain Dangerous Cargoes.

§160.201 General.
This subpart contains requirements and procedures for submitting Notices of Arrival (NOA) and Notice of Hazardous Condition. The sections in this subpart describe:
(a) Applicability and exemptions from requirements in this subpart;
(b) Required information in a NOA;
(c) Required changes to a NOA;
(d) Methods and times for submission of a NOA and changes to a NOA;
(e) How to obtain a waiver; and
(f) Requirements for submission of the Notice of Hazardous Conditions.

§160.202 Applicability.
(a) This subpart applies to US and foreign vessels bound for and departing from ports or places in the United States.
(b) This subpart does not apply to recreational vessels under 46 U.S.C. *4301 et seq.*
(c) Unless otherwise specified in this subpart, the owner, agent, master, operator, or person in charge of a vessel regulated by this subpart is responsible for compliance with the requirements in this subpart.
(d) Towing vessels controlling a barge or barges required to submit a NOA under this subpart must submit only one NOA containing the information required for the towing vessel and each barge under its control.

§160.203 Exemptions.
(a) Except for reporting notice of hazardous conditions, the following vessels are exempt from requirements in this subpart:
(1) Passenger and supply vessels when they are employed in the exploration for or in the removal of oil, gas, or mineral resources on the continental shelf.
(2) Oil Spill Recovery Vessels (OSRVs) when engaged in actual spill response operations or during spill response exercises.
(3) Vessels operating upon the following waters:
(i) Mississippi River between its sources and mile 235, Above Head of Passes;
(ii) Tributaries emptying into the Mississippi River above mile 235;
(iii) Atchafalaya River above its junction with the Plaquemine-Morgan City alternate waterway and the Red River; and
(iv) The Tennessee River from its confluence with the Ohio River to mile zero on the Mobile River and all other tributaries between those two points.
(b) If not carrying certain dangerous cargo or controlling another vessel carrying certain dangerous cargo, the following vessels are exempt from NOA requirements in this subpart:
(1) Vessels 300 gross tons or less, except for foreign vessels entering any port or place in the Seventh Coast Guard District as described in 33 CFR 3.35-1(b).
(2) Vessels operating exclusively within a Captain of the Port Zone.
(3) Vessels arriving at a port or place under force majeure.
(4) Towing vessels and barges operating solely between ports or places in the continental United States.
(5) Public vessels.
(6) Except for tank vessels, US vessels operating solely between ports or places in the United States on the Great Lakes.
(c) Vessels less than 500 gross tons need not submit the International Safety Management (ISM) Code Notice (Entry (7) in Table 160.206).
(d) [Suspended]
(e) [Suspended]
(f) US vessels need not submit the International Ship and Port Facility Code (ISPS) Notice Information (Entry (9) in Table 160.206)

§160.204 Definitions
As used in this subpart:
Agent means any person, partnership, firm, company or corporation engaged by the owner or charterer of a vessel to act in their behalf in matters concerning the vessel.
Barge means a non-self propelled vessel engaged in commerce.
Carried in bulk means a commodity that is loaded or carried on board a vessel without containers or labels and received and handled without mark or count.
Certain dangerous cargo (CDC) includes any of the following:
(1) Division 1.1 or 1.2 explosives as defined in 49 CFR 173.50.
(2) Division 1.5D blasting agents for which a permit is required under 49 CFR 176.415, or for which a permit is required as a condition of a Research and Special Programs Administration exemption.
(3) Division 2.3 "poisonous gas", as listed in 49 CFR 172.101 that is also a "material poisonous by inhalation" as defined in

49 CFR 171.8, and that is in a quantity in excess of 1 metric ton per vessel.
(4) Division 5.1 oxidizing materials for which a permit is required under 49 CFR 176.415 or for which a permit is required as a condition of a Research and Special Programs Administration exemption.
(5) A liquid material that has a primary or subsidiary classification of Division 6.1 "poisonous material" as listed in 49 CFR 172.101 that is also a "material poisonous by inhalation" as defined in 49 CFR 171.8 and that is in a bulk packaging, or that is in a quantity in excess of 20 metric tons per vessel when not in a bulk packaging.
(6) Class 7, "highway route controlled quantity" radioactive material, or "fissile material, controlled shipment," as defined in 49 CFR 173.403.
(7) All bulk liquefied gas cargo carried under 46 CFR 151.50-31 or listed in 46 CFR 154.7 that is flammable and/or toxic and that is not carried as certain dangerous cargo residue (CDC residue).
(8) The following bulk liquids except when carried as CDC residue:
  (i) Acetone cyanohydrin;
  (ii) Allyl alcohol;
  (iii) Chlorosulfonic acid;
  (iv) Crotonaldehyde;
  (v) Ethylene chlorohydrin;
  (vi) Ethylene dibromide;
  (vii) Methacrylonitrile;
  (viii) Oleum (fuming sulfuric acid); and
  (ix) Propylene oxide, alone or mixed with ethylene oxide.
(9) The following bulk solids:
  (i) Ammonium nitrate listed as Division 5.1 (oxidizing) material in 49 CFR 172.101 except when carried as CDC residue; and
  (ii) Ammonium nitrate based fertilizer listed as a Division 5.1 (oxidizing) material in 49 CFR 172.101 except when carried as CDC residue.

Certain dangerous cargo residue (CDC residue) includes any of the following:
(1) Ammonium nitrate in bulk or ammonium nitrate based fertilizer in bulk remaining after all saleable cargo is discharged, not exceeding 1,000 pounds in total and not individually accumulated in quantities exceeding two cubic feet.
(2) For bulk liquids and liquefied gases, the cargo that remains onboard in a cargo system after discharge that is not accessible through normal transfer procedures, with the exception of the following bulk liquefied gas cargoes carried under 46 CFR 151.50-31 or listed in 46 CFR 154.7:
  (i) Ammonia, anhydrous;
  (ii) Chlorine;
  (iii) Ethane;
  (iv) Ethylene oxide;
  (v) Methane (LNG);
  (vi) Methyl bromide;
  (vii) Sulfur dioxide; and
  (viii) Vinyl chloride.

Charterer means the person or organisation that contracts for the majority of the carrying capacity of a ship for the transportation of cargo to a stated port for a specified period. This includes "time charterers" and voyage charterers".

Crewmember means all persons carried on board the vessel to provide navigation and maintenance of the vessel, its machinery, systems, and arrangements essential for propulsion and safe navigation or to provide services for other persons on board.

Great Lakes means Lakes Superior, Michigan, Huron, Erie, and Ontario, their connecting and tributary waters, the Saint Lawrence River as far as Saint Regis, and adjacent port areas.

Gross tons means the tonnage determined by the tonnage authorities of a vessel's flag state in accordance with the national tonnage rules in force before the entry into force of the International Convention on Tonnage Measurement of Ships, 1969 ("Convention"). For a vessel measured only under Annex 1 of the Convention, gross tons means that tonnage. For a vessel measured under both systems, the higher gross tonnage is the tonnage used for the purposes of the 300 gross-ton threshold.

Hazardous condition means any condition that may adversely affect the safety of any vessel, bridge, structure, or shore area or the environmental quality of any port, harbor, or navigable waterway of the United States. It may, but need not, involve collision, fire, explosion, grounding, leaking, damage, injury or illness of a person on board, or manning shortage.

Nationality means the state (nation) in which a person is a citizen or to which a person owes permanent allegiance.

Operator means any person including, but not limited to, an owner, a charterer, or another contractor who conducts, or is responsible for, the operation of a vessel.

Persons in addition to crewmembers means any person onboard the vessel, including passengers, who are not included on the list of crewmembers.

Port or place of departure means any port or place in which a vessel is anchored or moored.

Port or place of destination means any port or place to which a vessel is bound to anchor or moor.

Public vessel means a vessel that is owned or demise (bareboat) chartered by the government of the United States, by a State or local government, or by the government of a foreign country and that is not engaged in commercial service.

Time charterer means the party who hires a vessel for a specific amount of time. The owner and his crew manage the vessel but the charterer selects the port of destination.

Voyage charterer means the party who hires a vessel for a single voyage. The owner and his crew manage the vessel but the charterer selects the port of destination.

§160.206 Information required in a NOA.
(a) Each NOA must contain all of the information items specified in Table 160.206.

APPENDIX II

TABLE 160.206. — NOA INFORMATION ITEMS

Required information	Vessels not carrying CDC	Vessels carrying CDC	
		Vessels	Towing vessels controlling vessels carrying CDC
(1) *Vessel information:*			
(i) Name;	X	X	X
(ii) Name of the registered owner;	X	X	X
(iii) Country of registry;	X	X	X
(iv) Call sign;	X	X	X
(v) International Maritime Organisation (IMO) international number or, if the vessel does not have an assigned IMO international number, substitute with official number;	X	X	X
(vi) Name of the operator;	X	X	X
(vii) Name of the charterer; and	X	X	X
(viii) Name of classification society.	X	X	X
(2) *Voyage information:*			
(i) Names of last five ports or places visited;	X	X	X
(ii) Dates of arrival and departure for last five ports or places visited;	X	X	X
(iii) For each port or place in the United States to be visited, list the names of the receiving facility, the port or place, the city, and the state;	X	X	X
(iv) For each port or place in the United States to be visited, the estimated date and time of arrival;	X	X	X
(v) For each port or place in the United States to be visited, the estimated date and time of departure;	X	X	X
(vi) The location (port or place and country) or position (latitude and longitude or waterway and mile marker) of the vessel at the time of reporting; and	X	X	X
(vii) The name and telephone number of a 24 hour point of contact.	X	X	X
(3) *Cargo information:*			
(i) A general description of cargo, other than CDC, onboard the vessel (e.g.: grain, container, oil, etc.);	X	X	X
(ii) Name of each certain dangerous cargo carried, including cargo UN number, if applicable; and		X	X
(iii) Amount of each certain dangerous cargo carried.		X	X
(4) *Information for each Crewmember Onboard:*			
(i) Full name;	X	X	X
(ii) Date of birth;	X	X	X
(iii) Nationality;	X	X	X
(iv) Passport or mariners document number (type of identification and number);	X	X	X
(v) Position or duties on the vessel; and	X	X	X
(vi) Where the crewmember embarked (list port or place and country)	X	X	X
(5) *Information for each Person Onboard in Addition to Crew:*			
(i) Full name;	X	X	X
(ii) Date of birth;	X	X	X
(iii) Nationality;	X	X	X
(iv) Passport number; and	X	X	X
(v) Where the person embarked (list port or place and country)	X	X	X
(6) *Operational condition of equipment required by §164.35.*	X	X	X

APPENDIX II

Required information	Vessels not carrying CDC	Vessels carrying CDC	
		Vessels	Towing vessels controlling vessels carrying CDC
(7) *International Safety Management (ISM) Code Notice:*			
(i) The date of issuance for the company's Document of Compliance certificate that covers the vessel;	x	x	x
(ii) The date of issuance for the vessel's Safety Management Certificate; and	x	x	x
(iii) The name of the Flag Administration, or the recognized organization(s) representing the vessel flag administration, that issued those certificates.	x	x	x
(8) [Suspended]			
(9) *International Ship and Port Facility Code (ISPS) Notice:*			
(i) The date of issuance for the vessel's International Ship Security Certificate (ISSC), if any;	x	x	x
(ii) Whether the ISSC, if any, is an initial Interim ISSC, subsequent and consecutive Interim ISSC, or final ISSC;	x	x	x
(iii) Declaration that the approved ship security plan, if any, is being implemented;	x	x	x
(iv) If a subsequent and consecutive Interim ISSC, the reasons therefor;	x	x	x
(v) The name and 24 hour contact information for the Company Security Officer; and;	x	x	x
(vi) The name of the Flag Administration, or the recognised security organisation(s) representing the vessel flag Administration that issued the ISSC	x	x	x

(b) Vessels operating solely between ports or places in the continental United States need submit only the name of and date of arrival and departure for the last port or places visited to meet the requirements in entries (2)(i) and (ii) in Table 160.206 of this section.

(c) You may submit a copy of INS Form 1-418 to meet the requirements of entries (4) and (5) in Table 160.206.

(d) Any vessel planning to enter two or more consecutive ports or places in the United States during a single voyage may submit one consolidated Notification of Arrival at least 96 hours before entering the first port or place of destination. The consolidated notice must include the name of the port or place and estimated arrival and departure date for each destination of the voyage. Any vessel submitting a consolidated notice under this section must still meet the requirements of §160.208 of this part concerning requirements for changes to a NOA.

§160.208 Changes to a submitted NOA.

(a) Unless otherwise specified in this section, when submitted NOA information changes, vessels must submit a notice of change within the times required in §160.212.

(b) Changes in the following information need not be reported:
 (1) Changes in arrival or departure times that are less than six (6) hours;
 (2) Changes in vessel location or position of the vessel at the time of reporting (entry (2)(vi) in Table 160.206);
 (3) Changes to crewmembers' positions or duties on the vessel (entry (5)(v) in Table 160.206).

(c) When reporting changes, submit only the name of the vessel, original NOA submission date, the port of arrival, the specific items to be corrected, and the new location or position of the vessel at the time of reporting. Only changes to NOA information need to be submitted.

§160.210 Methods for submitting a NOA.

(a) *Submission to the National Vessel Movement Center (NVMC).* Except as provided in paragraphs (b) and (c) of this section, vessels must submit NOA information required by §160.206 (entries 1-9 in Table 160.206) to the NVMC, United States Coast Guard, 408 Coast Guard Drive, Kearneysville, WV 25430, by:

(1) Electronic submission via the electronic Notice of Arrival and Departure (eNOAD) and consisting of the following three formats:
 (i) A Web site that can be used to submit NOA information directly to the NVMC, accessible from the NVMC web site at http://www.nvmc.uscg.gov;
 (ii) Electronic submission of Extensible Markup Language (XML) formatted documents via web service;
 (iii) Electronic submission via Microsoft Infopath; contact the NVMC at sans@nvmc.uscg.gov or by telephone at 1-800-708-9823 or 304-264-2502 for more information.

(2) E-mail at sans@nvmc.uscg.gov. Workbook available at http://www.nvmc.uscg.gov;

(3) Fax at 1-800-547-8724 or 304-264-2684. Workbook available at http://www.nvmc.uscg.gov; or,
(4) Telephone at 1-800-708-9823 or 304-264-2502.

(b) *Saint Lawrence Seaway transits.* Those vessels transiting the Saint Lawrence Seaway inbound, bound for a port or place in the United States, may meet the submission requirements of paragraph (a) of this section by submitting the required information to the Saint Lawrence Seaway Development Corporation and the Saint Lawrence Seaway Management Corporation of Canada by fax at 315-764-3235 or at 315-764-3200.

(c) *Seventh Coast Guard District.* Those foreign vessels 300 or less gross tons operating in the Seventh Coast Guard District must submit a NOA to the cognizant Captain of the Port (COTP).

(d) [Suspended]

§160.212 When to submit a NOA.

(a) *Submission of NOA.*
  (1) Except as set out in paragraph (a)(2) of this section, all vessels must submit NOAs within the times required in paragraph (a)(3) of this section.
  (2) Towing vessels, when in control of a vessel carrying CDC and operating solely between ports or places in the continental United States, must submit a NOA before departure but at least 12 hours before departure but at least 12 hours before entering the port or place of destination.
  (3) Times for submitting NOAs are as follows:

If your voyage time is:-	You must submit a NOA :-
(i) 96 hours or more; or	At least 96 hours before entering the port or place of destination; or
(ii) Less than 96 hours	Before departure but at least 24 hours before entering the port or place of destination.

(b) *Submission of changes to NOA.*
  (1) Except as set out in paragraph (b)(2) of this section, vessels must submit changes in NOA information within the times required in paragraph (b)(3) of this section.
  (2) Towing vessels, when in control of a vessel carrying CDC and operating solely between ports or places in the continental United States, must submit changes to a NOA as soon as practicable but at least 6 hours before entering the port or place of destination.
  (3) Times for submitting changes to NOAs are as follows:

If your remaining voyage time is :-	Then you must submit changes to a NOA :-
(i) 96 hours or more;	As soon as practicable but at least 24 hours before entering the port or place of destination;
(ii) Less than 96 hours but not less than 24 hours; or	As soon as practicable but at least 24 hours before entering the port or place of destination; or
(iii Less than 24 hours	As soon as practicable but at least 24 hours before entering the port or place of destination;

(c) [Suspended]

§160.214 Waivers.

The Captain of the Port may waive, within that Captain of the Port's designated zone, any of the requirements of this subpart for any vessel or class of vessels upon finding that the vessel, route, area of operations, conditions of the voyage, or other circumstances are such that application of this subpart is unnecessary or impractical for purposes of safety, environmental protection, or national security.

§160.215 Notice of hazardous conditions.

Whenever there is a hazardous condition either aboard a vessel or caused by a vessel or its operation, the owner, agent, master, operator, or person in charge shall immediately notify the nearest Coast Guard Sector Office or Group Office. (Compliance with this section does not relieve responsibility for the written report required by 46 CFR 4.05-10).

APPENDIX III

CODE OF FEDERAL REGULATIONS TITLE 33 — NAVIGATION AND NAVIGABLE WATERS

PART 161 — VESSEL TRAFFIC MANAGEMENT

Appendix III contains extracts from the above regulations issued by the United States Department of Commerce. For a complete description of this part see 33 CFR 161.

Subpart A — Vessel Traffic Services
General Rules

§161.1 Purpose and Intent.
(a) The purpose of this part is to promulgate regulations implementing and enforcing certain sections of the Ports and Waterways Safety Act (PWSA) setting-up a national system of Vessel Traffic Services that will enhance navigation, vessel safety, and marine environmental protection, and promote safe vessel movement by reducing the potential for collisions, rammings and groundings, and the loss of lives and property associated with these incidents within VTS areas established hereunder.

(b) Vessel Traffic Services provide the mariner with information related to the safe navigation of a waterway. This information, coupled with the mariner's compliance with the provisions set forth in this part, enhances the safe routing of vessels through congested waterways or waterways of particular hazard. Under certain circumstances, a VTS may issue directions to control the movement of vessels in order to minimize the risk of collision between vessels, or damage to property or the environment.

(c) The owner, operator, charterer, master or person directing the movement of a vessel remains at all times responsible for the manner in which the vessel is operated and maneuvered, and is responsible for the safe navigation of the vessel under all circumstances. Compliance with these rules or with a direction from the VTS is at all times contingent upon the exigencies of safe navigation.

(d) Nothing in this part is intended to relieve any vessel, owner, operator, charterer, master, or person directing the movement of a vessel from the consequences of any neglect to comply with this part or any other applicable law or regulations (e.g. the International Regulations for Prevention of Collisions at Sea, 1972 (72 COLREGS) or the Inland Navigation Rules) or of the neglect of any precaution which may be required by the ordinary practice of seamen, or by the special circumstances of the case.

§161.2 Definitions.
For the purposes of this part:

Cooperative Vessel Traffic Services (CVTS) means the system of vessel traffic management established and jointly operated by the United States and Canada within adjoining waters. In addition, CVTS facilitates traffic movement and anchorages, avoids jurisdictional disputes, and renders assistance in emergencies in adjoining United States and Canadian waters.

Hazardous Vessel Operating Condition means any condition related to a vessel's ability to safely navigate or maneuver, and includes, but is not limited to:

(1) The absence or malfunction of vessel operating equipment, such as propulsion machinery, steering gear, radar system, gyrocompass, depth sounding device, automatic radar plotting aid (ARPA), radiotelephone, Automatic Identification System equipment, navigational lighting, sound signalling devices or similar equipment.

(2) Any condition on board the vessel likely to impair navigation, such as lack of current nautical charts and publications, personnel shortage, or similar condition.

(3) Vessel characteristics that affect or restrict maneuverability, such as cargo or tow arrangement, trim, loaded condition, underkeel or overhead clearance, speed capabilities, power availability, or similar characteristics, which may affect the positive control or safe handling of the vessel or the tow.

Precautionary Area means a routing measure comprising an area within defined limits where vessels must navigate with particular caution and within which the direction of traffic may be recommended.

Navigable waters means all navigable waters of the United States, including the territorial sea of the United States, extending to 12 nautical miles from United States baselines, as described in Presidential Proclamation No 5928 of December 27, 1988.

Towing Vessel means any commercial vessel engaged in towing another vessel astern, alongside, or by pushing ahead.

Vessel Movement Center (VMC) means the shore-based facility that operates the vessel tracking system for a Vessel Movement Reporting System (VMRS) area or sector within such an area. The VMC does not necessarily have the capability or qualified personnel to interact with marine traffic, nor does it necessarily respond to traffic situations developing in the area, as does a Vessel Traffic Service (VTS).

Vessel Movement Reporting System (VMRS) means a mandatory reporting system used to monitor and track vessel movements. This is accomplished by a vessel providing information under established procedures as set forth in this part in the areas defined in Table 161.12 (c) (VTS and VMRS Centers, Call Signs/MMSI, Designated Frequencies, and Monitoring Areas).

Vessel Movement Reporting System (VMRS) User means a vessel, or an owner, operator, charterer, master, or person directing the movement of a vessel, that is required to participate in a VMRS.

Vessel Traffic Center (VTC) means the shore-based facility that operates the vessel traffic service for the Vessel Traffic Service area or sector within such an area.

Vessel Traffic Service (VTS) means a service implemented by the United States Coast Guard designed to improve the safety and efficiency of vessel traffic and to protect the environment. The VTS has the capability to interact with marine traffic and respond to traffic situations developing in the VTS area.

Vessel Traffic Service Area or VTS Area means the geographical area encompassing a specific VTS area of service. This area of service may be subdivided into sectors for the purpose of allocating responsibility to individual Vessel Traffic Centers or to identify different operating requirements.

> **Note:** Although regulatory jurisdiction is limited to the navigable waters of the United States, certain vessels will be encouraged or may be required, as a condition of port entry, to report beyond this area to facilitate traffic management within the VTS area.

VTS Special Area means a waterway within a VTS area in which special operating requirements apply.

VTS User means a vessel, or an owner, operator, charterer, master, or person directing the movement of a vessel, that is:
  (a) Subject to the Bridge-to-Bridge Radiotelephone Act; or
  (b) Required to participate in a VMRS within a VTS area (VMRS User).

VTS User's Manual means the manual established and distributed by the VTS to provide the mariner with a description of the services offered and rules in force for that VTS. Additionally, the manual may include chartlets showing the area and sector boundaries, general navigational information about the area, and procedures, radio frequencies, reporting provisions and other information which may assist the mariner while in the VTS area.

§161.3 Applicability.

The provisions of this subpart shall apply to each VTS User and may also apply to any vessel while underway or at anchor on the navigable waters of the United States within a VTS area, to the extent the VTS considers necessary.

§161.4 Requirement to carry the rules.

Each VTS User shall carry on board and maintain for ready reference a copy of these rules.

> **Note:** These rules are contained in the applicable U.S. Coast Pilot, the VTS User's Manual which may be obtained by contacting the appropriate VTS, and periodically published in the Local Notice to Mariners. The VTS User's Manual and the World VTS Guide, an International Maritime Organisation (IMO) recognised publication, contain additional information which may assist the prudent mariner while in the appropriate VTS area.

§161.5 Deviations from the rules.

(a) Requests to deviate from any provision in this part, either for an extended period of time or if anticipated before the start of a transit, must be submitted in writing to the appropriate District Commander. Upon receipt of the written request, the District Commander may authorize a deviation if it is determined that such a deviation provides a level of safety equivalent to that provided by the required measure or is a maneuver considered necessary for safe navigation under the circumstances. An application for an authorized deviation must state the need and fully describe the proposed alternative to the required measure.

(b) Requests to deviate from any provision in this part due to circumstances that develop during a transit or immediately preceding a transit, may be made verbally to the appropriate VTS Director. Requests to deviate shall be made as far in advance as practicable. Upon receipt of the request, the VTS Director may authorize a deviation if it is determined that, based on vessel handling characteristics, traffic density, radar contacts, environmental conditions and other relevant information, such a deviation provides a level of safety equivalent to that provided by the required measure or is a maneuver considered necessary for safe navigation under the circumstances.

Services, VTS measures, and Operating Requirements

§161.10 Services.

To enhance navigation and vessel safety, and to protect the marine environment, a VTS may issue advisories, or respond to vessel requests for information, on reported conditions within the VTS area, such as:
  (a) Hazardous conditions or circumstances;
  (b) Vessel congestion;
  (c) Traffic density;
  (d) Environmental conditions;
  (e) Aids to navigation status;
  (f) Anticipated vessel encounters;
  (g) Another vessel's name, type, position, hazardous vessel operating conditions, if applicable, and intended navigational movements, as reported;
  (h) Temporary measures in effect;
  (i) A description of local harbor operations and conditions, such as ferry routes, dredging, and so forth;
  (j) Anchorage availability; or
  (k) Other information or special circumstances.

§161.11 VTS measures.

(a) A VTS may issue measures or directions to enhance navigation and vessel safety and to protect the marine environment, such as, but not limited to:
  (1) Designating temporary reporting points and procedures;
  (2) Imposing vessel operating requirements; or
  (3) Establishing vessel traffic routing schemes.
(b) During conditions of vessel congestion, restricted visibility, adverse weather, or other hazardous circumstances, a VTS may control, supervise, or otherwise manage traffic, by specifying times of entry, movement, or departure to, from or within a VTS area.

APPENDIX III

§161.12 Vessel operating requirements.
(a) Subject to the exigencies of safe navigation, a VTS User shall comply with all measures established or directions issued by a VTS.

(b) If, in a specific circumstance, a VTS User is unable to safely comply with a measure or direction issued by the VTS, the VTS User may deviate only to the extent necessary to avoid endangering persons, property or the environment. The deviation shall be reported to the VTS as soon as is practicable.

(c) When not exchanging voice communications, a VTS User must maintain a listening watch as required by §26.04(e) of this chapter on the VTS frequency designated in Table 161.12(c) (VTS and VMRS Centers, Call Signs/MMSI, Designated Frequencies, and Monitoring Areas). In addition, the VTS User must respond promptly when hailed and communicate in the English language.

Note to §161.12(c): As stated in 47 CFR 80.148(b), a very high frequency watch on Channel 16 (156.800 Mhz) is not required on vessels subject to the Vessel Bridge-to-Bridge Radiotelephone Act and participating in a Vessel Traffic Service (VTS) system when the watch is maintained on both the vessel bridge-to-bridge frequency and a designated VTS frequency.

(d) As soon as practicable, a VTS User shall notify the VTS of any of the following:
  (1) A marine casualty as defined in 46 CFR 4.05-1;
  (2) Involvement in the ramming of a fixed or floating object;
  (3) A pollution incident as defined in §151.15 of this chapter;
  (4) A defect or discrepancy in an aid to navigation;
  (5) A hazardous condition as defined in §160.203 of this chapter;
  (6) Improper operation of vessel equipment required by Part 164 of this chapter;
  (7) A situation involving hazardous materials for which a report is required by 49 CFR 176.48; and
  (8) A hazardous vessel operating condition as defined in §161.2.

§161.13 VTS Special Area Operating Requirements.
The following operating requirements apply within a VTS Special Area:
  (a) A VTS User shall, if towing astern, do so with as short a hawser as safety and good seamanship permits.
  (b) A VMRS User shall:
    (1) Not enter or get underway in the area without prior approval of the VTS;
    (2) Not enter a VTS Special Area if a hazardous vessel operating condition or circumstance exists;
    (3) Not meet, cross or overtake any other VMRS User in the area without prior approval of the VTS; and
    (4) Before meeting, crossing or overtaking any other VMRS User in the area, communicate on the designated vessel bridge-to-bridge radiotelephone frequency, intended navigation movements, and any other information necessary in order to make safe passing arrangements. This requirement does not relieve a vessel of any duty prescribed by the International Regulations for Prevention of Collisions at Sea, 1972 (72 COLREGS) or the Inland Navigation Rules.

Subpart B — Vessel Movement Reporting System

§161.15 Purpose and intent.
(a) A Vessel Movement Reporting System (VMRS) is a system used to monitor and track vessel movements within a VTS or VMRS area. This is accomplished by requiring that vessels provide information under established procedures as set forth in this part, or as directed by the Center.

(b) To avoid imposing an undue reporting burden or unduly congesting radiotelephone frequencies, reports shall be limited to information which is essential to achieve the objectives of the VMRS. These reports are consolidated into three reports (sailing plan, position, and final).

§161.16 Applicability.
Unless otherwise stated, the provisions of this subpart shall apply to the following vessels and VMRS Users:
  (a) Every power-driven vessel of 40 meters (approximately 131 feet) or more in length, while navigating;
  (b) Every towing vessel of 8 meters (approximately 26 feet) or more in length, while navigating; or
  (c) Every vessel certificated to carry 50 or more passengers for hire, when engaged in trade.

§161.17 Definitions.
As used in this subpart:
  Center means a Vessel Traffic Center or Vessel Movement Center.
  Published means available in a widely distributed and publicly available medium (e.g., VTS User's Manual, ferry schedule, Notice to Mariners).

§161.18 Reporting requirements.
(a) A Center may:
  (1) Direct a vessel to provide any of the information set forth in Table 161.18(a) (IMO Standard Ship Reporting System);
  (2) Establish other means of reporting for those vessels unable to report on the designated frequency; or
  (3) Require reports from a vessel in sufficient time to allow advance vessel traffic planning.

(b) All reports required by this part shall be made as soon as is practicable on the frequency designated in Table 161.12(c) (VTS and VMRS Centers, Call Signs/MMSI, Designated Frequencies, and Monitoring Areas).

(c) When not exchanging communications, a VMRS User must maintain a listening watch as described in § 26.04(e) of this chapter on the frequency designated in Table 161.12(c) (VTS and VMRS Centers, Call Signs/MMSI, Designated Frequencies, and Monitoring Areas). In addition, the VMRS User must respond promptly when hailed and communicate in the English language.

Note: As stated in 47 CFR 80.148(b), a VHF watch on Channel 16 (156.800 Mhz) is not required on vessels subject to the Vessels Bridge-to-Bridge Radiotelephone Act and participating in a Vessel Traffic Service (VTS) system when the watch is maintained on both the vessel bridge-to-bridge frequency and a designated VTS frequency.

(d) A vessel must report:
  (1) Any significant deviation from its Sailing Plan, as defined in §161.19, or from previously reported information; or
  (2) Any intention to deviate from a VTS issued measure or vessel traffic routeing system.
(e) When reports required by this part include time information, such information shall be given using the local time zone in effect and the 24 hour military clock system.

§161.19 Sailing Plan (SP).

Unless otherwise stated, at least 15 minutes before navigating a VTS area, a vessel must report the:
  (a) Vessel name and type;
  (b) Position;
  (c) Destination and ETA;
  (d) Intended route;
  (e) Time and point of entry; and
  (f) Dangerous cargo on board, or in its tow, as defined in §160.203 of this chapter, and other required information as set out in §160.211 and §160.213 of this chapter, if applicable.

§161.20 Position Report (PR).

A vessel must report its name and position:
  (a) Upon point of entry into a VMRS area;
  (b) At designated points as set forth in Subpart C; or
  (c) When directed by the Center.

§161.21 Automated reporting.

(a) Unless otherwise directed, vessels equipped with an Automatic Identification System (AIS) are required to make continuous, all stations, AIS broadcasts, in lieu of voice position reports, to those Centers denoted in Table 161.12(c) of this part.
(b) Should an AIS become non-operational, while or prior to navigating a VMRS area, it should be restored to operating condition as soon as possible, and, until restored a vessel must:
  (1) Notify the Center;
  (2) Make voice radio position reports at designated reporting points as required by §161.20(b) of this part; and
  (3) Make any other reports as directed by the Center.

§161.22 Final Report (FR).

A vessel must report its name and position:
  (a) On arrival at its destination; or
  (b) When leaving a VTS area.

§161.23 Reporting exemptions.

(a) Unless otherwise directed, the following vessels are exempted from providing Position and Final Reports due to the nature of their operation:
  (1) Vessels on a published schedule and route;
  (2) Vessels operating within an area of a radius of three nautical miles or less; or
  (3) Vessels escorting another vessel or assisting another vessel in maneuvering procedures.
(b) A vessel described in paragraph (a) of this section must:
  (1) Provide a Sailing Plan at least 5 minutes but not more than 15 minutes before navigating within the VMRS area; and
  (2) If it departs from its promulgated schedule by more than 15 minutes or changes its limited operating area, make the established VMRS reports, or report as directed.

APPENDIX IV

CODE OF FEDERAL REGULATIONS TITLE 33 — NAVIGATION AND NAVIGABLE WATERS

PART 164 — NAVIGATION SAFETY REGULATIONS

Appendix IV contains extracts from the above regulations issued by the United States Department of Commerce. For a complete description of this part see 33 CFR 164.

§164.01 Applicability.

(a) This part (except as specifically limited by this section) applies to each self-propelled vessel of 1600 or more gross tons (except as provided in paragraphs (c) and (d) of this section or for foreign vessels described in §164.02) when it is operating in the navigable waters of the United States except the St. Lawrence Seaway.

(c) Provisions of §164.11(a)2 and (c), §164.30, §164.33 and §164.46 do not apply to warships or other vessels owned, leased, or operated by the United States Government and used only in government non-commercial service when these vessels are equipped with electronic navigation systems that have met the applicable agency regulations regarding navigation safety.

(d) Provisions of §164.46 apply to some self-propelled vessels of less than 1600 gross tonnage.

§164.02 Applicability exception for foreign vessels.

(a) Except as provided in §164.46(a)(2), §§164.38 and 164.39 this part does not apply to vessels that:
  (1) Are not destined for, or departing from, a port or place subject to the jurisdiction of the United States; and
  (2) Are in:
    (i) Innocent passage through the territorial sea of the United States; or
    (ii) Transit through navigable waters of the United States which form a part of an international strait.

§164.03 Incorporation by reference. (See 33 CFR 164.)

§164.11 Navigation underway: General.

The owner, master, or person in charge of each vessel underway shall ensure that:
  (a) The wheelhouse is constantly manned by persons who:
    (1) Direct and control the movement of the vessel; and
    (2) Fix the vessel's position;
  (b) Each person performing a duty described in paragraph (a) of this section is competent to perform that duty;
  (c) The position of the vessel at each fix is plotted on a chart of the area and the person directing the movement of the vessel is informed of the vessel's position;
  (d) Electronic and other navigational equipment, external fixed aids to navigation, geographic reference points, and hydrographic contours are used when fixing the vessel's position;
  (e) Buoys alone are not used to fix the vessel's position;

Note: Buoys are aids to navigation placed in approximate positions to alert the mariner to hazards to navigation or to indicate the orientation of a channel. Buoys may not maintain an exact position because strong or varying currents, heavy seas, ice, and collisions with vessels can move or sink them or set them adrift. Although buoys may corroborate a position fixed by other means, buoys cannot be used to fix a position: however, if no other aids are available, buoys alone may he used to establish an estimated position.

  (f) The danger of each closing visual or each closing radar contact is evaluated and the person directing the movement of the vessel knows the evaluation;
  (g) Rudder orders are executed as given;
  (h) Engine speed and direction orders are executed as given;
  (i) Magnetic variation and deviation and gyrocompass errors are known and correctly applied by the person directing the movement of the vessel;
  (j) A person whom he has determined is competent to steer the vessel is in the wheelhouse at all times (See also 46 U.S.C. 8702 (d), which requires an able seaman at the wheel on US vessels of 100 gross tons or more in narrow or crowded waters or during low visibility);
  (k) If a pilot other than a member of the vessel's crew is employed, the pilot is informed of the draft, maneuvering characteristics, and peculiarities of the vessel and of any abnormal circumstances on the vessel that may affect its safe navigation.
  (l) Current velocity and direction for the area to be transited are known by the person directing the movement of the vessel;
  (m) Predicted set and drift are known by the person directing the movement of the vessel;
  (n) Tidal state for the area to be transited is known by the person directing the movement of the vessel;
  (o) The vessel's anchors are ready for letting go;
  (p) The person directing the movement of the vessel sets the vessel's speed with consideration for:
    (1) The prevailing visibility and weather conditions;
    (2) The proximity of the vessel to fixed shore and marine structures;
    (3) The tendency of the vessel underway to squat and suffer impairment of maneuverability when there is small underkeel clearance;

(4) The comparative proportions of the vessel and the channel;
(5) The density of marine traffic;
(6) The damage that might be caused by the vessel's wake;
(7) The strength and direction of the current; and
(8) Any local vessel speed limit;
(q) The tests required by §164.25 are made and recorded in the vessel's log; and
(r) The equipment required by this part is maintained in operable condition.
(s) Upon entering US waters, the steering wheel or lever on the navigating bridge is operated to determine if the steering equipment is operating properly under manual control, unless the vessel has been steered under manual control from the navigating bridge within the preceding 2 hours, except when operating on the Great Lakes and their connecting and tributary waters.
(t) At least two of the steering gear power units on the vessel are in operation when such units are capable of simultaneous operation, except when operating on the Great Lakes and their connecting and tributary waters.
(u) On each passenger vessel meeting the requirements of the International Convention for the Safety of Life at Sea, 1960 (SOLAS 60) and on each cargo vessel meeting the requirements of SOLAS 74 as amended in 1981, the number of steering gear power units necessary to move the rudder from 35° on either side to 30° on the other in not more than 28 seconds must be in simultaneous operation.

§164.13 Navigation underway: tankers.

(b) Each tanker must have an engineering watch capable of monitoring the propulsion system, communicating with the bridge, and implementing manual control measures immediately when necessary. The watch must be physically present in the machinery spaces or in the main control space and must consist of at least an engineer with an appropriately endorsed license or merchant mariner credential.
(c) Each tanker must navigate with at least two deck officers with an appropriately endorsed license or merchant mariner credential on watch on the bridge, one of whom may be a pilot. In waters where a pilot is required, the second officer must be an individual holding an appropriately endorsed license or merchant mariner credential and assigned to the vessel as master, mate, or officer in charge of a navigational watch, who is separate and distinct from the pilot.
(d) Except as specified in paragraph (e) of this section a tanker may operate with an auto pilot engaged only if all of the following conditions exist:
(1) The operation and performance of the automatic pilot conforms with the standards recommended by the International Maritime Organisation in IMO Resolution A.342(IX).

(2) A qualified helmsman is present at the helm and prepared at all times to assume manual control.
(3) The tanker is not operating in any of the following areas:
   (i) The areas of the traffic separation schemes specified in subchapter P of this chapter.
   (ii) The portions of a shipping safety fairway specified in part 166 of this chapter.
   (iii) An anchorage ground specified in part 110 of this chapter.
   (iv) An area within one-half nautical mile of any US shore.
(e) A tanker equipped with an integrated navigation system, and complying with paragraph (d)(2) of this section, may use the system with the auto pilot engaged while in the areas described in paragraphs (d)(3)(i) and (ii) of this section.

§164.15 Navigation bridge visibility. (See 33 CFR 164.)

§164.19 Requirements for vessels at anchor.

The master or person in charge of each vessel that is anchored shall ensure that:
(a) A proper anchor watch is maintained;
(b) Procedures are followed to detect a dragging anchor; and
(c) Whenever weather, tide, or current conditions are likely to cause the vessel's anchor to drag, action is taken to ensure the safety of the vessel, structures, and other vessels, such as being ready to veer chain, let go a second anchor, or get underway using the vessel's own propulsion or tug assistance.

§164.25 Tests before entering or getting underway.

(a) Except as provided in paragraphs (b) and (c) of this section no person may cause a vessel to enter into or get underway on the navigable waters of the United States unless no more than 12 hours before entering or getting underway, the following equipment has been tested:
(1) Primary and secondary steering gear. The test procedure includes a visual inspection of the steering gear and its connecting linkage, and, where applicable, the operation of the following:
   (i) Each remote steering gear control system.
   (ii) Each steering position located on the navigating bridge.
   (iii) The main steering gear from the alternative power supply, if installed.
   (iv) Each rudder angle indicator in relation to the actual position of the rudder.
   (v) Each remote steering gear control system power failure alarm.
   (vi) Each remote steering gear power unit failure alarm.
   (vii) The full movement of the rudder to the required capabilities of the steering gear.
(2) All internal vessel control communications and vessel control alarms.
(3) Standby or emergency generator, for as long as necessary to show proper functioning, including steady state temperature and pressure readings.

(4) Storage batteries for emergency lighting and other systems in vessel control and propulsion machinery spaces.

(5) Main propulsion machinery, ahead and astern.

(b) Vessels navigating on the Great Lakes and their connecting and tributary waters, having once completed the test requirements of this sub-part, are considered to remain in compliance until arriving at the next port call on the Great Lakes.

(c) Vessels entering the Great Lakes from the St. Lawrence Seaway are considered to be in compliance with this sub-part if the required tests are conducted preparatory to or during the passage of the St. Lawrence Seaway or within one hour of passing Wolfe Island.

(d) No vessel may enter, or be operated on the navigable waters of the United States unless the emergency steering drill described below has been conducted within 48 hours prior to entry and logged in the vessel's logbook, unless the drill is conducted and logged on a regular basis at least once every three months. This drill must include at a minimum the following:

(1) Operation of the main steering gear from within the steering gear compartment.

(2) Operation of the means of communication between the navigating bridge and the steering compartment.

(3) Operation of the alternative power supply for the steering gear if the vessel is so equipped.

§164.30 Charts, publications and equipment: General.

No person may operate or cause the operation of a vessel unless the vessel has the marine charts, publications, and equipment as required by §§164.33 through 164.41 of this part.

§164.33 Charts and publications.

(a) Each vessel must have the following:

(1) Marine charts of the area to be transited, published by the National Ocean Service, US Army Corps of Engineers, or a river authority that:

(i) Are of a large enough scale and have enough detail to make safe navigation of the area possible; and

(ii) Are currently corrected.

(2) For the area to be transited, a currently corrected copy of, or applicable currently corrected extract from, each of the following publications:

(i) US Coast Pilot.

(ii) Coast Guard Light List.

(3) For the area to be transited, the current edition of, or applicable current extract from:

(i) Tide tables published by private entities using data provided by the National Ocean Service.

(ii) Tidal current tables published private entities using data provided by the National Ocean Service, or river current publication issued by the US Army Corps of Engineers, or a river authority.

(b) As an alternative to the requirements for paragraph (a) of this section, a marine chart or publication, or applicable extract, published by a foreign government may be substituted for a US chart and publication required by this section. The chart must be of large enough scale and have enough detail to make safe navigation of the area possible, and must be currently corrected. The publication, or applicable extract, must singly or in combination contain similar information to the US Government publication to make safe navigation of the area possible. The publication or applicable extract must be currently corrected, with the exception of tide and tidal current tables, which must be the current editions.

(c) As used in this section, "currently corrected" means corrected with changes contained in all Notices to Mariners published by National Imagery and Mapping Agency, or an equivalent foreign government publication, reasonably available to the vessel, and that is applicable to the vessel's transit.

§164.35 Equipment: All vessels.

Each vessel must have the following:

(a) A marine radar system for surface navigation.

(b) An illuminated magnetic steering compass, mounted in a binnacle, that can be read at the vessel's main steering stand.

(c) A current magnetic compass deviation table or graph or compass comparison record for the steering compass, in the wheelhouse.

(d) A gyrocompass.

(e) An illuminated repeater for the gyrocompass required by paragraph (d) of this section that is at the main steering stand, unless that gyrocompass is illuminated and is at the main steering stand.

(f) An illuminated rudder angle indicator in the wheelhouse.

(g) The following maneuvering information prominently displayed on a fact sheet in the wheelhouse:

(1) A turning circle diagram to port and starboard that shows the time and distance and advance and transfer required to alter course 90 degrees with maximum rudder angle and constant power settings, for either full and half speeds, or for full and slow speeds. For vessels whose turning circles are essentially the same for both directions, a diagram showing a turning circle in one direction, with a note on the diagram stating that turns to port and starboard are essentially the same, may be substituted.

(2) The time and distance to stop the vessel from either full and half speeds, or from full and slow speeds, while maintaining approximately the initial heading with minimum application of rudder.

(3) For each vessel with a fixed propeller, a table of shaft revolutions per minute for a representative range of speeds.

(4) For each vessel with a controllable pitch propeller, a table of control settings for a representative range of speeds.

(5) For each vessel that is fitted with an auxiliary device to assist in maneuvering,

such as a bow thruster, a table of vessel speeds at which the auxiliary device is effective in maneuvering the vessel.
(6) The maneuvering information for the normal load and normal ballast condition for:
  (i) Calm weather—wind 10 knots or less, calm sea;
  (ii) No current;
  (iii) Deep water conditions-water depth twice the vessel's draft or greater; and
  (iv) Clean hull.
(7) At the bottom of the fact sheet, the following statement:

Warning. The response of the (name of the vessel) may be different from that listed above if any of the following conditions, upon which the maneuvering information is based, are varied:
(1) Calm weather-wind 10 knots or less, calm sea;
(2) No current;
(3) Water depth twice the vessel's draft or greater;
(4) Clean hull; and
(5) Intermediate drafts or unusual trim.

(h) An echo depth sounding device.
(i) A device that can continuously record the depth readings of the vessel's echo depth sounding device except when operating on the Great Lakes and their connecting and tributary waters.
(j) Equipment on the bridge for plotting relative motion.
(k) Simple operating instructions with a block diagram, showing the changeover procedures for remote steering gear control systems and steering gear power units, permanently displayed on the navigating bridge and in the steering gear compartment.
(l) An indicator readable from the centerline conning position showing the rate of revolution of each propeller, except when operating on the Great Lakes and their connecting and tributary waters.
(m) If fitted with controllable pitch propellers, an indicator readable from the centerline conning position showing the pitch and operational mode of such propellers, except when operating on the Great Lakes and their connecting and tributary waters.
(n) If fitted with lateral thrust propellers, an indicator readable from the centerline conning position showing the direction and amount of thrust of such propellers, except when operating on the Great Lakes and their connecting and tributary waters.
(o) A telephone or other means of communication for relaying headings to the emergency steering station. Also, each vessel of 500 gross tons and over and constructed on or after June 9th 1995 must be provided with arrangements for supplying visual compass readings to the emergency steering station.

§164.37 Equipment: Vessels of 10,000 gross tons or more.

(a) Each vessel of 10,000 gross tons or more must have, in addition to the radar system under §164.35(a), a second marine radar system that operates independently of the first.

Note: Independent operation means two completely separate systems, from separate branch power supply circuits or distribution panels to antennas, so that failure of any component of one system will not render the other system inoperative.

(b) On each tanker of 10,000 gross tons or more that is subject to 46 U.S.C. 3708, the dual radar system required by this part must have a short range capability and a long range capability; and each radar must have true north features consisting of a display that is stabilized in azimuth.

§164.38 Automatic radar plotting aids (ARPA). (See 33 CFR 164.)

§164.39 Steering Gear: Foreign Tankers. (See 33 CFR 164).

§164.40 Devices to indicate speed and distance.

(a) Each vessel required to be fitted with an Automatic Radar Plotting Aid (ARPA) under §164.38 must be fitted with a device to indicate speed and distance of the vessel either through the water, or over the ground.

§164.41 Electronic position fixing devices.

(a) Each vessel calling at a port in the continental United States, including Alaska south of Cape Prince of Wales, except each vessel owned or bareboat chartered and operated by the United States, or by a state or its political subdivision, or by a foreign nation, and not engaged in commerce, must have a satellite navigation receiver with:
  (1) Automatic acquisition of satellite signals after initial operator settings have been entered; and
  (2) Position updates derived from satellite information during each usable satellite pass.
(b) A system that is found by the Commandant to meet the intent of the statements of availability, coverage, and accuracy for the U.S. Coastal Confluence Zone (CCZ) contained in the U.S. "Federal Radionavigation Plan" (Report No. DOD–NO 4650.4–P, I or
No. DOT–TSC–RSPA–80–16, I). A person desiring a finding by the Commandant under this subparagraph must submit a written application describing the device to the Coast Guard Deputy Commander for Operations (CG–DCO), 2100 2nd St. SW., Stop 7471, Washington, DC 20593-7471. After reviewing the application, the Commandant may request additional information to establish whether or not the device meets the intent of the Federal Radionavigation Plan.

Note.—The Federal Radionavigation Plan is available from the National Technical Information Service, Springfield, Va. 22161, with the following Government Accession Numbers:

    Vol 1, ADA 116468
    Vol 2, ADA 116469
    Vol 3, ADA 116470
    Vol 4, ADA 116471

§164.42 Rate of turn indicator.

Each vessel of 100,000 gross tons or more shall be fitted with a rate of turn indicator.

§164.46 Automatic Identification System (AIS).

(a) The following vessels must have a properly installed, operational, type approved AIS as of the date specified:
  (1) Self-propelled vessels of 65 ft or more in length, other than passenger and fishing vessels, in commercial service and on an international voyage, not later than December 31st 2004.
  (2) Notwithstanding paragraph (a)(1) of this section, the following self-propelled vessels, that are on an international voyage must also comply with SOLAS, as amended, Chapter V, regulation 19.2.1.6, 19.2.4, and 19.2.3.5 or 19.2.5.1 as appropriate (Incorporated by reference, see §164.03):
    (i) Passenger vessels, of 150 gross tonnage or more, not later than July 1st 2003;
    (ii) Tankers, regardless of tonnage, not later than the first safety survey for safety equipment on or after July 1st 2003.
    (iii) Vessels, other than passenger vessels or tankers, of 50,000 gross tonnage or more, not later than July 1st 2004; and
    (iv) Vessels, other than passenger vessels or tankers, of 300 gross tonnage or more but less than 50,000 gross tonnage, not later than the first safety survey for safety equipment on or after July 1st 2004, but not later than December 31st 2004.
  (3) Notwithstanding paragraphs (a)(1) and (a)(2) of this section, the following vessels, when navigating an area denoted in table 161.12(c) of §161.12, not later than December 31st 2004.
    (i) Self-propelled vessels of 65 ft or more in length, other than fishing vessels and passenger vessels certificated to carry less than 151 passengers for hire, in commercial service;
    (ii) Towing vessels of 26 ft or more in length and more than 600 horsepower, in commercial service;
    (iii) Passenger vessels certificated to carry more than 150 passengers for hire.

§164.51 Deviations from rules: Emergency.

Except for the requirements of §164.53(b), in an emergency, any person may deviate from any rule in this part to the extent necessary to avoid endangering persons, property, or the environment.

§164.53 Deviations from rules and reporting: Non-operating equipment.

(a) If during a voyage any equipment required by this part stops operating properly, the person directing the movement of the vessel may continue to the next port of call, subject to the directions of the District Commander or the Captain of the Port, as provided by 33 CFR 160.
(b) If the vessel's radar, radio navigation receivers, gyrocompass, echo depth sounding device, or primary steering gear stops operating properly, the person directing the movement of the vessel must report or cause to be reported that it is not operating properly to the nearest Captain of the Port, District Commander, or, if participating in a Vessel Traffic Service, to the Vessel Traffic Center, as soon as possible.

§164.55 Deviations from rules: Continuing operation or period of time.

The Captain of the Port, upon written application, may authorize a deviation from any rule in this part if he determines that the deviation does not impair the safe navigation of the vessel under anticipated conditions and will not result in a violation of the rules for preventing collisions at sea. The authorization may be issued for vessels operating in the waters under the jurisdiction of the Captain of the Port for any continuing operation or period of time the Captain of the Port specifies.

§164.61 Marine casualty reporting and record retention.

When a vessel is involved in a marine casualty as defined in 46 CFR 4.03-1, the master or person in charge of the vessel shall:
  (a) Ensure compliance with 46 CFR 4.05, "Notice of Marine Casualty and Voyage Records," and
  (b) Ensure that the voyage records required by 46 CFR 4.05-15 are retained for:
    (1) 30 days after the casualty if the vessel remains in the navigable waters of the United States; or
    (2) 30 days after the return of the vessel to a United States port if the vessel departs the navigable waters of the United States within 30 days after the marine casualty.

§164.70 Definitions. (See 33 CFR 164.)

§164.72 Navigational safety equipment, charts or maps, and publications required on towing vessels. (See 33 CFR 164.)

§164.74 Towline and terminal gear for towing astern. (See 33 CFR 164.)

§164.76 Towline and terminal gear for towing alongside and pushing ahead. (See 33 CFR 164.)

§164.78 Navigation underway: Towing vessels. (See 33 CFR 164.)

§164.80 Tests, inspections and voyage planning. (See 33 CFR 164.)

§164.82 Maintenance, failure and reporting. (See 33 CFR 164.)

APPENDIX V

CODE OF FEDERAL REGULATIONS TITLE 33 — NAVIGATION AND NAVIGABLE WATERS

PART 165 — REGULATED NAVIGATION AREAS AND LIMITED ACCESS AREAS — EXTRACTS

Appendix V contains extracts from the above regulations issued by the United States Department of Commerce.

Regulations specific to this volume are given by title only where the area concerned falls wholly within pilotage waters; where the regulation affects an area outside pilotage waters, a summary of the regulation is given.

For a complete description of this part see 33 CFR 165.

Subpart A — General

§165.5 Establishment procedures

(a) A safety zone, security zone, or regulated navigation area may be established on the initiative of any authorised Coast Guard official.

(b) Any person may request that a safety zone, security zone, or regulated navigation area may be established. Except as provided in paragraph (c) of this section, each request must be submitted in writing to either the Captain of the Port or District Commander.

(c) Safety Zones and Security Zones. If, for good cause, the request for a safety zone or security zone is made less than 5 working days before the zone is to be established, the request may be made orally, but it must be followed by a written request within 24 hours.

§165.7 Notification

(a) The establishment of these limited access areas and regulated navigation areas is considered rule making. The procedures used to notify persons of the establishment of these areas vary depending upon the circumstances and emergency conditions. Notification may be made by marine broadcasts, local notice to mariners, local news media, distribution in leaflet form, and on-scene oral notice, as well as publication in the Federal Register.

(b) Notification normally contains the physical boundaries of the area, the reasons for the rule, its estimated duration, and the method of obtaining authorization to enter the area, if applicable, and special navigational rules, if applicable.

§165.8 Geographic coordinates

Geographic coordinates expressed in terms of latitude or longitude, or both, are not intended for plotting on maps or charts whose referenced horizontal datum is the North American Datum of 1983 (NAD 83), unless such geographic coordinates are expressly labelled NAD 83. Geographic coordinates without the NAD 83 reference may be plotted on maps or charts referenced to NAD 83 only after application of the appropriate corrections that are published on the particular map or chart being used.

§165.9 Geographic application of limited and controlled access areas and regulated navigation areas.

(a) *General.* The geographic application of the limited and controlled access areas and regulated navigation areas in this part are determined based on the statutory authority under which each is created.

(b) *Safety zones and regulated navigation areas.* These zones and areas are created under the authority of the Ports and Waterways Safety Act, 33 U.S.C. 1221-1232.

(c) *Security zones.* These zones have two sources of authority — the Ports and Waterways Safety Act, 33 U.S.C. 1221-1232, and the Act of June 15, 1917, as amended by both the Magnuson Act of August 9, 1950 ("Magnuson Act"), 50 U.S.C. 191-195, and sec. 104 of the Maritime Transportation Security Act of 2002.

(d) *Naval vessel protection zones.* These zones are issued under the authority of 14 U.S.C. 91 and 633 and may be established in waters subject to the jurisdiction of the United States as defined in §2.38 of this chapter, including the territorial sea to a seaward limit of 12 nautical miles from the baseline.

Subpart B — Regulated Navigation Areas

§165.10 Regulated navigation area.

A regulated navigation area is a water area within a defined boundary for which regulations for vessels navigating within the area have been established under this part.

§165.11 Vessel operating requirements (regulations).

Each District Commander may control vessel traffic in an area which is determined to have hazardous conditions, by issuing regulations:

(a) Specifying times of vessel entry, movement, or departure to, from, within, or through ports, harbors, or other waters;

(b) Establishing vessel size, speed, draft limitations, and operating conditions; and

(c) Restricting vessel operation, in a hazardous area or under hazardous conditions, to vessels which have particular operating characteristics or capabilities which are considered necessary for safe operation under the circumstances.

§165.13 General Regulations.

(a) The master of a vessel in a regulated navigation area shall operate the vessel in accordance with the regulations contained in Subpart F.

(b) No person may cause or authorize the operation of a vessel in a regulated navigation area contrary to the regulations in this part.

Subpart C — Safety Zones

§165.20 Safety zones.

A safety zone is a water area, shore area, or water and shore area, to which, for safety or environmental purposes, access is limited to authorised persons, vehicles, or vessels. It may be stationary and described by fixed limits or it may be described as a zone around a vessel in motion.

§165.23 General regulations.

Unless otherwise provided for in this part:
(a) No person may enter a safety zone unless authorised by the Captain of the Port or the District Commander;
(b) No person may bring or cause to be brought into a safety zone any vehicle, vessel or object unless authorised by the Captain of the Port or the District Commander;
(c) No person may remain in a safety zone or allow any vehicle, vessel or object to remain in a safety zone unless authorised by the Captain of the Port or the District Commander; and
(d) Each person in a safety zone who has notice of a lawful order or direction shall obey the order or direction of the Captain of the Port or District Commander issued to carry out the purposes of this subpart.

Subpart D — Security Zones

§165.30 Security zones.

(a) A security zone is an area of land, water, or land and water which is so designated by the Captain of the Port or District Commander for such time as is necessary to prevent damage or injury to any vessel or waterfront facility, to safeguard ports, harbors, territories, or waters of the United States or to secure the observance of the rights and obligations of the United States.
(b) The purpose of a security zone is to safeguard from destruction, loss or injury from sabotage or other subversive acts, accidents, or other causes of a similar nature:
(1) Vessels,
(2) Harbors,
(3) Ports and
(4) Waterfront facilities in the United States and all territory, continental or insular, that is subject to the jurisdiction of the United States.

§165.33 General regulations.

Unless otherwise provided in the special regulations in Subpart F of this part:
(a) No person or vessel may enter or remain in a security zone without the permission of the Captain of the Port;
(b) Each person and vessel in a security zone shall obey any direction or order of the Captain of the Port;
(c) The Captain of the Port may take possession and control of any vessel in the security zone;
(d) The Captain of the Port may remove any person, vessel, article, or thing from a security zone;
(e) No person may board, or take or place any article or thing on board, any vessel in a security zone without the permission of the Captain of the Port; and
(f) No person may take or place any article or thing upon any waterfront facility in a security zone without the permission of the Captain of the Port.

Subpart E — Restricted Waterfront Areas

§165.40 Restricted Waterfront Areas.

The Commandant, may direct the COTP to prevent access to waterfront facilities, and port and harbor areas, including vessels and harbor craft therein. This section may apply to persons who do not possess the credentials outlined in 33 CFR 125.09 when certain shipping activities are conducted that are outlined in 33 CFR 125.15.

Subpart F — Specific Regulated Navigation Areas and Limited Access Areas

§165.100 Regulated navigation area: Navigable waters within the First Coast Guard District.

§165.101 Regulated navigation area: Kittery, Maine.

§165.102 Security Zone: Walkers Point, Kennebunkport, Maine.

§165.103 Safety and Security Zones; LPG Vessel Transits in Portland, Maine, Captain of the Port Zone, Portsmouth Harbor, Portsmouth, New Hampshire.

§165.105 Security Zones; Passenger Vessels, Portland, Maine, Captain of the Port Zone.

§165.110 Safety and Security Zone; Liquefied Natural Gas Carrier Transits and Anchorage Operations, Boston, Massachusetts.

(b) *Location.* The following areas are safety and security zones:
(1) *Vessels underway.* All navigable waters of the United States within the Captain of the Port (COTP) Boston zone, as defined in 33 CFR 3.05-10, two miles ahead and one mile astern, and 500 yards on each side of any liquified natural gas carrier (LNGC) vessel while underway.
(2) *Vessels anchored in Broad Sound.* All waters within a 500 yard radius of any anchored LNGC vessel located in the waters of Broad Sound bounded by a line starting at position 42°25′N 070°58′W; then running SE to 42°22′N 070°56′W; then running E to 42°22′N 070°50′W; then running N to 42°25′N 070°50′W; then running W back to the starting point (NAD 83).
(3) *Vessels moored at the Distrigas LNG facility.* All waters within a 400 yard radius of any LNGC vessel moored at the Distrigas LNG facility in Everett, Ma.
(4) *Vessels calling on a deepwater port.* All waters within a 500 metre radius of any LNGC vessel engaged in regasification or transfer, or otherwise moored, anchored, or affixed to a deepwater port listed in 33 CFR 150.490 and falling within the waters of the Boston COTP Zone, as defined in 33 CFR 3.05-10.

(c) *Regulations.*
  (1) In accordance with the general regulations in §§165.23 and 165.33 of this part, entry into or movement within these zones is prohibited unless authorized by the Captain of the Port, Boston, or his/her authorized representative.
  (2) No person or vessel may enter the waters within the boundaries of the safety and security zones described in paragraph (b) of this section unless previously authorized by the COTP Boston, or his/her authorized representative. However, LNGCs and support vessels, as defined in 33 CFR 148.5, operating in the vicinity of NEGDWP are authorized to enter and move within such zones in the normal course of their operations following the requirements set forth in 33 CFR 150.340 and 150.345, respectively.
  (3) All vessels operating within the safety and security zones described in paragraph (b) of this section must comply with the instructions of the COTP or his/her authorized representative.

§165.111 Safety Zone; Boston Harbor; Boston, Massachusetts.

§165.112 Safety Zone; USS CASSIN YOUNG, Boston, Massachusetts.

§165.114 Safety and Security Zones; Escorted Vessels - Boston Harbor, Massachusetts.

§165.115 Safety and Security Zones; Pilgrim Nuclear Power Plant, Plymouth, Massachusetts.

(a) *Location.* All waters of Cape Cod Bay and land adjacent to those waters enclosed by a line beginning at position:
  41°56′59·3″N 70°34′58·5″W, thence to:
  41°57′12·2″N 70°34′41·9″W, thence to:
  41°56′42·3″N 70°34′00·1″W, thence to:
  41°56′29·5″N 70°34′14·5″W.
(b) *The regulations:*
  (1) In accordance with the general regulations in §§165.23 and 165.33 of this part, entry into or movement within these zones this zone is prohibited unless authorized by the Captain of the Port, Boston.

§165.116 Safety and Security Zones; Salem and Boston Harbors, Massachusetts.

§165.117 Regulated Navigation Areas, Safety and Security Zones: Deepwater Ports, First Coast Guard District.

(a) *Location.*
  (1) *Regulated navigation areas.* All waters within a 1000 meter radius of the geographical positions set forth in paragraph (a)(3) of this section are designated as regulated navigation areas.
  (2) *Safety and security zones.* All waters within a 500 meter radius of the geographic positions set forth in paragraph (a)(3) of this section are designated as safety and security zones.
  (3) *Coordinates.*
    (i) The geographic coordinates forming the loci for the regulated navigation areas, safety and security zones for the Northeast Gateway Deepwater Port are: 42°23′38″N, 070°35′31″W; and 42°23′56″N, 070°37′00″W. (NAD 83).
    (ii) [Reserved]
(b) *Definitions.* As used in this section—
  Authorized representative means a Coast Guard commissioned, warrant, or petty officer or a Federal, State, or local law enforcement officer assisting the Captain of the Port (COTP) Boston.
  Deepwater port means any facility or structure meeting the definition of deepwater port 33 CFR 148.5.
  Dredge means fishing gear consisting of a mouth frame attached to a holding bag constructed of metal rings or mesh.
  Support vessel means any vessel meeting the definition of support vessel in 33 CFR 148.5.
  Trap means a portable, enclosed device with one or more gates or entrances and one or more lines attached to surface floats used for fishing. Also called a pot.
(c) *Applicability.* This section applies to all vessels operating in the regulated navigation areas set forth in paragraph (a) of this section, except—
  (1) Those vessels conducting cargo transfer operations with the deepwater ports whose coordinates are provided in paragraph (a)(3) of this section.
  (2) Support vessels operating in conjunction therewith, and
  (3) Coast Guard vessels or other law enforcement vessels operated by or under the direction of an authorized representative of the COTP Boston.
(d) *Regulations.*
  (1) No vessel may anchor, engage in diving operations, or commercial fishing using nets, dredges, traps (pots), or use of remotely operated vehicles (ROVs) in the regulated navigation areas set forth in paragraph (a)(1) of this section.
  (2) In accordance with the general regulations in §§165.23 and 165.33 of this part, entry into or movement within the safety and security zones designated in paragraph (a)(2) of this section is prohibited unless authorized by the COTP Boston, or his/her authorized representative.
  (3) Notwithstanding paragraph (d)(2) of this section, tankers and support vessels, as defined in 33 CFR 148.5, operating in the vicinity of NEGDWP are authorized to enter and move within such zones in the normal course of their operations following the requirements set forth in 33 CFR 150.340 and 150.345, respectively.
  (4) All vessels operating within the safety and security zones described in paragraph (a)(2) of this section must comply with the instructions of the COTP or his/her authorized representative.

§165.120 Safety Zone: Chelsea River, Boston Inner Harbor, Boston, Massachusetts.

§165.121 Safety and Security Zones: High Interest Vessels, Narragansett Bay, Rhode Island.

§165.122 Regulated Navigation Area: Navigable waters within Narragansett Bay and the Providence River, Rhode Island

§165.125 Regulated Navigation Area; EPA Superfund Site, New Bedford Harbor, Massachusetts.

§165.130 Security Zone; Sandy Hook Bay, New Jersey.

§165.141 Safety Zone: Sunken vessel EMPIRE KNIGHT, Boon Island, Maine.

(a) *Location.* The following area is a safety zone: All waters of the Atlantic Ocean within a 1000 yard radius of the stern section of the sunken vessel EMPIRE KNIGHT, in approximate position 43°06′19″N 70°27′09″W (NAD 1983) and extending from the water's surface to the seabed floor.

(c) *The regulations:*
   (1) The general regulations contained in 33 CFR 165.23 apply.
   (2) All vessels and persons are prohibited from anchoring, diving, dredging, dumping, fishing, trawling, laying cable, or conducting salvage operations in this zone except as authorized by the Coast Guard Captain of the Port, Portland, Maine. Innocent transit through the area within the safety zone is not affected by this regulation and does not require the authorization of the Captain of the Port.

§165.150 Regulated Navigation Area; New Haven Harbor, Quinnipiac River, Mill River.

§165.153 Regulated Navigation Area: Long Island Sound Marine Inspection and Captain of the Port Zone.

(a) *Regulated Navigation Area location.* All waters of the Long Island Sound Marine Inspection and Captain of the Port (COTP) Zone, as delineated in 33 CFR 3.05-35, extending seaward 12 nautical miles from the territorial sea baseline, are established as a regulated navigation area (RNA).

(b) *Applicability.* This section applies to all vessels operating within the RNA excluding public vessels.

(c) *Definitions.* The following definitions apply to this section:

Commercial service means any type of trade or business involving the transportation of goods or individuals, except service performed by a combatant vessel.

Ferry means a vessel that:
   (1) Operates in other than ocean or coastwise service;
   (2) Has provisions only for deck passengers or vehicles, or both;
   (3) Operates on a short run on a frequent schedule between two points over the most direct water route; and
   (4) Offers a public service of a type normally attributed to a bridge or tunnel.

Public vessels means vessels owned or bareboat chartered and operated by the United States, or by a State or political subdivision thereof, or by a foreign nation, except when such vessel is engaged in commercial service.

Territorial sea baseline means the line defining the shoreward extent of the territorial sea of the United States drawn according to the principles, as recognized by the United States, of the Convention on the Territorial Sea and the Contiguous Zone, 15 U.S.T. 1606, and the 1982 United Nations Convention on the Law of the Sea (UNCLOS), 21 I.L.M. 1261. Normally, the territorial sea baseline is the mean low water line along the coast of the United States.

(d) *Regulations.*
   (1) Speed restrictions in the vicinity of Naval Submarine Base New London and Lower Thames River. Unless authorized by the Captain of the Port (COTP), vessels of 300 gross tons or more may not proceed at a speed in excess of eight knots in the Thames River from New London Harbor channel buoys 7 and 8 (Light List numbers 21875 and 21880 respectively) north through the upper limit of the Naval Submarine Base New London Restricted Area, as that area is specified in 33 CFR 334.75(a). The U.S. Navy and other Federal, State and municipal agencies may assist the U.S. Coast Guard in the enforcement of this rule.
   (2) Enhanced communications. Vessels of 300 gross tons or more and all vessels engaged in towing barges must issue securité calls on marine band or Very High Frequency (VHF) radio channel 16 upon approach to the following locations:
      (i) Inbound approach to Cerberus Shoal; and
      (ii) Outbound approach to Race Rock Light (USCG Light List No. 19815).
   (3) All vessels operating within the RNA that are bound for a port or place located in the United States or that must transit the internal waters of the United States, must be inspected to the satisfaction of the U.S. Coast Guard, before entering waters within three nautical miles from the territorial sea baseline. Vessels awaiting inspection will be required to anchor in the manner directed by the COTP. This section does not apply to vessels operating exclusively within the Long Island Sound Marine Inspection and COTP Zone, vessels on single voyage which depart from and return to the same port or place within the RNA, all towing vessels engaged in coastwise trade, vessels in innocent passage not bound for a port or place subject to the jurisdiction of the United States, and all vessels not engaged in commercial service whose last port of call was in the United States. Vessels requiring inspection by the COTP may contact the COTP via marine band or Very High Frequency (VHF) channel 16, telephone at

(203) 468-4401, facsimile at (203) 468-4418, or letter, addressed to Captain of the Port, Long Island Sound, 120 Woodward Ave., New Haven, CT 06512.

(4) All vessels operating within the RNA that are bound for a port or place located in the United States or that must transit the internal waters of the United States, must obtain authorization from the Captain of the Port (COTP) before entering waters within three nautical miles from the territorial sea baseline. Vessels awaiting COTP authorization to enter waters within three nautical miles from the territorial sea baseline will be required to anchor in the manner directed by the COTP. This section does not apply to vessels operating exclusively within the Long Island Sound Marine Inspection and COTP Zone, vessels on a single voyage which depart from and return to the same port or place within the RNA, all towing vessels engaged in coastwise trade, vessels in innocent passage not bound for a port or place subject to the jurisdiction of the United States, and all vessels not engaged in commercial service whose last port of call was in the United States. Vessels may request authorization from the COTP by contacting the COTP via marine band or Very High Frequency (VHF) channel 16, telephone at (203) 468-4401, facsimile at (203) 468-4418, or letter addressed to Captain of the Port, Long Island Sound, 120 Woodward Ave., New Haven, CT 06512.

(5) Vessels over 1,600 gross tons operating in the RNA within three nautical miles from the territorial sea baseline that are bound for a port or place located in the United States or that must transit the internal waters of the United States must receive authorization from the COTP prior to transiting or any intentional vessel movements, including, but not limited to, shifting berths, departing anchorage, or getting underway from a mooring. This section does not apply to vessels in innocent passage not bound for a port or place subject to the jurisdiction of the United States.

(6) Ferry vessels. Vessels of 300 gross tons or more are prohibited from entering all waters within a 1200-yard radius of any ferry vessel transiting in any portion of the Long Island Sound Marine Inspection and COTP Zone without first obtaining the express prior authorization of the ferry vessel operator, licensed, COTP, or the designated COTP on-scene patrol.

(7) Vessels engaged in commercial service. No vessel may enter within a 100-yard radius of any vessel engaged in commercial service while that vessel is transiting, moored, or berthed in any portion of the Long Island Sound Marine Inspection and COTP zone without the express prior authorization of the vessel's operator, master, COTP, or the designated COTP on-scene representative.

(8) Bridge foundations. Any vessel operating beneath a bridge must make a direct, immediate and expeditious passage beneath the bridge while remaining within the navigable channel. No vessel may stop, moor, anchor or loiter beneath a bridge at any time. No vessel may approach within a 25-yard radius of any bridge foundation, support, stanchion, pier or abutment except as required for the direct, immediate and expeditious transit beneath a bridge.

(9) This section does not relieve any vessel from compliance with applicable navigation rules.

§165.154 Safety and Security Zones; Captain of the Port Long Island Sound Zone Safety and Security Zones.

§165.156 Regulated navigation area: East Rockaway Inlet to Atlantic Beach Bridge, Nassau County, Long Island, New York.

§165.164 Security Zones: Dignitary Arrival/Departure and United Nations Meetings New York, NY.

§165.169 Safety and Security Zones: New York Marine Inspection Zone and Captain of the Port Zone.

(a) *Safety and security zones.* The following waters within the New York Marine Inspection Zone and Captain of the Port Zone are safety and security zones:

(12) *Approaches to New York, Atlantic Ocean.*
  (i) *Location.* The following area is a security zone: All waters of the Atlantic Ocean between the Ambrose to Hudson Canyon Traffic Lane and the Barnegat to Ambrose Traffic Lane bound by the following points:
  40°21′29.9″N 73°44′41.0″W;
  40°21′04.5″N 73°45′31.4″W;
  40°15′28.3″N 73°44′13.8″W;
  40°15′35.4″N 73°43′29.8″W;
  40°19′21.2″N 73°42′53.0″W;
  40°21′29.9″N 73°44′41.0″W. (NAD 1983)
  (ii) *Enforcement period.* Enforcement periods for the zone in paragraph (a)(12) of this section will be announced through marine information broadcast or other appropriate method of communication and the zone is activated whenever a vessel is anchored in the area described in paragraph (a)(12)(i) or a Coast Guard patrol vessel is on scene.
  (iii) *Regulations.*
    (A) The area described in paragraph (a)(12) of this section is not a Federal Anchorage Ground. Only vessels directed by the Captain of the Port or his or her designated representative to enter this zone are authorized to anchor here.
    (B) Vessels do not need permission from the Captain of the Port to transit the area described in paragraph (a)(12) of this section during periods when that security zone is not being enforced.

(b) *Regulations.*
  (1) Entry into or remaining in a safety or security zone is prohibited unless authorized by the Coast Guard Captain of the Port, New York.

Subpart G — Protection of Naval Vessels

§165.2010 Purpose.

This subpart establishes the geographic parameters of naval vessel protection zones surrounding US naval vessels in the navigable waters of the United States.

§165.2015 Definitions.

The following definitions apply to this subpart:

Large US naval vessel means any US naval vessel greater than 100 feet in length overall.

Naval vessel protection zone is a 500 yard regulated area of water surrounding large US naval vessels that is necessary to provide for the safety or security of these US naval vessels.

Official patrol means those personnel designated and supervised by a senior naval officer present in command.

Senior naval officer present in command is, unless otherwise designated by competent authority, the senior line officer of the US Navy on active duty, eligible for command at sea, who is present and in command of any part of the Department of Navy in the area.

US naval vessel means any vessel owned, operated, chartered, or leased by the US Navy; and any vessel under the operational control of the US Navy or a Combatant Command.

§165.2020 Enforcement authority.

(a) Coast Guard.
(b) Senior naval officer present in command.

§165.2025 Atlantic Area.

(a) This section applies to any vessel or person in the navigable waters of the United States within the boundaries of the US Coast Guard Atlantic Area which includes the First, Fifth, Seventh, Eighth, and Ninth US Coast Guard Districts.

Note to paragraph (a): The boundaries of the US Coast Guard Atlantic Area and the First, Fifth, Seventh, Eighth, and Ninth US Coast Guard Districts are set out in 33 CFR part 3.

(b) A naval vessel protection zone exists around US naval vessels greater than 100 feet in length overall at all times in the navigable waters of the United States, whether the large US naval vessel is underway, anchored, moored, or within a floating drydock, except when the large naval vessel is moored or anchored within a restricted area or within a naval defensive sea area.

(c) The Navigation Rules shall apply at all times within a naval vessel protection zone.

(d) When within a naval vessel protection zone, all vessels shall operate at the minimum speed necessary to maintain a safe course, unless required to maintain speed by the Navigation Rules, and shall proceed as directed by the Coast Guard, the senior naval officer present in command, or the official patrol. When within a naval vessel protection zone, no vessel or person is allowed within 100 yards of a large US naval vessel unless authorized by the Coast Guard, the senior naval officer present in command, or official patrol.

(e) To request authorization to operate within 100 yards of a large US naval vessel, contact the Coast Guard, the senior naval officer present in command, or official patrol on VHF-FM channel 16.

(f) When conditions permit, the Coast Guard, senior naval officer present in command, or the official patrol should:

(1) Give advance notice on VHF-FM channel 16 of all large US naval vessel movements;

(2) Permit vessels constrained by their navigational draft or restricted in their ability to maneuver to pass within 100 yards of a large US naval vessel in order to ensure a safe passage in accordance with the Navigation Rules; and:

(3) Permit commercial vessels anchored in a designated anchorage area to remain at anchor when within 100 yards of passing large US naval vessels; and:

(4) Permit vessels that must transit via a navigable channel or waterway to pass within 100 yards of a moored or anchored large US naval vessel with minimal delay consistent with security.

Note to paragraph (f): The listed actions are discretionary and do not create any additional right to appeal or otherwise dispute a decision of the Coast Guard, the senior naval officer present in command, or the official patrol.

APPENDIX VI

CODE OF FEDERAL REGULATIONS TITLE 33 — NAVIGATION AND NAVIGABLE WATERS

PART 334 — DANGER ZONES AND RESTRICTED AREA REGULATIONS — EXTRACTS

Appendix VI contains extracts from the above regulations issued by the United States Department of Commerce.

Regulations specific to this volume are given by title only where the area concerned falls wholly within pilotage waters; where the regulation affects an area outside pilotage waters, a summary of the regulation is given.

For a complete description of this part see 33 CFR 334.

§334.1 Purpose.

The purpose of this part is to:
(a) Prescribe procedures for establishing, amending and disestablishing danger zones and restricted areas.
(b) List the specific danger zones and restricted areas and their boundaries; and
(c) Prescribe specific requirements, access limitations and controlled activities within the danger zones and restricted areas.

§334.2 Definitions.

(a) *Danger zone.* A defined water area (or areas) used for target practice, bombing, rocket firing or other especially hazardous operations, normally for the armed forces. The danger zones may be closed to the public on a full time or intermittent basis, as stated in the regulations.

(b) *Restricted area.* A defined water area for the purpose of prohibiting or limiting public access to the area. Restricted areas generally provide security for Government property and/or protection to the public from the risks of damage or injury arising from the Government's use of that area.

There are danger zones and/or restricted areas in the following areas:

§334.10 Gulf of Maine off Seal Island, Maine; Naval aircraft bombing target area.

(a) *The danger zone.* A circular area with a radius of 1·5 nautical miles, having its centre just easterly of Seal Island at latitude 43°53'00'' and longitude 68°44'00''.

(b) *The regulations:*
(1) No aerial bombing practice will take place in the danger zone after 5:00 p.m. Mondays through Saturdays, at any time on Sundays, or during foggy or inclement weather.
(2) Vessels or other watercraft will be allowed to enter the danger zone any time there are no aerial bombing exercises being conducted.
(3) No live ammunition or explosives will be dropped in the area.
(5) Prior to the conducting of each bombing practice, the area will be patrolled by a naval aircraft or surface vessel to ensure that no persons or watercraft are within the danger zone. Vessels may be requested to veer off when drops are to be made, however, drops will be made only when the area is clear. The patrol aircraft will employ the method of warning known as "buzzing" which consists of low flight by the airplane and repeated opening and closing of the throttle.
(6) Any such watercraft shall, upon being so warned, immediately leave the designated area and, until the conclusion of the practice, shall remain at such distance that it will be safe from falling projectiles.

§334.20 Gulf of Maine off Cape Small, Maine; Naval aircraft practice mining range area.

(a) *The danger zone.* Within an area bounded as follows:
43°43'00"N 69°46'00"W.
43°38'30"N 69°46'00"W.
43°38'30"N 69°49'30"W.
43°42'10"N 69°49'30"W.

(b) *The regulations.*
(1) Test drops from aircraft will be made within the area at intermittent periods from noon until sunset local time and only during periods of good visibility.
(2) Testing will not restrict any fishing, recreational, or commercial activities in the testing area.
(3) Aircraft will patrol the area prior to and during test periods to insure that no surface vessels are within the area. No test drops will be made while surface vessels are transitting the area.
(4) No live ammunition or explosives will be dropped in the area.

§334.30 Gulf of Maine off Pemaquid Point, Maine; Naval Sonobuoy Test Area.

(a) *The area.* The test area or "Foul Area" encompasses a circular area one nautical mile in radius, the centre of which is located 7·9 nautical miles, bearing 187° magnetic from Pemaquid LIght.

(b) *The regulations:*
(1) Sonobuoy drops will be made only in the designated area and when visibility is at least three miles.
(2) Sonobuoy drop tests will normally be conducted at intermittent periods on a five day week basis, Monday through Friday. However, on occasions tests may be conducted intermittently on a seven day week basis.
(3) Prior to and during the period when sonobuoys are being dropped, an escort vessel or naval aircraft will be in the

vicinity to ensure that no persons or vessels are in the testing area. Vessels may be requested to veer off when sonobuoys are about to be dropped, however, drops will be made only when the area is clear.

(5) No live ammunition or explosives will be dropped in the area.

§334.40 Atlantic Ocean in vicinity of Duck Island, Maine, Isles of Shoals; Naval aircraft bombing target area.

(a) *The danger zone.* A circular area with a radius of 500 yards having its centre on Shag Rock in the vicinity of Duck Island at latitude 43°00′12″, longitude 70°36′12″.

(b) *The regulations:*
   (1) No person or vessel shall enter or remain in the danger zone from 8:00 a.m. to 5:00 p.m. (local time) daily, except as authorized by the enforcing agency.

§334.45 Kennebec River, Bath Iron Works Shipyard, Bath, Maine; Naval restricted area.

§334.50 Piscataqua River at Portsmouth Naval Shipyard, Kittery, Maine; restricted areas.

§334.60 Cape Cod Bay south of Wellfleet Harbor, Massachusetts; Naval aircraft bombing target area.

(a) *The danger zone.* A circular area with a radius of 1000 yards having its centre on the aircraft bombing target hulk James Longstreet in Cape Cod Bay at latitude 41°49′46″, longitude 70°02′54″.

(b) *The regulations:*
   (1) No person or vessel shall enter or remain in the danger zone at any time, except as authorized by the enforcing agency.

§334.70 Buzzards Bay and adjacent waters, Massachusetts; danger zones for naval operations.

(a) Atlantic Ocean in vicinity of Nomans Land:-
   (1) *The area.* The waters surrounding Nomans Land within an area bounded as follows:
      41°12′30″N 70°50′30″W.
      41°15′30″N 70°51′30″W.
      41°17′30″N 70°50′30″W.
      41°16′00″N 70°47′30″W.
      41°12′30″N 70°47′30″W.
   (2) *The regulations.* No vessel or person shall at any time enter or remain within a rectangular portion of the area bounded on the north by latitude 41°16′00″, on the east by longitude 70°47′30″, on the south by latitude 41°12′30″, and on the west by longitude 70°50′30″, or within the remainder of the area between November 1 and April 30, inclusive, except by permission of the enforcing agency.

§334.75 Thames River, Naval Submarine Base New London; restricted area.

§334.80 Narragansett Bay, Rhode Island; restricted area.

§334.81 Narragansett Bay, East Passage, Coddington Cove, Naval Station Newport, Newport, Rhode Island; Naval restricted area.

§334.82 Narragansett Bay, East Passage, Coasters Harbor Island, Naval Station Newport, Newport, Rhode Island; Restricted area.

§334.85 New York Harbor, adjacent to the Stapleton Naval Station, Staten Island, New York; restricted area.

§334.102 Sandy Hook Bay, Naval weapons station EARLE, Piers and Terminal Channel, Middletown, New Jersey; restricted area.

APPENDIX VII

NAVIGATION RULES FOR UNITED STATES INLAND WATERS

Following the signing of the Convention on the International Regulations for Preventing Collisions at Sea, 1972, a new effort was made to unify and update the various inland navigation rules. This effort culminated in the enactment of the Inland Navigation Rules Act of 1980. This leglisation sets out Rules 1 to 38 - the main body of the Rules. The five Annexes were published as regulations. It is important to note that with the exception of Annex V to the Inland Rules, the International and Inland Rules and Annexes are very similar in both content and format.

Appendix VII contains the rules but not the diagrams and annexes associated with them. For full details see http://www.navcen.uscg.gov/?pageName=navRulesContent

PART A—GENERAL

RULE 1

Application

(a) These Rules apply to all vessels upon the inland waters of the United States, and to vessels of the United States on the Canadian waters of the Great Lakes to the extent that there is no conflict with Canadian law.

(b) (i) These Rules constitute special rules made by an appropriate authority within the meaning of Rule 1(b) of the International Regulations.

　(ii) All vessels complying with the construction and equipment requirements of the International Regulations are considered to be in compliance with these Rules.

(c) Nothing in these Rules shall interfere with the operation of any special rules made by the Secretary of the Navy with respect to additional station or signal lights and shapes or whistle signals for ships of war and vessels proceeding under convoy, or by the Secretary with respect to additional station or signal lights and shapes for fishing vessels engaged in fishing as a fleet. These additional station or signal lights and shapes or whistle signals shall, so far as possible, be such that they cannot be mistaken for any light, shape, or signal authorized elsewhere under these Rules. Notice of such special rules shall be published in the Federal Register and, after the effective date specified in such notice, they shall have effect as if they were a part of these Rules.[1]

(d) Traffic separation schemes may be established for the purposes of these Rules. Vessel traffic service regulations may be in effect in certain areas.

(e) Whenever the Secretary determines that a vessel or class of vessels of special construction or purpose cannot comply fully with the provisions of any of these Rules with respect to the number, position, range, or arc of visibility of lights or shapes, as well as to the disposition and characteristics of sound-signaling appliances, the vessel shall comply with such other provisions in regard to the number, position, range, or arc of visibility of lights or shapes, as well as to the disposition and characteristics of sound-signaling appliances, as the Secretary shall have determined to be the closest possible compliance with these Rules. The Secretary may issue a certificate of alternative compliance for a vessel or class of vessels specifying the closest possible compliance with these Rules. The Secretary of the Navy shall make these determinations and issue certificates of alternative compliance for vessels of the Navy.

(f) The Secretary may accept a certificate of alternative compliance issued by a contracting party to the International Regulations if he determines that the alternative compliance standards of the contracting party are substantially the same as those of the United States.

[1] Submarines may display, as a distinctive means of identification, an intermittent flashing amber (yellow) beacon with a sequence of operation of one flash per second for three (3) seconds followed by a three (3) second off-period. Other special rules made by the Secretary of the Navy with respect to additional station and signal lights are found in Part 706 of Title 32, Code of Federal Regulations (32 CFR 706).

RULE 2

Responsibility

(a) Nothing in these Rules shall exonerate any vessel, or the owner, master, or crew thereof, from the consequences of any neglect to comply with these Rules or of the neglect of any precaution which may be required by the ordinary practice of seamen, or by the special circumstances of the case.

(b) In construing and complying with these Rules due regard shall be had to all dangers of navigation and collision and to any special circumstances, including the limitations of the vessels involved, which may make a departure from these Rules necessary to avoid immediate danger.

RULE 3

General definitions

For the purpose of these Rules and this Chapter, except where the context otherwise requires:

(a) The word "vessel" includes every description of water craft, including nondisplacement craft and seaplanes, used or capable of being used as a means of transportation on water;

(b) The term "power-driven vessel" means any vessel propelled by machinery;
(c) The term "sailing vessel" means any vessel under sail provided that propelling machinery, if fitted, is not being used;
(d) The term "vessel engaged in fishing" means any vessel fishing with nets, lines, trawls, or other fishing apparatus which restricts maneuverability, but does not include a vessel fishing with trolling lines or other fishing apparatus which do not restrict maneuverability;
(e) The word "seaplane" includes any aircraft designed to maneuver on the water;
(f) The term "vessel not under command" means a vessel which through some exceptional circumstance is unable to maneuver as required by these Rules and is therefore unable to keep out of the way of another vessel;
(g) The term "vessel restricted in her ability to maneuver" means a vessel which from the nature of her work is restricted in her ability to maneuver as required by these Rules and is therefore unable to keep out of the way of another vessel; vessels restricted in their ability to maneuver include, but are not limited to:
  (i) a vessel engaged in laying, servicing, or picking up a navigation mark, submarine cable, or pipeline;
  (ii) a vessel engaged in dredging, surveying, or underwater operations;
  (iii) a vessel engaged in replenishment or transferring persons, provisions, or cargo while underway;
  (iv) a vessel engaged in the launching or recovery of aircraft;
  (v) a vessel engaged in mineclearance operations; and
  (vi) a vessel engaged in a towing operation such as severely restricts the towing vessel and her tow in their ability to deviate from their course.
(h) The word "underway" means that a vessel is not at anchor, or made fast to the shore, or aground;
(i) The words "length" and "breadth" of a vessel means her length overall and greatest breadth;
(j) Vessels shall be deemed to be in sight of one another only when one can be observed visually from the other;
(k) The term "restricted visibility" means any condition in which visibility is restricted by fog, mist, falling snow, heavy rainstorms, sandstorms, or any other similar causes;
(l) "Western Rivers" means the Mississippi River, its tributaries, South Pass, and Southwest Pass, to the navigational demarcation lines dividing the high seas from harbors, rivers, and other inland waters of the United States, and the Port Allen-Morgan City Alternate Route, and that part of the Atchafalaya River above its junction with the Port Allen-Morgan City Alternate Route including the Old River and the Red River;
(m) "Great Lakes" means the Great Lakes and their connecting and tributary waters including the Calumet River as far as the Thomas J. O'Brien Lock and Controlling Works (between mile 326 and 327), the Chicago River as far as the east side of the Ashland Avenue Bridge (between mile 321 and 322), and the Saint Lawrence River as far east as the lower exit of Saint Lambert Lock;
(n) "Secretary" means the Secretary of the department in which the Coast Guard is operating;
(o) "Inland Waters" means the navigable waters of the United States shoreward of the navigational demarcation lines dividing the high seas from harbors, rivers, and other inland waters of the United States and the waters of the Great Lakes on the United States side of the International Boundary;
(p) "Inland Rules" or "Rules" mean the Inland Navigational Rules and the annexes thereto, which govern the conduct of vessels and specify the lights, shapes, and sound signals that apply on inland waters; and
(q) "International Regulations" means the International Regulations for Preventing Collisions at Sea, 1972, including annexes currently in force for the United States.

PART B—STEERING AND SAILING RULES

SUBPART I—CONDUCT OF VESSELS IN ANY CONDITION OF VISIBILITY

RULE 4

Application
Rules in this subpart apply in any condition of visibility.

RULE 5

Look-out
Every vessel shall at all times maintain a proper look-out by sight and hearing as well as by all available means appropriate in the prevailing circumstances and conditions so as to make a full appraisal of the situation and of the risk of collision.

RULE 6

Safe Speed
Every vessel shall at all times proceed at a safe speed so that she can take proper and effective action to avoid collision and be stopped within a distance appropriate to the prevailing circumstances and conditions.

In determining a safe speed the following factors shall be among those taken into account:
(a) By all vessels:
  (i) the state of visibility;
  (ii) the traffic density including concentration of fishing vessels or any other vessels;
  (iii) the maneuverability of the vessel with special reference to stopping distance and turning ability in the prevailing conditions;
  (iv) at night, the presence of background light such as from shore lights or from back scatter of her own lights;

(v) the state of wind, sea, and current, and the proximity of navigational hazards;
(vi) the draft in relation to the available depth of water.
(b) Additionally, by vessels with operational radar:
(i) the characteristics, efficiency and limitations of the radar equipment;
(ii) any constraints imposed by the radar range scale in use;
(iii) the effect on radar detection of the sea state, weather, and other sources of interference;
(iv) the possibility that small vessels, ice and other floating objects may not be detected by radar at an adequate range;
(v) the number, location, and movement of vessels detected by radar; and
(vi) the more exact assessment of the visibility that may be possible when radar is used to determine the range of vessels or other objects in the vicinity.

RULE 7

Risk of Collision
(a) Every vessel shall use all available means appropriate to the prevailing circumstances and conditions to determine if risk of collision exists. If there is any doubt such risk shall be deemed to exist.
(b) Proper use shall be made of radar equipment if fitted and operational, including long-range scanning to obtain early warning of risk of collision and radar plotting or equivalent systematic observation of detected objects.
(c) Assumptions shall not be made on the basis of scanty information, especially scanty radar information.
(d) In determining if risk of collision exists the following considerations shall be among those taken into account:
(i) such risk shall be deemed to exist if the compass bearing of an approaching vessel does not appreciably change; and
(ii) such risk may sometimes exist even when an appreciable bearing change is evident, particularly when approaching a very large vessel or a tow or when approaching a vessel at close range.

RULE 8

Action to avoid collision
(a) Any action taken to avoid collision shall, if the circumstances of the case admit, be positive, made in ample time and with due regard to the observance of good seamanship.
(b) Any alteration of course or speed to avoid collision shall, if the circumstances of the case admit, be large enough to be readily apparent to another vessel observing visually or by radar; a succession of small alterations of course or speed should be avoided.
(c) If there is sufficient sea room, alteration of course alone may be the most effective action to avoid a close-quarters situation provided that it is made in good time, is substantial and does not result in another close-quarters situation.
(d) Action taken to avoid collision with another vessel shall be such as to result in passing at a safe distance. The effectiveness of the action shall be carefully checked until the other vessel is finally past and clear.
(e) If necessary to avoid collision or allow more time to assess the situation, a vessel shall slacken her speed or take all way off by stopping or reversing her means of propulsion.
(f) (i) A vessel which, by any of these rules, is required not to impede the passage or safe passage of another vessel shall, when required by the circumstances of the case, take early action to allow sufficient sea room for the safe passage of the other vessel.
(ii) A vessel required not to impede the passage or safe passage of another vessel is not relieved of this obligation if approaching the other vessel so as to involve risk of collision and shall, when taking action, have full regard to the action which may be required by the rules of this part.
(iii) A vessel, the passage of which is not to be impeded remains fully obliged to comply with the rules of this part when the two vessels are approaching one another so as to involve risk of collision.

RULE 9

Narrow channels
(a) (i) A vessel proceeding along the course of a narrow channel or fairway shall keep as near to the outer limit of the channel or fairway which lies on her starboard side as is safe and practicable.
(ii) Notwithstanding paragraph (a)(i) and Rule 14(a), a power-driven vessel operating in narrow channels or fairways on the Great Lakes, Western Rivers, or waters specified by the Secretary, and proceeding downbound with a following current shall have the right-of-way over an upbound vessel, shall propose the manner and place of passage, and shall initiate the maneuvering signals prescribed by Rule 34(a)(i), as appropriate. The vessel proceeding upbound against the current shall hold as necessary to permit safe passing.
(b) A vessel of less than 20 meters in length or a sailing vessel shall not impede the passage of a vessel that can safely navigate only within a narrow channel or fairway.
(c) A vessel engaged in fishing shall not impede the passage of any other vessel navigating within a narrow channel or fairway.
(d) A vessel shall not cross a narrow channel or fairway if such crossing impedes the passage of a vessel which can safely navigate only within that channel or fairway. The latter vessel shall use the danger signal prescribed in Rule 34(d) if in doubt as to the intention of the crossing vessel.
(e) (i) In a narrow channel or fairway when overtaking, the power-driven vessel intending to overtake another power-driven vessel shall

indicate her intention by sounding the appropriate signal prescribed in Rule 34(c) and take steps to permit safe passing. The power-driven vessel being overtaken, if in agreement, shall sound the same signal and may, if specifically agreed to take steps to permit safe passing. If in doubt she shall sound the danger signal prescribed in Rule 34(d).
    (ii) This Rule does not relieve the overtaking vessel of her obligation under Rule 13.
(f) A vessel nearing a bend or an area of a narrow channel or fairway where other vessels may be obscured by an intervening obstruction shall navigate with particular alertness and caution and shall sound the appropriate signal prescribed in Rule 34(e).
(g) Every vessel shall, if the circumstances of the case admit, avoid anchoring in a narrow channel.

RULE 10

Traffic Separation Schemes
(a) This Rule applies to traffic separation schemes and does not relieve any vessel of her obligation under any other Rule.
(b) A vessel using a traffic separation scheme shall:
    (i) proceed in the appropriate traffic lane in the general direction of traffic flow for that lane;
    (ii) so far as practicable keep clear of a traffic separation line or separation zone;
    (iii) normally join or leave a traffic lane at the termination of the lane, but when joining or leaving from either side shall do so at as small an angle to the general direction of traffic flow as practicable.
(c) A vessel shall, so far as practicable, avoid crossing traffic lanes but if obliged to do so shall cross on a heading as nearly as practicable at right angles to the general direction of traffic flow.
(d) (i) A vessel shall not use an inshore traffic zone when she can safely use the appropriate traffic lane within the adjacent traffic separation scheme. However, vessels of less than 20 meters in length, sailing vessels, and vessels engaged in fishing may use the inshore traffic zone.
    (ii) Notwithstanding subparagraph (d) (i), a vessel may use an inshore traffic zone when en route to or from a port, offshore installation or structure, pilot station, or any other place situated within the inshore traffic zone, or to avoid immediate danger.
(e) A vessel other than a crossing vessel or a vessel joining or leaving a lane shall not normally enter a separation zone or cross a separation line except:
    (i) in cases of emergency to avoid immediate danger; or
    (ii) to engage in fishing within a separation zone.
(f) A vessel navigating in areas near the terminations of traffic separation schemes shall do so with particular caution.
(g) A vessel shall so far as practicable avoid anchoring in a traffic separation scheme or in areas near its terminations.
(h) A vessel not using a traffic separation scheme shall avoid it by as wide a margin as is practicable.
(i) A vessel engaged in fishing shall not impede the passage of any vessel following a traffic lane.
(j) A vessel of less than 20 meters in length or a sailing vessel shall not impede the safe passage of a power-driven vessel following a traffic lane.
(k) A vessel restricted in her ability to maneuver when engaged in an operation for the maintenance of safety of navigation in a traffic separation scheme is exempted from complying with this Rule to the extent necessary to carry out the operation.
(l) A vessel restricted in her ability to maneuver when engaged in an operation for the laying, servicing, or picking up of a submarine cable, within a traffic separation scheme, is exempted from complying with this Rule to the extent necessary to carry out the operation.

SUBPART II—CONDUCT OF VESSELS IN SIGHT OF ONE ANOTHER

RULE 11

Application
Rules in this subpart apply to vessels in sight of one another.

RULE 12

Sailing Vessels
(a) When two sailing vessels are approaching one another, so as to involve risk of collision, one of them shall keep out of the way of the other as follows:
    (i) when each has the wind on a different side, the vessel which has the wind on the port side shall keep out of the way of the other;
    (ii) when both have the wind on the same side, the vessel which is to windward shall keep out of the way of the vessel which is to leeward; and
    (iii) if a vessel with the wind on the port side sees a vessel to windward and cannot determine with certainty whether the other vessel has the wind on the port or on the starboard side, she shall keep out of the way of the other.
(b) For the purpose of this Rule the windward side shall be deemed to be the side opposite to that on which the mainsail is carried or, in the case of a square-rigged vessel, the side opposite to that on which the largest fore and aft sail is carried.

RULE 13

Overtaking
(a) Notwithstanding anything contained in Rules 4 through 18, any vessel overtaking any other shall keep out of the way of the vessel being overtaken.

(b) A vessel shall be deemed to be overtaking when coming up with another vessel from a direction more than 22.5 degrees abaft her beam; that is, in such a position with reference to the vessel she is overtaking, that at night she would be able to see only the sternlight of that vessel but neither of her sidelights.
(c) When a vessel is in any doubt as to whether she is overtaking another, she shall assume that this is the case and act accordingly.
(d) Any subsequent alteration of the bearing between the two vessels shall not make the overtaking vessel a crossing vessel within the meaning of these Rules or relieve her of the duty of keeping clear of the overtaken vessel until she is finally past and clear.

RULE 14

Head-on Situation
(a) Unless otherwise agreed, when two power-driven vessels are meeting on reciprocal or nearly reciprocal courses so as to involve risk of collision each shall alter her course to starboard so that each shall pass on the port side of the other.
(b) Such a situation shall be deemed to exist when a vessel sees the other ahead or nearly ahead and by night she could see the masthead lights of the other in a line or nearly in a line or both sidelights and by day she observes the corresponding aspect of the other vessel.
(c) When a vessel is in any doubt as to whether such a situation exists she shall assume that it does exist and act accordingly.
(d) Notwithstanding paragraph (a) of this Rule, a power-driven vessel operating on the Great Lakes, Western Rivers, or waters specified by the Secretary, and proceeding downbound with a following current shall have the right-of-way over an upbound vessel, shall propose the manner of passage, and shall initiate the maneuvering signals prescribed by Rule 34(a)(i), as appropriate.

RULE 15

Crossing Situation
(a) When two power-driven vessels are crossing so as to involve risk of collision, the vessel which has the other on her starboard side shall keep out of the way and shall, if the circumstances of the case admit, avoid crossing ahead of the other vessel.
(b) Notwithstanding paragraph (a), on the Great Lakes, Western Rivers, or water specified by the Secretary, a power-driven vessel crossing a river shall keep out of the way of a power-driven vessel ascending or descending the river.

RULE 16

Action by Give-way Vessel
Every vessel which is directed to keep out of the way of another vessel shall, so far as possible, take early and substantial action to keep well clear.

RULE 17

Action by Stand-on Vessel
(a) (i) Where one of two vessels is to keep out of the way, the other shall keep her course and speed.
 (ii) The latter vessel may, however, take action to avoid collision by her maneuver alone, as soon as it becomes apparent to her that the vessel required to keep out of the way is not taking appropriate action in compliance with these Rules.
(b) When, from any cause, the vessel required to keep her course and speed finds herself so close that collision cannot be avoided by the action of the give-way vessel alone, she shall take such action as will best aid to avoid collision.
(c) A power-driven vessel which takes action in a crossing situation in accordance with subparagraph (a)(ii) of this Rule to avoid collision with another power-driven vessel shall, if the circumstances of the case admit, not alter course to port for a vessel on her own port side.
(d) This Rule does not relieve the give-way vessel of her obligation to keep out of the way.

RULE 18

Responsibilities Between Vessels Except where Rules 9, 10, and 13 otherwise require:
(a) A power-driven vessel underway shall keep out of the way of:
 (i) a vessel not under command;
 (ii) a vessel restricted in her ability to maneuver;
 (iii) a vessel engaged in fishing; and
 (iv) a sailing vessel.
(b) A sailing vessel underway shall keep out of the way of:
 (i) a vessel not under command;
 (ii) a vessel restricted in her ability to maneuver; and
 (iii) a vessel engaged in fishing.
(c) A vessel engaged in fishing when underway shall, so far as possible, keep out of the way of:
 (i) a vessel not under command; and
 (ii) a vessel restricted in her ability to maneuver.
(d) A seaplane on the water shall, in general, keep well clear of all vessels and avoid impeding their navigation. In circumstances, however, where risk of collision exists, she shall comply with the Rules of this Part.

SUBPART III—CONDUCT OF VESSELS IN RESTRICTED VISIBILITY

RULE 19

Conduct of Vessels in Restricted Visibility
(a) This Rule applies to vessels not in sight of one another when navigating in or near an area of restricted visibility.
(b) Every vessel shall proceed at a safe speed adapted to the prevailing circumstances and conditions of restricted visibility. A power-driven vessel shall have her engines ready for immediate maneuver.

(c) Every vessel shall have due regard to the prevailing circumstances and conditions of restricted visibility when complying with Rules 4 through 10.
(d) A vessel which detects by radar alone the presence of another vessel shall determine if a close-quarters situation is developing or risk of collision exists. If so, she shall take avoiding action in ample time, provided that when such action consists of an alteration of course, so far as possible the following shall be avoided:
  (i) an alteration of course to port for a vessel forward of the beam, other than for a vessel being overtaken; and
  (ii) an alteration of course toward a vessel abeam or abaft the beam.
(e) Except where it has been determined that a risk of collision does not exist, every vessel which hears apparently forward of her beam the fog signal of another vessel, or which cannot avoid a close-quarters situation with another vessel forward of her beam, shall reduce her speed to the minimum at which she can be kept on course. She shall if necessary take all her way off and, in any event, navigate with extreme caution until danger of collision is over.

PART C—LIGHTS AND SHAPES

RULE 20

Application
(a) Rules in this Part shall be complied with in all weathers.
(b) The Rules concerning lights shall be complied with from sunset to sunrise, and during such times no other lights shall be exhibited, except such lights as cannot be mistaken for the lights specified in these Rules or do not impair their visibility or distinctive character, or interfere with the keeping of a proper look-out.
(c) The lights prescribed by these Rules shall, if carried, also be exhibited from sunrise to sunset in restricted visibility and may be exhibited in all other circumstances when it is deemed necessary.
(d) The Rules concerning shapes shall be complied with by day.
(e) The lights and shapes specified in these Rules shall comply with the provisions of Annex I of these Rules.

RULE 21

Definitions
(a) "Masthead light" means a white light placed over the fore and aft centerline of the vessel showing an unbroken light over an arc of the horizon of 225 degrees and so fixed as to show the light from right ahead to 22.5 degrees abaft the beam on either side of the vessel, except that on a vessel of less than 12 meters in length the masthead light shall be placed as nearly as practicable to the fore and aft centerline of the vessel.
(b) "Sidelights" mean a green light on the starboard side and a red light on the port side each showing an unbroken light over an arc of the horizon of 112.5 degrees and so fixed as to show the light from right ahead to 22.5 degrees abaft the beam on its respective side. On a vessel of less than 20 meters in length the sidelights may be combined in one lantern carried on the fore and aft centerline of the vessel, except that on a vessel of less than 12 meters in length the sidelights when combined in one lantern shall be placed as nearly as practicable to the fore and aft centerline of the vessel.
(c) "Sternlight" means a white light placed as nearly as practicable at the stern showing an unbroken light over an arc of the horizon of 135 degrees and so fixed as to show the light 67.5 degrees from right aft on each side of the vessel.
(d) "Towing light" means a yellow light having the same characteristics as the "sternlight" defined in paragraph (c) of this Rule.
(e) "All-round light" means a light showing an unbroken light over an arc of the horizon of 360 degrees.
(f) "Flashing light" means a light flashing at regular intervals at a frequency of 120 flashes or more per minute.
(g) "Special flashing light" means a yellow light flashing at regular intervals at a frequency of 50 to 70 flashes per minute, placed as far forward and as nearly as practicable on the fore and aft centerline of the tow and showing an unbroken light over an arc of the horizon of not less than 180 degrees nor more than 225 degrees and so fixed as to show the light from right ahead to abeam and no more than 22.5 degrees abaft the beam on either side of the vessel.

RULE 22

Visibility of Lights
The lights prescribed in these Rules shall have an intensity as specified in Annex I to these Rules, so as to be visible at the following minimum ranges:
(a) In a vessel of 50 meters or more in length:
  —a masthead light, 6 miles;
  —a sidelight, 3 miles;
  —a sternlight, 3 miles;
  —a towing light, 3 miles;
  —a white, red, green or yellow all-round light, 3 miles;
  —a special flashing light, 2 miles.
(b) In a vessel of 12 meters or more in length but less than 50 meters in length:
  —a masthead light, 5 miles; except that where the length of the vessel is less than 20 meters, 3 miles;
  —a sidelight, 2 miles;
  —a sternlight, 2 miles;
  —a towing light, 2 miles;
  —a white, red, green or yellow all-round light, 2 miles;
  —a special flashing light, 2 miles.
(c) In a vessel of less than 12 meters in length:
  —a masthead light, 2 miles;

—a sidelight, 1 mile;
—a sternlight, 2 miles;
—a towing light, 2 miles;
—a white, red, green or yellow all-round light, 2 miles;
—a special flashing light, 2 miles.
(d) In an inconspicuous, partly submerged vessel or object being towed:
—a white all-round light, 3 miles.

RULE 23

Power-driven Vessels Underway
(a) A power-driven vessel underway shall exhibit:
  (i) a masthead light forward;
  (ii) a second masthead light abaft of and higher than the forward one; except that a vessel of less than 50 meters in length shall not be obliged to exhibit such light but may do so;
  (iii) sidelights; and
  (iv) a sternlight.
(b) An air-cushion vessel when operating in the nondisplacement mode shall, in addition to the lights prescribed in paragraph (a) of this Rule, exhibit an all-round flashing yellow light where it can best be seen.
(c) A power-driven vessel of less than 12 meters in length may, in lieu of the lights prescribed in paragraph (a) of this Rule, exhibit an all-round white light and sidelights.
(d) A power-driven vessel when operating on the Great Lakes may carry an all-round white light in lieu of the second masthead light and sternlight prescribed in paragraph (a) of this Rule. The light shall be carried in the position of the second masthead light and be visible at the same minimum range.

RULE 24

Towing and Pushing
(a) A power-driven vessel when towing astern shall exhibit:
  (i) instead of the light prescribed either in Rule 23(a)(i) or 23(a)(ii), two masthead lights in a vertical line. When the length of the tow, measuring from the stern of the towing vessel to the after end of the tow exceeds 200 meters, three such lights in a vertical line;
  (ii) sidelights;
  (iii) a sternlight;
  (iv) a towing light in a vertical line above the sternlight; and
  (v) when the length of the tow exceeds 200 meters, a diamond shape where it can best be seen.
(b) When a pushing vessel and a vessel being pushed ahead are rigidly connected in a composite unit they shall be regarded as a power-driven vessel and exhibit the lights prescribed in Rule 23.
(c) A power-driven vessel when pushing ahead or towing alongside, except as required by paragraphs (b) and (i) of this Rule, shall exhibit:
  (i) instead of the light prescribed either in Rule 23(a)(i) or 23(a)(ii), two masthead lights in a vertical line;
  (ii) sidelights; and
  (iii) two towing lights in a vertical line.
(d) A power-driven vessel to which paragraphs (a) or (c) of this Rule apply shall also comply with Rule 23(a)(i) and 23(a)(ii).
(e) A vessel or object being towed, other than those mentioned in paragraph (g) of this Rule shall exhibit:
  (i) sidelights;
  (ii) a sternlight; and
  (iii) when the length of the tow exceeds 200 meters, a diamond shape where it can best be seen.
(f) Provided that any number of vessels being towed alongside or pushed in a group shall be lighted as one vessel, except as provided in paragraph (iii):
  (i) a vessel being pushed ahead, not being part of a composite unit, shall exhibit at the forward end sidelights, and a special flashing light;
  (ii) a vessel being towed alongside shall exhibit a sternlight and at the forward end, sidelights and a special flashing light; and
  (iii) when vessels are towed alongside on both sides of the towing vessels a sternlight shall be exhibited on the stern of the outboard vessel on each side of the towing vessel, and a single set of sidelights as far forward and as far outboard as is practicable, and a single special flashing light.
(g) An inconspicuous, partly submerged vessel or object being towed shall exhibit:
  (i) if it is less than 25 meters in breadth, one all-round white light at or near each end;
  (ii) if it is 25 meters or more in breadth, four all-round white lights to mark its length and breadth;
  (iii) if it exceeds 100 meters in length, additional all-round white lights between the lights prescribed in subparagraphs (i) and (ii) so that the distance between the lights shall not exceed 100 meters: Provided, that any vessels or objects being towed alongside each other shall be lighted as one vessel or object;
  (iv) a diamond shape at or near the aftermost extremity of the last vessel or object being towed; and
  (v) the towing vessel may direct a searchlight in the direction of the tow to indicate its presence to an approaching vessel.
(h) Where from any sufficient cause it is impracticable for a vessel or object being towed to exhibit the lights prescribed in paragraph (e) or (g) of this Rule, all possible measures shall be taken to light the vessel or object towed or at least to indicate the presence of the unlighted vessel or object.
(i) Notwithstanding paragraph (c), on the Western Rivers (except below the Huey P. Long Bridge on the Mississippi River) and on waters specified by the Secretary, a power-driven vessel when pushing ahead or towing alongside, except as paragraph (b) applies, shall exhibit:
  (i) sidelights; and

(ii) two towing lights in a vertical line.
(j) Where from any sufficient cause it is impracticable for a vessel not normally engaged in towing operations to display the lights prescribed by paragraph (a), (c) or (i) of this Rule, such vessel shall not be required to exhibit those lights when engaged in towing another vessel in distress or otherwise in need of assistance. All possible measures shall be taken to indicate the nature of the relationship between the towing vessel and the vessel being assisted. The searchlight authorized by Rule 36 may be used to illuminate the tow.

RULE 25

Sailing Vessels Underway and Vessels Under Oars
(a) A sailing vessel underway shall exhibit:
  (i) sidelights; and
  (ii) a stern light.
(b) In a sailing vessel of less than 20 meters in length the lights prescribed in paragraph (a) of this Rule may be combined in one lantern carried at or near the top of the mast where it can best be seen.
(c) A sailing vessel underway may, in addition to the lights prescribed in paragraph (a) of this Rule, exhibit at or near the top of the mast, where they can best be seen, two all-round lights in a vertical line, the upper being red and the lower green, but these lights shall not be exhibited in conjunction with the combined lantern permitted by paragraph (b) of this Rule.
(d) (i) A sailing vessel of less than 7 meters in length shall, if practicable, exhibit the lights prescribed in paragraph (a) or (b) of this Rule, but if she does not, she shall have ready at hand an electric torch or lighted lantern showing a white light which shall be exhibited in sufficient time to prevent collision.
  (ii) A vessel under oars may exhibit the lights prescribed in this Rule for sailing vessels, but if she does not, she shall have ready at hand an electric torch or lighted lantern showing a white light which shall be exhibited in sufficient time to prevent collision.
(e) A vessel proceeding under sail when also being propelled by machinery shall exhibit forward where it can best be seen a conical shape, apex downward. A vessel of less than 12 meters in length is not required to exhibit this shape, but may do so.

RULE 26

Fishing Vessels
(a) A vessel engaged in fishing, whether underway or at anchor, shall exhibit only the lights and shapes prescribed in this Rule.
(b) A vessel when engaged in trawling, by which is meant the dragging through the water of a dredge net or other apparatus used as a fishing appliance, shall exhibit:
  (i) two all-round lights in a vertical line, the upper being green and the lower white, or a shape consisting of two cones with their apexes together in a vertical line one above the other;
  (ii) a masthead light abaft of and higher than the all-round green light; a vessel of less than 50 meters in length shall not be obliged to exhibit such a light but may do so; and
  (iii) when making way through the water, in addition to the lights prescribed in this paragraph, sidelights and a sternlight.
(c) A vessel engaged in fishing, other than trawling, shall exhibit:
  (i) two all-round lights in a vertical line, the upper being red and the lower white, or a shape consisting of two cones with apexes together in a vertical line one above the other;
  (ii) when there is outlying gear extending more than 150 meters horizontally from the vessel, an all-round white light or a cone apex upward in the direction of the gear; and
  (iii) when making way through the water, in addition to the lights prescribed in this paragraph, sidelights and a sternlight.
(d) The additional signals described in Annex II to these Rules apply to a vessel engaged in fishing in close proximity to other vessels engaged in fishing.
(e) A vessel when not engaged in fishing shall not exhibit the lights or shapes prescribed in this Rule, but only those prescribed for a vessel of her length.

RULE 27

Vessels Not Under Command or Restricted in Their Ability to Maneuver
(a) A vessel not under command shall exhibit:
  (i) two all-round red lights in a vertical line where they can best be seen;
  (ii) two balls or similar shapes in a vertical line where they can best be seen; and
  (iii) when making way through the water, in addition to the lights prescribed in this paragraph, sidelights and a sternlight.
(b) A vessel restricted in her ability to maneuver, except a vessel engaged in mineclearance operations, shall exhibit:
  (i) three all-round lights in a vertical line where they can best be seen. The highest and lowest of these lights shall be red and the middle light shall be white;
  (ii) three shapes in a vertical line where they can best be seen. The highest and lowest of these shapes shall be balls and the middle one a diamond;
  (iii) when making way through the water, masthead lights, sidelights and a sternlight, in addition to the lights prescribed in subparagraph (b)(i); and
  (iv) when at anchor, in addition to the lights or shapes prescribed in subparagraphs (b)(i) and (ii), the light, lights or shapes prescribed in Rule 30.
(c) A vessel engaged in a towing operation which severely restricts the towing vessel and her tow in their ability to deviate from their course shall, in addition to the lights or shapes prescribed in subparagraphs (b)(i) and (ii) of this Rule, exhibit the lights or shape prescribed in Rule 24.

(d) A vessel engaged in dredging or underwater operations, when restricted in her ability to maneuver, shall exhibit the lights and shapes prescribed in subparagraphs (b)(i), (ii), and (iii) of this Rule and shall in addition, when an obstruction exists, exhibit:
   (i) two all-round red lights or two balls in a vertical line to indicate the side on which the obstruction exists;
   (ii) two all-round green lights or two diamonds in a vertical line to indicate the side on which another vessel may pass; and
   (iii) when at anchor, the lights or shape prescribed by this paragraph, instead of the lights or shapes prescribed in Rule 30 for anchored vessels.
(e) Whenever the size of a vessel engaged in diving operations makes it impracticable to exhibit all lights and shapes prescribed in paragraph (d) of this Rule, the following shall instead be exhibited:
   (i) Three all-round lights in a vertical line where they can best be seen. The highest and lowest of these lights shall be red and the middle light shall be white;
   (ii) A rigid replica of the international Code flag "A" not less than 1 meter in height. Measures shall be taken to insure its all-round visibility.
(f) A vessel engaged in mineclearance operations shall, in addition to the lights prescribed for a power-driven vessel in Rule 23 or to the lights or shape prescribed for a vessel at anchor in Rule 30, as appropriate, exhibit three all-round green lights or three balls. One of these lights or shapes shall be exhibited near the foremast head and one at each end of the foreyard. These lights or shapes indicate that it is dangerous for another vessel to approach within 1000 meters of the mineclearance vessel.
(g) A vessel of less than 12 meters in length, except when engaged in diving operations, is not required to exhibit the lights or shapes prescribed in this Rule.
(h) The signals prescribed in this Rule are not signals of vessels in distress and requiring assistance. Such signals are contained in Annex IV to these Rules.

RULE 29

Pilot Vessels
(a) A vessel engaged on pilotage duty shall exhibit:
   (i) at or near the masthead, two all-round lights in a vertical line, the upper being white and the lower red;
   (ii) when underway, in addition, sidelights and a sternlight; and
   (iii) when at anchor, in addition to the lights prescribed in subparagraph (i), the light, lights, or shape prescribed in Rule 30 for anchored vessels.
(b) A pilot vessel when not engaged on pilotage duty shall exhibit the lights or shapes prescribed for a vessel of her length.

RULE 30

Anchored Vessels and Vessels Aground
(a) A vessel at anchor shall exhibit where it can best be seen:
   (i) in the fore part, an all-round white light or one ball; and
   (ii) at or near the stern and at a lower level than the light prescribed in subparagraph (i), an all-round white light.
(b) A vessel of less than 50 meters in length may exhibit an all-round white light where it can best be seen instead of the lights prescribed in paragraph (a) of this Rule.
(c) A vessel at anchor may, and a vessel of 100 meters or more in length shall, also use the available working or equivalent lights to illuminate her decks.
(d) A vessel aground shall exhibit the lights prescribed in paragraph (a) or (b) of this Rule and in addition, if practicable, where they can best be seen:
   (i) two all-round red lights in a vertical line; and
   (ii) three balls in a vertical line.
(e) A vessel of less than 7 meters in length, when at anchor, not in or near a narrow channel, fairway, anchorage, or where other vessels normally navigate, shall not be required to exhibit the lights or shape prescribed in paragraphs (a) and (b) of this Rule.
(f) A vessel of less than 12 meters in length when aground shall not be required to exhibit the lights or shapes prescribed in subparagraphs (d)(i) and (ii) of this Rule.
(g) A vessel of less than 20 meters in length, when at anchor in a special anchorage area designated by the Secretary, shall not be required to exhibit the anchor lights and shapes required by this Rule.

RULE 31

Seaplanes
Where it is impracticable for a seaplane to exhibit lights and shapes of the characteristics or in the positions prescribed in the Rules of this Part she shall exhibit lights and shapes as closely similar in characteristics and position as is possible.

PART D—SOUND AND LIGHT SIGNALS

RULE 32

Definitions
(a) The word "whistle" means any sound signaling appliance capable of producing the prescribed blasts and which complies with specifications in Annex III to these Rules.
(b) The term "short blast" means a blast of about 1 second's duration.
(c) The term "prolonged blast" means a blast of from 4 to 6 seconds' duration.

APPENDIX VII

RULE 33

Equipment for Sound Signals

(a) A vessel of 12 meters or more in length shall be provided with a whistle and a bell and a vessel of 100 meters or more in length shall, in addition, be provided with a gong, the tone and sound of which cannot be confused with that of the bell. The whistle, bell and gong shall comply with the specifications in Annex III to these Rules. The bell or gong or both may be replaced by other equipment having the same respective sound characteristics, provided that manual sounding of the prescribed signals shall always be possible.

(b) A vessel of less than 12 meters in length shall not be obliged to carry the sound signaling appliances prescribed in paragraph (a) of this Rule but if she does not, she shall be provided with some other means of making an efficient signal.

RULE 34

Maneuvering and Warning Signals

(a) When power-driven vessels are in sight of one another and meeting or crossing at a distance within half a mile of each other, each vessel underway, when maneuvering as authorized or required by these Rules:

 (i) shall indicate that maneuver by the following signals on her whistle: one short blast to mean "I intend to leave you on my port side"; two short blasts to mean "I intend to leave you on my starboard side"; and three short blasts to mean "I am operating astern propulsion".

 (ii) upon hearing the one or two blast signal of the other shall, if in agreement, sound the same whistle signal and take the steps necessary to effect a safe passing. If, however, from any cause, the vessel doubts the safety of the proposed maneuver, she shall sound the danger signal specified in paragraph (d) of this Rule and each vessel shall take appropriate precautionary action until a safe passing agreement is made.

(b) A vessel may supplement the whistle signals prescribed in paragraph (a) of this Rule by light signals:

 (i) These signals shall have the following significance: one flash to mean "I intend to leave you on my port side"; two flashes to mean "I intend to leave you on my starboard side"; three flashes to mean "I am operating astern propulsion";

 (ii) The duration of each flash shall be about 1 second; and

 (iii) The light used for this signal shall, if fitted, be one all-round white or yellow light, visible at a minimum range of 2 miles, synchronized with the whistle, and shall comply with the provisions of Annex I to these Rules.

(c) When in sight of one another:

 (i) a power-driven vessel intending to overtake another power-driven vessel shall indicate her intention by the following signals on her whistle: one short blast to mean "I intend to overtake you on your starboard side"; two short blasts to mean "I intend to overtake you on your port side"; and

 (ii) the power-driven vessel about to be overtaken shall, if in agreement, sound a similar sound signal. If in doubt she shall sound the danger signal prescribed in paragraph (d).

(d) When vessels in sight of one another are approaching each other and from any cause either vessel fails to understand the intentions or actions of the other, or is in doubt whether sufficient action is being taken by the other to avoid collision, the vessel in doubt shall immediately indicate such doubt by giving at least five short and rapid blasts on the whistle. This signal may be supplemented by a light signal of at least five short and rapid flashes.

(e) A vessel nearing a bend or an area of a channel or fairway where other vessels may be obscured by an intervening obstruction shall sound one prolonged blast. This signal shall be answered with a prolonged blast by any approaching vessel that may be within hearing around the bend or behind the intervening obstruction.

(f) If whistles are fitted on a vessel at a distance apart of more than 100 meters, one whistle only shall be used for giving maneuvering and warning signals.

(g) When a power-driven vessel is leaving a dock or berth, she shall sound one prolonged blast.

(h) A vessel that reaches agreement with another vessel in a head on, crossing, or overtaking situation, as for example, by using the radiotelephone as prescribed by the Vessel Bridge-to-Bridge Radiotelephone Act (85 Stat. 164; 33 U.S.C. 1201 et seq.), is not obliged to sound the whistle signals prescribed by this Rule, but may do so. If agreement is not reached, then whistle signals shall be exchanged in a timely manner and shall prevail.

RULE 35

Sound Signals in Restricted Visibility

In or near an area of restricted visibility, whether by day or night, the signals prescribed in this Rule shall be used as follows:

(a) A power-driven vessel making way through the water shall sound at intervals of not more than 2 minutes one prolonged blast.

(b) A power-driven vessel underway but stopped and making no way through the water shall sound at intervals of not more than 2 minutes two prolonged blasts in succession with an interval of about 2 seconds between them.

(c) vessel not under command; a vessel restricted in her ability to maneuver, whether underway or at anchor; a sailing vessel; a vessel engaged in fishing, whether underway or at anchor; and a vessel engaged in towing or pushing another vessel shall, instead of the signals prescribed in paragraphs (a) or (b) of this Rule, sound at intervals of not more than 2 minutes, three blasts in succession; namely, one prolonged followed by two short blasts.

(d) A vessel towed or if more than one vessel is towed the last vessel of the tow, if manned, shall at intervals of not more than 2 minutes sound

four blasts in succession; namely, one prolonged followed by three short blasts. When practicable, this signal shall be made immediately after the signal made by the towing vessel.
(e) When a pushing vessel and a vessel being pushed ahead are rigidly connected in a composite unit they shall be regarded as a power-driven vessel and shall give the signals prescribed in paragraphs (a) or (b) of this Rule.
(f) A vessel at anchor shall at intervals of not more than 1 minute ring the bell rapidly for about 5 seconds. In a vessel of 100 meters or more in length the bell shall be sounded in the forepart of the vessel and immediately after the ringing of the bell the gong shall be sounded rapidly for about 5 seconds in the after part of the vessel. A vessel at anchor may in addition sound three blasts in succession; namely, one short, one prolonged and one short blast, to give warning of her position and of the possibility of collision to an approaching vessel.
(g) A vessel aground shall give the bell signal and if required the gong signal prescribed in paragraph (f) of this Rule and shall, in addition, give three separate and distinct strokes on the bell immediately before and after the rapid ringing of the bell. A vessel aground may in addition sound an appropriate whistle signal.
(h) A vessel of less than 12 meters in length shall not be obliged to give the above-mentioned signals but, if she does not, shall make some other efficient sound signal at intervals of not more than 2 minutes.
(i) A pilot vessel when engaged on pilotage duty may in addition to the signals prescribed in paragraphs (a), (b) or (f) of this Rule sound an identity signal consisting of four short blasts.
(j) The following vessels shall not be required to sound signals as prescribed in paragraph (f) of this Rule when anchored in a special anchorage area designated by the Secretary:
  (i) a vessel of less than 20 meters in length; and
  (ii) a barge, canal boat, scow, or other nondescript craft.

RULE 36

Signals to Attract Attention

If necessary to attract the attention of another vessel, any vessel may make light or sound signals that cannot be mistaken for any signal authorized elsewhere in these Rules, or may direct the beam of her searchlight in the direction of the danger, in such a way as not to embarrass any vessel.

RULE 37

Distress Signals

When a vessel is in distress and requires assistance she shall use or exhibit the signals described in Annex IV to these Rules. The distress signals for inland waters are the same as those displayed for international waters with the following additional signal described:

A high intensity white light flashing at regular intervals from 50 to 70 times per minute.

PART E—EXEMPTIONS

RULE 38

Exemptions

Any vessel or class of vessels, the keel of which is laid or which is at a corresponding stage of construction before December 24, 1980, provided that she complies with the requirements of—
(a) The Act of June 7, 1897 (30 Stat. 96), as amended (33 U.S.C. 154-232) for vessels navigating the waters subject to that statute;
(b) Section 4233 of the Revised Statutes (33 U.S.C. 301-356) for vessels navigating the waters subject to that statute;
(c) The Act of February 8, 1895 (28 Stat. 645), as amended (33 U.S.C. 241-295) for vessels navigating the waters subject to that statute; or
(d) Sections 3, 4, and 5 of the Act of April 25, 1940 (54 Stat. 163), as amended (46 U.S.C. 526 b, c, and d) for motorboats navigating the waters subject to that statute; shall be exempted from compliance with the technical Annexes to these Rules as follows:
  (i) the installation of lights with ranges prescribed in Rule 22, until 4 years after the effective date of these Rules, except that vessels of less than 20 meters in length are permanently exempt;
  (ii) the installation of lights with color specifications as prescribed in Annex I to these Rules, until 4 years after the effective date of these Rules, except that vessels of less than 20 meters in length are permanently exempt;
  (iii) the repositioning of lights as a result of conversion to metric units and rounding off measurement figures, are permanently exempt; and
  (iv) the horizontal repositioning of masthead lights prescribed by Annex I to these Rules:
    (1) on vessels of less than 150 meters in length, permanent exemption.
    (2) on vessels of 150 meters or more in length, until 9 years after the effective date of these Rules.
  (v) the restructuring or repositioning of all lights to meet the prescriptions of Annex I to these Rules, until 9 years after the effective date of these Rules;
  (vi) power-driven vessels of 12 meters or more but less than 20 meters in length are permanently exempt from the provisions of Rule 23(a)(i) and 23(a)(iv) provided that, in place of these lights, the vessel exhibits a white light aft visible all round the horizon; and
  (vii) the requirements for sound signal appliances prescribed in Annex III to these Rules, until 9 years after the effective date of these Rules.

APPENDIX VIII

WILDLIFE, FISHERIES AND THE NORTH ATLANTIC RIGHT WHALE

Appendix VIII contains, in Part 1, extracts from parts 222, 224, 226 and 622 of the Code of Federal Regulations issued by the United States Department of Commerce; and in Part 2, information and guidance specific to the protection of North Atlantic (or northern) right whales, including mandatory speed restrictions, mandatory reporting, and recommended two-way whale avoidance routes.

PART 1: CODE OF FEDERAL REGULATIONS TITLE 50 – WILDLIFE AND FISHERIES

For the complete text of these parts see Title 50 of the Code of Federal Regulations (CFR).

Part 222 – General Endangered and Threatened Marine Species

Subpart A — Introduction and General Provisions

§222.101 Purpose and scope of regulations.

(a) The regulations of parts 222, 223, and 224 of this chapter implement the Endangered Species Act (Act), and govern the taking, possession, transportation, sale, purchase, barter, exportation, importation of, and other requirements pertaining to wildlife and plants under the jurisdiction of the Secretary of Commerce and determined to be threatened or endangered pursuant to section 4(a) of the Act. These regulations are implemented by the National Marine Fisheries Service, National Oceanic and Atmospheric Administration, US Department of Commerce. This part pertains to general provisions and definitions. Specifically, parts 223 and 224 pertain to provisions to threatened species and endangered species, respectively. Part 226 enumerates designated critical habitat for endangered and threatened species. Certain of the endangered and threatened marine species enumerated in §§224.102 and 223.102 are included in Appendix I or II to the Convention on International Trade of Endangered Species of Wild Fauna or Flora. The importation, exportation, and re-exportation of such species are subject to additional regulations set forth in 50 CFR part 23, chapter 1.

(b) For rules and procedures relating to species determined to be threatened or endangered under the jurisdiction of the Secretary of the Interior, see 50 CFR parts 10 through 17. For rules and procedures relating to the general implementation of the Act jointly by the Departments of the Interior and Commerce and for certain species under the joint jurisdiction of both the Secretaries of the Interior and Commerce, see 50 CFR Chapter IV. Marine mammals listed as endangered or threatened and subject to these regulations may also be subject to additional requirements pursuant to the Marine Mammal Protection Act (for regulations implementing that act, see CFR part 216).

(c) No statute or regulation of any state shall be construed to relieve a person from the restrictions, conditions, and requirements contained in parts 222, 223, and 224 of this chapter. In addition, nothing in parts 222, 223, and 224 of this chapter, including any permit issued pursuant thereto, shall be construed to relieve a person from any other requirements imposed by a statute or regulation of any state or of the United States, including any applicable health, quarantine, agricultural, or customs laws or regulations or any other National Marine Fisheries Service enforced statutes or regulations.

Part 224 – Endangered Marine and Anadromous Species

§224.103 Special prohibitions for endangered marine mammals.

(c) *Approaching right whales*
  (1) *Prohibitions*. Except as provided under paragraph (c)(3) of this section, it is unlawful for any person subject to the jurisdiction of the United States to commit, attempt to commit, to solicit another to commit, or cause to be committed any of the following acts:
    (i) Approach (including by interception) within 500 yards (460 m) of a Right Whale by vessel, aircraft, or any other means;
    (ii) Fail to undertake required right whale avoidance measures specified under paragraph (c)(2) of this section.
  (2) *Right Whale avoidance measures*. Except as provided under paragraph (c)(3) of this section, the following avoidance measures must be taken if within 500 yards (460 m) of a right whale:
    (i) If underway, a vessel must steer a course away from the right whale and immediately leave the area at a slow safe speed;
    (ii) An aircraft must take a course away from the right whale and immediately leave the area at a constant airspeed.
  (3) *Exceptions*. The following exceptions apply to this section, but any person who claims the applicability of an exception has the burden of proving that the exception applies:
    (i) Paragraphs (c)(1) and (c)(2) of this section do not apply if a right whale approach is authorized by the National Marine Fisheries Service through a permit issued under part 222, subpart C, of this chapter (General Permit

Procedures) or through a similar authorization.

(ii) Paragraphs (c)(1) and (c)(2) of this section do not apply where compliance would create an imminent and serious threat to a person, vessel, or aircraft.

(iii) Paragraphs (c)(1) and (c)(2) of this section do not apply when approaching to investigate a right whale entanglement or injury, or to assist in the disentanglement or rescue of a right whale, provided that permission is received from the National Marine Fisheries Service or designee prior to the approach.

(iv) Paragraphs (c)(1) and (c)(2) of this section do not apply to an aircraft unless the aircraft is conducting whale watch activities.

(v) Paragraph (c)(2) of this section does not apply to the extent that a vessel is restricted in her ability to manoeuvre, and because of the restriction, cannot comply with paragraph (c)(2) of this section.

§224.105 Speed restrictions to protect North Atlantic Right Whales.

(a) The following restrictions apply to all vessels greater than or equal to 19·8 m (65 ft) in overall length and subject to the jurisdiction of the United States, and all other vessels greater than or equal to 19·8 m (65 ft) in overall length entering or departing a place subject to the jurisdiction of the United States. These restrictions shall not apply to US vessels owned or operated by, or under contract to, the Federal Government. This exemption extends to foreign sovereign vessels when they are engaging in joint exercises with the US Department of the Navy. In addition, these restrictions do not apply to law enforcement vessels of a state, or political subdivision thereof, when engaged in law enforcement or search and rescue duties.

(1) *Southeast US* (south of St. Augustine, FL to north of Brunswick, GA). Vessels shall travel at a speed of 10 knots or less over ground during the period of November 15 to April 15 each year in the area bounded by the following:
Beginning at 31°27′00·0″N 80°51′36·0″W; then west to charted mean high water line, then south along mean high water line and inshore limits of COLREGS limit to a latitude of 29°45′00·0″N, thence east to 29°45′00·0″N 80°51′36·0″W; thence back to starting point.

(2) *Mid-Atlantic US* (from north of Brunswick, Georgia to Rhode Island). Vessels shall travel at a speed of 10 knots or less over ground during the period of November 1 to April 30 each year in the area bounded by the following:

(i) Beginning at 33°56′42·0″N 77°31′30·0″W; thence along a NW bearing of 313·26° to charted mean high water line then south along mean high water line and inshore limits of COLREGS limit to a latitude of 31°27′00·0″N; thence east to:
31°27′00·0″N 80°51′36·0″W; thence to
31°50′00·0″N 80°33′12·0″W; thence to
32°59′06·0″N 78°50′18·0″W; thence to
33°28′24·0″N 78°32′30·0″W; thence to
33°36′30·0″N 77°47′06·0″W; thence back to starting point.

(ii) Within a 20 mile (37 km) radius (as measured seaward from COLREGS delineated coast lines and the center point of the port entrance) at the:
 (A) Ports of New York/New Jersey: 40°29′42·2″N 73°55′57·6″W; and
 (B) Ports of Philadelphia and Wilmington: 38°52′27·4″N 75°01′32·1″W; and
 (C) Ports of Hampton Roads and Baltimore: 37°00′36·9″N 75°57′50·5″W; and
 (D) Ports of Morehead City and Beaufort: 34°41′32·0″N 76°40′08·3″W

(iii) In Block Island Sound, in the area bounded by the following coordinates:
40°51′53·7″N 70°36′44·9″W; thence to:
41°20′14·1″N 70°49′44·1″W; thence to:
41°04′16·7″N 71°51′21·0″W; thence to:
40°35′56·5″N 71°38′25·1″W; thence back to starting point.

(3) *Northeast US* (north of Rhode Island).

(i) *In Cape Cod Bay*. Vessels shall travel at a speed of 10 knots or less over ground during the period of January 1 to May 15 in the area bounded by the following:
Beginning at 42°04′56·5″N 70°12′00·0″W; thence north to 42°12′00·0″N 70°12′00·0″; thence due west to charted mean high water line; thence along charted mean high water line within Cape Cod Bay back to the beginning point.

(ii) *Off Race Point*. Vessels shall travel at a speed of 10 knots or less over ground during the period of March 1 to April 30 each year in waters bounded by straight lines connecting the following points in the order stated:
42°30′00·0″N 69°45′00·0″W; thence to
42°30′00·0″N 70°30′00·0″W; thence to
42°12′00·0″N 70°30′00·0″W; thence to
42°12′00·0″N 70°12′00·0″W; thence to
42°04′56·5″N 70°12′00·0″W; thence along charted mean high water line and inshore limits of COLREGS limit to a latitude of 41°40′00·0″N, thence due east to 41°40′00·0″N 69°45′00·0″W; thence back to starting point.

(iii) *Great South Channel*. Vessels shall travel at a speed of 10 knots or less over ground during the period of April 1 to July 31 each year in all waters bounded by straight lines connecting the following points in the order stated:
42°30′00·0″N 69°45′00·0″W.
41°40′00·0″N 69°45′00·0″W.
41°00′00·0″N 69°05′00·0″W.
42°09′00·0″N 67°08′24·0″W.
42°30′00·0″N 67°27′00·0″W.
42°30′00·0″N 69°45′00·0″W.

(b) Except as noted in paragraph (c) of this section, it is unlawful under this section:
  (1) For any vessel subject to the jurisdiction of the United States to violate any speed restriction established in paragraph (a) of this section; or
  (2) For any vessel entering or departing a port or place under the jurisdiction of the United States to violate any speed restriction established in paragraph (a) of this section;
(c) A vessel may operate at a speed necessary to maintain safe manoeuvring speed instead of the required ten knots only if justified because the vessel is in an area where oceanographic, hydrographic and/or meteorological conditions severely restrict the manoeuvrability of the vessel and the need to operate at such speed is confirmed by the pilot on board or, when a vessel is not carrying a pilot, the master of the vessel. If a deviation from the ten knot speed limit is necessary, the reasons for the deviation, the speed at which the vessel is operated, the latitude and longitude of the area, and the time and duration of such deviation shall be entered into the logbook of the vessel. The master of the vessel shall attest to the accuracy of the the logbook entry by signing and dating it.

Part 226 — Designated Critical Habitat

§226.101 Purpose and scope.

The regulations contained in this part identify those habitats designated by the Secretary of Commerce as critical under section 4 of the Act, for endangered and threatened species under the jurisdiction of the Secretary of Commerce. Those species are enumerated at §223.102 of this chapter if threatened, and at §224.101 of this chapter if endangered. For regulations pertaining to the designation of critical habitat, see part 424 of this title, and for regulations pertaining to prohibition against the adverse modification or destruction of critical habitat, see part 402 of this title. Maps and charts identifying designated critical habitat that are not provided in this section may be obtained upon request to the Office of Protected Resources (see §222.102, definition of "Office of Protected Resources").

§226.203 Critical habitat for Northern Right Whales.

(a) *Great South Channel*. The area bounded by 41°40′N 69°45′W; 41°00′N 69°05′W; 41°38′N 68°13′W; and 42°10′N 68°31′W.
(b) *Cape Cod Bay, Massachusetts*. The area bounded by 42°04·8′N 70°10′W; 42°12′N 70°15′W; 42°12′N 70°30′W; and 41°46·8′N 70°30′W and on the south and east by the interior shore line of Cape Cod, Massachusetts.
(c) *Southeastern United States*. The coastal waters between 31°15′N and 30°15′N from the coast out 15 nautical miles; and the coastal waters between 30°15′N and 28°00′N from the coast out 5 nautical miles.

Part 622 Fisheries of the Caribbean, Gulf, and South Atlantic

The regulations in this part govern the conservation and management of species. For a complete description of this part see 50 CFR 622.

PART 2: NORTH ATLANTIC RIGHT WHALES

1. North Atlantic right whales

The North Atlantic (or northern) right whale is one of the world's most endangered large whale species. North Atlantic right whales are found primarily in continental shelf waters between Florida and Nova Scotia. They migrate annually along the east coast between the feeding grounds off New England and Canada and the calving grounds off Florida, Georgia and South Carolina. Because right whales mate, rest, feed and nurse their young at the surface, and often do not move out of the way of oncoming ships, they are highly vulnerable to being struck. Pregnant females and females with nursing calves appear to be particularly vulnerable to collision with ships. Ship strikes and fishing gear entanglements are the two known sources of human related mortality. Intentionally approaching within 500 yards of right whales is prohibited and is a violation of federal law. (See Appendix CFR Title 50, Part 224 (above) for limits, regulations and exceptions).

2. Description of North Atlantic right whale

Right whales are large baleen whales. Adults are generally 45 to 55 ft in length and can weigh up to 70 tons. The body is mostly black, but irregularly shaped white patches may be present on the ventral surface. The best field identification marks are a broad back with no dorsal fin, irregularly bumpy white patches (callosities) on the head, and a distinctive two-column V-shaped blow when viewed from directly behind or in front of the whale. The whales have broad, paddle-shaped flippers and a broad, deeply notched tail. Right whales are slow moving and seldom travel faster than 5 or 6 kn. They can stay submerged for 10 to 20 minutes and may appear suddenly when surfacing to breathe. They are often seen alone or in small groups. At times, right whales form large courtship groups of 20 to 30 animals.

3. Seasonal occurrence of North Atlantic right whales

During seasons and in areas where right whales may occur, vessel operators should maintain a sharp lookout for whales and reduce speeds when consistent with safe navigation. In any given year oceanographic variability may affect the seasonal distribution of right whales. In 1986, right whales were frequently sighted within the Stellwagen Bank National Marine Sanctuary throughout the summer, and in the early spring of of 1998 a large number of right whales were documented near the Narragansett/Buzzards Bay Traffic Separation Scheme. Three areas in US waters have been designated as critical habitats for North Atlantic right whales. The northern critical habitats, the Great South Channel (east of Cape Cod) and Cape Cod Bay extending into Massachusetts Bay, are feeding and nursery grounds. The southern critical habitat, off coastal Florida and Georgia (Sebastian Inlet, Florida to the Altamaha River, Georgia) is a calving area. (See CFR Title 50, Part 224 (above) for regulations, limitations, and exceptions and complete description of the SMAs).

Northern Right Whale

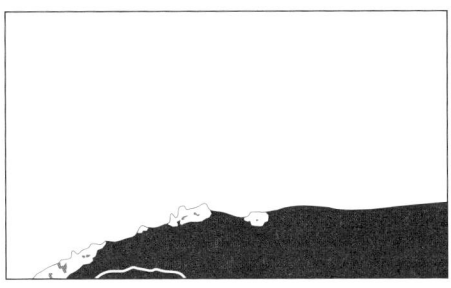

1. Whitish patches of raised and roughened skin (callosities) on top of the head.

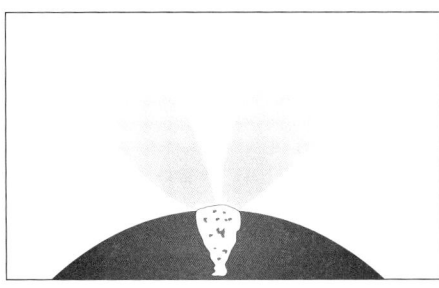

2. V - shaped blow easily visible from in front or behind the whale.

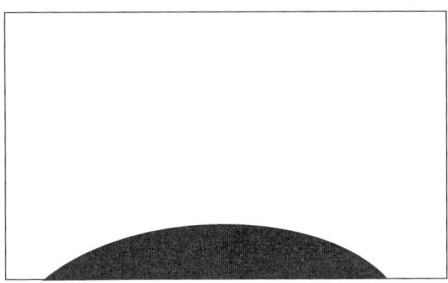

3. No dorsal fin on the back.

4. Tail flukes often lifted vertically when the whale dives.

5. All black tail on the top and underside.

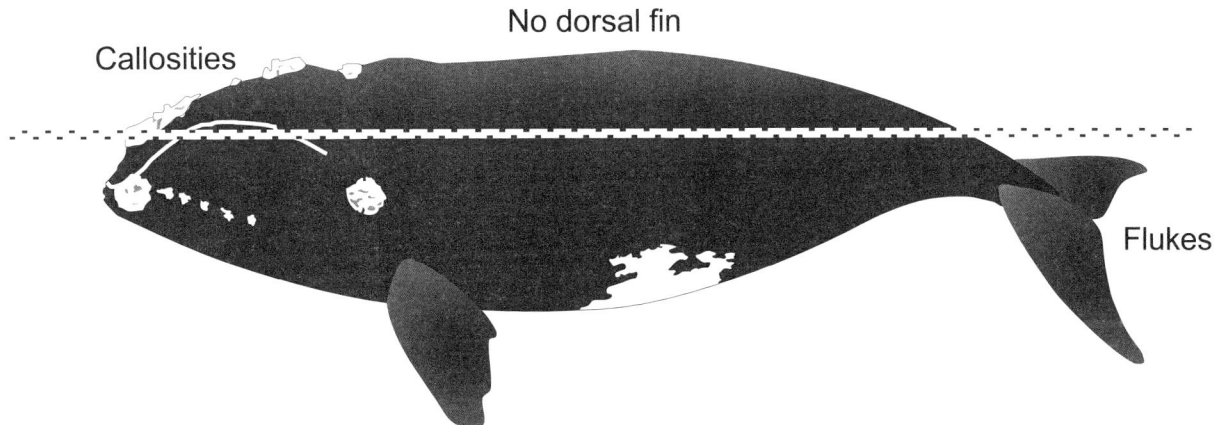

Location	Season	Comments
Central Gulf of Maine (Jordan Basin, Cashes Ledge)	April - June October - December	
Cape Cod Bay	December - May	
Great South Channel, N edge of Georges Bank	March - July	
Bay of Fundy, Scotian Shelf (Browns Bank, Roseway Basin)	July - October	Most of the population can be found in this area during this time
Jeffreys Ledge	October - December	Whales are frequently sighted in this area
Stellwagen Bank National Marine Sanctuary	Year-round	Peak sightings occur in the early spring with infrequent sightings in the summer
New York to N Carolina	November - April	The migration corridor between right whale habitats is within 30 miles of the coast
S Carolina, Georgia and Florida Calving Area	November - April	Calving right whales have been sighted as far north as Cape Fear, NC and as far south as Miami, FL with rare sightings in the Gulf of Mexico

4. Mandatory Speed Restrictions

4   Vessels 65 ft or greater in length overall (LOA) are subject to mandatory speed restrictions of 10 kn or less in seasonal management areas (SMA) along the US East Coast during times when right whales are likely to be present (See following maps for locations of SMAs).

The Northeastern SMA speed restrictions are in place from January 1st through May 15th in Cape Cod Bay, from March 1st through April 30th off Race Point, and from April 1st through July 31st in the Great South Channel.

5   In the Mid-Atlantic US SMAs speed restrictions are in place from November 1st to April 30th and include Block Island Sound, entry into the Ports of New York/New Jersey, Delaware Bay, Entrance to Chesapeake Bay, and the Ports of Morehead City and Beaufort, NC, and within a continuous boundary approximately 20 nautical miles from shore around the major ports of Wilmington, NC, Charleston, SC and Savannah, GA.

6   In the Southeastern US SMA speed restrictions are in place from November 15th to April 15th; this area extends from shore approximately 30 nautical miles eastward and contains the major ports of Brunswick, GA, Fernandina Beach, FL and Jacksonville, FL.

7   See CFR Title 50, Part 224 (above) for regulations, limitations, and exceptions and complete description of the SMAs. NOAA Fisheries may also establish voluntary Dynamic Management Areas (DMAs) when right whales are present in areas and times not covered by the SMAs. Information about established DMAs will be announced over NOAA's customary maritime communication media. Mariners are encouraged to avoid or reduce speed to 10 kn or less while transiting through DMAs.

5. Area To Be Avoided

8   In order to significantly reduce ship strikes to the North Atlantic right whale an area to be avoided was established in the Great South Channel, east of the Boston Harbor traffic lanes. Ships of 300 gross tons and above should avoid the area bounded by lines connecting the following geographical positions:
   41°44′08″N   69°34′50″W
   42°10′00″N   68°31′00″W
   41°24′53″N   68°31′00″W and:
   40°50′28″N   68°58′40″W between the period of April 1st through July 31st.

6. Early Warning and Sighting Advisory Systems

9   As weather and conditions permit, dedicated seasonal programmes of aerial and vessel surveys are conducted in the Northeast and Southeast US to provide whale sighting information to mariners. Surveys typically occur in the following locations at the specified times:
   a) Cape Cod Bay, the Gulf of Maine, the Great South Channel, and Rhode Island, Block Island, and Long Island Sounds from January through July.
   b) South Carolina/North Carolina border south to Crescent Beach, FL from December through March.

10   Survey planes occasionally use VHF-FM channel 16 to contact ships directly if whales have been spotted in close proximity to that vessel. However, many right whales go undetected by surveys. Seasonal right whale advisories and sighting reports are broadcast periodically for these and surrounding areas by Coast Guard Broadcast Notice to Mariners, NAVTEX, NOAA Weather Radio, Cape Cod Canal Vessel Traffic Control, the Bay Of Fundy Vessel Traffic Control, and are included in the return message from the Right Whale Mandatory Ship Reporting (MSR) systems. General sighting information may be obtained by sending an e-mail to ne.rw.sightings@noaa.gov (Northeast) or se.rw.sightings@noaa.gov (Southeast).

7. Precautions when transiting right whale habitat and areas of recently reported right whale sightings

11   NOAA recommends the following precautionary measures be taken to avoid adverse interactions with North Atlantic right whales:
   Before entering right whale habitat (See "Seasonal Occurrence" table), check Coast Guard Broadcast Notices to Mariners, NAVTEX, NOAA Weather Radio, Mandatory Ship Reporting (MSR) system, Cape Cod Canal Vessel Traffic Control, the Bay of Fundy Vessel Traffic Control, as well as other sources for recent right whale sighting reports. Local ship pilots also have information on whale sightings and safe local operating procedures.

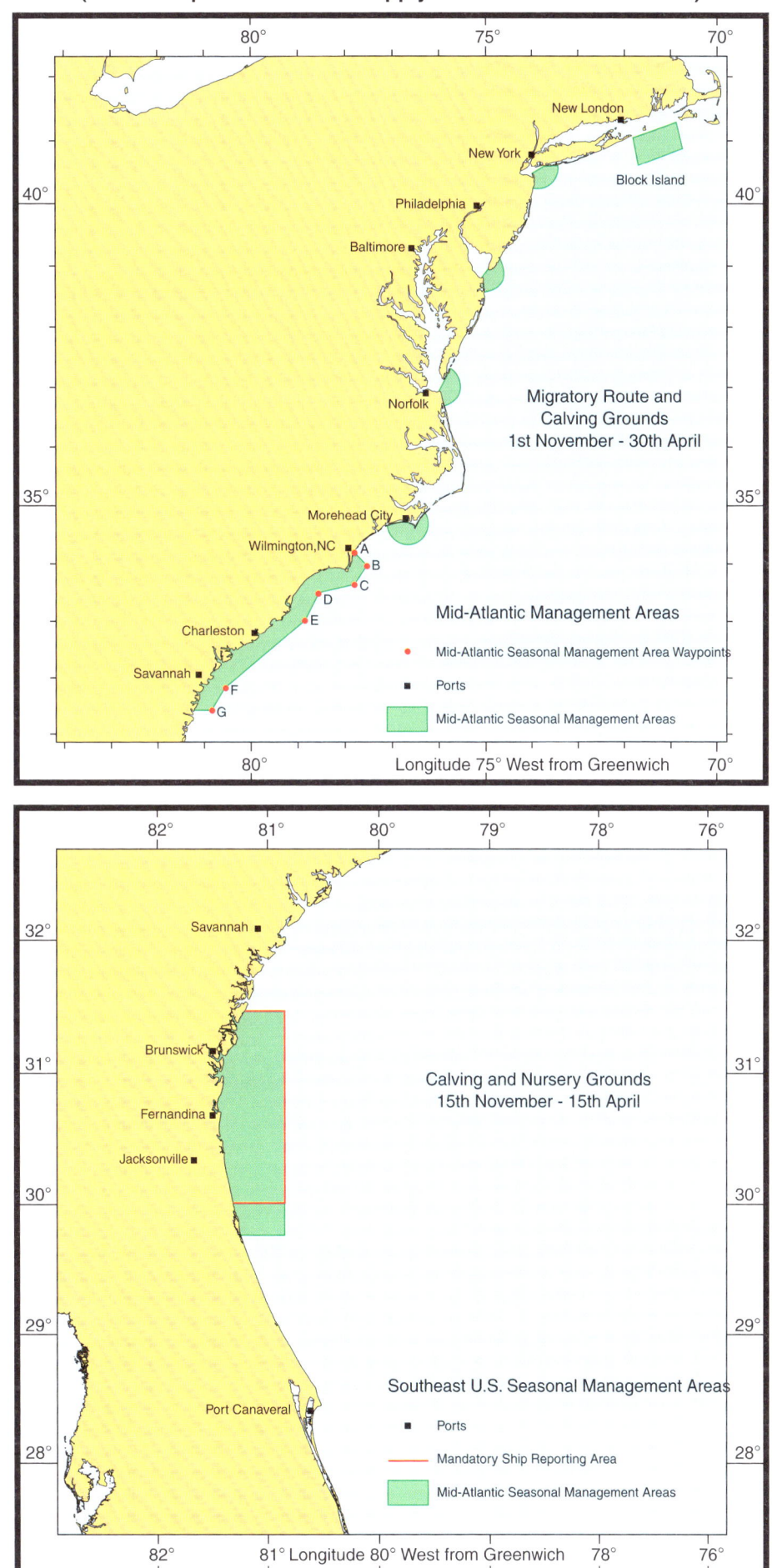

12 Review right whale identification materials and maintain a sharp watch with lookouts familiar with spotting whales. Although right whales are large, their dark colour and lack of a dorsal fin can make them difficult to spot.

Avoid transiting through the right whale habitats and areas where right whales have recently been sighted. If transiting between ports within critical habits, minimize transit distance. Route around observed or recently reported right whales and anticipate delays due to prudent seamanship in response to whale sightings. Avoid transits at night or during periods of low visibility.

13 If a right whale is sighted from the ship or reported along the intended track of the ship, mariners should exercise caution, post a lookout and reduce speed to 10 kn when consistent with safe navigation. If a right whale is sighted, a vessel must steer a course away from the right whale and immediately leave the area at slow safe speed. Do not assume right whales will move out of the way of an approaching vessel. Mariners should keep in mind that it is illegal to approach closer than 500 yards. (See CFR Title 50, Part 224 (above) for limits, regulations and exceptions).

14 Any whale accidentally struck, dead whale carcass, and sighting of an injured or entangled whale should be reported immediately to the Coast Guard or NOAA National Marine Fisheries Service noting the precise location, date, time and time of the accident or sighting. Call 978-281-9351 for reports to NOAA for the area from Virginia to Maine, or 877-433-8299 for the area from North Carolina to Florida. In the event of a strike or sighting of a dead, injured or entangled whale, the following information should be provided:

- Location, date and time of the accident or sighting of a carcass or an entangled whale,
- Speed and course of the vessel,
- Vessel specifications such as size and propulsion,
- Water depth,
- Environmental conditions such as visibility, wind speed and direction,
- Description of the impact,
- Fate of the animal, and
- Species and size, if known.

8. Recommended Two-Way Routes to Avoid Whales

15 To reduce the possibility of vessel strikes with right whales, Two-Way Routes were developed for vessels entering and transiting through Cape Cod Bay and arriving and departing the ports of Brunswick, GA, Fernandina Beach, FL and Jacksonville, FL. The routes were developed from an analysis of historical right whale sightings and are designed to reduce the likelihood of adverse interactions between large vessels and right whales. The routes are found on the latest BA and NOAA nautical charts. In July 2007, the northern leg of the Boston Traffic Separation Scheme (TSS) was shifted to direct ship traffic away from an area of high whale density. Use of the modified TSS is expected to considerably reduce the risk of striking a whale.

9. Mandatory Ship Reporting Systems (MSR) WHALESNORTH and WHALESSOUTH

16 Mandatory Ship Reporting (MSR) systems require all vessels, 300 gross tons or greater, to report to the US Coast Guard upon entering two designated reporting areas off the east coast of the United States. (See *Admiralty List of Radio Signals Volume 6(5)* for limits and regulations). Sovereign immune vessels are exempt from the requirement to report, but are encouraged to participate.

17 The two reporting systems will operate independently of each other. The system in the northeastern United States will operate year round and the system in the southeastern United States will operate each year from November 15th through April 15th. Reporting ships are only required to make reports when entering a reporting area during a single voyage (that is, a voyage in which a ship is in the area). Ships are not required to report when leaving a port in the reporting area nor when exiting the system.

18 Mariners should check all MSR messages carefully before transmittal to ensure the message includes the correct address and format. Additional greetings or comments in the message will preclude message receipt by the MSR system. Failure to receive a timely return message from the MSR system that provides locations of recent right whale sightings and precautionary guidance should be reported to the local Marine Safety Office of the US Coast Guard.

APPENDIX IX

CODE OF FEDERAL REGULATIONS TITLE 33 — NAVIGATION AND NAVIGABLE WATERS

PART 207 — NAVIGATION REGULATIONS – CAPE COD CANAL

Appendix IX contains extracts from the above regulations issued by the United States Department of commerce. For a complete description of this part see 33 CFR 207.

§207.20 Cape Cod Canal, Massachusetts; use, administration, and navigation.

(a) *Limit of Canal*. The canal, including approaches, extends from the Canal Station Minus 100 in Cape Cod Bay, approximately one and six-tenths (1.6) statute miles seaward of the Canal Breakwater Light, through dredged channels and land cuts to Cleveland Ledge Light in Buzzards Bay approximately four (4) statute miles southwest of Wings Neck.

(b) *Supervision*.
  (1) The movement of ships, boats and craft of every description through the canal and the operation and maintenance of the waterway and all property of the United States pertaining thereto shall be under the supervision of the Division Engineer, U.S. Army Engineer Division, New England, Corps of Engineers, Waltham, Massachusetts, or the authorized representative of the division engineer, the Engineer-In-Charge of the Cape Cod Canal. The division engineer or the Engineer-In-Charge from time to time will prescribe rules governing the dimensions of vessels which may transit the waterway, and other special conditions and requirements which will govern the movement of vessels using the waterway.
  (2) The Engineer-In-Charge, through the marine traffic controller on duty, will enforce these regulations and monitor traffic through the canal. The marine traffic controller on duty is the individual responsible for interpretation of these regulations with respect to vessels transiting the canal. Vessels transiting the canal must obey the orders of the marine traffic controller.
  (3) The government has tugs stationed at the West Boat Basin for emergency use on an on-call basis. A patrol vessel is manned and operational 24-hours a day.

c) *Communications*. There is a marine traffic controller on duty 24 hours a day, seven days a week, in the traffic control center located at the Canal Administrative Office. The primary method of communications between the canal and vessels transiting will be by VHF-FM Marine radio. The traffic controller can also be contacted by telephone.
  (1) For radio communications, call the traffic controller on channel 16 to establish contact. The transmissions will then be switched to channel 12 or 14 as the working channel to pass information. Channel 13 is also available at the canal office; however, the use of channel 13 should be limited to emergency situations or whenever vessels do not have one of the other channels. All four channels are monitored continuously by the traffic controller. Radio discipline will be adhered to in accordance with FCC rules and regulations.
  (2) For telephone communications with the traffic controller, call (617) 759-4431.
  (3) Vessels shall maintain a radio guard on Marine VHF-FM channel 13 during the entire passage through the canal.
  (4) All radio communications in the vicinity of the canal are tape recorded for future reference.

(d) *Vessels allowed passage*. The canal is open for passage to all adequately powered vessels properly equipped and seaworthy, of sizes consistent with safe navigation as governed by the controlling depths and widths of the channel and the vertical and horizontal clearances of the bridges over the waterway. The granting of permission for any vessel to proceed through the waterway shall not relieve the owners, agents and operators of full responsibility for its safe passage. No vessel having a greater draft forward than aft will be allowed to transit the canal. Craft of low power and wind driven are required to have and use auxiliary power during passage throughout the canal as defined in paragraph (a) of this section. Low powered vessels will be required to await slack water or favorable current for canal transit.

(e) *Tows*.
  (1) Tows shall be made-up outside the canal entrances. All vessels engaged in towing other vessels not equipped with a rudder shall use two lines or a bridle and one tow line. If the vessel in tow is equipped with a rudder or a ship shaped bow, one tow line may be used. All tow lines of hawsers must be hauled as short as practicable for safe handling of the tows. No towboat will be allowed to enter the waterway with more than two barges in tow unless prior approval is granted by the Engineer-In-Charge; requests must be submitted 12 hours in advance of the passage.
  (2) The maximum length of pontoon rafts using the canal will be limited to 600 feet, and the maximum width to 100 feet. Pontoon rafts exceeding 200 feet in length will be required to have an additional tug on the stern to insure that the tow is kept in line. The tugs used must have sufficient power to handle the raft safely.
  (3) Dead ships are required to transit the canal during daylight hours and must be provided with the number of tugs sufficient to afford safe passage through the canal. (A dead ship will not be allowed to enter the canal unless

prior approval is granted by the Engineer-In-Charge; requests must be submitted 12 hours in advance of the passage).

(f) *Dangerous cargoes.* The master or pilot of any vessel or tow carrying dangerous cargoes must notify the Marine Traffic Controller prior to entering the canal. Dangerous cargoes are defined as those items listed in 33 CFR 126.10 when carried in bulk (i.e., quantities exceeding 110 U.S. gallons in one tank) plus Class A explosives (commercial or military) as listed in 49 CFR 173.53 (commercial) and 46 CFR 146.29-100 (military), liquified natural gas and liquified petroleum gas. Transportation of dangerous cargoes through the canal shall be in strict accordance with existing regulations prescribed by law. In addition, vessels carrying dangerous cargoes shall comply with the following requirements.

(1) They must have sufficient horsepower to overcome tidal currents or they will be required to wait for favorable current conditions.
(2) Transits will be during daylight hours.
(3) No transit will be permitted when visibility conditions are unstable or less than 2 miles at the approaches and throughout the entire length of the canal.
(4) Transits must await a clear canal for passage.

(g) *Obtaining clearance.*
(1) Vessels under 65 feet in length may enter the canal without obtaining clearance. All craft are required to make a complete passage through the canal except excursion craft which may operate and change direction within the canal in accordance with procedures coordinated with the marine traffic controller on duty. When the railroad bridge span is in the closed (down) position, all vessels are directed not to proceed beyond the points designated by stop signs posted east and west of the railroad bridge. Vessels proceeding with a fair tide (with the current) should turn and stem the current at the designated stop points until the railroad bridge is in the raised (open) position.
(2) Vessels 65 feet in length and over shall not enter the canal until clearance has been obtained from the marine traffic controller by radio. See paragraph (c) *"Communications"* for procedures. If a vessel, granted prior clearance, is delayed or stops at the mooring basins, state pier, or the Sandwich bulkhead, a second clearance must be obtained prior to continuing passage through the canal.
(3) Vessels will be given clearance in the order of arrival, except when conditions warrant one-way traffic, or for any reason an order of priority is necessary, clearance will be granted in the following order.
   (i) First—To vessels owned or operated by the United States, including contractors' equipment employed on canal maintenance or improvement work.
   (ii) Second—To passenger vessels.
   (iii) Third—To tankers and barges docking and undocking at the Canal Electric Terminal.
   (iv) Fourth—To merchant vessels, towboats, commercial fishing vessels, pleasure boats and miscellaneous craft.
(4) Procedures in adverse weather: Vessels carrying flammable or combustible cargoes as defined in 46 CFR 30.25 will be restricted from passage through the canal when visibility is less than ½ mile. Other vessels may transit the canal in thick weather by use of radar with the understanding that the U.S. Government will assume no responsibility: And provided, That clearance has been obtained from the marine traffic controller.

(h) *Traffic lights.* There are three sets of traffic lights showing red, green, and yellow that are operated on a continuous basis at the canal. The traffic lights apply to all vessels 65 feet in length and over. The traffic lights are a secondary system that is operated in support of the radio communications system. The traffic lights are located at the easterly canal entrance, Sandwich, and at the westerly entrance to Hog Island Channel at Wings Neck. A third traffic light is located at the Canal Electric Terminal basin on the south side of the canal in Sandwich, and applies only to vessels arriving and departing that terminal.

(1) Westbound traffic. When the green light is on at the eastern (Cape Cod Bay) entrance, vessels may proceed westward through the canal. When the red light is on, any type of vessel 65 feet in length and over must stop clear of the Cape Cod Bay entrance channel. When the yellow light is on, vessels 65 feet in length and over and drawing less than 25 feet may proceed as far as the East Mooring Basin where they must stop. Prior to continuing passage through the canal, clearance must be obtained from the marine traffic controller.
(2) Eastbound traffic. When the green light is on at Wings Neck, vessels may proceed eastward through the canal. When the red light is on, vessels 65 feet and over in length and drawing less than 25 feet must keep southerly of Hog Island Channel Entrance Buoys Nos. 1 and 2 and utilize the general anchorage areas adjacent to the improved channel. Vessel traffic drawing 25 feet and over are directed not to enter the canal channel at the Cleveland Ledge Light entrance and shall lay to or anchor in the vicinity of Buzzards Bay Buoy No. 11 (FLW & Bell) until clearance is granted by the canal marine traffic controller or a green traffic light at Wings Neck is displayed. When the yellow light is on, vessels may proceed through Hog Island Channel as far as the West Mooring Basin where they must stop. Prior to continuing passage through the canal, clearance must be obtained from the marine traffic controller.

(i) *Railroad Bridge Signals.* The following signals at the Buzzards Bay Railroad Bridge will be given strict attention.
(1) The vertical lift span on the railroad bridge is normally kept in the raised (open) position except when it is lowered for the passage of trains, or for maintenance purposes.

Immediately preceding the lowering of the span, the operator will sound two long blasts of an air horn. Immediately preceding the raising of the span, the operator will sound one long blast of an air horn. When a vessel or craft of any type is approaching the bridge with the span in the down (closed) position and the span cannot be raised immediately, the operator of the bridge will so indicate by sounding danger signals of four short blasts in quick succession.

(2) When the lift span is in the down (closed) position in foggy weather or when visibility is obscured by vapor, there will be four short blasts sounded from the bridge every two minutes.

(j) *Speed*. All vessels are directed to pass mooring and boat basin facilities, the state pier, and all floating plant engaged in maintenance operations of the waterway at a minimum speed consistent with safe navigation. In order to coordinate scheduled rail traffic with the passage of vessels, to minimize erosion of the canal banks and dikes from excessive wave wash and suction, and for the safety of vessels using the canal, the following speed regulations must be observed by vessels of all types, including pleasure craft. The minimum running time for the land cut between the East Mooring Basin (Station 35) and the Administration Office in Buzzards Bay (Station 388) is prescribed as follows:

Head Tide—60 Minutes
Fair Tide—30 Minutes
Slack Tide—45 Minutes

The minimum running time between the Administration Office (Station 388) and Hog Island Channel westerly entrance Buoy No. 1 (Station 661) is prescribed as follows:

Head Tide—46 Minutes
Fair Tide—23 Minutes
Slack Tide—35 Minutes

The running time at slack water will apply to any vessel which enters that portion of the canal between stations 35 and 661, within the period of one-half hour before or after the predicted time of slack water as given in the National Ocean Survey publication "Current Tables, Atlantic Coast, North America." The minimum running time during a head tide or a fair tide shall apply to any vessel which enters that portion of the canal between Station 35 and 661 at any time other than designated above for time requirements at slack tide. Vessels of any kind unable to make a through transit of the land cut portion of the canal against a head current of 6.0 knots within a maximum time limit of 2 hours 30 minutes shall be required to obtain the assistance of a helper tug at the vessel owner's expense or await favorable tide conditions prior to receiving clearance from the marine traffic controller. In the event vessels within the confines of the canal fail to perform and are unable to make sufficient headway against the currents, the marine traffic controller may activate a helper tug in accordance with paragraph (k) of this section.

(k) *Management of vessels*.
  (1) Vessels within the limits of the canal shall comply with applicable navigation rules.
  (2) Vessels within the limits of the canal shall comply with the applicable requirements for the use of pilots established by the Coast Guard, including but not limited to those contained in 46 CFR 157.20-40. Vessels will not be granted clearance to enter the canal until the marine traffic controller has been notified of the name of the pilot who will be handling the vessel.
  (3) The master of a vessel will be responsible for notifying the marine traffic controller as soon as an emergency situation appears to be developing. When in the opinion of the marine traffic controller an emergency exists, he/she can require the master to accept the assistance of a helper vessel. Whether or not assistance is provided by a government vessel or by a private firm under contract to the government, the government reserves the right to seek compensation from the vessel owners for all costs incurred.
  (4) Right-of-Way: All vessels proceeding with the current shall have the right-of-way over those proceeding against the current. All craft up to 65 feet in length shall be operated so as not to interfere with the navigation of vessels of greater length.
  (5) Passing of vessels: The passing of one vessel by another when proceeding in the same direction is prohibited except when a leading low powered ship is unable to make sufficient headway. However, extreme caution must be observed to avoid collision, and consideration must be given to the size of the ship to be overtaken, velocity of current and wind, and atmospheric conditions. Masters of vessels involved shall inform the marine traffic controller on duty of developing situations to facilitate coordination of vessel movement. Meeting or passing of vessels at the easterly end of the canal between Station Minus 40 and Station 60 will not be permitted, except in cases of extreme emergency, in order to allow vessels to utilize the center line range to minimize the effects of hazardous eddies and currents. Due to bank suction and tidal set, meeting and passing of vessels at the following locations will be avoided:
    (i) Sagamore Bridge.
    (ii) Bourne Bridge.
    (iii) Railroad Bridge.
    (iv) Mass Maritime Academy.
  (6) Unnecessary delay in canal: Vessels and other type crafts must not obstruct navigation by unnecessarily idling at low speed when entering or passing through the canal.
  (7) Stopping in the waterway: Anchoring in the Cape Cod Canal Channel is prohibited except in emergencies. For the safety of canal operations it is mandatory that the masters of all vessels anchoring in or adjacent to the canal channel (Cape Cod Bay to Cleveland

Ledge Light) for any reason, immediately notify the marine traffic controller.

(8) Utilization of mooring and boat basins and the Sandwich Bulkhead: Vessels mooring or anchoring in the mooring or boat basins at the Sandwich bulkhead must do so in a manner not to obstruct or impede vessel movements to and from facilities. These facilities are of limited capacity and permission to occupy them for periods exceeding 24 hours must be obtained in advance from the marine traffic controller. Mooring in the West Boat Basin at Buzzards Bay, near the railroad bridge, is not permitted except in an emergency. Fishing boats, yachts, cabin cruisers and other craft utilizing the East Boat Basin on the south side of the canal at Sandwich, Massachusetts are not permitted to tie up at the Corps of Engineers landing float or anchor in a manner to prevent canal floating plant from having ready access to the float. All vessels or barges left unattended must be securely tied with adequate lines or cables. The United States assumes no liability for damages which may be sustained by any craft using the bulkhead at Sandwich or the canal mooring or boat basin facilities. Vessels shall not be left unattended along the face of the government bulkhead. A responsible person with authority to authorize and/or accomplish vessel movement must remain onboard at all times.

(l) *Grounded, wrecked or damaged vessels*. In the event a vessel is grounded, or so damaged by accident as to render it likely to become an obstruction and/or hazard to navigation in the waterway, the division engineer or the division engineer's authorized representative shall supervise and direct all operations that may be necessary to remove the vessel to a safe locality.

(m) [Reserved]

(n) *Deposit of refuse*. No oil or other allied liquids, ashes, or materials of any kind shall be thrown, pumped or swept into the canal or its approaches from any vessel or craft using the waterway, nor shall any refuse be deposited on canal grounds, marine structures, or facilities.

(o) *Trespass to property*. Subject to the provisions of paragraph (q) of this section trespass upon the canal property is prohibited.

(p) *Bridges over the canal*. The government owns, operates and maintains all bridges across the canal which include one railroad bridge and two highway bridges. The division engineer or his/her authorized representative may establish rules and regulations governing the use of these bridges.

APPENDIX X

CODE OF FEDERAL REGULATIONS TITLE 33 — NAVIGATION AND NAVIGABLE WATERS

PART 166 — SHIPPING SAFETY FAIRWAYS

Appendix X contains extracts from the above regulations issued by the United States Department of Commerce.

Regulations specific to this volume are given by title only where the area concerned falls wholly within pilotage waters; where the regulation affects an area outside pilotage waters, a summary of the regulation is given.

For a complete description of this part see 33 CFR 166.

Subpart A — General

§166.100 Purpose.

The purpose of these regulations is to establish and designate shipping safety fairways and fairway anchorages to provide unobstructed approaches for vessels using US ports.

§166.103 Geographic coordinates.

Geographic coordinates expressed in terms of latitude or longitude, or both, are not intended for plotting on maps or charts whose referenced horizontal datum is the North American Datum of 1983 (NAD 83), unless such geographic coordinates are expressly labelled NAD 83. Geographic coordinates without the NAD 83 reference may be plotted on maps or charts referenced to NAD 83 only after application of the appropriate corrections that are published on the particular map or chart being used.

§166.105 Definitions.

(a) *Shipping safety fairway* or *fairway* means a lane or corridor in which no artificial island or fixed structure, whether temporary or permanent, will be permitted. Temporary underwater obstacles may be permitted under certain conditions described for specific areas in Subpart B. Aids to navigation approved by the US Coast Guard may be established in a fairway.

(b) *Fairway anchorage* means an anchorage area contiguous to and associated with a fairway, in which fixed structures may be permitted within certain spacing limitations, as described for specific areas in Subpart B.

§166.110 Modification of areas.

Fairways and anchorages are subject to modification in accordance with 33 U.S.C. 1223(c); 92 Stat.1473.

Subpart B — Designations of Fairways and Fairway Anchorages

§166.500 Areas along the Atlantic Coast.

(a) *Purpose.* Fairways as described in this section are established to control the erection of structures therein to provide safe vessel routes along the Atlantic Coast.

(b) *Designated areas:*

 (1) Off New York Shipping Safety Fairway.

  (i) *Ambrose to Nantucket Safety Fairway.* The area enclosed by rhumb lines, (North American Datum of 1927 (NAD-27)), joining points at:

   40°32′20″N 73°04′57″W
   40°30′58″N 72°58′25″W
   40°34′07″N 70°19′23″W
   40°35′37″N 70°14′09″W
   40°30′37″N 70°14′00″W
   40°32′07″N 70°19′19″W
   40°28′58″N 72°58′25″W
   40°27′20″N 73°04′57″W

  (i) *Nantucket to Ambrose Safety Fairway.* The area enclosed by rhumb lines, NAD-27, joining points at:

   40°24′20″N 73°04′58″W
   40°22′58″N 72°58′26″W
   40°26′07″N 70°19′09″W
   40°27′37″N 70°13′46″W
   40°22′37″N 70°13′36″W
   40°24′07″N 70°19′05″W
   40°20′58″N 72°58′26″W
   40°19′20″N 73°04′58″W

INDEX

Abner Point	3.121
Acabonack Harbor	6.54
Acushnet River	5.150
Adams, Fort	5.203
Agamenticus, Mount	3.211
Aids to navigation	1.21
Beacons	1.23
Buoyage	1.25
IALA	1.25
ODAS	1.26
Winter buoyage	1.27
Daymarks	1.24
Landmarks	1.22
Lights	1.21
Albany	7.173
Alden Rock	3.177
Aldridge Ledge	4.94
Allen Cove	2.84
Allen Island	3.22
Allen Rock	5.222
Light	5.222
Allerton, Point	4.97
Alley Island	2.89
Ambrose Channel	7.65
Amesbury Point	2.186
Ammen Rock	3.7
Anchorage Channel	7.91
Anderson Ledge	3.250
Andrews Point	3.256
Angelica Point	5.129
Ann, Cape	3.246
Light	3.249
Appledore Island	3.253
Apponagansett Bay	5.127
Archer Rock	4.37
Arey Ledges	2.180
Arnold Point	5.258
Arthur Kill	7.101
Anchorages	7.107
Directions	7.105
General information	7.101
Harbours and terminals	7.108
Arundel, Cape	3.208
Asbury Park	7.28
Ash Creek	6.154
Asia Rip	4.68
Atlantic	2.88
Atlantic Point	2.159
Atlantis Canyon	5.5
Augusta	3.94
Avery Ledge	3.256
Avery Point	6.97
Babbidge Island	2.121
Babson Ledge	4.21
Bache Rock	3.175
Back Beach	4.48
Badgers Island	3.232
Bagaduce River	2.134
Bailey Island	3.120
Bailey Ledge	3.33
Bailey Point	3.33
Baker Island	2.41
Light	2.24
Bakers Island	4.36
Light	4.34
Bald Head Cliff	3.210
Bald Head: Cape Small	3.107
Bald Head: Kennebec River	3.98
Bald Island	2.122
Bald Porcupine Island	2.42
Bald Rock	2.28
Bangor	2.217
Bangs Island	3.150
Bantam Rock	3.74
Bar Beach	6.242
Bar Island	2.70
Bar Island Ledge	3.47
Bar Ledge	3.212
Barker Point	6.96
Barnegat Bay	7.28
Barnegat Inlet	7.35
Barnegat Light	7.32
Barnstable	4.150
Airport Light	5.48
Harbor	4.150
Barren Island	7.22
Barretto Point	7.146
Barrington	5.222
River	5.222
Barter Shoal	3.20
Barters Island	3.91
Bartlett Harbor	2.187
Bartlett Island	2.70
Bartlett Reef:	
Fishers Island Sound	6.39
Bartlett Reef: Niantic Bay	6.161
Basin Point: Broad Sound	3.132
Basin Point:	
New Meadows River	3.112
Basket Island	3.158
Bass Harbor	2.87
Bar	2.73
Head	2.65
Light	2.71
Bass Point	4.55
Bass River: Beverly Harbor	4.47
Bath	3.102
Battery, The	7.135
Bay Head	7.28
Bay Ledge	2.143
Bay Ridge Channel	7.93
Bay Ridge Flats	7.91
Bayonne	7.115
Beach Island	2.116
Beach Ledge	2.74
Beach Point	4.150
Beacon Hill	5.184
Beals	2.12
Bean Point	2.62
Bear Island:	
New Meadows River	3.111
Bear Island: Southwest Harbor	2.44
Bearse Rock	5.85
Bearse Shoal	5.38
Beauchamp Point	2.145
Beaufort Point	6.218
Beaver Neck	5.194
Beaverhead	5.207
Beavertail Light	5.186
Beavertail Point	5.194
Belden Point	6.221
Belfast Bay	2.169
Belfast Harbor	2.169
Bellport Bay	7.25
Belmont Island	7.144
Benjamin River	2.85
Bergen Point	7.122
Berkley	5.252
Bernard	2.87
Beverly	4.47
Channel	4.47
Harbor	4.47
Biddeford	3.213
Pool	3.214
Big Black Ledge	2.31
Big Moose Island	2.41
Billings Cove	2.85
Billingsgate Shoal	4.149
Birch Harbor	2.33
Birch Island	3.133
Birch Islands	2.16
Birch Point: Cousins Island	3.164
Birch Point:	
New Meadows River	3.112
Bird Island	5.143
Bishop and Clerks	5.50
Bishop Rock Shoal	5.204
Black Bess Point	4.22
Black Island: Blue Hill Bay	2.69
Black Island: Casco Passage	2.75
Black Island: Muscongus Bay	3.46
Black Ledge: Narraguagus Bay	2.18
Black Ledge:	
New London Harbor	6.111
Black Point: Long Island Sound	6.159
Black Rock Channel	4.99
Black Rock Harbor	6.154
Black Rock: Black Rock Harbor	6.156
Black Rock: Blue Hill Bay	2.91
Black Rock: Gloucester Harbor	4.21
Black Rock: Niantic Bay	6.161
Black Rock: Western Bay	2.10
Black Rocks, The	3.85
Blackboys	6.173
Blacksnake Ledge	3.114
Block Canyon	7.8
Block Island	5.184
North Reef	6.16
Sound	6.7
South–east Light	5.186
Blubber Island	3.21
Blue Hill Bay	2.65
Blue Hill Harbor	2.92
Blue Point Hill	3.209
Bluefish Shoal	6.211
Bluff Head: East Penobscot Bay	2.121
Bluff Head: Kennebec River	3.100
Bluff Island	3.212
Boat Rock	2.83
Bois Bubert Island	2.18
Bold Dick, Rock	3.114
Bold Island	2.80
Bonney Chess Ledge	2.25
Boon Island	3.210
Ledge	3.210
Light	3.209
Booth Bay	3.73
Boothbay Harbor	3.76
Borden Flats	5.259
Boston Harbor	4.77
Alongside berths	4.107
Arrival information	4.85
Directions for entrance	
channels	4.91
General information	4.77
Harbour	4.89
Limiting conditions	4.81
Main anchorages	4.102
Other channels	4.99
Port services	4.113
Boston Island	3.89
Boston Ledge	4.97
Boston Light	4.91
Boston Main Channel	4.96
Boston Neck	5.193
Boston, City of	4.77
Bostwick Bay	6.52
Bostwick Point	6.52
Bowden Ledge	2.44
Bowditch Ledge	4.36
Bowery Bay	7.153
Bracy Cove	2.48
Bradbury Island	2.116

Bradford Point	3.33
Bragdon Rock	3.112
Branch	5.100
Brandies, The	2.115
Branford Harbor	6.179
Branford Reef	6.88
Brant Point	5.65
Light	5.68
Brayton Point	5.260
Breakers, The	2.180
Breaking Rocks	3.258
Bremen Long Island	3.48
Brenton Cove	5.215
Brenton Point	5.193
Brewer	2.217
Brickyard Point	6.241
Bridgeport Harbor	6.138
Arrival information	6.143
Berths	6.149
Directions	6.147
General information	6.138
Harbour	6.145
Limiting conditions	6.140
Port services	6.151
Brightman Street Bridge	5.252
Brimbles	4.38
Brimstone Island:	
Blue Hill Bay Approaches	2.78
Brimstone Island:	
East Penobscot Bay	2.111
Brimstone Point	3.213
Bristol	5.221
Harbor	5.221
Neck	5.221
Point	5.221
Broad Cove: Muscongus Bay	3.58
Broad Cove: Saint George River	3.30
Broad Sound: Casco Bay	3.130
Broad Sound:	
Massachusetts Bay	4.55
Broadway	5.100
Broken Ground	5.50
Broken Part of Pollock Rip	5.38
Bronx	7.40
River	7.154
Brooklyn	7.40
Bridge	7.142
Brooklyn Rock	5.164
Brothers, The: Port Clyde	3.20
Brothers, The: Portland Harbor	3.194
Brown Cow, The	2.115
Browney Island	2.10
Browns Bank	4.132
Browns Head: Muscongus Bay	3.47
Ledge	3.47
Browns Head:	
West Penobscot Bay	2.169
Browns Ledge	5.120
Browns Reef	6.88
Brush Islet	4.125
Bucks Harbor	2.86
Bucksport	2.205
Bull Ledge	3.86
Bull Point	5.203
Bullock Point	5.240
Reach	5.240
Bulwark Shoal	3.175
Bunkers Harbor	2.33
Bunkers Ledge	2.33
Burnham Rocks	4.13
Burnt Coat Harbor	2.82
Burnt Island: Booth Bay	3.76
Light	3.74
Burnt Island: Georges Islands	2.144
Burnt Porcupine Island	2.42
Burton Point	3.35
Bushy Islet	3.112
Bustins Island	3.140
Butler Flats	5.165
Butler Hole	5.38
Butter Ball Rock	5.203
Butter Island	2.116
Buttermilk Channel	7.95
Buzzards Bay	5.111
Entrance Light	5.118
Byard Point	2.81
Byram	6.213
Point	6.213
River	6.213
Cabbage Island	3.75
Cable and Anchor Reef	6.94
Cadillac Mountain	2.35
Calderwood Point	2.115
Caldwell Island	3.22
Calf Pasture Point:	
Narragansett Bay	5.209
Calf Pasture Point:	
Norwalk River	6.196
Camden Harbor	2.164
Camel Ground	3.97
Cameron Point	3.89
Canal Land Cut	5.145
Canapitsit Channel	5.91
Cape Island:	
Cape Porpoise Harbor	3.217
Captain Harbor	6.208
Captains Hill	4.133
Carrying Place Head	3.109
Carrying Place Island	2.13
Carter, Cape	2.85
Cartwright Island	6.27
Carver Cove	2.125
Carvers Harbor	2.180
Light	2.180
Casco Bay	3.104
Casco Passage	2.75
Cashes Ledge	3.3
Castine	2.134
Harbor	2.134
Castle Hill	5.203
Castle Island: Boston Harbor	4.96
Anchorage	4.105
Castle Island: Narragansett Bay	5.221
Castle, The	2.25
Cat Ledges	3.86
Cataumet	5.131
Rock	5.131
Catumb Passage	6.32
Cedar Creek	6.154
Cedar Island	3.254
Ledge	3.250
Cedar Island Point	5.144
Cedar Ledges:	
New Meadows River	3.112
Cedar Ledges: Quahog Bay	3.114
Cedar Point:	
Massachusetts Bay	4.122
Cedar Point: Saugatuck River	6.223
Cedar Point:	
Shelter Island Sound	6.61
Centerport Harbor	6.236
Centerville Harbor	5.85
Centre Island	6.239
Cerberus Shoal	6.16
Chandler Cove	3.153
Channel Rock: Nantucket Sound	5.85
Channel Rock:	
Saint George River	3.24
Channel Rocks	3.161
Chapel Hill Channel	7.68
Chappaquiddick Island	5.49
Chappel Ledge	4.37
Charles M. Braga Jr.	
Memorial Bridge	5.252
Charles Reef	6.88
Charlestown	4.96
Charts	1.15
Admiralty charts	1.15
Datums	1.18
Horizontal	1.18
Vertical	1.19
Depth terms in US waters	1.20
Foreign charts	1.16
Chatham	5.55
Light	4.66
Roads	5.55
Chatham Harbor	4.70
Chebeague Point	3.131
Chelsea River	4.89
Cherry Harbor	6.53
Cherry Hill Point	6.52
Chester Harbor, Port	6.213
Childrens Island	4.37
Channel	4.38
Chimney Corner Reef	6.88
City Island	6.220
Harbor	6.220
Clapboard Island	3.158
Clark Point: Prospect Harbor	2.32
Clarks Cove	5.128
Clarks Island: Duxbury Bay	4.137
Clarks Island:	
Portsmouth Harbor	3.228
Clarks Point	5.151
Clason Point	7.155
Cleaves Point	6.63
Cleveland East Ledge Light	5.118
Cleveland Ledge Channel	5.143
Cliff Island	3.147
Climate and Weather	1.112
Air temperature	1.133
Anticyclones	1.117
Cloud	1.127
Depressions	1.119
Fog and visibility	1.132
Fronts	1.121
General conditions	1.113
General information	1.112
Precipitation	1.128
Pressure	1.114
Relative humidity	1.136
Winds	1.122
Clinton Harbor	6.176
Clous Ledge	3.87
Coasters Harbor Island	5.198
Coatue Beach	5.65
Coatue Point	5.65
Cockenoe Harbor	6.194
Cockenoe Island	6.193
Cod Rock	3.238
Cod, Cape	4.61
Bay	4.118
Breakwater Head Light	4.130
Canal	5.133
Light; see Highland Light	4.66
Coddington Cove	5.219
Coddington Point	5.219
Coecles Harbor	6.56
Coggeshall Point	5.220
Cohasset Harbor	4.125
Colby Cove	3.92
Cold Spring Harbor	6.240
Coles Ledge	2.16
College Island	3.155
College Point	7.160
Reef	7.147
Colt Ledge: Jericho Bay	2.24
Colt Ledge: Vinalhaven Island	2.180
Comfort, Point	7.76
Commissioners Ledge	4.94
Common Fence Point	5.260
Common Flat	5.55
Conanicut Island	5.193
Conanicut Point	5.208

Conary Nub	2.91
Conary Point	2.91
Condon Point	2.86
Coney Island: New York	7.65
Channel	7.72
Light	7.63
Coney Ledge	4.37
Conimicut Point	5.227
Reach	5.240
Connecticut River	6.163
Connecticut Turnpike Bridge	6.141
Constable Hook	7.119
Reach	7.119
Constellation Rock	6.49
Contention Cove	2.90
Cooper Bluff	6.240
Corea Harbor	2.29
Corlears Hook	7.144
Cormorant Reef	6.211
Cornfield Point	6.87
Shoal	6.87
Corwin Rock	3.177
Cos Cob Harbor	6.227
Cotuit Bay	5.48
Countries,	
United States of America,	
General description	1.62
Cousins Island	3.158
Cove Neck	6.239
Cove Point	6.241
Cow and Calf Ledge	2.70
Cow Island: Hussey Sound	3.155
Ledge	3.162
Cow Island: Muscongus Bay	3.48
Cows, The	6.206
Cowyard	4.137
Cox Head	3.98
Coxens Ledge	5.124
Crab Island	3.141
Crabtree Neck	2.62
Cradle Cove	2.190
Cranberry Harbor	2.49
Cranberry Point	2.31
Crane Island	3.43
Crane Neck Point	6.232
Crane Reef	6.87
Criehaven Harbor	2.107
Crockett Point:	
Fox Islands Thorofare	2.151
Cross Point	3.87
Cross Rip Shoal	5.49
Cross River	3.87
Crotch Island	2.80
Crow Island: Chandler Cove	3.153
Crow Island: Hussey Sound	3.155
Crow Island: Luckse Sound	3.150
Crow Island: Mackerel Cove	2.88
Crow Point: Buzzards Bay	5.130
Crow Shoal	6.53
Crowninshield Point	2.48
Crumple Island	2.9
Cuban Ledge	6.230
Cuckolds, The	3.74
Culloden Point	6.26
Cultivator Shoal	3.7
Cundy Harbor	3.112
Currents, tidal streams and flow	1.92
Currents	1.93
Sea level and tides	1.97
Curtis Island	2.166
Light	2.166
Curtis Point	4.41
Cutchogue Harbor	6.69
Cutthroat Shoal	4.38
Cuttyhunk	5.126
Harbor	5.125
Island	5.88
Pond	5.126

Damariscotta	3.63
River	3.63
Damariscove Island	3.74
Dansbury Reef	3.215
Danvers River	4.47
Dark Harbor	2.190
Darling Island	2.91
Darling Ledge	2.91
Dartmouth Rock	5.127
Dauntless Rock	6.217
Davenport Neck	6.218
Davids Island	6.219
Davis Bank	4.68
Davis Island	3.26
Davis Neck	3.260
Davis Strait	3.26
Davisville Depot	5.225
Decatur Rock	5.165
Deep Cove	3.34
Deer Island	4.55
Deer Island Thorofare	2.80
Deer Isle	2.77
Deer Point	3.153
Delancey Point	6.216
Democrat Point	7.21
Dering Harbor	6.64
Devils Back: Boston Harbor	4.94
Devils Back: Muscongus Bay	3.46
Devils Bridge	5.96
Devils Elbow	3.46
Devon	6.168
Diamond Cove	3.157
Diamond Island Ledge	3.193
Diamond Island Pass	3.156
Diamond Island Roads	3.195
Dice Head	2.134
Dillingham Ledge	2.145
Dillingham Point	2.166
Distress and Rescue	1.57
General information	1.57
Global Maritime Distress and	
Safety System (GMDSS)	1.58
Rescue services	1.60
United States Coast Guard	1.60
Ship reporting systems	1.59
Automated Mutual-assistance	
Vessel Rescue System	1.59
Dix Island	3.98
Dix Island Harbor	2.184
Dodge Point	2.189
Dodge Rock	3.257
Dog Bar	4.19
Channel	4.19
Dogfish Head	3.86
Dolliver Neck	4.20
Dorchester Bay	4.89
Doubling Point	3.100
Douglas Island Harbor	2.19
Douglas Islands	2.19
Dread Ledge	4.53
Drisko Island	2.10
Drums, The	2.69
Drunkers Ledges	3.120
Dry Salvages	3.250
Duck Island Harbor	6.236
Duck Island: Isles of Shoals	3.250
Duck Island: Long Island Sound	6.175
Roads	6.175
Ducktrap Harbor	2.191
Dumpling Islands	2.186
Dumpling Rocks	5.165
Dumplings, The	5.203
Dunbar Point	5.62
Dutch Island	5.224
Harbor	5.224
Duxbury	4.137
Bay	4.137
Beach	4.127

Dyer Bay	2.25
Dyer Island: Narragansett Bay	5.205
Dyer Island: Pleasant Bay	2.16
Narrows	2.17
Dyer Point	2.25
Eagle Bar	4.37
Eagle Island: Casco Bay	3.131
Eagle Island:	
East Penobscot Bay	2.116
Eagle Island: Saco Bay	3.212
Eagle Island: Salem Sound	4.33
Channel	4.38
East Bank	7.65
East Beach	6.235
East Blue Hill	2.91
East Boothbay	3.70
East Boston	4.96
East Branch: Black Rock Harbor	6.154
East Branch: Stamford Harbor	6.203
East Brown Cow	3.109
East Bunker Ledge	2.44
East Chop	5.49
Light	5.82
East Clump	6.38
East Cod Ledge	3.165
East Fort Point	6.235
East Hue and Cry Rock	3.177
East Neck	6.237
East Norwalk	6.196
East Passage	5.194
East Penobscot Bay	2.111
East Point: Blue Hill Bay	2.69
East Point: Fishers Island	6.31
East Point: Frenchmans Bay	2.43
East Point: Nahant Bay	4.53
East Reef	6.178
East River	7.135
Anchorages and harbours	7.156
Directions	7.144
General information	7.135
Side channels	7.148
East Rockaway Inlet	7.26
East Shoal	5.86
Eastchester Bay	6.230
Eastern Bay	2.64
Eastern Drunkers Ledge	3.120
Eastern Ear Ledge	2.24
Eastern Egg Rock	3.42
Eastern Harbor	2.14
Eastern Head	2.24
Eastern Island	2.28
Eastern Passage	2.69
Eastern Point: Gloucester Harbor	4.17
Light	4.18
Eastern Point:	
New London Harbor	6.111
Eastern Point: Southwest Harbor	2.44
Eastern Way: Gouldsboro Bay	2.28
Eastern Way: Southwest harbor	2.43
Easton Point	5.180
Eaton Point	2.167
Eatons Neck	6.94
Light	6.92
Point	6.231
Ebenecook Harbor	3.89
Echo Bay	6.218
Edgartown	5.71
Harbor	5.71
Light	5.75
Edgartown Great Pond	5.18
Edgewater	7.83
Edgewater Point	6.217
Eel Grass Ground	6.42
Egg Island	5.62
Egg Rock North Ledge	3.42
Egg Rock: Frenchman Bay	2.42
Light	2.39

INDEX

Egg Rock: Nahant Bay	4.53
Egg Rock: Pigeon Hill Bay	2.21
Egg Rock: Western Bay	2.9
Eggemoggin Reach	2.81
Eldridge Shoal	5.51
Elizabeth	7.114
Elizabeth Islands	5.88
Elizabeth, Cape	3.165
Light	3.172
Elizabethport	7.114
Ellingwood Rock	3.97
Ellis Island	7.91
Ellis Reef	6.42
Elm Islands	3.114
Elm Point	6.250
Emerson Point	3.250
Emery Cove	2.64
Endeavor Shoals	6.18
English Kills	7.149
Ensign Islands	2.190
Eustis Rock	5.132
Execution Rocks	6.95
Light	6.92
Fairhaven	5.150
Falkner Island	6.86
Fall River	5.261
Harbor	5.261
Falmouth Harbor	5.86
False Hook Channel	7.69
Fanning Point	6.60
Farnham Point	3.67
Farnham Rock	4.124
Farrel Island	2.119
Fayerweather Island	6.156
Felix Ledge	5.106
Fernald Point	2.51
Ferry Point	7.106
Fessenden Ledge	2.12
Fiddler Ledge	2.151
Fiddler Reach	3.100
Fields Point	5.241
Fifteen Foot Rock	4.37
Fippennies Ledge	3.3
Fire Island	7.25
Inlet	7.25
Light	7.20
First Cliff	4.126
Fish Hawk Island	3.75
Fish Island	5.162
Fish Islands	6.225
Fish Point: East Penobscot Bay	2.127
Fish Point: Portland	3.179
Fisherman Island: Booth Bay	3.66
Passage	3.66
Fisherman Island: West Penobscot Bay	2.144
Passage	2.149
Fisherman Island: Western Bay	2.10
Fishers Island	6.31
Sound	6.31
Fishing Rip	4.68
Fiske Rock	5.205
Fitch Point	6.197
Fivemile River	6.224
Flag Island	3.110
Flanders Bay	2.61
Flash Island	3.116
Flat Island: West Penobscot Bay	2.192
Flat Island: Western Bay	2.10
Flat Neck Point	6.211
Fletcher Neck	3.214
Flint Island	2.16
Narrows	2.16
Flip Rock	4.55
Flushing Bay	7.159
Flushing Creek	7.159
Flying Passage	3.48
Flying Point: Marblehead Neck	4.51
Flynns Knoll	7.66
Fogland Point	5.183
Folly Cove	3.261
Folly Point	3.261
Fore River	3.178
Fort Island	3.67
Fort Knox	2.203
Fort Pickering Light	4.43
Fort Point: Gloucester Harbor	4.21
Fort Point: New Meadows River	3.111
Fort Point: Penobscot River	2.195
Cove	2.199
Ledge	2.203
Light	2.202
Fort Point: Portsmouth Harbor	3.237
Fort Pond Bay	6.26
Fort Scammel Point	3.193
Foster Island	2.17
Foster Point	3.67
Fourfoot Rocks	6.211
Fourteen Foot Channel	7.71
Fowle Point	3.87
Fowler Rock	5.208
Fox Island: West Passage	5.208
Fox Island: Port Chester	6.214
Fox Islands Thorofare	2.121
Fox Point: Providence River	5.230
Reach	5.241
Fox Point: Vineyard Sound	5.91
Frankfort Flats	2.204
Franklin Island	3.39
Light	3.39
French Island	3.137
Frenchman Bay	2.35
Fresh Kills	7.111
Friendship	3.52
Harbor	3.51
Long Island	3.51
Frohock Point	2.191
Frost Point: Portsmouth Harbor	3.231
Frost Point: Southport Harbor	6.222
Fuller Rock	3.107
Light	3.15
Fuller Rock Reach	5.241
Gales Ledge	4.35
Gales Point	4.26
Gallatin Rock	5.85
Gallops Island	4.99
Gammon, Point	5.48
Gangway Ledge: Booth Bay	3.66
Gangway Ledge: Muscongus Bay	3.42
Gangway Rock	6.96
Gannet Ledge	5.85
Gap Head	3.257
Gardiners Bay	6.47
Gardiners Island	6.7
Gardiners Point	6.49
Garrison Island	3.51
Gaspee Point	5.240
Gay Cove Ledge	3.41
Gay Head	5.88
Light	5.93
Gay Island	3.44
Gazelle Rock	5.61
General Edwards Bridge	4.57
George Washington Bridge	7.172
Georges Bank	3.3
Georges Island	4.97
Georges Islands: Saint George River	3.22
Georges Islands: West Penobscot Bay	2.144
Georges Rock	6.193
Georges Shoal	3.7
Gig Rock	3.27
Gilbert Canyon	5.5
Gilbert Head	3.98
Gilkey Harbor	2.190
Gilley Thorofare	2.45
Glen Cove Harbor	6.243
Glen Cove Landing	6.244
Glen Island	6.219
Glenwood Landing	6.244
Gloucester	4.14
Harbor	4.14
Goat Island: Cape Porpoise	3.210
Goat Island: Kennebec River	3.99
Goat Island: Newport	5.213
Googins Ledge	2.64
Goose Island	6.194
Goose Nest	3.150
Ledge	3.150
Goose Point	4.138
Goose Rock	3.41
Ledge	3.41
Goose Rock Passage	3.88
Goose Rocks Light	2.121
Goose Rocks Shoals	6.88
Gooseberry Island	3.215
Gooseberry Island Ledge	3.109
Gooseberry Neck	5.111
Gorges, Fort	3.193
Goshen Point	6.97
Gosport	3.254
Harbor	3.254
Goudy Ledge	3.110
Gould Island	5.204
Gouldsboro	2.27
Gouldsboro Bay	2.27
Governors Island: Boston Harbor	4.96
Governors Island: New York Harbor	7.91
Gowanus Bay	7.100
Gowanus Flats	7.94
Grape Island	4.98
Grass Ledge	2.122
Graves, The: Boston Harbor	4.93
Light	4.91
Graves, The: West Penobscot Bay	2.145
Gravesend Bay	7.82
Great Beds Reach	7.73
Great Brewster	4.91
Spit	4.99
Great Captain Island	6.208
Light	6.92
Great Captain Rocks	6.214
Great Chebeague Island	3.147
Great Cranberry Island	2.49
Great Diamond Island	3.154
Great Duck Island	2.24
Light	2.23
Great Egg Rock	4.35
Great Gott Island	2.73
Great Gull Island	6.14
Great Harbor	5.103
Great Haste	4.33
Great Island	4.149
Great Kills Harbor	7.81
Great Ledge: New Bedford Harbor	5.165
Great Ledge: Woods Hole	5.101
Great Mark Island	3.121
Great Misery Island	4.36
Great Neck: Buzzards Bay	5.149
Great Neck: Long Island Sound	6.250
Great Peconic Bay	6.70
Great Pig Rocks	4.51
Great Point	5.32
Light	5.39
Great Rock	5.61
Great Round Shoal	5.39
Channel	5.39
Great Salt Pond	6.22
Great South Bay	7.25
Great South Beach	7.25

Great South Channel	4.64
Great Spoon Island	2.24
Great Spruce Head	2.146
Great Wass Island	2.7
Green Harbor	4.122
Green Island	2.78
Green Island Ledge	3.131
Green Island Passage	3.145
Green Island Reef	3.145
Green Island: Boston Harbor	4.95
Green Island: Western Bay	2.10
Green Islands: Sheepscot River	3.89
Green Islands: Blue Hill Bay Approach	2.69
Green Jacket Shoal	5.242
Green Ledge	2.116
Greening Island	2.47
Greenport	6.60
Harbor	6.60
Greens Ledge: Sheffield Harbor, Light	6.92
Greens Ledge: Sheffield Island Harbor	6.199
Greens Ledge: Penobscot Bay Approaches	2.143
Greenwich	6.228
Harbor	6.228
Greenwich Bay	5.226
Greenwich Cove: Captain Harbor	6.226
Greenwich Point	6.208
Griffin Ledge	3.26
Griffith Head	3.82
Ledge	3.85
Grindel Point	2.190
Grindstone Ledge	2.58
Grindstone Neck	2.57
Groton	6.97
Guilford Harbor	6.177
Gull Island: Buzzards Bay	5.125
Gull Island: Massachusetts Bay	4.125
Gull Ledge	2.131
Gull Rock	3.46
Gull Rocks: Newport Harbor	5.213
Gull Rocks: Pigeon Hill Bay	2.21
Gun Point	3.115
Cove	3.117
Gunboat Shoal	3.236
Gunning Rocks	3.20
Gurnet Point	4.118
Light	4.133
Gut, The	3.69
Hackensack River	7.130
Haddock Island	3.47
Haddock Ledge	2.191
Hadley Harbor	5.100
Hadlock Cove	2.49
Hale, Fort	6.128
Halfmoon Shoal	5.49
Halftide Ledge	3.47
Halftide Rock	4.95
Halfway Ledge	5.208
Halfway Rock: Casco Bay	3.120
Light	3.13
Halfway Rock: Marblehead Channel	4.37
Halfway Rock: Narragansett Bay	5.204
Halibut Point	3.256
Halibut Rocks	3.97
Halibut Rocks: Jericho Bay	2.78
Hall Island	3.43
Hallets Cove	7.156
Hallets Point	7.145
Hallets Rock	5.50
Hamilton, Fort	7.83
Hamlin Point	5.118
Hammonasset Point	6.88
Hammonasset River	6.176
Hancock Point	2.62
Handkerchief Shoal	5.38
Harbor Bluff	5.62
Harbor Cove	4.17
Harbor Island Rock	3.46
Harbor Island: Eggemoggin Reach	2.86
Harbor Island: Swans Island	2.82
Harbor Ledge	6.206
Harbor Ledge: Penobscot Bay Approaches	2.109
Hardhead Island	2.116
Harding	3.111
Harding Beach	5.56
Harding Ledge	3.86
Hardwood Island: Blue Hill Bay	2.70
Hardwood Island: Moosabec Reach	2.12
Hardy Rocks	4.38
Harlem River	7.148
Harpswell Harbor	3.122
Harpswell Neck	3.104
Harpswell Sound	3.119
Harraseeket River	3.140
Harrington Bay	2.17
Harrington River	2.17
Harrys Rock	4.98
Hart Island: Long Island Sound	6.220
Roads	6.220
Hart Island: Port Clyde Approach	3.24
Hartford	6.163
Harwich Port	5.55
Haskell Island	3.119
Haste Shoal	4.43
Hatchet Cove	3.53
Hatchett Point	6.87
Hatchett Reef	6.87
Haut, Isle au	2.112
Bay	2.111
Thorofare	2.118
Haverhill	3.258
Hawes Shoal	5.54
Hay Ledge	3.20
Head of the Harbor	5.69
Heart Island	2.131
Hedge Fence	5.49
Hell Gate	7.145
Hempstead Bay	7.26
Hempstead Harbor	6.242
Hen and Chickens Reef	6.217
Hen and Chickens: Buzzards Bay	5.111
Hen and Chickens: Captain Harbor	6.211
Hen and Chickens: Long Island Sound	6.87
Hen Island	6.216
Hen Island Ledge	3.112
Hen Islet	3.112
Henderson Ledge	3.35
Henderson Point	3.238
Hendricks Head	3.86
Henrietta Rock	5.164
Henry Cove	2.59
Henry Point	2.136
Heron Neck Light	2.143
Hewes Ledge	2.132
Hewes Point	2.132
Hewett Island	2.184
Hewlett Point	6.96
Hicks Ledge	6.218
High Cliff	4.136
High Head: Blue Hill Bay	2.90
High Hill Point	5.183
Highland Light	4.66
Highlands of Navesink	7.32
Hingham Bay	4.89
Hoadley Point	6.88
Hoboken	7.83
Hockamock Head	2.82
Hockomock Bay	3.88
Hockomock Channel	3.48
Hockomock Point	3.47
Hodgdon Ledge	3.87
Hodges Rock	5.85
Hodgkins Cove	3.260
Hoffman Island	7.65
Hog Back	7.145
Hog Creek Point	6.47
Hog Island Shoal	5.258
Lighthouse	5.201
Hog Island: Cape Cod Canal	5.144
Channel	5.144
Hog Island: Muscongus Bay	3.47
Hog Island: Narragansett Bay	5.221
Hog Neck	5.149
Holbrook Ledge	3.75
Holmes Rock	7.145
L'Hommedieu Shoal	5.51
Hook of the Cape	4.61
Hope Island: Luckse Sound	3.149
Hope Island: Narragansett Bay	5.208
Horns Hook	7.145
Horse Island	3.132
Horseshoe Cove	7.78
Horseshoe Shoal	5.49
Horton Point	6.86
Hospital Island	2.136
Hospital Point	4.36
Housatonic River	6.168
House Island	3.193
Howard Point	3.33
Howland Hook Container Terminal	7.113
Hudson	7.182
Hudson Canyon	7.8
Hudson River	7.165
Anchorages and harbours	7.178
General information	7.165
Hull	4.87
Bay	4.89
Gut	4.98
Hungry Island	3.48
Hunters Point	7.144
Huntington	6.237
Bay	6.235
Harbor	6.237
Hunts Point	7.161
Hupper Island	3.18
Hupper Point	3.21
Hurricane Sound	2.185
Hussey Sound	3.154
Hussey, The	3.144
Hutchinson River	6.230
Hyannis	5.58
Harbor	5.58
Point	5.58
Port	5.58
Hydrographer Canyon	5.5
Hypocrite Channel	4.95
Hypocrites, The	3.66
Ida Lewis Rock	5.213
Indian Hill	4.131
Indian Island	2.145
Indian Point	3.153
Indian River	2.145
Inez Rock	5.165
Inner Green Island	3.144
Inner Harbor: Boston Harbor	4.106
Inner Harbor: Gloucester Harbor	4.21
Inner Harbor: Prospect Harbor	2.32
Inner Heron Island	3.67
Berths	3.68
Inner Heron Ledge	3.67
Inner Ledges	2.166
Inner Sand Island	2.10

INDEX

Interval Shoal	3.121
Intrepid Rock	6.38
Iron Point	2.121
Ironbound Island	2.42
Island Beach	7.28
Isle of Springs	3.87
Isles of Shoals	3.251
Light	3.250
Islesboro Harbor	2.132
Islesboro Island	2.94
Islesboro Ledge	2.117
Jackknife Ledge	3.97
Jacobs Point	6.181
Jaffrey Point	3.237
Jamaica Bay	7.22
Jamaica Island	3.231
Jameson Point: Muscongus Bay	3.51
Jameson Point: West Penobscot Bay	2.152
Jamestown	5.217
Jamestown Bridge	5.199
Jamison Ledge	3.109
Jaquish Island	3.105
Jed Islands	2.91
Jefferson, Port	6.186
Harbor	6.186
Jeffreys Bank	3.3
Jellison, Cape	2.194
Jenks Ledge	3.41
Jeremy Point	4.149
Jericho Bay	2.77
Jerry Point	3.154
Jersey City	7.83
Jersey Flats	7.91
Jessup Neck	6.68
Jewell Island	3.144
Job Island	2.190
Joe Beach Ledge	4.56
John Ledge	4.36
Johns Bay	3.62
Johns Island Sunken Ledge	2.78
Johns Island: Blue Hill Bay approaches	2.74
Johns Island: Johns Bay	3.62
Johns Ledge	3.149
Johns River	3.62
Johnson Rock	3.145
Johnson, Port	7.121
Johnsons Creek	6.141
Jones Beach	7.26
Jones Garden Island	3.46
Jones Inlet	7.26
Jones Ledge: Casco Bay	3.163
Jones Ledge: Narragansett Bay	5.207
Jones Point	3.67
Jones Rocks	6.211
Jonesport	2.12
Jordan Island	2.60
Jordan Reef	3.192
Jordans Delight Ledge	2.18
Joshua Cove	6.178
Judith, Point	5.173
Juniper Point: Beverly Harbor	4.47
Juniper Point: Woods Hole	5.101
Junk of Pork	3.144
Junken Ledge	2.143
Kearny Point	7.122
Kegs, The	3.41
Kelp Ledges	3.24
Kelsey Point	6.175
Breakwater	6.175
Kennebec River	3.94
Kennebunk River	3.218
Kennebunkport	3.218
Kent Cove	2.126
Kettle Bottom Rock	5.203
Kettle Island	4.35
Ledge	4.35
Kettle Point	5.241
Keyser Point	6.199
Kibby Ground	5.182
Kill Pond Bar	5.56
Kill Van Kull	7.115
Directions	7.119
General information	7.115
Terminals and harbours	7.120
Kimball Head	2.115
Kimball Island	2.118
Kimball Rock	2.115
Kimberly Reef	6.88
Kings Point: Long Island Sound	6.250
Kings Point: Southwest Harbor	2.47
Kingston	7.181
Kingston Bay	4.138
Kittery	3.219
Kitts Rocks	3.237
Knubble Bay	3.88
La Guardia Airport	7.159
Lagoon Pond	5.78
Larchmont Harbor	6.217
Latimer Reef	6.37
Light	6.37
Lawrence Cove	2.204
Lawrence Point	7.146
Ledge	7.146
Lee Island	3.99
Leetes Rocks	6.178
Leonardo	7.74
Lewis Bay	5.58
Lewis Rock	2.44
Liberty Island	7.91
Lighthouse Point	6.130
Limits of the book	1.1
Lincoln House Point	4.54
Lincolnville	2.191
Linekin Bay	3.75
Linekin Neck	3.63
Lion Head	5.203
Little Bay: East River	7.164
Little Birch Island	3.132
Little Black Ledge	2.31
Little Brewster Island	4.97
Little Bustins Island	3.141
Little Calf Island	4.95
Little Captain Island	6.208
Little Chebeague Island	3.153
Little Cows, The	6.156
Little Cranberry Island	2.49
Little Diamond Island	3.156
Little Egg Rock	3.41
Little Georges Shoals	5.8
Little Goshen Reef	6.160
Little Gull Island Light	6.14
Little Harbor: Portsmouth Harbor	3.237
Little Harbor: Woods Hole	5.104
Little Mark Island	3.120
Little Misery Island	4.36
Little Moose Island	2.41
Little Nahant	4.53
Little Narragansett Bay	6.44
Little Neck	6.236
Little Peconic Bay	6.57
Little Pig Rocks	4.51
Little River, Rock	3.212
Little Sheepscot River	3.88
Little Whaleboat Island	3.133
Littlejohn Island	3.162
Lloyd Harbor	6.238
Lloyd Neck	6.95
Lloyd Point	6.95
Locust Island	3.49
Logan International Airport	4.91
Londoner	3.250
Lone Rock: Nomans Land	5.106
Lone Rock: Quicks Hole	5.105
Long Beach Point: Shelter Island Sound	6.63
Long Beach: Nahant Bay	4.53
Long Beach: New York Approach	7.26
Long Branch	7.28
Long Cove: Penobscot Bay	2.178
Long Cove: Muscongus Bay	3.54
Long Island	6.72
Sound	6.71
Long Island: Blue Hill Bay	2.70
Long Island: Blue Hill Bay Approach	2.24
Long Island: Boston Harbor	4.93
Anchorage	4.103
Head	4.93
Long Island: Luckse Sound	3.147
Long Ledge: Deer Island Thorofare	2.80
Long Ledge: New Meadows River	3.110
Long Neck Point	6.195
Long Point: Cape Cod Bay	4.142
Long Point: Marshall Island	2.79
Long Pond Shoal	2.44
Long Porcupine Island	2.42
Long Sand Shoal	6.87
Lookout: village	2.124
Lopaus Head	2.87
Lords Passage	6.32
Louds Island	3.47
Lovell Island	4.99
Lowell Cove	3.118
Lowell Rock	2.145
Light	2.161
Lower Basket Ledge	3.162
Lower Bay	7.58
Anchorage areas	7.76
Lower Cape	4.61
Lower Clapboard Island Ledge	3.163
Lower Goose Island	3.133
Lower Hell Gate	3.88
Lower Mark Island	3.86
Lower Middle Ground	2.19
Lower Middle: Boston	4.96
Lower Narrows	3.47
Lucas Shoal	5.96
Luce Cove	2.204
Luckse Sound	3.147
Lumbo Ledge	3.15
Lydonia Canyon	5.5
Lynde Point	6.163
Lynn	4.57
Harbor	4.57
Mack Point	2.175
Mackerel Cove	2.88
Mackerel Cove: Merriconeag Sound	3.121
Mackerel Rock	2.18
MacMahan Island	3.88
Madison Reef	6.177
Magnetic anomalies, local	
Cape Ann	3.248
Gloucester Harbor	4.10
Jordan Island	2.38
Kennebec River	3.95
Lower Bay	7.62
Magnolia Harbor	4.35
Mahoney Island	2.81
Main Channel	5.42
Maine, Gulf of	3.3
Malaga Island	3.254
Malcolm Ledge	2.103
Mamaroneck	6.216
Harbor	6.216
Manana Island	2.102

INDEX

Manasquan Inlet	7.36
Manasquan River	7.36
Manchester Bay	4.36
Manchester Channel	4.46
Manchester Harbor	4.46
Manchester Point	2.51
Manhasset Bay	6.245
Manhasset Neck	6.95
Manhattan	7.40
Bridge	7.142
Island	7.40
Manomet Hill	4.131
Manomet Point	4.127
Manresa Island	6.196
Manursing Island	6.208
Reef	6.214
Maple Juice Cove	3.35
Maquoit Bay	3.139
Marblehead	4.48
Channel	4.37
Harbor	4.48
Neck	4.48
Rock	4.37
Mariner Ledge	3.161
Maritime Topography	1.89
General remarks	1.89
Seabed	1.90
Seismic and volcanic activity	1.91
Mark Island Ledge:	
Merriconeag Sound	3.120
Mark Island:	
Deer Island Thorofare	2.120
Mark Island:	
West Penobscot Bay	2.145
Mark Island: Winter Harbor	2.57
Mark Island:	
New meadows River	3.110
Ledge	3.110
Marsh Cove Head	2.118
Marshall Island	2.77
Marshall Ledge	3.20
Marshall Point: Port Clyde	3.18
Light	3.20
Marshall Point:	
West Penobscot Bay	2.146
Martha's Vineyard	5.18
Martin Point	3.48
Martin Rock	4.38
Mary Ann Rocks	4.131
Mashnee Island	5.144
Mason Island	6.45
Maspeth Creek	7.149
Massachusetts Bay	4.1
Matinecock Point	6.95
Matinicus Harbor	2.109
Matinicus Island	2.109
Matinicus Rock Light	2.102
Mattapoisett Harbor	5.129
Mattapoisett Neck	5.129
Mayflower Ledge	4.20
McBlair Shoal	5.39
McFarland Island	3.76
McHeard Cove	2.91
McIntosh Ledge	2.117
McKown Point	3.77
Meadow Cove	3.71
Meadow Point	2.63
Medomak River	3.48
Meduncook River	3.44
Megansett	5.131
Harbor	5.131
Melville	5.220
Menemsha	5.108
Basin	5.108
Bight	5.107
Creek	5.108
Menunketesuck Island	6.174
Merchant Row	2.79
Mere Point	3.138

Merepoint	3.138
Bay	3.138
Neck	3.138
Merriconeag Sound	3.119
Merrimack River	3.258
Merriman Ledges	3.122
Metedeconk River	7.36
Metinic Island	2.144
Ledge	2.144
Miacomet Rip	5.16
Mianus	6.227
River	6.227
Middle Bay	3.133
Middle Breakers	4.35
Middle Breakwater	6.131
Middle Brewster	4.95
Middle Clump	6.38
Middle Ground Rock	3.114
Middle Ground Shoal	5.76
Middle Ground: Blue Hill Bay	2.92
Middle Ground:	
Fishers Island Sound	6.41
Middle Ground: Plum Gut	6.85
Middle Ground:	
Salem Sound approaches	4.35
Middle Ground: Vineyard Sound	5.96
Middle Ledge: Buzzards Bay	5.165
Middle Ledge: Sheepscot River	3.86
Middle Mark Island	3.86
Middle Rip	4.68
Middle Rock:	
East Penobscot Bay	2.116
Middle Rock: Somes Sound	2.51
Midway Shoal	6.85
Milbridge	2.20
Mile Ledge	3.15
Milford Harbor	6.180
Milford Point	6.168
Mill Neck Creek	6.241
Mill Point	3.88
Mill River: Southport Harbor	6.222
Mill River:New Haven Harbor	6.118
Mill Rock	7.145
Millstone Point	6.161
Ministerial Island	3.131
Mink Point	5.102
Mishaum Ledge	5.124
Mitchell Point	2.19
Mitchell Rock	3.177
Monhegan Harbor	2.110
Monhegan Island	2.102
Light	2.102
Monks Hill	4.133
Monomoy Island	5.32
Monomoy Point	5.32
Monomoy Shoals	5.33
Monroe Island	2.144
Montauk	6.26
Harbor	6.30
Lake	6.30
Point	6.9
Light	6.14
Shoal	7.21
Montgomery Point	3.71
Moon Head	4.101
Moore Point	3.140
Moores Harbor	2.123
Moosabec Reach	2.12
Moose Island: Blue Hill Bay	2.70
Moose Island:	
Deer Island Thorofare	2.80
Moose Neck	2.10
Moose Peak Light	2.8
Moose Point	2.169
Morgan Bay	2.91
Moriches	
Bay	7.24
Inlet	7.24
Morris Island	5.56

Morris, Port	7.157
Morse Island	3.44
Moser Ledge	3.39
Moses Point	6.241
Mosher Ledge	5.164
Moshier Island	3.140
Moshier Ledge	3.141
Mosquito Island	2.144
Mosquito Ledge	3.20
Mott Point	6.242
Moulton Ledge	2.24
Mount Battie	2.166
Mount Desert Island	2.3
Mount Desert Narrows	2.64
Mount Desert Rock	2.24
Light	2.23
Mount Hope	5.259
Bay	5.247
Bridge	5.252
Point	5.259
Mount Misery Point	6.186
Mount Misery Shoal	6.190
Mouse Island	3.76
Moxy Reef	2.145
Murray Ledge	3.24
Murray Rock	3.211
Muscle Ridge Channel	2.147
Muscongus Bay	3.37
Muscongus Harbor	3.57
Muscongus Sound	3.47
Muskeget Channel	5.52
Muskeget Island	5.52
Mussel Point	4.17
Musselbed Shoals	5.258
Mutton Shoal	5.54
Mystic	6.45
Harbor	6.45
River	6.45
Mystic River: Boston Harbor	4.89
Nahant	4.53
Bay	4.53
Harbor	4.56
Rock	4.55
Nantasket Beach	4.91
Nantasket Roads	4.104
Nantucket	5.65
Harbor	5.65
Island	5.16
Shoals	5.19
Sound	5.41
Napatree Beach	6.44
Napatree Point Ledge	6.37
Napeague Bay	6.27
Napeague Harbor	6.27
Narragansett Bay	5.172
Narraguagus Bay	2.18
Narraguagus River	2.20
Narrow Bay	7.25
Narrows, The: Boston Harbor	4.99
Narrows, The:	
Damariscotta River	3.67
Narrows, The: New York Harbor	7.83
Narrows: Saint George River	3.33
Nash Island	2.15
Nashawena Island	5.88
Naskeag Point	2.65
Natural conditions	1.89
Climate and Weather	1.112
Climate information	1.139
Currents, tidal streams	
and flow	1.92
Maritime topography	1.89
Sea and swell	1.99
Sea water characteristics	1.105
Naugus Head	4.39
Nauset Beach, Light	4.66
Nauset Harbor	4.70

Naushon Island . . . 5.88
Nautilus Island . . . 2.134
Navesink River . . . 7.79
Navigation and Regulations . . . 1.1
Navigational dangers and hazards . . . 1.2
Coastal conditions . . . 1.2
Coastal dangers . . . 1.3
Former mined areas . . . 1.5
Natural conditions . . . 1.4
Overhead cables . . . 1.6
Nayatt Point . . . 5.227
Ned Point . . . 5.129
Neddick, Cape . . . 3.211
Nubble . . . 3.211
Negro Island: Booth Bay . . . 3.75
Negro Island: Saco Bay . . . 3.214
Ledge . . . 3.215
Negro Ledge . . . 5.164
Negro Point . . . 7.145
Neptune LNG Deepwater Port . . . 4.76
New Bedford . . . 5.150
Harbor . . . 5.162
New Brighton . . . 7.121
New Brunswick . . . 7.73
New Castle Island . . . 3.237
New Haven Harbor . . . 6.118
Arrival information . . . 6.125
Berths . . . 6.133
Directions . . . 6.130
General information . . . 6.118
Harbour . . . 6.128
Limiting conditions . . . 6.121
Port services . . . 6.135
New Inlet . . . 4.122
New Jersey . . . 7.3
New Jersey Intracoastal Waterway . . . 7.37
New London Harbor . . . 6.97
Arrival information . . . 6.103
Berths . . . 6.113
Directions . . . 6.109
Entrance Light . . . 6.109
General information . . . 6.97
Harbour . . . 6.107
Limiting conditions . . . 6.99
Port services . . . 6.115
New London Ledge . . . 6.111
New Meadows . . . 3.111
New Meadows River . . . 3.111
New Rochelle . . . 6.218
Harbor . . . 6.219
New Suffolk . . . 6.69
New York and New Jersey Port of . . . 7.40
New York City . . . 7.40
New York Harbor . . . 7.39
Anchorages . . . 7.4
Approaches . . . 7.2
Arrival information . . . 7.45
Berths . . . 7.52
General information . . . 7.39
Harbour . . . 7.50
Limiting conditions . . . 7.42
Pilotage . . . 7.5
Port services . . . 7.55
Traffic regulations . . . 7.5
Newagen, Cape . . . 3.73
Newark Bay . . . 7.122
Anchorages . . . 7.131
Directions . . . 7.128
General information . . . 7.122
Side channels . . . 7.129
Terminals . . . 7.132
Newburgh . . . 7.179
Newbury Neck . . . 2.90
Newburyport . . . 3.258
Newcastle . . . 3.63
Newcomb Ledge . . . 4.35
Newport . . . 5.210
Bridge . . . 5.199
Harbor . . . 5.210
Newport Neck . . . 5.203
Newtown Creek . . . 7.149
Niantic Bay . . . 6.159
Nightcap Island . . . 2.16
Ninigret Pond . . . 6.29
Nissequogue River . . . 6.232
Noank . . . 6.45
Nobska Point . . . 5.86
Nomans Land . . . 5.88
Nonamesset Island . . . 5.97
Nonamesset Shoal . . . 5.101
Norman's Woe Rock . . . 4.18
Noroton Point . . . 6.199
North Brother Island . . . 7.146
North Channel . . . 5.42
North Dumpling . . . 6.38
North Falmouth . . . 5.131
North Haven Island . . . 2.94
North Haven Peninsula . . . 6.68
North Islesboro . . . 2.133
North Jenny Ledge . . . 3.110
North Ledge . . . 5.165
North Point: Swans Island . . . 2.88
North Point: Western Bay . . . 2.89
North River: Beverly Harbor . . . 4.47
North Sugarloaf . . . 3.98
North Tiverton . . . 5.264
North Weymouth . . . 4.31
Northeast Gateway Deepwater Ports . . . 4.71
Northeast Harbor . . . 2.50
Northeast Ledge: Camden Harbor . . . 2.164
Northeast Ledge: Blue Hill Bay . . . 2.69
Northeast Point . . . 2.164
Light . . . 2.166
Northern Island . . . 2.182
Northport . . . 6.236
Bay . . . 6.236
Harbor . . . 6.236
Northport Basin . . . 6.234
Northport Offshore Terminal . . . 6.233
Northwest Harbor: East Penobscot Bay . . . 2.131
Northwest Harbor: Shelter Island Sound . . . 6.66
Northwest Point . . . 5.209
Norton Island Ledge . . . 2.16
Norton Point . . . 7.65
Norwalk . . . 6.196
Cove . . . 6.197
Harbor . . . 6.196
Islands . . . 6.193
River . . . 6.196
Norwich . . . 6.107
Noyack Bay . . . 6.68
Noyes Rock . . . 6.42
Noyes Shoal . . . 6.41
Nubbin, The . . . 3.163
Nubble Channel . . . 4.100
NW Bluff . . . 6.239
Nyes Neck . . . 5.130

Oak Bluffs Harbor . . . 5.87
Oak Island . . . 2.122
Oak Neck . . . 6.241
Oak Point: Penobscot River . . . 2.200
Oak Point: Western Bay . . . 2.90
Obeds Rock . . . 3.149
Oceanographer Canyon . . . 5.5
Odiornes Point . . . 3.237
Odom Ledge . . . 2.203
Ohio Ledge . . . 5.206
Old Anthony Rock . . . 3.165
Old Cilly Ledge . . . 2.144
Old Cock . . . 5.122
Old Ferry Point . . . 7.162
Old Field Beach . . . 6.189
Old Field Point . . . 6.94
Light . . . 6.94
Old Harbor . . . 5.189
Point . . . 5.189
Old Horse Ledge . . . 3.24
Old Hump Channel . . . 3.42
Old Hump Ledge . . . 3.42
Old Man . . . 5.105
Old Man Ledge: Muscongus Bay . . . 3.41
Old Man Ledge: Penobscot Bay . . . 2.144
Old Man Shoal . . . 5.16
Old Orchard Beach . . . 3.212
Old Orchard Shoal . . . 7.76
Light . . . 7.67
Old Tom . . . 2.45
Old Whale Ledge . . . 2.42
Old Woman . . . 2.31
Onset . . . 5.149
Bay . . . 5.149
Orcutt Harbor . . . 2.86
Orient . . . 6.63
Harbor . . . 6.63
Orient Point . . . 6.47
Light . . . 6.14
Orion Shoal . . . 5.39
Orono Island . . . 2.75
Orrington . . . 2.201
Orrs Island . . . 3.117
Osterville, Point . . . 5.85
Otis Cove . . . 3.34
Otter Cliff Ledge . . . 2.41
Otter Cove . . . 2.14
Otter Island . . . 3.41
Otter Ledge . . . 2.69
Otter Point . . . 2.41
Otter Rock Shoal . . . 2.134
Outer Bar Island . . . 2.29
Outer Breakers . . . 4.51
Outer Brewster . . . 4.95
Outer Green Island . . . 3.175
Outer Heron Island . . . 3.65
Ledge . . . 3.65
Outer Sand Island . . . 2.10
Outer Steamboat Rock . . . 6.216
Overset Island . . . 3.154
Owls Head . . . 2.145
Bay . . . 2.150
Harbor . . . 2.189
Light . . . 2.142
Oyster Bay . . . 6.239
Harbor . . . 6.241
Village . . . 6.241
Oyster Pond Reef . . . 6.85
Light . . . 6.14
Oyster Shell Point . . . 6.197

Padanaram Breakwater . . . 5.127
Palmer Island . . . 5.162
Pancake Ground . . . 4.22
Parker Flats . . . 3.98
Parker Head . . . 3.98
Parker Point: Blue Hill Bay . . . 2.92
Parsonage Point . . . 6.229
Pasque Island . . . 5.88
Passagassawakeag River . . . 2.169
Passaic . . . 7.129
River . . . 7.129
Patchogue River . . . 6.175
Paterson Point . . . 2.173
Patience Island . . . 5.209
Patten Bay . . . 2.90
Pawcatuck River . . . 6.44
Pawtuxet Neck . . . 5.240

Peaked Cliff	4.127	
Peaks Island	3.154	
Pecks Point	2.63	
Peconic River	6.57	
Peddocks Island	4.98	
Pemaquid Neck	3.37	
Pemaquid Point	3.39	
Light	3.39	
Pemaquid River	3.62	
Pendleton Point	2.117	
Penfield Reef	6.156	
Light	6.92	
Penikese Island	5.125	
Penobscot Bay	2.94	
Penobscot River	2.195	
Penzance	5.102	
Point	5.102	
Pequonnock River	6.145	
Perch Island	3.75	
Perkins Island	3.98	
Ledge	3.98	
Perry Ledge	2.143	
Perth Amboy	7.108	
Petit Manan Island	2.9	
Light	2.8	
Petit Manan Point	2.25	
Pettis Rocks	3.99	
Phelps Bank	4.68	
Phillips Point	4.53	
Phoenix, Fort	5.164	
Pickering Island	2.116	
Pierces Island	3.238	
Pierhead Channel	7.96	
Pigeon Cove	3.257	
Pigeon Hill Bay	2.21	
Pigeon Hill: Pigeon Hill Bay	2.21	
Pigeon Hill: Cape Ann	3.257	
Pilgrim Ledge	4.35	
Pilgrim Monument	4.144	
Pilgrim Nuclear Power Plant	4.132	
Pilotage	1.28	
United States	1.28	
Pine Creek Point	6.222	
Pine Hill Point	5.208	
Pine Point	6.85	
Pines River	4.57	
Pinetree Ground	5.182	
Pinkham Island	3.121	
Piscataqua River	3.219	
Placentia Island	2.69	
Platts Bank	3.3	
Playland	6.229	
Pleasant Bay	2.15	
Pleasant Point	3.33	
Pleasant River	2.15	
Pleasure Beach	6.147	
Plum Gut	6.85	
Plum Island: Long Island Sound	6.85	
Plum Island: Merrimack River	3.258	
Light	3.250	
Plum Point: Manhasset Bay	6.245	
Plum Point: Oyster Bay	6.241	
Plummer Island	2.10	
Plymouth	4.136	
Bay	4.132	
Beach	4.132	
Harbor	4.136	
Light	4.133	
Pocasset Harbor	5.132	
Poge, Cape	5.49	
Bay	5.71	
Point Francis	2.28	
Point Judith	6.7	
Point Judith Harbor of Refuge	6.19	
Point Judith Light	5.186	
Point Judith Pond	6.19	
Point Pleasant Canal	7.36	
Point Rip	5.39	
Poland North Ledge	3.47	
Poland South Ledge	3.47
Pollock Rip	5.38
Channel	5.38
Pomham Rocks	5.240
Pomp Island	2.12
Ponce Landing	3.155
Pond Island: Blue Hill Bay	2.76
Passage	2.76
Pond Island: Kennebec River	3.98
Shoal	3.97
Pond Point	2.9
Pool Hill	3.246
Poor Shoal	3.74
Popasquash Neck	5.221
Popasquash Point	5.206
Pope Head	4.38
Popes Island	5.162
Popham, Fort	3.98
Porcupine Islands	2.35
Port Chester	6.213
Harbor	6.213
Port Clyde	3.18
Port Elizabeth	7.133
Port Newark	7.134
Porterfield Ledge	2.160
Portland Harbor	3.178
Arrival information	3.185
Berths	3.195
Directions	3.191
General information	3.178
Harbour	3.189
Head Light	3.172
Limiting conditions	3.181
Port services	3.199
Portsmouth Harbor	3.219
Arrival information	3.227
Berths	3.239
Directions	3.235
General Information	3.219
Harbour	3.232
Limiting conditions	3.221
Port services	3.242
Pot Rock	2.16
Potato Ledge	2.80
Potts Harbor	3.132
Potts Point	3.132
Poughkeepsie	7.180
Pound of Tea Islet	3.140
Powderhorn Island	3.87
Powderhorn Ledge	3.87
Powers Rock	4.36
Prairie Ledge	4.20
Pralls Island	7.107
Premium Point	6.218
President Roads	4.102
Prince Head	4.98
Prince Point Ledge	3.163
Promised Land	6.27
Channel	6.27
Prospect Harbor	2.31
Point	2.31
Prospect Point:	
Hempstead Harbor	6.242
Prospect Point: Prospect Harbor	2.31
Prouts Neck	3.212
Providence	5.227
Arrival information	5.233
Berths	5.242
Directions	5.239
General information	5.227
Harbour	5.237
Limiting conditions	5.230
Port services	5.244
Providence Point	5.209
Providence River	5.227
Provincetown	4.142
Harbor	4.142
Prudence Island	5.193
Pulpit Harbor	2.188
Pulpit Rock	2.188
Pumpkin Island	3.65
Pumpkin Nob	3.155
Quahog Bay	3.115
Queens	7.40
Queensboro Bridge	7.142
Quicks Hole	5.106
Quincy Bay	4.89
Quinnipiac River	6.118
Quonochontaug Pond	6.29
Quonset Point	5.225
Race Point: Cape Cod	4.59
Lighthouse	4.66
Race Point: Long Island Sound	6.84
Race Rock	6.84
Light	6.14
Race, The	6.84
Radio Facilities	
Radio aids to navigation	1.30
Radio medical advice	1.34
Radio navigational warnings	1.31
Local warnings	1.32
Long range warnings	1.31
Radio weather reports	1.33
Ragged Island: Quahog Bay	3.114
Ragged Island:	
Penobscot Bay Approaches	2.107
Ram Head	4.94
Flats	4.95
Ram Island Ledge	3.215
Ram Island Reef	6.38
Ram Island: Booth Bay	3.66
Ram Island: Kennebec River	3.99
Ram Island: Marblehead Neck	4.51
Ram Island: Portland	3.192
Ledge	3.192
Ram Island:	
Tibbett Narrows	2.10
Ram Island: Western Bay	2.11
Ram Islet	3.87
Raritan Bay	7.73
Channel	7.67
Raritan River	7.73
Cutoff	7.73
Raspberry Island	3.18
Rat Island	6.221
Reach, The	2.180
Reading, Port	7.110
Red Bank Reach	7.67
Red Brook Harbor	5.132
Red Hook Channel	7.94
Red Point	2.74
Regulations	1.35
International regulations	1.35
Pollution	1.37
Submarine cables	1.35
Submarine pipelines	1.36
Traffic separation schemes	1.38
National regulations	1.39
Code of Federal Regulations	1.40
Communication	
between vessels	1.46
Danger Zones and	
restricted areas regulations	1.49
National Marine Sanctuaries	1.42
National Terrorism	
Advisory System	1.50
Navigation Rules for	
US Inland Waters	1.44
Navigation safety regulations	1.43
North Atlantic Right Whale	1.51
Notifications	1.47
Pollution of the sea	1.41
Quarantine and customs	1.53
Regulated Navigation Areas	1.48

Special anchorage areas	1.45
United States Coast Guard	1.39
Vessel arrival inspections	1.52
Pollution	1.37
Revere Beach	4.57
Rhode Island	5.193
Sound	5.9
Rich Hill	3.112
Richmond	7.40
Richmond Island	3.210
Richmond, Port	7.121
Richmond: Kennebec River	3.94
Richs Head	2.69
Ricketsons Point	5.128
Ridley Cove	3.116
Rikers Island	7.146
Channel	7.153
Ripley Neck	2.17
Riverhead	6.57
Roaring Bull Ledge	2.24
Roaring Bull: Marblehead Neck	4.51
Roaring Bull: Metinic Island	2.144
Roaring Bulls	4.95
Robins Island	6.58
Robinson Point	2.115
Robinson Rock	2.145
Rockaway Beach	7.22
Rockaway Inlet	7.22
Rockaway Point	7.16
Rockland Breakwater Head Light	2.155
Rockland Harbor	2.152
Rockport Harbor: West Penobscot Bay	2.160
Rocky Neck	4.21
Rocky Point: Block Island Sound	6.26
Rocky Point: Long Island Sound, East part	6.86
Rocky Point: Oyster Bay	6.239
Rocky Point: Plymouth Bay	4.132
Rodman Neck	6.220
Rodman, Fort	5.164
Rogue Island	3.110
Rogues Island	3.149
Romer Shoal	7.65
Light	7.63
Roosevelt Island	7.145
Rose Island	5.204
Rosier, Cape	2.116
Roslyn	6.242
Round Pond	3.55
Round Rock Shoal	4.18
Round Rock: Casco Bay	3.114
Round Rock: Greenwich Bay	5.226
Rumstick Neck Reach	5.206
Rumstick Point	5.222
Rutherford Island	3.62
Rye Beach	6.229
Sabbathday Harbor	2.133
Sabin Point	5.240
Reach	5.240
Sachem Head	6.177
Sachuest Point	5.183
Saco	3.213
Bay	3.212
River	3.213
Saddleback Ledge: Casco Bay	3.114
Saddleback Ledge: Isle au Haut Bay	2.115
Sag Harbor	6.61
Cove	6.62
Sagamore Beach	4.131
Saint George	7.119
Saint George River	3.29
Sakonnet Point	5.183
Sakonnet River	5.183

Salem	4.39
Channel	4.36
Harbor	4.39
Neck	4.39
Sound	4.26
Sally Islands	2.27
Salsbury Cove	2.64
Salter Island	3.82
Salters Point Rock	5.165
Salvages, The	3.250
Sammy Rock	4.51
Sand Cove: Prospect Harbor	2.32
Sand Cove: Winter Harbor	2.59
Sand Island	3.149
Sand Point	2.64
Sands Point	6.95
Sandspit, The	5.165
Sandy Bay	3.256
Ledge	3.257
Sandy Beach	4.150
Sandy Hook	7.58
Bay	7.76
Channel	7.66
Light	7.32
Point	7.76
Light	7.63
Sandy Point Ledges	3.163
Sandy Point: Block Island	6.16
Light	6.16
Sandy Point: Greenwich Bay	5.226
Sandy Point: Little Narragansett Bay	6.44
Sandy Point: Narragansett Bay	5.205
Sandy Point: New Haven Harbor	6.128
Breakwater Light	6.132
Sandy Point: Penobscot River	2.203
Sankaty Head, Light	5.22
Saquish Head	4.132
Saquish Neck	4.137
Sargentville	2.85
Sasanoa River	3.88
Satan Rock	4.38
Saturday Night Ledge	4.13
Saugatuck	6.223
River	6.223
Saugus River	4.57
Sawyer Island	3.90
Saybrook Outer Bar	6.166
Saybrook Point	6.165
Scarborough River	3.212
Schoodic Harbor	2.34
Schoodic Head	2.41
Schoodic Island	2.24
Schoodic Peninsula	2.35
Schoodic Point	2.41
Schuyler, Fort	7.163
Scituate Harbor	4.126
Scituate Neck	4.125
Sconticut Neck	5.151
Scott Cove	6.225
Scraggy Island	2.119
Scraggy Neck	5.131
Sculpin Ledge	4.101
Channel	4.101
Sculpin Point	2.92
Sea and Swell	1.99
Sea conditions	1.100
Swell conditions	1.101
Seaflower Reef	6.38
Seal Cove: Ragged Island	2.108
Seal Harbor: Frenchman Bay	2.48
Seal Harbor: Isleboro Island	2.192
Seal Harbor: Muscle Ridge Channel	2.183
Seal Island	2.103
Seal Ledge	2.91
Seal Ledges	3.41
Seal Rock: Linekin Bay	3.75
Seal Rocks	3.98

Searle Rock	4.35
Sears Island	2.175
Searsport Harbor	2.175
Seavey Island	3.232
Sebascodegan Island	3.113
Seekonk River	5.227
Seguin Island	3.13
Light	3.13
Seguin Ledges	3.96
Seguin SSW Ledge	3.15
Seguine Point	7.67
Bend	7.67
Sellers Rock	2.116
Seven Hundred Acre Island	2.146
Sewall, Fort	4.48
Seymour Point	6.223
Shabbit Island	2.12
Ledge	2.12
Shag Rock: Isles of Shoal	3.252
Shag Rock: Kennebec River	3.98
Shag Rocks	4.56
Shagwong Reef	6.18
Shagwong Rock	6.18
Shark Island	3.42
Shark River Inlet	7.38
Shea Island	6.195
Sheep Island: Boston Harbor	4.98
Sheep Island: Dyer Bay	2.26
Sheep Island: Gouldsboro Bay	2.28
Sheep Island: West Penobscot Bay	2.150
Sheep Porcupine Island	2.42
Sheephead Island	2.129
Sheephead Island Ledges	2.129
Sheepscot Bay	3.82
Sheepscot River	3.82
Sheffield Island	6.193
Harbor	6.195
Shelter Island: Gardiners Bay	6.57
Sound	6.57
Shelter Island: Middle Bay	3.133
Shinnecock Bay	7.23
Shinnecock Canal	7.23
Shinnecock Inlet	7.23
Ship and Barges Ledge	2.70
Ship Island	2.70
Ship Rock	6.216
Shippan Point	6.203
Shipstern Island	2.18
Shoals, Isles of	3.251
Shooters Island	7.116
Shovelful Shoal	5.38
Shrewsbury River	7.79
Sias Point	5.149
Signals	1.54
National signals Naval vessels	1.54
Submarines	1.55
Survey vessels and Buoy tenders	1.56
Simms Rock	2.9
Sister Island	3.139
Sister Islands	2.74
Sisters Ground	3.110
Sisters, The: Casco Bay	3.110
Sisters, The: Georges Islands	3.27
Sisters, The: Kennebec River Approaches	3.85
Sixmile Reef	6.86
Skillings River	2.63
Small Point	3.107
Small, Cape	3.107
Smalley Bar	4.149
Smith Cove: East Penobscot Bay	2.136
Smith Cove: Gloucester Harbor	4.17
Smith Cove: Shelter Island Sound	6.67
Smithtown Bay	6.232

INDEX

Smuttynose Island	3.250
Snippershan Ledge	2.143
Socony, Port	7.109
Soldier Ledge	3.155
Somes Harbor	2.51
Somes Sound	2.51
South Amboy	7.80
Reach	7.73
South Boston	4.96
South Brewer	2.217
South Bristol	3.69
South Brooksville	2.86
South Brother Island	7.151
Channel	7.152
Ledge	7.153
South Channel	4.38
South Ferry: Narragansett Bay	5.207
South Ferry: Shelter Island Sound	6.67
South Freeport	3.141
South Gouldsboro	2.60
South Harpswell	3.132
South Norwalk	6.196
South Oyster Bay	7.25
South Portland	3.178
Southeast Breakers	4.35
Southeast Harbor: Deer Island Thorofare	2.83
Southeast Harbor: Gloucester Harbor	4.22
Southeast Ledge	5.209
Southeast Point	5.186
Southeast Rock	2.9
Southeast Shoal	3.210
Southern Harbor	2.186
Southern Island	2.182
Southern Mark Island	2.79
Ledge	2.79
Southold	6.65
Bay	6.65
Southport Harbor	6.222
Southport Island	3.73
Southwest Approach	2.74
Southwest Harbor: East Penobscot Bay	2.129
Southwest Harbor: Frenchman Bay	2.47
Southwest Ledge: Block Island	6.17
Southwest Ledge: New Haven Harbor	6.131
Southwest Point: Hog Island, Narragansett Bay	5.206
Southwest Point: Southwest Approach	2.74
Southwest Shoal	5.95
Sow and Pigs Reef	5.96
Spar Island	5.259
Sparrow Island	2.119
Spectacle Island	4.96
Spectacle Islands	3.89
Spindle Rock	5.85
Spindle, The	4.56
Spoon Ledge	2.122
Spring Point	3.193
Spruce Head	2.146
Spruce Island	2.190
Spruce Point: Booth Bay	3.76
Ledges	3.75
Spruce Point: Cousins Island	3.162
Spruce Point: Prospect Harbor	2.31
Spurling Rock	2.45
Squash Meadow	5.46
Squaw Point	2.194
Squibnocket Point	5.105
Squirrel Island	3.74
Squirrel Point	3.98
Stage Harbor	5.55
Light	5.56
Stage Head	4.22
Stage Island: Kennebec River	3.98
Stage Island: Wood Island Harbor	3.214
Stamford	6.203
Harbor	6.203
Stand-in Point	2.151
Standish Monument	4.133
Stanley Point	2.26
Staple Ledge	2.69
Staple Point	2.84
Staples Cove	3.142
Stapleton Naval Station	7.85
Star Island	3.254
Star Island: Montauk Harbor	6.30
Staten Island	7.50
Light	7.63
Statue of Liberty	7.89
Stave Island: Casco Bay	3.150
Ledge	3.150
Stave Island: Frenchman Bay	2.60
Harbor	2.60
Steets Ledge	2.172
Stellwagen Bank	4.3
National Marine Sanctuary	4.3
Stellwagen Ledges	4.122
Stellwagen Rock	4.131
Stepping Stones	3.149
Light	6.96
Steuben	2.27
Stevens Island	2.10
Stielman Rocks	3.237
Stills Point	2.92
Stinson Neck	2.83
Stinson Point	2.116
Stirling Basin	6.60
Stockbridge Point	3.140
Stockman Island	3.131
Stockton Harbor	2.194
Stone Horse Shoal	5.38
Stone Island	6.175
Stones Point	3.33
Stonington: Deer Island Thorofare	2.84
Stonington: Fishers Island Sound	6.39
Harbor	6.39
Point	6.39
Stony Brook Harbor	6.232
Stony Point Dike	5.144
Stover Ledge	3.87
Stover Point	3.121
Strait, The	5.100
Straitsmouth Island	3.256
Light	3.257
Stratford	6.168
Point	6.168
Light	6.147
Stratford Shoal Middle Ground	6.86
Stratton Island	3.212
Strawberry Point: Buzzards Bay	5.129
Strawberry Point: Massachusetts Bay	4.122
Strout Island	2.17
Narrows	2.17
Sturdivant Island	3.158
Stuyvesant	7.178
Succonnesset Point	5.51
Succonnesset Shoal	5.51
Sugar Loaves	2.151
Sugar Reef	6.37
Passage	6.32
Sugarloaf	3.98
Sullivan Falls	2.62
Sullivan Harbor	2.62
Summer Harbor	2.60
Sunken Duck Rock	2.144
Sunset	2.129
Sutton Island	2.44
Swampscott	4.54
Swans Island	2.69
Swash Channel	7.70
Swinburne Island	7.65
Sylvester Cove	2.130
Tarpaulin Cove	5.109
Light	5.96
Taunton	5.252
River	5.247
Taunton Bay	2.62
Taylor Point: Cape Cod Canal	5.145
Taylor Point: Narragansett Bay	5.199
Temple Ledge	3.15
Tenants Harbor	2.182
Tenpound Island	4.20
Ledge	4.20
Terminal Channel	7.74
Thacher Island	3.250
Thames River	6.97
The Graves Light	4.91
Thieves Ledge	4.97
Thimbles, The	6.178
Thomaston	3.36
Thompson Island	3.26
Thompson Rock	3.41
Three and One–Half Fathoms Ledge	4.97
Three Fathom Ledge	2.103
Threefoot Rock	6.161
Threemile Harbor	6.55
Throgs Neck	7.135
Thrumcap	3.132
Thrumcap Island	3.63
Thrumcap, The	2.42
Tibbett Island	2.12
Tibbett Narrows	2.12
Tibbett Rock	2.9
Tibbits Ledge	3.75
Tinker Island	2.70
Tinkers Island	4.51
Tinkers Ledge	4.37
Tom Rock	3.85
Tomlinson Bridge	6.122
Tommy Island	2.18
Toms Point	6.248
Tongue Point	6.145
Toothacher Bay	2.78
Totten, Fort	7.147
Tottenville	7.101
Town River Bay	4.107
Townsend Gut	3.77
Townshend Ledge	6.88
Tracey Ledge	5.213
Traffic and operations	1.7
Exercise areas Firing practice	1.12
Naval exercises	1.11
Fishing Fish traps	1.10
General remarks	1.9
Submarine exercises, Submarine operating areas	1.13
Traffic Ferries	1.7
Pleasure craft	1.8
Trafton Halftide Ledge	2.19
Trafton Island	2.18
Trotts Rock	3.194
Troy Dam	7.165
Troy Lock	7.165
Trumbull, Fort	6.99
Trumpet Island	2.70
Truro	4.144
Tuckernuck Shoal	5.49
Tumbler Island	3.76
Tupper Ledge	2.90
Turkey Cove	3.34
Turkey Point	3.34

282

Turnip Island 3.120	Watts Point 3.33	White Head 3.194
Ledge 3.120	Weaver Cove 5.220	White Island: Isles of Shoals 3.250
Turtle Head 2.146	Weaver Ledge 2.87	White Island: Middle Bay 3.133
Cove 2.193	Webber Sunken Ledge 3.47	White Islands 3.65
Turtle Island 2.57	Webster Head 2.188	Ledge 3.65
Twenty-Eight Foot Shoal 6.86	Wee Captain Island 6.208	White Ledge 3.96
Two Bush Channel 2.138	Weehawken 7.83	White Rock:
Two Bush Island Light 2.142	Weekapaug Breachway 6.29	Fishers Island Sound 6.42
Two Bush Island: Quahog Bay ... 3.114	Weeks Point 6.242	White Rock: Niantic Bay 6.161
Twomile Ledge 5.182	Welker Canyon 5.5	Whitehead Island 2.147
Twomile Rock 5.182	Wellfleet 4.149	Light 2.148
Twotree Island 6.161	Harbor 4.149	Whitehead Passage 3.194
Channel 6.161	Wequetequock Cove 6.44	Whitmore Neck 2.83
	West Bank 7.65	Whittum Island 3.88
	Light 7.63	Wickets Island 5.149
Umbrella Point 6.217	West Beach 6.235	Wicopesset Island 6.37
Umbrella Rock 6.217	West Branch:	Wicopesset Passage 6.32
Uncas Point 6.178	Black Rock Harbor 6.154	Widow Island 2.125
Underwood Ledge 3.163	West Branch: Stamford Harbor ... 6.203	Wilbur Point 5.151
Union River 2.90	West Breakwater 6.133	Wild Harbor 5.130
Bay 2.90	West Brown Cow 3.131	Wilkes Ledge 5.124
Unionport 7.155	West Chop 5.49	Willets Point 7.135
United Riverhead Terminal 6.182	Light 5.82	Williamsburg Bridge 7.142
Upper Basket Ledge 3.162	West Cod Ledge 3.165	Wilson Point: Penobscot River ... 2.195
Upper Bay 7.83	Rock 3.177	Windmill Point 4.97
Upper Cape 4.61	West Cundy Point 3.116	Winnapaug Pond 6.29
Upper Clapboard Island Ledge ... 3.162	West Harbor: Fishers Island 6.46	Winnegance Bay 3.112
Upper Flag Island 3.132	West Harbor: Oyster Bay 6.241	Winter Harbor 2.57
Upper Goose Island 3.133	West Head 4.101	Winter Island 4.39
Upper Green Islets 3.131	West Hue and Cry 3.177	Winterport 2.211
Upper Hell Gate 3.88	West Mark Island Ledge 2.120	Winthrop Head 4.91
Upper Mark Island 3.87	West Neck 6.237	Winthrop Point 6.100
Usher Point 5.221	West Passage 5.194	Wiscasset 3.93
Usher Rocks 5.221	West Penobscot Bay 2.137	Witch Rock 3.192
	West River: Moosabec Reach ... 2.12	Wohoa Bay 2.12
	West River: New Haven Harbor .. 6.119	Wood End 4.145
Vaill Island 3.144	West Shoal 5.86	Wood Island: Casco Bay 3.109
Valiant Rock 6.84	West Southwest Ledge 5.50	South Ledge 3.109
Veatch Canyon 5.5	West Tremont 2.71	Wood Island:
Verrazano Narrows Bridge 7.86	Westbrook 6.174	Portsmouth Harbor 3.228
Veterans Memorial Bridge 5.252	Harbor 6.174	Wood Island: Saco Bay 3.214
Vinalhaven Island 2.94	Westchester 7.155	Harbor 3.214
Vineyard Haven 5.78	Creek 7.155	Light 3.209
Village 5.78	Western Bay 2.10	Wood Pond Point 2.21
Vineyard Sound 5.88	Western Channel 4.57	Wooden Ball Island 2.103
	Western Ear 2.115	Woods Hole 5.97
	Ledge 2.115	Passage 5.100
Wadsworth, Fort 7.91	Western Egg Rock 3.46	Directional Light 5.102
Waldoboro 3.59	Western Harbor 4.22	Town 5.97
Wamphassuc Point 6.39	Western Head 2.24	Woods Point 2.92
Ward Point 7.106	Western Island 2.29	Woolwich 3.103
Bend 7.67	Western Ledge 3.67	Wreck Island 3.46
Wards Island 7.145	Western Passage 2.28	Wreck Shoal 5.51
Warren 5.222	Western Reef 2.18	Wylie Rock 3.74
River 5.222	Western Way 2.46	Wyman Ledge 3.109
Warren Cove 4.135	Westport Harbor 5.182	
Warren Island 2.190	Westport Island 3.87	
Warren Point 5.182	Westport River 5.182	Yarmouth Island 3.115
Warwick Point 5.209	Weymouth Fore River 4.98	Yarmouth Ledges 3.114
Washers, The 2.115	Weymouth Great Hill 4.91	Yellow Birch Head 2.26
Washington Canal 7.73	Weymouth Point 2.90	Yellow Island 2.60
Washington Shoal 6.18	Whale Ledge 2.21	Yellow Mill Channel 6.145
Washington, Port 6.245	Whale Rock: Narragansett Bay ... 5.207	Yellow Rock 3.114
Washman Rock 3.215	Whaleback 4.36	York Ledge: Casco Bay 3.163
Wasque Point 5.18	Whaleback Ledge 2.80	York Ledge: York River 3.211
Wasque Shoal 5.54	Whaleback Light 3.237	York Narrows 2.75
Light 5.18	Whaleback Reef 3.237	Youngs Point 2.27
Watch Hill 6.16	Whaleback Rock 3.96	Youngs Rock 6.38
Cove 6.44	Whaleboat Island 3.135	
Light 6.14	Shoal 3.131	
Passage 6.37	Whaleboat Ledge 3.131	Zeke Point 2.121
Point 6.16	White Bull 3.110	Zephyr Rock 2.143
Waterman Cove 2.127		

NOTES

NOTES

NOTES

NOTES

NOTES

NOTES

PREVIOUS EDITIONS

Ports on the east coast of the United States

First published 1858
Second Edition 1874
Third Edition 1882

East Coast of the United States

First published 1899
Second Edition, Part I 1909
Third Edition, Volume I 1922
Fourth Edition 1934
Fifth Edition 1949
Sixth Edition 1960
Seventh Edition 1975
Eighth Edition 1995
Ninth Edition 1998
Tenth Edition 2001
Eleventh Edition 2004
Twelfth Edition 2006
Thirteenth Edition 2009

Produced in the United Kingdom
by UKHO